ACCA
STUDY TEXT

Paper 3.5

Strategic Business
Planning and Development

IN THIS JUNE 2004 EDITION

- Targeted to the syllabus and study guide

- Quizzes and questions to check your understanding

- Clear layout and style designed to save you time

- Plenty of exam-style questions with detailed guidance from BPP

- Chapter roundups and summaries to help revision

FOR EXAMS IN DECEMBER 2004 AND JUNE 2005

BPP Professional Education
June 2004

First edition 2001
Fourth edition June 2004

ISBN 07517 1671 5 (previous ISBN 07517 1160 8)

British Library Cataloguing-in-Publication Data
A catalogue record for this book is available from the British Library

Published by

BPP Professional Education
Aldine House, Aldine Place
London W12 8AW

www.bpp.com

Printed in Great Britain by Ashford Colour Press

We are grateful to the Association of Chartered Certified Accountants for permission to reproduce past examination questions and questions from the pilot paper. The answers have been prepared by BPP Professional Education.

(ii)

BPP
PROFESSIONAL EDUCATION

THE BPP STUDY TEXT

Aims of this Study Text

To provide you with the knowledge and understanding, skills and application techniques that you need if you are to be successful in your exams

This Study Text has been written around the **Advanced Corporate Reporting** syllabus.

- It is **comprehensive**. It covers the syllabus content. No more, no less.

- It is written at the **right level**. Each chapter is written with the ACCA's **study guide** in mind.

- It is targeted to the **exam**. We have taken account of the **pilot paper and all sittings so far,** questions put to the examiners at ACCA conferences and the assessment methodology.

To allow you to study in the way that best suits your learning style and the time you have available, by following your personal Study Plan (see page (viii))

You may be studying at home on your own until the date of the exam, or you may be attending a full-time course. You may like to (and have time to) read every word, or you may prefer to (or only have time to) skim-read and devote the remainder of your time to question practice. Wherever you fall in the spectrum, you will find the BPP Study Text meets your needs in designing and following your personal Study Plan.

To tie in with the other components of the BPP Effective Study Package to ensure you have the best possible chance of passing the exam (see page (vi))

Recommended period of use	Elements of the BPP Effective Study Package
From the outset and throughout	**Learning to Learn Accountancy** Read this invaluable book as you begin your studies and refer to it as you work through the various elements of the BPP Effective Study Package. It will help you to acquire knowledge, practise and revise, efficiently and effectively.
Three to twelve months before the exam	**Study Text and i-Learn** Use the Study Text to acquire knowledge, understanding, skills and the ability to apply techniques. Use BPP's **i-Learn** product to reinforce your learning.
Throughout	**Virtual Campus** Study, practise, revise and take advantage of other useful resources with BPP's fully interactive e-learning site with comprehensive tutor support.
Throughout	**MCQ cards and i-Pass** Revise your knowledge and ability to apply techniques, as well as practising this key exam question format, with 150 multiple choice questions. **i-Pass**, our computer-based testing package, provides objective test questions in a variety of formats and is ideal for self-assessment.
One to six months before the exam	**Practice & Revision Kit** Try the numerous examination-format questions, for which there are realistic suggested solutions prepared by BPP's own authors. Then attempt the two mock exams.
From three months before the exam until the last minute	**Passcards** Work through these short, memorable notes which are focused on what is most likely to come up in the exam you will be sitting.
One to six months before the exam	**Success Tapes** These audio tapes cover the vital elements of your syllabus in less than 90 minutes per subject. Each tape also contains exam hints to help you fine tune your strategy.

BPP
PROFESSIONAL EDUCATION

HELP YOURSELF STUDY FOR YOUR ACCA EXAMS

Exams for professional bodies such as ACCA are very different from those you have taken at college or university. You will be under **greater time pressure before** the exam, as you may be combining your study with work. There are many different ways of learning and so the BPP Study Text offers you a number of different tools to help you through. Here are some hints and tips: they are not plucked out of the air, but **based on research and experience**. (You don't need to know that long-term memory is in the same part of the brain as emotions and feelings – but it's a fact anyway.)

The right approach

1   The right attitude

Believe in yourself	Yes, there is a lot to learn. Yes, it is a challenge. But thousands have succeeded before and you can too.
Remember why you're doing it	Studying might seem a grind at times, but you are doing it for a reason: to advance your career.

2   The right focus

Read through the Syllabus and Study guide	These tell you what you are expected to know and are supplemented by exam focus points in the text.
Study the Exam Paper section	Past exam papers are likely to be a reasonable guide of what you should expect in the exam.

3   The right method

The big picture	You need to grasp the detail – but keeping in mind how everything fits into the big picture will help you understand better. • The **Introduction** of each chapter puts the material in context. • The Syllabus content, Study guide and Exam focus points show you what you need to grasp.
In your own words	To absorb the information (and to practise your written communication skills), it helps **put it into your own words.** • **Take notes.** • Answer the **questions** in each chapter. You will practise your written communication skills, which become increasingly important as you progress through your ACCA exams. • Draw **mind maps**. We have an example for the whole syllabus. • Try 'teaching' to a colleague or friend.

Give yourself cues to jog your memory	The BPP Study Text uses **bold text** to **highlight key points** and **icons** to identify key features, such as **Exam focus points** and **Key terms.**
	• Try **colour coding** with a highlighter pen.
	• Write **key points** on cards.

4   **The right review**

Review, review, review	It is a **fact** that regularly reviewing a topic in summary form can **fix it in your memory**. Because **review** is so important, the BPP Study Text helps you to do so in many ways.
	• **Chapter roundups** summarise the key points in each chapter. Use them to recap each study session.
	• The **Quick quiz** is another review tool to ensure that you have grasped the essentials.
	• Go through the **Examples** in each chapter a second or third time.

Developing your personal Study Plan

The BPP Learning to Learn Accountancy book emphasises is the need to prepare (and use) a study plan. Planning and sticking to the plan are key elements of learning success.

There are four steps you should work through.

Step 1. **How do you learn?**

First you need to be aware of your style of learning. The BPP Learning to Learn Accountancy book commits a chapter to this **self-discovery**. What types of intelligence do you display when learning? You might be advised to brush up on certain study skills before launching into this Study Text.

> BPP's **Learning to Learn Accountancy** book helps you to identify what intelligences you show more strongly and then details how you can tailor your study process to your preferences. It also includes handy hints on how to develop intelligences you exhibit less strongly, but which might be needed as you study accountancy.

Are you a **theorist** or are you more **practical**? If you would rather get to grips with a theory before trying to apply it in practice, you should follow the study sequence on page (ix). If the reverse is true (you need to know why you are learning theory before you do so), you might be advised to flick through Study Text chapters and look at questions, case studies and examples (Steps 7, 8 and 9 in the **suggested study sequence**) before reading through the detailed theory.

Step 2. **How much time do you have?**

Work out the time you have available per week, given the following.

- The standard you have set yourself
- The time you need to set aside later for work on the Practice & Revision Kit and Passcards
- The other exam(s) you are sitting
- Very importantly, practical matters such as work, travel, exercise, sleep and social life

Note your time available in box A.   A   [Hours]

Step 3. **Allocate your time**

- Take the time you have available per week for this Study Text shown in box A, multiply it by the number of weeks available and insert the result in box B.   B
- Divide the figure in Box B by the number of chapters in this text and insert the result in box C.   C

Remember that this is only a rough guide. Some of the chapters in this book are longer and more complicated than others, and you will find some subjects easier to understand than others.

Step 4. **Implement**

Set about studying each chapter in the time shown in box C, following the key study steps in the order suggested by your particular learning style.

This is your personal **Study Plan**. You should try and combine it with the study sequence outlined below. You may want to modify the sequence a little (as has been suggested above) to adapt it to your **personal style**.

BPP's *Learning to learn Accountancy* gives further guidance on developing a study plan, and deciding when and where to study.

Suggested study sequence

Tackle the chapters in the order you find them in the Study Text. Taking into account your individual learning style, you could follow this sequence.

Key study steps	Activity
Step 1 **Topic list**	Each numbered topic is a numbered section in the chapter.
Step 2 **Introduction**	This gives you the **big picture** in terms of the **context** of the chapter. The content is referenced to the **Study Guide**, and **Exam Guidance** shows how the topic is likely to be examined. In other words, it sets your **objectives for study.**
Step 3 **Knowledge brought forward boxes**	In these we highlight information and techniques that it is assumed you have 'brought forward' with you from your earlier studies. If there are topics which have changed recently due to legislation for example, these topics are explained in more detail.
Step 4 **Explanations**	Proceed methodically through the chapter, reading each section thoroughly and making sure you understand.
Step 5 **Key terms and Exam focus points**	• **Key terms** can often earn you *easy marks* if you state them clearly and correctly in an appropriate exam answer (and they are indexed at the back of the text). • **Exam focus points** give you a good idea of what has come up in the exam and how we think the examiner intends to examine certain topics.
Step 6 **Note taking**	Take brief notes if you wish, avoiding the temptation to copy out too much.
Step 7 **Examples**	Follow each through to its solution very carefully.
Step 8 **Case examples**	Study each one, and try to add flesh to them from your own experience – they are designed to show how the topics you are studying come alive (and often come unstuck) in the real world.
Step 9 **Questions**	Make a very good attempt at each one.
Step 10 **Answers**	Check yours against ours, and make sure you understand any discrepancies.
Step 11 **Chapter roundup**	Work through it very carefully, to make sure you have grasped the major points it is highlighting.
Step 12 **Quick quiz**	When you are happy that you have covered the chapter, use the **Quick quiz** to check how much you have remembered of the topics covered.
Step 13 **Question(s) in the Question bank**	Either at this point, or later when you are thinking about revising, make a full attempt at the **Question(s)** suggested at the very end of the chapter. You can find these at the end of the Study Text, along with the **Answers** so you can see how you did. We highlight those that are introductory, and those which are of the standard you would expect to find in an exam.

BPP
PROFESSIONAL EDUCATION

Short of time: *Skim study technique?*

You may find you simply do not have the time available to follow all the key study steps for each chapter, however you adapt them for your particular learning style. If this is the case, follow the **skim study** technique below (the icons in the Study Text will help you to do this).

- Study the chapters in the order you find them in the Study Text.

- For each chapter:

    - Follow the key study steps 1-3, and then skim-read through step 4. Jump to step 11, and then go back to step 5.

    - Follow through steps 7 and 8, and prepare outline answers to questions (steps 9/10).

    - Try the Quick Quiz (step 12), following up any items you can't answer, then do a plan for the Question (step 13), comparing it against our answers.

    - You should probably still follow step 6 (note-taking), although you may decide simply to rely on the BPP Passcards for this.

Moving on...

However you study, when you are ready to embark on the practice and revision phase of the BPP Effective Study Package, you should still refer back to this Study Text, both as a source of **reference** (you should find the list of key terms and the index particularly helpful for this) and as a **refresher** (the Chapter Roundups and Quick Quizzes help you here).

And remember to keep careful hold of this Study Text – you will find it invaluable in your work.

> More advice on Study Skills can be found in the BPP **Learning to Learn Accountancy** book

SYLLABUS

Aim

To ensure that candidates can exercise judgement and technique in strategic business management to enable them to contribute to the formulation of business strategy, the development of products and services and the maintenance of quality throughout the organisation.

Objectives

On completion of this paper candidates should be able to:

- identify and apply the principal concepts and ideas in the theory and practice of strategic management

- understand the internal and external factors affecting an organisation and apply the knowledge to evaluate its strategic position

- identify appropriate strategies based on the evaluation of the organisation's objectives and position

- identify the appropriate methods of implementing chosen strategies and evaluate their impact on organisational structures and operations

- understand the impact of globalisation on strategic business planning

- integrate knowledge effectively and use it creatively in applying concepts and techniques

- analyse, interpret and apply data and information and present reasoned conclusions

- communicate analyses and conclusions effectively and with sensitivity for different purposes and contrasting audiences with due emphasis on social expectations.

Position of the paper in the overall syllabus

Candidates should have a sound understanding of Paper 1.2 *Financial Information for Management*, Paper 1.3 *Managing People* and Paper 2.1 *Information systems*. The information in these papers will provide some of the basic material for strategy analysis and development.

Paper 3.5 builds upon the knowledge obtained in Paper 1.3 by

- reinforcing the importance of recruitment and selection processes and procedures

- examining the importance of training and development and motivation within a strategic context

- providing a more strategic view of human resource issues

- extending the coverage of work organisations.

Page 3.5 develops parts of the knowledge gained in Paper 1.2 by

- applying financial information to strategy evaluation and strategy recommendation
- giving more emphasis on pricing policies and procedures
- examining performance measurement criteria.

Paper 3.5 develops parts of the knowledge obtained in Paper 2.1 by

- reinforcing the knowledge of managing information systems at a strategic level.

Although much of the knowledge gained in Part 3 will be specific to the individual papers, Paper 3.5 will, by its very nature, provide integration with most of the other papers at this level.

In Paper 3.1 *Audit and Assurance Services* there will be links with professional and ethical considerations.

In Paper 3.3 *Performance Management* there will be strong relationships with areas on performance measurement and decision-making.

In Paper 3.4 *Business Information Management* there will be related material on information resource management and information systems and competition.

In Paper 3.7 *Strategic Financial Management* there will be relationships with objectives and corporate governance, strategy formulation and the global economic environment.

Syllabus content

1   Models of strategic management

(a) What is strategic management?

   (i)   corporate strategy
   (ii) business strategy

(b) Why is strategic management important?

(c) The process, content and context of strategic management

(d) Process of strategy development

   (i)   deliberate or prescriptive strategies
   (ii) emergent and incremental strategies

(e) Strategic content

   (i)   strategic analysis
   (ii)   strategic choice
   (iii) strategic implementation

(f) Strategic management in different contexts

   (i)   configuration
   (ii) culture

2   External environmental scanning

(a) Analysis of the general environment

   (i)   SLEPT analysis
   (ii)   Porter's diamond
   (iii) forecasting and scenarios

(b) Analysis of the customers and markets - marketing research

(c) Analysis of the competitive environment

   (i)   five forces model
   (ii)   competition and collaboration
   (iii) competitor intelligence for business advantage
   (iv)   sustainable competitive advantage and critical success factors

3   Internal assessment

(a) Resource audit
(b) Analysis of capabilities and core competences
(c) Adding competitive value - value chain and value system
(d) Analysis of human resources
(e) Analysis of financial resources
(f) Analysis of operations resources

4   The nature of strategy analysis and choice

(a) The purpose of the organisation

 (i)   stakeholder expectations
 (ii)   cultural context
 (iii) mission, objective and strategic intent

(b) Developing the strategy

 (i)   alternative directions for strategy development

 • resource based
 • market based
 • finance based

 (ii)   methods of strategy development

 • internal development
 • strategic alliances
 • mergers and acquisitions

(c) Strategy evaluation and selection

 (i)   analysis of suitability, feasibility and acceptability
 (ii)   corporate/business strategy selection

5   The nature of strategy implementation

(a) Marketing issues

 (i)   segmentation, targeting and positioning
 (ii)   strategies for market leaders, followers, challengers and nichers
 (iii) development and application of marketing mix strategies

(b) Finance issues

 (i)   performance evaluation
 (ii)   funding implementation and resource allocation

(c) Research and Development issues

 (i)   management of innovation
 (ii)   management and control of quality

(d) IS/IT issues

 (i)   IT/IS as a strategic resource
 (ii)   the management of information systems development Current   issues   and developments

6   Matching structures with strategy

7   The nature of global competition

(d) Managing a global company

    (i)   ethnocentric, polycentric or geocentric orientation

    (ii)   cross cultural management and leadership

(e) Reaching global customers

    (i)   international marketing research

    (ii)   international market segmentation

8   Outcomes of the strategic management process

(a) Corporate versus business performance

(b) Sustainable competitive advantage

(c) A learning organisation

(d) Alternative performance measures

    (i)   financial

    (ii)   non financial

    (iii) strategic

9   Ethical considerations

(a) The importance of social responsibility

(b) Corporate governance

(c) The attitude towards ethics on national and global scales

Excluded topics

The syllabus content outlines the areas for assessment. No areas of knowledge are specifically excluded from the syllabus.

Key areas of the syllabus

Although all the syllabus will be examined in some form the core areas will be focused on the strategy process. This comprises the identification of corporate objectives, strategic analysis, including internal and external reviews, strategy development, evaluation and implementation.

Paper 3.5(U)

Strategic Business Planning and Development Study Guide

SESSION 1

1 INTRODUCTION TO STRATEGIC MANAGEMENT

Syllabus reference 1a-c

(a) Strategic management defined

   (i)   corporate strategy

      - understand the strategic perspective

      - evaluate the overall purpose and scope

      - describe the expectations of owners

      - describe the expectations of stakeholders

      - explain the concept of added value

   (ii) business strategy

      - be aware of the role of business units

      - identify market competition

(b) The importance of strategic management

   - define strategy and strategic thinking

   - differentiate between policy, strategy, tactics

   - understand the need for a long term view

   - define long term objectives

   - understand long term efficiency

(c) The process, content and context of strategic management

   - describe the present position of the organisation

   - understand the external environment

   - understand the organisation at present

   - evaluate where does the organisation want to be

   - demonstrate how is the organisation going to get there

(d) The process of strategy development

   - identify deliberate strategies

   - identify prescriptive strategies

   - identify emergent and incremental strategies

   - understand strategic planning and strategic management

SESSION 2

(e) The rational model

   (i)   strategic analysis

      - assess the strategic position

      - evaluate expectations and influence of stakeholders

   (ii) strategic choice

      - define underlying influences which guide strategy

      - evaluate strategic options

      - understand evaluation and selection procedures

   (iii) strategic implementation

      - define resource planning

      - define corporate strategy

      - define operational and financial strategy

SESSION 3

Syllabus reference 1d and 1f

(f) Strategic management in different contexts

   (i)   strategic configuration

      - understand logical incremental model

      - understand rational command model

      - understand cultural political incremental

      - understand political choice

SESSION 4

   (ii) culture

      - define the meaning of culture

      - understand the determinants of culture: Schein

      - understand the implications of culture: Pümpin

      - describe the cultural web: Johnson and Scholes

      - link culture with structure

      - discuss models of culture: Handy, Miles and Snow, Peters and Waterman, Mintzberg

      - understand changing organisational culture: Kanter, Lewin

      - evaluate the link between culture and strategic leadership

      - identify regional and national culture

SESSION 5

EXTERNAL ENVIRONMENTAL SCANNING

Syllabus reference 2a, b, c

(a) Analysis of the general environment

  (i) SLEPT analysis

    - be aware the social impact on the organisation

    - be aware of the legal issues and implications

    - be aware of the role and influence of the economy

    - be aware of the political environment

    - be aware of the impact of technology

    - be aware of complexity, dynamism and uncertainty

    - understand systems thinking

    - analyse the organisation as an open system

    - understand the focal zone analysis

  (ii) Porter's diamond

    - explain firm strategy, structure and rivalry

    - explain demand conditions

    - explain related and supporting industries

  (iii) forecasting and scenarios

    - understand strategic life cycles

    - understand statistical forecasting techniques

    - understand the Delphi technique

    - understand scenario planning

SESSION 6

(b) Analysis of customers, markets and marketing research

  - explain aggregate and sectoral concentration

  - understand customer behaviour

  - understand the principles of marketing research

  - explain market research as a component of marketing research

  - discuss social change and social trends

  - discuss demographic factors

  - discuss population size

  - discuss demographic change

  - discuss social structure

  - discuss economic change

(c) Analysis of the competitive environment

  (i) the five forces model

    - understand the general model

    - discuss intensity of rivalry among existing competitors

    - discuss bargaining power of suppliers

    - discuss bargaining power of buyers

    - discuss the threat of new entrants

    - discuss the threat of substitutes

    - evaluate the weaknesses of the model

    - explain the threat of potential entrants

    - understand the connection with market structure

    - discuss the role of government and regulation

  (ii) competition and collaboration

    - review government regulation

    - discuss the competition commission

    - compare different market environments

    - discuss cartels, oligopolies

SESSION 7

  (iii) competitor intelligence for business advantage

    - understand the portfolio analysis approach

    - describe the Boston Consulting Group model

    - describe the Shell directional policy matrix/nine cell grid

    - understand the importance of understanding portfolio analysis

    - understand the product life cycle

    - explain competitor benchmarking

    - explain competitive positioning grid

  (iv) sustainable competitive advantage

    - define competitive advantage

- explain competitive advantage

- discuss generic strategies (Porter)

- understand different approaches by management

- evaluate branding, patents, copyrights and trademarks

- identify national advantage (Porter)

- evaluate the strategic role of the marketing mix

(v) critical success factors

- define how to measure success

- compare actual and relative success factors

- compare efficiency and effectiveness

- evaluate financial measures

- contract the expectations of stock holders and shareholders

- discuss quality issues

- evaluate success measurement for non profit making organisations

SESSION 8

INTERNAL ASSESSMENT

Syllabus reference 3a, b, c

(a) Resource audit

- identify quality, nature and extent of available resources

- identify physical, human and financial resources

- identify intangible resources

- understand unique resources and competitive advantage

- evaluate internal control systems

- analyse departmental organisation

(b) Analysis of capabilities and core competencies

- formulate a SWOT analysis

- interpret a SWOT analysis

- describe the product life cycle

- understand the seven 'S' approach

- demonstrate threshold competencies

- demonstrate core competencies

identify appropriate markets

review quality and reliability

explain product attributes

SESSION 9

(c) Adding competitive value

- understand the value chain

- link the value chain with organisational structure

- explain the value systems

- discuss product and market differentiation

- identify sources of differentiation

- assess innovation

understand technical development

identify new target markets

identify new distribution channels

identify new market segments

be aware of sudden environmental shocks

SESSION 10

Syllabus reference 3d, e, f

(d) Analysis of human resources

- understand skills and competencies

- discuss workforce adaptability

- assess innovative capability

(e) Analysis of operations resources

- evaluate the availability of resources

- understand management information and control systems

- understand production control systems

- understand process control

- describe resource utilisation and costs

SESSION 11

(f) analysis of financial resources

- understand financial control systems

- understand capital structure

- understand liquidity and gearing

- define the 'balanced scorecard': Kaplan and Norton

SESSION 12

THE NATURE OF STRATEGY ANALYSIS AND CHOICE

Syllabus reference 4a

(a) The purpose of the organisation

(i) stakeholder expectations

- understand stakeholder power and influence

- be able to carry out stakeholder mapping: Mendelow

(ii) the cultural context

- identify national and local culture

- understand organisational culture and objectives

SESSION 13

(iii) mission, objectives and strategic intent

- define policy, strategy and tactics

- define strategic vision

- define the mission statement

- define strategic intent: Hamel and Prahalad

- define strategic scope

- state implicit and explicit objectives

- evaluate the prime organisational objective

- evaluate the organisation's policy

- understand marginalist theories of organisational objectives

- explain the accounting concept of profit

- explain the economist's concept of profit

- explain behavioural theories of organisation

- identify the expectations of the owners

- evaluate the role of stakeholders

SESSION 14

Syllabus reference 4b

(b) Developing the strategy

(i) alternative directions for strategy development

evaluate PIMS analysis

- understand resource based

- understand product value and development

- explain withdrawal strategy

- explain consolidation strategy

- explain market based strategy

- explain market development and extension strategy

- explain market penetration strategy

- explain market positioning strategy

- understand growth vector analysis: Ansoff

- define the planning gap

- define finance based strategies

- understand the role of the budgetary process

SESSION 15

(ii) methods of strategy development

- compare level one and level two strategies

- evaluate internal development

- evaluate organic growth: Greiner's growth model

- analyse joint ventures and strategic alliances

- review mergers and acquisitions

- define concentric and conglomerate diversification

- define forward and backward integration

- be aware of the problems of diversification and acquisition

SESSION 16

Syllabus reference 1e, 4c

(c) Strategy evaluation and selection

(i) analysis of suitability, feasibility and acceptability

suitability

- understand life cycle analysis

- understand life cycle/portfolio matrix

- assess resources and competencies

- discuss business profile analysis

- be aware of decision trees

(ii) feasibility

- explain funds flow analysis

- explain break even analysis

- explain resource deployment analysis

(iii) acceptability

- identify, justify expected performance outcomes

- review profitability analysis

- review cost-benefit analysis

- review risk analysis

- evaluate shareholder value

- assess expectation of stakeholders

(iv) corporate and business strategy selection

- formulate the role of planning

- carry out a formal evaluation

- analyse enforced choice

- differentiate learning from experience

- be aware of dominant stakeholder selection

SESSION 17

THE NATURE OF STRATEGY IMPLEMENTATION

Syllabus reference 5a, b, c, d, e, f, g

(a) Marketing issues

(i) segmentation, targeting and positioning

- understand strategic group analysis

- define strategic groups and strategic space

- describe market segmentation analysis

- explain segmentation by factor, market or organisation

- describe targeting

- distinguish between product and market positioning

(ii) strategies for market leaders, followers, challengers and nichers

- understand the strategic clock: Bowman

- understand the market options matrix

- understand price based strategies

- understand added value and differentiation strategies

- explain hybrid strategy

- define focused differentiation

SESSION 18

(iii) development and application of marketing mix strategies

- discuss product strategy

- discuss price strategy

- discuss place strategy

- discuss promotion strategy

SESSION 19

(b) Finance issues

(i) performance evaluation

- explain ratio analysis

- be aware of financial measures

- understand ROCE, ROI, profitability

(ii) funding the implementation and the resource allocation

- explain financial sources

- explain capital allocation

- explain shareholders' funds

(c) Research and Development issues

(i) management of innovation

- assess the role of research and development in strategy

- evaluate acquisition of new technologies

- discuss exploitation of existing technologies

- discuss innovation and existing products

- discuss innovation and new products

- explain innovation and intrapreneurship

(ii) management and control of quality

- discuss the role of quality in strategy

- describe quality procedures

- explain quality assurance

- explain total quality management

(d) IS/IT issues

   (i)   IS/IT as a strategic resource

- understand organisation and control of the information strategy

- define usefulness and application of information technology

- assess monitoring advances and changes in information technology

- describe current good practice

- describe costs and benefits

- discuss information and organisational structure

   (ii)   the management of information systems development

- be aware of information as a strategic device

- assess project selection criteria

- understand the sue, planning and control of information technology

- evaluate the application of information technology

SESSION 20

(e)   Human Resource issues

   (i)   recruitment and selection

- define the strategic role of human resources

- formulate the human resource plan

- identify and evaluate appropriate recruitment methods

- advise on succession planning

   (ii)   motivation and discipline

- understand the appropriate motivational and supportive policies

- describe the links between objectives, appraisal, reward and motivation

   (iii)   appraisal and performance evaluation

- assess organisational and individual objectives

- assess appraisal methods

- discuss appraisal and competence assessment

   (iv)   staff training and development

- understand the importance of the management of change

- describe the management of diversity

- evaluate the role of teamworking and empowerment

SESSION 21

(f) (i)   Project management issues

- define the project life cycle

- understand the objectives of project management

- make and estimation of resource requirements

- assess the efficient use of resources

- understand operational research procedures

   (ii)   tools and techniques of project management

- understand statistical approaches

- describe statistical process control

   (iii)   operations management

- assess the strategic significance of operations

- link operations management and strategy

- understand purchasing and inbound logistics

- evaluate the manufacturing process

- understand distribution and outbound logistics

- describe quality and quality regimes

- have knowledge of just-in-time supply management

- discuss business process re-engineering

SESSION 22

(g) (i)   Management of change issues

- assess the motivation to change

- evaluate attitudes to change

- link together culture and change

- understand the managing of change: Lewin, System Intervention Strategy

(ii) Process of understanding types of strategic change and their causes

- identify external environmental change and shocks

- identify internal environmental change

- understand business relationships

- understand transformational change

- discuss enforced change

- identify technological change

- evaluate people issues

(iii) development of strategic change programme

- describe the Gemini 4Rs framework

- describe force field analysis

- describe power influence

- understand cultural influence

(iv) management roles in the strategy change process

- understand the importance of communication and education

- evaluate collaboration

- evaluate intervention

- assess the importance of direction

- describe routine change

(v) managing the strategic change process

- evaluate changing identity of the organisation

- understand co-ordination and transition

- appreciate the need for control

- describe the role of change strategists

- describe the role of change implementers

- describe the role of change recipients

SESSION 23

MATCHING STRUCTURES WITH STRATEGY

Syllabus reference 6a, b, c

(a) Types of organisation structures

- understand the determinants of structure

- evaluate the meaning of structure

- describe the simple organisation

- describe the entrepreneurial organisation

- describe the functional organisation

- describe the divisional organisation

- describe the matrix organisation

- describe the multinational organisation

- describe the global organisation

- understand the holding company

- evaluate the role of the strategic business unit

- assess intermediate and variations in structure

- discuss advantages and appropriateness of different structures

- understand the process stage towards globalisation: Kenichi Ohmai, Keegan

(b) Centralisation versus decentralisation

- evaluate issues in organisational structural change

- understand organic and mechanistic structures: Burns and Stalker

- describe contingency theory

- describe the virtual organisation

SESSION 24

(c) Organisational configurations

- compare structural configurations: Mintzberg

- make a comparison of organisational types

SESSION 25

THE NATURE OF GLOBAL COMPETITION

Syllabus reference 7a, b

(a) The internationalisation of business

- understand the motivations behind internationalisation

- be aware of the concept of globalisation as distinct from international marketing

- discuss the competitive advantage of nations: Porter

- understand absolute advantage and comparative advantage

- evaluate implications for organisational success

- explain internationalisation strategies

- understand single markets and trading blocks

- explain multinational organisations: Bartlett and Ghoshal

(b) The development of the global business

- discuss market convergence

- explain cost advantages

- explain government pressures

- understand currency volatility and trade barriers

- understand purchasing power parity

- understand the emergence of global competition

SESSION 26

Syllabus reference 7c, d, e

(c) Global strategies

- evaluate market entry strategies

- compare standardisation versus customisation

- understand product positioning

- discuss international channel management

- analyse the development of global brands

(d) Managing a global company

- describe the international planning process

- assess ethnocentric, polycentric and geocentric orientation

- explain cross cultural management and leadership

(e) Reaching global customers

(i) international marketing research

- be able to assess value of published statistics

- discuss comparability and reliability of data

- assess national and local information sources

- evaluate field sales force

(ii) international market segmentation

understand the following

- geographic

- ethnic

- economic

- technological capability

SESSION 27

OUTCOMES OF THE STRATEGIC PROCESS

Syllabus reference 8a, b, c, d

(a) Corporate and business performance

- discuss sustainable competitive advantage

- evaluate critical success factors

(b) A learning organisation

- assess shared purpose and vision

- understand challenging experiences

- explain the holistic view

(c) Alternative performance measures

- understand performance standards

- utilise financial indicators

- utilise non financial indicators

- formulate strategic success measurements

(d) Strategic failure

- assess strategic drift: the Icarus Paradox

- understand indicators of failure

- analyse weak or inappropriate strategic leadership

- discuss Z scores: Altman

SESSION 28

ETHICAL CONSIDERATIONS

(a) The importance of social responsibility

- evaluate the meaning of social responsibility

- discuss corporate social responsibility

- review business ethics

- review ethical dilemmas

- describe the ethical spectrum: Reidenbach and Robin

(b) Corporate governance

- assess corporate conduct

- assess the governance framework

- discuss governance change

- distinguish between rights, duties and expectations of stakeholders

(c) The attitude towards ethics on national and global scales

(i) the ethical stance

- discuss at the national and international level

- explain at the corporate level

- explain at the manager level

- evaluate the cultural context

THE EXAM PAPER

The examination is a **three hour paper** divided into **two sections**.

		Number of Marks
Section A:	One compulsory question	60
Section B:	Choice of 2 from 3 questions (20 marks each)	40
		100

Additional information

Candidates need to be aware that questions involving knowledge of new examinable regulations will not be set until at least six months after the last day of the month in which the regulation was issued.

The Study Guide provides more detailed guidance on the syllabus.

Section A will consist of a compulsory case study, usually with three questions dealing mainly with strategy formulation. Questions will include some quantitative information but will require answers in mainly discursive form.

Section B will offer a choice of two questions from three. They will not be linked to the scenario in Section A

Analysis of past papers

The analysis below shows the topics that were examined in all sittings of the current syllabus so far and in the Pilot Paper.

June 2004

Section A

1   A small entrepreneurial IT systems company has reached a crisis in its development
   (a)   Purpose and contributions of mission statement
   (b)   Report on current position of a company
   (c)   Assessment of owner's three exit options
   (d)   Distinguishing B2B from consumer marketing

Section B

2   Role of marketing in a small company supplying large supermarkets; 'niching' strategy
3   Corporate governance: autocratic and possible corrupt CEO; role of non-executive directors
4   Value of appraisal and performance management in a medium sized accounting firm.

December 2003

Section A

1   A small manufacturing company serving both industrial and consumer markets is suffering from fierce competition on price and innovation. The company has high overheads, and little interest or ability in marketing.
   (a)   Performance review of all three product groups
   (b)   Assess strategic options and make recommendation
   (c)   Changing from technology-led to marketing-led culture
   (d)   Creating a more effective new product development system

Section B

2   Understanding conflict with change theories and models; conflict resolution action plan
3   Importance of marketing in the financial services industry; measuring marketing performance
4   Organic growth method of entry to overseas markets.

June 2003

Section A

1 A small business buys supplies from overseas manufacturers and resells them to wholesalers and major retailers.
   (a)   Strategic and financial review of current position
   (b)   Possible strategies for future development
   (c)   Identifying and avoiding causes of corporate decline
   (d)   Account for current success using the value chain model

Section B

2 Product portfolio planning; benchmarking
3 Marketing strategy for a new market; creating and sustaining competitive advantage
4 Business ethics and legality; ensuring proper behaviour; implementing change in a dysfunctional organisation.

December 2002

Section A

1 Strategic review of manufacturing company; strategic evaluation; factors influencing success in mergers; ethical problems

Section B

2 Reasons why strategies fail; successful implementation of strategy

3 Manufacturing or buying in goods for resale; problems of outsourcing non-core activities

4 Polycentrism and geocentrism in international operations; factors encouraging a policy of customisation

June 2002

Section A

1 Stakeholders' goals and objectives in a hospital; identification of strategic problems; assessment of strategic options; social responsibility in the context of health care

Section B

2 Overseas marketing; obtaining and using market intelligence

3 Acquisition: potential problems; integrating a new business into a group

4 Package holiday operations: critical success factors and performance indicators

BPP
PROFESSIONAL EDUCATION

Introduction

OXFORD BROOKES BSc (Hons) IN APPLIED ACCOUNTING

The standard required of candidates completing Part 2 is that required in the final year of a UK degree. Students completing Parts 1 and 2 will have satisfied the examination requirement for an honours degree in Applied Accounting, awarded by Oxford Brookes University.

To achieve the degree, you must also submit two pieces of work based on a **Research and Analysis Project.**

- A 5,000 word **Report** on your chosen topic, which demonstrates that you have acquired the necessary research, analytical and IT skills.

- A 1,500 word **Key Skills Statement**, indicating how you have developed your interpersonal and communication skills.

BPP was selected by the ACCA and Oxford Brookes University to produce the official text *Success in your Research and Analysis Project* to support students in this task. The book pays particular attention to key skills not covered in the professional examinations.

THE OXFORD BROOKES PROJECT TEXT CAN BE ORDERED USING THE FORM AT THE END OF THIS STUDY TEXT.

OXFORD INSTITUTE OF INTERNATIONAL FINANCE MBA

The Oxford Institute of International Finance (OXIIF), a joint venture between the ACCA and Oxford Brookes University, offers an MBA for finance professionals.

For this MBA, credits are awarded for your ACCA studies, and entry to the MBA course is available to those who have completed their ACCA professional stage studies. The MBA was launched in 2002 and has attracted participants from all over the world.

The qualification features an introductory module (*Markets, Management and Strategy*). Other modules include *Global Business Strategy, Managing Self Development,* and *Organisational Change & Transformation.*

Research Methods are also taught, as they underpin the **research dissertation**.

The MBA programme is delivered through the use of targeted paper study materials, developed by BPP, and taught over the Internet by OXIIF personnel using BPP's virtual campus software.

For further information, please see the Oxford Institute's website: www.oxfordinstitute.org.

CONTINUING PROFESSIONAL DEVELOPMENT

ACCA is introducing a new continuing professional development requirement for members from 1 January 2005. Members will be required to complete and record 40 units of CPD annually, of which 21 units must be verifiable learning or training activity.

BPP has an established professional development department which offers a range of relevant, professional courses to reflect the needs of professionals working in both industry and practice. To find out more, visit the website: www.bpp.com/pd or call the client care team on 0845 226 2422.

SYLLABUS MINDMAP

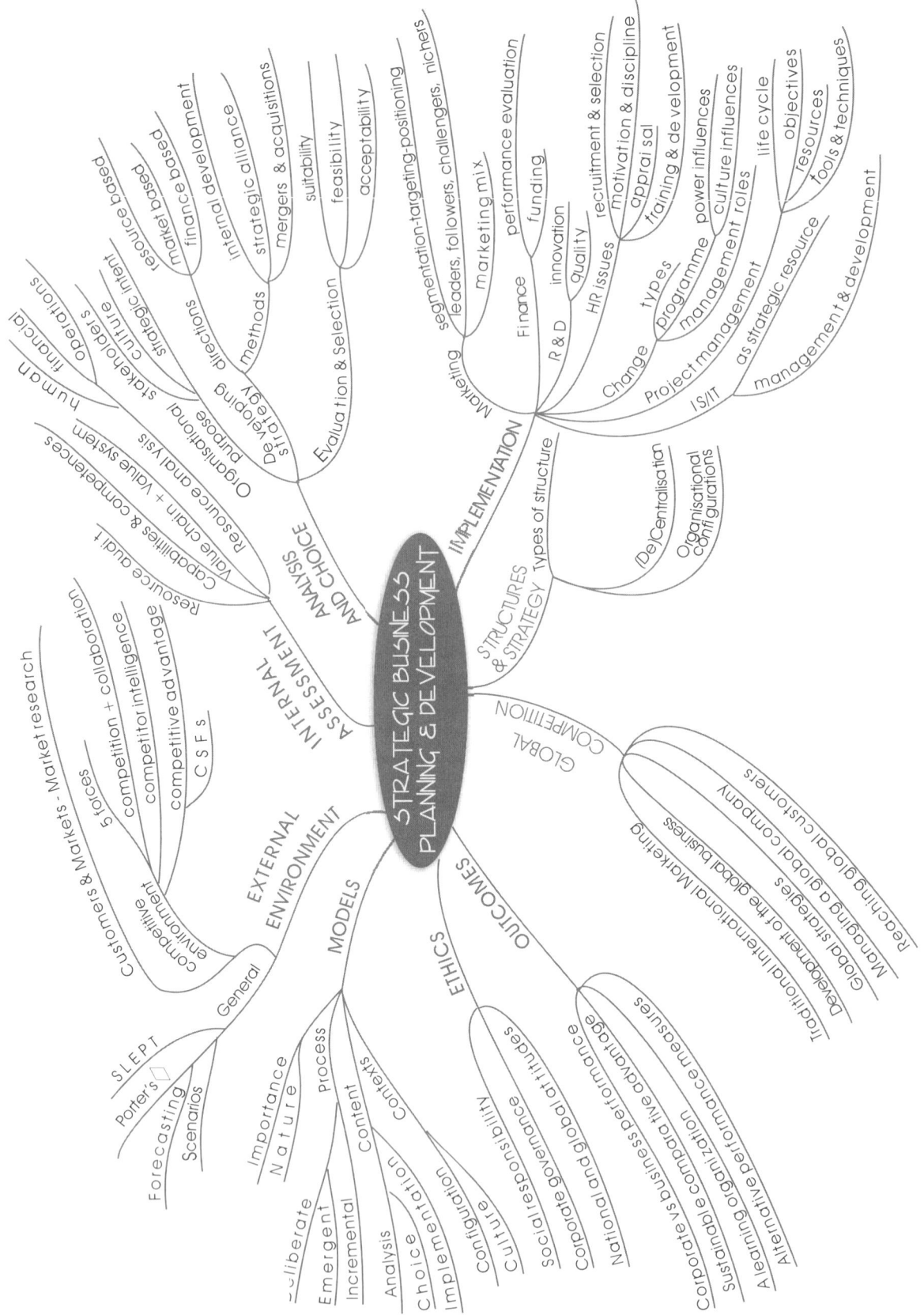

Part A
Models of strategic management

Chapter 1

STRATEGIC MANAGEMENT: THE TRADITIONAL APPROACH

Topic list	Syllabus reference
1 What is strategy?	1(a), 1(b)
2 Levels of strategy in an organisation	1(a)
3 The roles of marketing	1(c)
4 Making strategies: the rational model	1(d), 1(c)
5 For the rational model	1(d)
6 Against the rational model	1(a)

Introduction

This chapter outlines the framework of the book by describing the **rational model** approach to strategic management. Once we have outlined what strategic management is, we see how it applies at different **levels** of business. We then describe the **process of planning** and outline the criticisms of this model. This is an important chapter, especially Section 4, as it **offers a framework for this Study Text** and is applicable to many exam questions.

Study guide

Section 1 – Models of strategic management

- What is strategic management?

- Why is strategic management important?

- The process, content and context of strategic management

- Process of strategy development

Exam guide

This chapter covers material that is essential basic knowledge and may underlie any question in the exam.

1 WHAT IS STRATEGY?

1.1 This book is about strategy and strategic management as it is practised in profit-seeking organisations. Many of the ideas and techniques can be applied in the public sector and in not-for-profit organisations, but you should bear in mind throughout your studies that Paper 3.5 is concerned with **businesses**.

e.g

Case example

Hong Kong Telecom

Hongkong Telecom is a subsidiary of Cable & Wireless. The Chinese telecoms market is conservatively estimated to be worth more than £368 billion: only one in six Chinese households currently possesses a land-based phone line. The company has seen double-digit growth over the past three years in a highly competitive market, and is, according to chief executive Linus Chiang, 'poised on the cusp of a reincarnation'.

Competition

The company lost its domestic monopoly in 1995. 'We were printing money,' Cheung says. 'Suddenly we were faced with competition and huge technological advances. We were good technically and technologically, but not in terms of service and efficiency.'

'Rather than trying to fight off the competition by legalities and by making life more difficult for customers by forcing different dialling codes and so forth onto them, we have embraced competition and taken advantage of it. In the short term that approach is not helpful. But we are taking a long-term view and using competition as a driving force, an agent for change.'

Culture and human resources

The key to success, he asserts, is attitude, a performance culture and a service culture. Hongkong Telecom employees are judged against three key criteria: 'One, are you bold and decisive? Two, are you results-rather than activity-oriented? Three, are you effective – in other words, do you make things simple for internal and external audiences?'. There have been 2,500 voluntary redundancies over the past three years, and they are increasingly demanding on remaining managers. 'We are de-layering and fast-tracking and weeding out incompetence,' says Cheung.

Cheung introduced Operation Excel, a programme that focuses on revenue enhancement and cost control, and rewards initiative, performance, teamwork and results, as an antidote to the complacency bred by monopoly. The programme has helped effect transition to a dynamic performance culture.

There have been some novel initiatives. Cheung jokes that he is the Postmaster General as well as the CEO. 'I looked at the way we were distributing our four million telephone bills each month, and my boyhood newspaper delivery experience came in handy. I found we could achieve significant savings by utilising our employees to deliver some of our bills. Staff are able to make additional income too.' What's more, he has galvanised the entire workforce to sell mobile phones. And he leads by example, travelling business rather than first class on his frequent trips abroad.

Product/service innovation

Most significantly, the company has switched its focus from international direct dialling to other areas, including fixed line, mobile, and interactive services. They won the licence for video-on-demand and home shopping in November, and it is a world first, using complex technology to deliver laser disk quality movies, karaoke, gambling, computer games, TV shopping, etc. Accessible by anyone with a telephone and a TV set using a single controller, the service has the potential to reach Hong Kong's 1.5 million households over the next five years. Another innovation is Netvigator, an Internet access service launched into a marketplace of 80 competitors. To differentiate their offering, they focused on the customer interface, delivering useful, immediate information.

Competitive strategy

Hongkong Telecom's competitive differentiator is to respond to customer needs. Finance director David Prince explains: 'In telecoms, competitors tend to start from price, because what we have are effectively commodity products. We are trying to bring more creativity in marketing and customer service to telecoms. We differentiate ourselves from the competition on quality rather than price, by providing a total package to suit individuals' lifestyles.' When it lost its lead to Hutchison in the mobile phone market, Hongkong Telecom held its prices but improved its technology so that, for example, mobiles work in tunnels and underground trains.

KEY TERMS

Strategy: a course of action including the specification of resources required to meet a specific objective.

Tactics: the deployment of resources to execute an agreed strategy.

Policy: a general statement providing guidelines for management of decision making.

1.2 The terminology of strategic management is not universally defined. There is a number of words that are used almost interchangeably in daily life: strategy, tactics, mission, object, aim, target, goal, policy. We will develop our definitions as we progress through the subject matter of this Study Text. There are several points to note about the Hongkong Telecom case example.

- The **objective** is survival and growth.

- The **strategy** is a changed approach to products and markets. (Other strategies could have been chosen to meet this objective.)

- A **policy** is that senior managers travel business class rather than first class.

- The **resources** include the technological infrastructure and getting better performance out of existing personnel.

Case example

A government's *objective* of reducing road traffic accidents might be achieved in a number of ways, for example: stricter policing; traffic calming; lower speed limits; tougher driving tests etc.

KEY TERM

Strategic management: the development, implementation and control of agreed strategies. There is more to strategy than merely **deciding** what you want to achieve and how you are to achieve it.

1.3 Strategic management involves:

Phase	Application in Hong Kong telecom case example
Analysis	Discerning trends in the environment, looking at competitors
Choice	Embrace change rather than resisting it
Implementation	The *process* of changing the culture and organisation, and bringing the new products and services on-stream
Control	After the strategies have been implemented, how successful have they been?

1.4 **Strategy** is defined *by Johnson and Scholes* in this way.

'the direction and scope of an organisation over the long term which achieves advantage for the organisation through its configuration of resources within a changing environment to meet the needs of markets and to fulfil stakeholder expectations.'

BPP
PROFESSIONAL EDUCATION

2 LEVELS OF STRATEGY IN AN ORGANISATION

2.1 Any level of the organisation can have objectives and devise strategies to achieve them. The strategic management process is multi-layered.

2.2 *Hofer and Schendel* refer to three levels of strategy: corporate, business and functional/operational. The distinction between corporate and business strategy arises because of the development of the **divisionalised** business organisation, which typically has a corporate centre and a number of strategic business units (SBUs). *Chandler* described how four large US corporations found that the best way to divide strategic responsibility was to have the corporate HQ allocate resources and exercise overall financial control while the SBUs were each responsible for their own product-market strategies. Functional operational strategies are then developed for component parts of SBUs.

Corporate strategies

> **KEY TERM**
>
> **Corporate strategy** is concerned with what types of business the organisation is in. It 'denotes the most general level of strategy in an organisation' (Johnson and Scholes).

Levels of strategy

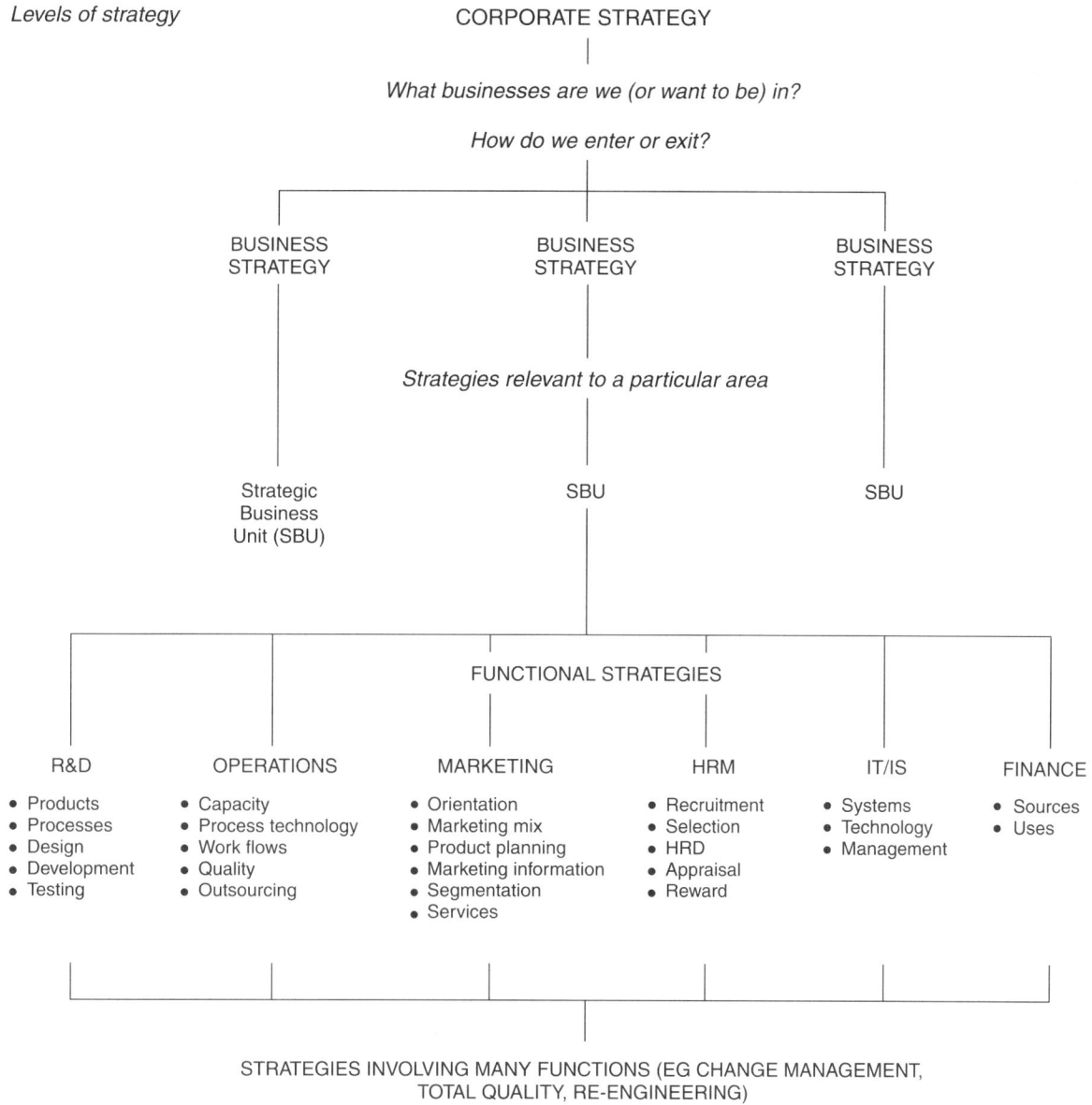

CORPORATE STRATEGY

What businesses are we (or want to be) in?

How do we enter or exit?

BUSINESS STRATEGY	BUSINESS STRATEGY	BUSINESS STRATEGY

Strategies relevant to a particular area

Strategic Business Unit (SBU)	SBU	SBU

FUNCTIONAL STRATEGIES

R&D	OPERATIONS	MARKETING	HRM	IT/IS	FINANCE
• Products • Processes • Design • Development • Testing	• Capacity • Process technology • Work flows • Quality • Outsourcing	• Orientation • Marketing mix • Product planning • Marketing information • Segmentation • Services	• Recruitment • Selection • HRD • Appraisal • Reward	• Systems • Technology • Management	• Sources • Uses

STRATEGIES INVOLVING MANY FUNCTIONS (EG CHANGE MANAGEMENT, TOTAL QUALITY, RE-ENGINEERING)

2.3 Defining aspects of corporate strategy

Characteristic	Comment
Scope of activities	Strategy and strategic management impact upon the whole organisation: all parts of the business operation should support and further the strategic plan.
Environment	The organisation counters threats and exploits opportunities in the environment (customers, clients, competitors).
Resources	Strategy involves choices about allocating or obtaining corporate resources now and in future.
Values	The value systems of people with power in the organisation influence its strategy.
Timescale	Corporate strategy has a long-term impact.
Complexity	Corporate strategy involves uncertainty about the future, integrating the operations of the organisation and change.

Business strategy

KEY TERM

Business strategy: how an organisation approaches a particular product market area.

2.4 Business strategy can involve decisions such as whether to segment the market and specialise in particularly profitable areas, or to compete by offering a wider range of products.

Case example

Mercedes-Benz wished to expand its product range to include four wheel drive vehicles and smaller cars, culminating in the merger with Chrysler.

2.5 Some large, diversified firms have separate **strategic business units** (SBUs) dealing with particular areas. Business strategy for such large organisations is strategy at the SBU level.

Functional/operational strategies

2.6 Functional/operational strategies deal with specialised areas of activity.

Functional area	Comment
Marketing	Devising products and services, pricing, promoting and distributing them, in order to satisfy customer needs at a profit. Marketing and corporate strategies are interrelated.
Production	Factory location, manufacturing techniques, outsourcing and so on
Finance	Ensuring that the firm has enough financial resources to fund its other strategies by identifying sources of finance and using them effectively
Human resources management	Secure personnel of the right skills in the right quantity at the right time, and to ensure that they have the right skills and values to promote the firm's overall goals
Information systems	A firm's information systems are becoming increasingly important, as an item of expenditure, as administrative support and as a tool for competitive strength. Not all information technology applications are strategic, and the strategic value of IT will vary from case to case.
R&D	New products and techniques

Question 1

Ganymede Ltd is a company selling widgets. The finance director says: 'We plan to issue more shares to raise money for new plant capacity - we don't want loan finance - which will enable us to compete better in the vital and growing widget markets of Latin America. After all, we've promised the shareholders 5% profit growth this year, and trading is tough.'

Identify the **corporate**, **business** and **functional** strategies in the above statement.

Answer

The corporate objective is profit growth. The corporate strategy is the decision that this will be achieved by entering new markets, rather than producing new products. The business strategy suggests that those markets include Latin America. The operational or functional strategy involves the decision to invest in new plant (the production function) which is to be financed by shares rather than loans (the finance function).

2.7 Section summary

- Corporate strategies are for the organisation as a whole.
- Business, operational and functional strategies flow from the corporate strategy.

3 THE ROLES OF MARKETING 12/03

3.1 This Study Text is largely about corporate strategy. As we mentioned earlier, the terminology used is sometimes rather imprecise. An important area of potential confusion arises in the relationship between 'strategic management' and 'marketing'. A number of ideas and models are shared between the two activities (to the extent that they are, in fact, separate activities), and many marketing authors write as though 'marketing' encompasses all of 'strategic management'. In this text we will reject this view: for our purposes, 'marketing' is an important area of business activity that makes a particular contribution to strategic management, but is ultimately subordinate to it.

3.2 What then is marketing?

Marketing is the management process responsible for identifying, anticipating and satisfying customer requirements profitably. *(Chartered Institute of Marketing)*

While useful in its way, the CIM definition is not the only one we might consider; in fact there are many. Here is what *Dibb, Simkin, Pride and Ferrel* have to say:

Marketing consists of individual and organisational activities that facilitate and expedite satisfying exchange relationships in a dynamic environment through the creation, distribution, promotion and pricing of goods, services and ideas.

This is a more detailed definition and has the advantage of being very specific about the activities it includes under the umbrella term 'marketing'.

3.3 There is one important problem with both of these approaches to marketing and that is their tendency towards **over-inclusiveness**. We see this most clearly when we think about the activity we know as **production**. Taking the CIM definition first, if we ask 'Does the production function have anything to do with satisfying customer requirements profitably?' we must, if we are fair, answer 'Yes, it does.' If production is to the wrong standard, or at too great a cost, or late, customer satisfaction will be reduced. A very similar question could be asked about the phrase 'creation ... of goods...' in the definition of Dibb *et al*, and it would have to be answered in the same way. Now, it is clear that it would be going too far to suggest that production is a core marketing activity and should be controlled by the Marketing Director.

3.4 While it is not so obvious in the case of functions such as finance and human resource management, the same argument applies to them, if to a lesser extent. We are driven to the conclusion that neither definition we have looked at is much good at explaining the relationship between marketing as an activity and the other activities to be found in any given organisation.

3.5   The related term 'marketing concept' is worth looking at if we wish to understand more deeply. *Philip Kotler*, one of the best known of writers on marketing subjects says this:

> The marketing concept holds that the key to achieving organisational goals lies in determining the needs and wants of target markets and delivering the desired satisfactions more efficiently and effectively than the competition.

3.6   In Kotler's statement we see a clue to resolving the problem we have identified. It is necessary for us to strike a clear distinction between marketing as an **activity** and marketing as a **concept** of how an organisation should go about its business.

Models of marketing

3.7   The material in paragraphs 3.8 to 3.9 is taken from the introduction to the syllabus for Stage 2 of the CIM qualification. It therefore represents an authoritative view of just what marketing is.

3.8   The type, or model, of marketing practised in any organisation depends on a number of factors, not least of which are the activities to be performed according to the nature of the business and the organisation's dominant orientation. Marketing activities in organisations can be grouped broadly into four roles.

(a)   **Sales support**: the emphasis in this role is essentially reactive: marketing supports the direct sales force. It may include activities such as telesales or telemarketing, responding to inquiries, co-ordinating diaries, customer database management, organising exhibitions or other sales promotions, and administering agents. These activities usually come under a sales and marketing director or manager.

(b)   **Marketing communications**: the emphasis in this role is more proactive: marketing promotes the organisation and its product or service at a tactical level. It typically includes activities such as providing brochures and catalogues to support the sales force.

(c)   **Operational marketing**: the emphasis in this role is for marketing to support the organisation with a co-ordinated range of marketing activities including marketing research; brand management; product development and management; corporate and marketing communications; and customer relationship management. Given this breadth of activities, planning is also a function usually performed in this role but at an operational or functional level.

(d)   **Strategic marketing**: the emphasis in this role is for marketing to contribute to the creation of competitive strategy. As such, it is practised in customer-focused and larger organisations. In a large or diversified organisation, it may also be responsible for the coordination of marketing departments or activities in separate business units.

3.9   **Operational marketing activities**.

- Research and analysis
- Contributing to strategy and marketing planning
- Managing brands
- Implementing marketing programmes
- Measuring effectiveness
- Managing marketing teams

The operational marketing role, where it exists, will be performed by a marketing function in a business.

3.10 So, what is the relationship between marketing and strategic management? The two are closely linked since there can be no corporate plan which does not involve products/services and customers.

3.11 **Corporate strategic plans** aim to guide the overall development of an organisation. Marketing planning is subordinate to corporate planning but makes a significant contribution to it and is concerned with many of the same issues. The marketing department is probably the most important source of information for the development of corporate strategy. The corporate audit of product/market strengths and weaknesses, and much of its external environmental analysis is directly informed by the **marketing audit**.

3.12 Specific marketing strategies will be determined within the overall corporate strategy. To be effective, these plans will be interdependent with those for other functions of the organisation.

(a) The **strategic** component of marketing planning focuses on the direction which an organisation will take in relation to a specific market, or set of markets, in order to achieve a specified set of objectives.

(b) Marketing planning also requires an **operational** component that defines tasks and activities to be undertaken in order to achieve the desired strategy. The **marketing plan** is concerned uniquely with **products** and **markets**.

3.13 Marketing management aims to ensure the company is pursuing effective policies to promote its products, markets and distribution channels. This involves exercising strategic control of marketing, and the means to apply strategic control is known as the **marketing audit**. Not only is the marketing audit an important aspect of **marketing control**, it can be used to provide much information and analysis for the **corporate planning process**.

4 MAKING STRATEGIES: THE RATIONAL MODEL

4.1 In this and the next chapter, we discuss different approaches to making strategies.

4.2 First we outline the **rational model** which forms the structure for the rest of the text. Here is a case example as to how it applies in practice.

Case example

Goold and Quinn (in *Strategic Control*) cite Ciba-Geigy, a Swiss-based global firm with chemicals and pharmaceuticals businesses, as an example of formal strategic control and planning processes.

(a) Strategic planning starts with the identification of strategic business sectors, in other words, areas of activity where there are identifiable markets and where profit, management and resources are largely independent of the other sectors.

(b) Strategic plans are drawn up, based on a 'comprehensive analysis of market attractiveness', competitors and so on. There are three important aspects to these plans.

- Long term objectives
- Key strategies
- Funds requirements

(c) At corporate level, these plans are reviewed. Head office examines all the different plans, and, with a 7-10 year planning horizon, the total risk, profitability, cash flow and resource requirements are assessed. Business sectors are allocated specific targets and funds.

> ## KEY TERM
>
> **Planning:** 'the establishment of objectives and the formulation, evaluation and selection of the policies, strategies, tactics and action required to achieve these objectives. Planning comprises long-term/strategic planning, and short-term operations planning.'

4.3 Characteristics of strategic plans

- Documented (written down)

- The result of a formal, systematised process with a start and end point

- Determined or endorsed by senior managers, with little direct involvement from operational managers, although they may be consulted

Strategic planning model

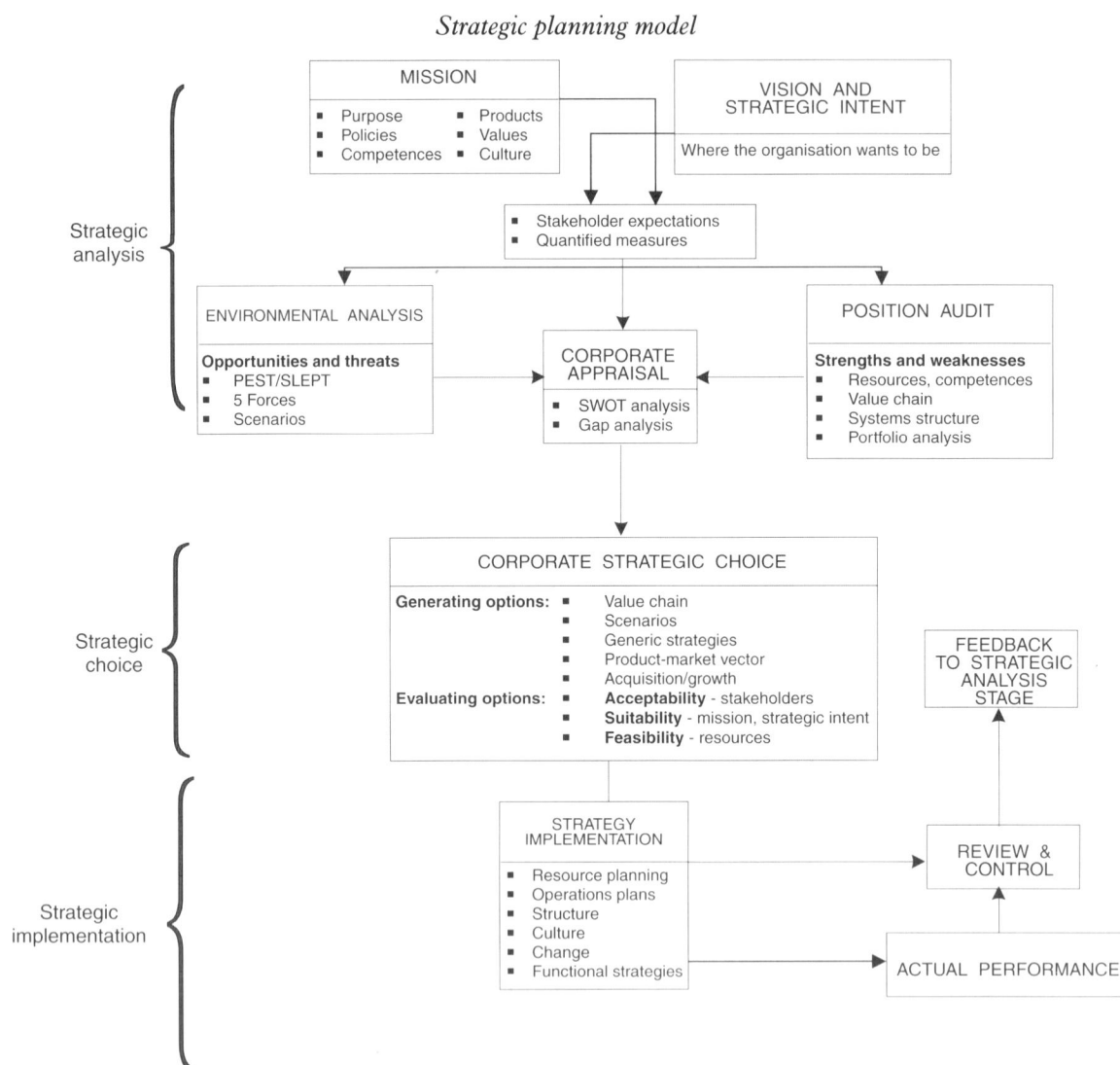

4.4 The diagram above outlines the process of strategic planning. At each stage, the process involves the use of various techniques, tools and **models** to make sense of the situation. You will be expected to show familiarity with these models in your answers to exam questions.

4.5 The rational model of strategic planning moves from the theoretical to the practical; from thinking about what the organisation exists for to doing something concrete about it. It is also an iterative process: it is **not** done once and for all. In large organisations there may be a planning department which produces a revised plan at regular intervals; work will continue on some or all of the processes at all times. It is a process of refinement, of **adaptation to the environment**.

4.6   We now summarise each of the three main parts of this continuing process.

4.7   **Strategic analysis**

	Stage	Comment	Key tools, models, techniques
Step 1.	Mission and/or vision	Mission denotes values, the business's rationale for existing; vision refers to where the organisation intends to be in a few years time	• Mission statement
Step 2.	Goals	Interpret the mission to different stakeholders	• Stakeholder analysis
Step 3.	Objectives	Quantified embodiments of mission	• Measures such as profitability, time scale, deadlines
Step 4.	Environmental analysis	Identify opportunities and threats	• PEST analysis • Porter's 5 force analysis and competitive advantage of nations • Scenario building
Step 5.	Position audit or situation analysis	Identify strengths and weaknesses Firm's **current** resources, products, customers, systems, structure, results, efficiency, effectiveness	• Resource audit • Distinctive competence • Value chain • Product life cycle • Boston (BCG) matrix • General Electric business screen • Shell directional policy matrix • Marketing audit For IT: • Nolan's stage model • McFarlan's grid • Awareness frameworks
Step 6.	Corporate appraisal	Combines Steps 4 and 5	• SWOT analysis charts
Step 7.	Gap analysis	Compares outcomes of Step 6 with Step 3	• Gap analysis

4.8   **Strategic choice**

Stage	Comment	Key tools, models, techniques
Strategic options generation	Come up with new ideas • How to compete (competitive advantage) • Where to compete • Method of growth	• Value chain analysis • Scenario building • Porter's generic strategic choices • Ansoff's growth vector • Acquisition vs organic growth
Strategic options evaluation	Normally, each strategy has to be evaluated on the basis of • Acceptability • Suitability • Feasibility	• Stakeholder analysis • Risk analysis • Decision-making tools such as decision trees, matrices, ranking and scoring methods • Financial measures (eg ROCE, DCF) For IT: Opportunity Frameworks

4.9   **Implementation and functional strategies**

Stage	Comment	Key tools, models, techniques
Resource planning	Deploying the resources to achieve the strategy	• Critical success factors • Outsourcing
Operations plans		• Activity schedules • Budgets • Project management • For IT, systems development methodologies
Organisation structure and culture	Designing the organisation to implement the strategy	• Mintzberg's five element model • Departmentation
Change	Implement changes	• Force field analysis • Unfreeze-change-refreeze • Negotiation
Functional strategies	HRM	• Personnel planning • Motivation (eg Maslow) • Appraisal schemes
	Production	• TQM
	Marketing	• Marketing information systems • Marketing mix • Segmentation • Product life cycle (again)

4.10 **Control**

Stage	Comment	Key tools, models, techniques
Control	Review performance and amend	• Critical success factors
		• Balanced scorecard
	Performance indicators	• Marketing information system
		• Budgets

4.11 Don't worry – all these will be described in the appropriate chapter in the text. You can use these tables as checklists. Many of the models can be used in all phases of the strategic management process.

4.12 **Contents of a strategic plan**

Context

- Results of environmental appraisal
- Results of position audit

Long-term plan

- Mission statement
- Long-term objectives (eg market share, volume sales, position in industry)
- Critical success factors

The year ahead

- Annual goals
- Major strategic projects (eg new organisation structure, IT systems etc)

Implementation

- Schedules
- Budgets
- Performance measures

4.13 **Section summary**

- According to the rational model, strategic management is a process of analysis, choice, implementation and control.

- Strategic plans are documents indicating what is to be done in the year ahead and further into the future.

5 **FOR THE RATIONAL MODEL**

5.1 **Assumptions of the rational model**

(a) **Top down**. Senior managers, or planning departments, 'think great thoughts'. The results of their deliberations are documented in a plan, and are refined into greater and greater detail.

(b) **Corporate first**. Strategies for the organisation as a whole are developed prior to strategies for individual business units or functions.

(c) **Breakdown**. Strategic planning can be broken down into its subcomponents, in the same way as manual work can be.

(d) **Objective evaluation**. Strategies are evaluated objectively on their merits, unclouded by bias.

Ansoff

5.2 *Ansoff* supports the theory of strategic planning.

(a) Businesses **pursue objectives**, which are orientated to the future (in terms of future results).

(b) **Partial ignorance**. In principle, the future is uncertain and the variables cannot be known, so conventional investment appraisal techniques (DCF) are of little use.

(c) Strategy provides consistency in what the organisation does, a **common thread**.

(i) Similar products (eg motor cars)

(ii) Similar customers (eg gas companies now sell electricity to customers, combining both sources of power on one bill)

(iii) A conglomerate might operate in many markets, but might concentrate on product made with simple technology

(iv) Same **customer needs**. An oil company might describe itself as being in the 'energy' business and hence might invest in wind-power, solar power or, more conventionally, natural gas.

Drucker

5.3 *Peter Drucker* takes a similar position.

(a) 'The continuous process of making **taking risky decisions systematically** and with **greatest knowledge** of their future effect'.

(i) This covers what the organisation **intends to do** in the environment, how it is to respond to opportunities or threats, what new things need to be done and when.

(ii) Because they are made in conditions of partial ignorance, strategies involve risk. Strategic planning cannot avoid risk, but it can **avoid unnecessary risk**.

(iii) **Decisions taken now have implications for the future.**

(b) **Organising systematically the efforts** needed to carry out these decisions, ie ensuring that everything 'degenerates into work'. The aim of strategic planning is action **now**, and its realisation in **processes, behaviour, or organisation structure** and **resource allocation**.

(c) '**Measuring the results** of these decisions ... through organised, systematic feedback'.

5.4 The emphasis on doing things in a **systematic way** naturally leads to the importance of planning, deciding what things to do, the order in which they are done, and when they should be done.

5.5 Formal strategic planning can take several months, and might even be the responsibility of a **separate department**.

Case example

Oil firms typically have long lead times between deciding to invest in a new field and bringing the investment on stream so that it can earn money.

Therefore, they must think 20 years ahead, in order to maintain supplies in future and keep in business at present.

Some oil firms are investing in renewable energy sources such as solar power, because they assume that pressure to reduce CO_2 emissions (for which petrol usage is responsible) will hit demand.

5.6 Advantages of a formal system of strategic planning

Advantages	Comment
Identifies risks	Strategic planning helps in managing these risks.
Forces managers to think	Strategic planning can encourage creativity and initiative by tapping the ideas of the management team.
Forces decision-making	Companies cannot remain static - they have to cope with changes in the environment. A strategic plan draws attention to the need to change and adapt, not just to 'stand still' and survive.
Better control	Management control can be better exercised if targets are explicit.
Enforces consistency at all levels	Long-term, medium-term and short-term objectives, plans and controls can be made consistent with one another. Otherwise, strategies can be rendered ineffective by budgeting systems and performance measures which have no strategic content.
Public knowledge	Drucker has argued that an entrepreneur who builds a long-lasting business has 'a theory of the business' which informs his or her business decisions. In large organisations, that the theory of the business has to become public knowledge, as decisions cannot be taken only by one person.
Time horizon	Some plans are needed for the long term.
Co-ordinates	Activities of different business functions need to be directed towards a common goal.
Clarifies objectives	Managers are forced to define what they want to achieve.
Allocates responsibility	A plan shows people where they fit in.

Case example

The UK defence industry faces lower government spending and greater competition as contracts are put out to open tender. There is greater competition in export markets. Having failed to diversify into civil areas, companies are changing the way they work.

Planning

A number of assumptions can be made about the environment and customer demands.

(a)   Military needs are for mobile and flexible forces.

(b)   For economic reasons, reliability and maintainability are desired.

(c)   There should be military applications of civilian technology.

(d)   The Ministry of Defence has also tightened up on procurement, replacing cost-plus contracts with competitive tenders.

Defence firms are undertaking strategic management. All firms are concerned with cash flow and productivity. Strategic planning departments have been set up to provide necessary inputs and analyses. The planners emphasise the threat from arms manufacturers in Russia, Germany and Japan. Analysts have identified that improvements in productivity and quality, to ensure the systems work, are of key importance.

Description or prescription?

5.7 Much of the literature on strategy falls into one of two types.

- **Description**, saying what businesses **actually do**
- **Prescription**, which tells businesses what they **ought to do**.

5.8 Planning appears like common sense; when it fails in practice, it is assumed that this is because people did not follow the rational model well enough. But there are more powerful criticisms, which we outline in the next section.

5.9 Section summary

- The rational model forces people to think in a systematic way, in conditions of partial ignorance.

- It ensures consistency and control by publicly outlining what the business should do, and by ensuring departmental resources are marshalled to the corporate plan.

6 AGAINST THE RATIONAL MODEL

6.1 Criticisms of the rational model concern how it has worked in **practice,** and more fundamental problems of **theory.** *Mintzberg* is prominent among the critics.

6.2 Criticisms of strategic planning in practice

Problem	Comments
Practical failure	Empirical studies have not proved that **formal planning** processes ('the delineation of steps, the application of checklists and techniques') contribute to success.
Routine and regular	Strategic planning occurs often in an **annual cycle**. But a firm 'cannot allow itself to wait every year for the month of February to address its problems.'
Reduces initiative	Formal planning discourages **strategic thinking**. Once a plan is locked in place, people are unwilling to question it. Obsession with particular performance indicators mean that managers focus on fulfilling the plan rather than concentrating on developments in the environment.
Internal politics	The assumption of **objectivity** in evaluation ignores political battles between different managers and departments.
Exaggerates power	**Managers are not all-knowing**, and there are **limits** to the extent to which they can control the behaviour of the organisation.

6.3 **Criticism of the rational model in theory** (Mintzberg, John Kay)

Criticism	Comment
Formalisation	'We have no evidence that any of the strategic planning systems - no matter how elaborate - succeeded in capturing (let alone improving on) the messy informal processes by which strategies really do get developed.'
Detachment: divorcing planning from operations	This implies that managers do not really need day to day knowledge of the product or market. But strategic thinking is necessary to detect the strategic messages **within** the nitty gritty of operations (eg like finding gold dust in a stream).
Formulation precedes implementation	A strategy is planned - then it is implemented. But **defining** strengths and weaknesses is actually very difficult in advance of **testing** them. 'The detached assessment of strengths and weaknesses may be unreliable, all bound up with aspirations, wishes and hopes'. Discovering strengths and weaknesses is a **learning process**. Implementing a strategy is necessary for learning - to see if it works.
Predetermination	Planning assumes that the environment can be forecast, and that its future behaviours can be controlled, by a strategy planned in advanced and delivered on schedule. In conditions of stability, forecasting and extrapolation make sense. But forecasting cannot cope with discontinuities (eg the change from mainframe computing to PCs).
The military analogy (John Kay)	An army's objective is to beat the enemy; the strategy describes how. This analogy is easy to grasp, but it may not be particularly relevant to **business** organisations. Their objectives are more complex and perhaps more ill-defined than an army's. They compete with other organisations for customers. They are less able to **command** resources than an army. Their employees want the organisation (and their jobs in it) to remain in permanent existence.

Where do we go from here?

6.4 Mintzberg's critique has not been fully accepted. Although the idea that planning is the **only** means by which strategies can be **made** is flawed, planning does have many uses. These are supporting roles; they cannot fully account for the making of strategy itself.

- It can force people to **think**.
- It can **publicise** strategic decisions.
- It can help **direct** activities in some cases.
- It can **focus debate**.

6.5 Section summary

- The rational model has not conspicuously succeeded in practice.
- There are theoretical problems with formalisation, detachment and predetermination.

Chapter roundup

- **Strategy** is a course of action, specifying the resources required, to achieve an objective. There are many levels of strategy in an organisation.

  ° **Corporate**: the general direction of the whole organisation
  ° **Business**: how the organisation or its SBUs tackle particular markets
  ° **Operational/functional**: specific strategies for different departments of the business

- According to the rational model, strategy is about the achievement of goals and objectives.

  ° **Mission, goals and objectives**. An organisation's mission answers the question 'what business are we in?' Goals and objectives determine what the business should achieve if it is to satisfy its mission.

  ° **Analysis of the environment** of the organisation and its internal position

  ° **Generation of alternative options** to satisfy objectives

  ° **Choice of preferred option**, based on rational and objective criteria of evaluation

- The rational model implies that strategies are best generated from the **top down**. It provides a **common thread** and enables decisions to be taken in conditions of **partial ignorance** (Ansoff), where **risk** (Drucker) is inevitable.

- The rational model might work in **stable environments.** There are practical and theoretical problems in asserting that a planning process is the only or best way of generating strategy. Criticisms include: its failure in practice; over reliance on **formalisation, detachment** and **predetermination**; the implication that firms can know what their strengths are **before testing** them.

Quick quiz

1 What is strategic management?

2 State two defining aspects of corporate strategy.

3 Distinguish between corporate and business strategy.

4 What are the stages in the rational model of strategic planning?

5 What aspects of strategy are outlined in the strategy generation process?

6 What are the bases of strategic choice?

7 Why do Ansoff and Drucker support the rational model?

8 What might be the *real* use of planning in strategic management?

Answers to quick quiz

1 Development, implementation and control of strategy

2 Scope is organisation wide; it relates to the corporate environment; it deals with corporate resources; it reflects prevailing corporate value systems; it has a long term impact; it deals with the most complex corporate problems.

3 Corporate strategy relates to the highest level of decision making. Business strategy concerns SBUs and their product-market areas

4 Strategic analysis; strategic choice; strategic implementation

5 How to compete; where to compete; method of growth

6 Acceptability; suitability; feasibility

7 Both believe in doing things in a systematic way

8 Forces people to think; publicises strategic decisions; helps direct activities; focuses debate

Now try the question below from the Exam Question Bank

Number	Level	Marks	Time
Q1	Introductory	20	36 mins

Chapter 2

OTHER MODELS OF STRATEGIC MANAGEMENT

Topic list	Syllabus reference
1 The need for new models	1(d)
2 Patterns and competences	1(d)
3 Emergent strategies and how to craft them	1(d)
4 Strategy and managerial intent	1(d)
5 Incrementalism	1(d)
6 Strategic thinking	1(d)
7 Environmental fit	1(d)
8 Competition	1(d)
9 Learning based strategy	1(d)
10 An overview?	1(d)

Introduction

This chapter contains some alternative approaches to the rational model. The **incrementalist model** suggests that small scale adjustments are preferred to wholesale reviews. Both the incrementalists and *Johnson and Scholes* recognise the political and **behavioural context.** *Mintzberg's* **emergent strategies** model suggests that some strategies develop by accident, and strategic management involves shaping or **crafting** these developments. *Ohmae* and *Porter* describe strategy in **competitive** terms - but unlike Porter, Ohmae assumes that **strategic thinking** is a matter of intuition rather than rational analysis. The final section of this chapter describes the many uses of the concept of strategy, as an 'integrative concept'.

Study guide

Section 1 – Models of strategic management

- Process of strategy development

Exam guide

This is another chapter full of fundamental ideas.

1   THE NEED FOR NEW MODELS

1.1   The case example below puts into a radically different perspective the issues raised in the previous chapter. It will show one reason why the common sense rational model is not the final word in corporate strategy.

Case example

Honda

Honda is now one of the leading manufacturers of motorbikes. The company is credited with identifying and targeting an untapped market for small 50cc bikes in the US, which enabled it to expand, trounce European competition and severely damage indigenous US bike manufacturers. By 1965, Honda had 63% of the US market. But this occurred by accident.

On entering the US market, Honda's **planned strategy** was to compete with the larger European and US bikes of 250ccs and over. These bikes had a defined market, and were sold through dedicated motorbike dealerships. Disaster struck when Honda's larger machines developed faults - they had not been designed for the hard wear and tear imposed by US motorcyclists. Honda had to recall the larger machines.

Honda had made little effort to sell its small 50 cc motorbikes - its staff rode them on errands around Los Angeles. Sports goods shops and ordinary bicycle and department stores had expressed an interest, but Honda did not want to confuse its image in its 'target' market of men who bought the larger bikes.

The faults in Honda's larger machines meant that reluctantly, Honda had no alternative to sell the small 50cc bikes just to raise money. They proved very popular with people who would never have bought motorbikes before. Eventually the company adopted this new market with enthusiasm with the slogan: 'You meet the nicest people on a Honda.'

The strategy had **emerged**, against managers' conscious intentions, but they eventually responded to the new situation.

2 PATTERNS AND COMPETENCES

2.1 There are other examples of radically different approaches to making business strategy. Here are three brief discussions to make you think.

Strategies as patterns of management decisions

2.2 *Andrews* does not separate **objectives** from the **strategies** designed to achieve them, as strategy arises out of the **general management process** whereby **senior** managers direct and control the business. This general management process generates **consistent** decisions. For example, a firm's managers may prefer certain types of market opportunities (eg low risk) than others.

2.3 For Andrews, **corporate strategy** is: 'the **pattern** of decisions in a company that determines and reveals its objectives, purposes, or goals, that produces the principal policies and plans for achieving those goals, and defines the range of business the company is to pursue, the kind of economic and human organisation it is or intends to be, and the nature of the economic and non economic contribution it intends to make to its shareholders, employees, customers and communities'.

Case example

Philips

'Philips, Europe's largest consumer electronics group, is to limit the extent to which it stakes its future on product breakthroughs - aiming for predictability in growth rather than seeking rewards in expensive and risky innovations.

The company - in earlier years inventor both of the compact disk and the failed V2000 video system - came close to bankruptcy in 1991 but recovered to achieve record net profits of Fl 2.52bn ($1.33bn) four years later before sliding back into a Fl 590m loss last year.

Mr Boonstra, new president for the company adds, 'Again and again we have proved vulnerable to market fluctuations, to the trade cycle, to success or lack of success with a particular product. 'We then put all our faith in a new invention, a new product, as if it is some magic wand that will solve all our problems with the market, the competition and price erosion. And if it fails to live up to its promise, we suffer setbacks. We are now seeking to break out of this cycle of all-or-nothing offensives. Under Mr Boonstra's cuts a number of projects from the Timmer era have been abandoned.'

(Financial Times, 25 March 1997)

In other words, Mr Boonstra is recognising that the **pattern of decision making** the firm had employed was no longer relevant or useful.

Strategy as the exploitation of competences

2.4 Strategic opportunities must be related to the firm's resources. A strategic approach involves identifying a firm's **competences**. The **distinctive competence** of an organisation is what it does well, uniquely, or better than rivals. Andrews says that, for a relatively undifferentiated product like cement, the ability of a maker to 'run a truck fleet more effectively' than its competitors will give it competitive strengths (if, for example, it can satisfy orders quickly). These competences may come about in a variety of ways.

- **Experience** in making and marketing a product or service
- The talents and potential of **individuals** in the organisation
- The **quality of co-ordination**

This is similar to the idea of **resource-based strategy**. This theory suggests that strategies are most likely to succeed if they are based on the possession of a unique, valuable resource. A simple example would be a source of a raw material or a proprietary technology. If you think in these terms it is not difficult to regard a **competence** as a valuable resource to be exploited.

Freewheeling opportunism

2.5 **Freewheeling opportunism** is a pattern of strategy that displays little apparent coherence or forethought. It is common among highly entrepreneurial individuals who are prepared to seize opportunities and back hunches. It can be present in larger, highly innovatory businesses, but is a high risk approach, depending for it's success on a combination of experience, talent and market awareness.

3 EMERGENT STRATEGIES AND HOW TO CRAFT THEM 12/01

3.1 In the Honda case example at the beginning of this chapter, we mentioned that the planned strategy of selling large bikes had to give way to a strategy which had emerged by accident, almost. *Mintzberg* develops this theme further.

3.2 **Emergent strategies** do not arise out of conscious strategic planning, but from a number of *ad hoc* choices, perhaps made lower down the hierarchy. They may not initially be recognised as being of strategic importance. Emergent strategies develop out of **patterns of behaviour,** in contrast to planned strategies or senior management decisions which are imposed from above. An exercise will make the point clearer.

Question 1

Aldebaran Ltd is a public relations agency founded by an entrepreneur, Estella Grande, who has employed various talented individuals from other agencies to set up in business. Estella Grande wants Aldebaran Ltd to become the largest public relations agency in North London. Management consultants, in a planning document, have suggested growth by acquisition. In other words, Aldebaran should buy up the other public relations agencies in the area. These would be retained as semi-independent business units, as the Aldebaran Ltd group could benefit from the goodwill of the newly acquired agencies. When Estella presents these ideas to the Board there is general consensus with one significant exception. Livia Strange, the marketing director, is horrified. 'How am I going to sell this to my staff? Ever since we've been in business, we've won business by undercutting and slagging off the competition. My team have a whole culture based on it. I give them champagne if they pinch a high value client. Why acquire these new businesses - why not stick to pinching their clients instead?'

What is the source of the conflict?

Answer

Livia Strange's department has generated its own pattern of competitive behaviour. It is an emergent strategy. It conflicts directly with the planned strategy proposed by the consultants. This little case history also makes the additional point that strategies are not only about numbers, targets and grand plans, but about the organisational cultures influencing a person's behaviour.

Deliberate and emergent strategies

3.3 The diagram below should help explain the point.

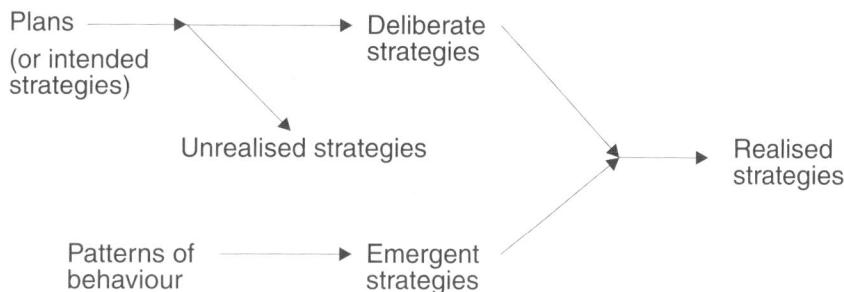

(a) **Intended strategies** are plans. Those plans or aspects of plans which are actually realised are called **deliberate strategies**.

(b) **Emergent strategies** are those which develop out of patterns of behaviour.

3.4 The task of **strategic management** is to control and shape these emergent strategies as they develop.

Case example

BPP began life as a training company. Lecturers had to prepare course material. This was offered for sale in a bookshop in the BPP building. Owing to the demand, BPP began offering its material to other colleges, in the UK and world-wide. BPP Publishing, which began as a small offshoot of BPP's training activities, is now a leading publisher in the market for targeted study material for the examinations of several professional bodies. It is unlikely that this development was anticipated when the course material was first prepared.

3.5 No realised strategy will be *wholly* deliberate or *wholly* emergent. The line between deliberate and emergent elements within each strategy will be in part influenced by organisation structure and culture.

Implicit or explicit strategies

3.6　We already mentioned the fact that entrepreneurs have a theory of the business which they may or may not document.

- Implicit strategies may exist only in the chief executive's head.
- Explicit strategies are properly documented.

Some plans are more explicit than others.

3.7　With these in mind, Mintzberg identified eight styles of strategic management.

Style	Comment
Planned strategies	• Precise intentions • Explicit intentions (ie written down, documented) • Imposed by central leadership • Large number of controls • Maximises predictability
Entrepreneurial strategies	• Intended strategy derives from the vision of strong leadership • Not always explicit
Ideological strategies	• Intended strategy is the collective vision of the organisation's members • Control is through shared values • These strategies involve changing the environment
Umbrella strategies	• Strategic targets ('ends') are defined and deliberate • How they are achieved ('means') is emergent
Process strategies	• Processes are formal (eg hiring) and deliberate • Content of strategies (what is done) is emergent
Disconnected strategies	• Members of subunits 'do their own thing' • Strategies are emergent for the whole organisation, deliberate for subunits
Consensus strategies	• Groups in the organisation converge on common patterns of activity
Imposed strategies	• Strategy is imposed by the environment (eg a strong customer) - which pre-empts the organisation's own choice

Crafting emergent strategies

3.8　Managers cannot simply let emerging strategies take over. Why?

- **Direction.** The emergent strategy may be **inappropriate** for the long-term direction of the organisation and may have to be corrected.

- **Resources.** It may have future implications for **resource use** elsewhere: in most organisations, different parts of the business compete for resources.

- Managers might wish to build on the strategy by **actively devoting more resources** to it.

3.9　Mintzberg uses the metaphor of **crafting strategy** to help understand the idea. Strategies are shaped as they develop, with managers giving help and guidance, devoting more resources to some, exploiting new opportunities and **responding** to developments. For example,

Honda's management reacted to the emergent strategy, eventually, and shaped its development.

3.10 Separating 'thinking' and 'doing' has the following result.

(a) A **purely deliberate strategy hampers rapid learning from experience** (once the formulators have stopped formulating). For example it is hard with deliberate strategies stumble by accident into strategic growth.

(b) A **purely emergent strategy defies control.** It may in fact be a bad strategy, dysfunctional for the organisation's future health.

3.11 Deliberate strategies introduce strategic change as a sort of quantum leap in some organisations. In this case, a firm undergoes only a few strategic changes in a short period but these are very dramatic.

Case example

In other organisations, however, strategic change can be **haphazard**. Mintzberg mentions the example of the Canadian National Film Board. This used to make short documentaries but ended up by chance with a feature film. This forced it to learn the marketing of such films, and so it eventually became much more involved in feature length productions than before - strategy by accident.

3.12 The strategist must be able to **recognise** patterns and to manage the process by which emergent strategies are created. In other words, the strategist must be able to **find strategies** as well as **invent them**.

How to craft strategy

3.13 Mintzberg lists these activities in crafting strategy.

Activity	Comment
Manage stability	• Most of the time, managers should be implementing the strategies, not planning them.
	• Obsessions with change are dysfunctional. Knowing *when* to change is more important.
	• Formal planning is the detailed working out of the agreed strategy.
Detect discontinuity	• Environments do not change regularly, nor are they always turbulent, though managers should be on the lookout for changes. *Some* small environmental changes are more significant for the long term than others, though guessing which these are is a problem.
Know the business	• An intimate feel for the business has to include an awareness and understanding of operations.
Manage patterns	• Detect emerging patterns and to help them take shape. Some emergent strategies must be uprooted, others nurtured.
Reconciling change and continuity	• 'Crafting strategy .... requires a natural synthesis of the future, present and past.' Obsessions with change and/or continuity can be counterproductive.

3.14 Section summary

- Strategy can emerge from patterns of behaviour, perhaps at operational level.

- Managers have to craft emergent strategies, accepting some and giving them resources, and rejecting others.

- An organisation's realised strategy will be a mix of emergent and intended strategies.

Question 2

Britannia Hospital has just appointed a new director, Florian Vole, imported from the private sector, where he had run 'Hanky House' a niche retail operation specialising in handkerchiefs and fashion accessories. The recession put the business into receivership, but Mr Vole was sought out to inject his private sector expertise in running a public sector institution. He calls a meeting of the hospitals senior managerial, medical and nursing staffs. 'What the public sector has been missing too long is vision, and when you're eyeball-to-eyeball with change, it's vision that you need, not planning documents and statistics. We need to be nimble and quick to adapt to our customer's ever changing needs. That is our strategy!'

What do think of Florian Vole's approach?

Answer

Mr Vole hasn't quite made the transition from the fashion industry, where desire for silk handkerchiefs is relatively fickle, to an institution like Britannia Hospital. Here planning is necessary. Resources must be obtained to cope with future needs. Customer needs are likely to be fairly basic (ie security, comfort, medical attention, stimulation). However, in the actual delivery of care and services, Florian Vole has a point: experimentation with new care techniques might improve the hospital's service to its patients.

4 STRATEGY AND MANAGERIAL INTENT

4.1   *Johnson and Scholes* discuss two other ways in which strategy can arise through deliberate management intent rather than simply emerging.

The command view

4.2   'Here strategy develops through the direction of an individual or group, but not necessarily through formal planning.' In this model there is a person or group with acknowledged strategic power and responsibility. The mechanisms by which this authority arises are reminiscent of *Weber's* analysis of **legitimate authority** into **legal-rational, charismatic** and **traditional.** Johnson and Scholes mention the autocratic leader; the charismatic leader whose reputation or personality gives control of strategic direction; and the making of economic and social strategy in the public sector by elected politicians.

Paradigm and politics.

4.3   (a)   The word **paradigm** may be used to signify the basic assumptions and beliefs that an organisation's decision-makers hold in common. Note that this is a slightly different concept from **culture**. The paradigm represents **collective experience** and is used to make sense of a given situation; it is thus essentially conservative and inhibiting to innovation, while an innovative **culture** is entirely feasible.

(b)   The **politics** of the organisation may also influence strategy.

'The political view of strategy development is that strategies develop as the outcome of processes of bargaining and negotiation among powerful internal or external interest groups (or stakeholders).'

4.4 Johnson and Scholes describe the processes by which paradigm and politics influence the process of strategy development.

Step 1. **Issue awareness**

- Internal results, customer responses or environmental changes can make **individuals** aware of a problem.
- A **trigger** alerts the **formal** information system to the problem, so that organisational activity takes over from the individual's consideration of the problem.

Step 2. **Issue formulation.** Managers try to analyse and get to the root of the problem. Information may be used to rationalise, rather than challenge, management's existing view of the situation. **Formal analysis** in practice plays a little role.

Step 3. **Solution development.** Some possible solutions are developed and one is selected.

- **Memory search**: solutions which worked in the past.
- **Passive search**: wait for a solution to suggest itself.

Solutions begin with a vague idea, which is further refined and explored by internal discussion.

Step 4. **Solution selection**

- **Eliminate unacceptable plans.** This screening process involves bargaining, diplomacy and judgement rather than formal evaluation according to the business case. ('Unacceptable' might mean unacceptable in terms of organisational politics, rather than in terms of business sense.)
- **Endorsements.** Many strategic decisions **originate from management subsystems**, which senior managers authorise. Junior managers might filter strategic information, or ignore certain options, to protect themselves.

Case example

Enron

Enron is now notorious for its unethical practices. However, its collapse is traceable to a failure of strategic control. In the early 1990s, Enron was extremely successful as a market maker in the supply of gas and electricity. Its strategy was 'asset light': it did not produce gas, or very much electricity, but it used its financial expertise and its control of gas pipe lines and electricity grids to make large profits from the integration of supply and demand.

Unfortunately, early success bred hubris and quite junior executives were allowed to make major investments in industries whose characteristics were totally different from the homogeneity of product and ease of distribution of gas and electricity. In each case, the strategies failed because they made large demands for capital and low utilisation of Enron's core trading competences.

4.5 Johnson and Scholes are less averse to planning than Mintzberg, but instead of assuming a rational objectivity, they anchor plans in the behaviour of the organisation and the people in it.

5   INCREMENTALISM

Bounded rationality

5.1   In practice, managers are limited by time, by the information they have and by their own skills, habits and reflexes.

- Strategic managers do **not** evaluate all the possible options open to them in a given situation, but choose from a small number of possibilities.

- Strategy making necessitates compromises with interested groups through political bargaining. This is called **partisan mutual adjustment**.

- The manager **does not optimise** (ie get the best possible solution).

- Instead **the manager satisfices.** The manager carries on searching until he or she finds an option which appears tolerably satisfactory, and adopts it, even though it may be less than perfect. This approach *Herbert Simon* characterised as **bounded rationality**.

Incrementalism

5.2   *Lindblom* described another approach. **Incrementalism** involves small scale extensions of past practices.

- It avoids major errors.

- It is more likely to be acceptable, because consultation, compromise and accommodation are built into the process.

5.3   **Disadvantages of incrementalism**

- Incrementalism does not work where radical new approaches are needed, and it has a built-in conservative bias. Forward planning does have a role.

- Even as a descriptive model of the public sector, it does not always fit. Some changes do not seem incremental, but involve dramatic shifts.

- Incrementalism ignores the influence of corporate culture, as it filters out unacceptable choices.

- It might only apply to a stable environment.

Question 3

Sir Humphrey Appleby pops in to see his boss, the Minister for Administrative Affairs. The Minister has a proposal. 'I've examined all the options, and I believe that strategy C is the best. My planners have done a great job, don't you agree?' 'Yes, Minister,' Sir Humphrey replies, 'But I'll have to run it past Horace in the Treasury, and of course, the Prime Minister's office - I hesitate to predict what the European Commissioner in Brussels will think ... do you want me to suggest to your planners that we try again'.

What models of strategic planning and management are discussed here?

Answer

The Minister is a planner: he's describing the rational model. Sir Humphrey is advocating the partisan mutual adjustment model. See Paragraph 5.1 for details.

A middle way? Logical incrementalism

> **KEY TERM**
>
> **Logical incrementalism:** managers have a vague notion as to where the organisation should go, but strategies should be tested in small steps, simply because there is too much uncertainty about actual outcomes.

5.4 Strategy is best described as a **learning process**. Logical incrementalism has the best of both worlds.

- The broad outlines of a strategy are developed by an in-depth review.
- There is still practical scope for day-to-day incremental decision making.

Contrasts

5.5 The implications of rationality and incrementalism can be expressed in diagrammatic form.

(a) *Rational planning model*

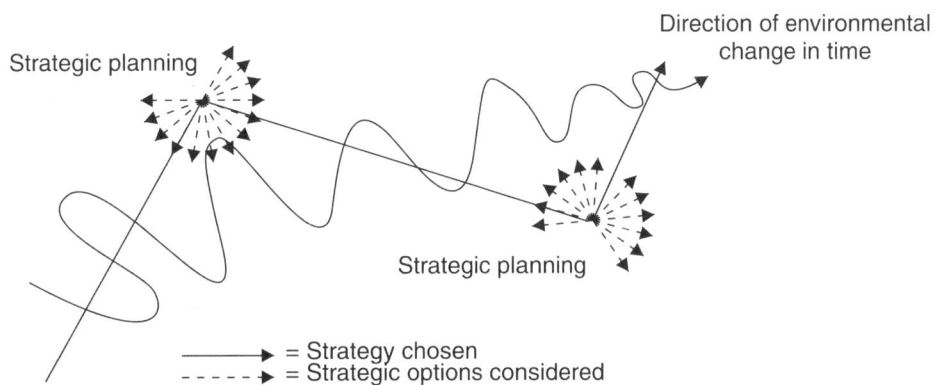

The dangers of the rational model are that the environment may change too quickly for the planning processes to react. All directions are considered, however.

(b) *Incremental model*

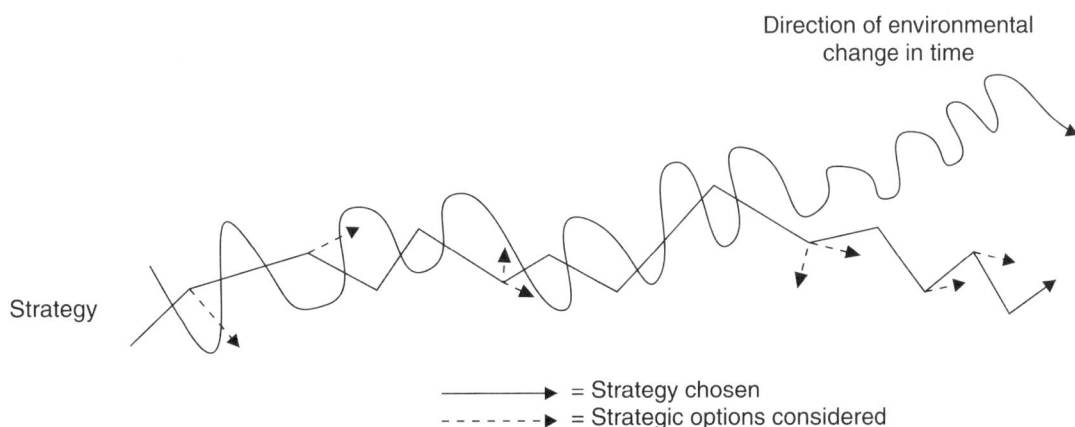

Incremental change may not be enough as the number of strategic options considered may be insufficiently radical to cope with environmental shift.

5.6 Section summary

- Managers do not take optimal (ie the best) decisions but satisfactory ones (decisions which will 'do').

- Managers do not pursue the whole rational model, but take small-scale decisions, building on what has gone before (incrementalism).

6 STRATEGIC THINKING

Strategic thinking as an intuitive process

6.1 *Kenichi Ohmae* (in *The Mind of the Strategist*) argues that **formal strategic planning processes have withered strategic thinking.** Strategy is essentially a creative process.

- **Successful strategists** 'have an idiosyncratic **mode of thinking** in which company, customers and competition merge in a dynamic interaction out of which a comprehensive set of objectives and plans for action eventually crystallises'.

- 'Successful business strategies result not from rigorous analysis but from a **particular state of mind**'. For Ohmae, the challenge to strategic management is to try to reproduce this ability in organisational structures, forms and cultures.

6.2 A strategist should be able to see beyond the present. There are several aspects to **strategic thinking.**

- Flexible thinking (what if? questions)
- Avoiding wrongly-focused perfectionism
- Keeping details in perspective (especially **uncertain details**)
- Focusing on key factors and the essentials (or **distinctive competences**) of a business

6.3 **How successful strategic thinking operates**

(a) **Ask the right question.** Find a **solution to a problem** rather than a **remedy to a symptom.** (Analogy: painkillers reduce a headache, they do not go to the underlying problem which may be poorly made spectacles, bad lighting or whatever.)

(b) **Observe the problems.**

(c) **Group** problems together by a process of **abstraction** (eg brainstorming) to see what they have in common (the **key factors**).

(d) Ohmae gives an example from an organisation's personnel system.

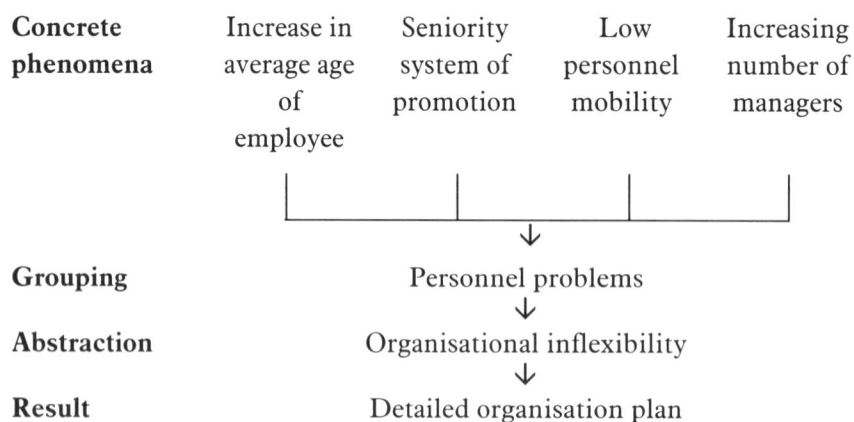

Concrete phenomena	Increase in average age of employee	Seniority system of promotion	Low personnel mobility	Increasing number of managers

Grouping	Personnel problems
	↓
Abstraction	Organisational inflexibility
	↓
Result	Detailed organisation plan

7 ENVIRONMENTAL FIT

7.1 For *Hofer and Schendel*, effective strategies must fit the characteristics of the firm and the environment together. In particular, **financial** and **physical resources** must be adequate if a strategy is to succeed.

(a) The environment is a key factor in the behaviour of any organisation, as organisations derive their **inputs** from it and distribute their **outputs** to it.

(b) **Fit or suitability** suggests that 'organisations are successful when they intentionally achieve **internal harmony** and **external adaptation** to their environment. Managers should use analytical techniques to identify the relationship between the organisation's internal capability and competences, and the external outputs. In very basic terms, the need for the fit is identified by the **SWOT** analysis and strategies are undertaken to secure the fit.'

(c) Hofer and Schendel suggest that strategy is a **mediating force** between the organisation and the environment.

7.2 Thus, although a strategy might be acceptable or feasible **in principle**, this does not necessarily make it the right one to choose. Arguably, the choice of strategy should follow a **strategic logic**. According to *Stacey* (*Strategic Management and Organisational Dynamics*), **strategic logic** requires that a proposed sequence of actions satisfy two conditions.

• It must be consistently related to the **objectives** of the organisation.

• It must match the organisation's **capability** (including its structure, control systems and culture) to its **environment**.

The idea is that all the pieces of the strategic puzzle should fit together in a predetermined manner.

The organisation in its ecological setting

7.3 Some writers have applied the ideas of evolution and natural selection to organisations. This 'ecology model' suggests that as an organisation's environment changes, it will only survive if it adapts and evolves. Business history is littered with the corpses of once powerful companies that failed to adapt. In this theory, an organisation survives if it finds a **niche** that provides both demand for its outputs and resources for it to use. Change plays an important role in determining whether or not an organisation finds a viable niche.

The future orientation: Hamel and Prahalad

7.4 There are two approaches to the future.

• The future will change incrementally (eg global warning, demographic trends).
• The future will be radically different (we do not know which inventions will succeed).

7.5 *Hamel and Prahalad* make two suggestions.

• The future is not just something that happens to organisations.
• Organisations can create the future.

7.6 Some management teams are simply more farsighted than others. Some are capable of imagining products, services and entire industries that do not yet exist and then giving them birth. Such managers seem to spend less time worrying about how to position the firm in **existing** competitive space and more time creating fundamentally **new** competitive space. Hamel and Prahalad suggest, however, that some companies are better 'prepared' to shape the future than others, and that this future-orientated stance is somehow embodied in the corporate culture.

7.7 Hamel and Prahalad offer a 'diagnostic' to indicate how future-orientated a company is.

Diagnostic statement	Protect the past	Create the future
Senior management, viewpoint about the future	Conventional, reactive	Distinctive, far-signed
Senior management spend most of their time on	Re-engineering current processes	Regenerating core strategies
Within the industry, the company...	Follows the rules	Makes the rules
The company is better at...	Operational efficiency	Building new businesses
To what extent do we pursue competitive advantage by...	Catching up with competitors	Creating new sources of competitive advantage
How is the company's agenda for change actually set?	By competitors	By a vision of the future
Are managers ...	Engineers of the present	Architects of the future
Are employees ...	Anxious	Hopeful

Case example

In the 1980s, Coca-Cola decided to change its flavour to compete with Pepsi. Market research, taster tests and so forth elicited favourable responses to the change, and so the new formulation was introduced.

A small group of consumers vociferously opposed the change; and this opposition spread suddenly and rapidly like an epidemic, forcing Coca-Cola to re-introduce the old formula. It was hard to detect the reasons for this, but if some consumers perceived Coke to symbolise American values, then changing the formula appeared to be an assault on them.

This case illustrates four issues.

(a) The limitations of planning.

(b) The seemingly unpredictable behaviour of the environment (as it became fashionable *not* to drink the new formula).

(c) Small causes (a few disaffected Coke-drinkers) can generate major consequences, by amplification, almost.

(d) The limitations to organisational gathering of information.

Consumers, who had initially favoured the product, turned against it, for reasons that could not be predicted by market researchers.

7.8 *Stacey* outlines a very different view.

(a) **The environment is not always predictable**. The environment is a **feedback system**, in which some effects can be amplified such as the rapidly expanding boycott of new Coke.

(b) Organisations can **shape their environment** (eg by moulding customer expectations) rather than just respond to it.

(c) Too much of a **good thing can lead to failure**.

- Successful firms embody incremental *and* revolutionary change.

- Companies do not exist in a state of equilibrium, but instead exist between stability and instability, and it is this creative tension that enables innovation.

(d) Managers' attempts to plan or impose a vision do not always shape up to the reality of emergent strategies. But too much emergent strategy leads to anarchy.

8 COMPETITION

8.1 Most businesses face competitors. According to Ohmae, what counts is performance in **relative terms**. 'A good business strategy' is 'one by which a firm can gain significant ground on its competitors at an acceptable cost'.

Method	Comment
Re-adjust current resources	Identify the key factors for success (or distinctive competence) and concentrate resources on these activities.
Relative superiority	A *relative* advantage can still be achieved by exploiting the competitors' actual or potential weaknesses.
Challenge assumptions	Challenge the accepted assumptions of doing business in a particular market (eg telephone banking challenges the need for branch networks in banks).
Degrees of freedom	Finding new ways of exploit markets (eg by segmentation, product/service differentiation etc).

8.2 In all cases, direct competition on the competitors' own turf is avoided. Successful strategy is the interplay of three Cs: **customers**, **competitors** and the **corporation**. This Ohmae calls the **strategic triangle**.

8.3 *Porter* defines strategy in similar competitive terms.

KEY TERM

Competitive strategy is 'the taking of offensive or defensive actions to create a defendable position within an industry ... and ... a superior return on investment'.

8.4 Porter highlights the importance of taking a competitive viewpoint. Porter suggests that over the past twenty years, firms have been learning to play to a new set of rules: benchmarking, outsourcing and the nurture of a few basic core competences. **The assumption is that rivals can easily copy any position, and so many companies are competing destructively** with each other in a state of **hyper-competition**. 'The root of the problem is the **failure to distinguish operational effectiveness and strategy**.

8.5 **Creating a sustainable strategic position**

Task	Comment
Operational effectiveness is not the same as strategy	Operational effectiveness involves doing the **same** things better than other firms. Improvements here can be imitated.
Strategy rests on unique activities	Competitive strategy is about being **different** ... choosing to perform activities differently or to perform different activities than rivals.'

Task	Comment
A sustainable strategic position requires trade-offs	Trade-offs limit what a company does. Trade-offs occur in three ways. • When activities are not compatible (eg an airline can offer a cheap no-meals service, or offer meals; doing both results in inefficiencies). • Where there will be inconsistencies in image and reputation. • Where an activity is over or underdesigned for its use (eg overqualified staff in menial positions).
Strategy is about combining activities	This is hard to imitate. (Operational effectiveness is about being good at *individual* activities.)
Strategy is about choices, not blindly imitating competitors	Many firms operate inefficiently, and so can benefit by improving operational effectiveness, but industry leaders at productivity frontier need to make choices and trade-offs.

8.6 Ohmae and Porter make three assumptions.

- The **survival** of a business is impossible without a **competitive strategy**.
- The **actual strategy** chosen will be **unique** to the organisation.
- The market place is sometimes like a **battlefield**.

8.7 Section summary

- For businesses, strategy must address competitors.
- The best strategies are distinctive, not imitations of what other firms do.
- Strategy is not the same as operational effectiveness.
- Strategy is about choices: including choices of what **not** to do.

9 LEARNING BASED STRATEGY

9.1 There has been considerable theoretical attention paid to the concept of a **learning organisation**, but as yet there is no single coherent model available. In this section we shall attempt to draw together some of the ideas related to strategy.

Knowledge as a resource

9.2 With the transformation of advanced economies away from manufacturing and towards ever more complex service industries, there has been a growing awareness of the importance of the **knowledge worker**, whose input is based on a high degree of skill and learning, and of the **knowledge-intensive firm**, which employs large numbers of such workers. A firm of accountants is a good example of a knowledge-based firm.

9.3 There is an obvious requirement for such firms and workers to maintain, develop and exploit their knowledge, collectively and individually. With this requirement comes recognition of the human resource as a source of competitive advantage.

9.4 *Nonaka* identifies two types of knowledge.

(a) **Tacit** knowledge may be compared to individual skills. It is personal and rooted in a specific context.

(b) **Explicit** knowledge is formal, systematised and easily shared. An example would be the specification for a technical process.

Knowledge creation

9.5 The exploitation of knowledge requires that its acquisition or creation is organised in a rational fashion. *Argyris* was one of the early exponents of the need for business learning. He used the term **double loop learning** to describe this process. The term is derived from **control theory**, in which a feedback control system that incorporates the option of changing the target is called a double loop system.

9.6 In double loop learning, knowledge is not only acquired, organised, stored and retrieved, but the purposes for which this is done are constantly reviewed. This involves regular examination of the organisation's purpose and objectives in the light of the knowledge already acquired.

The learning organisation

9.7 *Lynch* quotes *Garvin's* definition.

> An organisation skilled at creating, acquiring and transferring knowledge, and at modifying its behaviour to reflect new knowledge and insights.

This clearly reflects Argyris's double loop approach. *Senge* has proposed that strategy development should be seen as a learning process. The essential nature of organisational learning in this sense is **active creativity**. Senge suggests that this is best undertaken by co-operative groups.

9.8 **Implications for strategy**. The learning organisation will generate a flow of fresh ideas and insights. This will promote renewal and prevent stagnation. Increased openness to the environment will enhance the quality of response to events. However, none of this will happen if there is a rigid, prescriptive, **top-down** approach to the strategy-making process. There must be a wide range of inputs and a commitment to **discussion and debate**.

9.9 The potential advantages of the learning approach must not be allowed to seduce the organisation into endless, unfocused debate. Senior management must guide the process in order to keep it on track. They must also be prepared to take decisions without consultation when circumstances require them to do so.

10 AN OVERVIEW?

10.1 By now, you may be wishing for some kind of **integrative overview** of all the various theories, models and approaches we have mentioned. Unfortunately, there is no single diagram or family tree that can clarify these rather muddy waters. As is so often the case, we can make a good start by considering one of Mintzberg's ideas.

10.2 Henry Mintzberg's overview of the work of many writers on strategy suggests five ways in which the term strategy is used. A strategy can be a plan, ploy pattern, position or perspective. They are not mutually exclusive.

'P'	Comment
Plan	A 'consciously intended course of action'. See Chapter 1.
Ploy	A manoeuvre in a competitive game (Ohmae or Porter). For example a firm might add unnecessary plant capacity. The strategy is not to produce the goods but to **discourage a competitor** from entering the market.
Pattern	Andrews' and Mintzberg's ideas of emergent strategies.
Position	**Environmental fit** and relationships with other organisations. A position might be a distinctive niche, whereby the firm makes distinctive products or services or exploits a **distinct competence**.
Perspective	A unique way of looking at the world, of interpreting information from it, judging its opportunities and choices and acting. Different strategic perspectives might respond to the same environmental stimulus in different ways.

10.3 If we look at the various models we have discussed in this chapter, it will become apparent that it is difficult to improve on Mintzberg's analysis.

10.4 We might, for instance, try to split the models according to some helpful criteria. Here are a few examples of what we might come up with.

10.5 **Descriptive/prescriptive.** Some models might be regarded as being simply **descriptions** of what has been observed actually happening in organisations, while others could be taken as **guides** to the development of effective strategies. If we used this analysis, we might decide that the paradigm, politics, patterns of decisions, opportunistic, command, bounded rationality and incremental approaches fitted into the descriptive category, while the rational model, strategic thinking, learning based, environmental and competence or resource-based models were more prescriptive. However, this is not really a satisfactory classification, because some models, not least Mintzberg's emergent idea, would be difficult to classify in this way, since they appear to partake of both descriptive and prescriptive elements.

10.6 **Top down or bottom up.** Another approach might be to ask to what extent the models describe managerial control or input from lower down the hierarchy. Clearly, the rational model is the ultimate top down approach, with the opportunistic, command, paradigm, politics, pattern of decisions, bounded rationality, incremental and strategic thinking models representing other ways in which managers guide companies. The emergent strategy idea, once again, is difficult to classify, since it exploits developments that appear anywhere in the organisation, but depends on the fostering of a suitable culture by senior management. Learning-based and competence-based strategies are also likely to have an element of this dichotomy also.

10.7 **Internal or external bias.** An important line of analysis can be summed up in terms of SWOT: which does the regard as more critical, strengths and weaknesses or opportunities and threats? The company that pursues **environmental fit** is starting its planning with opportunities and threats. We would include the opportunistic approach, here, and probably the logical incremental and rational models also. The competence or resource-based idea and, possibly, learning-based strategy, on the other hand, are built on strengths and weaknesses.

10.8 **Usefulness**. Perhaps we can resolve our problem by asking which models are likely to be most useful in the search for a practical approach to business strategy. This will have the advantage that it will help us in the exam.

(a) The **rational model,** while ponderous in practice, has the virtue of covering all the ground. The actions and decisions it incorporates represent things that ought to be going on somewhere and to some extent in any business, if not quite in that exhaustive, step-by-step fashion. If we think of it less as a single, integrated strategic method and more as a **strategic checklist,** we will then see that many of the other theories link quite nicely to it.

(b) In particular, the apparently opposing ideas of **environmental fit** and **competence/resource-based strategy** may be regarded as differing emphases at the **SWOT analysis** stage.

(c) **Logical incrementalism,** the **command view** and **opportunism** may be seen as incomplete versions of the rational model, in which decisions are taken without the benefit of exhaustive prior research or even an awareness of what questions that research might answer. Despite this, they may well produce a strategy that is **good enough**.

(d) The **emergent** approach seems to contrast sharply with the rational model but we may think of it this way: environmental and internal analysis have been done *informally* by a kind of trial-and-error and almost without thinking about them; after all, the new strategy can only work if it suits both the environment and the company's resources. The possibility of something good turning up should be kept at the back of the mind. The trick is to recognise when a strategy is emerging without benefit of planning and then to make the most of it. This requires an open-minded approach and an organisation that is not over-fond of status, bureaucracy and hierarchy. The **learning** approach is similar.

Question 4

Here are some issues of strategy. Which of Mintzberg's categories (plan, position, ploy, perspective, pattern) do you think they fit into?

(a) The general manager of the Beardsley Hospital prepares a strategy. To minimise the time doctors spend walking from place to place she has rearranged the hospital so that services are clustered around patients. She has the resources so that this change will be phased in over three years, firstly Ophthalmology, secondly Oncology, thirdly Paediatrics, and so on.

(b) Two market traders sell fruit and vegetables. One decides to specialise in exotic fruits, as he feels there are enough well-off and/or experimentally minded people in his area to make it worth his while.

Answer

(a) This is probably strategy as *plan*. A document is being prepared by senior management.

(b) This is strategy as *position*. The market trader specialising in exotic fruit is trying to carve himself a niche.

Chapter roundup

- According to Andrews, strategy is a **pattern of senior management decisions**.

- Johnson and Scholes suggest an approach which follows a similar outline to the rational model, but which accounts for the '**political**' **and cultural influences on managers.**

- The rational approach also fails to identify **emergent strategies**, or allow for them, according to Mintzberg. Operations level can be a source of strategic change. Emergent strategies arise out of **patterns of behaviour**. They are not the result of the conscious intentions of senior managers. They have to be shaped or **crafted**. **Realised strategies** include intended and emergent strategies.

- Approaches to strategic management differ in the extent to which they are **deliberate or emergent**, and the extent to which they are **explicit or implicit.**

- Ohmae argues that successful **strategic thinking** involves a **creative and intuitive** approach to the business, not just logic. However, Johnson and Scholes emphasise the **paradigm.**

- Porter and Ohmae see business strategy is **competitive terms.** Competitive **advantage is always relative** to competitors.

- Many businesses, concentrating on improving operational effectiveness, have lost sight of the fact that strategy is **unique.** It involves making **trade-offs, choices** and **combining activities.**

- Mintzberg suggests that 'strategy' is used to mean **plan**, a **ploy**, a **pattern**, a **position** and a **perspective**.

- Managers are not able to take all factors into account. **Bounded rationality** forces them to satisfice not optimise.

- Incrementalism involves small scale adjustments to current policies, as they are less risky.

- **Learning based** strategy-making recognises the need to exploit the input of the **knowledge worker**. The flow of fresh ideas challenges the **paradigm.**

Quick quiz

1 How does Andrews describe corporate strategy?

2 What is a distinctive competence?

3 How does strategy emerge?

4 How does Mintzberg suggest strategy is crafted?

5 According to Johnson and Scholes, what is the paradigm?

6 What is meant by satisficing and bounded rationality?

7 What is incrementalism?

8 What is Ohmae's view of the origin of successful strategy?

9 What is environmental fit?

10 What are the three sides of the strategic triangle?

Answers to quick quiz

1 As a pattern of decisions

2 Something the organisation does well, uniquely or better than rivals

3 It develops out of patterns of behaviour

4 Managers respond to developments, exploit opportunities and allocate resources

5 Basic assumptions and beliefs held in common by an organisation's decision makers

6 Satisficing is accepting an imperfect but tolerable solution. Bounded rationality is the intellectual stance that accepts satisficing as an appropriate course of action

7 Small scale extensions of past practices

8 Strategy-making is a creative thought process

9 Adaptation of the organisation to its environment

10 Corporation, customers, competition

Now try the question below from the Exam Question Bank

Number	Level	Marks	Time
Q2	Exam	20	36 mins

Part B
Strategic analysis and options

Chapter 3

MISSION

Topic list	Syllabus reference
1 Vision and strategic intent	4(a)
2 Mission	4(a)
3 Goals and objectives: introduction	4(a)
4 Commercial goals and objectives	4(a)
5 Stakeholders' goals and objectives	4(a)
6 The role of culture	1(f)

Introduction

An organisation's **mission** - why it exists in society at all - is the guiding idea behind the organisation's activities. **Goals and objectives** are devised to fulfil the mission. Some, but not all, are quantified and so are easily measurable. Goals and objectives also interpret the organisation's mission to a number of different client groups or **stakeholders**, all of whom have an interest in what the organisation does. Mission can be easily subverted, or is given only lip service.

Mission must reflect the legitimate expectations of appropriate stakeholders. It will inevitably be influenced by the culture of the organisation.

Study guide

Section 4 – The nature of strategy analysis and choice

- The purpose of the organisation

Section 1 – Models of strategic management

- Strategic management in different contexts

Exam guide

Mission and culture are two basic areas upon which a wide range of questions could be created.

1   VISION AND STRATEGIC INTENT

1.1 A strategic thinker should have a **vision** for the future. This has three aspects.

- What the business *is* now
- What it *could* be in an ideal world
- What the ideal world would be like

1.2 A vision gives a general sense of direction to the company, even if there is not too much attention to detail. A vision, it is hoped, enables **flexibility** to exist in the context of a guiding idea. A company with two choices would move to B rather than A. The strategy draws on the vision. A vision might provide the boundaries (in Simon's description of bounded rationality) for the firm's direction.

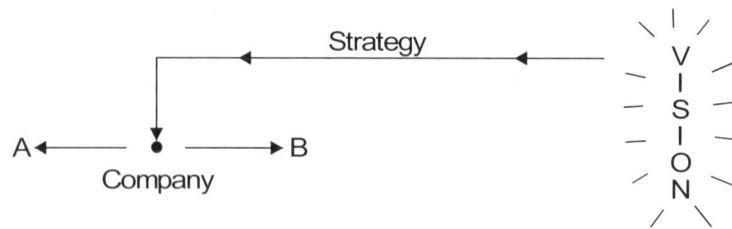

Case example

Nokia

What factors distinguish the top companies in the FT European performance league table this year?

Generalisations are dangerous, because the reasons for individual success vary greatly. But focusing on the best performers over five years – a period sufficient to overcome many of the vagaries of the market – suggests that the most important factors include strong, innovative managements with a track record of international success. The outright winner exemplifies these traits. Nokia, the Finnish mobile phone manufacturer, has produced a total shareholder return of 1,660 per cent over the past five years, well ahead of second Gruppo Editoriale L'Espresso, with a TSR of 1,238 per cent.

The figures were calculated for the five years until the end of March – a period ending well before a profits warning from Nokia earlier this month which hurt its share price.

Ten years ago a company from a remote country on the fringe of Europe would have seemed an unlikely global leader of the mobile handset market, but Nokia has overtaken Motorola of the US to head the sector and it keeps extending its advantage. Analysts estimate that in the fourth quarter of last year it commanded 35 per cent of global mobile unit sales, three times that of second placed Motorola.

Probably the most important factor behind its success is its strong management, which had the strategic vision to focus on the mobile phone market when it was in its infancy – a decision helped by the fact that Finland took an early lead in telecoms deregulation and mobile phone standards. It also helped that Nokia approached the market with a consumer electronics viewpoint, rather than that of an established telecommunications equipment manufacturer like rival Ericsson of Sweden.

Martin Dickson, Financial Times, 29 June 2001

1.3 Nebulous concepts of vision, by its nature undefined, seem to take us a long way from strategy and planning as discussed in Chapter 1. We began with a simple process of strategic management: problem identification, analysis, solution. We end up with processes of observation and abstraction, guided by a creative insight into vision.

1.4 Problems with vision

- It ignores real, practical problems.
- It can degenerate into wishful thinking.

Strategic intent

1.5 *Hamel and Prahalad* suggest that **strategic intent** is similar to vision, but it should to have an emotional core.

a company.
- It implies a 'stretch' beyond current competences.
- Like vision it gives a sense of **direction** and discovery.
- It entails a sense of discovery, as employers learn new things.

- It gives coherence to plans.

1.6 Effectively, it aims to enthuse employees with the business strategy. As such, it is possibly less powerful a motivator than mission.

Case example

General Motors in the US had a collective vision, resulting in huge investment in automation and technology to become the *21st Century Corporation*. Whereas its European operations have been notably successful in beating off the Japanese, the American parent, despite its huge investment stumbled in the face of Japanese and US domestic competition for a while in the 1980s, although the company has now improved.

---

2 MISSION

KEY TERM

Mission 'describes the organisation's basic function in society, in terms of the products and services it produces for its clients' (Mintzberg).

Elements of mission

2.1 **Purpose.** Why does the company exist?

- To create wealth for shareholders?

- To satisfy the needs of **all stakeholders** (including employees, society at large, for example)?

Case example

The Co-op

The Co-operative Wholesale Society and Co-operative Retail Society are business organisations, but their purpose is not simply profit. Rather, being owned by their suppliers/customers rather than external shareholders, they have always, since the foundation, had a wider social concern.

The Co-op has been criticised by some analysts on the grounds that it is insufficiently profitable, certainly in comparison with supermarket chains such as Tescos. However, the Co-op has explicit **social** objectives. In some cases it will retain stores which, although too small to be as profitable as a large supermarket, provide an important social function in the communities which host them.

Of course, the Co-op's performance as a retailer can be improved, but judging it on the conventional basis of profitability ignores its social objectives.

2.2 **Strategy.** Mission provides the commercial logic for the organisation, and so defines two things

- The **products or services** it offers and therefore its competitive position.
- The **competences** by which it hopes to prosper, and its way of competing.

2.3 **Strategic scope.** An organisation's strategic scope is defined by the **boundaries** its managers set for it. These boundaries may be set in terms of geography, market, business method, product or any other parameter that **defines the nature of the organisation**.

2.4 **Policies and standards of behaviour.** The mission needs to be converted into everyday performance. For example, a firm whose mission covers excellent customer service must deal with simple matters such as politeness to customers, speed at which phone calls are answered and so forth.

2.5 **Values and culture.** Values are the basic, perhaps unstated, beliefs of the people who work in the organisation.

(a) **Principles of business**

- Commitment to suppliers and staff
- Social policy eg on non-discrimination or ecology
- Commitments to customers

(b) **Loyalty and commitment.** A sense of mission may inspire employees to sacrifice their own personal interests for the good of the whole. This however has to be reciprocated by company loyalty to its staff (eg long-term staff retention).

(c) **Guidance for behaviour.** A sense of mission helps create a work environment where there is a sense of **common purpose**.

2.6 The values of the business as a **collective entity** are in tune with the **personal values** of the individuals working for it. In conflicts of ethics, clashes between organisational and personal values are hard to resolve if someone's principles disagree with what the organisation wants. Whistle blowers are people who give information to the government or the press about those activities of their employers which they think are immoral. Whistle blowers rarely gain in financial or career terms from doing so. An employee's sense of mission (eg to the patients, in the case of NHS whistle blowers) or code of professional ethics (eg ethical guidelines for accountants) may be stronger than mere loyalty to management if the whistle blower disagrees with management decisions.

2.7 For there to be a strong, motivating sense of mission, the four elements above must be mutually reinforcing.

Case examples

- The most obvious example is a religious organisation where an individual's faith and organisational teaching and purpose are the same.

- Sometimes employees can have a sense of mission even where there is chaos in management. For example, a doctor's dedication to his or her patients may be strong despite poor management, say, by the health authority or hospital trust.

The importance of mission

2.8 Although hard to quantify (and hence, from an accounting viewpoint, of dubious value) mission is taken seriously by many firms.

(a) Values and feelings are integral elements of **consumers' buying decisions**, as evidenced by advertising, branding and market research. Customers not only ask 'What do you sell?' but 'What do you stand for?'

(b) A respect for quantifiable information is part of the professional culture and training of the accountant; other people have different values and priorities.

(c) Studies into organisational behaviour suggest that employees are **motivated** by more than money. A sense of mission and values can help to motivate employees.

(d) Many firms take mission seriously in strategic management.

Case example

Some writers believe there is an empirical relationship between strong *corporate values* and profitability. The *Financial Times* reported (22 February 1993) the result of research by the Digital Equipment Corporation into a sample of 429 company executives.

(a) 80% of the sample have a formal mission statement.

(b) 80% believed mission contributes to profitability.

(c) 75% believe they have a responsibility to implement the mission statement.

(d) *Only* 6% admitted, openly, that corporate values make *little* difference in practice, although 30% believed that 'values' should be subordinated to commercial gain in case of conflict.

Mission statements

2.9 **Mission statements** are formal statements of an organisation's mission. They might be reproduced in a number of places (eg at the front of an organisation's annual report, on publicity material, in the chairman's office, in communal work areas and so on). There is no standard format, but they should possess certain characteristics.

- **Brevity** - easy to understand and remember
- **Flexibility** - to accommodate change
- **Distinctiveness** - to make the firm stand out

Mission and planning

2.10 Although the mission statement might be seen as a set of abstract principles, it can play an important **role in the planning process**.

(a) **Plans should outline the fulfilment of the organisation's mission**. To take the example of a religious organisation (the best example of a 'missionary organisation'), the mission of spreading the gospel might be embodied in plans to send individuals as missionaries to various parts of the world, plans for fund-raising activities, or even targets for the numbers of new converts.

(b) **Evaluation and screening.** Mission also acts as a yardstick by which plans are judged.

- The mission of an ethical investment trust would preclude investing in tobacco firms.

- Mission helps to ensure consistency in decisions.

(c) **Implementation.** Mission also affects the implementation of a planned strategy, in the culture and business practices of the firm.

2.11 **Problems with mission**

Problem	Comment
Ignored in practice	The inherent danger of mission is that it will not be implemented. Their *official* goals often do not correspond with the end they actually seem to pursue'.

Problem	Comment
Public relations	Sometimes, of course, mission is merely for public consumption, not for internal decision making.
'Post hoc'	Missions are sometimes produced to *rationalise* its existence to particular audiences'. In other words, mission does not drive the organisation, but what the organisation actually does is assumed to be a mission.
Full of generalisations	'Best', 'quality', 'major': is just a wish list.

Case examples

Enron

What is so striking about interviews with former employees is how many of them suspected that all was not right with Enron long before it collapsed into bankruptcy last December.

Enron's culture, employees say, came straight from the top. Ken Lay, its former chairman, designated Enron's core values: Respect, Integrity, Communication and Excellence, words emblazoned on enormous banners that hung in the lobby of its Smith Street headquarters in Houston.

But employees say Mr Lay's true interest was performance. The flaw was that performance, as defined by Enron, was limited to actions that boosted the company's bottom line – and ultimately its stock price.

"There were no rewards for saving the company from a potential loss. There were only rewards for doing a deal that could outwardly be reported as revenue or earnings," says one former employee.

Mr Lay would dangle large financial rewards before bright young employees and then step out of the way and allow them to show what they could do.

Joshua Chaffin and Stephen Fidler, Financial Times, 9 April 2002

2.12 **System goals** are those which organisations as **systems** pursue. These goals have a habit of **subverting mission,** by making mission subordinate to them.

Systems goal	Comment
Survival	Individuals benefit from the organisation's existence (as their employer, for their social life), irrespective of what the organisation actually does. There is a strong incentive for an organisation to survive simply because it keeps its managers in work.
Efficiency	This is the greatest benefit for a given cost. However, an organisation can be **efficient** (doing things well) as opposed to being **effective** (doing the right things). Efficiency takes precedence over effectiveness because it means doing more of the same, and does not require consideration of other stakeholders.
Control	Organisations try 'to exercise some control over their own environments'. Examples of control are vertical integration (eg to control supply), diversification (to reduce uncertainty).
Growth	**Managers** benefit directly from growth, in terms of salaries and status. Growth is the natural goal of the manager as it reduces vulnerability to the environment and other organisations.

These goals are interrelated: growth can bring efficiency. Of course, growth often does benefit shareholders and fulfils the mission, but not always.

2.13 Section summary

The functions of 'mission'

- Provides a focus for strategic decisions
- Creates values to guide discretionary decision-taking
- Replaces national or divisional subcultures with a corporate culture
- Communicates the nature of the organisation to insiders and outsiders

3 GOALS AND OBJECTIVES: INTRODUCTION

3.1 From the vision and mission, **goals** are derived.

> **KEY TERMS**
>
> Mintzberg defines **goals** as 'the intentions behind decisions or actions, the states of mind that drive individuals or collectives of individuals called organisations to do what they do.'
>
> **Operational goals** can be expressed as objectives. Here is an example.
>
> Operational goal: 'Cut costs'. The objective: 'Reduce budget by 5%'
>
> **Non-operational goals** A university's goal might be to 'seek truth'.
>
> Not all goals can be measured.

3.2 In practice most organisations set themselves **quantified objectives** in order to enact the corporate mission. Many objectives are:

- **S**pecific
- **M**easurable
- **A**ttainable
- **R**esults-orientated
- **T**ime-bounded

3.3 There should be **goal congruence**. The goals set for different parts of the organisation should be consistent with each other.

> **KEY TERM**
>
> CIMA defines **goal congruence** as follows:
>
> 'The state which leads individuals to take action which are in their self interest and also in the best interest of the entity'.

Primary and secondary objectives

3.4 Some objectives are more important than others. In the hierarchy of objectives, there is a **primary corporate objective** and other **secondary objectives** which should combine to ensure the achievement of the overall corporate objective.

3.5 For example, if a company sets itself an objective of growth in profits, as its primary aim, it will then have to develop strategies by which this primary objective can be achieved. An objective must then be set for each individual strategy. Secondary objectives might then be concerned with sales growth, continual technological innovation, customer service, product quality, efficient resource management or reducing the company's reliance on debt capital.

Long-term objectives and short-term objectives

3.6 Objectives may be long-term and short-term. A company that is suffering from a recession in its core industries and making losses in the short term might continue to have a long term primary objective of achieving a growth in profits, but in the short term its primary objective might be survival.

3.7 **Types of goal**

Goal	Comment
Ideological goals	These goals focus on the organisation's mission. They are shared sets of beliefs and values.
Formal goals	Such goals are imposed by a dominant individual or group such as shareholders. People work to attain these goals as a route to their personal goals.
Shared personal goals	Individuals reach a consensus about what they want out of an organisation (eg a group of academics who decide they want to pursue research).
System goals	Derive from the organisation's existence as an organisation, independent of mission.

3.8 **Section summary**
- Goals can be objectives (quantified and SMART) or aims (not quantified).
- There should be goal congruence. There are many different levels of goal which people work towards.

4 COMMERCIAL GOALS AND OBJECTIVES

4.1 Objectives are normally **quantified** statements of what the organisation actually intends to achieve over a period of time.

4.2 **Uses of objectives**
- Objectives **orientate the activities** of the organisation towards the fulfilment of the organisation's mission, in theory if not always in practice.
- The mission of a **business**, whether stated or not, must include **profitability**.
- Objectives can also be used as standards **for measuring the performance** of the organisation and departments in it.

The nature of profit

4.3 To an economist, cost includes an amount for normal profit which is the reward for entrepreneurship. **Normal profit is the opportunity cost of entrepreneurship,** because it is the amount of profit that an entrepreneur could earn elsewhere, and so it is the profit that he must earn to persuade him to keep on with his investment in his current enterprise.

4.4 **Accounting profits** consist of sales revenue minus the **explicit costs** of the business. Explicit costs are those which are clearly stated and recorded; some examples are given below.

- Materials costs - prices paid to suppliers
- Labour costs - wages paid
- Depreciation costs on fixed assets
- Other expenses, such as rates and building rental

4.5 **Economic profit** consists of sales revenue minus both the explicit costs and the **implicit costs** of the business. Implicit costs are benefits forgone by not using the factors of production in their next most profitable way. The most important implicit cost is the cost of **entrepreneurship**. You will recall from your economics studies that **normal profit** is the overall return to the owner of a firm that leads him or her to continue participating in the industry. If this level of profit is not achieved, the owner will close the business and try something else. Exactly the same idea applies to large companies financed by shares: if shareholders do not receive what they perceive to be an adequate return on their investment they will take their money elsewhere.

4.6 This concept of profit is important to the strategist. If profitability is to be an organisation's primary objective, it must be specified in **quantified terms**. That is, a specific target rate of profit must be set. Effectively, this rate can only be determined by examining the **opportunity cost** of investing in the business: this is given by the **rate of profit available on alternative investments** with similar characteristics, particularly risk. This is then the **minimum** rate of return acceptable to the shareholders.

Corporate and unit objectives

4.7 **Corporate objectives** concern the firm as **a whole**, for example:

- Profitability
- Market share
- Growth
- Cash flow
- Return on capital employed
- Risk

- Customer satisfaction
- Quality
- Industrial relations
- Added value
- Earnings per share

4.8 Similar objectives can be developed for each **strategic business unit (SBU)**. (An SBU is a part of the company that for all intents and purposes has its own distinct products, markets and assets.)

4.9 **Unit objectives** are specific to individual units of an organisation.

(a) **Commercial**

- Increase the number of customers by x% (an objective of a sales department)

- Reduce the number of rejects by 50% (an objective of a production department)

- Produce monthly reports more quickly, within 5 working days of the end of each month (an objective of the management accounting department)

(b) **Public sector**

- Introduce x% more places at nursery schools (an objective of a borough education department)

- Respond more quickly to calls (an objective of a local police station, fire department or hospital ambulance service)

(c) **General**

- Resources (eg cheaper raw materials, lower borrowing costs, 'top-quality college graduates')

- Market (eg market share, market standing)

- Employee development (eg training, promotion, safety)

- Innovation in products or processes

- Productivity (the amount of output from resource inputs)

- Technology

Primary and secondary objectives

4.10 Some objectives are more important than others. There is a **primary corporate objective** (restricted by certain constraints on corporate activity) and other **secondary objectives** which are strategic objectives which should combine to ensure the achievement of the primary corporate objective.

(a) For example, if a company sets itself an objective of growth in profits, as its primary objective, it will then have to develop strategies by which this primary objective can be achieved.

(b) Secondary objectives might then be concerned with sales growth, continual technological innovation, customer service, product quality, efficient resource management (eg labour productivity) or reducing the company's reliance on debt capital.

Trade-off between objectives

4.11 When there are several key objectives, some might be achieved only **at the expense of others**. For example, a company's objective of achieving good profits and profit growth might have adverse consequences for the cash flow of the business, or the quality of the firm's products.

4.12 There will be a **trade-off** between objectives when strategies are formulated, and a choice will have to be made. For example, there might be a choice between the following two options.

Option A 15% sales growth, 10% profit growth, a £2 million negative cash flow and reduced product quality and customer satisfaction.

Option B 8% sales growth, 5% profit growth, a £500,000 surplus cash flow, and maintenance of high product quality/customer satisfaction.

If the firm chose option B in preference to option A, it would be trading off sales growth and profit growth for better cash flow, product quality and customer satisfaction. The long-term effect of reduced quality has not been considered.

4.13 **EXAMPLE**

A company's primary objective might be to increase its earnings per share from 30p to 50p in the next five years.

(a) **Strategies** for achieving the objective might be selected.

- Increase profitability in the next twelve months by cutting expenditure.
- Increase export sales over the next three years.
- Develop a successful new product for the domestic market within five years.

(b) **Secondary objectives** might then be re-assessed.

- Improve manpower productivity by 10% within twelve months.
- Improving customer service in export markets with the objective of doubling the number of overseas sales outlets in selected countries within the next three years.
- Investing more in product-market research and development, with the objective of bringing at least three new products to the market within five years.

Case example

On Easter Sunday 1997, the UK saw the launch of a new commercial TV station, Channel 5 (C5). The following objectives are relevant.

(a) *Primary objectives* - profit for its various shareholders.

(b) *Secondary objectives*

C5 sells advertising time. The rates it can charge are often determined by audience share. To satisfy advertisers, C5 has to have *audience share objectives*.

(c) These audience share objectives affect various operational aspects of the business.

    (i) *Coverage.* C5 had to ensure that enough of the population can receive C5.

    (ii) *Availability.* Before the launch, many people's video recorders had to be *retuned*: up to 11m households were believed to be affected by interference from the new station. Retuning problems delayed the initial launch of the channel. This was a *short term*, but critical, *operational objective*.

    (iii) *Programming.* Finally, audience share targets set priorities for programming

---

Conflict between goals

4.14 Dealing with conflicts between different types of goals

(a) **Rational evaluation** according to financial criteria

(b) **Bargaining.** Managers with different goals will compete and will form alliances with other managers to achieve their goals.

(c) **Satisficing.** Organisations do not aim to maximise performance in one area if this leads to poor performance elsewhere. Rather they will accept satisfactory, if not excellent, performance in a number of areas.

(d) **Sequential attention.** Goals are dealt with one by one in a sequence.

(e) **Priority setting.** Certain goals get priority over others. This is determined by senior managers, but there are quite complicated systems to link goals and strategies according to certain criteria.

4.15 Section summary

- Primary objectives for a business are essential financial.
- Secondary objectives support the primary objectives.
- In practice, objectives conflict and a variety of methods are used to establish which are most important.

5   STAKEHOLDERS' GOALS AND OBJECTIVES

Case example

Hoechst

Shares in Hoechst, the world's largest drugs and chemicals group, tumbled 8 per cent yesterday after the German company revealed it had abandoned plans to seek a separate listing for its pharmaceuticals business. It also revealed fourth-quarter results well below expectations.

Pharmaceutical companies are traditionally more profitable than chemicals companies, and their shares usually attract a higher rating. For conglomerates spanning both activities, the value of the drugs business tends to be disproportionately diminished by the chemicals arm.

Last year Hoechst said a public offering for MHR, its drugs business, was a priority and hinted at a listing this year. However, Mr Jürgen Dormann, chairman, said yesterday the group no longer planned to list HMR. Meanwhile, the group is accelerating its exit from chemicals.

The Lex column commented: 'Hoechst's U-turn is astounding. The group's rationale for the new strategy is sketchy. It argues borrowings have fallen faster than planned, so an HMR flotation is no longer a financial necessity - but debt will rise in 1997. Hoechst also makes much of keeping full control of drugs and linking it with its other life science businesses. But two of these, agrochemicals and diagnostics, are themselves joint ventures. This about-face seems to have more to do with *management's desire to keep on running the more attractive pharmaceutical business* than with anything else'. (BPP italics)

Financial Times, 13 March 1997

Stakeholders

5.1   We mentioned stakeholders briefly in Chapter 2 when we discussed strategy and managerial intent and we will return to them when we discuss the evaluation of strategic options in Chapter 8.

KEY TERM

Stakeholders: groups or individuals whose interests are directly affected by the activities of a firm or organisation

5.2   Here are some stakeholder groups.

Stakeholder group	Members
• Internal stakeholders	Employees, management
• Connected	Shareholders, customers, suppliers, lenders
• External	The government, local government, the public

5.3   Stakeholder groups can exert influence on strategy. The greater the power of a stakeholder group, the greater its influence will be. Each stakeholder group has different expectations about what it wants, and the expectations of the various groups will conflict. To some extent, the expectations of stakeholders will influence the organization's mission. We will return to the subject of stakeholder expectations in Chapter 8 when we discuss the evaluation of strategic options.

Stakeholders' objectives

5.4   Here is a checklist of stakeholders' objectives. It is not comprehensive.

(a) **Employees and managers**

- Job security (over and above legal protection)
- Good conditions of work (above minimum safety standards)
- Job satisfaction
- Career development and relevant training

(b) **Customers**

- Products of a certain quality at a reasonable price
- Products that should last a certain number of years
- A product or service that meets customer needs.

(c) **Suppliers**: regular orders in return for reliable delivery and good service

(d) **Shareholders**: long-term wealth

(e) **Providers of loan capital (stock holders)**: reliable payment of interest due and maintenance of the value of any security.

(f) **Society as a whole**

- Control pollution
- Financial assistance to charities, sports and community activities
- Co-operate with government in identifying and preventing health hazards

---

Case example

British Airways

British Airways publicity once indicated the following corporate goals.

- Safety and security
- Strong and consistent financial performance
- Global reach
- Superior services

- Good value for money
- Healthy working environment
- Good neighbourliness

'Overall, our aim is to be the best and most successful company in the airline industry.'

(1) BA's success is measured according to its standing in comparison with *other* airlines. BA was one of the industry's few profit-makers shortly after the Gulf War: although it may not top all league tables, quality of service has improved massively. It has operated effectively over a large number of its goals, in comparison with competitors.

(2) BA has also achieved consistent performance over a variety of its goals. Had it plunged into loss, there would be some doubts about its effectiveness.

5.5 Section summary

- Stakeholders have an interest in an organisation, but it is debatable whether they have rights over it.

- Stakeholders pursue their own goals.

6   THE ROLE OF CULTURE

Organisational culture

> **KEY TERM**
>
> The word, **culture** is used by sociologists and anthropologists to encompass 'the sum total of the beliefs, knowledge, attitudes of mind and customs to which people are exposed in their social conditioning.'

6.1   Through contact with a particular culture, individuals learn a language, acquire values and learn habits of behaviour and thought.

(a)   **Beliefs and values**. Beliefs are what we feel to be the case on the basis of objective and subjective information (eg people can believe the world is round or flat). Values are beliefs which are relatively enduring, relatively general and fairly widely accepted as a guide to culturally appropriate behaviour.

(b)   **Customs.** Customs are modes of behaviour which represent culturally accepted ways of behaving in response to given situations.

(c)   **Artefacts.** Artefacts are all the physical tools designed by human beings for their physical and psychological well-being, including works of art, technology, products.

(d)   **Rituals.** A ritual is a type of activity which takes on symbolic meaning; it consists of a fixed sequence of behaviour repeated over time.

The learning and sharing of culture is made possible by **language** (both written and spoken, verbal and non-verbal).

6.2   Knowledge of the culture of a society is clearly of value to businesses in a number of ways.

(a)   **Marketers** can adapt their products accordingly, and be fairly sure of a sizeable market. This is particularly important in export markets.

(b)   **Human resource managers** may need to tackle cultural differences in recruitment. For example, some ethnic minorities have a different body language from the majority, which may be hard for some interviewers to interpret.

6.3   Culture in a society can be divided into **subcultures** reflecting social differences. Most people participate in several of them.

> **KEY TERM**
>
> **Organisational culture** consists of the beliefs, attitudes, practices and customs to which people are exposed during their interaction with the organisation.

6.4   Culture is both internal to an organisation and external to it. The culture of an organisation is embedded in the culture of the wider society. Its importance to strategy is that it can predispose the organisation towards or away from a particular course of action.

6.5   All organisations will generate their own cultures, whether spontaneously or under the guidance of positive managerial strategy. *Schein* suggests that three levels of culture can be distinguished in organisations.

(a) **Basic, underlying assumptions** which guide the behaviour of the individuals and groups in the organisation. These may include customer orientation, or belief in quality, trust in the organisation to provide rewards, freedom to make decisions, freedom to make mistakes and the value of innovation and initiative at all levels.

(b) **Overt beliefs** expressed by the organisation and its members, which can be used to condition the assumptions mentioned above. These beliefs and values may emerge as sayings, slogans and mottoes, such as IBM's motto, 'think'. They may emerge in a rich mythology of jokes and stories about past successes and heroic failures.

(c) **Visible artefacts** - the style of the offices or other premises, dress rules, visible structures or processes, the degree of informality between superiors and subordinates and so on.

Management can encourage this by selling a sense of the corporate mission, or by promoting the corporate image. It can reward the right attitudes and punish (or simply not employ) those who are not prepared to commit themselves to the culture.

6.6   An organisation's culture is influenced by many factors.

(a) **The organisation's founder**. A strong set of values and assumptions is set up by the organisation's founder, and even after he or she has retired, these values have their own momentum. Or, to put it another way, an organisation might find it hard to shake off its original culture. *Peters and Waterman* believed that 'excellent' companies began with strong leaders.

(b) **The organisation's history**. *Johnson and Scholes* state that the way an organisation works reflects the era when it was founded. Farming, for example, sometimes has a craft element to it. The effect of history can be determined by stories, rituals and symbolic behaviour. They legitimise behaviour and promote priorities. (In some organisations certain positions are regarded as intrinsically more 'heroic' than others.)

(c) **Leadership and management style**. An organisation with a strong culture recruits managers who naturally conform to it.

(d) **Structure and systems** affect culture as well as strategy.

6.7   The **McKinsey 7-S** model was designed to show how the various aspects of a business relate to one another. It is a useful illustration of the way culture fits into an organisation. In particular, it shows the links between the organisation's behaviour and the behaviour of individuals within it. The model was developed by Peters and Waterman while working as McKinsey consultants.

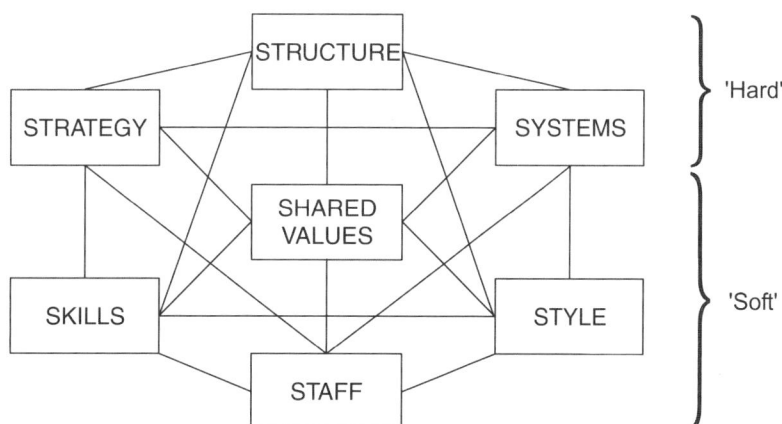

6.8 Three of the elements are considered 'hard'.

(a) **Structure**. The organisation structure determines division of tasks in the organisation and the hierarchy of authority from the most senior to junior.

(b) **Strategy**. Strategy is way in which the organisation plans to outperform its competitors, if it is a business, or how it intends to achieve its objectives.

(c) **Systems**. Systems include the technical systems of accounting, personnel, management information and so forth.

These 'hard' elements are easily quantified or defined, and deal with **facts and rules.**

6.9 However, the McKinsey model suggests that certain 'soft' elements are equally important.

(a) **Shared values** are the guiding beliefs of people in the organisation as to why it exists. (For example, people in a hospital seek to save lives.) It forms part of the corporate culture.

(b) **Staff** are the people in the organisation. They have their own complex concerns and priorities.

(c) **Style** is another aspect of the **corporate culture,** which includes the shared assumptions, ways of working and attitudes of management.

(d) **Skills** refer to those things that the organisation does well. For example, BT is good at providing a telephone service, but even if the phone network is eventually used as a transmission medium for television/film programmes, BT is unlikely to make those programmes itself.

The importance of the 'soft' elements for success was emphasised by Peters and Waterman in their study of 'excellent' companies.

The organisational iceberg

6.10 *French and Bell* described the **organisational iceberg** in which formal aspects are **overt** and informal aspects are **covert** or hidden, rather as the bulk of an iceberg is underwater. The formal aspects are similar to the McKinsey 'hard' elements while the informal aspects correspond to the 'soft' elements in the 7-S model.

6.11 **Formal aspects**

- Goals
- Terminology
- Structure
- Policies and procedures
- Products
- Financial resources

6.12 **Informal aspects**

- Beliefs and assumptions
- Perceptions
- Attitudes   } about the formal systems
- Feelings
- Values
- Informal interactions
- Group norms

The cultural web

6.13 Johnson and Scholes use the term cultural web to mean a combination of the assumptions that make up the **paradigm**, together with the **physical manifestations** of culture. They suggest that the paradigm may be reinforced by such manifestations.

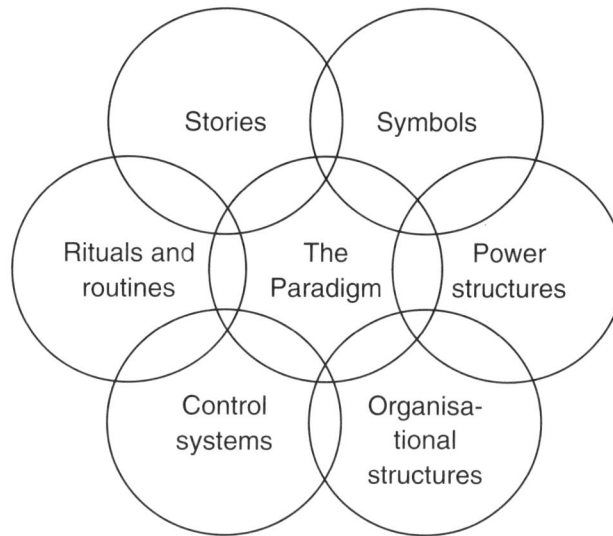

The cultural web

Culture and structure

6.14 Writing in 1972, *Roger Harrison* suggested that organisations could be classified into four types. His work was later popularised by *Charles Handy* in his book 'Gods of Management'. The four types are differentiated by their structures, processes and management methods. The differences are so significant as to create distinctive cultures, to each of which Handy gives the name of a Greek god.

6.15 **Zeus** is the god representing the **power culture**. Zeus is a dynamic entrepreneur who rules with snap decisions. Power and influence stem from a central source, perhaps the owner-directors or the founder of the business. The degree of formalisation is limited, and there are few rules and procedures, though this does not prevent the power-holders from exercising strict control. Such a firm is likely to be organised on a **functional** basis.

(a) The organisation is capable of adapting quickly to meet change.

(b) Personal influence decreases as the size of an organisation gets bigger. **The power culture is therefore best suited to smaller entrepreneurial organisations, where the leaders have direct communication with all employees**.

(c) Subordinates succeed by successfully guessing how their superiors would want them to act.

6.16 **Apollo** is the god of the **role culture** or **bureaucracy**. Everything is orderly and legitimate. There is a presumption of **logic and rationality**.

(a) These organisations have a formal hierarchical structure, and operate by well-established rules and procedures. Individuals are required to perform their job to the full, but not to overstep the boundaries of their authority. Individuals who work for such organisations tend to learn an expertise without experiencing risk; many do their job adequately, but are not over-ambitious.

(b) **The bureaucratic style can be very efficient** in a stable environment, when the organisation is large and when the work is predictable.

6.17 **Athena** is the goddess of the **task culture.** Management is dedicated to achieving the current goal. Performance is judged by results.

(a) The task culture is reflected in project teams and task forces. In such organisations, **there is no dominant or clear leader. The principal concern in a task culture is to get the job done.** Therefore the individuals who are important are the **experts** with the ability to accomplish a particular aspect of the task.

(b) The task culture is well suited to complex, unstable environments.

(c) Task cultures are expensive, as experts demand a market price.

(d) Task cultures also depend on variety, and to tap creativity requires a tolerance of perhaps costly mistakes.

6.18 **Dionysus** is the god of the **existential culture.** In the three other cultures, the individual is subordinate to the organisation or task. **An existential culture is found in an organisation whose purpose is to serve the interests of the individuals within it.** These organisations are rare, although an example might be a partnership of a few individuals who do all the work of the organisation themselves (with perhaps a little secretarial or clerical assistance).

(a) Barristers (in the UK) work through chambers. The clerk co-ordinates their work and hands out briefs, but does not control them.

(b) Management in these organisations are often lower in status than the professionals and are labelled secretaries, administrators, bursars, registrars and chief clerk.

(c) The organisation depends on the **talent of the individuals;** management is derived from the consent of the managed, rather than the delegated authority of the owners.

6.19 The descriptions above interrelate four different strands.

- The individual
- The type of the work the organisation does
- The culture of the organisation
- The environment

Organisational effectiveness perhaps depends on an appropriate fit of all of them.

Case example

Handy cites a pharmaceutical company which at one time had all its manufacturing subcontracted, until turnover and cost considerations justified a factory of its own. The company hired nine talented individuals to design and run the factory. Result:

(a) The *design team* ran on a task culture, with a democratic/consultative leadership style, using project teams for certain problems. This was successful while the factory was being built.

(b) After its opening, the factory, staffed by 400, was run on similar lines. There were numerous problems. Every problem was treated as a project, and the workforce resented being asked to help sort out 'management' problems. In the end, the factory was run in a slightly more autocratic way. Handy states that this is a classic case of an *Athenian* culture to create a factory being superseded by an *Apollonian* culture to run it. Different cultures suit different businesses.

Question 1

Which of Handy's cultures would you say is prevalent in your office?

Question 2

Review the following statements. Ascribe each of them to one of the four approaches.

People are controlled and influenced by:

- the personal exercise of rewards, punishments or charisma;
- the impersonal exercise of economic and political power to enforce procedures and standards of performance;
- communication and discussion of task requirements leading to appropriate action, motivated by personal commitment, to achieve the goal;
- intrinsic interest and enjoyment in the activities to be done, and/or concern and caring for the needs of the other people involved.

Answer

- Power
- Role
- Task
- Existential

Culture, the environment and strategy

6.20   Culture is an important filter of information and an interpreter of it, as suggested in the diagrams below.

- Ignoring culture

- Including culture

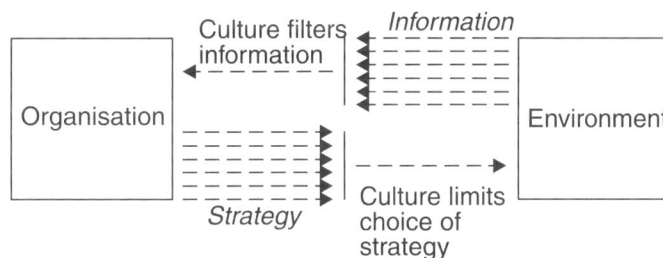

Culture filters and reconfigures environmental information. (A tragic example is the events in Waco, where members of the Branch Davidian cult interpreted environmental information about the FBI as presaging the end of the world.) At the same time culture filters out a number of strategic choices. For example, a firm might have a cultural predisposition against embarking on risky ventures. Another culture might have an ingrained 'Buy British' approach. Finally, **if culture is embodied in *behaviour*, existing behaviour may make a strategy incompatible with the culture and so impossible to implement.**

6.21   A model of culture which focuses specifically on a firm's approach to strategy was suggested by *Miles and Snow*, who outlined three strategic cultures, and a fourth 'non-strategic' culture.

(a) **Defenders like low risks, secure niche markets, and tried and trusted solutions**. These companies have cultures whose stories and rituals reflect historical continuity and consensus. Decision-taking is relatively formalised. There is emphasis on correct procedure. Personnel are drawn from within the industry.

(b) **Prospectors are organisations where the dominant beliefs are more to do with results** (doing the right things ie effectiveness). They seek to expand and increase market presence, and move into new areas.

(c) **Analysers try to balance risk and profits**. They use a core of stable products and markets as a source of earnings, like defenders, but move into areas that prospectors have already opened up. Analysers follow change, but do not initiate it.

(d) **Reactors**, unlike the three above, **do not have viable strategies**, other than living from hand to mouth.

Case example

Miles and Snow's analysis was applied to the responses by the regional electricity companies (RECs) to takeover bids in the Autumn of 1995. (The RECs are responsible for supplying and distributing electricity.) As at October 1995, seven of the 12 RECs in England and Wales had received takeover bids. (*Financial Times,* 4 October 1995).

At privatisation they 'shared a common heritage and hence ... greater similarities than would be found in more well-established private sector market places'.

- The largest REC, Eastern Group, 'embraced' the possibility of an alliance with Hanson. Eastern exhibits the characteristics of a 'prospector'. Its chief executive is 'non-REC' 'with a North American corporate pedigree and a greater interest in activities outside the traditional REC field'.

- Norweb and Midlands were 'cautious prospectors' which allow significant degrees of decentralisation, and a 'willingness to bring in executives with experience external to the industry'. They countenance 'strategic alliances'.

- Many of the RECs 'have demonstrated classical defender strategies'. They have specific features.

  ○ Hierarchical company structures

  ○ Board membership drawn from within the industry

  ○ Incremental growth, rather than more rapid growth by entering new business areas; little enthusiasm for diversification

---

6.22 *Denison's* model uses a grid to assess the relationship of culture with the environment. There are two dimensions.

(a) How orientated is the firm to the environment rather than to its internal workings? (An internal orientation is not always a bad thing, eg maintaining the safety of a nuclear installation.)

(b) To what extent does the environment offer stability or change?

		Organisation's strategic orientation	
		Internal	*External*
Environmental responses Required	*Stability*	Consistency	Mission
	Change/flexibility	Involvement	Adaptability

6.23 There are thus four possible cultures.

(a) **Consistency culture**. This exists in a stable environment, and its structure is well integrated. Management are preoccupied with efficiency. Such cultures are characterised by formal ways of behaviour. Predictability and reliability are valued. This has some features in common with the Apollonian culture.

(b) **Mission culture**. The environment is relatively stable, and the organisation is orientated towards it (eg 'customers'). A mission culture, whereby members' work activities are given meaning and value, is appropriate. For example, hospitals are preoccupied with the sick: inevitably their values are 'customer' orientated. A church is concerned with saving souls.

(c) **Involvement culture**. This is similar to clan control identified in an earlier chapter. The basic premise behind it is that the satisfaction of employees' needs is necessary for them to provide optimum performance. An example might be an orchestra, whose performance depends on each individual. Involvement and participation, as discussed in an earlier chapter, are supposed to create a greater sense of commitment and hence performance. For example, if you train people well enough, it is assumed that they will perform well. An involvement culture might take a 'human relations' approach to management.

(d) **Adaptability culture**. The company's strategic focus is on the external environment, which is in a state of change. Corporate values encourage inquisitiveness and interest in the external environment. Fashion companies are an example: ideas come from a variety of sources. Customer needs are fickle and change rapidly.

Question 3

(a) What do you think is the most significant contrast between Denison's model and Harrison's model?

(b) Which is better?

Answer

(a) Handy's model places much more emphasis on organisation structure and systems, which both determine and are determined by culture. Handy's model describes actual cultures. Denison's model describes *ideal* cultures, and is more concerned with the environment and a firm's external orientation than its structure. Denison suggests that if the environment is stable *and* the business is most effective with an internal orientation, *then* a consistency culture will be *best* etc.

(b) It depends on what you wish to use each model for.

Culture and risk

6.24 *Deal and Kennedy (Corporate Cultures)* consider cultures to be a function of the willingness of employees to take **risks**, and how quickly they get **feedback** on whether they got it right or wrong.

High risk

BET YOUR COMPANY CULTURE ('Slow and steady wins the race') Long decision-cycles: stamina and nerve required eg oil companies, aircraft companies, architects	**HARD 'MACHO' CULTURE** ('Find a mountain and climb it') eg entertainment, management consultancy, advertising
PROCESS CULTURE ('It's not what you do, it's the way that you do it') Values centred on attention to excellence of technical detail, risk management, procedures, status symbols eg banks, financial services, government	**WORK HARD/PLAY HARD CULTURE** ('Find a need and fill it') All action - and fun: team spirit eg sales and retail, computer companies, life assurance companies

Slow feedback (left)   *Fast feedback* (right)

Low risk

Excellence, culture and motivation

6.25 *Peters and Waterman*, in their book *In Search of Excellence*, found that the 'dominance and coherence of culture' was an essential feature of the 'excellent' companies they observed. A 'handful of guiding values' was more powerful than manuals, rule books, norms and controls formally imposed (and resisted). They commented: 'If companies do not have strong notions of themselves, as reflected in their values, stories, myths and legends, people's only security comes from where they live on the organisation chart.'

6.26 Peters and Waterman also discuss the central importance of *positive reinforcement* in any method of motivation as critical. 'Researchers studying motivation find that the prime factor is simply the self-perception among motivated subjects that they are in fact doing well ... Mere association with past personal success apparently leads to more persistence, higher motivation, or something that makes us do better.'

6.27 Peters and Waterman argue that employees can be 'switched on' to extraordinary loyalty and effort in the following cases.

(a) **The cause is perceived to be in some sense great**. Commitment comes from believing that a task is inherently worthwhile. Devotion to the *customer*, and the customer's needs and wants, is an important motivator in this way.

(b) **They are treated as winners**. 'Label a man a loser and he'll start acting like one.' Repressive control systems and negative reinforcement break down the employee's self-image.

(c) **They can satisfy their dual needs, both to** be a conforming, secure part of a successful team to be stars in their own right.

6.28 This means applying control (through firm central direction, and shared values and beliefs) but also allowing maximum individual autonomy (at least, the illusion of control) and even competition between individual or groups within the organisation. Peters and Waterman call this *loose-tight* **management**. Culture, peer pressure, a focus on action, customer-orientation and so on are 'non-aversive' ways of exercising control over employees. In other words, the control system used is **cultural control**.

Cultural characteristics of dynamic companies

6.29 *Pümpin* defines a dynamic company as one that 'considerably increases the benefits for its stakeholders within a relatively short time.' He notes that the culture of such firms emphasises four main aspects of business.

- **Expansion**. Rapid growth is eagerly sought.
- **Speed**. Time is seen as a vital resource.
- **Productivity**. Management is lean.
- **Risk-taking**. The possibility of failure is accepted.

6.30 Since it is not possible to emphasise everything, dynamic companies often display weaknesses in other important areas of culture.

- Customer service
- Innovation
- Technology
- Attitude to the workforce, including trust and respect
- Company spirit, including loyalty and identification

Strategic excellence positions and culture

6.31 Pümpin calls a specific superior capability a **strategic excellence position** (SEP). This is similar to what is generally known as a **competence**. SEPs fall into three categories.

- **Product-related,** such as technical superiority
- **Market-related,** such as an excellent image
- **Functional,** such as a cost-cutting production method

Once again, Pümpin asserts that it is not possible to be excellent at everything and that companies must decide where they will aim to excel.

6.32 There is a close relationship between a company's culture and its SEPs in that a SEP can only be developed if the company has an appropriate system of values. The aim of developing a SEP is to achieve above average capability in a specific field. This can only be done if the corporate culture emphasises the importance of that field.

Case example

In the 1960s, John De Lorean, then working for General Motors, emphasised the importance of developing smaller cars. This was an accurate strategic analysis but the strategy was never properly implemented because of GM's then prevailing corporate culture, which emphasised full-sized cars.

Chapter roundup

- **Mission** describes an organisation's **purpose** (ie its **basic function in society**). Mission directs strategy, embodies values, and influences policies and standards of behaviour.

- A **mission statement** should be brief, flexible and distinctive.

- The mission has to be translated into actual business practice. This is achieved by **goals** covering all areas of the business and most, if not all, stakeholder groups.

- People use the words **goal and objective interchangeably**, it is useful to keep in mind the difference between those goals which can be expressed as **objectives** (quantitative and SMART) and **aims** which are not quantitative.

- An organisation has many goals and objectives. A business has **profitability** or **return** as an overriding goal. However each **stakeholder group** has its own expectations of the business. Managers have to satisfy stakeholders, but this depends on the power different stakeholders have.

- **Systems** goals are those which the organisation's existence as an organisation encourages it to pursue. They are independent of the organisation's basic mission. Managers, as a stakeholder group, are capable of **subverting the organisation's mission**, as they have day to day control. Technical experts (eg work study analysts) are less concerned with *mission* than exercising their specialisation for whoever is interested. They have less interest in the survival of the organisation than do line managers.

- Culture is important both in organisations and in the wider world. It is the knowledge, beliefs, customs and attitudes which people adhere to. In wider society it is affected by factors such as age, class, race and religion, while in organisations it is defined by assumptions, beliefs and artefacts. These, in turn, are influenced by history, management, structure and systems. The McKinsey 7-S model shows how culture relates to other aspects of the organisation.

- Harrison's four-fold classification of organisations, popularised by Handy, is a useful analysis of some common aspects of culture.

    o The **power** culture depends on the holder of centralised power.
    o The **role** culture is associated with bureaucracy and emphasises rules and procedures.
    o The **task** culture is focused on delivering the current goal.
    o The **existential** culture supports individual independence and aspiration.

- Culture colours the organisation's view of its environment and hence influences its strategy. **Defenders** like low risk solutions and niche markets. **Prospectors** are more adventurous and concerned with results. **Analysers** try to balance risk and profits. **Reactors** do not have viable strategies. Deal and Kennedy analyse culture in terms of inherent risk in the industry and the speed with which feedback is available on strategic decisions.

- Pümpin emphasises that companies cannot be good at everything. Hence their cultures must support their chosen **strategic excellence positions**.

Quick quiz

1   What is vision?

2   What do you understand by 'strategic intent'?

3   What is the role of mission in organisations?

4   What should characterise a mission statement?

5   Name three stakeholder groups.

6   What constitutes culture in a general sense?

7   What are the main aspects of organisational culture?

8   What influences organisational culture?

9   Describe Harrison's analysis of organisations.

10 How did Miles and Snow analyse strategic culture?

11 What is the relationship between culture and SEPs?

Answers to quick quiz

1   A view of what the business is now, what it could be in an ideal world; and what that ideal world would be

2   Vision with an emotional core to energise and stretch

3   Mission provides the commercial logic for the organisation

4   Brevity, flexibility, distinctiveness

5   Internal; external; connected

6   Beliefs, values, customs, artefacts, rituals

7   Underlying assumptions, overt beliefs and visible artefacts

8   Many factors, including the founder, history, management style, structure, systems

9   Harrison analysed organisations into four types based on their structure and culture

   • Organisations structured around a dynamic leader display a power culture

   • The role culture is typical of bureaucracy.

   • Organisations that are run by project teams or have a matrix structure tend to display the task culture.

   • The existential culture pervades the loose organisation which exists to serve the interests of its principal members.

10 Defenders like low risks and secure markets. Prospectors constantly seek improved results. Analysers try to balance risk and profit. Reactors live from hand to mouth

11 SEPs can only be developed if they are supported by the culture of the organisation.

Now try the question below from the Exam Question Bank

Number	Level	Marks	Time
Q3	Introductory	n/a	30 mins

Chapter 4

ETHICAL CONSIDERATIONS

Topic list	Syllabus reference
1 Ethics and the organisation	9(c)
2 Social responsibility	9(a)
3 Corporate governance	9(b)

Introduction

Organisations are part of human society and, like individual people, are subject to rules that govern their conduct towards others. Some of these rules are **law** and enforced by legal sanction. Other rules fall into the realm of **ethics** or morality and are enforced only by the strength of society's approval or disapproval. Under a system of government that enjoys a measure of political legitimacy, law is generally a matter of consensus. Legal rules are therefore largely a matter of enforcing broadly acceptable standards of behaviour in a practical way. Ethics is more concerned with **absolute standards** of **right and wrong** and, human nature being what it is, individuals have widely divergent views on what those standards should be. Inevitably, therefore, ethical conduct is a matter of continuing debate. The first section of this chapter is concerned with the strategic impact of ethical ideas on organisations.

The behaviour of organizations may also be considered in the light of notions of **corporate social responsibility**. This is a rather poorly defined concept and the subject of continuing debate. However, there does now seem to be widespread acceptance that commercial organizations should devote some of their resources to the promotion of wider social aims that are not necessarily mandated by either law or the rules of ethics.

The final section of this chapter is concerned with **corporate governance** and the mechanisms that may be installed to promote fair and honest behaviour at the strategic apex.

Study guide

Section 9 – Ethical considerations

- The importance of social responsibility

- Corporate governance

- The attitude towards ethics on national and global scales

Exam guide

The importance of the topics covered in this chapter is indicated by there having been a part question on ethics in the pilot paper and a complete Section B question in June 2003. The examiner has expressed his shock at the level of ignorance of ethics and corporate governance in late 2003: look out for more questions on these topics! Ethics is something that is relevant to all behaviour, so it could be included in a question on any topic.

1 ETHICS AND THE ORGANISATION 12/02, 6/03

Fundamentals of ethical theory

1.1 Ethics is concerned with right and wrong and how conduct should be judged to be good or bad. It is about how we should live our lives and, in particular, how we should behave towards other people. It is therefore relevant to all forms of human activity.

1.2 Business life is a fruitful source of ethical dilemmas because its whole purpose is material gain, the making of profit. Success in business requires a constant, avid search for potential advantage over others and business people are under pressure to do whatever yields such advantage.

Non-cognitivism, ethical relativism and intuitionism

1.3 The approach called **non-cognitivism** denies the possibility of acquiring objective knowledge of moral principles. It suggests that all moral statements are essentially subjective and arise from the culture, belief or emotion of the speaker.

1.4 Non-cognitivism recognises the differences that exist between the rules of behaviour prevailing in different cultures. The view that right and wrong are culturally determined is called **ethical relativism** or **moral relativism**. This is clearly a matter of significance in the context of international business. Managers encountering cultural norms of behaviour that differ significantly from their own may be puzzled to know what rules to follow.

Cognitivism

1.5 **Cognitivist** approaches to ethics are built on the principle that objective, universally applicable moral truths exist and can be known. There are four important cognitivist theories to consider after we have looked at **law** and **religion** in relation to ethics.

Ethics and religion

1.6 Religions are based on the concept of universally applicable principle. However, they not only provide endless examples to support the moral relativist approach, both in their rules and their statements of fundamental belief; they are also vulnerable to criticism on logical rounds. Specifically, how does God decide what is right and what is wrong? Presumably, it is not mere whim and **moral principles** are involved. The implication is that it is proper to seek to understand these reasons for ourselves and to use them as the basis of our moral code.

Ethics and law

1.7 Cognitivist ethics and law can be seen as parallel and connected systems of rules for regulating conduct. Both are concerned with right conduct and the principles that define it. However, ethics and law are not the same thing.

1.8 Law must be free from ambiguity. However, unlike law, ethics can quite reasonably be an arena for debate, about both the principles involved and their application in specific rules. The law must be certain and therefore finds it difficult to deal with problems of conduct that are subject to opinion and debate.

1.9   Another difference is that many legal rules are only very remotely connected with ethics, if at all, and some laws in some countries have been of debateable moral stature, to say the least.

Consequentialist ethics: utilitarianism

1.10   The **consequentialist** approach to ethics is to make moral judgements about courses of action by reference to their outcomes or consequences. Right or wrong becomes a question of benefit or harm.

1.11   **Utilitarianism** is the best-known formulation of this approach and can be summed up in the '**greatest good**' principle. This says that when deciding on a course of action we should choose the one that is likely to result in the greatest good for the greatest number of people.

1.12   There is an immediate problem here, which is how we are to define what is good for people. *Bentham* considered that **happiness** was the measure of good and that actions should therefore be judged in terms of their potential for promoting happiness or relieving unhappiness. Others have suggested that longer lists of harmful and beneficial things should be applied.

1.13   The utilitarian approach may also be questioned for its potential effect upon minorities. A situation in which a large majority achieved great happiness at the expense of creating misery among a small minority would satisfy the 'greatest good' principle. It could not, however, be regarded as ethically desirable. A linked problem arises when we consider the nature of happiness and unhappiness, in that pain can be very much more intense than pleasure. We must therefore be very cautious in our netting-off of total happiness against total unhappiness.

1.14   However, utilitarianism can be a useful guide to conduct. It has been used to derive wide ranging rules and can be applied to help us make judgements about individual, unique problems.

Deontological ethics

1.15   **Deontology** is concerned with the application of universal ethical principles in order to arrive at rules of conduct, the word deontology being derived from the Greek for 'duty'. Whereas the consequentialist approach judges actions by their outcomes, deontology lays down *a priori* criteria by which they may be judged in advance. The definitive treatment of deontological ethics is found in the work of *Immanuel Kant*.

1.16   Kant's approach to ethics is based on the idea that facts themselves are neutral: they are what is; they do not give us any indication of what should be. If we make moral judgements about facts, the criteria by which we judge are separate from the facts themselves. Kant suggested that the criteria come from within ourselves and are based on a sense of what is right; an intuitive awareness of the nature of good.

1.17   Kant spoke of motivation to act in terms of 'imperatives'. A **hypothetical imperative** lays down a course of action to achieve a certain result. For instance, if I wish to pass an examination I must study the syllabus. A **categorical imperative**, however, defines a course of action without reference to outcomes. For Kant, moral conduct is defined by categorical imperatives. We must act in certain ways because it is right to do so – right conduct is an end in itself.

1.18 Kant arrived at two formulations of the categorical imperative with which we should be familiar.

(a) 'So act that the maxim of your will could hold as a principle establishing universal law.'

In other words, never act in a way that you would condemn in others. This is very close to the common sense maxim called the 'golden rule' that is found in many religious teachings. It appears in the Bible as

'Therefore all things whatsoever ye would that men should do to you, do ye even so to them: for this is the law and the prophets' (Matthew 7:12)

(b) 'Do not treat people simply as means to an end but as an end in themselves.'

The point of this rule is that it distinguishes between **people** and **objects**. We use objects as means to achieve an end: a chair is for sitting on, for instance. People are different. Human dignity requires that we regard people differently from the way we regard objects, since they have unique intellects, feelings, motivations and so on of their own. Note, however, that this does not preclude us from using people as means to an end as long as we, at the same time, recognise their right to be treated as autonomous beings. Clearly, organisations and even society itself could not function if we could not make use of other people's services.

Natural law

1.19 Natural law approaches to ethics are based on the idea that a set of objective or 'natural' moral rules exists and we can come to know what they are.

1.20 At one time natural law theory time was concerned with the rights of the citizen against arbitrary acts by powerful rulers. This was subsequently developed into a more democratic concept of government by consent, with a prominent position occupied by what are now called 'human rights'.

1.21 In terms of business ethics, the natural law approach deals mostly with rights and duties. Where there is a right, there is also a duty to respect that right. Clearly, this idea is not limited in its application to matters of law and government. It implies that we all must respect one another's rights of all kinds. For those concerned with business ethics there are undeniable implications for behaviour towards individuals. Unfortunately, the implications about duties can only be as clear as the rights themselves and there are wide areas in which disagreement about rights persists.

Duty and consequences

1.22 In their pure form, neither the duties of natural law nor Kant's categorical imperative will admit consideration of the consequences of our actions: we act in a certain way because we are obeying inflexible moral rules. Unfortunately, such an approach can have undesirable results. If people have absolute rights that we must respect whatever the circumstances, we may find that our actions in doing so harm the common good. An example is the accused person who commits an offence while on bail. The potential threat to public safety has to be balanced against the right of the individual to liberty. There is thus a great potential for conflict between courses of action based on the consequentialist approach and those based on deontology or natural law.

1.23 While individual cases are bound to provoke debate, it would be reasonable to suggest that an inflexible approach to rules of conduct is likely to produce ethical dilemmas. Deciding what to do when the arguments point in opposite directions is always going to be difficult. However, generally we do not have the option of doing nothing, and this is particularly true of business. We discuss some specific business related dilemmas later in this chapter.

Virtue ethics

1.24 The idea of pursuing a harmonious or virtuous life was first expressed by Aristotle. His approach was based on gentlemanly behaviour and a rational judgement about what constitutes good. To some extent this consists of avoiding extremes of any kind, since moderation will lead to virtue. For example, courage lies between cowardice at one end of the scale and foolhardiness at the other.

1.25 We need not concern ourselves too closely with the detail of Aristotle's approach, except to note that the cultivation of appropriate virtues has been proposed as a route to ethical behaviour in business. For example, managers might cultivate a range of virtues such as those listed below.

- Courage
- Fairness
- Empathy
- Persistence
- Honesty
- Politeness
- Receptivity to new ideas
- Determination
- Firmness

Ethics and strategy

1.26 In this Study Text we have emphasised that what the organisation wishes to achieve – its **mission** – is fundamental to any focussed control of its activities. When we discussed the concept of mission we made passing reference to **policies and standards of behaviour**.

1.27 It is important to understand that if ethics is applicable to corporate behaviour at all, it must therefore be a fundamental aspect of **mission**, since everything the organisation does flows from that. Managers responsible for strategic decision making cannot avoid responsibility for their organisation's ethical standing. They should consciously apply ethical rules to all of their decisions in order to filter out potentially undesirable developments.

The scope of corporate ethics

1.28 Corporate ethics may be considered in three contexts.

- The organisation's interaction with **national** and **international society**
- The effects of the organisation's **routine operations**
- The behaviour of **individual members** of staff

1.29 **Influencing society**. The organisation operates within and interacts with the political, economic and social framework of wider society. It is both inevitable and proper that it will both influence and be influenced by that wider framework. Governments, individual politicians and pressure groups will all make demands on such matters as employment prospects and executive pay. Conversely, organisations themselves will find that they need to make their own representations on such matters as monetary policy and the burden of regulation. International variation in such matters and in the framework of **corporate governance** will affect organisations that operate in more than one country. It is appropriate that the organisation develops and promotes its own policy on such matters.

1.30 **Corporate behaviour.** The organisation should establish **corporate policies** for those issues over which it has direct control. Examples of matters that should be covered by policy include health, safety, labelling, equal opportunities, environmental effects, political activity, bribery and support for cultural activities.

1.31 **Individual behaviour.** Policies to guide the behaviour of individuals are likely to flow from the corporate stance on the matters discussed above. The organisation must decide on the extent to which it considers it appropriate to attempt to influence individual behaviour. Some aspects of such behaviour may be of strategic importance, especially when managers can be seen as representing or embodying the organisation's standards. Matters of financial rectitude and equal treatment of minorities are good examples here.

Exam focus point

.The December 2002 examination offered 8 marks for a discussion of an ethical problem involving a corrupt business proposal. The examiner was ' very disappointed with the narrow and naïve answers… candidates need to be more aware of this area because it will not go away!' And lo! The June 2003 examination duly contained a question about a mis-managed company that, among other abuses, had been the scene of accounting irregularities and the bribery of foreign customers.

1.32 **Corporate ethical codes**. Organizations often publish corporate codes of ethical standards. Fundamentally, this is a good idea and can be a useful way of disseminating the specific policies we have discussed above. However, care must be taken over such a document.

(a) It should not be over-prescriptive or over-detailed, since this encourages a legalistic approach to interpretation and a desire to seek loopholes in order to justify previously chosen courses of action.

(b) It will only have influence if senior management adhere to it consistently in their own decisions and actions.

Case example

Ethics panel assails Third World placebo studies

Boston, July 11 (Reuters) – It is unethical for US researchers to test expensive treatments on people in Third World countries who would be unable to afford those drugs, a bioethics commission warned on Thursday in a published report. In an article in the New England Journal of Medicine, the National Bioethics Advisory Commission also said it was unethical to give volunteers placebos instead of treatments that are known to work.

These warnings by Harold Shapiro and Eric Meslin, the chairman and executive director respectively of the presidential commission, mark the latest round in a debate over the rules for conducting studies in countries where ethical standards may be less stringent than in the United States.

The issue surfaced in the Journal in 1997 when Drs. Peter Lurie and Sidney M Wolfe of Public Citizen's Health Research Group cited 15 government-financed studies that, they said, were using unethical methods to test whether various treatments could block the spread of the AIDS virus from a woman to her newborn child. All were being done in developing countries.

Some of the women in those studies were given placebos, even though the GlaxoSmithKline drug AZT had been shown to prevent babies from contracting AIDS from their infected mothers. At the time, it was regarded as unethical in the United States and other countries to test alternative AIDS treatments by giving pregnant volunteers a placebo.

Supporters of the studies had argued that giving placebos was valid because the radically different economic conditions in developing countries, where AZT was not widely available, made it virtually impossible to do the type of research that had become the standard in developed countries.

Shapiro and Meslin, who lead the 17 member advisory council established by former President Bill Clinton in 1995, wrote in the Journal that the experimental treatment should be tested against the best established treatment, "whether or not that treatment is available in the host country."

Giving placebos when an effective treatment exists "is not ethically acceptable," they said.

Shapiro and Meslin also said it was important to "avoid the exploitation of potentially vulnerable populations in developing countries."

If an experiment is testing a drug or device that " is not likely to be affordable in the host country or if the health care infrastructure cannot support its proper distribution and use, it is unethical to ask persons in that country to participate in the research, since they will not enjoy any of its potential benefits," they said.

There have been suggestions that researchers or drug companies may be testing products in poor countries because the cost is less and the rules are less stringent.

"Conducting a trial in a developing country because it is more convenient or efficient or less troublesome to do is never a sufficient justification," said Shapiro and Meslin.

The two also said that if tests show that the experimental treatment turns out to be more effective, it should be made available to all the people who participated in the study.

Researchers should not abandon their volunteers after the study is completed, they said.

---

2 SOCIAL RESPONSIBILITY 6/02

Corporate social responsibility

2.1 Businesses, particularly large ones, are subject to increasing expectations that they will exercise **social responsibility**. This is an ill-defined concept, but appears to focus on the provision of specific benefits to society in general, such as charitable donations, the creation or preservation of employment, and spending on environmental improvement or maintenance. A great deal of the pressure is created by the activity of minority action groups and is aimed at businesses because they are perceived to possess extensive resources. The momentum of such arguments is now so great that the notion of social responsibility has become almost inextricably confused with the matter of ethics. It is important to remember the distinction. Social responsibility and ethical behaviour are not the same thing.

2.2 In this context, you should remember that a business managed with the sole objective of maximising shareholder wealth can be run in just as ethical a fashion as one in which far wider stakeholder responsibility is assumed. On the other hand, there is no doubt that many large businesses have behaved irresponsibly in the past and some continue to do so.

Against corporate social responsibility

2.3 *Milton Friedman* argued against corporate social responsibility along the following lines.

(a) Businesses do not have responsibilities, only people have responsibilities. Managers in charge of corporations are responsible to the owners of the business, by whom they are employed.

(b) These employers may have charity as their aim, but 'generally [their aim] will be to make as much money as possible while conforming to the basic rules of the society, both those embodied in law and those embodied in ethical custom.'

(c) If the statement that a manager has social responsibilities is to have any meaning, 'it must mean that he is to act in some way that is not in the interest of his employers.'

(d) If managers do this they are, generally speaking, spending the owners' money for purposes other than those they have authorised; sometimes it is the money of customers or suppliers that is spent and, on occasion, the money of employees. By doing this, the manager is, in effect, both raising taxes and deciding how they should be spent, which are functions of government, not of business. There are two objections to this.

   (i) Managers have not been democratically elected (or selected in any other way) to exercise government power.

   (ii) Managers are not experts in government policy and cannot foresee the detailed effect of such social responsibility spending.

Friedman argues that the social responsibility model is politically collectivist in nature and deplores the possibility that collectivism should be extended any further than absolutely necessary in a free society.

2.4 A second argument against the assumption of corporate social responsibility is that the **maximisation of wealth is the best way that society can benefit from a business's activities**.

(a) Maximising wealth has the effect of increasing the tax revenues available to the state to disburse on socially desirable objectives.

(b) Maximising shareholder value has a 'trickle down' effect on other disadvantaged members of society.

(c) Many company shares are owned by pension funds, whose ultimate beneficiaries may not be the wealthy anyway.

The stakeholder view

2.5 The **stakeholder view** is that many groups have a stake in what the organisation does. This is particularly important in the business context, where shareholders own the business but employees, customers and government also have particularly strong claims to having their interests considered. This is fundamentally an argument derived from **natural law theory** and is based on the notion of individual and collective **rights**.

2.6 It is suggested that modern corporations are so powerful, socially, economically and politically, that unrestrained use of their power will inevitably damage other people's rights. For example, they may blight an entire community by closing a major facility, thus enforcing long term unemployment on a large proportion of the local workforce. Similarly, they may damage people's quality of life by polluting the environment. They may use their purchasing power or market share to impose unequal contracts on suppliers and customers alike. And they may exercise undesirable influence over government through their investment decisions. Under this approach, the exercise of corporate social responsibility constrains the corporation to act at all times as a good citizen.

2.7 Another argument points out that corporations exist within society and are dependent upon it for the resources they use. Some of these resources are obtained by direct contracts with suppliers but others are not, being provided by government expenditure. Examples are such things as transport infrastructure, technical research and education for the workforce. Clearly, corporations contribute to the taxes that pay for these things, but the relationship is rather tenuous and the tax burden can be minimised by careful management. The implication is that corporations should recognise and pay for the facilities that society provides by means of socially responsible policies and actions.

2.8 *Henry Mintzberg* (in *Power In and Around Organisations*) suggests that simply viewing organisations as vehicles for shareholder investment is inadequate.

(a) In practice, he says, organisations are rarely controlled effectively by shareholders. Most shareholders are passive investors.

(b) Large corporations can manipulate markets. Social responsibility, forced or voluntary, is a way of recognising this.

(c) Moreover, as mentioned above, businesses do receive a lot of government support. The public pays for roads, infrastructure, education and health, all of which benefits businesses. Although businesses pay tax, the public ultimately pays, perhaps through higher prices.

(d) Strategic decisions by businesses always have wider social consequences. In other words, says Mintzberg, the firm produces two kinds of outputs: **goods and services** and the **social consequences of its activities** (eg pollution).

Externalities

2.9 If it is accepted that businesses do not bear the total social cost of their activities, then the exercise of social responsibility is a way of compensating for this. An example is given by the environment. Industrial pollution is injurious to health: if someone is made ill by industrial pollution, then arguably the polluter should pay the sick person, as damages or in compensation, in the same way as if the business's builders had accidentally bulldozed somebody's house.

2.10 In practice, of course, while it is relatively easy to identify statistical relationships between pollution levels and certain illnesses, mapping out the chain of cause and effect from an individual's wheezing cough to the dust particles emitted by Factory X, as opposed to Factory Y, is quite a different matter.

2.11 Of course, it could be argued that these external costs are met out of general taxation: but this has the effect of spreading the cost amongst other individuals and businesses. Moreover, the tax revenue may be spent on curing the disease, rather than stopping it at its source. Pollution control equipment may be the fairest way of dealing with this problem. Thus advocates of social responsibility in business would argue that business's responsibilities then do not rest with paying taxes.

2.12 Is there any justification for social responsibility outside remedying the effects of a business's direct activities. For example, should businesses give to charity or sponsor the arts? Several arguments have been advanced suggesting that they should.

(a) If the **stakeholder concept** of a business is held, then the public is a stakeholder in the business. A business only succeeds because it is part of a wider society. Giving to charity is one way of encouraging a relationship.

(b) Charitable donations and artistic sponsorship are a useful medium of **public relations** and can reflect well on the business. It can be regarded, then, as another form of promotion, which like advertising, serves to enhance consumer awareness of the business, while not encouraging the sale of a particular brand.

2.13 The arguments for and against social responsibility of business are complex ones. However, ultimately they can be traced to different assumptions about society and the relationships between the individuals and organisations within it.

> **Exam focus point**
>
> The June 2002 examination approached the idea of social responsibility from an unusual direction, asking for a discussion of the topic in relation to a hospital, rather than the usual commercial organisation. The problem here is that it becomes necessary to stand most of the arguments on their heads, since there is no doubt that considerations other than economic success are crucial to such an organisation. You must be prepared to **think** in the exam hall.

The ethical stance

> **KEY TERM**
>
> An organisation's **ethical stance** is defined by *Johnson and Scholes* as the extent to which it will exceed its minimum obligation to stakeholders.

2.14 Johnson and Scholes illustrate the range of possible ethical stances by giving four illustrations.

- **Short-term shareholder interest**
- **Long-term shareholder interest**
- **Multiple stakeholder obligations**
- **Shaper of society**

Short-term shareholder interest

2.15 An organisation might limit its ethical stance to taking responsibility for **short-term shareholder interest** on the grounds that it is for **government** alone to impose wider constraints on corporate governance. This minimalist approach would accept a duty of obedience to the demands of the law, but would not undertake to comply with any less substantial rules of conduct. This stance can be justified on the grounds that going beyond it can **challenge government authority**; this is an important consideration for organisations operating in developing countries.

Long-term shareholder interest

2.16 There are two reasons why an organisation might take a wider view of ethical responsibilities when considering the **longer-term interest of shareholders**.

(a) The organisation's **corporate image** may be enhanced by an assumption of wider responsibilities. The cost of undertaking such responsibilities may be justified as essentially promotional expenditure.

Case example

The *Cooperative Bank* has estimated that it made £40m profit in 2003 as a result of its ethical policies.

Research showed that the Bank's ethical stance attracted business far in excess of that lost by turning away customers with poor human rights records or weak environmental performance.

(b) The responsible exercise of corporate power may prevent a build-up of social and political **pressure for legal regulation**. Freedom of action may be preserved and the burden of regulation lightened by acceptance of ethical responsibilities.

Multiple stakeholder obligations

2.17 An organisation might accept the **legitimacy of the expectations of stakeholders other than shareholders** and build those expectations into its stated purposes. This would be because without appropriate relationships with groups such as suppliers, employers and customers, the organisation would not be able to function.

2.18 A distinction can be drawn between **rights** and **expectations**. The *Concise Oxford Dictionary* defines a right as 'a legal or moral entitlement'. One is on fairly safe interpretative ground with legal rights, since their basis is usually clearly established, though subject to development and adjustment. The concept of *moral* entitlement is much less well defined and subject to partisan argument, as discussed above in the context of **natural law**. There is, for instance, an understandable tendency for those who feel themselves aggrieved to declare that their *rights* have been infringed. Whether or not this is the case is often a matter of opinion. For example, in the UK, there is often talk of a 'right to work' when redundancies occur. No such right exists in UK law, nor is it widely accepted that there is a moral basis for such a right. However, there is a widespread acceptance that governments should make the prevention of large-scale unemployment a high priority.

2.19 Clearly, organisations have a duty to respect the **legal rights** of stakeholders other than shareholders. These are extensive in the UK, including wide-ranging **employment law** and **consumer protection law**, as well as the more basic legislation relating to such matters as contract and property. Where **moral entitlements** are concerned, organisations need to be practical: they should take care to establish just what *expectations* they are prepared to treat as *obligations*, bearing in mind their general ethical stance and degree of concern about bad publicity.

2.20 Acceptance of obligations to stakeholders implies that **measurement of the organisation's performance** must give due weight to these extra imperatives. For instance, as is widely known, *Anita Roddick* does not care to have the performance of *Body Shop* assessed in purely financial terms.

Shaper of society

2.21 It is difficult enough for a commercial organisation to accept wide responsibility to stakeholders. The role of **shaper of society** is even more demanding and largely the province of public sector organisations and charities, though some well-funded private organisations might act in this way. The legitimacy of this approach depends on the framework of corporate governance and accountability. Where organisations are clearly set up for such a role, either by government or by private sponsors, they may pursue it. However, they must also satisfy whatever requirements for financial viability are established for them.

Ethical dilemmas

2.22 There are a number of areas in which the various approaches to ethics and conflicting views of a business's responsibilities can create **ethical dilemmas** for managers. These can impact at the highest level, affecting the development of policy, or lower down the hierarchy, especially if policy is unclear and guidance from more senior people is unavailable.

2.23 Dealing with **unpleasantly authoritarian governments** can be supported on the grounds that it contributes to economic growth and prosperity and all the benefits they bring to society in both countries concerned. This is a consequentialist argument. It can also be opposed on consequentialist grounds as contributing to the continuation of the regime, and on deontological grounds as fundamentally repugnant.

2.24 **Honesty in advertising** is an important problem. Many products are promoted exclusively on image. Deliberately creating the impression that purchasing a particular product will enhance the happiness, success and sex-appeal of the buyer can be attacked as dishonest. It can be defended on the grounds that the supplier is actually selling a fantasy or dream rather than a physical article.

2.25 Dealings with **employees** are coloured by the opposing views of corporate responsibility and individual rights. The idea of a job as property to be defended has now disappeared from UK labour relations, but there is no doubt that corporate decisions that lead to redundancies are still deplored. This is because of the obvious impact of sudden unemployment on aspirations and living standards, even when the employment market is buoyant. Nevertheless, it is only proper for businesses to consider the cost of employing labour as well as its productive capacity. Even employers who accept that their employees' skills are their most important source of competitive advantage can be reduced to cost cutting in order to survive in lean times.

2.26 Another ethical problem concerns **payments by companies to officials** who have power to help or hinder the payers' operations. In *The Ethics of Corporate Conduct, Clarence Walton* discusses to the fine distinctions which exist in this area.

(a) **Extortion**. Foreign officials have been known to threaten companies with the complete closure of their local operations unless suitable payments are made.

(b) **Bribery**. This is payments for services to which a company is not legally entitled. There are some fine distinctions to be drawn; for example, some managers regard political contributions as bribery.

(c) **Grease money**. Multinational companies are sometimes unable to obtain services to which they are legally entitled because of deliberate stalling by local officials. Cash payments to the right people may then be enough to oil the machinery of bureaucracy.

(d) **Gifts**. In some cultures (such as Japan) gifts are regarded as an essential part of civilised negotiation, even in circumstances where to Western eyes they might appear ethically dubious. Managers operating in such a culture may feel at liberty to adopt the local customs.

2.27 Business ethics are also relevant to competitive behaviour. This is because a market can only be free if competition is, in some basic respects, fair. There is a distinction between competing aggressively and competing unethically. The dispute between British Airways and Virgin centred around issues of business ethics.

3   CORPORATE GOVERNANCE

> **KEY TERM**
>
> The conduct of an organisation's senior officers constitutes its **corporate governance**.

3.1   *Lynch* says that the field of corporate governance includes the **selection** of the organisation's senior officers and 'their relationships with owners, employees and other stakeholders'. He points out that the influence of those officers over the future direction of the organisation makes corporate governance a matter of **strategic importance.**

3.2   Senior managers' influence amounts, in fact, to considerable **power**, and it is a matter of wide concern that power is wielded responsibly. Within the organisation, whatever the formal **ethical stance**, management decisions affect interests other than the purely financial. The effect on employment of short-term cost cutting is an example. Externally, the public interest may be affected. Lynch gives the example of the directors of privatised UK utility companies that awarded themselves large rewards, effectively at the taxpayer's expense.

3.3   Other recent examples include the deception and fraud committed by *Robert Maxwell* and, in the USA, the corrupt accounting policies pursued at *Enron Corporation*.

3.4   *Michel Albert* distinguishes three typical forms of corporate governance: the **Anglo-Saxon**, the **Rhine** and the **Japanese**. The first differs from the other two in that it is managed by a small number, often one or two, of senior managers who are responsible only to a fluctuating body of shareholders. In the other two models, top management is more **collective** in nature involving a larger team, and is responsible to a more stable body representing outside interests, such as trade unions in the Rhine model and large institutions in the Japanese models. The Anglo Saxon model thus has fewer constraints on top management wrong-doing.

3.5   Extensive abuses have led to a variety of measures intended to improve the quality of corporate governance.

    (a)   The development of **accounting standards** has been driven in part by the need to prevent abuses in financial reporting.

    (b)   The various professional bodies all have their own **codes of professional conduct**.

    (c)   A series of major financial scandals has led to government intervention in the UK in the form of **commissions on standards of behaviour**, each producing its code of conduct.

3.6   In April 2004, *Student Accountant* reported on the proposed new directive on statutory audit: this

> ... would clarify the duties of statutory auditors and underpin these with ethical principles to ensure ... objectivity and independence. There would be an option for member states to require the rotation of auditors every seven years ... companies themselves would be obliged to strengthen their own corporate governance ... set up an audit committee comprising independent members ... communicating directly with the auditor. That committee will have responsibility for selecting the auditor ...

3.7   Lynch points out that an important check on the abuse of power by senior managers is the **free flow of information to stakeholders**: 'wrongdoing will go unchecked as long as it remains unknown or unreported'. However, there are legitimate concerns about commercial confidentiality to be addressed here. The **auditor** has an important role to play, reviewing internal information on a confidential basis.

3.8   A second group of controls centres on the **non-executive director**. The various UK reports on corporate governance all emphasised the importance of the independent non-executive director. It is now usual for large companies to have committees at board level with strong non-executive director representation to deal with such matters as ethics, audit and senior manager remuneration. However, Lord Young, a former trade minister and successful businessman, believes that it is 'patent nonsense' to suggest that people who hold several non-executive directorships are capable of supervising full time directors.

3.9   **Whistle-blowing** is the disclosure by an employee of illegal, immoral or illegitimate practices on the part of the organisation. In theory, the public ought to welcome the public trust: however, confidentiality is very important in the accountants' code of ethics. Whistle-blowing frequently involves **financial loss** for the whistleblower.

(a)   Whistle-blowers may lose their jobs.

(b)   A whistle-blower who is a member of a professional body cannot, sadly, rely on that body to take a significant interest, or even offer a sympathetic ear. Some professional bodies have narrow interpretations of what is meant by ethical conduct. For many the duties of **commercial confidentiality** are felt to be more important.

In the UK, the Public Interest Disclosure Act 1998 offers some protection to whistle-blowers, but both the subject of the disclosure and the way in which it is made must satisfy the requirements of the Act.

Chapter roundup

- Ethics is not the same thing as law or the rules of religion

- Ethical theory is not integrated: consequentialist, deontological and natural law based rules are capable of pointing to different conclusions. Partly as a result of this, **ethical dilemmas** can exist at all levels in the organisation.

- **Mission** should incorporate recognition of the ethical dimension.

  Corporate ethics has three contexts.

  - ○ Interaction with national and international society
  - ○ Effects of routine operations
  - ○ Behaviour of individuals

- An organisation's **ethical stance** is the extent to which it will exceed its minimum obligations to stakeholders. There are four typical stances.

  - ○ Short-term shareholder interest
  - ○ Long-term shareholder interest
  - ○ Multiple stakeholder obligations
  - ○ Shaper of society

- There is a fundamental split of views about the nature of corporate responsibility.

  - ○ The **strong stakeholder view** that a range of goals should be pursued
  - ○ The view that the business organisation is a purely **economic force**, subject to law

- Expectations about the exercise of **social responsibility** by organisations are subject to the same split of views as corporate ethical responsibility.

- There is particular concern over **externalities**, or the social and environmental costs of corporate activities.

- **Corporate governance** is the conduct of the organisation's senior officers. Abuses have led to a range of measures to improve corporate governance. Non-executive directors have a particular role to play.

Quick quiz

1   What is an organisation's **ethical stance**?

2   Why might an organisation act to secure long-term shareholder interests?

3   What is a right?

4   When should ethical considerations be included in performance measures?

5   What is bribery?

6   What is corporate governance?

7   What is the role of the auditor in corporate governance?

8   What is an externality?

Answers to quick quiz

1 The extent to which it will exceed its minimum obligation to shareholders.

2 To improve corporate image and forestall legal regulation.

3 A legal or moral entitlement.

4 When moral expectations are accepted as obligations.

5 Payment for services for which there is no entitlement.

6 The conduct of the organisation's senior officers.

7 The independent review of confidential information.

8 A social or environmental cost of the organisation's activities not borne by the organisation.

Now try the question below from the Exam Question Bank

Number	Level	Marks	Time
Q4	Exam	20	36 mins

Chapter 5

ENVIRONMENTAL ANALYSIS

Topic list	Syllabus reference
1 The organisation as an open system	2(a)
2 The general environment	2(a)
3 Competitive forces	2(c)
4 Strategic intelligence	2(a)
5 Segmenting the market	5(a)
6 Buyer behaviour	2(b)
7 Marketing research	2(b)

Introduction

The aim of environmental analysis is to review the environment for **Opportunities** and **Threats**, and to secure environmental fit. An organisation has many interchanges with its environment. It draws inputs from it and outputs goods and services to it. The environment is a major **source of uncertainty**.

An organisation is affected by **general environmental trends** usefully summarised in the **PEST** model. Issues relating specifically to its particular industry reflect the **competitive environment**, and we discuss **Porter's five forces model** as a way of analysing it.

A thorough understanding of actual and potential markets is an essential prerequisite for the formulation of business strategy. We deal with the processes of **segmentation** and **product positioning** in this chapter and describe **buyer behaviour**. The chapter concludes with a discussion of market research.

Study guide

Section 2 – External environmental scanning

- Analysis of the general environment

- Analysis of customers and markets

Exam guide

The material in this chapter could form the background to a compulsory Section A question.

1 THE ORGANISATION AS AN OPEN SYSTEM

Systems theory

> ### KEY TERM
>
> *Curtis* defines a **system** as a collection of interrelated parts which taken together forms a whole such that:
>
> (a) The collection has some purpose
>
> (b) A change in any of the parts leads to or results from a change in some other part or parts.

1.1 An organisation is a type of system.

Open and closed systems

1.2 **General systems theory** makes a distinction between open, closed and semi-closed systems.

(a) **A closed system is isolated from its environment and independent of it,** so that no environmental influences affect the behaviour of the system, nor does the system exert any influence on its environment.

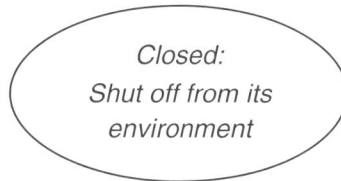

Closed:
Shut off from its
environment

(b) **An open system is connected to and interacts with its environment**. It takes in influences from its environment and also influences this environment by its behaviour. An open system is a stable system which is nevertheless continually changing or evolving.

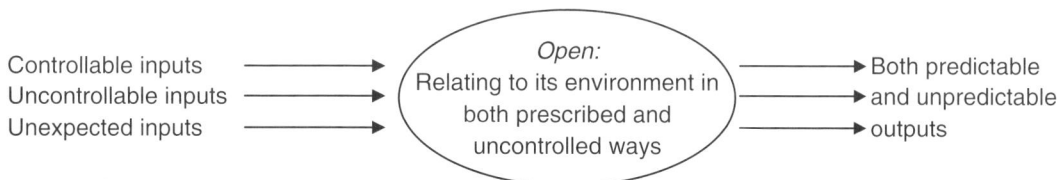

Controllable inputs
Uncontrollable inputs
Unexpected inputs
Open:
Relating to its environment in
both prescribed and
uncontrolled ways
Both predictable
and unpredictable
outputs

(c) **Few systems are entirely closed**. Many are **semi-closed,** in that their relationship with the environment is in some degree restricted. An example of a semi-closed system might be a pocket calculator. Its inputs are restricted to energy from its batteries and numerical information entered to it in a particular way (by the operator depressing a sequence of keys). The calculator is restricted in what it will do.

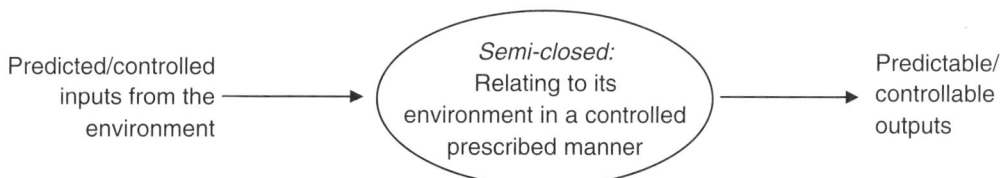

Predicted/controlled
inputs from the
environment
Semi-closed:
Relating to its
environment in a controlled
prescribed manner
Predictable/
controllable
outputs

BPP
PROFESSIONAL EDUCATION

1.3 **Social organisations, such as businesses and government departments, are by definition open systems.**

1.4 Organisations have a variety of interchanges with the environment, obtaining inputs from it, and generating outputs to it.

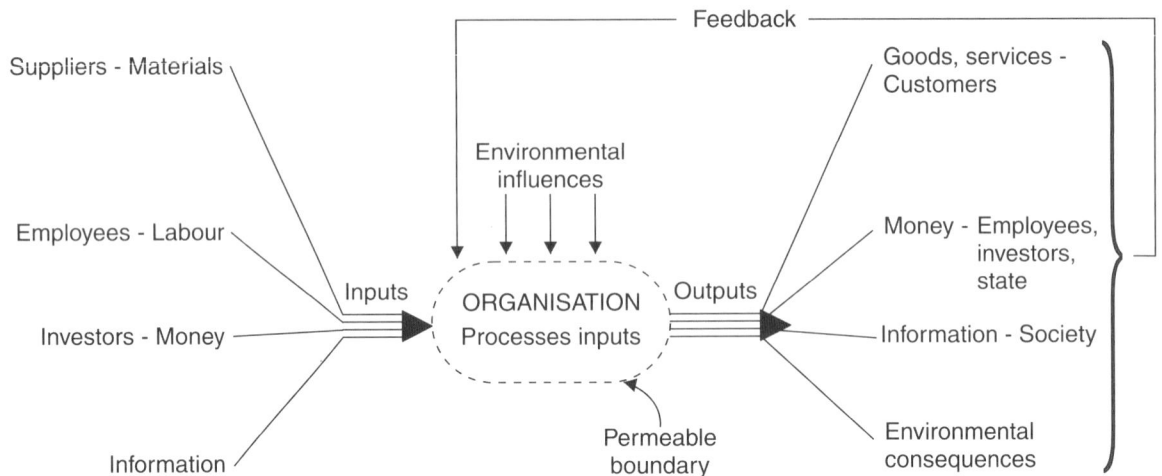

Environmental uncertainty

1.5 A large part of business strategy consists of making the organisation's interaction with its environment as efficient as possible. In the context of strategic management, therefore, the degree of **uncertainty** in the environment is of great importance. The greater the uncertainty, the greater the strategic challenge.

1.6 Uncertainty depends on **complexity** and **stability**: the more complex or dynamic the environment is, the more uncertain it is.

(a) An **uncomplicated, stable** environment can be dealt with as a matter of routine. The security and efficiency of a **mechanistic** or **bureaucratic** approach to management can be exploited. Since the future is likely to resemble the past, extrapolation from history is a satisfactory way of preparing for future events.

(b) Where the environment is **dynamic,** the management approach must emphasise response to rapid change. **Scenario planning, intuition** and a **learning approach** are all valid features of such a response.

(c) **Complexity** makes an environment difficult to understand. Diversity of operations and technological advance contribute to complexity. Complexity is difficult to analyse. It may be that it is best dealt with by a combination of **experience** and **extensive decentralisation.**

2 THE GENERAL ENVIRONMENT

2.1   The environment of an organisation is everything outside its boundaries.

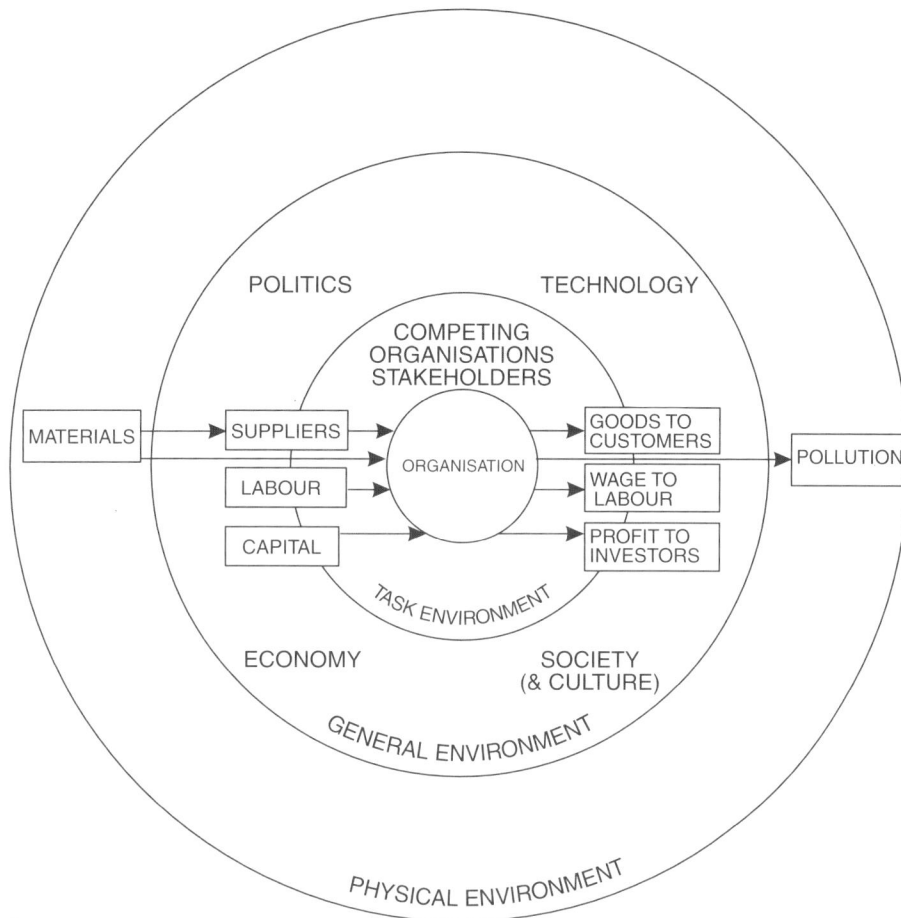

2.2   As you can see:

(a)   The **task** (or micro or near) **environment** is of immediate concern, and is uniquely configured for each organisation: no organisation has a network of suppliers, customers, competitors or stakeholders identical to another's.

(b)   The **general** (or macro or far) **environment** relates to PEST factors in the environment affecting all organisations.

- Political-legal factors
- Economic factors

- Social and cultural factors
- Technological factors

Exam focus points
The **PEST model** is a useful checklist for general environmental factors - in the real world they are all interlinked, of course.
Read a newspaper to keep yourself up with current relevant developments. We will offer a general framework here.
The acronym **PEST** is sometimes replaced by **SLEPT** (social, legal, economic, political, technological) or even STEEPLE, where the extra E stands for the **ethical** environment.

The political and legal environment

2.3   Laws come from common law, parliamentary legislation and government regulations derived from it, and obligations under EU membership and other treaties.

2.4   **Legal factors affecting all companies**

Factor	Example
General legal framework: contract, tort, agency	Basic ways of doing business; negligence proceedings; ownership; rights and responsibilities, property
Criminal law	Theft (eg of documents in Lanica's failed bid for the Co-op); insider dealing; bribery; deception
Company law	Directors and their duties; reporting requirements; takeover proceedings; shareholders' rights; insolvency
Employment law	Trade Union recognition; Social Chapter provisions; possible minimum wage; unfair dismissal; redundancy; maternity; Equal Opportunities
Health and Safety	Fire precautions; safety procedures
Data protection	Use of information about employees and customers
Marketing and sales	Laws to protect consumers (eg refunds and replacement, 'cooling off' period after credit agreements); what is or isn't allowed in advertising
Environment	Pollution control; waste disposal
Tax law	Corporation tax payment; Collection of income tax (PAYE) and National Insurance contributions; VAT
Competition law	General illegality of cartels

2.5   Some legal and regulatory factors affect **particular industries**, if the public interest is served. For example, electricity, gas, telecommunications, water and rail transport are subject to **regulators** who have influence over market access, competition and pricing policy (can restrict price increase).

2.6   This is for either of two reasons.

- The industries are, effectively, monopolies.
- Large sums of public money are involved (eg in subsidies to rail companies).

Case example

Gas deregulation

Government policy. Gas used to be a state monopoly in the UK. The industry was privatised as one company, British Gas. Slowly, the UK gas market has been opened to competition: now about 20 suppliers compete with British Gas.

Regulators. Ofgas regulates the gas industry. Ofgas has introduced a Code of Conduct requiring gas suppliers to train sales agents, allow for a cooling off period and so on.

Contracts. British Gas is vulnerable to competitors because of its prices. When it was privatised, it inherited 'take or pay contracts' requiring it to buy gas at a specific price from gas producers. Since that time, gas prices have fallen, and competitors have been able to benefit from this.

New markets. Government policy has also deregulated the electricity market, so that companies such as British Gas can now sell electricity.

Public policy on competition

2.7 Monopolies may have economic disadvantages and economic advantages.

(a) A **beneficial monopoly** achieves **economies of scale** in an industry where the **minimum efficient scale** is at a level of production that would mean having to achieve a large share of the total market supply.

KEY TERM

Economies of scale arise when a business grows to the extent that it is able to increase its input of all four types of productive resource: land, labour, capital and enterprise. The effect is to cause the whole structure of short-run costs to fall.

(b) A monopoly would be detrimental to the public interest if **cost efficiencies** are not achieved. *Oliver Williamson* suggested that monopolies might be inefficient if 'market power provides the firm with the opportunity to pursue a variety of other-than-profit objectives'. For example, managers might instead try to maximise sales, or try to maximise their own prestige.

2.8 *Consumer protection policies*

(a) Control over markets can arise by firms eliminating the opposition, either by merging with or taking over rivals or stopping other firms from entering the market. When a single firm controls a big enough share of the market it can begin to behave as a monopolist even though its market share is below 100%.

(b) Several firms could behave as monopolists by agreeing with each other not to compete. This could be done in a variety of ways - for example by exchanging information, by setting common prices or by splitting up the market into geographical areas and operating only within allocated boundaries. Such a **collusive oligopoly** is called a cartel.

Case example

In 2001 both VW and Michelin were made to pay heavy fines for monopolistic practices by the European Commission.

2.9 In a perfect monopoly, there is only one firm that is the sole producer of a good that has no closely competing substitutes, so that the firm controls the supply of the good to the market. The definition of a monopoly in practice is wider than this, because governments seeking to control the growth of monopoly firms will probably choose to regard any firm that acquires a certain share of the market as a potential monopolist.

The Competition Commission in the UK

2.10 The Director General of Fair Trading may ask the Competition Commission (CC) to investigate if any firm or group of firms controls 25% or more of the market, or the Secretary of State may do the same if any proposed takeover or merger would create a firm that controlled 25% or more of the market. The CC may also investigate proposed mergers where the assets involved exceed £70 million in value. The Commission will then investigate the proposed merger or takeover and recommend whether or not it should be allowed to proceed.

2.11 The **public interest** includes the promotion of competition and the extension of consumer sovereignty, efficiency and enterprise.

2.12 The **interpretation** of the public interest leads to conflicts in many cases. For example, actions which enhance competition and consumer sovereignty may conflict with the objective of allowing firms to be large enough to take advantage of competitive conditions in the international economy.

   (a) The CC may agree to a merger, but set conditions which are designed to protect consumers, or it may require that some assets be sold by the merged enterprise in order to prevent a dominant market position being established in a particular area of its operations.

   (b) The CC will consider whether any **excessive profits** have been made. In the Roche Products case for example, a return on capital of 70% was deemed to be evidence of **excessive pricing.** In another case, Pedigree Petfoods, 44% was held to be **not excessive**.

   (c) The CC will also see whether there is on the face of it a **high degree of interdependence** between a small number of firms. This evidence could be in the form of parallel pricing, predatory pricing or price discriminating policies, sometime prevalent in oligopolies in which there are say only four or five firms.

   (d) A firm carrying out 'anti-competitive' practices will not be favoured. An example of this could be 'socially unproductive advertising', where firms in a dominant position have huge advertising spends with the objective of building a barrier over which firms unable to spend a lot on advertising cannot climb. If the merger involves any anti-competitive **distribution policies** such as single supplier agreements, it could be opposed.

   (e) The CC will wish to avoid splitting up large companies, thus depriving them of economies of sale. The CC may also throw out applications if they could aggravate unemployment in an area in which unemployment is already significantly high.

   (f) The CC will be mindful to protect the needs of merging firms to secure adequate returns for enterprise, risk taking, innovation, improved efficiency research and development, and the need to compete with multinational firms on a global scale. Supernormal profits will not in themselves be a reason to refer merger proposals.

The conflicts between objectives present one problem for the CC, while another problem is that governments may be motivated by other political and economic considerations in deciding whether to adopt CC recommendations.

2.13 **Anticipating changes in the law**

* The governing party's election **manifesto** is a guide to its political priorities, even if these are not implemented immediately.

* The government often publishes advance information about its plans (**green paper** or **white paper**) for consultation purposes.

* The **EU's single market programme** indicates future changes in the law.

Political risk and political change

2.14 The political environment is not simply limited to legal factors. Government policy affects the whole **economy**, and governments are responsible for enforcing and creating a **stable**

framework in which business can be done. A report by the World Bank indicated that the quality of **government policy is important in providing** three things.

- Physical infrastructure (eg transport).

- Social infrastructure (education, a welfare safety net, law enforcement, equal opportunities).

- Market infrastructure (enforceable contracts, policing corruption).

2.15 However, it is **political change** which complicates the planning activities of many firms. Here is a checklist for case study use. It shows a sequence of considerations.

Consideration	Example
Possibility of political change	Dissatisfaction with low prices at which utilities were sold to private sector
Likely nature of impact	Windfall tax
Consequences	How much will be paid
Coping strategies	Cash flow planning
Influence on decision making	Lobbying - BT said that, being no longer a monopoly, it should be excluded.

Political risk

2.16 The political risk in a decision is the risk that political factors will invalidate the strategy and perhaps severely damage the firm. Examples are wars, political chaos, corruption and nationalisation.

2.17 A **political risk checklist** was outlined by *Jeannet and Hennessey*. Companies should ask the following six questions.

> 1 How **stable** is the host country's political system?
>
> 2 How **strong** is the host government's commitment to specific rules of the game, such as ownership or contractual rights, given its ideology and power position?
>
> 3 How **long** is the government likely to remain in **power**?
>
> 4 If the present government is **succeeded**, how would the specific rules of the game change?
>
> 5 What would be the effects of any expected **changes** in the specific rules of the game?
>
> 6 In light of those effects, what **decisions and actions should be taken now**?

2.18 Another example of how matters can change is given below.

Case example

Indonesia was perceived as an Asian tiger economy, providing an attractive environment to British businesses and investors. The country was run autocratically and a system of 'crony capitalism' (where lucrative monopolies were given to members of the President's family) developed. Late in 1997, the exchange rate of Indonesia's currency the rupiah fell dramatically as investors fled: Indonesia's largest companies are heavily indebted, but this debt is denominated in UK dollars. Many people were killed in riots, there was widespread looting, and the Foreign Office advised British nationals to leave. Democratic legitimacy reduces political risk as it can accommodate change.

On 23 May 1998, the Financial Times reported that the new Indonesian government had cancelled – or put on hold – contracts with Thames Water and Lyonnaise Des Eaux for unspecified reasons relating to the old regime. By early June, the Thames contract was apparently reinstated. The Indonesian government had, effectively, assumed the currency risk of the indebted companies.

The economic environment

2.19 The economic environment is an important influence at local and national level.

Factor	Impact
Overall growth or fall in Gross Domestic Product	Increased/decreased demand for goods (eg dishwashers) and services (holidays).
Local economic trends	Type of industry in the area. Office/factory rents. Labour rates House prices.
Inflation	Low in most countries; distorts business decisions; wage inflation compensates for price inflation
Interest rates	How much it costs to borrow money affects **cash flow**. Some businesses carry a high level of debt. How much customers can afford to spend is also affected as rises in interest rates affect people's mortgage payments.
Tax levels	Corporation tax affects how much firms can invest or return to shareholders. Income tax and VAT affect how much consumers have to spend, hence demand.
Government spending	Suppliers to the government (eg construction firms) are affected by spending.
The business cycle	Economic activity is always punctuated by periods of growth followed by decline, simply because of the nature of trade. The UK economy has been characterised by periods of boom and bust. Government policy can cause, exacerbate or mitigate such trends, but cannot abolish the business cycle. (Industries which prosper when others are declining are called *counter-cyclical* industries.)

2.20 The **forecast state of the economy** will influence the planning process for organisations which operate within it. In times of boom and increased demand and consumption, the overall planning problem will be to **identify** the demand. Conversely, in times of recession, the emphasis will be on cost-effectiveness, continuing profitability, survival and competition.

2.21 **Key issues for the UK economy**

(a) The **service sector** accounts for most output. Services include activities such as restaurants, tourism, nursing, education, management consultancy, computer consulting, banking and finance. Manufacturing is still important, especially in exports, but it employs fewer and fewer people (20% of the labour force in 1995, accounting for 25% of GDP).

(b) The **housing market** is a key factor for people in the UK. Most houses are owner-occupied, and most people's wealth is tied up in their homes. UK borrowers generally borrow at variable rates of interest, so are vulnerable to changes in interest rates.

(c) **Tax and welfare.** Although headline rates of tax have fallen, people have to spend more on private insurance schemes for health or pensions. The government aims to target welfare provision on the needy and to reduce overall welfare spending by getting people into work.

(d) **Productivity**. An economy cannot grow faster than the underlying growth in productivity, without risking inflation. UK manufacturing productivity is still lower than that of its main competitors, but in services, the UK is relatively efficient.

2.22 Impact of international factors

Factor	Impact
Exchange rates	Cost of imports, selling prices and value of exports; cost of hedging against fluctuations
Characteristics of overseas markets	Desirable overseas markets (demand) or sources of supply.
Capital, flows and trade	Investment opportunities, free trade, cost of exporting

Case examples

In 1997, the volume of global merchandise trade grew by 9.5%, over three times more than world output, not untypical of the period since 1950.

The growth in trade has affected the *logistics industry (transport, warehouse, etc)* (worth US $130bn of which £31.6bn is outsourced). Total logistics expenditure in the EU is likely to rise from £130bn in 1996 to $155bn in 2001.

The social environment

Demography

> **KEY TERM**
>
> **Demography** is the study of human population and population trends.

2.23 Factors of importance to organisational planners

Factor	Comment
Growth	The rate of growth or decline in a national population and in regional populations.
Age	Changes in the age distribution of the population. In the UK, there will be an increasing proportion of the national population over retirement age. In developing countries there are very large numbers of young people.
Geography	The concentration of population into certain geographical areas.
Ethnicity	A population might contain groups with different ethnic origins from the majority. In the UK, about 5% come from ethnic minorities, although most of these live in London and the South East.
Household and family structure	A household is the basic social unit and its size might be determined by the number of children, whether elderly parents live at home and so on. In the UK, there has been an *increase* in single-person households and lone parent families.

Factor	Comment
Social structure	The population of a society can be broken down into a number of subgroups, with different attitudes and access to economic resources. Social class, however, is hard to measure (as people's subjective perceptions vary).
Employment	In part, this is related to changes in the workplace. Many people believe that there is a move to a casual flexible workforce; factories will have a group of **core employees**, supplemented by a group of insecure **peripheral employees**, on part time or temporary contracts, working as and when required. Some research indicates a 'two-tier' society split between '**work-rich**' (with two wage-earners) and '**work-poor**'. However, despite some claims, **most employees are in permanent, full-time employment.**
Wealth	Rising standards of living lead to increased demand for certain types of consumer good. This is why developing countries are attractive as markets.

2.24 **Implications of demographic change**

(a) **Changes in patterns of demand**: an ageing population suggests increased demand for health care services: a young growing population has a growing demand for schools, housing and work.

(b) **Location of demand**: people are moving to the suburbs and small towns.

(c) **Recruitment policies**: there are relatively fewer young people so firms will have to recruit from less familiar sources of labour.

(d) **Wealth and tax**. Patterns of poverty and hence need for welfare provisions may change. The tax base may alter.

Culture

2.25 Through contact with a particular culture, individuals learn a language, acquire values and learn habits of behaviour and thought.

(a) **Beliefs and values**. Beliefs are what we feel to be the case on the basis of objective and subjective information (eg people can believe the world is round or flat). **Values** are beliefs which are relatively enduring, relatively general and fairly widely accepted as a guide to culturally appropriate behaviour.

(b) **Customs:** modes of behaviour which represent culturally accepted ways of behaving in response to given situations.

(c) **Artefacts:** all the physical tools designed by human beings for their physical and psychological well-being: works of art, technology, products.

(d) **Rituals**. A ritual is a type of activity which takes on symbolic meaning, consisting of a fixed sequence of behaviour repeated over time.

The learning and sharing of culture is made possible by **language** (both written and spoken, verbal *and* non-verbal).

2.26 **Underlying characteristics of culture**

(a) **Purposeful**. Culture offers order, direction and guidance in all phases of human problem solving.

(b) **Learned.** Cultural values are transferred in institutions (the family, school and church) and through on-going social interaction and mass media exposure in adulthood.

(c) **Shared.** A belief or practice must be common to a significant proportion of a society or group before it can be defined as a cultural characteristic.

(d) **Cumulative.** Culture is handed down to each new generation. There is a strong traditional/historical element to many aspects of culture (eg classical music).

(e) **Dynamic.** Cultures adapt to changes in society: eg technological breakthrough, population shifts, exposure to other cultures.

Case example

Islamic banking

Islamic banking is a powerful example of the importance of culture in an economy. The Koran abjures the charging of interest, which is usury. However whilst interest is banned, profits are allowed. A problem is that there is no standard interpretation of the sharia law regarding this. Products promoted by Islamic banks include:

- Leasing (the Islamic Bank TII arranged leases for seven Kuwait Airways aircraft)
- Trade finance
- Commodities trading

The earlier Islamic banks offered current accounts only, but depositors now ask for shares in the bank profits. To tap this market, Citibank, the US bank, opened an Islamic banking subsidiary in Bahrain.

2.27 Knowledge of the culture of a society is clearly of value to businesses in a number of ways.

(a) **Marketers** can adapt their products accordingly, and be fairly sure of a sizeable market. This is particularly important in export markets.

(b) **Human resource managers** may need to tackle cultural differences in recruitment. For example, some ethnic minorities have a different body language from the majority, which may be hard for some interviewers to interpret.

2.28 Culture in a society can be divided into **subcultures** reflecting social differences. Most people participate in several of them.

Subculture	Comment
Class	People from different social classes might have different values reflecting their position of society.
Ethnic background	Some ethnic groups can still be considered a distinct cultural group.
Religion	Religion and ethnicity are related.
Geography or region	Distinct regional differences might be brought about by the *past* effects of physical geography (socio-economic differences etc). Speech accents most noticeably differ.
Age	Age subcultures vary according to the period in which individuals were socialised to an extent, because of the great shifts in social values and customs in this century. ('Youth culture'; the 'generation gap').

Subculture	Comment
Sex	Some products are targeted directly to women or to men.
Work	Different organisations have different corporate cultures, in that the shared values of one workplace may be different from another.

Case example

Consider the case of a young French employee of *Eurodisney*.

(a)   The employee speaks the French language - part of the national culture - and has participated in the French education system.

(b)   As a youth, the employee might, in his or her spare time, participate in various 'youth culture' activities. Music and fashion are emblematic of youth culture.

(c)   As an employee of Eurodisney, the employee will have to participate in the corporate culture, which is based on American standards of service with a high priority put on friendliness to customers.

2.29   Cultural change might have to be planned for. There has been a revolution in attitudes to female employment, despite the well-publicised problems of discrimination that still remain.

Question 1

Club Fun is a UK company which sells packaged holidays. Founded in the 1960s, it offered a standard 'cheap and cheerful' package to resorts in Spain and, more recently, to some of the Greek islands. It was particularly successful at providing holidays for the 18-30 age group.

What do you think the implications are for Club Fun of the following developments?

- A fall in the number of school leavers
- The fact that young people are more likely now than in the 1960s to go into higher education
- Holiday programmes on TV which feature a much greater variety of locations
- Greater disposable income among the 18-30 age group

Answer

The firm's market is shrinking. There is an absolute fall in the number of school leavers. Moreover, it is possible that the increasing proportion of school leavers going to higher education will mean there will be fewer who can afford Club Fun's packages. That said, a higher disposable income in the population at large might compensate for this trend. People might be encouraged to try destinations other than Club Fun's traditional resorts if these other destinations are publicised on television.

Business ethics

2.30   The conduct of an organisation, its management and employees will be measured against **ethical standards** by the customers, suppliers and other members of the public with whom they deal.

2.31   We considered business ethics in detail in Chapter 4.

Technological factors

2.32   The word 'technology' is used to mean three rather different things.

(a) **Apparatus or equipment** such as a TV camera

(b) **Technique:** for instance how to use the TV camera to best effect, perhaps in conjunction with other equipment such as lights.

(c) **Organisation:** for example the grouping of camera-operators into teams, to work on a particular project

2.33 **Technology contributes to overall economic growth**. The **production possibility curve** describes the total production in an economy. There are three ways in which technology can increase total output.

- Gains in productivity (more output per units of input)
- Reduced costs (eg transportation technology, preservatives)
- New types of product

2.34 **Effects of technological change on organisations**

(a) **The type of products or services that are made and sold.**

(b) **The way in which products are made** (eg robots, new raw materials)

(c) **The way in which services are provided.** For example companies selling easily transportable goods - for instance, books and CDs - can offer much greater consumer choice and are enjoying considerable success over the internet.

(d) **The way in which markets are identified.** Database systems make it much easier to analyse the market place.

(e) **The way in which firms are managed.** IT encourages 'delayering' of organisational hierarchies, homeworking, and better communication.

(f) **The means and extent of communications with external clients.** The financial sector is rapidly going electronic - call centres are now essential to stay in business, PC banking is on the way, and the Internet and interactive TV are starting to feature in business plans.

2.35 The impact of recent technological change also has potentially important social consequences, which in turn have an impact on business.

(a) **Homeworking.** Whereas people were once collected together to work in factories, home working will become more important.

(b) **Intellective skills.** Certain sorts of skill, related to interpretation of data and information processes, are likely to become more valued than manual or physical skills.

(c) **Services.** Technology increases manufacturing productivity, releasing human resources for service jobs. These jobs require **greater interpersonal skills** (eg in dealing with customers).

The physical environment

2.36 **The importance of physical environmental conditions**

(a) **Resource inputs.** Managing physical resources successfully (eg oil companies, mining companies) is a good source of profits.

(b) **Logistics.** The physical environment presents logistical problems or opportunities to organisations. Proximity to road and rail links can be a reason for siting a warehouse in a particular area.

(c) **Government.** The physical environment is under the control of other organisations.

    (i)   Local authority town planning departments can influence where a building and necessary infrastructure can be sited.

    (ii)   Governments can set regulations about some of the organisation's environmental interactions.

(d) **Disasters.** In some countries, the physical environment can pose a major threat to organisations. The example of the earthquake in Kobe, Japan, springs to mind.

An interrelationship between environmental factors and strategic planning

2.37   Issues relating to the effect of an organisation's activities on the physical environment have come to the fore in recent years.

2.38   **How environmental issues will impinge on business**

- **Consumer demand** for products that appear to be environmentally friendly.

- Demand for **less pollution** from industry.

- Greater **regulation** by government and the EU (eg recycling targets).

- **Polluter pays.** Demand that businesses be charged with the external cost of their activities.

- Possible requirements to conduct **environmental audits**.

- Opportunities to develop **products and technologies** which are environmentally friendly.

- **Taxes** (eg landfill tax).

2.39   The consumer demand for products which claim environmental soundness has waxed and waned, with initial enthusiasm replaced by cynicism as to 'green' claims.

(a) **Marketing.** Companies such as *Body Shop* have exploited environmental friendliness as a marketing tool.

(b) **Publicity.** Perhaps companies have more to fear from the impact of bad publicity (relating to their environmental practices) than they have to benefit from positive environmental messages as such. Public relations is a vital competitive weapon.

(c) **Lifestyles.** There may be a limit to which consumers are prepared to alter their lifestyles for the sake of environmental correctness.

(d) Consumers may be **imperfectly educated** about environmental issues. For example, much recycled paper has simply replaced paper produced from substantially developed forests. In short, companies may have to educate consumers as to the environmental impact of their products.

Exam focus point
You might need to use environmental analysis later in the strategic planning process, when discussing strategic options.

2.40 **Section summary**
- Use PEST as a checklist.
- Not all environmental factors are equally relevant to all firms at all times.

3 COMPETITIVE FORCES

12/01

> **Exam focus point**
>
> It is unusual in an exam at this level to be asked specifically about theoretical models. However, in the December 2001 case study 10 marks were available for a discussion of environmental models in relation to the specific case scenario. This question could have been answered using the SLEPT (or PEST) model, which has been discussed above, together with Porter's fire forces and strategic group analysis, both of which are discussed below.

3.1 In discussing competition, *Porter* (*Competitive Strategy*) distinguishes between factors which characterise the nature of competition.

(a) **In one industry compared with another** (eg in the chemicals industry compared with the clothing retail industry, some factors make one industry as a whole potentially more profitable than another (ie yielding a bigger return on investment).

(b) Factors **within a particular industry** lead to the competitive strategies that individual firms might select.

3.2 Five **competitive forces** influence the state of competition in an industry, which collectively determine the profit (ie long-run return on capital) potential of the industry as a whole. **Learn them.**

- The threat of **new entrants** to the industry
- The threat of **substitute** products or services
- The bargaining power of **customers**
- The bargaining power of **suppliers**
- The **rivalry** amongst current competitors in the industry

The threat of new entrants (and barriers to entry to keep them out)

3.3 A new entrant into an industry will bring extra capacity and more competition. The strength of this threat is likely to vary from industry to industry and depends on two things.

- The strength of the **barriers to entry**. Barriers to entry discourage new entrants.
- The likely **response of existing competitors** to the new entrant.

3.4 **Barriers to entry**

(a) **Scale economies**. High fixed costs often imply a high breakeven point, and a high breakeven point depends on a large volume of sales. If the market as a whole is not growing, the new entrant has to capture a large slice of the market from existing competitors. This is expensive (although Japanese companies have done this in some cases).

(b) **Product differentiation**. Existing firms in an industry may have built up a good brand image and strong customer loyalty over a long period of time. A few firms may promote a large number of brands to crowd out the competition.

Case example

The *UK detergent industry*

Complete newcomers (eg Ecover) had to go for niches or unusual distribution channels at first. New entrants would have to spend heavily to overcome the existing brand loyalties and to build up a brand image of their own. These high 'start-up' losses might deter would-be competitors.

(c) **Capital requirements**. When capital investment requirements are high, the barrier against new entrants will be strong, particularly when the investment would possibly be high-risk.

Case example

Telecommunications

The capital requirements for entering the telecommunications business are falling. Although many telecommunications firms had invested in optical fibre networks for trunk (eg long-distance calls), the final connection to the household is almost a monopoly for BT because of the expense of duplicating it, though TV Cable companies have slowly dented this.

(d) **Switching costs**. Switching costs refer to the costs (time, money, convenience) that a customer would have to incur by switching from one supplier's products to another's. Although it might cost a **consumer** nothing to switch from one brand of frozen peas to another, the potential costs for the **retailer or distributor** might be high.

(e) **Access to distribution channels**. Distribution channels carry a manufacturer's products to the end-buyer. New distribution channels are difficult to establish, and existing distribution channels hard to gain access to.

(f) **Cost advantages of existing producers, independent of economies of scale** include:

- Patent rights
- Experience and know-how (the learning curve)
- Government subsidies and regulations
- Favoured access to raw materials

Case example

Japanese firms

A little while ago, it was assumed that, following the success of Japanese firms worldwide in motor vehicles (Nissan, Honda, Toyota) and consumer electronics (eg Sony, JVC, Matsushita), *no* Western companies were safe from Japanese competition. Kao (household goods), Suntory (drinks), Nomura (banking and securities) were seen as successors to firms such as Procter and Gamble, Heineken etc.

This has not happened: for example, Japanese pharmaceutical firms, such as Green Cross, have not achieved the world domination (anticipated in 1982). US and European firms are still dominant in this industry.

Perhaps cars and consumer electronics are the exception rather than the rule. The reason for this might be distribution. Normally, outsiders do not find it easy to break into established distribution patterns. However, distribution channels in cars and consumer electronics offered outsiders an easy way in.

(a) The *car industry* is vertically integrated, with a network of exclusive dealerships. Given *time* and *money*, the Japanese firms could simply build their own dealerships and run them as they liked, with the help of local partners. This barrier to entry was not inherently *complex*.

(b) *Consumer electronics*

    (i) In the early years, the consumer electronics market was driven by *technology*, so innovative firms such as Sony and Matsushita could overcome distribution weaknesses with innovative products, as they had plenty to invest. This lowered entry barriers.

    (ii) Falling prices changed the distribution of hifi goods from small specialist shops to large cut-price outlets, such as *Comet*. Newcomers to a market are the natural allies of such new outlets: existing suppliers prefer to shun 'discount' retailers to protect margins in their current distribution networks.

Japanese firms have *not* established dominant positions in:

(a) Healthcare, where national pharmaceuticals wholesalers are active as 'gatekeepers'
(b) Household products, where there are strong supermarket chains
(c) Cosmetics, where department stores and specialist shops offer a wide choice.

3.5 Entry barriers might be **lowered** by the impact of change.

- Changes in the environment
- Technological changes
- Novel distribution channels for products or services

The threat from substitute products

3.6 A **substitute product** is a good or service produced by **another industry** which satisfies the same customer needs.

Case example

The Channel Tunnel

Passengers have several ways of getting to London to Paris, and the pricing policies of the various industries transporting them there reflects this.

(a) 'Le Shuttle' carries cars in the Channel Tunnel. Its main competitors come from the *ferry* companies, offering a substitute service. Therefore, you will find that Le Shuttle sets its prices with reference to ferry company prices, and vice versa.

(b) Eurostar is the rail service from London to Paris/Brussels. Its main competitors are not the ferry companies but the *airlines*. Prices on the London-Paris air routes fell with the commencement of Eurostar services, and some airlines have curtailed the number of flights they offer.

The bargaining power of customers

3.7 Customers want better quality products and services at a lower price. Satisfying this want might force down the profitability of suppliers in the industry. Just how strong the position of customers will be depends on a number of factors.

- How much the **customer buys**
- How **critical** the product is to the customer's own business

- **Switching costs (ie the cost of switching supplier)**
- Whether the products are **standard items** (hence easily copied) or specialised
- The **customer's own profitability:** a customer who makes low profits will be forced to insist on low prices from suppliers
- Customer's **ability to bypass** the supplier (or take over the supplier)
- The **skills** of the customer **purchasing staff,** or the price-awareness of consumers
- When **product quality** is important to the customer, the customer is less likely to be price-sensitive, and so the industry might be more profitable as a consequence

---

Case example

Although the Ministry of Defence may wish to keep control over defence spending, it is likely as a customer to be more concerned that the products it purchases perform satisfactorily than with getting the lowest price possible for everything it buys.

The bargaining power of suppliers

3.8 Suppliers can exert pressure for higher prices. The ability of suppliers to get higher prices depends on several factors.

- Whether there are just **one or two dominant suppliers** to the industry, able to charge monopoly or oligopoly prices
- The threat of **new entrants** or substitute products to the **supplier's industry**
- Whether the suppliers have **other customers** outside the industry, and do not rely on the industry for the majority of their sales
- The **importance of the supplier's product** to the customer's business
- Whether the supplier has a **differentiated product** which buyers need to obtain
- Whether **switching costs** for customers would be high

The rivalry amongst current competitors in the industry

3.9 The **intensity of competitive rivalry** within an industry will affect the profitability of the industry as a whole. Competitive actions might take the form of price competition, advertising battles, sales promotion campaigns, introducing new products for the market, improving after sales service or providing guarantees or warranties. Competition can stimulate demand, expanding the market, or it can leave demand unchanged, in which case individual competitors will make less money, unless they are able to cut costs.

3.10 **Factors determining the intensity of competition**

(a) **Market growth.** Rivalry is intensified when firms are competing for a greater market share in a total market where growth is slow or stagnant.

(b) **Cost structure.** High fixed costs are a temptation to compete on price, as in the short run any contribution from sales is better than none at all. A perishable product produces the same effect.

(c) **Switching.** Suppliers will compete if buyers switch easily (eg Coke vs Pepsi).

(d) **Capacity.** A supplier might need to achieve a substantial increase in output capacity, in order to obtain reductions in unit costs.

(e) **Uncertainty.** When one firm is not sure what another is up to, there is a tendency to respond to the uncertainty by formulating a more competitive strategy.

(f) **Strategic importance.** If success is a prime strategic objective, firms will be likely to act very competitively to meet their targets.

(g) **Exit barriers** make it difficult for an existing supplier to leave the industry. These can take many forms.

    (i) Fixed assets with a low **break-up value** (eg there may be no other use for them, or they may be old)

    (ii) The cost of **redundancy payments** to employees

    (iii) If the firm is a division or subsidiary of a larger enterprise, the **effect of withdrawal on the other operations** within the group

    (iv) The **reluctance of managers** to admit defeat, their loyalty to employees and their fear for their own jobs

    (v) **Government pressures** on major employers not to shut down operations, especially when competition comes from foreign producers rather than other domestic producers

---

Question 2

The *tea industry* is characterised by oversupply, with a surplus of about 80,000 tonnes a year. Tea estates 'swallow capital, and the return is not as attractive as in industries such as technology or services'. Tea cannot be stockpiled, unlike coffee, keeping for two years at most. Tea is *auctioned* in London and prices are the same in absolute terms as they were 15 years ago. Tea is produced in Africa and India, Sri Lanka and China. Because of the huge capital investment involved, the most recent investments have been quasi-governmental, such as those by the Commonwealth Development Corporation in ailing estates in East Africa. There is no simple demarcation between buyers and sellers. Tea-bag manufacturers own their own estates, as well as buying in tea from outside sources.

In 1997 tea prices were described in India at least as being 'exceptionally firm ... The shortage and high prices of coffee have also raised demand for tea which remains the cheapest of all beverages in spite of the recent rise in prices. Demand from Russia, Poland, Iran and Iraq are expected to rise.'

(a) Carry out a five forces analysis.

(b) Thinking ahead, suggest a possible strategy for a tea-grower with a number of estates which has traditionally sold its tea at auction.

Answer

(a) Here are some ideas. Barriers to entry are high. There are plenty of substitute products (coffee), competitive rivalry is high because of the difficulty of stockpiling products. Customer bargaining power is high, but supplier power is low: all it needs is capital, the right sort of land and labour.

(b) *Williamson and Magor* has begun to switch from selling tea at auction to consumer marketing. The firm is aiming to build up its own brand image in the UK and Germany, by offering - by mail order - unblended, specialist teas from its Indian estates. It advertised via Barclays Premier Card magazine; replies were used to set up a customer database. When the company's Earl Grey tea was recommended on BBC2's *Food and Drink,* these existing customers were targeted with a letter and a sample.

The impact of information technology on the competitive forces

---

Case example

The *Internet* has had a variety of impacts.

In March 1996, the Financial Times reported that German companies were losing lucrative niche markets because the *Internet* made it easier for customers to compare prices from other suppliers by obtaining other information over the Internet. High prices made German retailers vulnerable in an age when a shopper with a credit card and computer could sit at home and could order from around the world. The Internet has *increased competition*. The Internet is a competitive weapon. Tesco's home shopping service is supported by internet technology.

3.11 **Barriers to entry and IT**

(a) **IT can raise entry barriers** by increasing economies of scale, raising the capital cost of entry (by requiring a similar investment in IT) or effectively colonising distribution channels by tying customers and suppliers into the supply chain or distribution chain.

(b) **IT can surmount entry barriers**. An example is the use of telephone banking, which sometimes obviates the need to establish a branch network.

3.12 **Bargaining power of suppliers and IT**

(a) **Increasing the number of** accessible **suppliers.** Supplier power in the past can derive from various factors such as geographical proximity and the fact that the organisation requires goods of a certain standard in a certain time. IT enhances supplier information available to customers.

(b) **Closer supplier relationships.** Suppliers' power can be *shared*. CAD can be used to design components in tandem with suppliers. Such relationships might be developed with a few key suppliers. The supplier and the organisation both benefit from performance improvement, but the relations are closer.

(c) **Switching costs.** Suppliers can be integrated with the firm's administrative operations, by a system of electronic data interchange.

3.13 **Bargaining power of customers.** IT can lock customers in.

(a) **IT can raise switching costs.**

(b) **Customer information systems** can enable a thorough analysis of marketing information so that products and services can be tailored to the needs of certain segments.

3.14 **Substitutes.** In many respects, **IT itself is the substitute product.** Here are some examples.

(a) Video-conferencing systems might substitute for air transport in providing a means by which managers from all over the world can get together in a meeting.

(b) IT is the basis for new leisure activities (eg computer games) which substitute for TV or other pursuits.

(c) E-mail might substitute for some postal deliveries.

3.15 **IT and the state of competitive rivalry**

(a) IT can be used in support of a firm's **competitive** strategy of cost leadership, differentiation or focus. These are discussed later in this text.

(b) IT can be used in a **collaborative** venture, perhaps to set up new communications networks. Some competitors in the financial services industry share the same ATM network.

Using the five forces model: a caution

3.16 The five forces model provides a comprehensive framework for analysing the competitive environment. However, it must be used with caution. Its very comprehensiveness can encourage a feeling of omniscience in those who use it: a sense that all factors have been duly considered and dealt with. Unfortunately, no one is actually omniscient. Any analysis must pursue as high a degree of **objectivity** as possible. If there is too much subjectivity, unfounded complacence will result.

3.17 The creation in the UK of direct motor insurance selling by Direct Line Insurance is a case in point. Existing motor insurers' view of the threat from new entrants was that the need to create a distribution network of local agents and brokers was an **effective barrier to entry**. Direct Line's centralised call-centre approach simply bypassed the barrier.

3.18 The effect of subjectivity appears at an early stage in any analysis using the five forces approach. It is necessary to define with great care just what **market** or **market segment** one is dealing with. For a large organisation, or one operating in a complex environment, this may be extremely difficult. BPP's provision of classroom training in accountancy is a good example. The market for training for potential chartered accountants is subject to considerable **customer** bargaining power, since there are a few large firms that predominate. ACCA and CIMA courses, on the other hand, are more subject to the rivalry of existing **competitors**, since, as well as other commercial training providers, universities and local technical colleges are also sources of competition.

3.19 The need for careful analysis is, perhaps, most demanding in the area of substitute products or services. It takes a particular alertness to discern potential substitutes in the early stages of their development.

Strategic group analysis

3.20 Five forces analysis deals with the competitive environment in broad **industry-wide** terms. It is possible to refine this by considering **strategic groups**. These are groups of close competitors following similar strategies. Such groups arise for a variety of reasons, such as barriers to entry or the attractiveness of particular market segments.

3.21 The **strategic space** pertaining to a strategic group is defined by two or three common strategic characteristics.

- Product diversity
- Geographical coverage
- Extent of branding
- Pricing policy
- Product quality
- Distribution method
- Target market segment

A series of 2-axis maps may be drawn using these characteristics to define both the extent of the strategic space and any unfilled gaps that exist within it. (A similar technique is used for specific products and is illustrated later in this chapter: this is **product positioning**.)

3.22 The identification of potential competitive advantage is the reason for analysing strategic groups. It improves knowledge of competitors and shows gaps in the organisation's current segments of operations. It may also reveal opportunities for migration to more favourable segments. Strategic problems may also be revealed.

3.23 Section summary

- The competitive environment of a firm is characterised by five forces: barriers to entry, substitute products, suppliers, customers and the intensity of competition.
- IT has implications for all these forces.
- Strategic group analysis refines five forces analysis.

Case example

AOL is a company that has defied environmental turbulence and the predictions of many industry analysts that it would fail. Unlike other ISPs (internet service providers), AOL has been marketing driven; its success in facing down Microsoft's Microsoft network (MSN) is considerable.

AOL began in 1980, going public in 1992. The initial service comprised games, email, chat, news, a browser and other information. It began as an on-line video-games service.

Unlike MSN, CompuServe and Prodigy, AOL's management realised that:

(a) The customer interface should not intimidate technophobes (ie it is a **mass** medium).
(b) AOL could be set apart by fostering a sense of community.

AOL faced competition from Microsoft whose CEO, Bill Gates, threatened to buy or bury AOL. In response, AOL:

(a) posted disks containing its software to huge number of households in the US;
(b) lobbied anti-trust regulators and teamed up with Microsoft's rival.

AOL has had some problems, especially service breakdowns owing to perceived under-investment in carrying capacity. Furthermore, to what extent will users continue to want managed content sites, when sites such as Yahoo! are free and offer increasing amounts of content?

AOL's chief executive believes AOL can become the Coca-Cola of the Internet - the Real Thing, standing out in a constantly shifting sea of imitators. A lot of investors are betting that he will pull it off.

(Economist, July 11 1998)

---

4   STRATEGIC INTELLIGENCE

KEY TERM

Strategic intelligence, according to Donald Marchand, is defined as 'what a company needs to know about its business environment to enable it to anticipate change and design appropriate strategies that will create business value for customers and be profitable in new markets and new industries in the future'.

4.1 **Many firms' intelligence gathering procedures reflect the organisation structure.** Each function of the organisation collected information relevant to its own concerns, without any wider corporate viewpoint.

(a) The data collected reflects the **restricted functional view,** not the overall corporate view.

(b) There are inevitable **gaps and blind-spots** in the information collected.

(c) Until recently (with the arrival of e-mail and intra-net applications) **sharing information** across functional departments **has been very difficult**.

4.2 **Why information should be shared**

(a) Not all strategic knowledge or decision-making capacity resides at the top of the firm.

(b) Sharing encourages 'a **diversity of interpretations** and views about the future'. For example, the marketing department may realise the commercial significance of new technology that may have escaped R&D.

(c) As companies delayer and lose management levels, the **organisation hierarchy** which used to distribute information is **less effective** at this task.

4.3 A model of the process of creating strategic intelligence is outlined below.

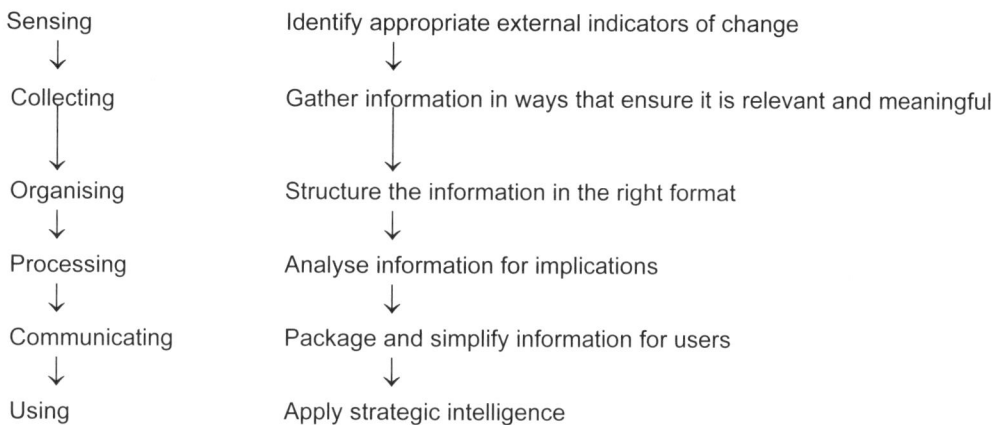

Sensing → Identify appropriate external indicators of change

↓

Collecting → Gather information in ways that ensure it is relevant and meaningful

↓

Organising → Structure the information in the right format

↓

Processing → Analyse information for implications

↓

Communicating → Package and simplify information for users

↓

Using → Apply strategic intelligence

It is easy to be overwhelmed by the volume and variety of relevant environmental information on offer. The temptation to ignore it completely is understandable, especially as managers are often more concerned with short-term issues relating to immediate production. Much environmental information cannot be easily quantified, and so is therefore harder to assimilate into decision making systems.

4.4 **Key dimensions of strategic intelligence**

Dimension	Comment
Information culture	What is the role of information in the organisation? Is it only distributed on a 'need to know basis' or do people have to give specific reasons for secrecy?
Future orientation	Is the focus on *specific* decisions and trade-offs, or a *general* attitude of enquiry?
The structure of information flows	Is communication vertical (up and down the hierarchy), or horizontal?
Processing strategic intelligence	Are 'professional' strategists delegated to this task or is it everybody's concern?
Scope	Is strategic intelligence dealt with by senior management only, or is it dispersed throughout the organisation?
Time horizon	Short-termist or orientated towards the long term?
The role of IT	Many firms are using IT to enhance communication across business functions.
Organisational memory	Do managers keep in mind the lessons of past successes or failures?

Sources of strategic intelligence

4.5   Strategic intelligence can be obtained internally (from the MIS or personnel) or externally (via media, trade associations, government, Internet).

Forecasts

4.6   Forecasting attempts to reduce the uncertainty managers face. In **simple/static conditions the past is a relatively good guide** to the future.

(a)   **Time series analysis.** Data for a number of months/years is obtained and analysed. The aim of time series analysis is to distinguish seasonal and other cyclical fluctuations from long term underlying trends.

An example of the use of this approach is the UK's monthly inflation statistics which show a headline figure and the underlying trend.

(b)   **Regression analysis** is a quantitative technique to check any underlying correlations between two variables (eg sales of ice cream and the weather). Remember that the relationship between two variables may only hold between certain values. (You would expect ice cream consumption to rise as the temperature becomes hotter, but there is probably a maximum number of ice creams an individual can consume in a day, no matter how hot it is.)

4.7   **Dynamic/complex conditions**

- **Future developments:** the past is not a reliable guide.

- Techniques such as **scenario building** are useful as they can propose a number of possible futures.

- **Complex environments** require techniques to reduce the effects of complexity on organisational structure and decision-making.

Technological forecasting

4.8   Technological change is a source of uncertainty, but can be countered in two ways.

- Ensuring that employees are kept up to date with relevant developments

- The **Delphi model**, which is explained in detail later in this section.

Econometric models for medium-term forecasting

4.9   Econometrics is the study of economic variables and their interrelationships.

(a)   **Leading indicators** are indicators which change *before* market demand changes. For example, a sudden increase in the birth rate would be an indicator of future demand for children's clothes.

(b)   The ability to predict the span of time between a change in the indicator and a change in market demand. Change in an indicator is especially useful for demand forecasting when they reach their highest or lowest points (when an increase turns into a decline or vice versa).

Scenario building

4.10 Because the environment is so complex, it is easy to become overwhelmed by the many factors. Firms therefore try to model the future and the technique is *scenario building*.

KEY TERM

A **scenario** is 'an internally consistent view of what the future might turn out to be'.

Macro scenarios

4.11 **Macro scenarios** use macro-economic or political factors, creating alternative views of the future environment (eg global economic growth, political changes, interest rates). Macro scenarios developed because the activities of oil and resource companies (which are global and at one time were heavily influenced by political factors) needed techniques to deal with uncertainties.

Case example

The *Guardian* (28 August 1995) identified three macro scenarios for the UK economy, as outlined in a study by Cash, Hughes and Hawthorn. In particular they contrast the UK's future in manufacturing and services (eg media, banking). The authors outline three possible scenarios.

(a) *Base projection*: Britain is stuck on a low growth path, with unemployment remaining at about 2m. This might be because the UK sucks in imports at a greater rate than it exports, and exports of financial and miscellaneous services are not enough to make up the gap.

(b) *Super-serv* scenario. This assumes that the UK's trend in manufacturing remains the same, but that the volume of financial and miscellaneous service exports doubles. If this occurs, unemployment would fall, by 2003, to 1 million. By that year UK exports of such services would exceed the USs.

(c) *Fast-man*. This assumes that businesses reinvest in manufacturing, so that manufactured exports rise by 14% more than the base projection, leading to a small manufacturing surplus in 2003.

These scenarios are based on a 5.5% annual growth in world trade. The article does not indicate whether one scenario more probable than the others.

Building scenarios

4.12 Keeping the scenario process simple is the way to get most out of scenario building.

(a) Normally a *team* is selected to develop scenarios, preferably of people from diverse backgrounds. The team should include 'dissidents' who challenge the consensus and some reference outsiders to offer different perspectives.

(b) Most participants in the team draw on both general reading and specialist knowledge.

4.13 **Steps in scenario planning (Mercer).**

Step 1. **Decide on the drivers for change**
- Environmental analysis helps determine key factors.
- **At least** a ten year time horizon is needed, to avoid simply extrapolating from the present.
- Identify and select the **important** issues and degree of certainty required.

Step 2. **Bring drivers together into a viable framework**
- This relies almost on an intuitive ability to make patterns out of 'soft' data, so is the hardest part of the process.
- Items identified can be brought together as mini-scenarios.
- There might be many trends, but these can be grouped together.

Step 3. • Produce seven to nine mini-scenarios. The underlying logic of the connections between the items can be explored.

Step 4. Group mini-scenarios into two or three larger scenarios containing all topics.

- This generates most debate and in likely to highlight fundamental issues.

- More than three scenarios will confuse people.

- The scenarios should be complementary not opposite. They should be equally likely. There is no 'good' or 'bad' scenario.

- The scenarios should be tested to ensure they hang together. If not, go back to Step 1.

Step 5. **Write the scenarios**

- The scenarios should be written up in the form most suitable for managers taking decisions based on them.

- Most scenarios are qualitative rather than quantitative in nature.

Step 6. **Identify issues arising**

- Determine the most critical outcomes, or branching points which are critical to the long term survival of the organisation.

- Role play can be used to test what the scenarios mean to key actors in the future of the business.

Industry scenarios

4.14 Porter believes that the most appropriate use for scenario analysis is if it is restricted to an industry. An **industry scenario** is an internally consistent view of an **industry's** future structure. It is not a forecast, but a possibility. Different competitive strategies may be appropriate to different scenarios.

4.15 **Using scenarios to formulate competitive strategy**

(a) A strategy built in response to only one scenario is **risky**, whereas one supposed to cope with them all might be **expensive**.

(b) Choosing scenarios as a basis for decisions about competitive strategy.

Approach	Comment
Assume the most probable	This choice puts too much faith in the scenario process and guesswork. A less probable scenario may be one whose **failure** to occur would have the **worst** consequences for the firm.
Hope for the best	A firm designs a strategy based on the scenario most attractive to the firm: this is wishful thinking.
Hedge	The firm chooses the strategy that produces **satisfactory** results under **all** scenarios. **Hedging, however, is not optimal**. The **low risk** is paid for by a **low reward**.
Flexibility	A firm taking this approach plays a 'wait and see' game. It is safer, but sacrifices first-mover advantages.
Influence	A firm will try and influence the future, for example by influencing demand for related products in order that its favoured scenario will be realised in events as they unfold.

Case example

Here are some of the issues facing manufacturers of personal computers over the next few years. The industry is likely to consolidate, thus increasing the advantage of the biggest brand name computer companies. Here's why.

(a) Small volume producers cannot achieve the **economies of scale** enjoyed by Dell and Hewlett Packard (HP), who can get cheaper components if they buy in bulk. Smaller manufacturers cannot then compete on price.

(b) Bigger manufacturers can insist on JIT supply, thereby lowering storage costs. They can form close ties with suppliers to get early access, to innovatory technology

(c) **Usage**. Intel chips not only power individual computers but are at the heart of many **networks**. They now power workstations. Smaller manufacturers cannot really compete in this market.

(d) There is a new segment of low-cost machines for use at home. This now accounts for 25% of the US market (in 1997). Prices will fall further thus encouraging first time buyers, and so expanding the total size of the market.

(e) Distribution channels favour larger producers. Internet sale of PCs favour firms with flexible logistics. Dell pioneered the build to order method.

Currently, the largest makers, Compaq and IBM are feeling squeezed by Dell and HP. In the second tier, Apple, NEC and AST have lost ground. In Europe, ICL and Olivetti have pulled out of the PC market. There are still hundreds of very small PC makers accounting for 25% of world sales, either reaching specialist or local markets. Their survival depends on offering high-touch service, responding in a quicker or more flexible way to the bigger and more remote suppliers.

For consumers, the prospect is less choice but lower prices.

Delphi

4.16 The Delphi technique was developed by the Rand Corporation to permit the best use to be made of **judgement** in forecasting. The technique overcomes the problems of **groupthink** and dominance by one or two individuals that commonly undermine the usefulness of expert panels. The technique is used **to answer specific questions** about the future.

4.17 A co-ordinator asks a number of experts to respond to a question. Their areas of expertise must all be relevant to the subject matter of the question, but they must bring differing perspectives to it. The experts never meet and they are unaware of each other's identity. Each expert gives an answer and justifies it with reasons.

4.18 The co-ordinator collates the answers and reasons and re-distributes them to the experts, still without attribution. The experts then re-consider their original views in the light of any divergent opinions, perhaps revising them, perhaps explaining why they do not accept the need for amendment. The co-ordinator then collates and redistributes as before.

4.19 After sufficient iterations of this process of reconsideration, it is likely that a reasonably consistent overall answer will emerge.

5 SEGMENTING THE MARKET   12/01

5.1 A market is not a mass, homogeneous group of customers, each wanting an identical product. Every market consists of potential buyers with different **needs** and different **buying behaviour**. These different customers may be **grouped into segments**. A different marketing approach will be taken by an organisation for each market segment.

> ### KEY TERM
>
> **Market segmentation** is 'the subdividing of a market into distinct and increasingly homogeneous subgroups of customers, where any subgroup can conceivably be selected as a target market to be met with a distinct marketing mix'.

5.2 **Reasons for segmenting markets**

(a) **Focus strategy:** a firm can build itself a niche. A segment is a group of customers whose special needs can be catered for in a focus strategy.

(b) **More money:** by catering specifically for segments and satisfying their needs better, customers will probably spend more than if they were offered a single product.

(c) **Convenience:** a firm cannot be all things to all people. In Chapter 1 we suggested that firms have to choose how to compete and who to serve - if only to survive in the face of competition.

The bases for segmentation

5.3 An important initial marketing task is the **identification of segments** within the market. One basis (or variable) will not be appropriate in every market, and sometimes two or more bases might be valid at the same time.

5.4 **Segmentation variables** fall into a small number of categories.

(a) **Psychographic or lifestyle** segmentation is based on variables such as interests, activities, personality and opinions. This is very useful for many consumer goods, since they can be designed and promoted to appeal on the basis of such variables.

(b) Consumer **behaviour** in relation to the product is a suitable segmentation basis for products that can be aimed at customers according to such variables as usage rate, impulse purchase, brand loyalty and sensitivity to marketing mix variables such as price, quality and promotion.

(c) **Socio-demographic** segmentation is based on social, economic and demographic variables such as those below.

- Age
- Sex
- Income
- Occupation
- Education

- Religion
- Ethnicity/national origin
- Social class
- Family size

(d) **Geographical** segmentation is very simple, but useful, especially in business-to-business marketing, which relies heavily on personal selling. It can be combined with socio-demographic segmentation.

Case example

Capital One

Capital One's competitive advantage comes not from the brand strength of American Express, or the economies of scale that Citibank enjoys, or from its links with affinity groups such as those that benefit MBNA Bank. Its strength is in gathering and using data. 'It is the best data mining shop anywhere in the US', is the assessment of Eric Clemons, professor of marketing at Wharton Business School at the University of Pennsylvania.

Its special skill is spotting the patterns that identify 'micro-segments' in the market for consumer credit. Last year, the company offered thousands of variations of credit card. It also conducted 64,000 marketing tests on small groups of customers to gauge how new varieties would be received.

The ability to segment the credit card market more finely than its competitors, and customise products accordingly, is what sets Capital One apart. Many companies talk about mass customisation. The Virginia-based company really does it.

Financial Times, 14 May 2002

5.5 Segmentation can also be applied to an **industrial market.**

- The **nature of the customer's business.** An accountant may choose to specialise in the accounts of retail businesses, and a firm of solicitors may specialise in conveyancing work for property development companies.

- **Size**

- **Location**

- **Industry:** components manufacturers specialise in the industries of the firms to which they supply components. In the motor car industry, there are companies which specialise in the manufacture of car components, possibly for a single firm.

Testing segment validity

5.6 A market segment will only be valid if it is **worth designing and developing a unique marketing mix** for that segment.

Question	Comment
Can the segment be measured?	It might be possible to conceive of a market segment, but it is not necessarily easy to measure it. For example, for a segment based on people with a conservative outlook on life, can conservatism of outlook be measured by market research?
Is the segment big enough?	There has to be a large enough potential market to be profitable.
Can the segment be reached?	There has to be a way of getting to the potential customers via the organisation's promotion and distribution channels.
Do segments respond differently?	If two or more segments are identified by marketing planners but each segment responds in the same way to a marketing mix, the segments are effectively one and the same and there is no point in distinguishing them from each other.

Targeting

5.7 Having analysed the market into viable segments and obtained information on them, the organisation must decide which segment or segments to **target**. This decision is taken after considering two main groups of factors.

(a) **The segment's attractiveness.** Attractiveness will be related to size, potential for growth and profitability and the potential influence of Porter's **five forces**.

(b) **The organisation's objectives and resources**.

5.8 Targeting a segment thus requires an understanding of the topics discussed in the next chapter, on internal analysis.

5.9 After the targeting decision has been taken, the organisation may consider **product positioning**.

Product positioning

5.10 A product's **positioning** defines how it is intended to be perceived by customers and how it differs from current and potential competing products.

5.11 It is not always possible to identify a market segment where there is no direct competitor, and a marketing problem for the firm will be the creation of some form of **product differentiation** (real or imagined) in the marketing mix of the product.

5.12 A perceptual map of product positioning can be used to identify **gaps in the market**. This example might suggest that there could be potential in the market for a low-price high-quality bargain brand. A company that carries out such an analysis might decide to conduct further research to find out whether there is scope in the market for a new product which would be targeted at a market position where there are few or no rivals. (A firm successfully pursuing **cost leadership** might be in a good position to offer a **bargain brand**.)

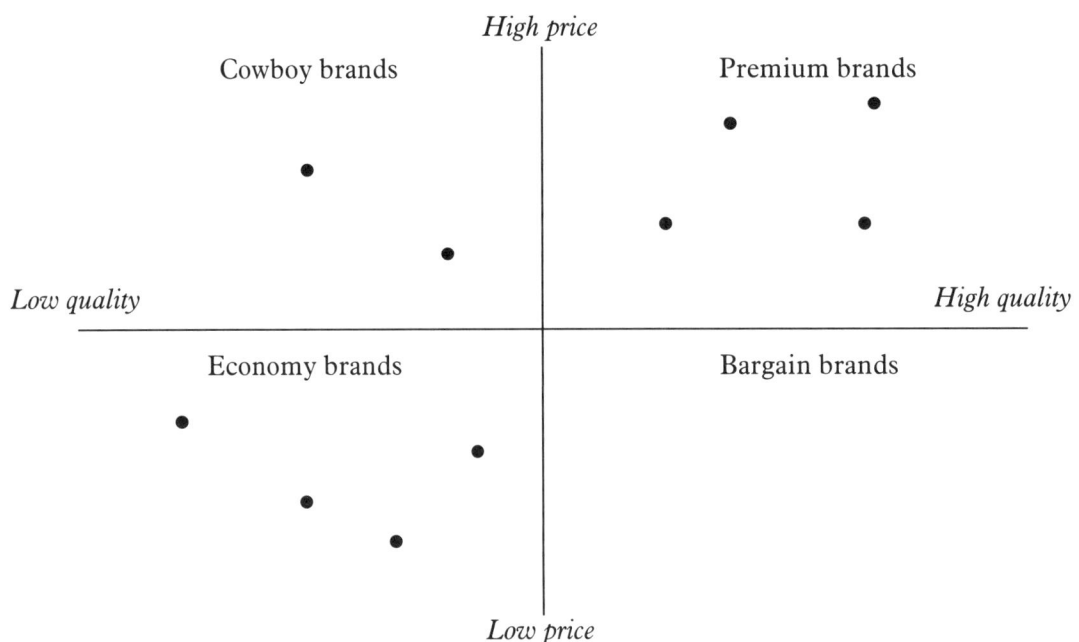

5.13 Similar matrices to explore possible product positions in terms of, for instance, attributes, applications, users, occasions for use and specific aspects of quality may be drawn to refine knowledge of product position.

Do not confuse product positioning with **competitive position**, which is dealt with in Chapter 8 of this Study Text.

5.14 Section summary

- Segmentation is the grouping of potential customers according to their common needs.
- A distinct marketing approach can be adopted for each segment.
- Positioning compares one product with another.

6 BUYER BEHAVIOUR

6.1 Goods are usually divided into two broad categories.

KEY TERMS

Consumer goods: these are goods made for the ultimate **household consumer** and they are in such a form that they can be used by the consumer **without the need for any further commercial processing.**

Industrial goods: these are goods which are used to make other goods or to render services. They are goods which are not consumer goods.

Customer behaviour in the consumer market

6.2 Once the needs of the segment have been identified, further analysis will be done as to how the segment can be induced to buy. Buyer behaviour is the process whereby customers identify a need and take a purchase decision.

The buying process

6.3 The psychological **process of buying**

Step 1. The consumer has an unconscious or conscious **need**, but is unaware of any product which would satisfy that need.

Step 2. The consumer then becomes **aware** of the product.

Step 3. If this awareness suggests that the product might satisfy his need, the consumer will show an **interest** and will wish to obtain more information about the product.

Step 4. The customer will **evaluate** this information, and this may create a **preference** for the product.

6.4 A buying decision might be taken entirely by one person. However, the buying process might be influenced by several different individuals. For example, a family's holiday destination is unlikely to be decided by one person alone.

6.5 The buying decision is not simply a result of a psychological process. It is also the **outcome of an interaction** between the **buyer**, the **seller**, the **product** and the **situation**.

Factor	Comment
Buyer	People's characteristics and experiences influence their buying decisions. Marketing managers may nevertheless be able to make generalisations about different types of consumer.
Seller	The characteristics of the seller will affect the consumer's decision to buy or not buy, because the seller will give an impression of the quality of the firm's after sales service, its experience in the field, its reliability and friendliness and so on.
Product	Management can control the characteristics of the goods sold by their organisation (eg quality, durability, price, design features etc).
Situation	The circumstances under which the decision to buy or not to buy is taken. Some aspects might be subject to management control (eg whether the products are available in supermarkets). Other factors may be outside the control of management (eg the weather, or discussions with a friend who has some opinions about the product).

Psychological influences on demand

6.6 **Psychological influences which affect consumer buying behaviour**

(a) **Motivation.** This is discussed in the context of work in Chapter 18.

(b) **Attitudes** to a product

(c) **Experience** of the type of product

(d) **Loyalty.** A consumer may demonstrate a loyalty towards a particular company's goods or to a brand, or even to a particular shop or retail chain. However **loyalty**, or even just **inertia**, is quite an important factor in the sale of financial services.

(e) **Personality.** Inevitably, a consumer's buying behaviour will be influenced by his or her personality.

(f) **Group influences.** An individual will also be influenced by other people in the groups to which he or she belongs (eg people at work).

Socio-economic influences on demand

6.7 Consumers' buying decisions will be influenced by a variety of social, economic and cultural factors.

- The **size of population.**
- The **family decision-making units.**
- **Regional preferences.**
- **Culture.**
- **Social class.**
- **Life style.**

Case example

After the high protein, low carbohydrate Atkins diet swept the US in 2003 and sales of its Slimfast foods fell dramatically, Unilever rapidly launched a new 'carb options' range of foods

---

The consumer's motivation mix

6.8 **Customer behaviour** is therefore determined by **economic, psychological** and **sociological considerations.** The reasons for buying a product or their relative importance may vary from person to person, or product to product. These reasons make up the **motivation mix** of the customer.

6.9 Complex models of buyer behaviour have been developed to take account of these influences on purchase decisions.

Buyer behaviour in industrial markets

6.10 Business-to-business markets have their own peculiarities.

- More demarcated than the consumer market (eg just look in the Yellow Pages)
- Rational in that customers should not buy beyond economic need
- Easier to forecast than the consumer market

The decision-making unit (DMU)

6.11 The decision-making unit (DMU) is a term used to describe the person or people who actually **take the decision** to buy a good or service.

> **KEY TERM**
>
> The **decision making unit** is defined in marketing management as a group containing every person who has some influence (positive or negative) at one or more stages in the purchasing process.

6.12 **People in the DMU**

(a) **Employees or managers** in sales and production might make recommendations about what type of supplies should be purchased.

(b) **Superiors** might authorise the recommendations of a junior buying manager.

(c) **Colleagues.** In large organisations, there will be several buying managers, who might work independently, but might also work closely together, either formally or informally.

(d) **Technical staff and engineers** provide **specifications** for component purchases.

(e) **Accountants** might be able to set a limit on the price the organisation will pay.

(f) The **board of directors** might approve major items.

(g) **User departments** are also involved.

(h) **Previous strategic or buying decisions** may constrain choices: the information technology strategy may require, say, that all computers should run Windows 97.

Factors in the motivation mix of industrial buyers

6.13 The motivation of industrial buyers is supposedly more rational than that of the domestic consumer.

Motive	Comment
Quality	Even where quality standards are imposed by an outside body (eg the British Standards Institution) or by customer specification, there can be some variation in the quality of goods of competing manufacturers.
Price	The economic value of industrial goods to the buyer depends on the price which the buyer can obtain for the product the buyer produces. Where profit margins in the final market are under pressure, the buyer of industrial goods will probably make price the main purchasing motivation. A supplier can reduce prices or help in other ways (by increasing quality, thereby reducing the usage cost to the customer).
Budgetary control	This will influence the purchaser's buying activities, and the buying department may look further afield (perhaps abroad) for potential suppliers to obtain a better price or quality of goods.
Fear of breakdown	Where a customer has a highly organised and costly production system, he will clearly want to avoid a breakdown in the system, due to a faulty machine or running out of stocks of materials.
Credit	The importance of credit could vary with the financial size of the buyer, but customers should always be attempting to obtain the best credit terms they can get.

6.14 **Types of buying situation**

Situation	Comment
Routinised buyer behaviour	Habitual buying where the buyer knows the offering, the item is frequently purchased, and the buyer has well developed supplier preferences. Deviation from habit behaviour is likely to be influenced by price and availability considerations.
Limited problem solving	The purchase of a new or unfamiliar product/service but where the suppliers are known and the product is in a familiar class of products - for instance a new type of packaging material.
Extensive problem solving	The purchase of unfamiliar products from unfamiliar suppliers. This is time-consuming.

6.15 *Webster and Wind* see **organisational buyer behaviour** as being affected by two influences.

(a) The **individual** characteristics of the members of the DMU

(b) The relationships between members of the DMU. For example, a **gatekeeper controls the flow of information** about the purchase. This role can be senior or junior.

7 MARKETING RESEARCH

7.1 Marketing managers, like all other managers, need information for planning and control. The **marketing information system** (MKIS) is a part of an organisation's overall management information system (MIS).

7.2 Many marketing decisions are taken on a continuous basis (eg decisions are taken on various aspects of the marketing mix - sales, advertising, sales promotion at least annually). A continuous plan of information is also required for control purposes. A marketing information system, normally part of the management information system, meets these needs.

(a) **Internal reports (and accounts) systems**

- Results data
- Measures of current performance
- Sales, costs, stock information
- Possible areas for improvement (including timeliness, availability and distribution of reports)

(b) **Marketing intelligence system**

- Happenings data (eg what competitors are doing)
- Information on developments in the environment
- It involves scanning and the dissemination of a wide range of intelligence
- Possible areas of improvement

(c) **Marketing research system** contains specific studies of marketing problems, opportunities and effectiveness.

(d) **Analytical marketing system**. This uses models to explain, predict and improve marketing processes. Models may be descriptive, decisional, verbal, graphical or mathematical.

All subsystems should be interactive.

7.3 The sources of marketing data will vary from organisation to organisation, but are both internal and external, including information provided by marketing research.

> **KEY TERM**
>
> **Marketing research** has been defined by the Chartered Institute of Marketing as the 'objective gathering, recording and analysing of all facts about problems relating to the transfer and sales of goods and services from producer to consumer or user'.

7.4 **The scope of marketing research**

(a) **Market research** covers sales forecasting, market trends, potential for current and new products.

(b) **Product research** covers consumers attitudes to product, comparative studies, test marketing and so on.

(c) **Price research** covering customer perceptions, the responsiveness of customer demand to changes in prices and so on.

(d) **Promotion research** covering how effective advertising has been, how sales staff work.

(e) **Distribution research** covering logistics, warehousing, packaging, and so on.

Marketing research procedure

7.5 Marketing research involves the following five stages of work.

Step 1. **Definition of the problem**. The marketing problem which management wishes to resolve must be properly defined.

Step 2. **Design of the research**. Once the research team knows what problem it must help to resolve, it will establish the type of data (secondary or primary), the collection method to be used (postal questionnaire, personal interview), the selection of a research agency (if appropriate) and if a sample is to be taken, the design of the sample. Any questions put to respondents must be carefully designed.

Step 3. **Collection of the data.**

Step 4. **Analysis of the data.**

Step 5. **Presentation of a report** which should then lead to a management marketing decision.

The sources of marketing research information

7.6 Marketing research data can be either primary data or secondary data.

> **KEY TERMS**
>
> **Primary data** is information collected specifically for the study by means of **field research**.
>
> **Secondary data** is 'data neither collected directly by the user nor specifically for the user, often under conditions that are not well known to the user' (American Marketing Association). The collection of secondary data for marketing research is sometimes known as **desk research.**

7.7 **Desk research** involves collecting data from the following sources.

  (a) **Records inside the firm**, gathered by another department or section for a different purpose to the research task in hand.

  (b) Published information from **external sources** such as government statistics, marketing statistics and so on.

7.8 **Field research is the collection of primary data**.

  * Experimentation
  * Sampling
  * Piloting
  * Observation
  * Questionnaires

  * Consumer panels
  * Trade audits
  * Pre-tests
  * Post-tests after
  * Attitude scales and methods of analysis

7.9 In a **controlled experiment,** a controlled research environment is established and selected stimuli are then introduced. Controlled experiments have been used to find the best advertising campaign, the best price level, the best incentive scheme, the best sales training method and so on.

7.10 In marketing research for consumer goods, it will be impossible to obtain data from *every* consumer in the market. A **sample provides an estimate of the characteristics of the entire population**.

  (a) To make a truly **random sample** we need a **sampling frame**. This is a list of every member of the target population. This is not always practical or available.

  (b) **Non-random sampling** is used to save money and increase practicability. Bias may be introduced.

7.11 **Observation** can be used as a means of obtaining sample data where quantitative data is required. For example, if data is needed about the volume of traffic passing along a road at a certain time of day, observers (either people or recording equipment) can be placed so as to count the traffic as it passes by. Observation can also be used to study consumer behaviour, although this is usually within a controlled experiment.

7.12 **Questionnaires** (eg over the phone, postal replies, street interviews) provide a quick, cheap method of conducting a survey, provided that necessary conditions are met.

  * The questions are unambiguous.
  * People return them, so that the sample is not biased.
  * Respondents answer truthfully.

7.13 **Consumer panels** consist of a representative cross-section of consumers who have agreed to give information about their attitudes or buying habits (through personal visits or mail questionnaires) at regular intervals of time.

7.14 **Trade audits** are carried out among panels of wholesalers and retailers, and the term 'retail audits' refers to panels of retailers only. A research firm sends 'auditors' to selected outlets at regular intervals to count stock and deliveries, thus enabling an estimate of throughput to be made. **Retail audits** provide continuous monitoring of retail activity.

Pre-testing and post testing

7.15 Marketing research may be carried out both **before, during** and **after** the marketing decision is implemented. Research for an advertising campaign attempts to measure both the communication effect and the sales effect of advertisements.

Question 3

How would you go about the market research for:

(a) A new type of tank;
(b) A new type of teapot?

Answer

(a) Desk research, followed by direct approaches to likely buyers.
(b) Desk research, then sample-based consumer research.

7.16 Section summary

- A marketing information system is a source of intelligence.
- Marketing research covers all aspects of marketing activities. Market research is more restricted in scope.
- Primary research collects data for a specific study. Secondary research collects background data.

Chapter roundup

- General system theory would see the organisation as an **open system**, interacting with its environment.

- Environmental uncertainty depends on the degree of **complexity** and the degree of **stability** present.

- The **organisation's environment** is a source of **uncertainty**, depending on how **complex** or **dynamic** it is. General factors (PEST) affect all organisations.

- The **physical** environment is important for logistical reasons, as a source of resources, and because of increasing regulation. The **economic** environment affects firms at national and international level, both in the *general* level of economic activity and in particular variables (eg exchange rates). The **law** impinges on organisations, defining what they can or cannot do. **Political change** is a source of environmental uncertainty.

- Public policy on **competition** and **consumer protection** is particularly relevant to business strategy.

- The **social and cultural** environment features long-term social trends and people's beliefs and attitudes (eg concern with ecological issues).

- The **competitive environment** is structured by five forces: **barriers to entry; substitute products**; the bargaining power of **customers**; the bargaining power of **suppliers**; **competitive rivalry**.

- There are many sources of environmental information. Analysing this information, much of which is not quantitative, is no easy task.

- Marketing analysis involves predicting **demand for products and services**. Market **segmentation** is a way of analysing the market. A **segment** is a homogeneous group of customers who can be offered a distinctive marketing mix. Identified segments must be tested to see if they can be reached.

- **Buyer behaviour** is a term used to describe why people (or firms) buy goods and services. The buying decision frequently involves several individuals (the decision making unit).

- **Marketing research** can be **secondary (desk)** or **primary** (samples, questionnaires etc). Secondary research involves analysing data (eg census information) not specifically collected by the marketer. Primary research is more focused on customer attitudes to particular product or service issues.

Quick quiz

1   What is the significance of the law?

2   What is political risk?

3   What is the business cycle?

4   What is demography?

5   How has IT development influenced the way organisations are managed?

6   In what way will environmental issues affect consumer demand?

7   What are the five competitive forces?

8   List some barriers to entry.

9   What is segmentation?

10   What is a DMU?

Answers to quick quiz

1   Law forms a strict framework of rules governing the conduct of organisations.

2   The risk that political factors will invalidate the planned strategy.

3   The historical pattern of variation in the level of economic activity.

4   The study of human population and population trends.

5   IT has removed much of the information processing role of middle management, making 'delayering' possible.

6   Increased demand for products that appear to be environmentally friendly.

7   Rivalry among existing firms; bargaining power of suppliers and customers; threat of substitutes and of new entrants.

8   Scale economies; product differentiation; capital requirements; switching costs; access to distribution channels; non-scale cost advantages.

9   Dividing a market into distinct, homogeneous subgroups, each of which may be targeted with a distinctly positioned product.

10   In industrial marketing, the group of people who collaborate to reach a buying decision.

Now try the question below from the Exam Question Bank

Number	Level	Marks	Time
Q5	Exam	20	36 mins

Chapter 6

INTERNAL ANALYSIS

Topic list	Syllabus reference
1 The position audit	3(a)
2 Resources and limiting factors	3(a)
3 Competences and critical success factors	3(b)
4 Converting resources: the value chain	3(c)
5 Outputs: the product portfolio	2(c)
6 Organisation structure	6(c)
7 The customer base	2(b)
8 Drawing the threads together	3(b)

Introduction

In this chapter we examine some of the key aspects of the organisation's current **position**. A **resource audit** identifies any gaps in resources and limiting factors on organisational activity. **Value chain** analysis identifies how the business adds value to the resources it obtains, and how it deploys these resources to satisfy customers. A **competence** is a skill which the organisation has which can ensure a fit between the environment and the organisation's capability. The internal appraisal should identify **strengths and weaknesses**.

We then review the organisation's current outputs, its **product portfolio.**

Organisation structure and culture are also strategic issues. Structure describes how the organisation controls its work, and culture describes the mind-set of managers and staff.

The purpose of all this activity is the customer, and a review of the **customer base** should identify trends and developments.

Study guide

Section 3 – Internal assessment

- Resource audit

- Analysis of capabilities and core competences

- Adding competitive value – value chain and value system

Section 2 – External environmental scanning

- Analysis of customers and markets – market research

- Analysis of the competitive environment

Section 6 – Matching structures with strategy

- Organisational configurations

Exam guide

In this chapter we introduce some specific models that you must become very familiar with. They are useful both for analysing data and structuring answers. They appear in Sections 4, 5 and 6. Other sections contain essential concepts and definitions.

1 THE POSITION AUDIT

KEY TERM

Position audit is part of the planning process which examines the current state of the entity. A wide range of factors is examined. Here are some examples.

- Resources of tangible and intangible **assets**
- Products, brands and markets
- Operating systems such as production and distribution
- Internal organisation
- Current results
- Financial resources

2 RESOURCES AND LIMITING FACTORS

2.1 A **resource audit** is a review of all aspects of the resources the organisation uses.

Resource	Example
Material inputs	Source, suppliers, waste, new materials, cost, availability, future provision
Human resources	Number, skills, efficiency, industrial relations, adaptability, innovatory capacity
Management	Size, skills, loyalty, career progression, structure.
Fixed assets	Age, condition, utilisation rate, value, replacement, technologically up-to-date? Cost
Finance	Short-term and long term capital, gearing levels, working capital, cashflow
Intangible assets	Patents, goodwill, brands, image
Organisation	Culture and structure
Knowledge	Ability to generate and disseminate ideas, innovation

Unique resources are particularly valuable and an important source of competitive advantage.

KEY TERM

A **unique resource** is one which is both better than its equivalent employed by competitors and difficult to imitate.

2.2 **Resources are of no value unless they are organised into systems,** and so a resource audit should go on to consider how well or how badly resources have been utilised, and whether the organisation's systems are effective and efficient.

Limiting factors

2.3 Every organisation operates under resource **constraints**.

> **KEY TERM**
>
> A **limiting factor** or **key factor** is 'a factor which at any time or over a period may limit the activity of an entity, often one where there is shortage or difficulty of supply.'

Examples

- A shortage of production capacity
- A limited number of key personnel, such as salespeople with technical knowledge
- A restricted distribution network
- Too few managers with knowledge about finance, or overseas markets
- Inadequate research design resources to develop new products or services
- A poor system of strategic intelligence
- Lack of money
- A lack of adequately trained staff

2.4 Once the limiting factor has been identified, the planners should do two things.

- In the short term, make best use of the resources available.
- Try to reduce the limitation in the long term.

Resource use

2.5 Resource use is concerned with the efficiency with which resources are used, and the effectiveness of their use in achieving the planning objectives of the business.

> **KEY TERMS**
>
> **Effectiveness** is the measure of achievement and is assessed by reference to goals.
>
> **Economy** is reduction or containment of cost.
>
> There will normally be a trade off between effectiveness and economy. **Efficiency** means being effective at minimum cost or controlling costs without losing operational effectiveness. **Efficiency** is therefore a **combination of effectiveness and economy.**

Case example

A key resource is capital. British and US firms have been accused of not making enough capital investment, in comparison with businesses in the Asian tiger economies. But investment has to be productive: much of the late 1980s investment boom in Japan resulted in massive over-capacity. Other investment capital was wasted in speculative property development.

American firms score highly on *capital productivity*. In other words, they get the best return from the capital invested.

3   COMPETENCES AND CRITICAL SUCCESS FACTORS   12/01, 6/02

3.1   A strategic approach involves identifying a firm's **competences**. 'Members of organisations develop judgements about what they think the company can do well - its core competence.' These competences develop in a variety of ways.

- **Experience** in making and marketing a product or service
- The talents and potential of individuals in the organisation
- The **quality of co-ordination.**

> **KEY TERM**
>
> **Core competences** critically underpin the organisation's competitive advantage.
>
> *Johnson & Scholes*

3.2   *Johnson & Scholes* divide competences into two types. An organisation must achieve at least a **threshold** level of competence in **everything** it does. The organisation's **core competences** are those where it **outperforms competitors** and that are **difficult to imitate**.

3.3   Competitiveness depends on **unique resources** or core competences. The organisation's level of performance in its core competences may be judged in three ways.

- Comparison with past results
- Comparison with industry norms
- Bench marking

3.4   **Tests for identifying a core competence.**

(a)   **It provides potential access to a wide variety of markets**. GPS of France developed a core competence in 'one-hour' processing, enabling it to process films and build reading glasses in one hour.

(b)   **It contributes significantly to the value enjoyed by the customer.** For example, for GPS, the waiting time restriction was very important.

(c)   **It should be hard for a competitor to copy.** This will be the case if it is technically complex, involves specialised processes, involves complex interrelationships between different people in the organisation or is hard to define.

In many cases, a company might choose to combine competences.

3.5   Bear in mind that **relying on a competence is no substitute for a strategy**. However, a core competence can form a basis for a strategy.

Preparing resource plans

Planning issues: critical success factors

3.6   Competences can be related to **critical success factors**.

KEY TERMS

Critical success factors (CSFs) 'are those factors on which the strategy is fundamentally dependent for its success'.

Key tasks are what must be done to ensure each critical success factor is satisfied.

Priorities indicate the order in which tasks are completed.

3.7 EXAMPLE

- Some CSFs are generic to the whole industry, others to a particular firm. The critical success factor to run a successful **mail order business** is speedy delivery.

- A CSF of a **parcel delivery service** is that it **must be quicker than the normal post.**

- Underpinning critical success factors are **key tasks**. If **customer care** is a CSF, then a key task, and hence a measure of performance, would include responding to enquires within a given time period. There may be a number of key tasks - but some might be more important than others, or must come first in a sequence.

Question 1

Draw up a list of four critical success factors for the strategy of the organisation for which you work.

Exam focus point

A part-question in the June 2002 examination asked you to identify and discuss the critical success factors in the package holiday industry. This is a good example of how you must be prepared to **apply** your theoretical knowledge in this exam.

3.8 Relationship between competences and CSFs

- A competence is what a organisation **has or is able to do.**
- A **CSF** is what is **necessary to achieve an objective.**

3.9 **Competences thus fulfil the CSF.** In the examples quoted, a competence of faster delivery supports a CSF that a courier service must be faster than a competitor.

4 CONVERTING RESOURCES: THE VALUE CHAIN 6/03

4.1 The **value chain** model of corporate activities, developed by Michael Porter, offers a bird's eye view of the firm and what it does. Competitive advantage, says Porter, arises out of the way in which firms organise and perform **activities**.

Activities

KEY TERM

Activities are the means by which a firm creates value in its products. (They are sometimes referred to as **value activities**.)

4.2   Activities incur costs, and, in combination with other activities, provide a product or service which earns revenue.

4.3   EXAMPLE

Let us explain this point by using the example of a **restaurant**. A restaurant's activities can be divided into buying food, cooking it, and serving it (to customers). There is no reason, in theory, why the customers should not do all these things themselves, at home. The customer however, is not only prepared to **pay for someone else** to do all this but also **pays more than the cost of** the resources (food, wages and soon). The ultimate value a firm creates is measured by the amount customers are willing to pay for its products or services above the cost of carrying out value activities. A firm is profitable if the realised value to customers exceeds the collective cost of performing the activities.

(a)   Customers **purchase value**, which they measure by comparing a firm's products and services with similar offerings by competitors.

(b)   The business **creates value** by carrying out its activities either more efficiently than other businesses, or by combining them in such a way as to provide a unique product or service.

Question 2

Outline different ways in which the restaurant can create value.

Answer

Here are some ideas. Each of these options is a way of organising the activities of buying, cooking and serving food in a way that customers will value.

(a)   It can become more efficient, by automating the production of food, as in a fast food chain.

(b)   The chef can develop commercial relationships with growers, so he or she can obtain the best quality fresh produce.

(c)   The chef can specialise in a particular type of cuisine (eg Nepalese, Korean).

(d)   The restaurant can be sumptuously decorated for those customers who value atmosphere and a sense of occasion, in addition to a restaurant's purely gastronomic pleasures.

(e)   The restaurant can serve a particular type of customer (eg celebrities).

4.4   Porter (in *Competitive Advantage*) grouped the various activities of an organisation into a **value chain**. Here is a diagram.

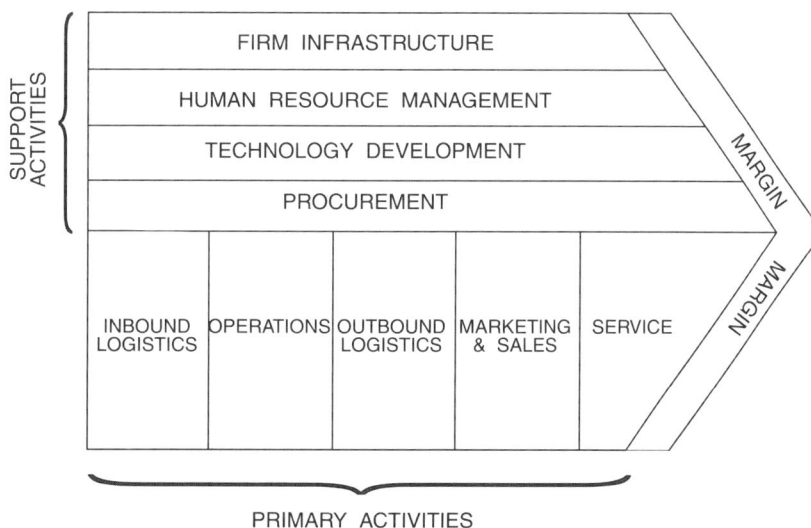

The **margin** is the excess the customer is prepared to **pay** over the **cost** to the firm of obtaining resource inputs and providing value activities. It represents the **value created** by the **value activities** themselves and by the **management of the linkages** between them.

> **Exam focus point**
> This diagram is worth committing to memory as it can be used both to analyse data and to structure answers.

Activity

4.5 **Primary activities** are directly related to production, sales, marketing, delivery and service.

	Comment
Inbound logistics	Receiving, handling and storing inputs to the production system: warehousing, transport, stock control and so on.
Operations	Convert resource inputs into a final product. Resource inputs are not only materials. People are a resource especially in service industries.
Outbound logistics	Storing the product and its distribution to customers: packaging, testing, delivery and so on.
Marketing and sales	Informing customers about the product, persuading them to buy it, and enabling them to do so: advertising, promotion and so on.
After sales service	Installing products, repairing them, upgrading them, providing spare parts and so forth.

4.6 **Support activities** provide purchased inputs, human resources, technology and infrastructural functions to support the primary activities.

Activity	Comment
Procurement	Acquire the resource inputs to the primary activities (eg purchase of materials, subcomponents equipment).
Technology development	Product design, improving processes and/or resource utilisation.
Human resource management	Recruiting, training, developing and rewarding people.
Management planning	Planning, finance, quality control: Porter believes they are crucially important to an organisation's strategic capability in all primary activities.

4.7 **Linkages** connect the activities of the value chain.

(a) **Activities in the value chain affect one another**. For example, more costly product design or better quality production might reduce the need for after-sales service.

(b) **Linkages require co-ordination**. For example, Just In Time requires smooth functioning of operations, outbound logistics and service activities such as installation.

> **Exam focus point**
> Question 1 in the June 2003 examination offered 10 marks for the analysis of a business's success using the value chain model.

Value system

4.8   Activities and linkages that add value do not stop at the organisation's **boundaries**. For example, when a restaurant serves a meal, the quality of the ingredients - although they are chosen by the cook - is determined by the grower. The grower has added value, and the grower's success in growing produce of good quality is as important to the customer's ultimate satisfaction as the skills of the chef. A firm's value chain is connected to what Porter calls a **value system**.

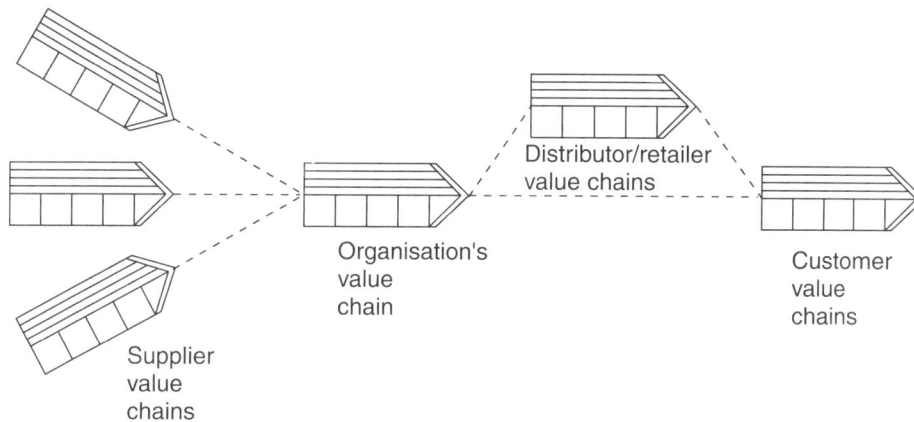

4.9   **Using the value chain.** A firm can secure competitive advantage in several ways.

- Invent new or better ways to do activities
- Combine activities in new or better ways
- Manage the linkages in its own value chain
- Manage the linkages in the value system

Question 3

Sana Sounds is a small record company. Representatives from Sana Sounds scour music clubs for new bands to promote. Once a band has signed a contract (with Sana Sounds) it makes a recording. The recording process is subcontracted to one of a number of recording studio firms which Sana Sounds uses regularly. (At the moment Sana Sounds is not large enough to invest in its own equipment and studios.) Sana Sounds also subcontracts the production of records and CDs to a number of manufacturing companies. Sana Sounds then distributes the disks to selected stores, and engages in any promotional activities required.

What would you say were the activities in Sana Sounds' *value chain*?

Answer

Sana Sounds is involved in the record industry from start to finish. Although recording and CD manufacture are contracted out to external suppliers, this makes no difference to the fact that these activities are part of Sana Sounds' own value chain. Sana Sounds earns its money by managing the whole set of activities. If the company grows then perhaps it will acquire its own recording studios.

4.10 Section summary

- The value chain models how activities can be deployed to add value for the customer.
- Value chains are part of a value system.
- Firms can benefit by performing activities in a unique way and/or exploiting linkages.

5 OUTPUTS: THE PRODUCT PORTFOLIO 12/03

The product life cycle

5.1 Many firms make a number of different products or services. Each product or service has its own financial, marketing and risk characteristics. The combination of products or services influences the attractiveness and profitability of the firm.

Case example

Glaxo has for many years produced *Zantac* an anti-ulcer drug. Patents expire after a defined perior' Glaxo has been anticipating this development for a while and has invested in new drugs to provide income when returns from Zantac fall.

5.2 The profitability and sales of a product can be expected to change over time. The **product life cycle** is an attempt to recognise distinct stages in a product's sales history. Marketing managers distinguish between different aspects of the product.

(a) **Product class:** this is a broad category of product, such as cars, washing machines, newspapers' also referred to as the **generic product**.

(b) **Product form:** within a product class there are different forms that the product can take, for example five-door hatchback cars or two-seater sports cars; twin tub or front loading automatic washing machines; national daily newspapers or weekly local papers and so on.

(c) **Brand:** the particular type of the product form (for example Ford Escort, Vauxhall Astra; Financial Times, Daily Mail, Sun).

5.3 The product life cycle applies in differing degrees to each of the three cases. A product-class (eg cars) may have a long maturity stage, and a particular make or brand *might* have an erratic life cycle (eg Rolls Royce) or not. Product forms however tend to conform to the classic life cycle pattern.

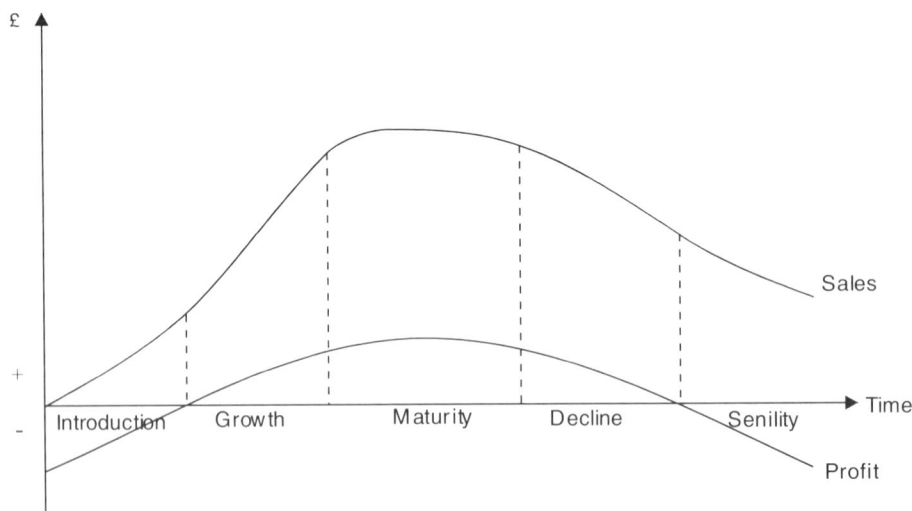

5.4 Introduction

- A new product takes time to find acceptance by would-be purchasers and there is a slow growth in sales. Unit costs are high because of low output and expensive sales promotion.

- There may be early teething troubles with production technology.

- The product for the time being is a loss-maker.

5.5 **Growth**

- If the new product gains market acceptance, sales will eventually rise more sharply and the product will start to make profits.

- Competitors are attracted. As sales and production rise, unit costs fall.

5.6 **Maturity.** The rate of sales growth slows down and the product reaches a period of maturity which is probably the longest period of a successful product's life. Most products on the market will be at the mature stage of their life. Profits are good.

5.7 **Decline**. Eventually, sales will begin to decline so that there is over-capacity of production in the industry. Severe competition occurs, profits fall and some producers leave the market. The remaining producers seek means of prolonging the product life by modifying it and searching for new market segments. Many producers are reluctant to leave the market, although some inevitably do because of falling profits.

The relevance of the product life cycle to strategic planning

5.8 In reviewing outputs, planners should assess products in three ways.

(a) The **stage of its life cycle** that any product has reached.

(b) The **product's remaining life**, ie how much longer the product will contribute to profits.

(c) How **urgent is the need to innovate**, to develop new and improved products?

Difficulties of the product life cycle concept

5.9 (a) **Recognition**. How can managers recognise where a product stands in its life cycle?

(b) **Not always true**. The theoretical curve of a product life cycle does not always occur in practice. Some products have no maturity phase, and go straight from growth to decline. Some never decline if they are marketed competitively.

(c) **Changeable**. Strategic decisions can change or extend a product's life cycle.

(d) **Competition varies** in different industries. The financial markets are an example of markets where there is a tendency for competitors to copy the leader very quickly, so that competition has built up well *ahead* of demand.

Case example

Airbus

Airbus is now, by some measures, the world's second largest manufacturer of aircraft. Airbus has launched aircraft which compete with Boeing in every sector of the market, save the Jumbo 747. Airbus is expected to be very profitable. It has a relatively modern range of aircraft in an industry with product life cycles of 25 years or more. Airbus is seeking to compete with the Boeing 747 perhaps by finding new partners in Asia to build a new super-jumbo. The carrot Airbus offers to potential partners is that it will be able to introduce new technology.

Portfolio planning

5.10 **Portfolio analysis** examines the current status of the organisation's products and their markets. Portfolio analysis is the first stage of **portfolio planning**, which aims to create a balance among the organisation's market offerings in order to maximise competitive advantage. The same approach is equally applicable to products, market segments and even SBUs.

5.11 Four **major strategies** can be pursued with respect to products, market segments and, indeed, SBUs.

(a) **Build**. A build strategy forgoes short term earnings and profits in order to increase market share.

(b) **Hold**. A hold strategy seeks to maintain the current position.

(c) **Harvest**. A harvesting strategy seeks short-term earning and profits at the expense of long-term development.

(d) **Divest**. Divestment reduces negative cash flow and releases resources for use elsewhere.

Market share, market growth and cash generation: the Boston classification

> **KEY TERM**
>
> **Market share:** 'One entity's sale of a product or service in a specified market expressed as a percentage of total sales by all entities offering that product or service.'

5.12 The **Boston Consulting Group** (BCG) developed a matrix based on empirical research that assesses a company's products in terms of potential cash generation and cash expenditure requirements. Products or SBUs are categorised in terms of market growth rate and relative market share.

(a) Assessing rate of **market growth** as high or low depends on the conditions in the market. No single percentage rate can be set, since new markets may grow explosively while mature ones grow hardly at all.

(b) **Relative market share** is assessed as a ratio: it is market share compared with the market share of the **largest competitor**. Thus a relative market share greater than unity indicates that the product or SBU is the market leader. (See Section 7 of Chapter 7 for an assessment of the importance of market share.)

		Market share	
		High	*Low*
Market growth	*High*	Stars	Question marks
	Low	Cash cows	Dogs

5.13 The **BCG Matrix**

(a) **Stars**. In the short term, these require capital expenditure in excess of the cash they generate, in order to maintain their market position, but promise high returns in the future. Strategy: **build**.

(b) In due course, stars will become **cash cows**. Cash cows need very little capital expenditure and generate high levels of cash income. Cash cows can be used to finance the stars. Strategy: **hold** or **harvest** if weak.

(c) **Question marks**. Do the products justify considerable capital expenditure in the hope of increasing their market share, or should they be allowed to die quietly as they are squeezed out of the expanding market by rival products? Strategy: **build** or **harvest**.

(d) **Dogs**. They may be ex-cash cows that have now fallen on hard times. Although they will show only a modest net cash outflow, or even a modest net cash inflow, they are cash traps which tie up funds and provide a poor return on investment. However, they may have a useful role, either to complete a product range or to keep competitors out. Strategy: **divest** or **hold**.

Question 4

The marketing manager of Juicy Drinks Ltd has invited you in for a chat. Juicy Drinks Ltd provides fruit juices to a number of supermarket chains, which sell them under their own label. 'We've got a large number of products, of course. Our freshly squeezed orange juice is doing fine - it sells in huge quantities. Although margins are low, we have sufficient economies of scale to do very nicely in this market. We've got advanced production and bottling equipment and long term contracts with some major growers. No problems there. We also sell freshly squeezed pomegranate juice: customers loved it in the tests, but producing the stuff at the right price is a major hassle: all the seeds get in the way. We hope it will be a winner, once we get the production right and start converting customers to it. After all the market for exotic fruit juices generally is expanding fast.'

What sort of products, according to the Boston classification, are described here?

Answer

(a)   Orange juice is a cash cow
(b)   Pomegranate juice is a question mark, which the company wants to turn into a star.

Case example

Unilever

Unilever reappraised its strategies in 1996, to revive sales in sated markets of Europe and America.

Unilever's cash cow is margarine. Unilever intends to focus on core product categories. Unilever says it know what it wanted to do but did not always succeed. 'Star' categories such as ice cream and cosmetics were identified, but sometimes they were denied sufficient financial and human resources.

Unilever has introduced a new analytical tool to assess its businesses. Unilever will reduce its huge portfolio by 'harvesting' some products (taking profits but reinvesting little), and selling or closing others. The group has already disposed of its processed meats and mass-market cosmetics businesses in the past 18 months.

With fewer businesses, Unilever can pour more financial, technical and human resources into those that remain. It can also concentrate its efforts on emerging markets. Two years ago Unilever said it planned to have 30% of its turnover from emerging markets by 2000. This goal has now been achieved.

The General Electric Business Screen

5.14   The approach of the GE Business Screen (GEBS) is similar to that of the BCG matrix. The GEBS includes a broader range of company and market factors. A typical example of the GE matrix is provided below. This matrix **classifies products (or businesses)** according to **industry attractiveness** and **company strengths**. The approach aims to consider a variety of factors which contribute to both these variables.

	Strong	Invest for growth	Invest selectively for growth	Develop for income
Business Strength	*Average*	Invest selectively and build	Develop selectively for income	Harvest or Divest
	Weak	Develop selectively Build on strengths	Harvest	Divest
		Attractive	*Average*	*Unattractive*

Market attractiveness

5.15 The broader approach of the GE matrix emphasises the attempt to match competences within the company to conditions within the market place. Difficulties associated with measurement and classification mean that again the results of such an exercise must be interpreted with care.

Exam focus point

10 marks were available in June 2003 for applying product portfolio models to a product divestment strategy.

The Shell directional policy matrix

5.16 There have been several other matrices designed as guides to strategy. The **Shell directional policy matrix** is similar to the GEBS in that its classifications depend upon **managerial judgement** rather than simple **numerical scores**, as in the BCG matrix. Its axes are **competitive capability** and **prospects for sector profitability**. Clearly, these measures are very similar to those used in the GEBS.

Prospects for sector profitability

		Unattractive	Average	Attractive
	Weak	Disinvest	Phased withdrawal	Double or quit
Enterprise's competitiveness capabilities	Average	Phased withdrawal	Custodial Growth	Try harder
	Strong	Cash generation	Growth Leader	Leader

The Shell directional policy matrix

5.17 Section summary

- Most organisations offer several products/services. These have different financial and marketing needs.

- Existing products generate cash for investment in newer products, which will in turn generate cash in future.

6 ORGANISATION STRUCTURE

6.1 Organisation structure determines how work is allocated, directed and controlled, in order to achieve the goals of the organisation. An organisation's structure must support its strategy. For instance, the classic division of large organisations into SBUs arose because of the **diversity** of the products and markets concerned. Central control of detail became impracticable.

Co-ordinating tasks

6.2 Mintzberg suggests **five methods of co-ordination**.

   (a) **Mutual adjustment.** People co-ordinate themselves.

   (b) **Direct supervision.** One person is responsible for co-ordinating the work of others. This person issues instructions and monitors performance.

   (c) **Standardisation of work processes.** The contents of work are 'specified or programmed' (eg standard procedures for carrying out an audit).

   (d) **Standardisation of outputs.** Outputs in this instance can mean a set level of profits (or level of performance) but the work process itself is not designed or programmed.

   (e) **Standardisation by skills and knowledge.** The kind of knowledge and training required to perform the work is specified. For example, doctors are trained in the necessary skills before being let loose on patients.

Components of organisation structure and systems

6.3 The **organisation structure** embodies mechanisms for co-ordinating work. Mintzberg believes that any organisation is based on the following principles.

- **Job specialisation** (the number of tasks in a given job, the division of labour)
- **Behaviour formalisation** (in other words, the standardisation of work processes)
- **Training** (to enforce work standardisation)
- **Indoctrination** of employees (in the organisation's culture)
- Unit **grouping** (eg organisation by function, geographical area, or product)
- Unit **size** (eg span of control)
- **Planning and control systems**
- **Liaison** and **communication** devices (networks, committees, matrix structures)

6.4 Mintzberg identifies five component parts.

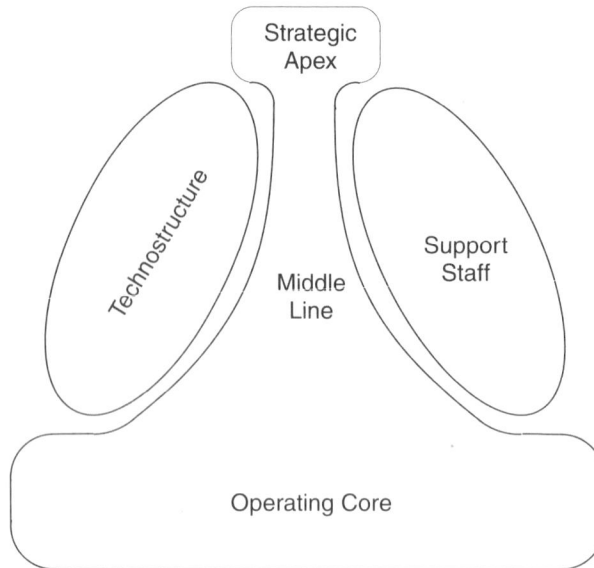

Component	Comment
Operating core	People directly involved in production (ie in securing inputs and processing them into outputs and distributing those outputs), perhaps the **primary activities** of the value chain.
Strategic apex	Owner, board of directors. This component ensures that the organisation follows its mission and serves the needs of its owners. Its job is supervision, control, boundary management and strategy.
Middle line	People in this area administer the work done. The chain of formal authority runs from senior managers at the apex through middle managers to front line supervisors at the operating core. It converts the wishes of the strategic apex into the work of the operating core.
Technostructure	Administrators and planners **standardise work**. Work-study analysts (eg engineers) standardise work processes by analysing and determining the most efficient method of doing a job. Planners (eg quality staff, accountants) standardise outputs. Personnel analysts standardise skills by arranging for training programmes.
Support staff	Ancillary services such as public relations, legal counsel, the cafeteria do not plan or standardise production. They function independently of the operating core.

6.5 These elements are linked in five ways.

(a) **Organisation hierarchy** (see below).

(b) **Flow of regulated activity**. Inputs are processed into outputs. The activities in the value chain are controlled and linked.

(c) **Informal communications** supplement or bypass the formal communication system.

(d) **System of work constellations**. Groups of people, permanent or temporary, work on distinct tasks. For example, the members of the accounts department work together. Some constellations are temporary: for example, in producing a set of annual financial statements, people from the finance department (for the numbers), the sales department (for detailed statistics) and public relations (for presentation) need to be involved.

(e) **Ad hoc decision processes**. A decision process involves recognising a problem, diagnosing its causes, finding a solution and implementing it. For any one decision, these activities occur in a number of different places in the organisation. For example, customer care personnel might first hear of a problem with faulty goods, but the decisions as to how to prevent the problem happening again will be taken in by the production department.

Influence of components

6.6 **Coalitions** of individuals 'may occur within departments, geographical locations, different levels in the hierarchy, different age groups'. Such groups might manipulate the direction it takes.

6.7 Each component has its own **preferred co-ordination mechanism.**

Hierarchy and span of control

6.8 A formal organisation structure has distinctive characteristics.

(a) A **division of labour**

(b) Planned **divisions of responsibility**

(c) **Power centres** which control its efforts

(d) **Substitution of personnel** (eg the position of Financial Controller does not disappear when the current occupant resigns)

(e) The ability to **group personnel** in different ways according to work

6.9 The existing organisation structure is **worth reviewing.**

(a) It can **help or hinder the mission** and effectiveness of the organisation.

(b) It might have to be **changed**, which takes time.

(c) It shapes the **deployment of value activities** and the management of the **linkages** between them.

(d) It **channels and filters information** from markets and personnel.

(e) It **is the arena for various political manoeuvrings** by management and other interest groups.

6.10 The **scalar chain** (or chain of command) is the organisation hierarchy, from the most junior to the most senior. A long scalar chain has many levels with many ranks between the most junior and the senior.

6.11 The **span of control** (unit size) is the number of subordinates working for a manager in the level immediately below the manager.

6.12 A **tall organisation** has a large number of management levels and small spans of control.

(a) These are held to be cumbersome and inflexible. People think they slow down communications and responsiveness to the market, and stifle initiative.

(b) They offer more secure **promotion paths.**

6.13 **Flat organisations** (few management levels) are becoming more popular, as they are supposed to be more flexible and responsive. They also save large costs in the form of management salaries.

(a) Information technology must be used in order to reduce the information processing function of middle management.

(b) Front line employees must accept much more responsibility. This is called **empowerment.**

6.14 **Delayering** is the removal of management layers. Many large organisations have shed large numbers of managerial staff in this way. We will come back to this in Chapter 10.

Authority and the technostructure

6.15 **Authority is the right** to do something, whereas **power relates to the ability** to exercise authority. Authority is normally derived from position in the hierarchy.

(a) **Line authority** reflects a manager's direct authority over a subordinate.

(b) **Staff authority** is the right to give advice and is normally exercised by one department over another.

(c) **Functional authority** is staff authority exercised through procedures which managers in other departments have to follow. The personnel department sets down recruitment procedures; the finance department lays down expenditure authorisation procedures.

6.16 Often, **members of the technostructure seek to expand their area of control** and expertise for reasons not necessarily connected with the organisation's well being (eg acquiring a costly state of the art computer system when this is not needed).

6.17 However, **managers in the middle line might ignore necessary controls** or ignore the productivity enhancements that the technostructure might suggest.

6.18 The **informal organisation** is those work and social relationships that exist outside the formal organisation structure. The informal organisation depends on individual personalities and, unlike the formal organisation structure, is affected when someone leaves.

(a) Certain individuals might have a **significant influence** outside of their formal authority (eg if one of the directors gets on particularly well with the MD).

(b) An inefficient formal organisation structure might force employees to rely on the informal organisation to get work done.

6.19 **Significance of organisation structure for strategy**.

(a) **Different coalitions** in the organisation have their own agendas to promote and sources of power.

(b) Structure and **culture are closely related** and culture influences how managers interpret the world.

(c) **Implementing a strategy sometimes requires a change to the structure** (see Chapter 10.)

(d) **Organisation structure** can influence managers' preferences for certain strategic choices. For example, an organisation which is very decentralised, and in which units actively compete with each other, may not take well to a strategy involving co-operation.

6.20 Section summary

(a) Organisation structure directs communication and deploys resources in order to co-ordinate work.

(b) Each component (apex, technostructure, operating core, middle line, support staff) prefers to co-ordinate work in a different way.

(c) Organisation hierarchy outlines formal authority, but there are other sources of power within the organisation which influence what it can do.

6.21 We return to organisation structure in Chapter 9.

7 THE CUSTOMER BASE

7.1 A **marketing audit** involves a review of an organisation's products and markets, the marketing environment, and its marketing system and operations. The profitability of each product and each market should be assessed, and the costs of different marketing activities established.

7.2 **Information obtained about markets**

(a) **Size of the customer base**. Does the organisation sell to a large number of small customers or a small number of big customers?

(b) **Size of individual orders**. The organisation might sell its products in many small orders, or it might have large individual orders. Delivery costs can be compared with order sizes.

(c) **Sales revenue and profitability**. The performance of individual products can be compared. Here is an example.

Product group	Sales revenue		Contribution to profits	
	£'000	% of total	£'000	% of total
B	7,500	35.7	2,500	55.6
E	2,000	9.5	1,200	26.7
C	4,500	21.4	450	10.0
A	5,000	23.8	250	5.6
D	2,000	9.5	100	2.2
	21,000	100.0%	4,500	100.0%

An imbalance between sales and profits over various product ranges can be potentially dangerous. In the figures above, product group A accounts for 23.8% of turnover but only 5.6% of total contribution, and product group D accounts for 9.5% of turnover but only 2.2% of total contribution.

(d) **Segments**. An analysis of sales and profitability into, for instance, export markets and domestic markets

(e) **Market share**. Estimated share of the market obtained by each product group

(f) **Growth**. Sales growth and contribution growth over the previous four years or so, for each product group

(g) Whether the **demand** for certain products is **growing, stable or likely to decline**

(h) Whether **demand is price sensitive** or not

(i) Whether there is a growing tendency for the market to become **fragmented**, with more specialist and custom-made products.

7.3 Information about current marketing activities

- Comparative pricing
- Advertising effectiveness
- Effectiveness of distribution network
- Attitudes to the product, in comparison with competitors

(Marketing is examined in depth in later chapters.)

Customers

7.4 Many firms, especially in business-to-business markets, sell to a relatively small number of customers. **Key customer analysis** calls for six main areas of investigation.

(a) **Key customer identity** (name, location, size, product market)

(b) **Customer history:** order size and frequency, reasons for purchase, key decision makers

(c) **Relationship of customer to product**

- Are the products purchased to be resold? If not, why are they bought?
- Do the products form part of the customer's service/product?

(d) **Relationship of customer to potential market**

- What is the size of the customer in relation to the total end-market?
- Is the customer likely to expand, or not? Diversify? Integrate?

(e) **Customer attitudes and behaviour**

- What interpersonal factors affect sales by the firm and by competitors?
- Does the customer also buy competitors' products?
- To what extent may purchases be postponed?
- What emotional factors exist in buying decisions?

(f) **The financial performance of the customer**

How successful is the customer in his own markets?

(g) **The profitability of selling to the customer**

(i) What profit/contribution is the organisation making on sales to the customer, after discounts and selling and delivery costs?

(ii) What would be the financial consequences of losing the customer?

(iii) Is the customer buying in order sizes that are unprofitable to supply?

(iv) What is return on investment in plant used?

(v) What is the level of inventory required specifically to supply these customers?

(vi) Are there any other specific costs involved in supplying this customer, such as technical and test facilities, R&D facilities, special design staff?

(vii) What is the ratio of net contribution per customer to total investment on both a historic and replacement cost basis?

7.5 **Not all customers are as important as others.** The checklist below can help identify the most important.

Strategic importance evaluation guide	High	Medium	Low	N/A
1 Fit between customer's needs and our capabilities, at present and potentially.				
2 Ability to serve customer compared with our major competitors, at present and potentially.				
3 'Health' of customer's industry, current and forecast.				
4 'Health' of the customer, current and forecast.				
5 Customer's growth prospects, current and forecast.				
6 What can we learn from this customer?				
7 Can the customer help us attract others?				
8 Relative *significance:* how important is the customer compared *with other* customers?				
9 What is the *profitability* of serving the customer?				

8   DRAWING THE THREADS TOGETHER

8.1   Organisational performance depends on the interplay of a range of elements. This interdependence is illustrated by the McKinsey 7S model, which we repeat here after its earlier explanation in Chapter 3 of this Study Text.

> **Exam focus point**
> The examiner for Paper 3.5 regards this diagram as a useful tool for understanding how strategic management is linked to other aspects of the organisations. Such linkages are an essential aspect of *implementing* strategy. A deficiency in any of the elements or mismatch between them will hamper success.

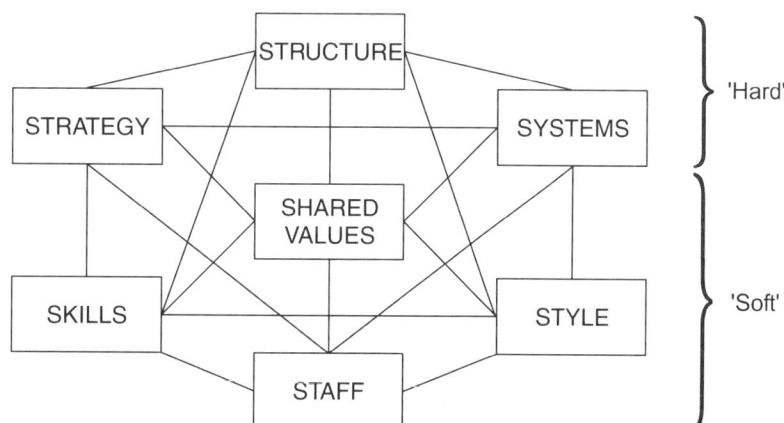

Chapter roundup

- A **position audit** reviews the organisation's current position.

- **Resource audits** identify physical human and material resources and how they are deployed into a **distinctive competence**, something it does uniquely well.

- The **value chain** describes those activities of the organisation which add value to purchased inputs. Primary activities are involved in the production of goods and services. Support activities provide necessary assistance. **Linkages** are the relationships between activities. Managing the value chain, which includes relationships with outside suppliers, can be a source of strategic advantage.

- The **product life cycle** concept holds that products have a life cycle, and that a product demonstrates different characteristics of profit and investment at each stage in its life cycle. The life cycle concept is a model, not a prediction. (Not all products pass through each stage of the life cycle.) It enables a firm to examine its portfolio of goods and services as a whole.

- The **Boston classification** classifies products in terms of their capacity for growth within the market and the market's capacity for growth as a whole. A firm should have a balanced **portfolio of products**.

- **Organisation structure** indicates how value activities are **co-ordinated** within the organisation. Organisations are characterised by formal division of labour, **hierarchies** of authority (scalar chains) and networks of **authority** and power. There are five components.

- The organisation structure influences strategy, as it is one of the ways in which power is deployed and **information** communicated.

- A **marketing audit** renews the customer base and effectiveness of marketing operations.

Quick quiz

1   What is a limiting factor?

2   What is a core competence?

3   What is the significance of the value chain?

4   Distinguish between product class and product form.

5   List the stages of the product life cycle.

6   What is a cash cow?

7   Describe the five component parts of the organisation identified by Mintzberg.

8   What is meant by scalar chain?

9   What is a marketing audit?

10   What is key customer analysis?

Answers to quick quiz

1 Any factor that limits activity, usually because of a shortage.

2 Competences where the organisation outperforms competitors and that are difficult to imitate.

3 The value chain illustrates how value is created by value activities and linkages.

4 Product class is a broad generic category, eg 'car'. Product form is a specific type within the class, eg 'executive saloon'.

5 Introduction, growth, maturity, decline.

6 A product that requires little expenditure but generates plentiful revenue.

7 Strategic apex; middle line; operating core; technostructure; support staff.

8 The chain of command.

9 A comprehensive review of products and markets, the marketing environment and marketing system.

10 Establishment of important date about important customers.

Now try the question below from the Exam Question Bank

Number	Level	Marks	Time
Q6	Exam	20	36 mins

Chapter 7

STRATEGIC OPTIONS

Topic list		Syllabus reference
1	Corporate appraisal (SWOT analysis)	3(b)
2	Gap analysis	3(b)
3	Generic competitive strategies: how to compete	4(b)
4	Using the value chain in competitive strategy	4(b)
5	Product-market strategy: direction of growth	4(b)
6	Method of growth	4(b)
7	Strategy and market position	5(a)
8	The marketing mix	5(a)

Introduction

Once the internal and external analyses are complete, the next task is to develop strategies. **SWOT analysis** is a way of identifying the extent to which an organisation has managed to obtain a fit with the environment: it identifies internal **strengths** and **weaknesses**, and external **opportunities** and **threats**. Strategies are developed to exploit strengths and opportunities, and to mitigate threats and weaknesses. **Gap analysis** is a technique of quantifying the extent to which new strategic projects are necessary. We can identify three basic strategic decisions.

How you compete: competitive strategy. Taking the **industry scenario** into account, it should be possible to identify the best way of competing. The value chain, which we encountered earlier, can be used here. The strategy clock summarises strategic options.

Where you compete. This decision relates to the products sold and the markets they are sold in: Ansoff's model or the market options matrix.

Method of growth. This decision relates to whether a firm grows by its own efforts (organic growth) or acquires other businesses (acquisition).

We also examine a range of strategies that have been proposed as suitable for market leaders, market followers, market challengers and market nichers.

Finally, this chapter considers market mix strategies.

Study guide

Section 3 – Internal assessment

- Analysis of capabilities and core competences

Section 4 – The nature of strategy analysis and choice

- Developing the strategy

Section 5 – The nature of strategy implementation

- Marketing issues

Exam guide

This chapter is concerned with several very specific techniques, any of which could form the basis for an answer concerning strategy formulation.

---

1 CORPORATE APPRAISAL (SWOT ANALYSIS)

1.1 A complete awareness of the organisation's environment and its internal capacities is *necessary* for a rational consideration of future strategy, but it is not *sufficient*. The threads must be drawn together so that potential strategies may be developed and assessed. The most common way of doing this is to analyse the factors into **strengths**, **weaknesses**, **opportunities** and **threats**. Strengths and weaknesses are diagnosed by the internal analysis, opportunities and threats by the environmental analysis.

> **KEY TERM**
>
> **Corporate appraisal (SWOT):** 'a critical assessment of the **strengths** and **weaknesses**, **opportunities** and **threats** in relation to the internal and environmental factors affecting the entity in order to establish its condition prior to the preparation of a long-term plan.'

1.2 A **strengths and weaknesses** analysis establishes strengths that should be exploited and weaknesses which should be improved. It may be thought of as a review in detail of **core competences**: those the organisation **has** and those it **needs.**

1.3 Here are some examples of opportunities and threats

(a) **Opportunities**

- What opportunities exist in the business environment?
- What is their inherent profit-making potential?
- What is the organisation's ability to exploit the worthwhile opportunities?

(b) **Threats**

- What threats might arise?
- How will competitors be affected?
- How will the company be affected?

The opportunities and threats might arise from the PEST and competitive factors.

Bringing them together

1.4 EXAMPLE

STRENGTHS	WEAKNESSES
£10 million of capital available	Heavy reliance on a small number of customers
Production expertise and appropriate marketing skills	Limited product range, with no new products and expected market decline. Small marketing organisation.

THREATS	OPPORTUNITIES
A major competitor has already entered the new market	Government tax incentives for new investment. Growing demand in a new market, although customers so far relatively small in number.

The company is in imminent danger of losing its existing markets and must diversify its products and markets. The new market opportunity exists to be exploited, and since the number of customers is currently small, the relatively small size of the existing marketing force would not be an immediate hindrance. A strategic plan could be developed to buy new equipment and use existing production and marketing to enter the new market, with a view to rapid expansion. Careful planning of manpower, equipment, facilities, research and development would be required and there would be an objective to meet the threat of competition so as to obtain a substantial share of a growing market. The cost of entry at this early stage of market development should not be unacceptably high.

1.5 The SWOT technique can also be used for specific areas of strategy such as IT and marketing.

1.6 Effective SWOT analysis does not simply require a categorisation of information, it also requires some **evaluation of the relative importance** of the various factors under consideration.

(a) These features are only of relevance if they are **perceived to exist by the consumers.** Listing corporate features that internal personnel regard as strengths/weaknesses is of little relevance if they are not perceived as such by the organisation's consumers.

(b) In the same vein, threats and opportunities are conditions presented by the external environment and they should be independent of the firm.

1.7   The SWOT can now be used guiding strategy formulation.

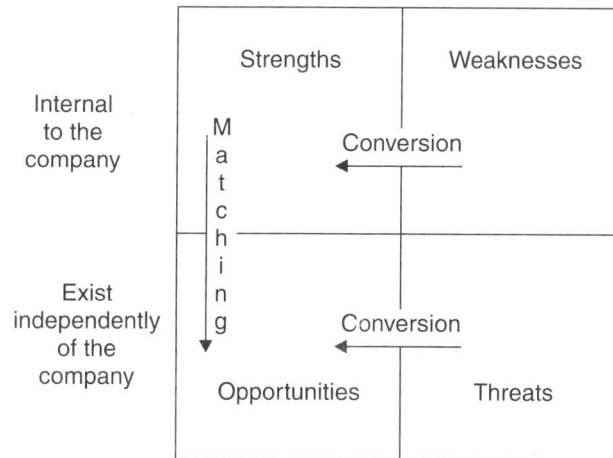

(a) **Match strengths with market opportunities**

Strengths which do not match any available opportunity are of limited use while opportunities which do not have any matching strengths are of little immediate value.

(b) **Conversion**

This requires the development of strategies which will convert weaknesses into strengths in order to take advantage of some particular opportunity, or converting threats into opportunities which can then be matched by existing strengths.

Question 1

Hall Faull Downes Ltd has been in business for 25 years, during which time profits have risen by an average of 3% per annum, although there have been peaks and troughs in profitability due to the ups and downs of trade in the customers' industry. The increase in profits until five years ago was the result of increasing sales in a buoyant market, but more recently, the total market has become somewhat smaller and Hall Faull Downes has only increased sales and profits as a result of improving its market share.

The company produces components for manufacturers in the engineering industry.

In recent years, the company has developed many new products and currently has 40 items in its range compared to 24 only five years ago. Over the same five year period, the number of customers has fallen from 20 to nine, two of whom together account for 60% of the company's sales.

Give your appraisal of the company's future, and suggest what it is probably doing wrong.

Answer

A general interpretation of the facts as given might be sketched as follows.

(a) Objectives: the company has no declared objectives. Profits have risen by 3% per annum in the past, which has failed to keep pace with inflation but may have been a satisfactory rate of increase in the current conditions of the industry. Even so, stronger growth is indicated in the future.

151   **BPP**
PROFESSIONAL EDUCATION

(b)

Strengths	Weaknesses
Many new products developed.	Products may be reaching the end of their life and entering decline.
Marketing success in increasing market share	New product life cycles may be shorter.
	Reduction in customers.
	Excessive reliance on a few customers.
	Doubtful whether profit record is satisfactory.
Threats	Opportunities
Possible decline in the end-product.	None identified.
Smaller end-product market will restrict future sales prospects for Hall Faull Downes.	

(c) Strengths: the growth in company sales in the last five years has been as a result of increasing the market share in a declining market. This success may be the result of the following.

- Research and development spending
- Good product development programmes
- Extending the product range to suit changing customer needs
- Marketing skills
- Long-term supply contracts with customers
- Cheap pricing policy
- Product quality and reliable service

(d) Weaknesses:

(i) The products may be custom-made for customers so that they provide little or no opportunity for market development.

(ii) Products might have a shorter life cycle than in the past, in view of the declining total market demand.

(iii) Excessive reliance on two major customers leaves the company exposed to the dangers of losing their custom.

(e) Threats: there may be a decline in the end-market for the customers' product so that the customer demands for the company's own products will also fall.

(f) Opportunities: no opportunities have been identified, but in view of the situation as described, new strategies for the longer term would appear to be essential.

(g) Conclusions: the company does not appear to be planning beyond the short-term, or is reacting to the business environment in a piecemeal fashion. A strategic planning programme should be introduced.

(h) Recommendations: the company must look for new opportunities in the longer-term.

(i) In the short term, current strengths must be exploited to continue to increase market share in existing markets and product development programmes should also continue.

(ii) In the longer term, the company must diversify into new markets or into new products and new markets. Diversification opportunities should be sought with a view to exploiting any competitive advantage or synergy that might be achievable.

(iii) The company should use its strengths (whether in R&D, production skills or marketing expertise) in exploiting any identifiable opportunities.

(iv) Objectives need to be quantified in order to assess the extent to which new long-term strategies are required.

2   GAP ANALYSIS

> **KEY TERMS**
>
> **Forecasting:** 'the identification of relevant factors and quantification of this effect on an entity as a basis for planning'.
>
> **Gap analysis** is the comparison of an entity's ultimate objective with the sum of projections and already planned projects.

2.1   Gap analysis compares two things.

(a)   The organisation's **targets** for achievement over the planning period

(b)   What would the organisation be **expected to achieve** if it carried on in the current way with the same products and selling to the same markets, with no major changes to operations. This is called an F_o **forecast,** by *Argenti.*

This difference is the gap. New strategies will then have to be developed which will close this gap, so that the organisation can expect to achieve its targets over the planning period.

Errors in the forecast

2.2   Forecasts can never be completely accurate - they might be misleading in cases of environmental turbulence. But in stable environments, they are valid, if adjusted for error. Errors can be accounted for in two ways.

(a)   Estimating **likely variations**: for example, 'in 1999 the forecast profit is £5 million with possible variations of plus or minus £2 million'.

(b)   Providing a **probability distribution** for profits: for example, 'in 1999 there is a 20% chance that profits will exceed £7 million, a 50% chance that they will exceed £5 million and an 80% chance that they will exceed £2½ million. Minimum profits in 1999 will be £2 million'.

2.3   The gap could be filled by new product-market growth strategies.

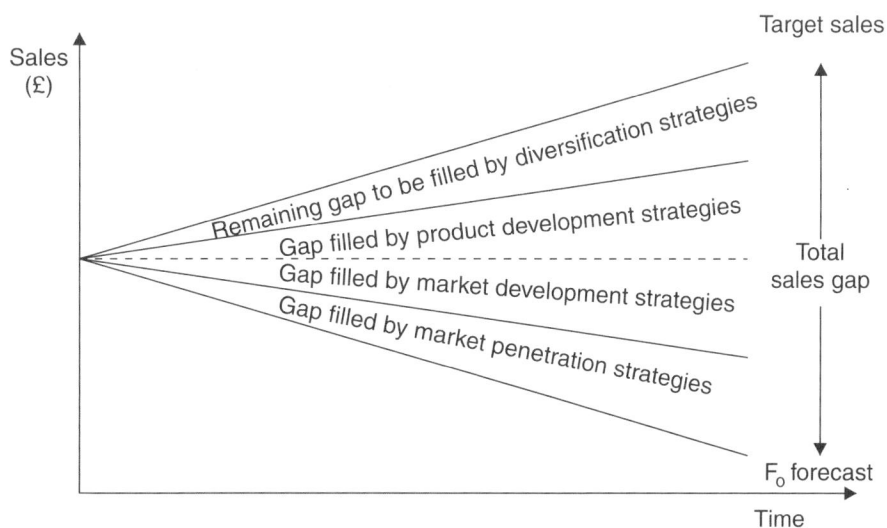

See Section 5 of this chapter for a discussion of the product-market growth strategies shown above.

Question 2

Gap analysis can be used to model a variety of factors in addition to sales and profit. How do you think you could use gap analysis for manpower?

Answer

(a) The F_0 forecast would start with current manpower levels, and would be projected into the future assuming natural wastage, no training and no new appointments.

(b) The organisation would have to assess its needs in terms of manpower *numbers* and *skills*.

(c) Strategies to fill the gap would include recruitment and training programmes.

3 GENERIC COMPETITIVE STRATEGIES: HOW TO COMPETE

3.1 Competitive advantage is anything which gives one organisation an edge over its rivals. *Porter* argues that a firm should adopt a competitive strategy which is intended to achieve some form of competitive advantage for the firm.

Competitive strategy means 'taking offensive or defensive actions to create a dependable position in an industry, to cope successfully with ... competitive forces and thereby yield a superior return on investment for the firm. Firms have discovered many different approaches to this end, and the best strategy for a given firm is ultimately a unique construction reflecting its particular circumstances'. (Porter)

The choice of competitive strategy

3.2 Porter believes there are three **generic strategies** for competitive advantage.

> **KEY TERMS**
>
> **Cost leadership** means being the lowest cost producer in the industry as a whole.
>
> **Differentiation** is the exploitation of a product or service which the *industry as a whole* believes to be unique.
>
> **Focus** involves a restriction of activities to only part of the market (a segment) through:
>
> - Providing goods and/or services at lower cost (**cost-focus**);
> - Providing a differentiated product or service (**differentiation-focus**)

3.3 **Cost leadership and differentiation are industry-wide strategies. Focus involves segmentation** but involves pursuing, **within the segment only,** a strategy of cost leadership or differentiation.

Cost leadership

3.4 A cost leadership strategy seeks to achieve the position of lowest-cost producer in the **industry as a whole**. By producing at the lowest cost, the manufacturer can compete on price with every other producer in the industry, and earn the higher unit profits, if the manufacturer so chooses.

3.5 **How to achieve overall cost leadership**

(a) Set up production facilities to obtain **economies of scale**.

(b) Use the **latest technology** to reduce costs and/or enhance productivity (or use cheap labour if available).

(c) In high technology industries, and in industries depending on labour skills for product design and production methods, exploit the **learning curve effect**. By producing more items than any other competitor, a firm can benefit more from the learning curve, and achieve lower average costs.

(d) Concentrate on **improving productivity**.

(e) **Minimise overhead costs**.

(f) **Get favourable access to sources of supply**.

Case example

Large out-of-town stores specialising in one particular category of product are able to secure cost leadership by economies of scale over other retailers. Such shops have been called **category killers**, an example of which is PC World.

Differentiation

3.6 A differentiation strategy assumes that competitive advantage can be gained through **particular characteristics** of a firm's products. Products may be divided into three categories.

(a) **Breakthrough products** offer a radical performance advantage over competition, perhaps at a drastically lower price (eg float glass, developed by *Pilkington*).

(b) **Improved products** are not radically different from their competition but are obviously superior in terms of better performance at a competitive price (eg microchips).

(c) **Competitive products** derive their appeal from a particular compromise of cost and performance. For example, cars are not all sold at rock-bottom prices, nor do they all provide immaculate comfort and performance. They compete with each other by trying to offer a more attractive compromise than rival models.

3.7 **How to differentiate**

(a) **Build up a brand image** (eg Pepsi's blue cans are supposed to offer different 'psychic benefits' to Coke's red ones).

(b) **Give the product special features** to make it stand out (eg Russell Hobbs' Millennium kettle incorporated a new kind of element, which boils water faster).

(c) **Exploit other activities of the value chain** (see Section 4 below).

3.8 **Generic strategies and the five forces**

Competitive force	Advantages		Disadvantages	
	Cost leadership	*Differentiation*	*Cost leadership*	*Differentiation*
New entrants	Economies of scale raise entry barriers	Brand loyalty and perceived uniqueness are entry barriers		
Substitutes	Firm is not so vulnerable as its less cost-effective competitors to the threat of substitutes	Customer loyalty is a weapon against substitutes		
Customers	Customers cannot drive down prices further than the next most efficient competitor	Customers have no comparable alternative Brand loyalty should lower price sensitivity		Customers may no longer need the differentiating factor Sooner or later customers become price sensitive
Suppliers	Flexibility to deal with cost increases	Higher margins can offset vulnerability to supplier price rises	Increase in input costs can reduce price advantages	
Industry rivalry	Firm remains profitable when rivals go under through excessive price competition	Unique features reduce direct competition	Technological change will require capital investment, or make production cheaper for competitors Competitors learn via imitation Cost concerns ignore product design or marketing issues	Imitation narrows differentiation

Focus (or niche) strategy

3.9 In a focus strategy, a firm concentrates its attention on one or more particular segments or niches of the market, and does not try to serve the entire market with a single product.

Case example

A good example of a niche strategy is that adopted by the makers of *Sibelius 7*, a computer system for composers of music. Contrary to most other developments in software, *Sibelius 7* requires dedicated hardware to work effectively: it cannot be run on a PC or Mac with a soundcard. Users of the software have to buy hardware too.

(a) A **cost-focus strategy:** aim to be a cost leader for a particular segment. This type of strategy is often found in the printing, clothes manufacture and car repair industries.

(b) A **differentiation-focus strategy:** pursue differentiation for a chosen segment. Luxury goods are the prime example of such a strategy.

3.10 Advantages

(a) A niche is more secure and a firm can insulate itself from competition.

(b) The firm does not spread itself too thinly.

(c) Both cost leadership and differentiation require **superior performance** – life is easier in a niche, where there may be little or no competition.

3.11 Drawbacks of a focus strategy

(a) The firm sacrifices economies of scale which would be gained by serving a wider market.

(b) Competitors can move into the segment, with increased resources (eg the Japanese moved into the US luxury car market, to compete with Mercedes and BMW).

(c) The segment's needs may eventually become less distinct from the main market.

Which strategy?

3.12 Although there is a risk with any of the generic strategies, Porter argues that a firm *must* pursue one of them. A **stuck-in-the-middle** strategy is almost certain to make only low profits. 'This firm lacks the market share, capital investment and resolve to play the low-cost game, the industry-wide differentiation necessary to obviate the need for a low-cost position, or the focus to create differentiation or a low-cost position in a more limited sphere.'

Question 3

The managing director of Hermes Telecommunications plc is interested in corporate strategy. Hermes has invested a great deal of money in establishing a network which competes with that of Telecom UK, a recently privatised utility. Initially Hermes concentrated its efforts on business customers in the South East of England, especially the City of London, where it offered a lower cost service to that supplied by Telecom UK. Recently, Hermes has approached the residential market (ie domestic telephone users) offering a lower cost service on long-distance calls. Technological developments have resulted in the possibility of a cheap mobile telecommunication network, using microwave radio links. The franchise for this service has been awarded to Gerbil phone, which is installing transmitters in town centres and stations etc.

What issues of competitive strategy have been raised in the above scenario, particularly in relation to Hermes Telecommunications plc?

Answer

(a) Arguably, Hermes initially pursued a cost-focus strategy, by targeting the business segment.

(b) It seems to be moving into a cost leadership strategy over the whole market although its competitive offer, in terms of lower costs for local calls, is incomplete.

(c) The barriers to entry to the market have been lowered by the new technology. Gerbil phone might pick up a significant amount of business.

Conceptual difficulties with generic strategy

3.13 In practice, it is rarely simple to draw hard and fast distinctions between the generic strategies as there are conceptual problems underlying them.

(a) **Cost leadership**

   (i) **Internal focus.** Cost refers to internal measures, rather than the market demand. It can be used to gain market share: but it is the **market share which is important,** not cost leadership as such.

   (ii) **Only one firm.** If cost leadership applies cross the whole industry, only one firm will pursue this strategy successfully. However, the position is not clear-cut.

   • More than one firm might **aspire** to cost leadership, especially in dynamic markets where new technologies are frequently introduced.

   • The boundary between cost leadership and cost focus might be blurred.

   • Firms competing market-wide might have different competences or advantages that confer cost leadership in different segments.

   (iii) **Higher margins can be used for differentiation.** Having low costs does *not* mean you have to charge lower prices or compete on price. A cost leader can choose to 'invest higher margins in R&D or marketing'. Being a cost leader arguably gives producers more freedom to choose *other* competitive strategies.

(b) **Differentiation.** Porter assumes that a differentiated product will always be sold at a *higher price*.

   (i) However, a **differentiated product** may be sold at the same price as competing products in order to **increase market share.**

   (ii) **Choice of competitor.** Differentiation from whom? Who are the competitors? Do they serve other market segments? Do they compete on the same basis?

   (iii) **Source of differentiation.** This can include **all** aspects of the firm's offer, not only the product. Restaurants aim to create an atmosphere or 'ambience', as well as serving food of good quality.

3.14 **Focus** probably has fewer conceptual difficulties, as it ties in very neatly with ideas of market segmentation. In practice most companies pursue this strategy to some extent, by designing products/services to meet the needs of particular target markets.

3.15 'Stuck-in-the-middle' is therefore what many companies actually pursue quite successfully. Any number of strategies can be pursued, with different approaches to **price** and the **perceived added value** (ie the differentiation factor) in the eyes of the customer.

The strategy clock

3.16 Porter's basic concept of generic strategies has been the subject of further discussion. *Johnson and Scholes*, quoting *Bowman*, describe the strategic options on the **strategy clock**.

The Strategy Clock

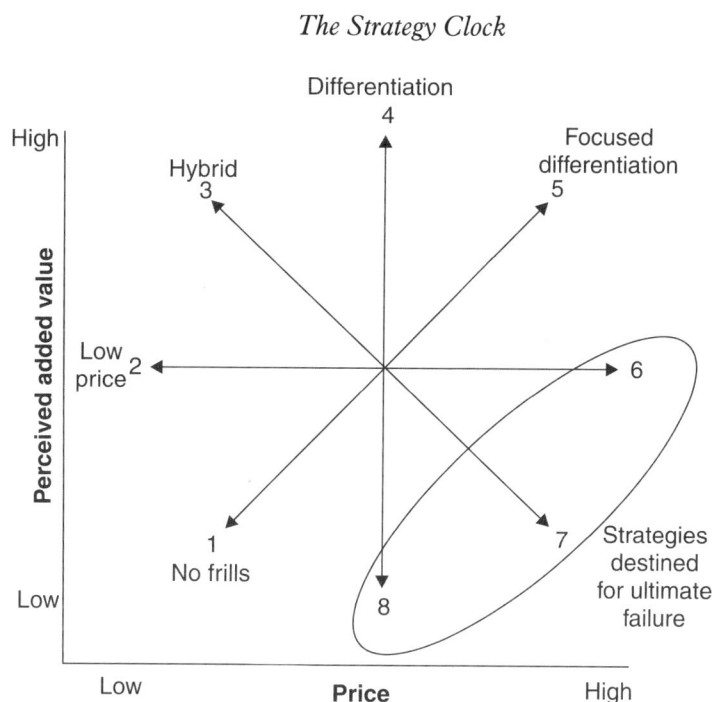

Price-based strategies

3.17 Strategies 1 and 2 are price-based strategies.

(a) A **no frills** strategy is aimed at the most price-conscious and can only succeed if this segment of the market is sufficiently large. This strategy may be used for market entry, to gain experience and build volume. This was done by Japanese car manufacturers in the 1960s.

(b) A **low price** strategy offers better value than competitors. This can lead to price war and reduced margins for all. Porter's generic strategy of **cost leadership** is appropriate to a firm adopting this strategy.

Differentiation strategies

3.18 Strategies 3, 4 and 5 are all differentiation strategies. Each one represents a different trade-off between market share (with its cost advantages) and margin (with its direct impact on profit). Differentiation can be created in three ways.

- Product features
- Marketing, including powerful brand promotion
- Core competences

3.19 The pursuit of any differentiation strategy requires detailed and accurate **market intelligence**. The customers and their preferences must be clearly identified, as must the competition and their likely responses. The chosen basis for differentiation should be inherently difficult to imitate, and will probably need to be developed over time.

3.20 The **hybrid** strategy seeks both differentiation and a lower price than competitors. The cost base must be low enough to permit reduced prices and reinvestment to maintain differentiation. This strategy may be more advantageous than differentiation alone under certain circumstances.

- If it leads to growth in market share
- If differentiation rests on core competences and costs can be reduced elsewhere

- If a low price approach is suited to a particular market segment
- Where it is used as a market entry strategy

3.21 The basic **differentiation** strategy comes in two variants, depending on whether a price premium is charged or a competitive price is accepted in order to build market share.

3.22 A strategy of **focussed differentiation** seeks a high price premium in return for a high degree of differentiation. This implies concentration on a well defined and probably quite restricted market segment. **Coherence** of offer will be very important under these circumstances. Johnson and Scholes give the example of a department store offering a range of products to a variety of customer types but failing to differentiate such matters as premises, décor and staff according to the particular segment served.

Failure strategies

3.23 Combinations 6, 7 and 8 are likely to result in failure.

3.24 Section summary

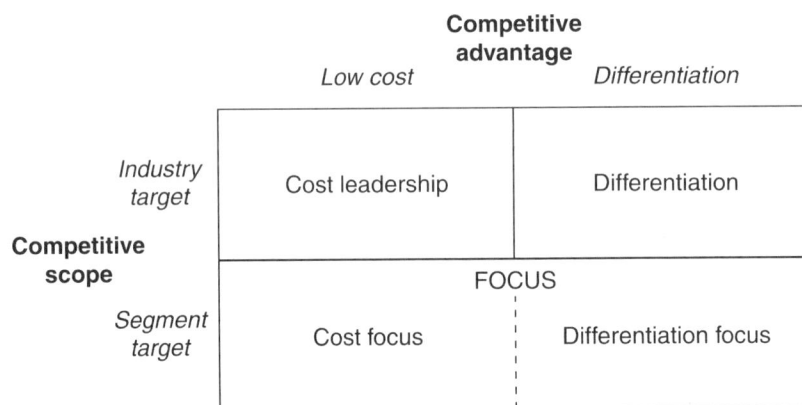

	Competitive advantage	
	Low cost	*Differentiation*
Industry target	Cost leadership	Differentiation
Segment target	Cost focus	Differentiation focus

The **strategy clock** explores Porter's generic strategies in more detail.

4 USING THE VALUE CHAIN IN COMPETITIVE STRATEGY 6/03

4.1 The value chain can be used to design a competitive strategy, by deploying the various activities strategically. The examples below are based on two supermarket chains, one concentrating on low prices, the other differentiated on quality and service. See if you can tell which is which.

(a)

Firm infrastructure	Central control of operations and credit control				
Human resource management	Recruitment of mature staff	Client care training	Flexible staff to help with packing		
Technology development		Recipe research	Electronic point of sale	Consumer research & tests	Itemised bills
Procurement	Own label products	Prime retail positions		Adverts in quality magazines & poster sites	
	Dedicated refrigerated transport	In store food halls Modern store design Open front refrigerators Tight control of sell-by dates	Collect by car service	No price discounts on food past sell-by dates	No quibble refunds
	INBOUND LOGISTICS	OPERATIONS	OUTBOUND LOGISTICS	MARKETING & SALES	SERVICE

(b)

Firm infrastructure	Minimum corporate HQ				
Human resource management		De-skilled store-ops	Dismissal for checkout error		
Technology development	Computerised warehousing		Checkouts simple		
Procurement	Branded only purchases big discounts	Low cost sites			Use of concessions
	Bulk warehousing	1,000 lines only Price points Basic store design		Low price promotion Local focus	Nil
	INBOUND LOGISTICS	OPERATIONS	OUTBOUND LOGISTICS	MARKETING & SALES	SERVICE

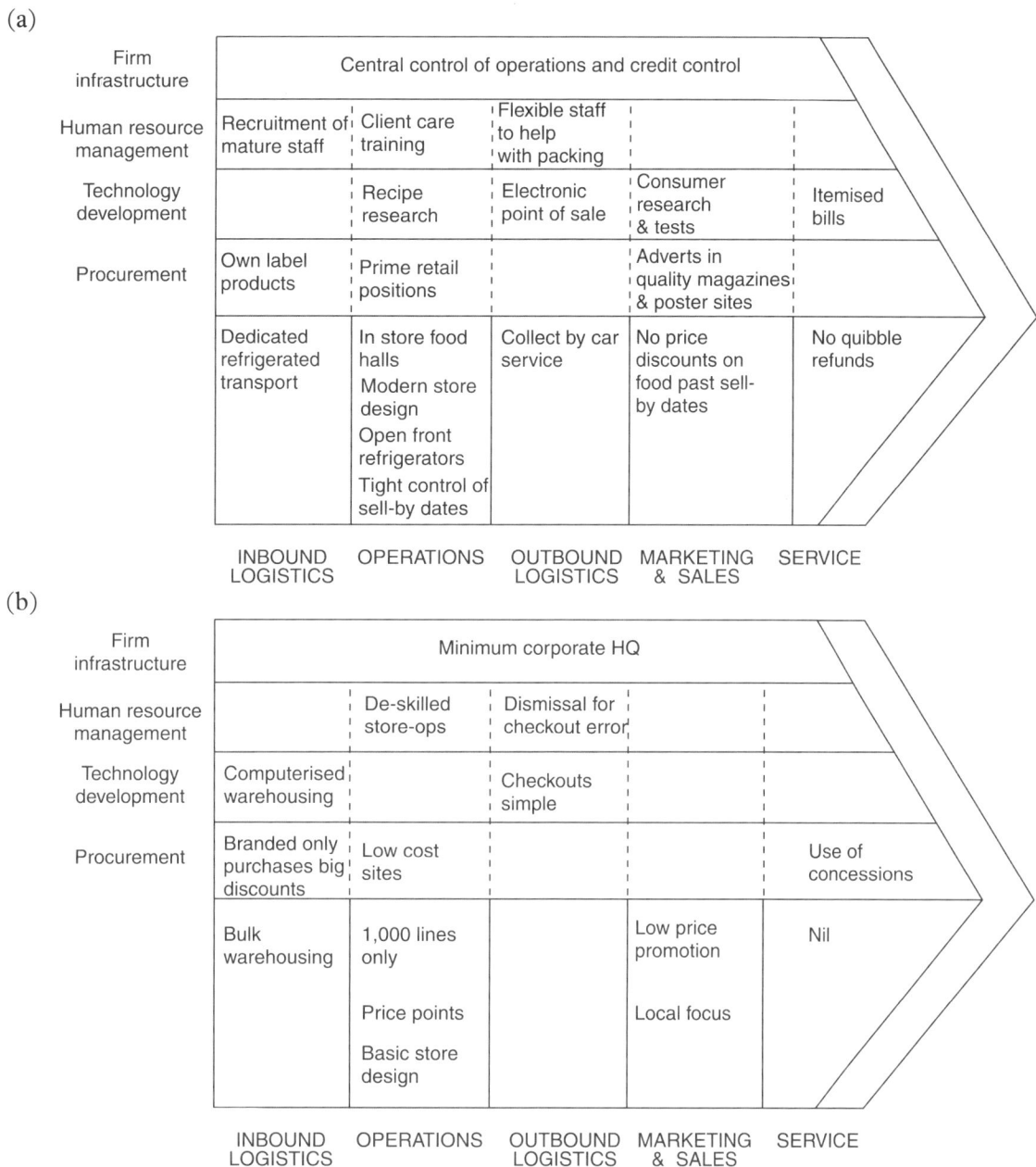

4.2 The two supermarkets represented are based on the following.

(a) The value chain in 4.1(a) is based on Marks and Spencer foods, which seeks to differentiate on quality and service. Hence the no quibble refunds, the use of prime retail sites, and customer care training.

(b) The value chain in 4.1(b) is similar to that of Lidl, a 'discount' supermarket chain which sells on price, pursuing a cost leadership, or perhaps more accurately, a cost-focus strategy. This can be seen in the limited product range and its low-cost sites.

(c) You can probably think of other innovations such as **loyalty cards** and home delivery.

5 PRODUCT-MARKET STRATEGY: DIRECTION OF GROWTH

KEY TERM

Product-market mix is a short hand term for the **products/services** a firm sells (or a service which a public sector organisation provides) and the **markets** it sells them to.

The importance of market share

5.1 The concepts behind **Profit Impact of Market Strategy** (PIMS) analysis were developed at General Electric in the 1960s. The PIMS database is now maintained by the Strategic Planning Institute, a consulting organisation. The database provides empirical evidence of the impact of various marketing strategies on corporate success.

5.2 Like some of the portfolio matrix tools we looked at in the last chapter, the PIMS framework regards **competitive strength** and **market attractiveness** as important determinants of profitability. However, perhaps the single most significant factor to emerge from the PIMS data is the link between profitability and **relative market share**. You will recall that relative market share was one of the axes of the **BCG matrix.**

5.3 There is a definite, observable correlation between market share and return on investment. This is probably the result of **economies of scale.** Economies of scale due to increasing market share are particularly evident in **purchasing** and the **utilisation of fixed assets.**

Product-market mix

5.4 *Ansoff* drew up a **growth vector matrix**, describing how a combination of a firm's activities in current and new markets, with existing and new products can lead to **growth**. Ansoff's original model was a 4 cell matrix based on product and market, shown as the heart of the diagram below. *Lynch (Corporate Strategy)* has produced an enhanced model that he calls the **market options matrix.** This adds the external options shown in the diagram. Withdrawal, demerger and privatisation are discussed at the end of this Section.

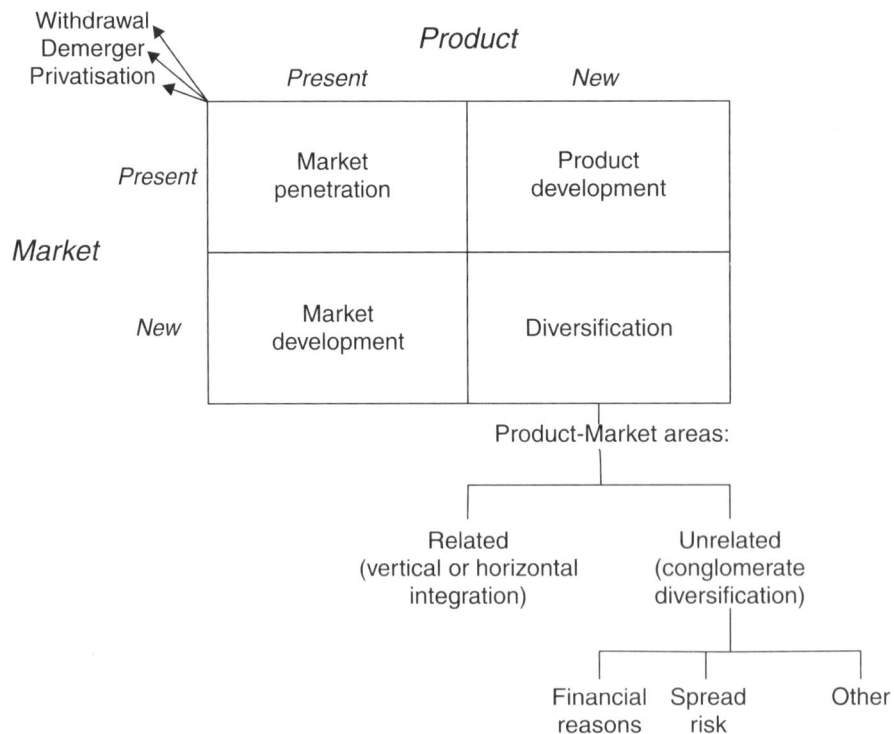

Current products and current markets: market penetration

5.5 **Market penetration**. The firm seeks to do four things.

(a) **Maintain or to increase its share** of current markets with current products, eg through competitive pricing, advertising, sales promotion

(b)   Secure dominance of growth markets

(c)   Restructure a mature market by driving out competitors

(d)   Increase usage by existing customers (eg airmiles, loyalty cards)

This is a relatively **low risk** strategy since it requires no capital investment. As such it is attractive to the unadventurous type of company.

Consolidation

5.6   To consolidate is to seek to maintain current market share. This may be an appropriate strategy when the firm is already the market leader; if availability of funds is limited; or when an owner-manager is approaching retirement or wishes to avoid the loss of personal control that is a likely consequence of growth. Also, if it seems that profitability does **not** correlate with market share, consolidation may be a sensible option.

(a)   Consolidation does not mean neglect. It is unlikely that competitors will halt their efforts, so the firm must continue to enhance its market offer in order to maintain its relative position.

(b)   PIMS data indicates that **high product quality** is important if a consolidation strategy is to succeed. It can compensate to some extent for both a low market share and a low level of marketing expenditure.

Present products and new markets: market development

5.7   **Market development** is the process by which the firm seeks new markets for its current products. There are many possible approaches. Here are some examples.

(a)   **New geographical areas** and export markets (eg a radio station building a new transmitter to reach a new audience).

(b)   **Different package sizes** for food and other domestic items so that both those who buy in bulk and those who buy in small quantities are catered for.

(c)   **New distribution channels** to attract new customers (eg organic food sold in supermarkets not just specialist shops

(d)   **Differential pricing policies** to attract different types of customer and create **new market segments**. For example, travel companies have developed a market for cheap long-stay winter breaks in warmer countries for retired couples.

This approach to strategy is also low in risk since it also requires little capital investment.

New products and present markets: product development

5.8   **Product development** is the launch of new products to existing markets. This has several advantages.

(a)   The company can exploit its existing marketing arrangements such as promotional methods and distribution channels at low cost.

(b)   The company should already have good knowledge of its customers and their wants and habits.

(c)   Competitors will be forced to respond.

(d)   The cost of entry to the market will go up.

This strategy is **riskier** than both market penetration and market development since it is likely to require **major investment** in the new product development process and, for physical products, in suitable production facilities.

Case example

Over the next few years, the UK will be saturated with huge number of TV channels as a result of digital TV. This gives the opportunity to enhance the services TV can provide, including new video on demand (NVOD – multiple showings of a film on different channels, starting 15 minutes apart).

New products: new markets (diversification)

5.9 **Diversification** occurs when a company decides to make **new products for new markets**. It should have a clear idea about what it expects to gain from diversification.

(a) **Growth.** New products and new markets should be selected which offer prospects for growth which the existing product-market mix does not.

(b) **Investing surplus** funds not required for other expansion needs, bearing in mind that the funds could be returned to shareholders. Diversification is a high risk strategy, having many of the characteristics of a new business start-up. It is likely to require the deployment of **new competences**.

Related diversification

> ### KEY TERM
>
> **Related diversification** is 'development beyond the present *product market*, but still within the broad confines of the industry ... [it] ... therefore builds on the assets or activities which the firm has developed' (Johnson and Scholes). It takes the form of vertical or horizontal integration.

5.10 **Horizontal integration** is to development into activities which are competitive with or directly **complementary** to a company's present activities.

5.11 **Vertical integration** occurs when a company becomes its own supplier or distributor. For example, **backward integration** would occur where a milk processing business acquires its own dairy farms rather than buying raw milk from independent farmers. If a manufacturer of synthetic yarn began to produce shirts from the yarn instead of selling it to other shirt manufacturers, that would be **forward integration**. Vertical integration has its greatest potential for success when the final customer's needs are not being properly satisfied. If there is potential for improving the satisfaction of the end user by improving the links in the value system, them an integration strategy may succeed. Examples would be where there is a premium on speed, as in the marketing of fresh foodstuffs, or when complex technical features require great attention to quality procedures.

5.12 **Advantages of vertical integration**

- A **secure supply of components** or **materials,** hence lower supplier bargaining power
- **Stronger relationships** with the final consumer of the product
- A share of the **profits** at all stages of the value chain
- More effective pursuit of a **differentiation strategy**
- Creation of **barriers to entry**

Case examples

Kumio Nakamura, president of Matsushita has said that, 'the vertical integration of Japanese manufacturers is a huge advantage because it enables us to move from development to production in a short time.'

5.13 Disadvantages of vertical integration

(a) **Overconcentration.** A company places 'more eggs in the same end-market basket' (Ansoff). Such a policy is fairly inflexible, more sensitive to instabilities and increases the firm's dependence on a particular aspect of economic demand.

(b) The firm **fails to benefit from any economies of scale or technical advances** in the industry into which it has diversified. This is why, in the publishing industry, most printing is subcontracted to specialist printing firms, who can work machinery to capacity by doing work for many firms.

Case examples

(a) **Horizontal integration**. Since water and electricity distribution were privatised in the UK, there have been a number of changes. Regional water companies have purchased **regional electricity distribution** firms. For example, *Norweb* has been bought by *North West Water*. Although the businesses are very different, they have a very similar customer base, and cost savings can be achieved by shared billing, accounts management and soon.

(b) **Vertical integration**. Before privatisation, the UK electricity industry was a state-owned monopoly, vertically integrated from power generation to distribution. Privatisation effectively split up these two businesses, to introduce competition in power generation, so that the regional distribution companies could buy from a number of suppliers. However, the power distribution companies sought to buy a regional distribution company, giving them a captive market: National Power was set to buy Southern Electric, but the bid was blocked by the government on the grounds that it would inhibit competition.

Unrelated diversification

> **KEY TERM**
>
> **Unrelated (or conglomerate) diversification** 'is development beyond the present *industry* into products/ markets which, at face value, may bear no close relation to the present product/market.'

5.14 Conglomerate diversification is now very unfashionable. However, it has been a key strategy for companies in Asia, particularly South Korea.

5.15 Advantages of conglomerate diversification

(a) **Risk-spreading.** Entering new products into new markets offers protection against the failure of current products and markets.

(b) **High profit opportunities**. An improvement of the **overall profitability and flexibility** of the firm through acquisition in industries which have better economic characteristics than those of the acquiring firms.

(c) **Escape** from the present business

(d) **Better access to capital** markets

(e) **No other way to grow**

(f) **Use surplus cash**

(g) **Exploit under-utilised resources**

(h) **Obtain cash,** or other financial advantages (such as accumulated tax losses)

(i) **Use a company's image and reputation** in one market to develop into another where corporate image and reputation could be vital ingredients for success

5.16 **Disadvantages of conglomerate diversification**

(a) The **dilution of shareholders' earnings** if diversification is into growth industries with high P/E ratios.

(b) **Lack of a common identity and purpose** in a conglomerate organisation. A conglomerate will only be successful if it has a high quality of management and financial ability at central headquarters, where the diverse operations are brought together.

(c) **Failure in one of the businesses will drag down the rest,** as it will eat up resources.

(d) **Lack of management experience.** Japanese steel companies have diversified into areas completely unrelated to steel such as personal computers, with limited success.

(e) **Poor for shareholders.** Shareholders can spread risk quite easily, simply by buying a diverse portfolio of shares. They do not need management to do it for them.

Diversification and synergy

5.17 **Synergy combined results** produce a better rate of return than would be achieved by the same resources used independently. Synergy is used to justify diversification.

5.18 **Obtaining synergy**

(a) **Marketing synergy:** use of common marketing facilities such as distribution channels, sales staff and administration, and warehousing. For example the AA offers loans to customers as well as breakdown services.

(b) **Operating synergy:** arises from the better use of operational facilities and personnel, bulk purchasing, a greater spread of fixed costs whereby the firm's competence can be transferred to making new products. For example, although there is very little in common between sausages and ice cream, both depend on a competence of refrigeration.

(c) **Investment synergy:** The wider use of a common investment in fixed assets, working capital or research, such as the joint use of plant, common raw material stocks and transfer of research and development from one product to another

(d) **Management synergy:** the advantage to be gained where management skills concerning current operations are easily transferred to new operations because of the similarity of problems in the two industries.

Case example

Pearson has four main businesses: consumer publishing (Penguin), TV production (Thames, Grundy), educational publishing (Addison Wesley, Longman and Simon & Schuster) and information (Financial Times, Economist). It is likely (at time of writing) that Pearson will focus its activities by disposing of its TV interests in order to concentrate on education. With the purchase of Simon & Schuster, Pearson now the biggest educational publisher in the world. There is some synergy between the publishing companies and Pearson's newspaper interests (eg FT).

5.19 Synergy is probably difficult to achieve in practice when one company takes over another. All too often, the expectations of synergy that help to justify a business combination fail to materialise. Synergy is probably more discussed in takeover bids than actually implemented.

Question 4

A large organisation in road transport operates nationwide in general haulage. This field has become very competitive and with the recent down-turn in trade, has become only marginally profitable. It has been suggested that the strategic structure of the company should be widened to include other aspects of physical distribution so that the maximum synergy would be obtained from that type of diversification.

Suggest two activities which might fit into the suggested new strategic structure, explaining each one briefly. Explain how each of these activities could be incorporated into the existing structure. State the advantages and disadvantages of such diversification.

Answer

The first step in a suggested solution is to think of how a company operating nationwide in general road haulage might diversify, with some synergistic benefits. Perhaps you thought of the following.

(a) To move from **nationwide to international haulage**, the company might be able to use its existing contacts with customers to develop an international trade. Existing administration and depot facilities in the UK could be used. Drivers should be available who are willing to work abroad, and the scope for making reasonable profits should exist. However, international road haulage might involve the company in the purchase of new vehicles (eg road haulage in Europe often involves the carriage of containerised products on large purpose-built vehicles). Since international haulage takes longer, vehicles will be tied up in jobs for several days, and a substantial investment might be required to develop the business. In addition, in the event of breakdowns, a network of overseas garage service arrangements will have to be created. It might take some time before business builds up sufficiently to become profitable.

(b) Moving from general haulage to **speciality types of haulage**, perhaps haulage of large items of plant and machinery, or computer equipment. The same broad considerations apply to speciality types of haulage. Existing depot facilities could be used and existing customer contacts might be developed. However, expertise in specialist work will have to be 'brought in' as well as developed within the company and special vehicles might need to be bought. Business might take some time to build up and if the initial investment is high, there could be substantial early losses.

Other strategies

5.20 **Withdrawal** may be an appropriate strategy under certain circumstances.

(a) Products may simply disappear when they reach the end of their life cycles.

(b) Underperforming products may be weeded out.

(c) Sale of subsidiary businesses for reasons of corporate strategy, such as finance, change of objectives, lack of strategic fit.

(d)   Sale of assets to raise funds and release other resources.

5.21   **Exit barriers** make this difficult.

(a)   Cost barriers include redundancy costs and the difficulty of selling assets.

(b)   Managers might fail to grasp the idea of decision-relevant costs ('we've spent all this money, so we must go on').

(c)   Political barriers include government attitudes. Defence is an example.

(d)   Marketing considerations may delay withdrawal. A product might be a loss-leader for others, or might contribute to the company's reputation for its breadth of coverage.

(e)   Psychology. Managers hate to admit failure, and there might be a desire to avoid embarrassment.

(f)   People might wrongly assume that carrying on is a low risk strategy.

5.22   **Demerger** can realise underlying asset values in terms of share valuation. ICI's demerger of its attractive pharmaceuticals business led to the shares in the two demerged companies trading at a higher combined valuation than those of the original single form.

5.23   **Privatisation** has been pursued by governments all over the world to raise funds and transform culture and performance.

5.24   **Section summary**

Product-market strategies

- Penetration: same products, same markets
- Product development: new products, same markets
- Market development: same products, new markets
- Diversification: new products, new markets
- Withdrawal, demerger or privatisation
- Any combination of the above, depending on the product portfolio

6   METHOD OF GROWTH   12/01

6.1   **Methods of growth**

- **Building up new businesses** from scratch and developing them
- **Acquiring** already existing businesses from their current owners
- **Merger** of two or more separate businesses
- Spreading the costs and risks by **joint ventures** or other forms of **co-operation**.

Organic growth

6.2   Organic growth (sometimes referred to as internal development) is the primary method of growth for many organisations, for a number of reasons. Organic growth is achieved through the development of internal resources.

6.3   **Reasons for pursuing organic growth**

(a)   **Learning.** The process of developing a new product gives the firm the best understanding of the market and the product.

(b) **Innovation.** It might be the only sensible way to pursue genuine technological innovations, and exploit them. (Compact disk technology was developed by Philips and Sony, who earn royalties from other manufacturers licensed to use it.)

(c) There is **no suitable target for acquisition.**

(d) Organic growth can be **planned more meticulously** and offers little disruption.

(e) It is often **more convenient** for managers, as organic growth can be financed easily from the company's current cash flows, without having to raise extra money.

(f) The **same style of management and corporate culture** can be maintained.

(g) **Hidden or unforeseen losses are less likely** with organic growth than with acquisitions.

(h) **Economies of scale** can be achieved from more **efficient use of central head office** functions such as finance, purchasing, personnel, management services etc.

6.4 **Problems with organic growth**

(a) **Time** – sometimes it takes a long time to descend a **learning curve.**

(b) **Barriers to entry** (eg distribution networks) are harder to overcome: for example a brand image may be built up from scratch.

(c) The firm will have to **acquire the resources independently.**

(d) Organic growth may be **too slow for the dynamics of the market.**

6.5 Organic growth is probably ideal for market penetration, and suitable for product or market development, but it might be a problem with extensive diversification projects.

Acquisitions and mergers 12/02

6.6 The purpose of acquisitions

(a) **Marketing advantages**

- Buy in a new product range
- Buy a market presence (especially true if acquiring a company overseas)
- Unify sales departments or to rationalise distribution and advertising
- Eliminate competition or to protect an existing market

(b) **Production advantages**

- Gain a higher utilisation of production facilities
- 'Buy in' technology and skills
- Obtain greater production capacity
- Safeguard future supplies of raw materials
- Improve purchasing by buying in bulk

(c) **Finance and management**

- Buy a high quality management team, which exists in the acquired company
- Obtain cash resources where the acquired company is very liquid
- Gain undervalued assets or surplus assets that can be sold off
- Obtain tax advantages (eg purchase of a tax loss company)

(d) **Risk-spreading**

(e) **Independence**. A company threatened by a take-over might take over another company, just to make itself bigger and so a more expensive target for the predator company.

(f) **Overcome barriers to entry**

6.7 Many acquisitions **do** have a logic, and the **acquired company can be improved** with the extra resources and better management. Furthermore, much of the criticisms of **takeovers** has been directed more against the notion of **conglomerate diversification** as a strategy rather than takeover as a **method of growth**.

Case example

Amersham/Nycomed

It does not take X-ray vision to spot the commercial sense in Amersham International's merger with Norway's Nycomed. The enlarged group will be the world's largest supplier of diagnostic imaging agents - which enhance X-rays and medical scans - with 30 per cent of a £3bn market. The fit, in products, technology and geography, is excellent. And the group is promising annual cost savings of £40m within three years. Amersham's timing looks impeccable. Its shares have jumped a fifth since it announced a merger with the biotech division of Pharmacia & Upjohn three weeks ago, while Nycomed's have been woeful performers. As a result, Amersham's shareholders will get 50 per cent of the new group, although their company if contributing less than 40 per cent of the profits. At yesterday's prices, Amersham is valued at around 19 times forecast 1997 earnings and Nycomed only 14 times.

That does not mean it is a bad deal for the Norwegians. Relief that Nycomed has found another partner, two years after its failed merger attempt with Ivax of the US and despite a poor record since, sent the shares up 23 per cent yesterday.

Investors will also want reassurance that price pressure in US contrast media, the source of Nycomed's problems, is stabilising. And the potential of Nycomed's new ultrasound technology is still unclear. But a rating of 16 times estimated 1998 earnings does not look expensive for a rapidly growing healthcare company.

Financial Times, 2 July 1997

6.8 **Problems with acquisitions and mergers**   6/02

(a) **Cost**. They might be too expensive, especially if resisted by the directors of the target company. Proposed acquisitions might be referred to the government under the terms of anti-monopoly legislation.

(b) **Customers** of the target company might resent a sudden takeover and consider going to other suppliers for their goods.

(c) **Incompatibility**. In general, the problems of assimilating new products, customers, suppliers, markets, employees and different systems of operating might create 'indigestion' and management overload in the acquiring company. A proposed merger between two UK financial institutions was called off because of incompatible information systems.

(d) **Asymmetric information**. *John Kay* suggests that the acquisitions market for companies is rarely efficient.

    (i) The existing management 'always knows more about what is for sale than the potential purchaser. ... Successful bidders are often only the people who were willing to pay too much - that is the reason why their bid succeeds'.

(ii)   'At the same time, good buys may be ignored, because there is no potential purchaser confident that he really is making a good buy.'

(e)   **Driven by the personal goals** of the acquiring company's managers, as a form of sport, perhaps.

(f)   **Corporate financiers and banks** have a stake in the acquisitions process as they can charge fees for advice.

(g)   **Poor success record of acquisitions.** Takeovers benefit the shareholders of the acquired company often more than the acquirer. According to the Economist Intelligence Unit, there is a consensus that fewer than half all acquisitions are successful.

(h)   **Firms rarely take into account non-financial factors**. A survey by London Business School examining 40 acquisitions (in the UK and USA) revealed some major flaws.

(i)   All acquirers conducted financial audits, but only 37% conducted anything approaching a management audit: despite detailed audits of equipment, property, finances etc, few bothered with people.

(ii)   Some major problems of implementation relate to **human resources and personnel issues** such as morale, performance assessment and culture. Especially in service industries and 'knowledge-based' or creative businesses, many of the firm's assets are effectively the staff. If key managers or personnel leave, the business will suffer.

Exam focus point

A question in the June 2002 examination asked specifically for the identification of major problems that might arise if an acquisition were not managed carefully. The suggested solution concentrated on the potential for managerial conflict but did mention problems arising from incompatibility of systems.

The second part of the question asked how to make an acquisition work. The solution emphasised the management of change.

In December 2002, Question 1 included 12 marks for the identification of factors that would contribute to the success of a merger. You would have been well prepared if you had been familiar with the material in the two pages above and applied it sensibly.

Joint ventures, alliances and franchising

6.9   Short of mergers and takeovers, there are other ways by which companies can co-operate.

6.10   **Consortia:** organisations co-operate on specific business areas such as purchasing or research.

6.11   **Joint ventures:** Two firms (or more) join forces for manufacturing, financial and marketing purposes and each has a share in both the equity and the management of the business.

(a)   **Share costs**. As the capital outlay is shared, joint ventures are especially attractive to smaller or risk-averse firms, or where very expensive new technologies are being researched and developed (such is the civil aerospace industry).

(b)   **Cut risk**. A joint venture can reduce the risk of government intervention if a local firm is involved (eg Club Méditerranée pays much attention to this factor).

(c)   Participating enterprises **benefit from all sources of profit**.

(d) **Close control** over marketing and other operations.

(e) Overseas joint ventures provide **local knowledge, quickly**.

(f) **Synergies**. One firm's production expertise can be supplemented by the other's marketing and distribution facility.

(g) **Learning**. Alliances can also be a 'learning' exercise in which each partner tries to learn as much as possible from the other.

(h) **Technology**. New technology offers many uncertainties and many opportunities. Such alliances provide funds for expensive research projects, spreading risk.

(i) **The alliance itself can generate innovations**

(j) The alliance can involve '**testing' the firm's core competence** in different conditions, which can suggest ways to improve it

6.12 **Disadvantages of joint ventures**

(a) Conflicts of interest between the different parties.

(b) Disagreements may arise over profit shares, amounts invested, the management of the joint venture, and the marketing strategy.

(c) One partner may wish to withdraw from the arrangement.

Case example

SGS-Thompson's semiconductor manufacturing facility in Shenzhen, China (cost US$110m) was a joint venture. There were many problems, including the unsuitable site, selected by the Chinese partner. By 1996, according to The Economist, morale was at rock bottom and the partners did not trust each other. 'Vendors were ripping us off, the government was robbing us blind, key employees were on the take.' The situation has now improved.

6.13 A **licensing agreement** is a commercial contract whereby the licenser gives something of value to the licensee in exchange for certain performances and payments.

(a) The licenser may provide rights to produce a patented product or to use a patented process or trademark as well as advice and assistance on marketing and technical issues.

(b) The licenser receives a **royalty**.

6.14 **Subcontracting** is also a type of alliance. Co-operative arrangements also feature in supply chain management, JIT and quality programmes.

6.15 **Franchising** is a method of expanding the business on less capital than would otherwise be possible. For suitable businesses, it is an **alternative business strategy to raising extra capital** for growth. Franchisers include Budget Rent-a-car, Dyno-rod, Express Dairy, Holiday Inn, Kall-Kwik Printing, KFC, Prontaprint, Sketchley Cleaners, Body Shop and even McDonald's. The franchiser and franchisee each provide different inputs to the business.

(a) The **franchiser**

- Name, and any goodwill associated with it
- Systems and business methods
- Support services, such as advertising, training and help with site decoration

(b) The **franchisee**

- Capital, personal involvement and local market knowledge

- Payment to the franchiser for rights and for support services

- Responsibility for the day-to-day running, and the ultimate profitability of the franchise.

6.16 Disadvantages of franchising

- The **search for competent candidates** is both costly and time consuming where the franchiser requires many outlets (eg McDonald's in the UK).

- **Control** over franchisees (McDonald's franchisees in New York recently refused to co-operate in a marketing campaign).

7 STRATEGY AND MARKET POSITION   12/01

7.1 So far in this chapter we have considered the broader aspects of strategy as they affect the overall stance of the organisation. In this section we will examine some of the options that apply most appropriately to the strategic management of individual products or brands. An appreciation of scale is important when considering strategy. The strategies we discuss below may be regarded as detailed strategy for a major global organisation. On the other hand, they may constitute the essence of corporate strategy for a smaller company.

7.2 Most of the material in this section is based on *Strategic Marketing Management* by *Wilson, Gilligan and Pearson*.

Strategies for market leaders

7.3 PIMS research has revealed the advantages of being the market leader. A company in this position may try to do three things.

(a) **Expand the total market** by seeking increased usage levels; and new uses and users. These aims correspond to market penetration and market development.

(b) **Protect the current market share**. The most common way of doing this is by means of continuous product innovation.

(c) **Expand market share**. This may be pursued by enhancing the attractiveness of the product offering in almost any way, including increased promotion, aggressive pricing and improved distribution.

7.4 **Military analogies** have been used to describe defensive strategies for market leaders.

(a) **Position defence** relies upon not changing anything. This does not work very well.

(b) **Mobile defence** uses market broadening and diversification.

(c) **Flanking defence** is needed to respond to attacks on **secondary markets** with growth potential.

(d) **Contraction defence** involves withdrawal from vulnerable markets and those with low potential. It may amount to surrender.

(e) **Pre-emptive defence** gathers information on potential attacks and then uses competitive advantage to strike first. Product innovation and aggressive promotion are important features.

(f) **Counter-offensive** defence reacts to an attack in one of three ways.

- Meeting it head on, for example entering a price war
- Exploiting a weakness in the attacker's strategy, perhaps by product innovation
- Attacking the attacker's base, perhaps by cutting price in its strongest market

Strategies for market challengers

7.5 The market challenger seeks to **build market share** in the hope of eventually overtaking the existing leader. However, this does not necessarily mean attacking the market leader head-on. This is a risky strategy in any case, because of the leader's resources in cash, promotion and innovation. Instead, the challenger may attack smaller regional firms or companies of similar size to itself that are vulnerable through lack of resources or poor management.

7.6 **Military analogies** have also been used to describe the challenger's attacking options.

(a) The **head-on attack** matches the target's marketing mix in detail, product for product and so on. A limited frontal attack may concentrate on selected desirable customers.

(b) The **flank attack** is mounted upon a market segment, geographic region or area of technology that the target has neglected.

(c) The **encirclement attack** consists of as large number of simultaneous flank attacks as possible in order to overwhelm the target.

(d) The **bypass attack** is indirect and unaggressive. It focuses on unrelated products, new geographic areas and technical leap-frogging to advance in the market.

(e) **Guerilla attack** consists of a series of aggressive, short-term moves to demoralise, unbalance and destabilise the opponent. Tactics include drastic price cuts, poaching staff, political lobbying and short bursts of promotional activity.

Strategies for market followers

7.7 The market follower accepts the status quo and thus avoids the cost and risk associated with innovation in product, price or distribution strategy. Such a **me-too** strategy is based on the leader's approach. This can be both profitable and stable. However, to be consistently successful, such a strategy must not simply imitate. The follower should compete in the most appropriate segments, maintain its customer base and ensure that its turnover grows in line with the general expansion of the market. It should be aware that it may constitute an attractive target for market challengers. The follower must therefore control its costs and exploit appropriate opportunities.

Strategies for market nichers

7.8 Avoiding competition by **niching** is a profitable strategy for small firms generally and for larger organisations where competition is intense. The key to niching is **specialisation**, but there are other considerations.

(a) The chosen market must have some growth potential while being uninteresting to major competitors.

(b) The firm must be able to serve its customers sufficiently well to build up sufficient goodwill to fend off any attacks.

(c) It must be possible to build up sufficient size to be profitable and purchase efficiently.

7.9 Serving a single niche can be risky: a sudden change in the market can lead to rapid decline. **Multiple niching** can overcome this problem.

8 THE MARKETING MIX

8.1 The marketing function aims to satisfy customer needs profitably through an appropriate **marketing mix.**

> **KEY TERM**
>
> **Marketing mix:** 'the set of controllable variables and their levels that the firm uses to influence the target market'. These are product, price, place and promotion and are sometimes known as the 4 Ps.

8.2 The design of the marketing mix will be decided on the basis of management intuition and judgement, together with information provided by marketing research (eg of the image of the product in the eyes of the customer, and the reasons which make customers buy a particular product).

8.3 **Elements in the marketing mix partly act as substitutes for each other** and they must be **integrated.** This is so the product can be positioned in the market to appeal to the customer. For example, a firm can raise the selling price of its products if it also raises product quality or advertising expenditure. Equally, a firm can perhaps reduce its sales promotion expenditure if it is successful in achieving a wider range and larger numbers of sales outlets for its product, etc.

Case example

Cat food wars

Pedigree Petfoods owns Whiskas, for many years the UK brand leader in cat food. Spillers' brand Felix was a minor player in a mature market: it faced the threat of delisting by the major supermarkets, which wanted to give greater space to the more profitable cat treat and own label sectors.

Felix responded to this threat by advertising in 1989. Between 1989 and 1996:

	1989	*1996*
Brand awareness	29%	57%
Volume share	6.7%	25.4%

By some calculations, £17m of advertising generated £108m increase in sales. By some measures, Felix outsold Whiskas in March 1996. Four elements contributed to Felix's success.

(a) *Product.* 'Palatability' - apparently cats liked it.

(b) *Price.* Keen pricing.

(c) *Promotion.* Advertising which emphasised cats' 'rogue-ish' nature and were less 'clinical' and idealised than *Whiskas* ads. 'The rational and idealised approach of competitors' advertising didn't reflect what most cat owners really appreciated about their pets'. Spillers made a little advertising go a long way.

(d) Felix had fewer lines, and was less confusing for shoppers.

Competitor response

In Autumn 1996, Whiskas was relaunched with TV advertising, the 'added cat-isfaction' slogan, new packaging and new product formulation. The re-launch cost £8m but, according to Marketing Week (November 22 1996), sales of Whiskas were static three months after the relaunch.

There are about 7.23m cats in the UK.

Although the cat food market may be fairly mature, recent evidence suggests that in the UK at least, cats are overtaking dogs in popularity and suitability as pets, especially for households where both partners work. Cats are seen as 'low maintenance'. Long-term growth might be expected from the market.

However, the Whiskas relaunch leaves some questions for Spillers. Will Spillers invest more to sustain its brands in the long term? Pedigree has done so: 'dominance and brand building being the key words in its lexicon'.

Product

8.4 From the firm's point of view the product element of the marketing mix is what is being sold, whether it be widgets, power stations, haircuts, holidays or financial advice. From the customer's point of view, a **product is a solution to a problem or a package of benefits.** Product issues in the marketing mix will include such factors as:

- Design (size, shape)
- Features
- Quality and reliability
- After-sales service (if necessary)
- Packaging

8.5 **Issues related to products**

(a) The **core product** is the most basic description of the product - a car is a means of personal transport. The **actual product** is the car itself, with all its physical features such as a powerful engine, comfortable seats and a sun roof. The **augmented product** is the car plus the benefits which come with it, such as delivery, servicing, warranties and credit facilities for buyers.

Case example

Barclays has launched its Additions bank account. As well as normal transaction processing, the account offers life assurance, a free will-writing service, an overdraft and other benefits, in return for a monthly fee.

(b) The **product range** consists of two dimensions.

(i) **Width.** A car maker may have products in all parts, known as segments, of the market: luxury cars, family cars, small cheap cars, and so on.

(ii) **Depth.** It may then offer a wide variety of options within each segment - a choice of engines, colours, accessories and so on.

(c) **Benefits offered to the customer.** Customers differ in their attitudes towards new products and the benefits they offer.

Place

8.6 Place deals with how the product is distributed, and how it reaches its customers. We discussed aspects of distribution from an operational perspective in Chapter 8.

(a) **Channel.** Where are products sold? In supermarkets, corner shops? Which sales outlets will be chosen?

(b) **Logistics.** The location of warehouses and efficiency of the distribution system is also important. A customer might have to wait a long time if the warehouse is far away. Arguably, the **speed of delivery** is an important issue in **place**.

Case example

The selling of motor insurance in the UK has been revolutionised by Direct Line insurance, which sells over the phone, rather than through a network of high street brokers. Others have copied this approach.

8.7   A firm can distribute the product itself (direct distribution) or distribute it through intermediary organisations such as retailers, brokers etc. Key issues are:

(a)   **Product push**: the firm directs its efforts to distributors to get them to stock the product.

(b)   **Customer pull**: the firm persuades consumers to demand the product from retailers and distributors, effectively pulling the product through the chain.

8.8   **In favour of direct distribution**

(a)   The need **to demonstrate** a technical product (especially in the sale of industrial goods).

(b)   **Lethargic intermediaries**. Wholesalers and retailers will try to sell all the products they handle, and will not favour one manufacturer's products.

(c)   **No intermediaries might be available to sell the product.**

(d)   **High intermediary profit margins** affect the final sale price to customers.

(e)   A **small market** with only a few target customers may make direct selling **cheap** (and a dealer network impracticable).

(f)   Direct selling maintains **good relations with end-users** and helps obtain feedback (ie market research information).

8.9   **In favour of using intermediaries**

(a)   **Cheaper**

(b)   Financial resources can be more profitably employed elsewhere.

(c)   A **lack of retailing expertise**

(d)   A **lack of a sufficiently wide assortment** of products to sell. Retailers obtain a wide variety of products from many different manufacturers and put them all on sale in one store.

(e)   A **wide geographical market** area makes the costs of direct selling very high.

(f)   There may be **no other way** of reaching the consumer

8.10   **Making the choice** between direct and indirect distribution.

(a)   **Economic factors:** the most profitable method will differ according to circumstances.

(b)   **Control:** the more intermediate stages in the channel, the less will be the extent of control which the manufacturer can exercise over selling to the customer.

(c)   **Adaptive:** a manufacturer might wish to adapt its channels to changing circumstances. Long-term contracts with a distributor or agent, or long-term supply arrangements with a major retail group might take away the scope for flexibility and change, and a manufacturer might prefer to avoid these, and go for direct selling instead.

Promotion

8.11 Many of the actual activities of the marketing department are related to **promotion**. Promotion is the element of the mix over which the marketing department generally has most control. A useful mnemonic is AIDA which summarises the aims of promotion.

- Arouse **Attention**
- Generate **Interest**
- Inspire **Desire**
- Initiate **Action** (ie buy the product)

8.12 Promotion in the marketing mix includes all marketing communications which let the public know of the product or service.

- Advertising (newspapers, billboards, TV, radio, direct mail, internet)
- Sales promotion (eg special displays in particular stores)
- Direct selling by sales personnel.
- Public relations

Advertising

8.13 Advertising draws **new products** to the public's attention, **reminds the public** that older products exist, and **positions** the product in the customer's mind.

(a) Advertising is frequently outsourced to agencies.

(b) **Media** include TV, posters, newspapers and radio. Firms try to increase the effectiveness of their advertising efforts by **targeting** them effectively by direct mail. **Internet websites** can also be used - the firm can offer more information than in normal advertising messages and websites are interactive.

Sales promotion

8.14 **Sales promotion** is an essentially **short-term technique,** used to boost sales over a particular period, to encourage customers to try the product and so on.

(a) **Consumer promotions** include free samples, coupon offers (money-off offers), catalogues (for mail order), competitions, free gifts (in exchange for packet tops), exhibitions and demonstrations, and so on.

(b) **Retailer or middleman promotions** include extended credit, merchandising facilities, contests for retailers or shop assistants.

(c) **Sales force promotions** include bonuses, contests between salesmen (based on volumes of sales) and sales motivators such as gifts linked to sales.

(d) **Industrial promotions** include sales literature and catalogues, special discounts, exhibitions and trade fairs, events (eg invitations to customers to visit the Wimbledon Tennis Championships), trade-in allowances, and so forth.

Personal selling

8.15 The sales force engages in personal selling, as compared with the non-personal selling of advertising and sales promotion activities. The **buyer-seller relationship** is critical and helps to make a sale.

8.16 Since the work of the sales force is only one element in the sales mix, **greater dependence on advertising and sales promotion can mean a lesser dependence on direct selling**. At one extreme, direct mail firms do not need any sales force. It is unlikely, however, that salespeople could sell without some advertising or sales promotion back-up.

Question 5

What sort of promotion would be most suitable to the following?

(a) A company building railway engines
(b) A company selling toothpaste

Answer

(a) Direct selling and/or consultancy
(b) Advertising (press or TV). Most people use toothpaste, so little advertising would be wasted.

Public relations and corporate communications

8.17 Some organisations have a small **public relations** department which is responsible for the image of the organisation and its products in the eyes of the general public as reported by newspapers. An important element of **public relations is free publicity.** Advertising must be paid for: publicity, in contrast, is not paid for directly.

8.18 Publicity can be a useful selling aid. Obtaining it depends on three things.

- The newsworthiness of any item
- Relations between the public relations department and the news media
- The credibility of the publicity

8.19 **Corporate communications** are concerned with influencing the way an organisation behaves and with communicating the benefits of this behaviour to clearly-identified public audiences. Market research by MORI has demonstrated two important facts.

(a) Two out of every three people in the UK believe that a company which has a good reputation would not sell poor quality products (this suggests that customers would be more willing to try a new product if it is promoted by a well known corporate name than if it is made by an unknown company).

(b) Nine times out of ten, the better known a company is, the more highly it is regarded.

8.20 Corporate communications might be targeted of audiences other than consumers.

- The government
- Shareholders (eg in takeover battles)
- Retailers, wholesalers and distributors
- Banks
- Local communities
- Employers

Sponsorship

8.21 **Sponsorship** is now used fairly widely by firms to promote their corporate image. The firm provides funds, for example, to a sports organisation in return for which the organisation gives publicity to the name of the firm. Sponsorship can be a low-cost method of promotion, and can therefore be a useful addition to a firm's marketing mix.

Price

8.22 The price element of the marketing mix is the only one which brings in revenue. Price is influenced by many factors.

(a) **Economic influences:** supply and demand; price and income elasticities

(b) **Competitors' prices.** Competitors include other firms selling the same type of product, as well as firm selling substitute products. Generally, firms like to avoid price wars.

(c) **Quality connotations.** High price is often taken as being synonymous with quality, so pricing will reflect the a product's image. (Stella Artois lager was once marketed in the UK as being 'reassuringly expensive'.)

(d) **Discounts**. These can make the product attractive to distributors.

(e) **Payment terms** (eg offering a period of interest free credit)

(f) **Trade-in allowances**

(g) The stage in the **product life cycle**.

    (i) **Penetration pricing** is charging a low price to achieve early market share advantages

    (ii) **Skimming pricing** charging high prices early on to reap the maximum profits.

Case examples

Contrast the marketing mix of these holiday firms. Each has been designed to appeal to a particular *market segment*.

(a) *British Museum Tours.* These are tours with an archaeological or cultural interest, and are accompanied by a leading academic. The tours are expensive and might include destinations such as Iran and Ethiopia. Hotels are the most comfortable available. Advertising is not high profile, and is often directed to those who are already members of the British Museum Society.

(b) *Explore.* This firm offers escorted holidays to small groups, in a variety of locations, which may involve some trekking and camping. Locations include isolated villages in northern Thailand. The firm advertises itself on the basis of 'You'll see more'. The firm advertises in newspapers, but also likes to generate repeat business by word of mouth recommendation. Poster or TV advertising is not used.

(c) *Club 18-30.* Targeted at a specific age group, these promise 'fun' holidays in or around beach resorts. A poster advertising campaign in 1994/5 had to be suspended owing to complaints that posters were too 'raunchy'. Holidays are fairly cheap.

The extended marketing mix

People

8.23 The importance of employees in the marketing mix is particularly important in **service marketing,** because of the **inseparability** of the service from the service provider: the creation and consumption of the service generally happen at the same moment, at the interface between the server and the served. Front-line staff must be selected, trained and motivated with particular attention to customer care and public relations.

8.24 In the case of some services, the **physical presence** of people performing the service is a vital aspect of customer satisfaction. The staff involved are performing or producing a service, selling the service and also liaising with the customer to promote the service, gather information and respond to customer needs.

Processes

8.25 Efficient **processes** can become a marketing advantage in their own right. If an airline, for example, develops a sophisticated ticketing system, it can offer shorter waits at check-in or wider choice of flights through allied airlines. Efficient order processing not only increases customer satisfaction, but cuts down on the time it takes the organisation to complete a sale.

8.26 Issues to be considered include the following.

- Policies, particularly with regard to ethical dealings (a key issue for many consumers)
- Procedures, for efficiency and standardisation
- Automation and computerisation of processes
- Queuing and waiting times
- Information gathering, processing and communication times
- Capacity management, matching supply to demand in a timely and cost effective way
- Accessibility of facilities, premises, personnel and services

8.27 Such issues are particularly important in service marketing; because of the range of factors and people involved, it is difficult to standardise the service offered. Quality in particular specifications will vary with the circumstances and individuals.

8.28 Services are also innately **perishable**: their purchase may be put off, but they cannot be stored. This creates a need for process planning for efficient work.

Physicals

8.29 Services are **intangible:** there is no physical substance to them. This means that even when money has been spent on them the customer has no **evidence of ownership**. These factors make it difficult for consumers to perceive, evaluate and compare the qualities of service provision, and may therefore dampen the incentive to consume.

8.30 Issues of intangibility and ownership can be tackled by making available a physical symbol or representation of the service product or of ownership, and the benefits it confers. For example, tickets and programs relating to entertainment; and certificates of attainment in training are symbolic of the service received and a history of past positive experiences.

8.31 Physical evidence of service may also be incorporated into the design and specification of the service environment by designing premises to reflect the quality and type of service aspired to. Such environmental factors include finishing, decor, colour scheme, noise levels, background music, fragrance and general ambience.

The product life cycle

8.32 The product life cycle (see Chapter 5) has implications for the marketing mix, which will differ according to each stage.

Phase of the product life cycle

		Introduction	Growth	Maturity	Decline
1	*Products*	Initially, poor quality. Product design and development are a key to success. No standard product and frequent design changes (eg microcomputers in the early 1980s).	Competitors' products have marked quality differences and technical differences. Quality improves. Product reliability may be important.	Products become more standardised and differences between competing products less distinct.	Products even less differentiated. Quality becomes more variable.
2	*Customers*	Initial customers willing to pay high prices. Customers need to be convinced about buying.	Customers increase in number.	Mass market. Market saturation. Repeat-buying of products becomes significant. Brand image also important.	Customers are `sophisticated' buyers of a product they understand well.
3	*Promotion*	High advertising and sales promotion costs. High prices possible.	High advertising costs in absolute terms, but falling as a % of sales. Prices falling.	Markets become segmented. Segmentation and extending the maturity phase of the life cycle can be key strategies.	Less money spent on advertising and sales promotion.
4	*Competition*	Few or no competitors.	More competitors enter the market. Barriers to entry can be important.	Competition at its keenest: on prices, branding, servicing customers, packaging etc.	Competitors gradually exit from the market. Exit barriers can be important.
5	*Profit margins and pricing*	High prices but losses due to high fixed costs.	High prices. High contribution margins, and increasing profit margins. High P/E ratios for quoted companies in the growth market.	Falling prices but good profit margins due to high sales volume. Higher prices in some market segments.	Still low prices but falling profits as sales volume falls, since total contribution falls towards the level of fixed costs. Some increase in prices may occur in
6	*Manufacturing and distribution*	Over-capacity. High production costs. Few distribution channels. High labour skill content in manufacture.	Under-capacity. Move towards mass production and less reliance on skilled labour. Distribution channels flourish and getting adequate distribution channels is a key to marketing success.	Optimum capacity. Low labour skills. Distribution channels fully developed, but less successful channels might be cut.	Over-capacity because mass production techniques are still used. Distribution channels dwindling.

8.33 Section summary

- The marketing mix is product, place, promotion and price.

- These elements sometimes act as substitutes for each other.

- A product involves features, quality and the benefits the customer gains.

- Place involves logistics and channels of distribution (eg intermediaries).

- Promotion involves all areas of communications from advertising, direct selling, point-of-sale promotions and corporate communications.

- Price is set relative to costs, competition and demand.

Chapter roundup

- The **SWOT analysis** combines the results of the environmental analysis and the internal appraisal into one framework for assessing the firm's current and future strategic fit, or lack of it, with the environment. It is an analysis of the organisation's strengths and weaknesses, and the opportunities and threats offered by the environment.

- **Gap analysis** quantifies what a firm must do to reach its objectives. Any gap between the firm's objectives and the forecast results of continuing with other activities must be met somehow.

- **Competitive strategy** involves a choice between being the lowest cost producer (**cost leadership**), making the product different from competitors' products in some way (**differentiation**) or specialising on a segment of the market (**focus**, by addressing that segment by a strategy of cost leadership or differentiation). **Porter** believes that a firm *must* choose one of these or be **stuck-in-the-middle**.

- The value chain can be used as a tool to devise competitive strategies **value chain**.

- **Product-market** strategies involve determining which products should be sold in which markets, by market penetration, market development, product development and diversification. Diversification is assumed to be risky, especially conglomerate diversification, which is entirely unrelated to current products and markets.

- The **method of growth** can vary.

  - Companies can grow **organically**, building up their own products and developing their own market.

  - They may choose to acquire these ready-made by buying other companies. **Acquisitions** are risky because of the incompatibility of different companies.

  - Many firms grow by other means, such as joint ventures or franchising.

- The **marketing mix** comprises **product, price, place** and **promotion**. For **services**, this is extended to include **people, processes** and **physical evidence**.

- Strategies may be based upon **market position**.

Quick quiz

1   Define corporate appraisal.

2   How can it be used to guide strategy formulation?

3   What is gap analysis?

4   What is required for a successful cost leadership strategy?

5   How do you differentiate?

6   Draw Ansoff's growth vector diagram.

7   How could an acquisition bring marketing advantages?

8   What is the marketing mix?

9   Why might an organisation employ direct distribution?

10   What is meant by public relations?

Answers to quick quiz

1   A critical appraisal of strengths, weaknesses, opportunities and threats.

2   Match strengths with market opportunities; convert weaknesses into strengths and threats into opportunities.

3   Comparison of the objective with the outcomes of already-planned activities.

4   Economies of scale; latest technology; learning curve effect; improved productivity; minimised overhead costs; favourable access to sources of supply.

5   Build brand image; create special features in the product; exploit the value chain.

6

	Product	
	Present	*New*
Present	Market penetration	Product development
New	Market development	Diversification

Market (label on left side between Present and New rows)

7   New products; market presence; rationalisation/exploitation of sales, distribution or promotion; reduce competition/protect market.

8   Product, price, promotion, distribution.

9   Need to demonstrate; lethargic intermediaries; intermediaries unavailable; high intermediary market; small market; good relations with end-users.

10   Corporate image promotion and obtaining free publicity.

Now try the question below from the Exam Question Bank

Number	Level	Marks	Time
Q7	Exam	20	36 mins

Chapter 8

EVALUATING OPTIONS

Topic list	Syllabus reference
1 Evaluation	4(c)
2 Financial evaluation: an example	4(c)
3 Ranking costs and benefits	4(c)
4 Risk and uncertainty	4(c)
5 Stakeholders	4(c)

Introduction

The techniques in this chapter aim to show how in some cases, a systematic and rational approach to evaluating and company strategic options can be achieved. Financial evaluation is likely to appear in the exam regularly, so we show you an example of some of the issues involved.

A number of techniques enable decision-making in conditions of partial ignorance to be quantified. **Decision trees** enable the different expected values of different options to be compared. **Decision matrices** enable management's basic optimism or pessimism to be taken into account. **Sensitivity analysis** demonstrates the extent to which an outcome will change if inputs to the situation change.

Finally, the views of **stakeholders** need to be taken into account: a strategy affects different stakeholders in different ways.

Study guide

Section 4 – The nature of strategy analysis and choice

- Strategy evaluation and selection

Exam guide

The compulsory question in Section A of the exam is likely to be regularly concerned with mainstream matters of practical strategy. The techniques in this chapter will be useful in analysing the scenarios of many such questions.

1   EVALUATION

1.1   According to the rational model, individual strategies have to be **evaluated,** according to a number of criteria, before a strategy or a mixture of strategies is chosen. Three criteria are **suitability, feasibility** and **acceptability**.

Suitability

1.2   **Suitability** relates to the **strategic logic** of the strategy. The strategy should fit the situation of the firm. It should satisfy a range of requirements.

- **Exploit** strengths: that is, **unique** resources and **core competences**
- **Rectify** company **weaknesses**
- **Neutralise** or deflect environmental **threats**
- Help the firm to **seize opportunities**
- **Satisfy the goals** of organisation
- **Fill the gap** identified by gap analysis
- Generate/maintain **competitive advantage**
- Involve an acceptable level of **risk**
- Suit the **politics** and corporate **culture**

1.3 A number of techniques can be used to assess suitability.

Life cycle analysis

1.4 The **product life cycle** concept may be used to assess potential strategies. This was discussed in Chapter 5.

1.5 The product life cycle approach may be combined with an appraisal of the company's strength in its markets using using a **life cycle/portfolio matrix**. This was originally designed by consultants **Arthur D Little**.

STAGES OF INDUSTRY MATURITY

		Embryonic	Growth	Mature	Ageing
	Dominant	Fast grow Start up	Fast grow Attain cost leadership Renew Defend position	Defend position Attain cost leadership Renew Fast grow	Defend position Focus Renew Grow with industry
COMPETITIVE POSITION	**Strong**	Start up Differentiate Fast grow	Fast grow Catch up Attain cost leadership Differentiate	Attain cost leadership Renew, focus Differentiate Grow with industry	Find niche Hold niche Hang in Grow with industry Harvest
	Favourable	Start up Differentiate Focus Fast grow	Differentiate, focus Catch up Grow with industry	Harvest, hang in Find niche, hold niche Renew, turnaround Differentiate, focus Grow with industry	Retrench Turnaround
	Tenable	Start up Grow with industry Focus	Harvest, catch up Hold niche, hang in Find niche Turnaround Focus Grow with industry	Harvest Turnaround Find niche Retrench	Divest Retrench
	Weak	Find niche Catch up Grow with industry	Turnaround Retrench	Withdraw Divest	Withdraw

1.6 The position of the company on the **industry maturity** axis of this matrix depends on the assessment of eight factors including market growth rate, growth potential and number of competitors. Each stage has its own strategic implications. For instance, an ageing market will be subject to falling demand, so heavy marketing expenditure is unlikely to be justified.

1.7 **Competitive position**

(a) A **dominant** position allows the company to exert influence over the behaviour of competitors. It is rare in the private sector.

(b) A **strong** position gives considerable freedom of choice over strategy.

(c) A **favourable** position arises in a fragmented market, often when the company has strengths to exploit.

(d) A **tenable** position is vulnerable to competition and profitability may depend on specialisation.

(e) A **weak** position arises from inability to compete effectively. Firms of any size can find themselves in this condition.

Business profile analysis

1.8 In **business profile analysis** the expected effects of a strategy on the corporation are forecast. A business profile is then created by scoring the forecast state against the favourable parameters established by the empirical findings of PIMS research. There are eleven of these parameters; they relate to market position, financial strength, quality and operational efficiency. The forecast profile may be compared with the current profile in order to assess the proposed strategy for suitability.

Strategy screening

1.9 It is not enough merely to assess strategies for suitability. Eventually choices must be made. Such choices may be assisted by **strategy screening** methods, which include **ranking, decision trees** and **scenario planning**. Ranking and decision trees are dealt with later in this chapter. Scenarios have been described earlier in this Study Text. Potential strategies may be screened by assessing their suitability against each potential scenario. This leads not so much to a choice as to the establishment of a series of **contingency plans**.

Feasibility

1.10 **Feasibility** asks whether the strategy can be implemented and, in particular, if the organisation has adequate **resources**.

- Enough **money**
- The **ability** to deliver the goods/services specified in the strategy
- The ability to deal with the likely **responses that competitors** will make
- Access to **technology, materials and resources**
- Enough **time** to implement the strategy

1.11 Strategies which do not make use of the existing competences and which therefore call for new competences to be acquired, might not be feasible, since gaining competences takes time and can be costly.

1.12 Two important financial approaches to assessing the feasibility of particular strategies are **funds flow** analysis and **breakeven** analysis. The principles of both should be familiar to you from your earlier studies in financial and management accounting.

1.13 **Resource deployment analysis** makes a wider assessment of feasibility in terms of **resources** and **competences.** The resources and competences required for each potential strategy are assessed and compared with those of the firm. A two stage approach may be followed.

(a) Does the firm have the necessary resources and competences to achieve the **threshold** requirements for each strategy?

(b) Does the firm have the core competences and **unique resources** to maintain **competitive advantage**?

When assessing feasibility in this way, it is important to remember that it may be possible to acquire new competences and resources or to stretch existing ones. Such innovation is likely to be difficult to imitate.

Acceptability (to stakeholders)

1.14 **The acceptability** of a strategy depends on the views of **stakeholders**.

(a) **Financial considerations**. Strategies will be evaluated by considering how far they contribute to meeting the dominant objective of increasing shareholder wealth.

- Return on investment
- Profits
- Growth
- EPS
- Cash flow
- Price/Earnings
- Market capitalisation
- Cost-benefit analysis

Profitability analysis techniques include **forecast ROCE**, **payback period** and **NPV**, all of which you should be familiar with. These methods should not be overemphasised.

(i) They are developed for assessing **projects** where cash flows are predictable. This is unlikely to be easy with wider **strategies**.

(ii) There may be **intangible** costs and benefits associated with a strategy, such as an enhanced product range or image or a loss of market share. **Cost-benefit analysis** is probably more appropriate for dealing with such development.

(b) **Customers** may object to a strategy if it means reducing service, but on the other hand they may have no choice.

(c) **Banks** are interested in the implications for cash resources, debt levels and so on.

(d) **Government**. A strategy involving a takeover may be prohibited under competition legislation.

(e) **The public**. The environmental impact may cause key stakeholders to protest. For example, out of town superstores are now frowned upon by national and local government in the UK.

(f) **Risk**. Different shareholders have different attitudes to risk. A strategy which changed the risk/return profile, for whatever reason, may not be acceptable.

Strategy selection

Planning and enforced choice

1.15 The techniques dealt with in this chapter are appropriate to the use of the rational model and may be useful when less formal approaches are taken. They also have a role when strategic developments are **imposed from outside** the organisation. This may come about, for instance, as a result of a major change in the environment, as when the oil shocks of the 1970s stimulated off-shore production, or because of the influence of a dominant stakeholder. A good example of the second possibility was the effect of Marks and Spencer's decision to cease buying from William Baird, a UK clothing manufacturer. This led to plant closures, reorganisation and a management buyout offer.

1.16 **Formal evaluation of imposed strategy**

(a) The first role of formal evaluation is to assess the degree of **risk** inherent in the imposed strategy. This may indicate that a medium-term programme to reduce risk is required; this could be incorporated into the overall plan.

(b) Secondly, techniques such as **scenario planning** can be used to establish contingency plans in case the imposed strategy leads to unacceptably low performance.

Learning from experience

1.17 The rational model is a heavily top-down approach. We have discussed the alternative, **emergent** or **incremental** approaches earlier in this Study Text. The danger associated with these approaches is **strategic drift**: the tendency for strategy to lose direction and coherence. This is especially likely in the divisionalised conglomerate, where SBU managers may strive for and attain increasing degrees of independence.

1.18 It is a desirable feature of the strategic apex of such a company that it is able to promote, nurture and exploit developments at the periphery as part of its strategic process. This combines bottom-up creativity with an element of control.

Real options

1.19 The analysis and use of financial options as business tools is covered in the syllabus for Paper 3.7 and is not examinable in paper 3.5. However, the option concept is very useful in the context of selecting strategies. The selection of a particular course of strategic action may offer **options for future strategy**. The availability of such an option should be considered when evaluating strategies.

1.20 A possible course of action may open up further possibilities: one important case is the possibility of making further, follow-on investments. This is equivalent to a call option in financial strategy. For example, if a manufacturing business decides to open a retail outlet, it acquires the option to stock complementary products from other manufacturers. If the NPV of the basic outlet strategy is assessed as negative, this negative sum represents the price of the option to expand the range at a future date.

1.21 Using this type of conceptual approach allows more subtle evaluation of possible strategies to be undertaken and permits more sophisticated choices to be made between alternatives. In particular, the option to abandon a chosen strategy at low cost will make that strategy more attractive than one with a high cost of abandonment. This choice might rise where there are two possible approaches to manufacturing a new product.

(a) Purchase of high efficiency, highly specialised machinery
(b) Purchase of lower efficiency, general purpose machinery

Option (a) may offer lower costs if the venture succeeds, but the ability to use option (b)'s machinery for another purpose reduces its cost of abandonment should the venture fail.

2 FINANCIAL EVALUATION: AN EXAMPLE

Exam focus point

In answering case study questions, you may be given financial (eg profit) data which you may be expected to use. By this stage in your studies you should be fully confident about basic profit and cash flow calculations - they won't be all that technically demanding in Paper 3.5.

2.1 Strategies are evaluated by their impact on future profits, but this is not a precise science. By now, however, you should feel able to use profit and DCF analysis, so answer the Question below.

Question 1

T plc is a well-established company providing telecommunications services both nationally and internationally. Its business has been concerned with telephone calls, the provision of telephone lines and equipment, and private telecommunication networks. T plc has supplemented these services recently by offering mobile phones, which is an expanding market world-wide.

The company maintains a diverse customer base, including residential users, multi-national companies, government agencies and public sector organisations. The company handles approximately 100 million calls each working day, and employs nearly 140,000 personnel.

Strategic development

The Chairman of T plc stated within the latest Annual Report that there are three main areas in which the company aims to develop in order to remain in a world leader in the telecommunications market. He believes that the three main growth areas reflect the evolving nature of the telecommunications market, and will provide scope for development.

Development is planned in three areas.

(1) Expansion of the telecommunications business in the national and overseas markets, both by the company acting on its own and through partnership arrangements with other suppliers.

(2) Diversification into television and multi-media services, providing the hardware to permit telephone shopping from home and broadcasting services.

(3) Extension of the joint ventures and strategic alliances which have already been established with companies in North America, Europe, India and the Far East.

The Chairman explained that the company is intent on becoming a world leader in communications. This will be achieved through maintaining its focus on long-term development by improving its services to customers, developing high-quality up-to-date products and being innovative, flexible and market-driven. His aim is to deliver a world-class service at competitive cost.

Financial information

Comparative statistics showing extracts from the company's financial performance in its national telecommunications market over the last two years are as follows:

	Last year £ million	Previous year £ million
Turnover	16,613	15,997
Profit before interest and tax	3,323	2,876
Capital employed	22,150	21,300

The company estimates its cost of capital to be approximately 11%.

The Chairman expressed satisfaction with the increase in turnover and stated that cost efficiencies were now being generated following completion of a staff reduction programme. This would assist the company in achieving a target return on capital employed (ROCE) in this market of 20% over the next three years.

Business opportunities

The Chief Executive of T plc has stated that the major opportunities for the company lie in three main areas.

- Encouraging greater use of the telephone

- Provision of advanced services, and research and development into new technology, including the Internet and systems integration

- The increasing freedom from government control of world-wide telecommunication services

An extensive television and poster advertising campaign has been used by the company. This was in order to penetrate further the residential market by encouraging greater use of the telephone with varying charging incentives being offered to residential customers.

To further the objective of increasing long-term shareholder value, the company is actively considering investment of £200 million in each of the next three years in new technology and quality improvements in its national market. Because of its specialist technical nature, the investment is not expected to have any residual value at the end of the three-year period.

Following the investment, the directors of T plc believe that its rate of profit before interest and tax to turnover in its national telecommunications market will remain constant. This rate will be at the same level as last year for each of the three years of the investment.

Markets and competition

The company is currently experiencing an erosion of its market share and faces increasingly strong competition in the mobile phone market. While T plc is the leader in its national market, with an 85% share of the telecommunications business, it has experienced a reduced demand for the supply of residential lines in the last five years as competition has increased.

The market for the supply of equipment in the national telecommunications market is perceived to be static. The investment of £200 million in each of the next three years is estimated to increase T plc's share of this market to a level of 95%. The full improvement of 10% is expected to be received by T plc next year and its market share will then remain at this level for the full three-year period. It is anticipated that unless further investment is made after the three-year period, T plc's market share will revert to its current level as a consequence of the expected competitive response.

Industry regulation

The government has established an industry regulatory organisation to promote competition and deter anti-competitive behaviour.

As a result of the activities of the regulator and aggressive pricing strategies, it is anticipated that charges to customers will remain constant for the full three-year period of the new investment.

All cash flows can be assumed to occur at the end of the year to which they relate. The cash flows and discount rate are in real terms.

Required

(a) Evaluate and comment on T plc's proposed investment in new technology and quality improvements in its national telecommunications market.

Assume that variable costs are 80% of the incremental revenue, and that fixed costs will not increase. Ignore working capital.

(b) Assess to what extent the investment in new technology and quality improvements in T plc's national telecommunications market contributes towards the closure of the company's planning gap in respect of its target ROCE.

Note: You may assume that the entire capital investment is written off at the end of the three-year period.

(c) Recommend a strategy which T plc could employ to close the planning gap and achieve the strategic development aims identified by the Chairman.

Answer

(a) T's proposed investment in technological improvements

Using DCF

Investment outflows. Size of investment: £200m per year for three years, or a total in cash terms of £600m. Using discount tables, the discount factor for three years at 11% (cost of capital) of 2.444 gives a present value of these cash outflows of £488.8m.

Revenue inflows. The assumption is that market share will increase from 85% to 95%. Currently, turnover, for 85% of the market is £16,613m. This will increase to £18,567m (£16,613 × 95/85), in other words an inflow of £1,954m pa or, applying the discount rate, £4,767m over three years.

Variable costs, according to the question, are 80% of the incremental revenue. This amounts to £1,954m × 80% = £1,563.2m or, applying the discount factor, £3,814.2m, over three years.

Net present value

	£m
Size of investment, NPV	(488.8)
Revenues	4,767.0
Variable costs	(3,814.2)
Net present value	464.0

Using ROCE

Whilst in cashflow terms, the scheme is a good one, being higher than T's cost of capital, T actually measures its performance in terms of return on investment, with a target ROI of 20%.

The investment is £200m per year, and annual revenues less variable costs increase by £391m (ie £1,954m less £1,563m). However, we must question whether the investment can be separated from the firm's other capital employed. In year 1 for example, total profit will be £3,323m plus £391m = £3,714m. For the sake of argument, as a percentage of capital employed (£22,150m) this amounts to 16.7%, an improvement on last year but not as high as target. (It is interesting that capital employed for last year was £850m more than the previous year, whereas the profit was only £447m higher – does this imply new capital was brought in?)

All these figures go to show is that the firm's targets are varied. The investment, whilst perfectly beneficial in cash terms, does not reflect the target ROCE even though it goes towards it.

Shareholders' objectives

It is slightly surprising that no objectives have been set for the share price or other performance indicators such as earnings per share, which are couched in terms more relevant to the investment community.

(b)   *Closing the planning gap*

The chairman hopes to achieve a target ROCE of 20%. On capital employed of £22,150, this suggests a *target annual profit* of £22,150 × 20% of £4,430m. In other words, annual profit will have to increase by £1,107m (£4,430m less £3,323m currently). The new investment, providing £391m per annum (£1,954m uncleared revenue × 20%, ie variable costs are 80%) amounts to 35% of the planning gap. Additional profit of £716m is needed to close the planning gap.

The calculation ignores the following issues.

(i)   The risk of regulatory response
(ii)   Competitor reaction
(iii)   The need for expenditure to maintain market share.

(c)   *Strategies to close the planning gap*

> *Tutorial note*. Ideas for suitable strategies are flagged throughout the question, and you could have happily built on your answer to (d). But remember that this part of the question does not address market share objectives or innovation objectives but is directly focused on increasing reported ROCE and hence profit over the next three years. Any strategies you suggest must, whatever else they do, be profitable and not require huge investments no matter how large the 'long-term' benefits will be.

To close the planning gap, T has to generate annual profits (in addition to the £391m already generated) of £716m. Furthermore, because the gap is expressed as ROCE, any new investment might affect the capital employed figure. Projects will be chosen which offer the highest possible return.

(i)   *More cost cutting?* To chose the remaining gap, T could cut its costs further by approximately 5% (being £716m /(£16,613m - £3,323m)). A 1% cut in costs would achieve savings of £143m. The Chairman wants T 'to deliver a world-class service at competitive cost' and, indeed, cost-cutting is specifically mentioned in the question: 'cost efficiencies were now being generated following completion of a successful staff reduction programme. This would assist the company in achieving a target return on capital employed in this market of 20% over the next three years)'. However, we are not given data as to the scale of the cost efficiencies.

(ii) *Penetration (domestic)*. T cannot simply increase its prices to raise revenue as its prices are regulated. The number of subscribers is likely to fall to competitors. T can encourage customers to make more use of the phone, simply to generate revenue, for the same level of fixed costs. (Friends and Family discounts are an example.) As argued earlier, attention to penetration strategies is necessary.

Penetration (overseas markets) This is a big opportunity – but this must not be achieved at the expense of a massive investment, which would decrease return on capital in the next three years, and take time to generate profits. It thus seems likely that T should concentrate its efforts on where it can best add value, in alliance with local firms. Such strategic alliance should generate revenue but with little pressure on costs or investments.

(iii) *Market development*

T already operates in a number of overseas markets. New markets can include *new overseas markets* or *new consumer markets*. T is already aiming to build a genuinely global presence, and so might be able to take advantage of opportunities in Latin America or Africa. Such investments need to be handled carefully. T does not need to install a fixed line network and can 'leapfrog' over older or intermediate technologies.

A genuinely global market is, in a way, a new market. Exploiting this global market with a *suitable alliance*, is also possible, firstly because of an increase in *telecommunications traffic*, and secondly because of world trade liberalisation in services. A potential problem is that prices will almost certainly fall, so T has to position itself to get revenue from increased volume or offer higher value-added services such as network management.

However, from the chairman's point of view, such *alliances can take time to develop*. They are also subject to heavy regulatory pressure. Whether they will be able to develop the increased revenue is open to question.

(iv) *Product development*. The chairman has already indicated new services, such as home shopping and *internet services*. The internet can be a source of revenue growth, simply because of the use of telecommunications traffic which can be charged to users. T can also gain more of the potential revenue by acting as a service provider (like AOL or Compuserve) in its own right. As the internet becomes more of a consumer than a specialist service, T's brand name should stand it in good stead.

(v) *Diversification* is, classically, the *highest risk strategy* which may offer the highest rewards providing it is related as opposed to conglomerate diversification. The chairman has not mentioned smaller scale initiatives – T after all has a huge subscriber base, and could use it to collect bills for other companies via the phone bill. T will never be a content provider for the multimedia groups it serves; others will do just as well, but as owner of the hardware and the communications system it stands to profit from the increased traffic.

Summary

Most of the chairman's suggestions offer the prospect of significant wealth – but they seem to be *long-term investments* rather than the focus on the relatively short-term profit and ROCE targets which the chairman is concerned with. Cost cutting and market penetration, in the UK and overseas, is the best way to deliver the targets.

3 RANKING COSTS AND BENEFITS

3.1 A strategy can be assessed on how it achieves the organisation's objectives, but some **objectives may conflict** and the choice may not be clear cut.

3.2 The approaches below compare strategies according to the way they support some objectives rather than others, or those whose benefits cannot be quantified easily.

Ranking and scoring

3.3 **Ranking and scoring methods** are best illustrated by means of a simple example. The **objectives are weighted** in relative **importance** (eg minimising competitive threats may be more important than other objectives). We assume for the example below that the strategic options cannot be realistically combined.

Objectives Strategic option	*Growth in profit by over 10%*	*Reduce dependence on suppliers*	*Minimise competitive threats*	*Score*	*Rank*
Objective weighting	4	3	5		
Do nothing	✗	✗	✗	–	–
Cut costs by subcontracting	✓	✗	✗	4	3rd
Expand product range	✓	✗	✓	9	1st
Offer discounts to customers for fixed term contract	✗	✗	✓	5	2nd

In the above example, expanding the product range would be chosen as the firm believes it will enhance profits and minimise competitive threats.

3.4 In many cases, the strategies may not be mutually exclusive, or it might be possible to implement all the strategic options above (other than doing nothing).

Cost/benefit analysis

3.5 **Cost/benefit analysis** (CBA) is a strategy evaluation technique often used in the public sector, where many of the costs and benefits of a project are **intangible** and where market forces do not capture all costs and benefits.

(a) The project and its overall objectives are defined.

(b) It is not always easy to put a value on **social costs**. For example, a new road might result in excessive noise for local residents. They can be asked how much, in principle, they would be able and prepared to pay to move to a quieter dwelling. This gives a very rough estimate of the value of tranquillity. Financial costs are easy to assess.

(c) The **net benefits** for the project are estimated, if possible. A road might reduce journey times, and so save money. These are compared with costs, and the project is appraised by discounted cash flow (NPV and IRR) or cost/benefit ratios.

3.6 Private sector companies might be interested in CBA because:

(a) CBA can be applied **internally** (eg assessing an information systems project).

(b) **It can help them negotiate with public sector officials**. For example, large building projects require permission from the local authority. Local government officials sometimes insist on certain social benefits to be included in a project, so that some of the potential nuisance costs can be covered.

4   RISK AND UNCERTAINTY

4.1   Strategies, by definition, deal with future events: the future cannot be predicted. We can make a distinction between **risk** and **uncertainty**, but often the terms are used **interchangeably**.

KEY TERMS

Risk is sometimes used to describe situations where outcomes are not known, but their **probabilities** can be estimated. (This is the underlying principle behind insurance.)

Uncertainty is present when the outcome cannot be predicted or assigned probabilities. (Many insurance policies exclude 'war damage, riots and civil commotion'.)

4.2   **Types of risk and uncertainty**

Risk	Comment
Physical risk	Earthquakes, fire, flooding, and equipment breakdown. In the long-term, climatic changes: global warming, drought (relevant to water firms).
Economic risk	Assumptions about the economic environment might turn out to be wrong. Not even the government forecasts are perfect.
Financial risk	This term has a specific technical meaning: **the risk to shareholders caused by debt finance**. The risk exists because the debt finance providers have first call on the company's profits. The need to pay interest might prevent capital growth or the payment of dividends, particularly when trading is difficult. The converse is that when business is buoyant, interest payments are easily covered and shareholders receive the benefit of the remaining profits.
Business risk	Lowering of entry barriers (eg new technology); changes in customer/supplier industries leading to changed relative power; new competitors and factors internal to the firm (eg its culture or technical systems); management misunderstanding of core competences; volatile cash flows; uncertain returns; changed investor perceptions increasing the required rate of return.
Political risk	Nationalisation, sanctions, civil war, political instability, can all have an impact on the business.

Exam focus point

The December 2001 exam included a question scenario in which an entrepreneur was considering replacing his overseas agents with wholly owned production an distribution facilities. The purpose of this more was to achieve greater **control** over quality and critical inputs. However, an important implication was that the plan required the commitment of increased **resources**, thereby increasing risk of all types. Generally speaking, if is likely that moves to **increase control** will lead to **increased risk**.

Adjusting for risk

4.3   Risk can be incorporated into evaluation by making targets more demanding. For instance, a firm might require that all investments make a return of, say, 5%.

(a)   **Return.** The target return could be raised to compensate for the risk.

(b) **Payback.** To protect cash flows, it might be made a condition of all new investment projects that the project should pay back within a certain period of time.

(c) **Finance.** It might be determined that the investment should be financed under strict conditions (eg only from profits).

This approach is crude but quite effective.

Risk appraisal in strategy evaluation

4.4 Planners try to **quantify the risk,** so as to compare the estimated riskiness of different strategies.

(a) **Rule of thumb** methods might express a range of values from worst possible result to best possible result with a best estimate lying between these two extremes.

(b) **Basic probability theory** expresses the likelihood of a forecast result occurring. This would evaluate the data given by informing the decision-maker that there is, for example, a 50% probability that the best estimate will be achieved, a 25% chance that the worst result will occur and a 25% chance that the best possible result will occur. This evaluation of risk might help the executive to decide between alternative strategies, each with its own risk profile.

(c) One way of measuring the dispersion or **spread of values** with different possible outcomes from a decision is to calculate a **standard deviation** of the expected value (EV) of profit. The higher the standard deviation, the higher the risk, as the EV is more volatile.

4.5 **Decision** rules are useful in strategic planning for two reasons.

(a) They can be applied in scenario analysis - remember that scenario analysis identifies alternative futures, one of the elements of a decision matrix.

(b) They embody managerial attitudes to uncertainty. The **maximax** approach is optimistic, while the **maximim** is pessimistic. Remember that these rules are used under conditions of **uncertainty**, as is the **minimax regret** rule. If risk can be quantified, probabilistic methods such as decision trees may be used.

4.6 The **role of decision trees in strategic planning** is to assess which choices are mutually exclusive, and to try to give them some quantitative value. As such they are useful for three purposes.

- Clarifying strategic decisions when they are complex
- Using risk (in probability terms) as an input to quantifying the decision options.
- Ranking the relative costs and benefits of the options

4.7 That said, many of the options in a decision may not be mutually exclusive, and the decision tree may inhibit a creative approach to a problem by assuming that they are. Finally, it is often easy to forget that an **expected value is only useful for comparative purposes,** taking probability into account. It is **not a prediction** of an actual outcome. (If you toss a coin, there is a 50:50 chance of it turning heads; but in any one throw it will be either heads or tails, not a bit of both.)

Sensitivity analysis

4.8 *Ansoff* suggests that decision theory is of limited relevance in measuring risk, and **sensitivity analysis** should be used in preference. This involves:

- **Identifying each variable factor** in the calculation
- **Assessing the effect on the result** if the variable was amended by x% up or down.

4.9 This will highlight those variables which are most likely to have a significant effect on the final result. This helps managers identify which strategies are the riskiest, as certain environmental variables might lead to great volatility in returns.

4.10 Sensitivity analysis involves asking 'what if?' questions, and so it can be used for strategic planning. By changing the value of different variables in the model, a number of different **scenarios** for the future will be produced.

4.11 EXAMPLE

Wage increases can be altered to 10% from 5%; demand for a product can be reduced from 100,000 to 80,000, the introduction of new processing equipment can be deferred by six months, on the revised assumption that there will be delays, and so on. Sensitivity analysis can be formalised by identifying key variables in the model and then changing the value of each, perhaps in progressive steps. For example, wage costs might be increased in steps by 5%, 7½%, 10%, 12½% and 15% and the effect on profits and cash flows under each of these five wage cost assumptions can be tested.

4.12 In this way, a full picture would emerge of how the achievement of planning targets would be affected by different values for each key variable. **Once the most critical variables have been established**, management then can:

(a) **Apply the most stringent controls** to the most critical variables.

(b) **Alter the plans** so that the most critical variables are no longer as critical. For example, if a car manufacturing company's marketing management are planning to stop producing an old model of car and switch production resources to an entirely new model, sensitivity analysis might show that its profitability will be critically dependent on the speed with which the new model gains acceptance in the market.

(c) **Choose a lower-risk plan**. For example, if a London-based company has the choice of expanding its operations into either the rest of the UK or into France and the Low Countries, it might find that Continental operations would offer prospects of bigger profits, but the risk of failure might be bigger too and so it might opt to expand in the UK instead.

4.13 Section summary

- There are many types of risk.

- Risk can be accounted for by raising the return.

- Decision trees, matrices and sensitivity analysis are all used to model risk, by incorporating probability assessments and management assumptions.

5 STAKEHOLDERS

5.1 Strategies are created and assessed by management. However, the various **stakeholder** groups have more or less influence over what is acceptable.

5.2 We may discern two extreme approaches to stakeholder theory for profit-orientated business organisations. These are similar to the extreme approaches to the concept of **social responsibility** and similar arguments apply.

Strong view	Weak view
Each stakeholder in the business has a legitimate claim on management attention. Management's job is to balance stakeholder demands.	Satisfying stakeholders such as customers *is* a good thing - but only because it enables the business to satisfy its primary purpose, the long term growth in owner wealth.

5.3 **Problems with the strong stakeholder view**

(a) Managers who are accountable to everyone are, in fact, accountable to none.

(b) If managers are required to balance different stakeholders' interests there is a danger that they will favour their own interests.

(c) It confuses a stakeholder's interest in a firm with a person's citizenship of a state.

(d) People have interests, but this does not give them rights.

5.4 Strategic options pose varying degrees of risk to the **interests** of the different stakeholders. It is possible that they may respond in such a way as to reduce the attractiveness of the proposed strategy.

5.5 **Stakeholder risks**

Stakeholder	Interests to defend	Response to risk
Internal managers and employees (eg restructuring, relocation)	• Jobs/careers • Money • Promotion • Benefits • Satisfaction	• Pursuit of systems goals rather than shareholder interests • Industrial action • Negative power to impede implementation • Refusal to relocate • Resignation
Connected Shareholders (corporate strategy)	• Increase in shareholder wealth, measured by profitability, P/E ratios, market capitalisation, dividends and yield • Risk	• Sell shares (eg to predator) or replace management
Bankers (cash flows)	• Security of loan • Adherence to loan agreements	• Denial of credit • Higher interest charges • Receivership
Suppliers (purchase strategy)	• Profitable sales • Payment for goods • Long-term relationship	• Refusal of credit • Court action • Wind down relationships
Customers (product market strategy)	• Goods as promised • Future benefits	• Buy elsewhere • Sue
External Government	• Jobs, training, tax	• Tax increases • Regulation • Legal action
Interest/pressure groups	• Pollution • Rights • Other	• Publicity • Direct action • Sabotage • Pressure on government

5.6 How stakeholders relate to the management of the company depends very much on what **type of stakeholder** they are - internal, connected or external - and on the **level in the management hierarchy** at which they are able to apply pressure. Clearly a company's management will respond differently to the demands of, say, its shareholders and the community at large.

5.7 The way in which the relationship between company and stakeholders is conducted is a function of the parties' **relative bargaining strength** and the philosophy underlying **each party's objectives**. This can be shown by means of a spectrum.

		Stakeholders' bargaining strength		
Weak				Strong

| Company's
conduct
of relation-
ship | Command/
dictated by
company | Consultation
and
consideration
of
stakeholders'
views | Negotiation | Participation
and
acceptance
of
stakeholders'
views | Democratic
voting by
stakeholders | Command/
dictated by
stakeholders |

Stakeholder mapping   6/02

5.8 *Mendelow* classifies stakeholders on a matrix whose axes are power held and likelihood of showing an interest in the organisation's activities. These factors will help define the type of relationship the organisation should seek with its stakeholders.

	Level of interest	
	Low	High
Low Power	A	B
High	C	D

(a) **Key players** are found in segment D: strategy must be *acceptable* to them, at least. An example would be a major customer.

(b) Stakeholders in segment C must be treated with care. While often passive, they are capable of moving to segment D. They should, therefore be **kept satisfied.** Large institutional shareholders might fall into segment C.

(c) Stakeholders in segment B do not have great ability to influence strategy, but their views can be important in influencing more powerful stakeholders, perhaps by lobbying. They should therefore be **kept informed.** Community representatives and charities might fall into segment B.

(d) Minimal effort is expended on segment A.

5.9 Stakeholder mapping is used to assess the significance of stakeholder groups. This in turn has implications for the organisation.

    (a) The framework of **corporate governance** should recognise stakeholders' levels of interest and power.

    (b) It may be appropriate to seek to **reposition** certain stakeholders and discourage others from repositioning themselves, depending on their attitudes.

    (c) Key **blockers** and **facilitators** of change must be identified.

5.10 Stakeholder mapping can also be used to establish **political priorities**. A map of the current position can be compared with a map of a desired future state. This will indicate critical shifts that must be pursued.

> ### Exam focus point
> Part (a) of Question 1 in June 2002 asked about stakeholder power and mentioned the Mandelow Matrix by name. It is always useful to at least mention specific theoretical models that are relevant to your answer if you can.

5.11 In *Power In and Around Organisations*, *Mintzberg* identifies groups that not only have an **interest** in an organisation but **power** over it.

The external coalition
- Owners (who hold legal title)
- Associates (suppliers, customers, trading partners)
- Employee associations (unions, professional bodies)
- Public (government, media)

The internal coalition
- The chief executive and board at the strategic apex
- Line managers
- Operators
- The technostructure
- Support staff
- Ideology (ie culture)

5.12 Each of these groups has three basic choices.

- **Loyalty**. They can do as they are told.

- **Exit**. For example by selling their shares, or getting a new job.

- **Voice**. They can stay and try to change the system. Those who choose **voice** are those who can, to varying degrees, influence the organisation. Influence implies a degree of power and willingness to exercise it.

5.13 Existing **structures and systems** can **channel stakeholder influence.**

    (a) They are the **location of power**, giving groups of people varying degrees of influence over strategic choices.

    (b) They are **conduits of information**, which shape strategic decisions.

    (c) They **limit choices** or give some options priority over others. These may be physical or ethical constraints over what is possible.

    (d) They **embody culture**.

    (e) They **determine the successful implementation** of strategy.

(f) The **firm has different degrees of dependency** on various stakeholder groups. A company with a cash flow crisis will be more beholden to its bankers than one with regular cash surpluses.

Question 2

Ticket and Budget International is a large multinational firm of accountants. The firm provides audit services, tax services, and consultancy services for its many clients. The firm has a strong Technical Department which designs standardised audit procedures. The firm has just employed a marketing manager. The marketing manager regards an audit as a 'product', part of the entire marketing mix including price (audit fees), place (usually on the client's premises) and promotion (advertising in professional journals) The marketing manager is held in high regard by the firm's senior partner. The marketing director and the senior partner have unveiled a new strategic plan, drawn up in conditions of secrecy, which involves a tie-up with an advertising agency. The firm will be a 'one-stop shop' for business services and advice to management on any subject. Each client, or 'customer' will have a dedicated team of auditors, consultants and advertising executives. Obviously, a member of staff will be a member of a number of different teams.

The firm has recently settled a number of expensive law suits for negligence (which it has, of course, 'contested vigorously') out of court, without admitting liability. The Technical Department is conducting a thorough review of the firm's audit procedures.

In the light of what we have covered in this section, what do you think will be the organisational and stakeholder influences on the proposed strategy?

Answer

Accountants have divided loyalties - to their firm, and to their profession.

The Technical Department will almost certainly resist such a change, as the proposals devalue audit to being one of many business services to management. An audit is undertaken for the benefit of shareholders, not the company management. The Technical Department (the firm's technostructure) is also powerful as enforcement of the standards it will suggest should reduce professional negligence costs. The technostructure will thus exert a powerful influence over the strategy and business practices. External influences include *professional associations* (eg the ACCA) which have a technostructural influence on the profession as a whole. The marketing manager may also be misled as to the degree to which *customers* want a 'one-stop shop' for accounting and advertising services. Perhaps he is overestimating the power of this factor in the external coalition.

This exercise also covers some of the issues discussed in Chapter 6.

5.14 Different stakeholders will have their own views as to strategy. As some stakeholders have **negative power,** in other words power to impede or disrupt the decision, their likely response might be considered. Note that this would be expected in the light of the **partisan mutual adjustment model** of decision making.

Chapter roundup

- Strategies are evaluated according to their **suitability** to the firm's situation, their **feasibility** in terms of resources and competences and their **acceptability** to key stakeholders groups (eg shareholders).

- The A D Little lifecycle/portfolio matrix assesses suitability in terms of **industry maturity** and **competitive position**.

- **Management** can use a number of **analytical techniques** to assess a firm's current situation, to suggest plans for the future, and to evaluate the viability of different strategic options. None of these techniques should be considered as anything other than 'tools to think with'. All aim to clarify strategic decision making by simplifying it.

- Much strategy evaluation is involved with reducing the **risk** of a particular course of action, or assessing what that risk is. **Risk** is classified as business, financial, economic, political and physical.

- **Ranking and scoring** methods enable the strategist to give weights to certain objectives, and to score a strategy or set of strategies accordingly.

- **Decision matrices** enable the organisation to develop a coherent approach to dealing with projects (ie to maximise potential profits or minimise losses).

- Risk can sometimes be quantified, using **probability theory.** The standard deviation of a number of outcomes is a measure of risk.

- **Decision trees** are used to map a number of mutually exclusive alternatives and determine some value for them, taking probability into account.

- **Sensitivity analysis** is a way of analysing the degree to which a strategy is vulnerable to changes in certain variables.

- Different **stakeholder groups** have different assessment of the risk a strategy poses to their interests. Some are able to exercise power over management.

- Stakeholder mapping may be used to analyse the various stakeholder groups.

Quick quiz

1   What three criteria are used to evaluate strategies?

2   Why do organisations use ranking and scoring methods?

3   List five types of risk and uncertainty.

4   What adjustments might a firm make for risk?

5   Why should decision trees be used with caution by strategists?

6   What is sensitivity analysis?

7   What is meant by 'voice'?

8   What constitutes the external coalition?

Answers to quick quiz

1   Suitability, acceptability, feasibility.

2   They allow comparisons to be made when benefits cannot be quantified easily or when not all objectives are supported.

3   Physical, economic, financial, business and political.

4   Targets could be made more demanding.

5   They assume options are mutually exclusive, which may not be true. Also the use of expected values is based on average performance, so it is of questionable value when assessing a one-off project.

6   Assessing the impact of changes in variable factors.

7   An attempt by a stakeholder group to influence the outcomes of strategic decision making.

8   Owners, associates, employee associations, the public.

Now try the question below from the Exam Question Bank

Number	Level	Marks	Time
Q8	Exam	20	36 mins

Part C
Implementing strategy

Chapter 9

ORGANISATION STRUCTURE

Topic list		Syllabus reference
1	Strategy and structure	6(a)
2	Structural configurations	6(c)
3	Departmentation	6(a)
4	Centralisation and decentralisation	6(b)
5	Multifocused hierarchies: hybrid and matrix designs	6(a)
6	Mechanistic and organic structures	6(b)

Introduction

The relationship between organisation structure and strategy has been touched upon, but in this chapter we see how, ultimately, **organisation structure can be led by the type of strategy** and work processes adopted. A key influence is the environment.

Five organisation **configurations** are described. These are models which describe how work is co-ordinated in an organisation, and indicate the influences that the various component parts of the organisation have on its structure. **Departmentation** and the pros and cons of **centralisation and decentralisation** are discussed, with the choices for organisation hierarchy.

More complex aspects of structure include global models and multifocused models.

We conclude with an examination of a classic analysis of the influence of environment upon organisation.

Study guide

Section 6 – Matching structures with strategy

- Types of organisation structure
- Centralisation versus decentralisation
- Organisational configurations

Exam guide

In this chapter we return to underlying theory that could be useful in many questions. However it is quite possible that organisation structure could form the basis for a part question in Section B.

Case example

The UK's National Health Service has suffered a number of reorganisations in the past few years, with a variety of objectives.

(a) An internal market was introduced in 1991: hospitals became self-governing trusts and regional health authorities and some general practitioners (fundholders) bought services from them: the purchaser/provider split. The objective was to cut costs and improve efficiency.

(b) The current government intends to end the internal market but retain the purchaser/provider split.

General practitioners will *have* to co-operate. (They did not *have* to become fundholders). Care will be purchased by primary care groups (PCGs) in a region, representing GPs, nurses, social services and so on, covering about 100,000 people. Some (PCGs) will merely advise the health authority; others will be in charge of the budget.

---

1 STRATEGY AND STRUCTURE 12/01

Exam Focus point

The December 2001 examination offered a part-question worth 10 marks on the topic of organisation structure. The problem was to integrate key activities across the functional departments of a high tech business white retaining customer awareness in dynamic markets. The examiner felt that a matrix or project team structure might work best, his answer explaining how the advantages of this approach would benefit the company concerned.

Influences on organisation structure

1.1 Organisational structure determines to how work is co-ordinated, how decisions are taken, how work and information flow through the organisation. It is thus a fundamental aspect of management. A top-down approach is very common and reflects the assumption that lower echelons are created to support top management in achieving their strategic goals. A less formal approach recognises that creativity, initiative and experience may be worth nurturing and exploiting throughout the organisation. Below we summarise the possible influences on organisation structure.

Influence	Comment
Age	• The older the organisation, the more formalised its behaviour. Work is repeated, so is more easily formalised and standardised.
	• Organisation structure reflects the age of the **industry's** foundation.
Size and growth	The larger the organisation, the **more elaborate** its structure will be, the larger the average size of the units within it, the more formalised its behaviour (for consistency).
Tasks	The complexity of the task (eg milking cows, designing drugs) affects the structure of the organisation.
Co-ordination	Mutual adjustment, direct supervision and standardisation all have consequences for organisation structure.
Skills of managers and workers	Can people be left alone to do the job, or do they require close supervision?
Job design	Are jobs broken down into discrete activities?
Geographic dispersion	An organisation with several sites will have a different organisation structure from one located in one place.

Influence	Comment
Fashion	Bureaucracies are deeply unfashionable, but they are often the best at doing certain kinds of work. Indeed, **Burns and Stalker**, who developed the concept of organic and mechanistic organisations held that neither type of organisation had any intrinsic merits, as the key variables were **product-markets** and **technology**.
Control	The more an organisation is subject to **external control** (eg by government, holding company) the more centralised and formalised its structure. The power needs of organisational members (to control others, or at least to control their own working conditions) can lead to centralisation.
Technology	• The stronger the technical system (ie the technology) the more formalised the work, and the more bureaucratic the structure of the operating core. • The more sophisticated the technology, the more elaborate and professional the support staff will be (eg specialists who understand it). • **Information technology** has a profound effect on organisation structure, especially with regard to delayering.
Environment and markets	See below
Strategy	See below

Lawrence and Lorsch: diversity, uniformity and the environment

1.2 *Lawrence and Lorsch* suggested that the structure which develops is likely to be a compromise between **diversity** and **uniformity**. These cover technical matters such as procedures, but also matters such as managers' psychological outlook, similarity of personality and so on.

- **Uniformity:** most parts of the organisation are managed in a similar way.
- **Diversity:** there are different management practices in different departments.

1.3 **Pressures for uniformity**

Pressure	Comment
Stability	The organisation can grow to such a size as to take advantage of economies of scale. This advantage is maximised if the firm makes use of standardised rules and procedures, which are indicators of uniformity.
Need for centralised control	Where the organisation is large, centralised control may only be effected by having standardised rules and procedures or a common organisation culture.
Personnel	A large organisation with a low-skilled workforce will find that uniformity will enable more to be produced. Set procedures also allow specialised skills, once developed, to be of benefit to the whole organisation.
Technology	Similar technologies generate similar organisation structures.
Public responsibility	Detailed rules and procedures enable the firm to cope with strict environmental constraints.

1.4 **Pressures for diversity**

- Differences in regional characteristics, markets, customers or products

- Differences in the technology used in various aspects of the organisation's work

- The greater readiness of individuals to identify with smaller work groups than with an entire organisation

- The desire of subordinates to have more authority

1.5 Organisations with **high diversity** needed **integration devices** - committees, liaison groups and so on, in order to co-ordinate their activities properly.

Structure follows strategy?

1.6 To what extent does an organisation's **structure** follow its strategy? *Alfred Chandler* conducted a detailed historical study of the development of four major US corporations: *Du Pont, General Motors, Standard Oil of New Jersey* and *Sears Roebuck*. He found that all four had evolved a decentralised structure based on operating divisions, though by different routes.

1.7 Chandler suggested that during the period 1850 to 1920 (which he describes as the formative years of modern capitalism), the development of high volume production to serve mass markets forced the replacement of entrepreneurial, owner management by innovative professional managers. These managers created the modern, multi-unit corporation as the best response to the administrative problems associated with growth. The divisionalised organisation is thus a response to strategy in its broadest sense.

1.8 Chandler discerned two main types of strategy, positive and negative. Positive strategy is aggressive, seeks new markets and leads to **growth by product diversification**. Negative strategy seeks to defend a current position and leads to **growth by vertical integration** based on mergers and acquisitions. In both cases, the initial structural response is likely to be centralised control based on functional departments. Both Du Pont and Sears Roebuck went through this stage.

1.9 Unfortunately, this approach has important disadvantages, especially where there is geographic dispersion. These disadvantages are discussed in Chapter 7. Du Pont therefore created an innovative decentralised structure of largely autonomous product-based business units co-ordinated rather than controlled by the corporate headquarters. General Motors copied the idea to overcome a lack of overall control in its loose federation of operating units. Standard Oil of New Jersey followed suit after a series of *ad hoc* responses to crises of control; its particular problem was the need to allocate and co-ordinate resources. Sears Roebuck went through essentially the same process as Du Pont.

1.10 The creation of the multi-unit structures was thus a logical managerial response to the problems associated with strategies that create very large organisations.

1.11 Chandler described four levels of management activity typical of this structure.

(a) The **general office** is the headquarters, responsible for overall performance. It allocates resources to the divisions and controls their performance by setting targets.

(b) The **divisional central office** is responsible to the general office. **Divisions** are responsible for a product line or sales region and are themselves organised internally on a functional basis.

(c) Each function, such as production or sales has a **departmental headquarters, which** manages **field units** such as manufacturing plants or a sales team. Only at field unit level do managers carry out day-to-day operational work.

1.12 It has been argued that an established and well-functioning structure can influence strategy, as, for instance, when two retail organisations merge because the geographical pattern of their branches is complementary. However, this is really an aspect of organisational strengths and weaknesses analysis. Structure should, if necessary, be adjusted to suit the chosen strategy.

Strategy follows structure?

1.13 The other side of the argument would suggest that **strategy is determined or influenced by the structure** of the organisation, or that the structure limits the choice of strategy.

(a) **Structure embodies key decision-making relationships**, as well as filtering information. It might therefore influence the construction of the information that determines strategic choice.

(b) Structure also gives certain departments more power than others, by raising the profile of certain activities within the organisation.

(c) Structure enables resources to be co-ordinated in new ways.

1.14 Section summary

- There are many contingent influences on organisation structure.
- Two important influences are environmental uncertainty and business strategy.

2 STRUCTURAL CONFIGURATIONS

2.1 *Henry Mintzberg's* theory of organisational configuration is a way of expressing the main features by which both formal structure and power relationships are expressed in organisations.

2.2 Mintzberg has written that there are five ideal types of organisation, each of which configures the five components in a significantly different way. Why should this be so?

2.3 Mintzberg believes that each component of the organisation has its own **dynamic**, which **leads to a distinct type of organisation**.

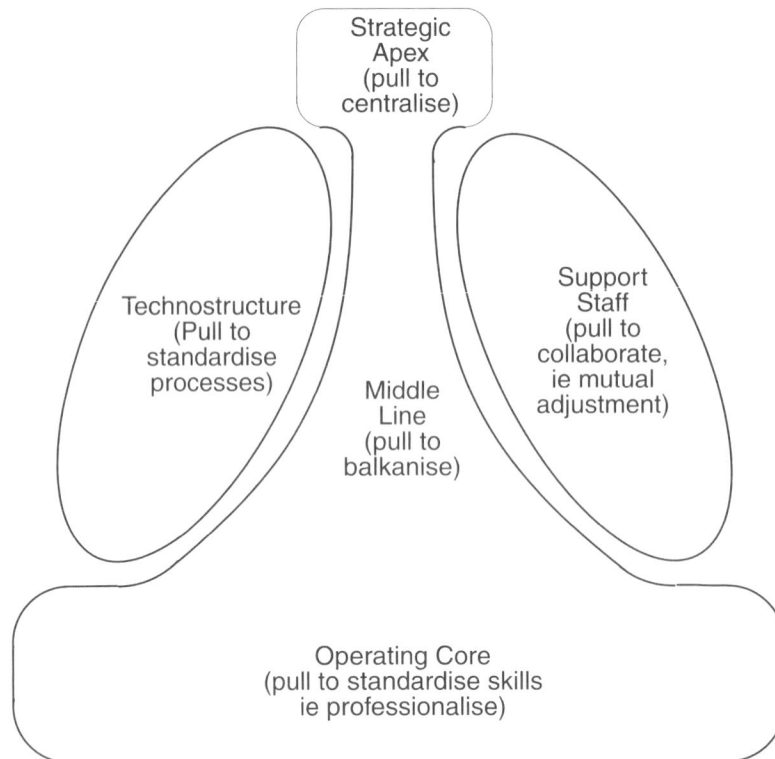

(a) The **strategic apex** wishes to retain control over decision-making. It achieves this when the co-ordinating mechanism is **direct supervision**. The force this most relates to is the **force for direction** (in other words for the need for people to be told what to do).

(b) The **technostructure's** reason for existence is the design of **procedures** and **standards**. For example, the preparation of accounts is highly regulated. This acts as a **force for efficiency**.

(c) The members of the **operating core** seek to minimise the control of administrators over what they do. They prefer to work autonomously, achieving what other co-ordination is necessary by **mutual adjustment**. As professionals, they rely on outside training (such as medical training) to standardise skills. This corresponds to the **force for proficiency**.

(d) The managers of the **middle line** seek to increase their **autonomy** from the strategic apex, and to increase their control over the operating core, so that they can concentrate on their own segment of the market or with their own products. This corresponds to the **force for concentration** (on individual product areas).

(e) **Support staff** only gain influence when their expertise is vital. **Mutual adjustment** is the co-ordinating mechanism. This corresponds to the **force for learning**.

The **forces for co-operation and competition** largely describe how these elements relate to each other.

The simple structure (or entrepreneurial structure)

2.4 The **strategic apex** wishes to retain control over decision-making, and so exercises what Mintzberg describes as a **pull to centralise**. Mintzberg believes that this leads to a **simple structure**.

Simple structure

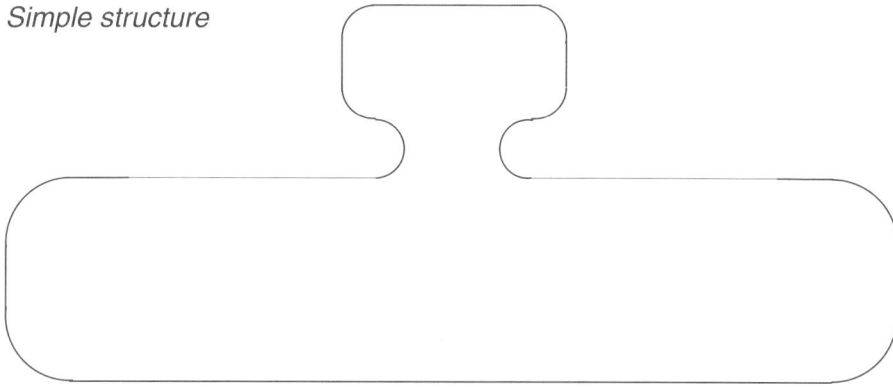

(a) **The simple structure is characteristic of small, young organisations**.

(b) In small firms, a single entrepreneur or management team will dominate (as in the power culture). If it grows, the organisation might need more managerial skills than the apex can provide. Strategies might be made on the basis of the manager's hunches.

(c) Centralisation is advantageous as it reflects management's full knowledge of the operating core and its processes. However, senior managers might intervene too much.

(d) It is risky as it depends on the expertise of one person. Such an organisation might be prone to **succession crises**. Who takes over if the boss dies? This problem is often encountered in family businesses.

(e) This structure can handle an environment that is relatively simple but fast moving, where standardisation cannot be used to co-ordinate activities.

(f) **Co-ordination is achieved by direct supervision,** with few formal devices. It is thus flexible.

(g) This structure has its own particular characteristics : wide span of control; no middle line and hence minimal hierarchy; and no technostructure, implying little formalisation or standardisation of behaviour.

The machine bureaucracy

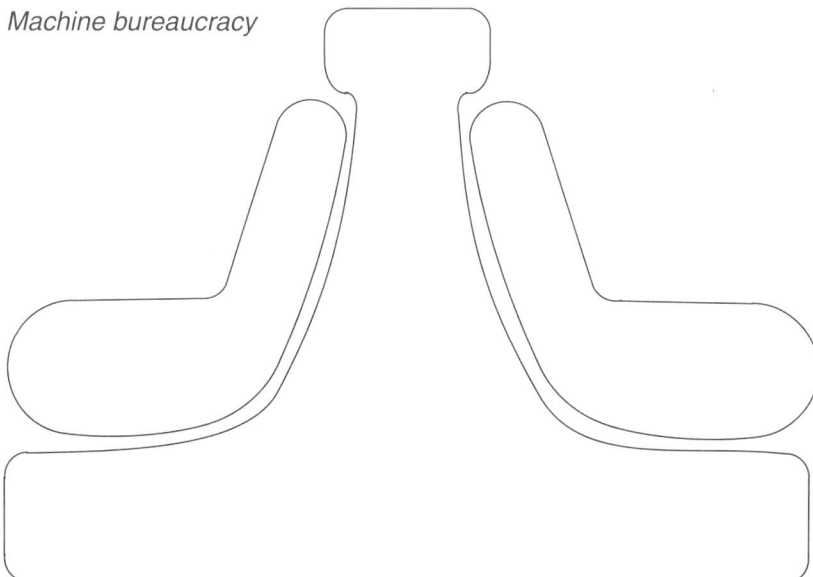

2.5 The **technostructure** exerts a pull for standardisation of work processes. It creates a **machine bureaucracy**.

Machine bureaucracy

(a) This is the classic bureaucracy, working on a sophisticated and well-tuned set of **rules and procedures**. Machine bureaucracies are associated with routine technical systems and repetitive tasks. The bureaucracy can function if people leave, as jobs are designed precisely.

(b) **The technostructure is the key part**. Power rests with analysts who standardise other people's work. The key management philosophy is **scientific management**.

(c) The work of the operating core is highly standardised. Direct supervision by the strategic apex is limited as **standardisation of work processes ensures co-ordination**.

(d) There is a strong emphasis on the **division of labour,** and in particular **on control**. Uncertainty has to be eliminated. The elaborate middle line monitors and directs the operating core. Outsourcing would be embraced reluctantly so the firm employs its own legal and PR specialists. (For example, many big firms have a central legal department.)

(e) Formal communication is most important. Authority is hierarchical.

(f) Conflict is rife between different departments, between line and staff, and between operating core and management.

(g) The environment must be simple and stable.

(h) The machine bureaucracy is the most efficient structure for integrating sets of simple and repetitive tasks.

(i) Machine bureaucracies cannot adapt rapidly they are designed for specialised purposes. They are driven by performance, not problem solving.

The professional bureaucracy

2.6 The **operating core** has a pull for standardisation, not of work processes but of **individual skills**. A machine bureaucracy would lay down exactly how financial transactions should be posted, whether people understood them or not. A **professional bureaucracy** would employ accountants who should know what is involved. The operating core seeks to minimise the influence of administrators (mainly the middle line and technostructure) over work. Examples are hospitals and accountancy firms.

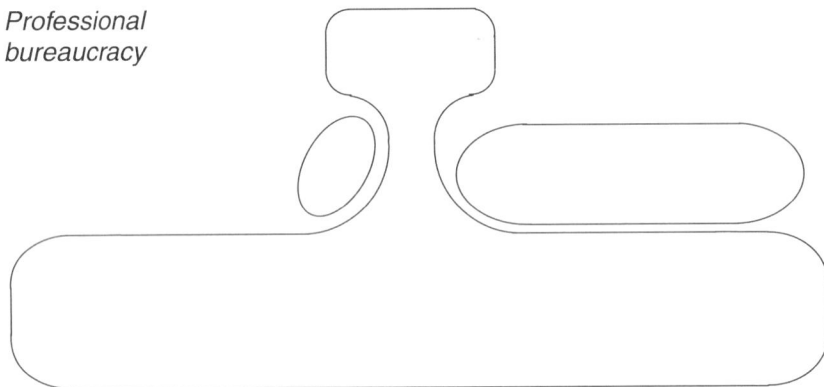

Professional bureaucracy

(a) It hires trained specialists who are all imbued with the skills and values of the profession. A school is an example. Teachers' work in the classroom is not directly supervised but all teachers are trained.

(b) **Co-ordination is achieved by standardisation of skills**, which originate outside its structure. (Teacher training occurs at independent colleges.)

(c) **Power is often based on expertise**, not formal position in the organisation hierarchy.

(d) Work processes are **too complex** to be standardised by a technostructure.

(e) The **operating core** is the key part. There is an elaborate support staff to service it. A technostructure might exist for budgeting, but not for designing work processes.

(f) Work is decentralised. **Professionals control their own work,** and seek collective control over the administrative decisions which affect them.

(g) There might be **two** organisation hierarchies: one, relatively informal, for the operating core doing the work; another, more formal for the support staff. An example is a barristers' chambers. Barristers are co-ordinated by their head clerk, but they retain collective authority over the clerk. The clerk, on the other hand, will exercise direct control over secretarial services.

(h) Professional administrators also manage much of the organisation's boundary.

(i) It can be democratic.

(j) The professional bureaucracy cannot always cope with any variations of standards, as control is exercised through training.

Question 1

How would a machine bureaucracy and a professional bureaucracy ensure that accounting transactions are correctly posted?

Answer

The machine bureaucracy would devise very precise procedures and rule-books telling untrained clerks exactly what to do in any situation.

The professional bureaucracy would employ trained and perhaps qualified accounts staff, whose professional training would give them the expertise to make the right decision.

The divisional form (or diversified form)

2.7 The middle line seeks as much autonomy for itself as possible. It exerts a **pull to balkanise** (ie to split into small self-managed units). The result is the **divisional form,** by which autonomy is given to managers lower down the line. The prime co-ordinating mechanism is **standardisation of outputs**: these are usually performance measures such as profit, which are set by the strategic apex.

Divisional form

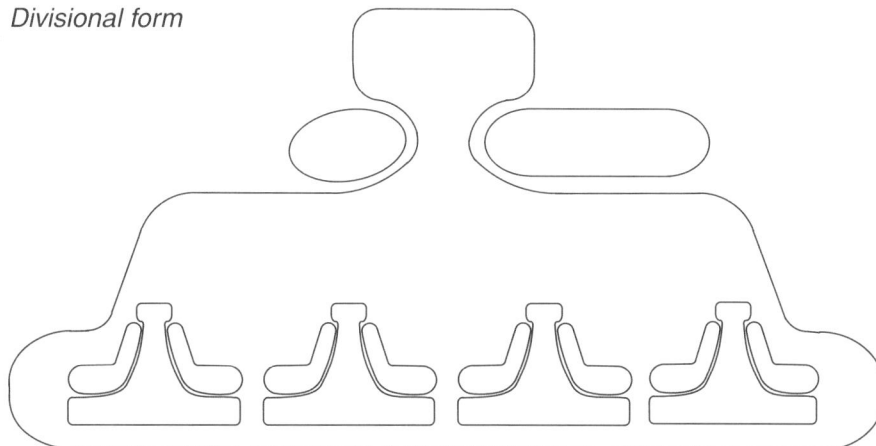

(a) Divisionalisation is the division of a business into **autonomous regions** or product businesses, each with its own revenues, expenditures and profits.

(b) Because each division is monitored by its objective performance towards a single integrated set of goals determined by the strategic apex, **each division is configured as a machine bureaucracy**.

(c) Communication between divisions and head office is restricted, formal and related to performance standards. Influence is maintained by headquarters' power to hire and fire the managers who are supposed to run each division.

(d) Divisionalisation is a function of organisation size, in numbers and in product-market activities.

Compare this analysis of Mintzberg's with Chandler's discussed in the previous section.

2.8 Mintzberg believes there are inherent problems in divisionalisation.

(a) A division is partly **insulated** by the holding company from shareholders and capital markets, which ultimately reward performance.

(b) It 'piggybacks on the machine bureaucracy in a simple stable environment, and may feel drawn back to that form'.

(c) The economic advantages it offers over independent organisations 'reflect fundamental inefficiencies in capital markets'. (In other words, different product-market divisions might function better as independent companies.)

(d) The divisions are **more bureaucratic** than they would be as independent corporations, owing to the performance measures imposed by the strategic apex.

(e) Big companies bring a threat to competitive markets.

(f) Headquarters management have a tendency to **usurp divisional profits** by management charges, cross-subsidies, head office bureaucracies and unfair transfer pricing systems.

(g) In some businesses, it is impossible to identify completely independent products or markets for which divisions would be appropriate.

(h) Divisionalisation is only possible at a fairly senior management level, because there is a limit to how much independence in the division of work can be arranged.

(i) It is a halfway house, relying on personal control over performance by senior managers and enforcing cross-subsidisation.

(j) Divisional performance is not directly assessed by the market.

(k) Many of the problems of divisionalisation are those of **conglomerate diversification**. Each business might be better run independently than with the others. The different businesses might offer different returns for different risks which shareholders might prefer to judge independently.

2.9 The multi-divisional structure might be implemented in one of two forms.

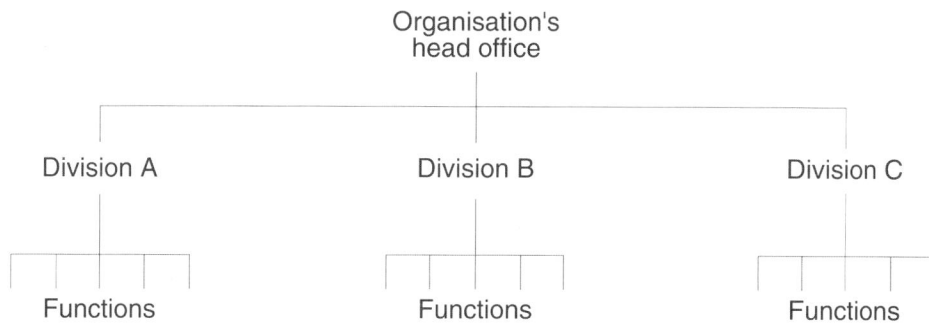

```
                        Organisation's
                         head office
                              |
        ┌─────────────────────┼─────────────────────┐
    Division A            Division B            Division C
        |                     |                     |
   ┌──┬──┬──┐            ┌──┬──┬──┐            ┌──┬──┬──┐
    Functions             Functions             Functions
```

This enables concentration on particular product-market areas, overcoming problems of functional specialisation at a large scale. Problems arise with the power of the head office, and control of the resources. Responsibility is devolved, and some central functions might be duplicated.

2.10 The **holding company** (group) structure is a radical form of divisionalisation. **Subsidiaries are separate legal entities**. The holding company can be a firm with a permanent investment or one which buys and sells businesses.

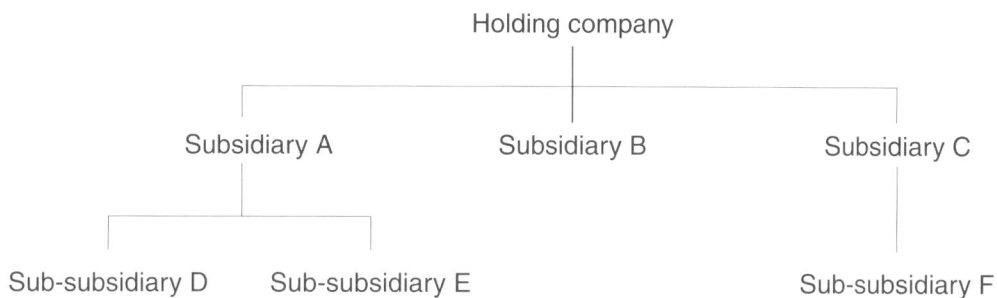

```
                      Holding company
                            |
        ┌───────────────────┼───────────────────┐
    Subsidiary A        Subsidiary B        Subsidiary C
        |                                        |
   ┌────┴────┐                                   |
Sub-subsidiary D   Sub-subsidiary E        Sub-subsidiary F
```

2.11 Divisionalisation has some advantages, despite the problems identified above.

(a) It focuses the attention of subordinate management on business performance and results.

(b) Management by objectives can be applied more easily. 'The manager of the unit knows better than anyone else how he is doing, and needs no one to tell him'.

(c) It gives more authority to junior managers, and therefore provides them with work which grooms them for more senior positions in the future.

(d) It tests junior managers in independent command early in their careers, and at a reasonably low level in the management hierarchy.

(e) It provides an organisation structure which reduces the number of levels of management. The top executives in each divisions should be able to report direct to the chief executive of the holding company.

2.12 **Rules for successful divisionalisation.**

(a) Divisional management should be free to use their authority to do what they think is right for their part of the organisation, but they must be held properly accountable to head office (eg for profits earned).

(b) A division must be large enough to support the quantity and quality of management it needs. It must not rely on head office for excessive management support.

(c) Each division must have a potential for growth in its own area of operations.

(d) There should be scope and challenge in the job for the management of the division.

(e) Division should exist side by side with each other. If they deal with each other, it should be as an arm's length transaction. Where they touch, it should be in competition with each other. There should be no insistence on preferential treatment to be given to a 'fellow unit' by another unit of the overall organisation.

The adhocracy

2.13 The **support staff** exert a pull of their own, towards **collaboration**. The **adhocracy** does not rely on standardisation to co-ordinate its activities, yet it is much more complex than the simple structure which also does not use standardisation.

Adhocracy

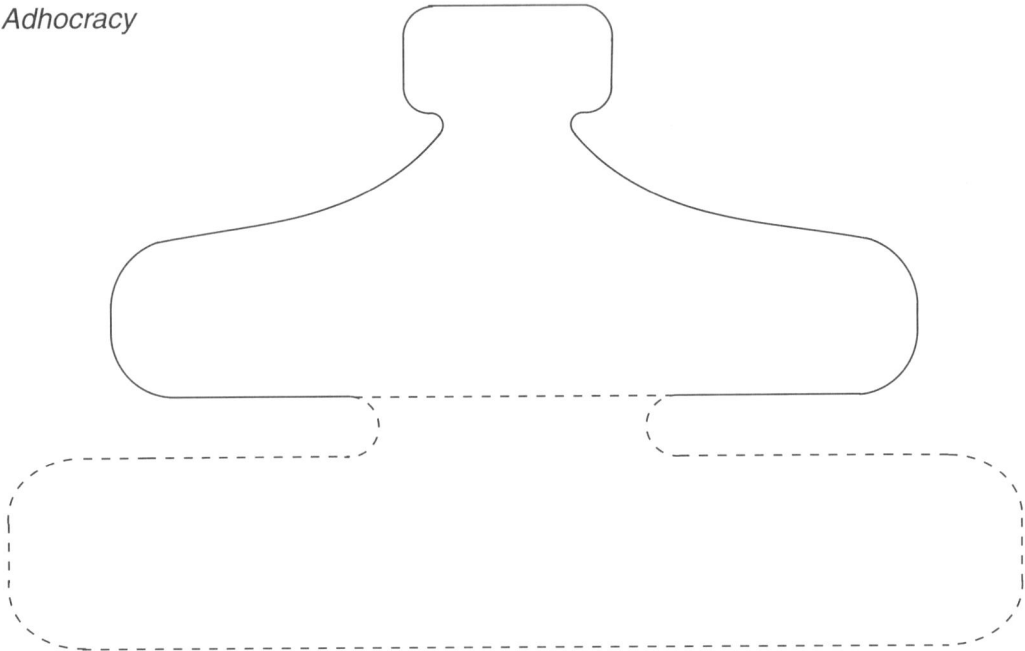

(a) The adhocracy is **complex and disorderly**. There is little formalisation of behaviour. Specialists are deployed in market-based project teams which group together and disperse as and when a project arises and ends. Co-ordination is informal, by mutual adjustment.

(b) The adhocracy relies on the expertise of its members, **but not through standardised skills**. Instead, the *mix* of skills is important. For example, a film is made by a director, actors, camera people, set designers and so on.

(c) A matrix structure might exist, but there are a large number of management roles such as project managers. Managers do not plan or supervise, but co-ordinate.

(d) Decision-making power depends on the type of decision and the situation in which it is made, rather than level in hierarchy. 'No-one ... monopolises the power to innovate'.

(e) Strategy is hard to determine in the adhocracy. It depends partly on the projects that come along (like a film studio). The strategic apex does not *formulate* strategies, but is engaged in battles over strategic *choices* (eg which films shall we make?) and liaisons with the outside parties.

(f) The adhocracy is positioned in a dynamic and complex environment.

(g) The adhocracy is driven to bureaucratise itself as it ages. The organisation will eventually **specialise in what it does best**, driving it to more stable environmental conditions and predictable work processes, leading perhaps to a professional bureaucracy.

2.14 The adhocracy is concerned with **innovation**.

(a) The **operating adhocracy** seeks to **innovate** to serve its clients, whereas the professional bureaucracy seeks perfection. (Mintzberg uses an analogy of a theatre company. An adhocratic theatre company produces new plays. A professional bureaucratic one would seek to produce ever more perfect renditions of Shakespeare.) The operating core is retained.

(b) The **administrative adhocracy** innovates to serve its **own convenience**. Note that the operating core is split off, frequently subcontracted or automated, or even forms a separate organisation. The support staff are important, a central pool of expert talent from which project teams are drawn.

2.15 Adhocracies sometimes exist because the complexity of their technical systems require a trained support staff to operate them.

(a) The adhocracy is an ambiguous environment for work. This elicits complex human responses, as many people dislike ambiguity.

(b) The adhocracy is not suitable for **standardised** work; it is better at dealing with unique projects.

(c) It has a high cost of communication, and workloads are unbalanced.

Concluding thoughts

2.16 The usefulness of Mintzberg's theory of structural configuration is that it covers many issues, over and above formal organisation structure.

- The type of work the organisation does (customised or standardised)
- The complexity it has to deal with (simple or complex)
- The environment (stable or dynamic)

We can summarise some of these in the table below.

Configuration	Co-ordination mechanism	Key part	Environment? (see Ch 6)	Possible characteristics
Simple	Direct supervision	Strategic apex	Simple/dynamic (even hostile)	Small, young, centralised, personality-driven. Crisis of leadership
Machine bureaucracy	Standardised work processes	Techno-structure	Simple/stable	Old, large, rule-bound, specialised
Professional bureaucracy	Standardised skills	Operating core	Complex/stable	Decentralised, emphasis on training
Divisional form	Standardised outputs	Middle line	Varies; each division is shielded to a degree	Old, large, divisions are quasi-autonomous, decentralised, bureaucratic
Adhocracy	Mutual adjustment	Support staff	Complex/dynamic	High automated, 'organic'

2.17   Mintzberg mentions one other co-ordinating factor: **mission**. A **missionary organisation** is one welded together by ideology or culture. There is job rotation, standardisation of values (*norms*) and little external control (eg like a religious sect). This relates to ideology, the **force for co-operation**.

2.18   As a cautionary note, these 'ideal types do not exist as such; they are **simplified models of real organisations**: most contain elements of all types.'

Question 2

Which organisation configurations are suggested in the following cases?

(a)   Creation Ltd provides public relations services to clients. It is run by five partners, with a staff of copy editors, designers, party-throwers and people with contacts in the press. Clients contact one of the partners who assembles a team to solve the client's problem, though the partner does not direct the solution.

(b)   The St Imelda Hospital is involved in providing physiotherapy to accident victims. It recruits trained physiotherapists, each of whom is allocated a patient. The hospital does not determine exactly what sort of treatments should be used.

Answer

(a)   Adhocracy
(b)   Professional bureaucracy

---

3   DEPARTMENTATION

KEY TERM

Departmentation: the division of an organisation into departments.

3.1   As an organisation grows in size, it employs more people and is able to specialise.

(a)   It is able to take advantage of economies of scale, which in turn may call for the establishment of departments of specialist or experts (eg research and development, management scientists).

(b)   The number of levels in the organisation hierarchy increases, so that problems of delegation of authority and control arise.

(c)   Specialist support teams (eg service and maintenance, quality control, corporate planning, organisation and methods, data processing) are created to ease the burdens and complexities of line management. Such support teams need to be slotted into the hierarchical structure.

(d)   Separate groups and departments continue to be formed as specialisation extends; new problems of communication and co-ordination (or integration) now arise.

3.2   The creation of departments is known as **departmentation**. Different patterns of departmentation are possible, and the pattern selected will depend on the individual circumstances of the organisation. Various methods of departmentation are described below.

Geographic departmentation

3.3 Some authority is retained at Head Office (organised, perhaps, on a functional basis) but day-to-day service operations are handled on a territorial basis. Within many sales departments, the sales staff are organised territorially.

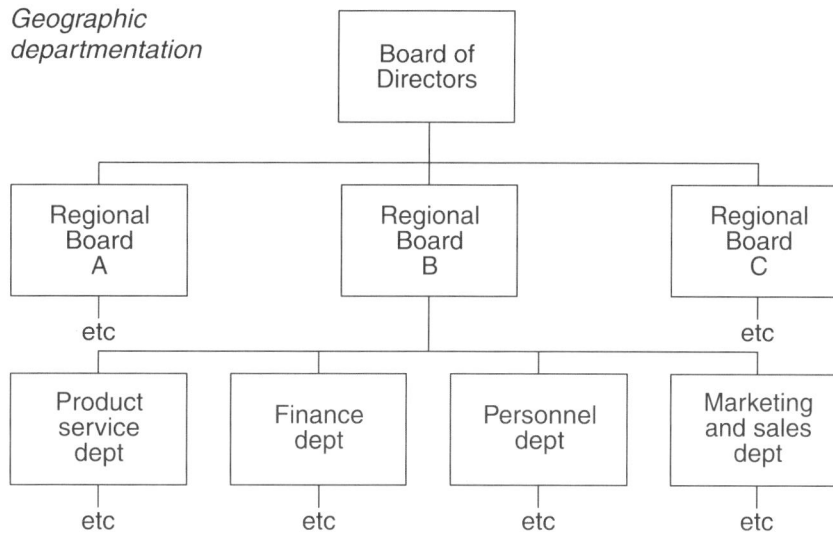

3.4 **Advantages of geographic departmentation**

(a) Better and quicker local decision making at the point of contact between the organisation (eg a salesman) and its customers.

(b) It may be less costly to establish area factories/offices than to run everything centrally (eg costs of transportation and travelling may be reduced).

(c) It might be essential for overseas operations.

3.5 The **disadvantage** of geographic departmentation is the duplication of management effort. For example, a national organisation divided into ten regions might have a customer liaison department in each regional office. If the organisation did all customer liaison work from head office it might need fewer managerial staff.

Functional departmentation

3.6 Functional organisation means that departments are defined by their **functions,** that is, the work that they do. It is a traditional, common sense approach and many organisations are structured like this. Primary functions in a manufacturing company might be production, sales, finance, and general administration. Sub departments of marketing might be selling, advertising, distribution and warehousing.

3.7 **Advantages of functional departmentation**

- It is based on work specialism and is therefore logical.
- The firm can benefit from economies of scale.
- It offers a career structure.

3.8 **Disadvantages**

- It does not reflect the actual business processes by which **value is created**.
- It is hard to identify where profits and losses are made on individual products.
- People do not have an understanding of how the *whole* business works.

- There are problems of co-ordinating the work of different specialisms.

Functional departmentation

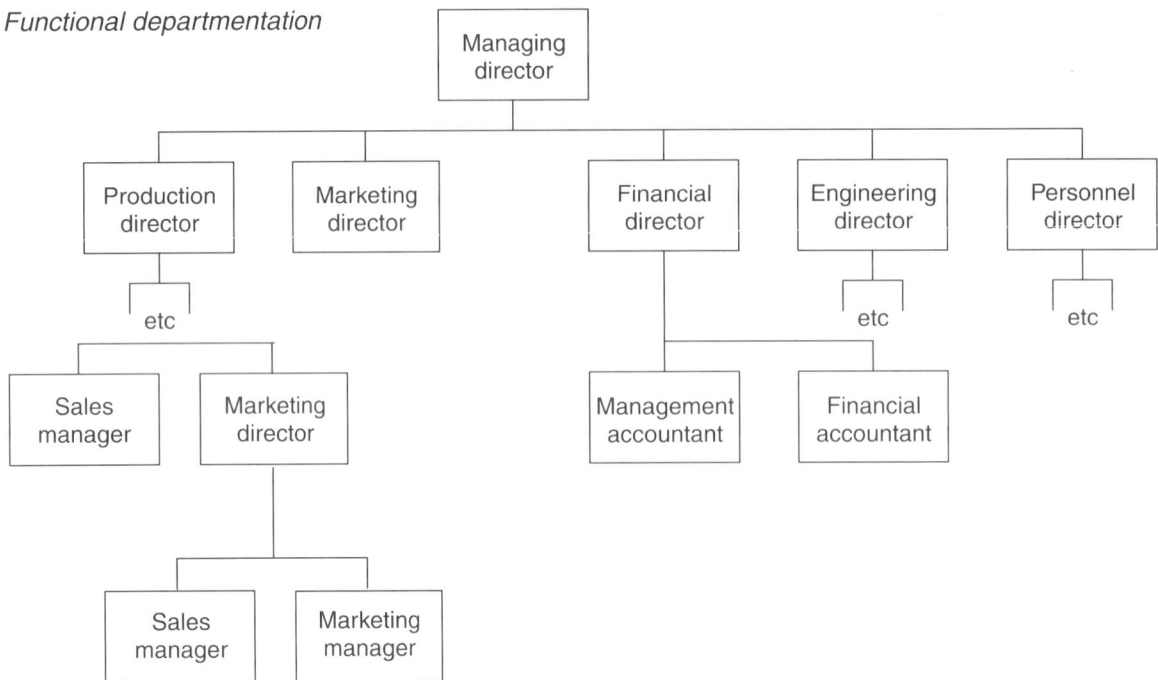

Product/brand departmentation

3.9 **Product.** Some organisations group activities on the basis of products or product lines. Some functional departmentation remains (eg manufacturing, distribution, marketing and sales) but a divisional manager is given responsibility for the product or product line, with authority over personnel of different functions. This is discussed in more detail later in this chapter.

3.10 **Advantages of product departmentation**

(a) Individual managers can be held accountable for the **profitability** of individual products.

(b) Specialisation can be developed. For example, some salesmen will be trained to sell a specific product in which they may develop technical expertise and thereby offer a better sales service to customers. Service engineers who specialise in a single product should also provide a better after sales service.

(c) The different functional activities and efforts required to make and sell each product can be co-ordinated and integrated by the divisional/product manager.

(d) It should be focused on how a business makes its profits.

3.11 The **disadvantage of product departmentation** is that it increases the overhead costs and managerial complexity of the organisation.

3.12 **Brand.** A brand is the name (eg 'Persil') or design which identifies the products or services of a manufacturer or provider and distinguishes them from those of competitors. Large organisations may produce a number of different brands of the same basic product, such as washing powder or toothpaste. This is viable because branding brings the product to the attention of buyers and creates brand loyalty - often the customers do not realise that two rival brands are in fact produced by the same manufacturer.

(a) Because branding is linked with unique marketing positions it becomes necessary to have brand departmentation. As with product departmentation, some functional departmentation remains (especially on the manufacturing side) but brand managers have responsibility for the brand's marketing and this can affect every function.

(b) Brand departmentation has similar advantages and disadvantages to product departmentation. In particular, overhead costs and complexity of the management structure are increased, the relationships of a number of different brand departments with the manufacturing department, if there is only one, being particularly difficult.

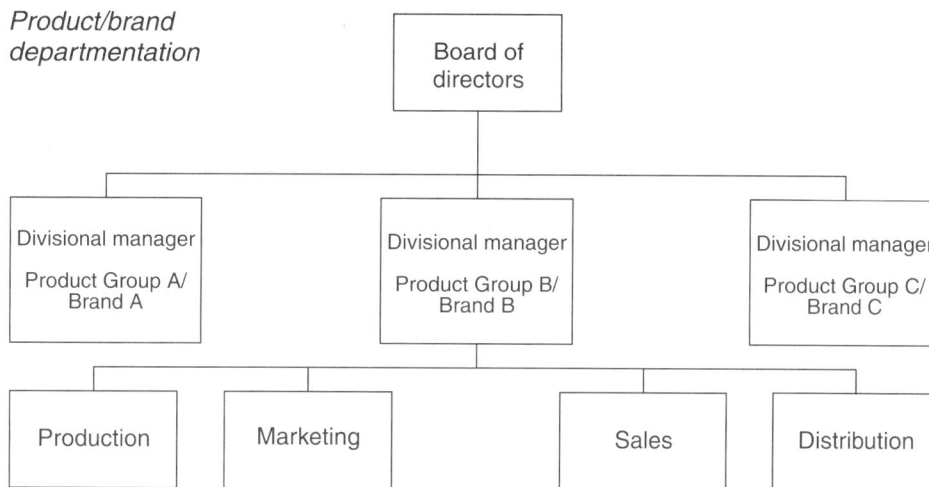

Product/brand departmentation

```
                        ┌─────────────┐
                        │  Board of   │
                        │  directors  │
                        └──────┬──────┘
          ┌────────────────────┼────────────────────┐
┌─────────────────┐  ┌─────────────────┐  ┌─────────────────┐
│ Divisional      │  │ Divisional      │  │ Divisional      │
│ manager         │  │ manager         │  │ manager         │
│                 │  │                 │  │                 │
│ Product Group A/│  │ Product Group B/│  │ Product Group C/│
│ Brand A         │  │ Brand B         │  │ Brand C         │
└────────┬────────┘  └────────┬────────┘  └─────────────────┘
    ┌────┴─────┐          ┌────┴─────┐
┌────────┐ ┌────────┐ ┌────────┐ ┌────────────┐
│Production│ │Marketing│ │ Sales │ │Distribution│
└────────┘ └────────┘ └────────┘ └────────────┘
```

Customer or market segment departmentation

3.13 **Customer or market segment**

(a) A manufacturing organisation may sell goods through wholesalers, export agents and by direct mail. It may therefore organise its sales, marketing and distribution functions on the basis of types of customer, or market segment. Departmentation by customer is commonly associated with sales departments and selling effort, but it might also be used by a jobbing or contracting firm where a team of managers may be given the responsibility of liaising with major customers.

(b) Another example is where firms distinguish between domestic consumers and business customers, with a different marketing and supply efforts for each.

Divisionalisation

3.14 **Divisionalisation** is the division of a very large enterprise into **autonomous** segments, each with its own revenues, expenditures and capital asset purchase programmes, and therefore each with its own profit and loss responsibility. Divisions of the organisation might be subsidiary companies under the holding company or profit or investment centres within a single company. Divisionalisation was discussed in Section 1 of this chapter.

4   CENTRALISATION AND DECENTRALISATION

KEY TERMS

Centralisation means a greater degree of central control.

Decentralisation means a greater degree of delegated authority to regions or sub-units.

4.1   Advantages of centralisation

Advantage	Comment
Control	Senior management can exercise greater control over the activities of the organisation and co-ordinate their subordinates or sub-units more easily.
Standardisation	Procedures can be standardised throughout the organisation.
Corporate view	Senior managers can make decisions from the point of view of the organisation as a whole, whereas subordinates would tend to make decisions from the point of view of their own department or section.
Balance of power	Centralised control enables an organisation to maintain a balance between different functions or departments.
Experience counts	Senior managers ought to be more experienced and skilful in making decisions.
Lower overheads	When authority is delegated, there is often a duplication of management effort (and a corresponding increase in staff numbers) at lower levels of hierarchy.
Leadership	In times of **crisis**, the organisation may need strong leadership by a central group of senior managers.

4.2   Advantages of decentralisation

Advantage	Comment
Workload	It reduces the stress and burdens of senior management.
Job	It provides subordinates with greater job satisfaction by giving them more say in making decisions which affect their work.
Local knowledge	Subordinates may have a better knowledge than senior management of 'local' conditions affecting their area of work.
Flexibility and speed	Delegation should allow greater flexibility and a quicker response to changing conditions. If problems do not have to be referred up a scalar chain of command to senior managers for a decision, decision-making will be quicker.
Training	Management at middle and junior levels are 'groomed' for eventual senior management positions.
Control	By establishing appropriate sub-units or profit centres to which authority is delegated, the system of control within the organisation might be improved.

4.3   **Contingency approach.** Centralisation suits some functions more than others.

- The **research and development function** might be centralised into a single unit, as a resource for each division.

- Sales departments might be decentralised on a terrorial basis.

Centralisation and strategic planning

4.4   *Goold and Campbell* categorised three types of strategic planning organisation, according to whether:

- Decisions are made at the centre or by subsidiaries

- How the centre measures and controls the performance of subsidiaries.

4.5 They identified **three strategic management styles**.

(a) **Strategic planners** (such as Cadbury-Schweppes) have a small number of core businesses. Head office plays a big part in making the strategic planning decisions for all its businesses, and subsidiaries are required to implement these global plans.

(b) **Strategic controllers** tend to be diversified. Headquarters are remote. Strategic planning involves general guidelines issued from head office, ongoing objectives and background assumptions.

(c) **Financial controllers** (such as GEC and Tarmac) are groups where most strategic decisions are made by the subsidiaries without head office interference. Head office exercises control over subsidiaries according to results - ie financial performance and success or failure in achieving financial targets.

Question 3

XYZ has over 500 profit centres (ranging from baggage handling equipment to stockings) and revenues of £7bn. Head office staff amount to 47. Each profit centre must provide the following.

(a) The *annual profit plan*. This is agreed in detail every year, after close negotiation. It is regarded as a commitment to a preordained level of performance.

(b) A *monthly management report*, which is extremely detailed (17 pages). Working capital is outlined in detail. Provisions (the easiest way to manipulate accounts) are highlighted.

Is XYZ a strategic planner, a strategic controller or a financial controller?

Answer
Financial controller.

4.6 **Influences on the choice of planning organisation**

(a) Highly diversified groups are much more difficult to control from the centre, and a **financial controller** system would probably be suitable.

(b) When **big capital investments** are planned, head office should be involved in the decision.

(c) When **cash flow** is tight, other strategies must be sacrificed to the paramount concern for short term survival and attention to cash flow.

(d) Organisations in a single industry which is fairly stable would perhaps be more efficiently managed by a hierarchical, centralised management system, structured perhaps on a functional basis (production, marketing etc).

(e) Top management might prefer one approach.

4.7 **Section summary**
- Centralisation offers control and standardisation.
- Decentralisation offers local knowledge.
- This applies also the strategic planning processes.

5 MULTIFOCUSED HIERARCHIES: HYBRID AND MATRIX DESIGNS

5.1 Many organisation hierarchies in practice combine elements of a number of these approaches. In the example below, research and development is centrally organised, but the operating activities of the firm are geographically arranged. This is an example of a **hybrid structure**.

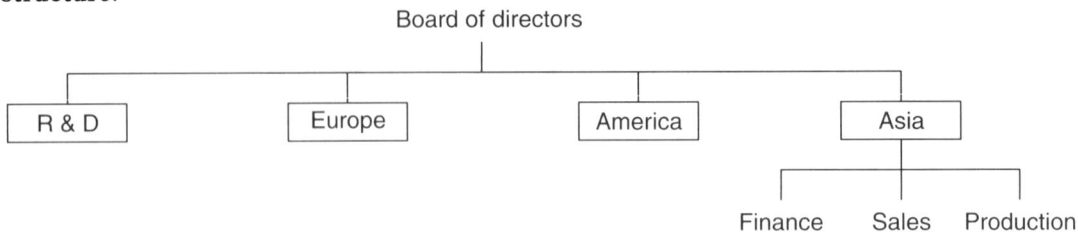

5.2 Another example is given below. R&D, human resources and finance are centralised functions: other activities are arranged on a product basis.

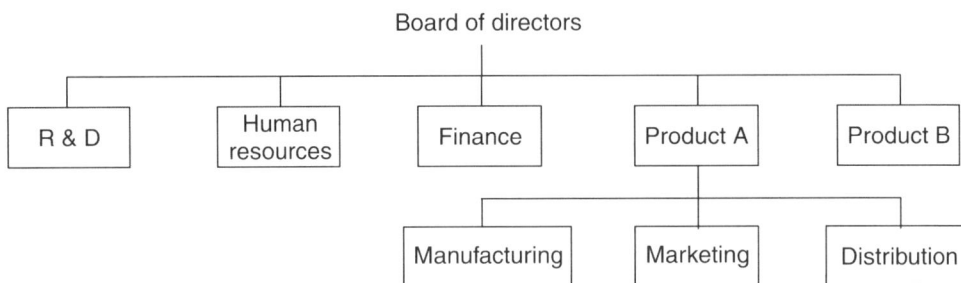

5.3 Most organisations contain features of the hybrid structure.

(a) Certain business activities are better arranged or centralised on a **functional basis** for reasons of **economies of scale,** and pooling of knowledge and efficiency (eg R&D).

(b) Other activities are best organised on a **product or territorial basis,** with the particular advantages of **specialisation, local knowledge,** and **flexibility** (eg marketing).

Question 4

The Erewhon Bank plc has branches in the UK, Eire, France, Germany and Denmark. It grew from the merger of a number of small local banks in these countries. These local banks were not large enough to compete single-handedly in their home markets. The Erewhon Bank hopes to attract both retail and corporate customers, through its use of home banking services and its heavily advertised Direct Bank service, which is a branchless bank to which customers telephone, fax or post their instructions. The bank also specialises in providing foreign currency accounts, and has set up a revolutionary service whereby participating customers can settle their own business transactions in Euros.

What sort of organisation structure do you think would be appropriate?

Answer

Although some of the technical details of the products described might have appeared daunting, you should have realised that the bank basically serves two markets, the personal sector and the corporate sector. However, you would perhaps be ill advised to organise the bank *solely* on that basis. Why?

(a) The banking needs of customers in the personal sector are likely to be quite distinct. This market is naturally segmented geographically. Users of the telephone banking service, for example, will want to speak in their own language. Also, despite the Single European Market, the competitive environment of financial services is likely to be different in each country (eg credit cards are widely used in France, but hardly used at all in Germany).

For the personal sector, a geographic organisation would be appropriate, although with the centralisation of common administrative and account processing functions and technological expertise, so that the bank gains from scale economies and avoids wasteful duplication.

(b) For the corporate sector, different considerations apply. If the bank is providing sophisticated foreign currency accounts, these will be of most benefit to multi-nationals or companies which regularly export from, or import to, their home markets. A geographical organisation structure may not be appropriate, and arguably the bank's organisation should be centralised on a Europe wide basis, with the country offices, of course, at a lower level.

Exam focus point

In practice, most organisation designs you come with are likely to be 'hybrid' in one way or another, because of the nature of the business and the factors affecting it. When asked to design a suitable organisation structure you should consider the nature of the business and the influences on it. For example, a firm with many retail outlets would naturally suit an area/geographical structure, although some activities, such as training, may be organised centrally.

Matrix and project organisation

5.4 Matrix organisation is a structure which provides for the formalisation of management control between different functions, whilst at the same time maintaining functional departmentation. It can be a mixture of a functional, product and territorial organisation.

5.5 A golden rule of classical management theory is **unity of command**: an individual should have one boss. (Thus, staff management can only act in an advisory capacity, leaving authority in the province of line management alone.) Matrix and project organisation may possibly be thought of as a reaction against the classical form of bureaucracy by establishing a structure of **dual command** either temporary (in the form of projects) or permanent (in the case of matrix structure).

Projects

5.6 A project normally has a defined task. Many projects are interdisciplinary, and might require, for instance the contributions of an engineer, a scientist, a statistician and a production expert, who would be appointed to the team while retaining membership and status within their own functional department.

(a) Members of the project team would provide formal lateral lines of communication and authority, superimposed on the functional departmental structure.

(b) Project teams are, essentially, temporary arrangements.

Matrix organisation

Case example

Matrix management first developed in the 1950s in the USA in the aerospace industry. Lockheed-California, the aircraft manufacturers, were organised in a functional hierarchy. Customers were unable to find a manager in Lockheed to whom they could take their problems and queries about their particular orders, and Lockheed found it necessary to employ 'project expediters' as customer liaison officials. From this developed *project co-ordinators*, responsible for co-ordinating line managers into solving a customer's problems. Up to this point, these new officials had no functional responsibilities.

Owing to increasingly heavy customer demands, Lockheed eventually created 'programme managers', with authority for project budgets and programme design and scheduling. These managers therefore had functional authority and responsibilities, thus a matrix management organisation was created.

5.7　The matrix organisation imposes the multi-disciplinary approach on a permanent basis. For example, it is possible to have a product management structure superimposed on top of a functional departmental structure in a matrix; product or brand managers may be responsible for the sales budget, production budget, pricing, marketing, distribution, quality and costs of their product or product line, but may have to co-ordinate with the R&D, production, finance, distribution, and sales departments in order to bring the product on to the market and achieve sales targets.

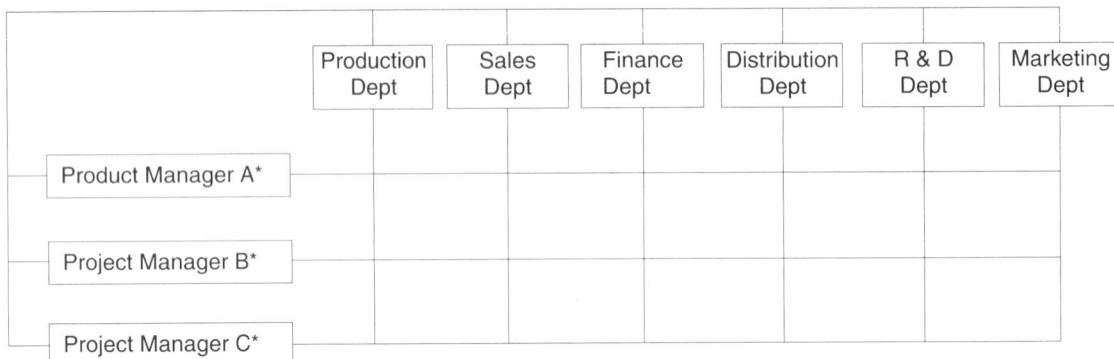

	Production Dept	Sales Dept	Finance Dept	Distribution Dept	R & D Dept	Marketing Dept
Product Manager A*						
Project Manager B*						
Project Manager C*						

* The product managers may each have their own marketing team; in which case the marketing department itself would be small or non-existent.

5.8　The authority of product managers may vary from organisation to organisation.

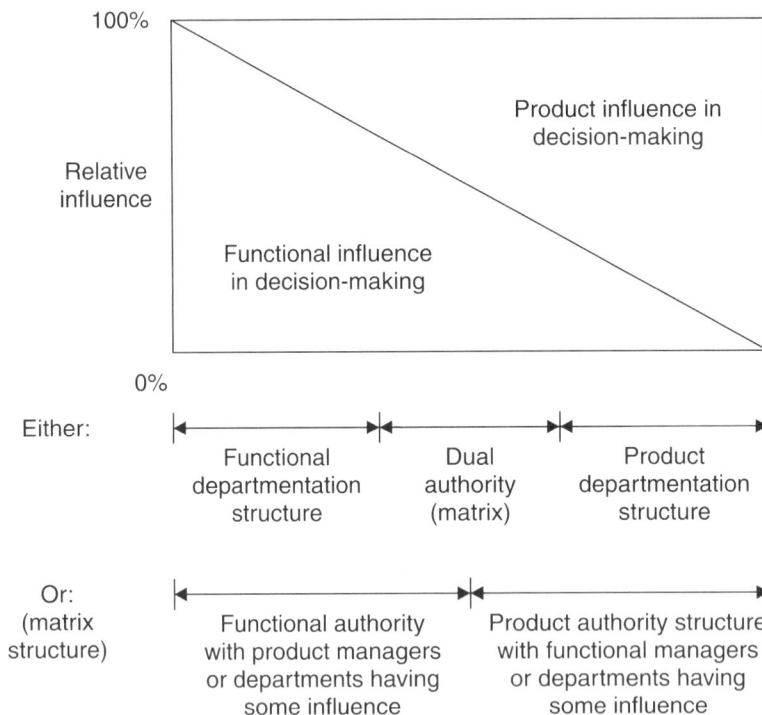

Once again, the division of authority between product managers and functional managers must be carefully defined.

5.9　Matrix management thus **challenges classical ideas** about organisation by rejecting the idea of one person, one boss.

5.10　A subordinate cannot easily take orders from two or more bosses, and so an arrangement has to be established, perhaps on the following lines.

(a) A subordinate takes orders from one boss (the functional manager) and the second boss (the project manager) has to ask the first boss to give certain instructions to the subordinate.

(b) A subordinate takes orders from one boss about some specified matters and orders from the other boss about different specified matters. The authority of each boss would have to be carefully defined. Even so, good co-operation between the bosses would still be necessary.

5.11 **Advantages of a matrix structure**

(a) It offers greater **flexibility**. This applies both to **people,** as employees adapt more quickly to a new challenge or new task, and develop an attitude which is geared to accepting change; and to **task and structure,** as the matrix may be short-term (as with project teams) or readily amended (eg a new product manager can be introduced by superimposing his tasks on those of the existing functional managers). Flexibility should facilitate efficient operations in the face of change.

(b) It should improve **communication** within the organisation.

(c) Dual authority gives the organisation **multiple orientation** so that functional specialists do not get wrapped up in their own concerns.

(d) It provides a **structure for allocating responsibility to managers for end-results**. A product manager is responsible for product profitability, and a project leader is responsible for ensuring that the task is completed.

(e) It provides for **inter-disciplinary co-operation** and a mixing of skills and expertise.

5.12 **A matrix organisation is most suitable in the following situations.**

(a) There is a fairly large number of different functions, each of great importance.

(b) There could be communications problems between functional management in different functions (eg marketing, production, R&D, personnel, finance).

(c) Work is supposed to flow smoothly between these functions, but the communications problems might stop or hinder the work flow.

(d) There is a need to carry out uncertain, interdependent tasks. Work can be structured so as to be **task centred**, with task managers appointed to look after each task, and provide the communications (and co-operation) between different functions.

(e) There is a need to achieve common functional tasks so as to achieve savings in the use of resources - ie product divisions would be too wasteful, because they would duplicate costly functional tasks.

(f) There are many geographic areas with distinct needs, but the firm wishes to exploit economies of scale.

5.13 **Disadvantages of matrix organisation**

(a) Dual authority threatens a **conflict** between managers. Where matrix structure exists it is important that the authority of superiors should not overlap and areas of authority must be clearly defined. A subordinate must know to which superior he is responsible for each aspect of his duties.

(b) One individual with two or more bosses is more likely to suffer **role stress** at work.

(c) It is sometimes more **costly** - eg product managers are additional jobs which would not be required in a simple structure of functional departmentation.

BPP
PROFESSIONAL EDUCATION

(d) It may be **difficult for the management to accept** a matrix structure. It is possible that a manager may feel threatened that another manager will usurp his authority.

(e) It required consensus and agreement which may slow down decision-making.

6 MECHANISTIC AND ORGANIC STRUCTURES

Bureaucracy and mechanistic structures

6.1 **Bureaucracy** is perhaps the term most commonly used to describe a hierarchical rule-bound organisation. Many of the organisational structures described earlier could be classified as bureaucracies. When the term was first coined, bureaucracy was regarded as a recipe for efficiency. There are still cases where a bureaucratic approach is well suited to an organisation's objectives.

6.2 *Weber* specified several general characteristics of bureaucracy, which he described as 'a continuous organisation of official functions bound by rules'.

6.3 Mintzberg, as we have seen, identifies two kinds of bureaucracy.

(a) Machine bureaucracy, similar to Weber's description, based on standardisation of work processes, functional groupings, size.

(b) Professional bureaucracy (eg hospitals) based on standardisation of skills.

Criticisms of bureaucracies

6.4 The very strength of some of the characteristics of bureaucracy may in some cases be turned into a cause of weakness. *Gouldner* argued that rules are **both functional** and **dysfunctional** in a bureaucracy.

(a) **Rules are functional**: they take away from subordinates the feeling that their superiors, in issuing orders, hold power over them. This in turn reduces the interpersonal tensions which otherwise exist between superiors and subordinates.

(b) **Rules are dysfunctional**: employees use rules to learn what is the **minimum** level of behaviour expected from them, and there is a tendency for employees to work at this minimum level of behaviour. This, in turn, suggested Gouldner, creates a requirement for close supervision. Greater pressure from supervisors will make subordinates more aware of the power the supervisor holds over them, thereby increasing tension within the work group.

6.5 **Undesirable features of bureaucracy**

(a) Committees and reports slow down the decision-making process.

(b) Conformity creates ritualism, formalism and 'organisation man'.

(c) Personal growth of individuals is inhibited - although bureaucracies tend to attract, select and retain individuals with a tolerance for such conditions.

(d) Innovation is discouraged.

(e) Control systems are frequently out of date. According to Michael Crozier, the control mechanism (whereby feedback on errors is used to initiate corrective action) is hampered by rigidity: bureaucracies cannot learn from their mistakes!

(f) Bureaucracies are slow to change. *Michael Crozier* stated that 'a system of organisation whose main characteristic is its rigidity will not adjust easily to change and will tend to resist change as much as possible'.

(g)   Over prescriptive rules produce a simplistic approach to problems.

6.6   The financial and technical advantages of bureaucratic organisations **usually outweigh** the disadvantages, especially in circumstances of slow change and a large customer/client base, to which bureaucracy is well suited. The dysfunctions, however, still need to be reduced to acceptable proportions.

Improving bureaucracy

6.7   The organisation should have some specific features.

- Small working groups (to promote group loyalty and purpose)
- Small working establishments (for the same reasons)
- As little centralisation as possible (to give junior management more scope)
- A highly developed two-way communication system

6.8   **Culture** may be used to increase the flexibility and humanity of the organisation. A less rule-bound structure/culture may be developed in particular units of the bureaucracy, such as those with direct customer/client contact.

6.9   Opportunities should be created for **individualism and innovation,** if only in certain units of the organisation. The bureaucracy may then be able to attract individuals of a less conforming type, better able to handle change, ambiguity and flexibility.

Bureaucracies and change

6.10 *Burns and Stalker* contrasted the **organic** structure of management (see below), which is more suitable to conditions of change, with a **mechanistic** system of management, which is more suited to stable conditions. A mechanistic structure, which appears very much like a bureaucracy, has the following characteristics.

(a)   Authority is delegated through a hierarchical, formal scalar chain, and **position power** is used in decision-making.

(b)   Communication is **vertical** (ie up and down the scalar chain) rather than **lateral**.

(c)   Individuals regard their own tasks as specialised and not directly related to the goals of the organisation as a whole.

(d)   There is a precise definition of duties in each individual job (rules, procedures, job definitions).

6.11 Mechanistic systems are **unsuitable in conditions of change** because they tend to deal with change by cumbersome methods.

(a)   The **ambiguous figure system**: in dealing with unfamiliar problems authority lines are not clear, matters are referred upwards and the top of the organisation becomes over-burdened by decisions.

(b)   **Mechanistic jungle**: jobs and departments are created to deal with the problems caused by change, creating further and greater problems.

(c)   **Committee system**: committees are set up to cope with the new problems. The committees can only be a temporary problem-solving device, but the situations which create the problems are not temporary.

However, for certain types of change this might be qualified.

Organic organisations: suitability for change

6.12 In contrast to mechanistic structures, Burns and Stalker identified an **organic structure** (also called an **organismic structure**). They believed organic structures were better suited to conditions of change than mechanistic structures. The mechanistic structures and the organic structure are contrasted in the table below.

Mechanistic	*Organic*
• Tasks are specialised and broken down into subtasks.	Specialist knowledge and expertise is seen to contribute to the 'common task' of the concern.
• Each individual task is 'abstract', pursued with techniques and purposes more or less distinct from that of the concern. People are concerned with task efficiency, not with how the task can be made to improve organisational effectiveness	Each task is seen and understood to be set by the total situation of the firm: people are concerned with the task insofar as it contributes to organisational effectiveness.
• Managers are responsible for co-ordinating tasks	Each task is adjusted and redefined through interaction with others. This is rather like co-ordination by mutual adjustment
• There are precise job descriptions and delineations of responsibility.	Job descriptions are less precise: it is harder to 'pass the buck'
• 'Doing the job' takes priority over serving the interests of the organisation.	'The spread of commitment to the concern beyond any technical definition'
• Hierarchic structure of control. An individual's performance assessment derives from a 'contractual relationship with an impersonal organisation.'	Network structure of control. An individual's job performance and conduct derive from a supposed community of interest between the individual and the organisation, and the individual's colleagues. (Loyalty to the 'team' is an important control mechanism.)
• Decisions are taken at the top, where knowledge is supposed to reside.	Relevant technical and commercial knowledge can be located anywhere 'omniscience is no longer imputed to the head of the concern.'
• Interaction is mainly vertical (up and down the scalar chain), and takes the form of commands and obedience.	Interaction is lateral and communication between people of different rank represents consultation, rather than command.
• Operations and working behaviour are governed by instructions issued by superiors.	Communication consists of information and advice rather than instructions and decisions.
• Insistence on loyalty to the concern and obedience to superiors.	Commitment to the concern's task (eg mission) is more highly valued than loyalty as such.
• Internal knowledge (eg of the organisation's specific activities) is more highly valued that general knowledge.	'Importance and prestige attach to affiliations and expertise valid in the industrial, technical and commercial milieux external to the firm'

6.13 **Four important points to note**

(a) Although organic systems are not hierarchical in the way that bureaucracies are, there are **differences of status**, determined by people's greater expertise, experience and so forth.

(b) The degree of **commitment to the concern** is more extensive in organic than mechanistic system. This is similar to the idea that an organisation's mission should motivate and inspire employees.

(c) The reduced importance of hierarchy is replaced by 'the development of shared beliefs and values'. In other words, corporate culture becomes very powerful. **Control is cultural rather than bureaucratic**.

(d) The two approaches represent **two ends of a spectrum**: there are intermediate stages between bureaucratic and organic organisations. Different departments of a business may be run on different lines. For example, the payroll department of a firm has a **well defined task** (eg paying salaries at the end of the month) with little variation. **Controls** are needed to ensure processing accuracy and to avoid fraud. A **mechanistic** system might be applied here. On the other hand, the '**creative** department' of an advertising agency, with a number of professional experts (copywriters, graphic designers, account executives), may be run on an **organic** basis.

6.14 Burns and Stalker recognised **that organic systems would only suit individuals with a high tolerance for ambiguity and the personal stresses involved in being part of such an organisation** – but the freedom of manoeuvre is considered worth this personal cost, for individuals who prize autonomy and flexibility.

Organic structures and innovation: the ambidextrous approach

6.15 A criticism levelled at organic organisations is that whilst they may be **good at creating ideas**, they might be **less good at exploiting** them. Decentralisation and loose structures encourage communication, but also perhaps make employees less likely to comply with a management instruction to exploit an innovation: in other words, there are problems of discipline at a basic level.

6.16 An organic structure might therefore be a drawback when certain types of things need to be done. For example, in warfare, a disciplined 'mechanistic' approach might be needed to fight certain kinds of battle: delays and indecision might be costly. (On the other hand, guerilla warfare might be conducted organically.)

6.17 To get round this problem some organisations employ what might be termed an **ambidextrous approach to organisation structure**. By this is meant that organisations employ the elements of both the organic *and* mechanistic structures in their operations.

(a) **Creative departments** may be developed, to deal with R&D and so forth, often as part of an organisation's support staff in the configuration, possibly to offer new ideas to the technostructure. Their precise location in the structural configuration will obviously depend on circumstances.

(b) Instead of creating a permanent arrangement, a mechanistic company might designate certain occasions for employees to behave as if they were in organic companies. Such occasions include brainstorming sessions and quality circles.

The dual core

6.18 In professional bureaucracies, the operating core is relatively unsupervised, and the professionals doing the work are, in an important sense, in charge of it. However, ensuring certain types of innovation is difficult. Innovation in **technical procedures**, such as experimental surgery, is perhaps best conducted within an **organic structure**, as the free flow of ideas is most important. Innovation might be 'bottom up' in this case.

6.19 However, not all innovation or change refers to technical procedures. Some organisations face the need for frequent administrative change, for example in response to environmental and legal change, whatever its purpose. For this a more 'top-down' **mechanistic approach** is needed to ensure innovations are actually achieved and implemented successfully.

Case example

An example of an administrative change in a professional bureaucracy is the UK's internal market for the National Health service. This is certainly administrative innovation, creating hospitals as autonomous units, and making (some) general practitioners responsible for their own budgets. Although, in theory, the changes were supposed to direct the resources of the NHS more efficiently, there is no doubt that the structure was imposed 'top-down' in a 'mechanistic way'

6.20 This is sometimes referred to as the **dual core approach** which recognises that administrative and technical changes are best effected by different organisation structures, a technical core and an administrative core.

The Shamrock Organisation

KEY TERM

Handy defines the **shamrock organisation** as a 'core of essential executives and workers supported by outside contractors and part-time help'. This structure permits the buying-in of services as needed, with consequent reductions in overhead costs.

6.21 The first leaf of the shamrock is the **professional core**. It consists of professionals, technicians and managers whose skills define the organisation's core competence. This core group defines what the company does and what business it is in. They are essential to the continuity and growth of the organisation. Their pay is tied to organisational performance and their relations will be more like those among the partners in a professional firm than those among superiors and subordinates in today's large corporation.

6.22 The next leaf is made up of **self-employed professionals or technicians** or smaller specialised organisations who are hired on contract, on a project-by-project basis. They are paid in fees for results rather than in salary for time. They frequently **telecommute**. No benefits are paid by the core organisation, and the worker carries the risk of insecurity.

6.23 The third leaf comprises the **contingent work force**, whose employment derives from the external demand for the organisation's products. There is no career track for these people and they perform routine jobs. They are usually temporary and part-time workers who will experience short periods of employment and long periods of unemployment. They are paid by the hour or day or week for the time they work.

6.24 A fourth leaf of the shamrock may exist, consisting of **consumers** who do the work of the organisation. Examples are shoppers who bag their own groceries and purchasers of assemble-it-yourself furniture.

6.25 **Outsourcing.** Many companies, without going as far as the shamrock model, have made significant use of **outsourcing** for a range of services. Outsourcing can be used for peripheral activities such as catering and, less commonly, for mission-critical ones such as IT services. Successful outsourcing depends on three things.

(a) The ability to specify with precision what is to be supplied

(b)   The ability to measure what is actually supplied and thus establish the degree of conformance with specification

(c)   The ability to make adjustments elsewhere if specification is not achieved.

The virtual organisation

6.26   The idea of a **virtual organisation** or **cybernetic corporation** has attracted considerable attention as the usefulness of IT for communication and control has been exploited. The essence of the virtual organisation is the electronic linking of spatially dispersed components.

6.27   While there is some disagreement among academics as to a precise definition of the virtual organisation, a consensus exists with regard to **geographical dispersion** and the centrality of **information technology** to the production process. Many also agree that the virtual organisation has a temporary character. Other characteristics are a flexible structure and a collaborative culture.

6.28   However, an organisation is not a virtual organisation merely because it uses IT extensively and has multiple locations. Many academics would exclude organisations that use communications extensively, but not in a way **critical to completing the production process**.

KEY TERM

A **virtual organisation** is a temporary or permanent collection of geographically dispersed individuals, groups, organisational units (which may or may not belong to the same organisation), or entire organisations that depend on electronic linking in order to complete the production process.

Chapter roundup

- Organisation structure is subject to many influences

- Each constituent part of the organisation exerts an influence on the organisation's configuration.

- The **strategic apex** exerts a pull to centralise, leading to the simple structure.

- The **technostructure** exerts a pull to standardise processes, leading to the machine bureaucracy.

- The **middle line** exerts a pull to balkanise leading to the divisional form.

- The **operating core** exerts a pull to standardise skills, and leads to a professional bureaucracy.

- The **support staff** exerts a pull to collaborate, leading to adhocracy.

- **Centralisation** offers control and standardisation; **decentralisation** utilises talent and local knowledge.

- An organisation's **formal hierarchy** can be arranged by territory, function, product, brand, customer/market, staff numbers and work patterns, and equipment specialisation.

- **Hybrid structures** contain elements of different kinds of departmentation.

- **Matrix structures** are formal mechanisms to ensure co-ordination across functional lines by the embodiment of dual authority in the organisation structure.

- **Mechanistic** or **bureaucratic** organisations are not ideally suited to conditions of change: their strict bureaucratic hierarchies and shallow decision making process do not encourage flexibility. **Organic** organisations are more flexible structures where roles are less well defined.

- The **shamrock organisation** consists of a core of essential executives and workers, supported by outside contractors and part-time help.

- The **virtual organisation** is geographically dispersed and uses information technology as a critical element of the production process.

Quick quiz

1   What are the characteristics of the simple structure?

2   Distinguish between machine bureaucracy and professional bureaucracy.

3   What component of the organisation leads a pull to divisionalisation?

4   What are the drawbacks to functional departmentation?

5   Why do many organisations adopt a hybrid structure?

6   What leads to the development of matrix structures?

7   Why are mechanistic systems unsuitable for conditions of change?

8   Describe the features of organic structures.

9   Why might a dual core approach be needed?

Answers to quick quiz

1   Centralisation, direct supervision, wide span of control, no technostructure

2   The machine bureaucracy works by rules and procedures laid down by the technostructure. It is most effective in a stable environment where tasks are simple and repetitive. The professional bureaucracy depends on the individual skills of the operating core rather than on a technostructure for its standards. It hires trained specialists who control their own work.

3   The middle line seeks to extend its authority.

4   It does not reflect the business processes by which value is created. This means that staff do not appreciate the way the organisation works. Also, it is difficult to identify where profits and losses are made, since traditional cost accounting bundles the costs of most functions together as overheads.

5   Different aspects of the organisation are often best-structured in different ways. For instance, sales may be best organised geographically or by product group, while purchasing and finance may be best centralised to achieve economies of scale.

6   Requirements for flexibility, improved communication, project accountability and interdepartmental co-operation.

7   They use cumbersome methods: problems are referred upwards; committees are formed; and new jobs and departments are overlaid on to the existing structure.

8   The structure is fluid and informal with extensive lateral interaction. Control is achieved through individual competence and co-ordination by mutual adjustment. There are few prescribed procedures.

9   The organic approach is appropriate when creativity and responsiveness to changing conditions are required. It depends on individual skill and community of interest. Where work is both routine and important and compliance with standards is required, a more mechanistic approach may be required. We might therefore see an organic structure in a marketing department and a more mechanistic structure in an accounts department.

Now try the question below from the Exam Question Bank

Number	Level	Marks	Time
Q9	Exam	20	36 mins

Chapter 10

PROJECT MANAGEMENT

Topic list	Syllabus reference
1 What is project management?	5(f)
2 Planning and resourcing techniques	5(f)
3 Project planning tools	5(f)
4 Management implications of project management techniques	5(f)
5 Research and development	5(c)
6 Innovation	5(c)

Introduction

Project management is a fairly well contained topic in the syllabus. The difference between project planning and other parts of planning is that a **project is not a repetitive activity**. That said, it encapsulates on a small scale many issues of planning and management, including the details of resource allocation.

This chapter also introduces strategic aspects of **innovation**, including research and development. You should be aware that innovation is widely regarded as an essential element of success. We have already discussed the nature of the **learning approach** to strategy; in this chapter we concentrate on some of the more practical aspects.

Study guide

Section 5 – The nature of strategy implementation

- Project management issues

- Research and development issues

Exam guide

While the subject matter of this chapter could be relevant to any question, we would expect it to appear as part of an optional question in Section B.

1   WHAT IS PROJECT MANAGEMENT?

> **KEY TERM**
>
> A **project** is 'an undertaking that has a beginning and an end and is carried out to meet established goals within cost, schedule and quality objectives' (Haynes, *Project Management*).

1.1 Characteristics of projects

- Specific start and end points
- Well-defined objectives
- Unique nature
- Cost and time constraints
- Cuts across organisational and functional boundaries

Unique features of project management

> **KEY TERM**
>
> **Project management** is directed at an end. It is not directed at maintaining or improving a continuous activity. It thus has a limited objective within a limited time span. According to Lock, 'the job of **project management** is to foresee as many dangers as possible, and to plan, organise and control activities so that they are avoided.'

1.2 Project management problems

Problem	Comment
Teambuilding	The work is carried out by a team of people usually assembled for one project, who must immediately be able to communicate effectively with each other.
Expected problems	**Expected** problems should be resolved by careful design and planning prior to commencement of work.
Unexpected problems	There should be mechanisms within the project to enable these problems to be resolved during the time span of the project without detriment to the objective, the cost or the time span.
Delayed benefit	**There is normally no benefit until the work is finished.** The 'lead in' time to this can cause a strain on the eventual recipient who is also faced with increasing expenditure for no immediate benefit.
Specialists	Contributions made by specialists are of differing importance at each stage.
Stakeholders	If the project involves several parties with different interests in the outcome, there might be disputes between them.

1.3 Many projects go wrong: this is usually manifested as a failure to complete on time, but this outcome can arise for a variety of reasons.

(a) **Unproven technology.** The use of new technological developments is likely to be a feature of any project. The range of such developments extends from fairly routine and non-critical improvements, through major innovations capable of transforming working practices, costs and time scales, to revolutionary techniques that make feasible projects that were previously quite impracticable. As the practical potential of a technical change moves from minor to major, so too moves its potential to cause disruption if something goes wrong with it. A classic example is *Rolls Royce's* attempt to use carbon fibre in the design of the RB211 engine in the early 1970s. Not only did the project fail to meet its objectives, its failure led to the company's financial failure, which necessitated its rescue by government.

(b) **Changing client specifications.** It is not unusual for clients' notions of what they want to evolve during the lifetime of the project. However, if the work is to come in on time and on budget, they must be aware of what is technically feasible, reasonable in their aspirations, prompt with their decisions and, ultimately, prepared to freeze the specification so that it can be delivered. The failure of the TSR2 aircraft project forty years ago was in large part caused by major, unrealistic changes to specification. Note that the term 'client' includes *internal* specifiers.

(c) **Politics.** This problem area includes politics of all kinds, from those internal to an organisation managing its own projects, to the effect of national (and even international) politics on major undertakings. Identification of a senior figure with a project; public interest and press hysteria; hidden agendas; national prestige; and political dogma can all have deleterious effects on project management. **Lack of senior management support** is an important political problem.

(d) **Poor project management.** This comes in several guises.

   (i) **Over optimism**. This can be particularly troublesome with new technology. Unrealistic deadlines may be accepted, for instance, or impossible levels of performance promised.

   (ii) **Over-promotion of technical staff**. It is common for people with a high level of technical skill to be promoted. Only then is it made clear that they lack management and leadership ability. This is a particular problem with IT projects.

   (iii) **Poor planning**. Realistic timescales must be established, use of shared resources must be planned and, most fundamental of all, jobs must be done in a sensible sequence.

   (iv) **Poor control**. Progress must be under continuous review and control action must be taken early if there are problems. The framework of control must provide for review at all levels of management and prompt reporting of problems.

The objectives of project management

1.4 The objectives, broadly speaking, of project management arise out of the deficiencies in para 1.3.

Objective	Comment
Quality	The end result should conform to the project specification. In other words, the result should achieve what the project was supposed to do.
Budget	The project should be completed without exceeding authorised expenditure.
Timescale	The progress of the project must follow the planned process, so that the result is ready for use at the agreed date. As time is money, proper time management can help contain costs.

The project life cycle

1.5 A typical project has a **project life cycle**.

- Conceiving and defining the project
- Planning the project

- Carrying out the plan (project implementation) and control
- Completing and evaluating the project

Conceiving and defining the project

1.6 A project often arises out of a perceived problem or opportunity. However, it is often not clear precisely what the problem is.

Step 1. **Analyse the problem.** The project team should study, discuss and analyse the project, from a number of different aspects (eg technical, financial).

Step 2. **Write the project definition**. There will be several stages, with each definition being more detailed and refined than before. The project might be defined in a:

- Contract
- Product specification
- Customer's specification

Step 3. **State the final objective of the project.** This clarifies what the project is trying to achieve (eg a sales system).

Step 4. **List the success criteria for a project**. These are the project's *basic* requirements and perhaps desirable enhancements. For the Channel Tunnel to be considered a success, the tunnel had to link the UK and France. If this was not done, the project would be a *total* failure.

Step 5. **Alternative strategies are identified** to find the best way to reach the project objective.

Step 6. **Evaluate alternatives** on the basis of technical and practical feasibility.

Step 7. **Assess the chosen strategy:** more detailed review and testing is carried out. A feasibility study examines the technical and financial aspects of the project, costing its critical assumptions and exposing possible flaws or unrealistic expectations.

Planning the project

1.7 A **project plan** aims to ensure that the project objective is achieved within the objectives of quality, cost and time. This involves three steps, once the basic project objective and the underlying activities have been agreed.

Step 1. **Break the project down into manageable units**. As a simple example, if your objective is to cook a dinner party for your friends, you will break down this task into preparing the starter, the main course, and then the dessert. If you were a stickler for planning, you could break these down further into detailed tasks (chop onions, peel potatoes). This is sometimes called establishing a **work breakdown structure**

Step 2. **For each unit, estimate the resources needed** (in materials, money and time).

Step 3. **Schedule and plan resource requirements and timings of each sub-unit. Gantt charts, network analysis** and so forth are ways by which this can be achieved. **Costing** is also part of the project planning stage.

Carrying out the plan: implementation and control

1.8 The project implementation stage is when the plans are put into action. Frequently a project is directed by a **project manager** (see below).

BPP
PROFESSIONAL EDUCATION

Step 1. **Review progress**

   (i)   **Control point, identification charts** indicate the sort of things that might go wrong, and the action taken to rectify them.

   (ii)   **Project control charts** use budget and schedule plans to give a status report on progress (eg cumulative time and cost) so that variances can be calculated.

Step 2. **Monitor performance**

• Inspection	• Quality testing
• Progress reviews (at regular stages)	• Financial audit

Step 3. **Take corrective action.** Falling behind schedule, because of some circumstance unforeseen at the planning stage, might require the rescheduling of the project or a change in resource configuration. If the project is over budget, cost savings can be found, or alternatively, more funds might be available from the client.

Completing and evaluating the project: post-audit

1.9   Finally, the project must be delivered to the customer, of course after final testing and review. Note that delivery might include subsidiary matters such as preparation of instruction manuals.

1.10   **Project evaluation** asks two questions.

   (a)   **Did the end result of the project meet the client's expectations?**

- The actual design and construction of the end product
- The timetable achieved: was the project achieved on time?
- The cost: was the project more or less within budget?

   (b)   Was the management of the project as successful as it might have been, or were there bottlenecks or problems?

- Problems that might occur on future projects with similar characteristics
- The performance of the team individually and as a group.

In other words, any project is an opportunity to learn how to manage future projects more effectively.

The role of the project manager

1.11   The project manager has to co-ordinate resources of time, money and staff.

Duty	Comment
Outline planning	Project planning (eg targets, sequencing)
	• Developing project targets such as overall costs or timescale needed (eg project should take 20 weeks).
	• Dividing the project into activities and placing these activities into the right sequence, often a complicated task if overlapping.
	• Developing a framework for the procedures and structures, manage the project (eg decide, in principle, to have weekly team meetings, performance reviews etc).

Duty	Comment
Detailed planning	**Work breakdown structure**, resource requirements, network analysis for scheduling.
Teambuilding	Brief superiors and team members.
Communication	The project manager must let superiors know what is going on, and ensure that members of the project team are properly briefed.
Co-ordinating project activities	Between the project team and users, and other external parties (eg suppliers of hardware and software).
Monitoring and control	The project manager should estimate the causes for each departure from the standard, and take corrective measures.
Problem-resolution	Even with the best planning, unforeseen problems may arise.
Quality control	There is often a short-sighted trade-off between getting the project out on time and the project's quality.

1.12 Section summary

- A project is not a continuous activity.
- Project objectives are quality, time and budget.
- Each project has a life cycle.
- Projects fail because of poor planning, poor management, political problems and vague or changing client specifications.
- Most projects are run by a project manager.

2 PLANNING AND RESOURCING TECHNIQUES

2.1 An accurate estimate of project costs provides a proper basis for management control.

(a) **Ball-park estimates** are made before a project starts. They might be accurate to within 25%.

(b) **Comparative estimates** accurate to within 15% are made if the project under consideration has some similarities with previous ones.

(c) **Feasibility estimates** (probably accurate to within 10%) arise from preliminary aspects of the design. Building companies use feasibility estimates.

(d) **Definitive estimates** (accurate to within 5%) are only made when *all* the design work has been done.

2.2 Any **estimate** must be accompanied by a proviso detailing its expected **accuracy**. It is unreasonable to expect exact accuracy, but the project manager should be able to keep within estimates, particularly for projects with no margin of safety and tight profits. Estimates can be improved in four ways.

- Learn from past mistakes.
- Ensure sufficient design information, is adequate.
- Ensure as detailed a specification as possible from the customer.
- Analyse the job into its constituent units properly.

Work breakdown structure (WBS)

> **KEY TERM**
>
> **Work breakdown structure** is the analysis of the work of a project into different units or tasks. It identifies the work that must be done, determines the resources required, sequences the work done, and allocates resources in the optimum way.

2.3 For example, building a house can be **sub-divided** into ground work, masonry, wiring, and roofing. Dealing with the foundations involves digging, filling, area marking and disposal of soil.

2.4 The process of work breakdown continues until the smallest possible sub-unit is reached. Digging the foundations for example would be analysed so that the number of labour hours needed, and hence the cost, could be determined. *Lock* recommends giving each sub-unit of work a code number to enable resources to be obtained and the work to be planned.

Question 1

Draw up a work breakdown structure for moving into a new house.

Cost estimation

2.5 **Use of WBS in devising estimates.**

(a) From the WBS it is possible to 'compile a complete **list of every item** that is going to attract expenditure.'

(b) **Checklists** can be used to ensure that all factors are be taken into account.

(c) **Estimation forms** can be designed to be based on the work breakdown structure, so that by each work unit number, there are columns for labour, materials and so forth.

2.6 **Costs** should be analysed.

(a) **Direct costs** of a project include labour, raw materials and sub-components.

(b) **Overhead costs** include heating, lighting and so forth, and can be fixed and/or variable. Overhead allocation can be difficult in some project environments, as a large element of the project costs might be fixed or sunk. (For example, a building company is unlikely to buy a brand new crane for every house it builds. An element of a crane's depreciation charge might be charged to a project.)

(c) **In-house costs** and **subcontracted** costs.

2.7 Collating the various costs identified with each unit of the work breakdown structure:

(a) Provides a useful cost analysis for various business functions.

(b) Assists cost control.

(c) Provides evidence, in any dispute with the client, that the costs are reasonable. (**Technical cost investigations** occur when the client sends technical cost officers to examine the books. The right to do so might be incorporated in the original contract.)

2.8 **Labour time estimates**

A project manager relies on the *personal* opinions of the individuals in each department.

(a) 'Estimates for any work will **more frequently be understated than overstated**'.

(i) Many people are **eager to please** the project manager.

(ii) People do **not** learn to estimate better. (In some companies, a rule of thumb is to add 50% on to the estimated time given by production or design staff.)

(b) On occasions when people's estimates are **over-pessimistic**, a cause might be a desire to **inflate departmental budgets**.

(c) Finally, some estimators are **inconsistent**. This is worst of all.

2.9 **Materials estimates**

(a) **Total materials cost**. Design engineers should prepare lists of materials required for each task. The purchasing department should indicate the costs.

(b) **Lead times for receipt**. Failure to receive materials on time can result in unexpected delay.

(c) **Estimating problems**

(i) **Contingencies**. Projects can be delayed because of design errors, production mistakes, material and component failures. An allowance is sometimes built in.

(ii) Additional work can be included in the contract price on a **provisional basis**.

(iii) **Increases in prices** will increase costs over the contract's life.

2.10 **Section summary**
- A project should be broken down into its constituent tasks (work breakdown structure).
- Cost, labour and materials estimates can be obtained, sometimes with difficulty, for each task.

3 PROJECT PLANNING TOOLS

3.1 The project manager thus needs to **schedule the activities** or tasks in the most efficient way given:

(a) The **dependency** of some activities on others. In other words, job B may need to be done before job C.

(b) **Constraints on resources**. Some resources will not be available at the ideal time or at the lowest price. For example, a computer project manager may have to compete with other project managers for the availability of skilled staff.

3.2 The project manager will have been given a broad time estimation for any activity based on three things.

- The **duration** of each sub-unit of work
- The **earliest time** work in a particular unit must be started
- The **latest time** it must be started

Gantt charts

3.3 A simple plan for a project is based on a **bar line chart** or **Gantt chart**.

(a) It can be used as a **progress control chart** with the lower section of each bar being completed as the activity is undertaken.

(b) A delay in a particular piece of work and its effect on other work can be shown in a **linked bar chart**. This shows the links between an activity and preceding activities which have to be completed before this particular activity can start.

(c) The requirement of each stage of the project for resources such as people and plant can also be shown on the Gantt chart. This can be done by entering numbers or by constructing a series of bar diagram along the bottom edge of the chart. This is similar to the resource histogram shown later in this section.

No.	DESCRIPTION OF WORK OR ACTIVITY	TIME (DAYS)													
		1	2	3	4	5	6	7	8	9	10	11	12	13	14
1	Excavate for foundations and services (drainage)														
2	Concrete foundations														
3	Build walls and soakaways for drainage														
4	Construct roof														
5	Fit garage doors														
6	Provide services (electric)														
7	Plaster														
8	Decorate														

- **Advantage:** easy to understand

- **Disadvantage:** limited when dealing with large complex projects in that they can only display a restricted amount of information and the links between activities are fairly crude.

3.4 To overcome these problems we use a more sophisticated technique known as network analysis.

Critical path analysis (CPA) or network analysis

3.5 CPA describes the **sequence** of activities, and how long they are going to take. These diagrams are drawn left to right.

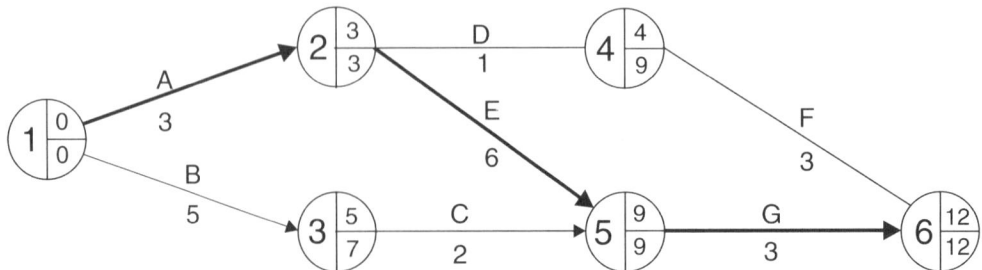

(a) **Events** (1 and 2) are represented by circles. **Activities** (eg A) connect events.

(b) The **critical path x**is represented by drawing double line or a thicker line between the activities on the path. It is the **minimum amount of time** that the project will take.

(c) It is the convention to note the earliest start date of any activity in the top right hand corner of the circle.

(d) We can then work backwards identifying the latest dates when activities have to start. These we insert in the bottom right quarter of the circle.

3.6 The **critical path** in paragraph 3.5 is AEG. Note the **float time** of five days for Activity F. Activity F can begin any time between days 4 and 9, thus giving the project manager a degree of flexibility.

Resource histograms

3.7 If all activities are started as soon as possible, the labour requirements can be shown on a bar chart. Bar charts such as these are sometimes called **resource histograms**.

No. of workers

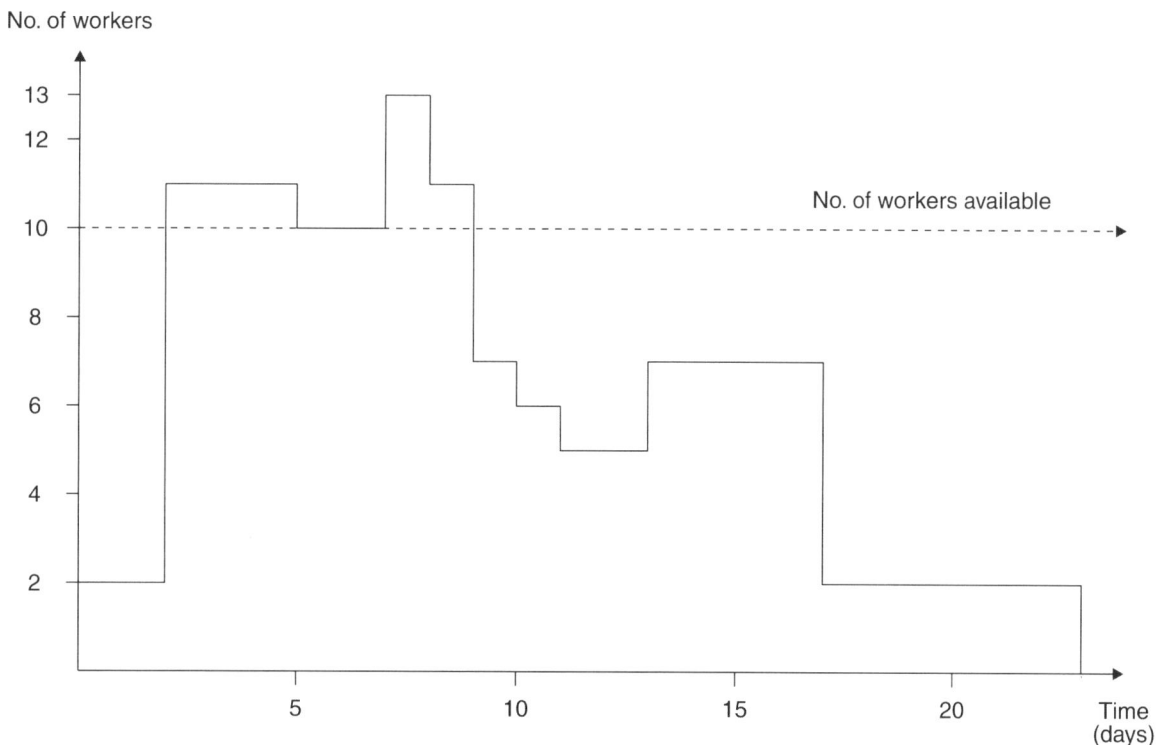

3.8 The number of workers required on the seventh day is 13. Can we re-schedule the non-critical activities to eliminate any excessive requirement? The various floats show whether we can move any activity. We might be able to re-arrange activities so that we can make use of the workers available from day 9 onwards.

Float times and costs

3.9 **Float time**, as we have seen, is slack time.

(a) Total float on a job is the time available (earliest start date to latest finish date) *less* time needed for the job. If, for example, job A's earliest start time was day 7 and its latest end time was day 17, and the job needed four days, total float would be:

$(17 - 7) - 4 = 6$ days

(b) **Free float** is the delay possible in an activity on the assumption that all preceding jobs start as early as possible and all subsequent jobs also start at the earliest time.

(c) **Independent float** is the delay possible if all preceding jobs have finished as late as was permissible, and all succeeding jobs start as early as possible.

3.10 Perhaps more important than cash flow consideration are the total expense and the expense involved in **crashing** a project.

(a) The **crash time** is the **minimum** time that an activity takes to be completed with **extra resources**.

(b) Crashing also has the affect of changing the critical path as extra resources can change the activity's duration.

3.11 It is possible therefore to draw up **two** sets of estimates identifying the cost, with or without crashing.

Criticisms of critical path/network analysis

3.12 (a) It is not always possible to devise an effective WBS for a project.

(b) **It assumes an essentially linear and sequential relationship** between activities: in other words it assumes that once Activity A is finished, Activity B proceeds, and that Activity B has no impact on Activity A. There may be complex and conditional relationships between what seem to be distinct and sequential activities, necessitating a much greater degree of analysis.

(c) There are inevitable **problems in estimation**. Where the project is completely new, the planning process may be conducted in conditions of relative ignorance.

(d) **Costs are based only on labour hours,** and all the problems relating to absorption of indirect overheads apply. Labour hours may only be a small proportion of the money involved in the project.

(e) Although network analysis plans the use of resources of labour and finance, it **does not appear to develop plans for contingencies, other than crashing time**.

(f) CPA **assumes a trade-off between time and cost** – but this does not really hold where a substantial portion of the cost is **indirect overheads** or where the direct labour proportion of the total cost of limited.

4 MANAGEMENT IMPLICATIONS OF PROJECT MANAGEMENT TECHNIQUES

4.1 Network analysis is a means of finding the best way to schedule activities, by highlighting the interrelationships between them. Central to the ideas are that work is broken down into units which can be analysed **independently** of each other.

Parallel engineering

4.2 Certain companies have taken this approach to product development. **Parallel engineering techniques** aim to speed the time taken to get a product to market. Once the overall idea of a design is agreed, individual development teams go ahead on **different aspects** of the project, in designing both the product and the production process and machinery.

Management by exception

4.3 Network planning facilitates management by exception, in which management attention is concentrated on items which deviate from plans. 'Critical operations usually make up about 20% of the project activities that can affect the overall progress'. Project management techniques enable management by exception by identifying, from the outset, those activities which might delay the others.

5 RESEARCH AND DEVELOPMENT

5.1 Here are some definitions culled from *Statement of Standard Accounting Practice 13.*

> **KEY TERMS**
>
> **Pure research** is original research to obtain new scientific or technical knowledge or understanding. There is no obvious commercial or practical end in view.
>
> **Applied research** is also original research work like (a) above, but it has a specific practical aim or application (eg research on improvements in the effectiveness of medicines etc).
>
> **Development** is the use of existing scientific and technical knowledge to produce new (or substantially improved) products or systems, prior to starting commercial production operations.

5.2 Many organisations employ **specialist staff** to conduct research and development (R&D). They may be organised in a separate functional department of their own. In an organisation run on a product division basis, R&D staff may be employed by each division.

Product and process research

5.3 There are two categories of R&D.

> **KEY TERMS**
>
> **Product research** is based on creating new products and developing existing ones, in other words the organisation's 'offer' to the market.
>
> **Process research** is based on improving the way in which those products or services are made or delivered, or the efficiency with which they are made or delivered.

Product research – new product development

5.4 The new product development process must be carefully controlled; new products are a major source of competitive advantage but can cost a great deal of money to bring to market. A screening process is necessary to ensure that resources are concentrated on projects with a high probability of success and not wasted on those that have poor prospects.

5.5 *Cooper* describes a typical modern screening process that he calls **Stage-Gate™**. This emphasises a cross-functional, prioritised, quality managed, project management approach consisting, typically, of five stages. Each stage begins with a **gate**; that is, a review meeting of managers who have the power either to kill the project or to allocate the resources necessary for it to progress to the next gate. Each gate incorporates the same three management elements.

(a) **Deliverables** are the results of the preceding stage's activity and are specified at its beginning.

(b) **Criteria** are applied by the decision makers to judge the progress of the project and decide whether or not to continue with it.

(c) **Outputs** are a **decision**, and such things as an **action plan**, a **budget** and a list of **deliverables** for the next gate.

5.6   A typical five stage process would look like this.

(a) The new idea is subjected to an initial screening to check such things as basic feasibility, strategic fit and marketability. Financial criteria are not usually applied at this stage. This is **Gate 1**.

(b) **Stage 1**. Preliminary investigation is likely to take less than a month and concentrates on preliminary assessment of market potential, technical implications and financial viability. Quick legal and risk assessments will also take place. This stage leads to **Gate 2**, which is similar to gate 1 in nature, but more rigorous. Gates 1 and 2 are probably operated by middle level managers since, in each case, the resources required to progress to the next stage are only moderate.

(c) **Stage 2**. It is now appropriate to **build a business case** for the project. The product is defined in detail and a full **marketing analysis** is carried out, featuring such processes as competitor analysis, user needs-and-wants studies, and value-in-use studies. There are also full **technical** and **manufacturing appraisals** and a detailed **financial analysis**. **Gate 3** assesses this business case and is probably operated by the company's senior management team, since approval at this stage will lead to heavy expenditure.

(d) **Stage 3**. The physical development of the product now proceeds, subject to a strict time schedule and budget of resources. Lengthy development phases may incorporate their own project management milestones to ensure control, but these are not formal gates in the Cooper sense. This stage leads to **Gate 4**, the **post development review**. The emphasis here is not on whether to proceed further but on ensuring that the project is on track and on reviewing the earlier work on feasibility using up to date information.

(e) **Stage 4**. This is the **testing and validation** stage and validates the entire commercial viability of the project. It may include **pilot production, field trials** and **test marketing. Gate 5** is **precommercialisation business analysis**. This gives top management the opportunity to check the work done in the testing and validation stage and apply final financial return and launch planning criteria.

(f) **Stage 5** is **full production** and **market launch**. Both must be carefully monitored and lead inexorably to the **post implementation review**, which considers the degree of success achieved by both the new product itself and the development process that led to its launch.

5.7   External to the **Stage-Gate™** management process are **idea generation** and **strategy formulation**.

(a) **Idea generation**, to be effective requires a system to promote, and reward creativity and innovative ideas. You will find lots of ideas elsewhere in this Study Text about how this can be done. Cooper suggests a four point plan.

(i)   Nominate one manager to be the **focal point for ideas**.

(ii) That manager establishes where ideas may **arise**.

(iii) Those sources are **encouraged**.

(iv) The ideas they produce are **captured**.

(b) **Strategy formulation**. A business should have a detailed new product strategy, specifying goals, priorities, funding and methods. This is a top management responsibility.

5.8 Cooper suggests that the basic process outlined above can be improved using features he calls the **six Fs**.

(a) **Flexibility** is incorporated by routing projects through an abbreviated process if they are small or low risk.

(b) **Fuzzy gates** have other conditions than open or closed: for example, a project may be given a **conditional approval** that depends on some future achievement, such as the receipt of a favourable legal report that is not yet available.

(c) **Fluidity** means that the stages are not sealed off from each other by the gates. For example, it may be permissible to order some long lead-time supplies needed for the next stage before the current one is complete. Assessment of **risk** is crucial here.

(d) **Focus** means considering portfolio management during the gate process, since resources saved by killing one project may then be redeployed to other, more promising ones.

(e) **Facilitation** of the whole process should be the full time responsibility of a manager who is charged with making the process (not the project) work.

(f) **Forever green**. The whole process can be used for other purposes than just new product development: it could, for instance be used on a proposal to extend premises.

5.9 Product research is not confined to dealing with new products. It has an important role in connection with **existing products**.

(a) **Value engineering** may be used to continue the development of existing products so that they use less costly components or processes without compromising the perceived value of the market offer.

(b) As products near the end of their **life cycle**, it may be possible to develop them for launch in a different market, or simply to extend their lives.

(c) Where products are being replaced by new versions it may be advantageous to ensure that the new products are **backwards compatible** with the installed base. This is an important consideration in software engineering, for example.

Process research

5.10 Process research involves attention to how the goods/services are produced. Process research has these aspects.

(a) **Processes** are crucial in service industries (eg fast food), where processes are part of the services sold.

(b) **Productivity**. Efficient processes save money and time.

(c) **Planning**. If you know how long certain stages in a project are likely to take, you can plan the most efficient sequence.

(d) **Quality management** for enhanced quality.

An important aspect of process research is that advances are much more difficult to imitate then are product developments. Competitors can purchase and **reverse engineer** new products. With good physical security in place, they will find it much more difficult to imitate new processes.

5.11 **The strategic role of R&D**. R&D should support the organisation's chosen strategy. To take a simple example, if a strategy of **differentiation** has been adopted, it would be inappropriate to expend effort on researching ways of minimising costs. If the company has a competence in R&D, this may form the basis for a strategy of product innovation. Conversely, where product lifecycles are short, as in consumer electronics, product development is fundamental to strategy.

5.12 **Problems with R&D**

(a) **Organisational.** Problems of authority relationships and integration arise with the management of R&D. The function will have to liase closely with marketing and with production, as well as with senior management responsible for corporate planning: its role is both strategic and technical.

(b) **Financial.** R&D is by nature not easily planned in advance, and financial performance targets are not easily set. Budgeting for long-term, complex development projects with uncertain returns can be a nightmare for management accountants.

(c) **Evaluation and control.** Pure research or even applied research may not have an obvious pay off in the short term. Evaluation could be based on successful application of new ideas, such as patents obtained and the commercial viability of new products.

(d) **Staff problems.** Research staff are usually highly qualified and profession-orientated, with consequences for the style of supervision and level of remuneration offered to them.

(e) **Cultural problems.** Encouraging innovation means trial and error, flexibility, tolerance of mistakes in the interests of experimentation, high incentives etc. If this is merely a subculture in an essentially bureaucratic organisation, it will not only be difficult to sustain, but will become a source of immense 'political' conflict. The R&D department may have an 'academic' or university atmosphere, as opposed to a commercial one.

5.13 **R&D should be closely co-ordinated with marketing.**

(a) Customer needs, as identified by marketers, should be a vital input to new product developments.

(b) The R&D department might identify possible changes to product specifications so that a variety of marketing mixes can be tried out and screened.

Case example

An example of the relationship of R&D to marketing was described in an article in the *Financial Times* (14 July 1992) about the firm Nestlé, which invests £46m a year in research (and approximately £190m on development). Nestlé had a central R&D function, but also regional development centres. The central R&D function was involved in basic research. 'Much of the lab's work was only tenuously connected with the company's business... When scientists joined the lab, they were told "Just work in this or that area. If you work hard enough, we're sure you'll find something"'. The results of this approach were:

(a) The research laboratory was largely cut off from development centres.
(b) Much research never found commercial application.

As part of Nestlé's wider reorganisation, which restructured the business into strategic business units (SBU's), formal links have been established between R&D and the SBUs. This means that research procedures have been changed so that a commercial time horizon is established for some projects.

6   INNOVATION

6.1   For many organisations, product innovation and being the **first mover** may be a major source of competitive advantage.

(a)   A reputation for innovation will attract **early adopters**, though it depends in part on promotional effort.

(b)   Customers may find they are locked in to innovative suppliers by unacceptable **costs of switching** to competitors.

(c)   The **learning** (or experience) **curve** effect may bring cost advantages .

(d)   The first mover may be able to **define the industry standard**.

(e)   A **price skimming** strategy can bring early profits that will be denied to later entrants.

(f)   Legal protection, such as patents, for intellectual property may bring important revenue advantages. This is particularly important in the pharmaceutical industry.

6.2   However, the first mover also has particular problems.

- Gaining regulatory approval where required
- Uncertain demand
- High levels of R&D costs
- Lower cost imitators
- Costs of introduction such as training sales staff and educating customers.

6.3   In particular, it is common for later entrants into a market to learn from the first mover's mistakes and achieve market dominance. A good example is the way Microsoft's Windows operating system has overtaken Apple's offering.

6.4   **Technology and the value chain**. *Porter* points out in 'Competitive Advantage' that 'every value activity uses some technology to combine purchased inputs and human resources to produce some output.' He goes on to discuss the varied role of **information technology** and emphasises the often-overlooked importance of **administrative** or **office technology**. The significance of this for strategy lies in the area of **core competences**. Just as **R&D** is as much concerned with processes as with products, so improvement in the linkages of the value chain will enhance competitive advantage.

6.5   **Intrapreneurship**. Intrapreneurship is entrepreneurship carried on within the organisation at a level below the strategic apex. The encouragement of intrapreneurship is an important way of promoting innovation. Such encouragement has many aspects.

(a)   Encouragement for individuals to achieve results in their own way without the need for constant supervision

(b)   A culture of risk-taking and tolerance of mistakes

(c)   A flexible approach to organisation that facilitates the formation of project teams

(d)   Willingness and ability to devote resources to trying out new ideas

(e)   Incentives and rewards policy that support intrapreneurial activity

Chapter roundup

- A **project** is an undertaking with a defined beginning and end, directed towards the achievement of a specified goal (eg building a house).

- **Project management** always involves dealing with the unexpected. Each project is in some respects new.

- The **objectives** of project management are to ensure that the end product conforms with customer specification and is produced on time and within budget.

- The **project life cycle** can be broken down into the stages of project definition, planning, implementation, completion and review.

- **Estimating** is always hazardous. Relatively small estimating errors can dent profits significantly.

- **Work breakdown structure** is the analysis of work into tasks. This can be used to estimate costs (by defining the resources needed for each task), and to schedule activities by determining which activities depend on which.

- **Project planning tools** include **network analysis**, **Gantt charts** and **resource histograms.**

- Research may be **pure, applied** or **development**. It may be intended to improve **products** or **processes**.

- R&D should support the organisation's strategy and be closely co-ordinated with marketing.

- **Innovation** can be a major source of competitive advantage but brings a burden of cost and uncertainty.

- **Intrapreneurship** is entrepreneurship carried on within the organisation at a level below the strategic apex.

Quick quiz

1   Define 'project'.

2   What are the distinctive problems of project management?

3   What are the objectives of project management?

4   What four different types of estimate can be given?

5   What is work breakdown structure?

6   What is technical cost investigation?

7   What is a Gantt Chart?

8   What is crashing?

9   What is the difference between pure and applied research?

10   What problems does innovation bring?

Answers to quick quiz

1   A project is 'an undertaking that has a beginning and an end and is carried out to meet established goals within cost, schedule and quality objectives' (Haynes, *Project Management*).

2   Teambuilding; expected problems; unexpected problems; delayed benefit; specialists; stakeholders.

3   Quality, budget, timescale.

4   Ball park; comparative; feasibility; definitive.

5   Analysis of a project into units or tasks to identify what must be done and in what sequence, and to identify the optimum allocation of resources.

6   Investigation of costs by the client's technical experts.

7   A horizontal bar chart relating tasks to time used for project control.

8   Crashing changes the critical path by devolving sufficient extra resources to finish the project in minimum time.

9   Pure research has no obvious commercial or practical end in view. Applied research does.

10   Regulatory approval; uncertain demand; R&D costs; lower cost imitators.

Now try the question below from the Exam Question Bank

Number	Level	Marks	Time
Q10	Exam	15	27 mins

Chapter 11

CHANGE

Topic list	Syllabus reference
1 What is change?	5(g)
2 Strategic change	5(g)
3 Change and the individual	5(g)
4 Models of the change process	5(g)
5 Force field analysis	5(g)
6 Overcoming resistance to change	5(g)
7 Managing conflict	5(g)
8 Changing corporate culture	5(g)

Introduction

Change is often an outcome of the strategic process, particularly when the environment is dynamic and market conditions are themselves changing. Unfortunately, the human reaction to proposals for change is often one of fear and opposition. Much effort has been expended on attempts to create models for the management of change and some of these are discussed in this chapter.

We also look specifically at cultural change. This is because cultural features like the **paradigm** and management style are frequently obstacles to necessary change in other aspects of the organisation's life and work.

Study guide

Section 5 – The nature of strategy implementation

- Management of change issues

Exam guide

Change is likely to feature regularly in the exam, both as an aspect of compulsory question scenarios and as a major topic in Section B questions.

1   WHAT IS CHANGE?

1.1   Change, in the context of organisation and management, can occur in many areas.

- The environment
- The products the organisation makes or the services it provides
- How products are made, or who makes them
- Management and working relationships
- Organisation structure or size

1.2 Some change is **transformational,** that is, extensive and crucial to the organisation.

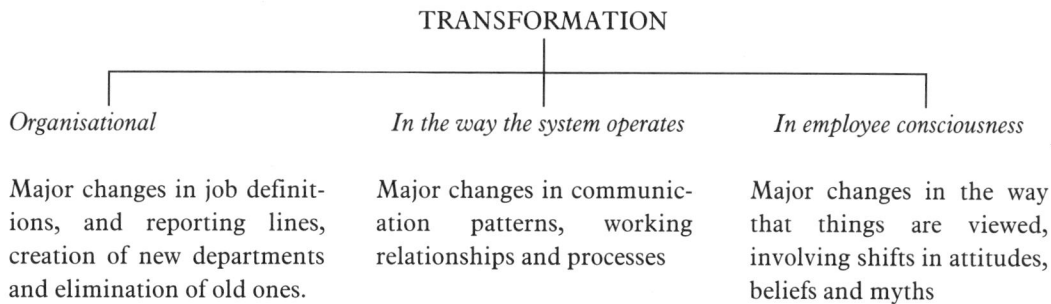

TRANSFORMATION

Organisational	*In the way the system operates*	*In employee consciousness*
Major changes in job definitions, and reporting lines, creation of new departments and elimination of old ones.	Major changes in communication patterns, working relationships and processes	Major changes in the way that things are viewed, involving shifts in attitudes, beliefs and myths

However, much change is incremental: there is steady development that may, over time, lead to the compete redesign of significant aspects of the organisation.

Case example

William Grant and Sons

People Management (September 1996) described how whisky distiller William Grant and Sons called on Jack Black, a 'business preacher,' to help a workforce struggling to come to terms with a major **change programme**.

Whisky producers like to emphasise **tradition** in their advertising: the centuries old recipes, the oak casks, the rural landscape around the distillery, the company's colourful founding fathers and their forelock-tugging workers.

William Grant and Sons, the Scottish distiller, in the last three years has put itself through a major programme of change. Until then, the image of tradition would have been nearer the truth. As David Nisbet, HR director at William Grants, puts it: 'We were benignly autocratic and paternalistic. Now we are team-based and non-hierarchical, but getting from one to the other proved difficult.'

The journey started with a **physical move** by the bottling plant and administrative headquarters from Paisley, west Glasgow, to Motherwell, east of the city. At the same time, the company **derecognised most of its unions**, retaining a purely representational agreement with one union at each site. Meanwhile, the whole workforce was being organised into **teams** of between three and 30 people each.

In short, it was the **big bang** approach to the management of change. For the restrained, Calvinist culture that predominated among the workforce, it was a little too much to absorb. To many people, quality circles were infra dig. Nisbet recalls: 'It was like pulling teeth. They sat round in these meetings and nothing happened. They weren't contributing.' What was needed was a massive injection of enthusiasm, an overnight **culture change**. It came from a Scottish consultant who has been making a name for himself over recent years as a kind of business preacher, a saver of commercial souls and the slayer of cynicism. Jack Black has been described as a cross between Billy Connolly and Billy Graham. It may seem strange that his 'mental fitness programme' could have enthused a workforce in a part of the world where the statement 'it's quite nice' is the ultimate accolade.

Black's programme, Mindstore, synthesises the ideas of many others - including Tony Buzan's mind-mapping techniques, neurolinguistic programming and the theories of Napoleon Hill, one of the first people to analyse leadership qualities - and delivers then in a humorous, chalk-and-talk style, interspersed with paper exercises which each participant does on their lap.

Since Mindstore, according to Nisbet, everyone in the organisation has been looking at their objective-setting. Each team has set three 'Smart goals' and is now moving to what they call 'Winner's goals'.

Initially, the **managers** took the course: then about a third of employees, from all levels, chose to go on it. But a drawback soon became apparent: 'some people still didn't have a positive **attitude to change** and didn't want to go on the course. They were finding it very difficult when their colleagues were coming back from it all fired up, positive and full of enthusiasm. They felt it put more pressure on them, and they were becoming more stressed and fearful.'

This manifested itself as absenteeism and an increase in visit to the occupational health department. The HR director made the decision to make it compulsory to attend Mindstore, despite the fact that the 'only way to really get it into the company culture is to make it mandatory.'

'You tend to find that when a company gives the workforce 'stretching' goals, they usually do that in an environment of fear, so people don't buy it. But if you train the people concerned to understand all this, which is what we do, they will set bigger goals than management would ever come up with.'

2 STRATEGIC CHANGE

2.1 Strategy can be seen as a process of adapting the organisation to its environment. This implies that any strategy is likely to require change to take place in the organisation. Further, the necessary rate of change is likely to be determined by the rate of change occurring in the environment. This is not, however, a full picture. While change itself may be divided into two types, **incremental** and **transformational**, so too may the management approach to change be divided into **reactive** and **proactive**. *Johnson and Scholes* suggest the model of change shown below.

Nature of change

		Incremental	Transformational
Management role	Proactive	Tuning	Planned
	Reactive	Adaptation	Forced

The importance of the **proactive management** role is that it implies that organisational change may be undertaken *before* it is imposed by events. It may, in fact, result from the process of forecasting and be response to *expected developments*. The organisation that does not take a proactive stance in the matter of change is likely to find itself in the **forced** quadrant of the diagram. **Forced change** is likely to be both painful and fraught with risk.

2.2 The need for change can affect any aspect of the organisation. The creation of new products and services is an obvious area for change, as is the development of the processes by which they are created and delivered. However, change can also become necessary in the **supporting activities** and **linkages** of the **value chain**, since **core competences** can be developed in these areas.

2.3 Inevitably, it is in these more amorphous areas, where human behaviour is of vital importance, that the management of change becomes most important and most difficult. **Cultural change** has been a preoccupation of senior managers for some time, reflecting the need to deliver significant improvements in quality, efficiency and service. We consider this further in Section 8 of this chapter.

Drivers of strategic change

2.4 **External developments**, whether or not forecast, are the most usual drivers of change. These can be analysed using the PEST approach.

(a) **Regulatory changes** must be complied with, but a proactive approach, including lobbying, may steer the change in a business friendly direction.

(b) Routine economic developments are unlikely to lead to transformational change, but the possibility of sudden **economic shock,** such as occurred in SE Asia in 1998, may do so.

(c) An interesting **social** development is the increasing number of women who wish to combine work with child-rearing. This has led to major changes in the labour market, including the expansion of job-sharing and part-time work

(d) **Technological** developments can lead to new products and processes, possibly making existing ones obsolete.

2.5 Change may also be driven by factors internal to the organisation including internal technical, administrative, financial and social developments.

3 CHANGE AND THE INDIVIDUAL

3.1 Effect of change on individuals

(a) There may be **physiological changes** in a person's life, both as the natural product of ageing, and as the result of external factors (a change in the pattern of shift-working).

(b) **Circumstantial changes** - living in a new house, establishing new relationships, working to new routines - will involve letting go of things, and learning new ways of doing things.

(c) Change affects individuals **psychologically.**

(i) **Disorientation** before new circumstances have been assimilated. A new set of models may have to be confronted, if the change involves a new roles set, new milieu, new relationships.

(ii) **Uncertainty** may lead to **insecurity**, especially acute in changes involving work (staying in employment) and/or fast acclimatisation (a short learning curve may lead to feelings of incapacity).

(iii) New expectations, challenges and pressures may generate **role stress** in which an individual feels discomfort in the role he or she plays.

(iv) **Powerlessness.** Change can be particularly threatening if it is perceived as an outside force or agent against which the individual is powerless.

Resistance to change at work

3.2 Resisting change means attempting to preserve the existing state of affairs against pressure to alter it. Despite the possibly traumatic effects of change most people do *not* in fact resist it on these grounds alone. Many people long for change, and have a wealth of ideas about how it should be achieved.

3.3 Sources of resistance to change

(a) **Attitudes or beliefs**, perhaps arising from cultural, religious or class influences (for example resistance to changes in the law on Sunday trading)

(b) **Loyalty to a group and its norms**, perhaps with an accompanying rejection of other groups or 'outsiders'

(c) **Habit or past norms**

(d) **Politics** - in the sense of resisting changes that might weaken the power base of the individual or group or strengthen a rival's position. Changes involving increased delegation may be strongly resisted by senior management, for example

(e) **The way in which any change** is put forward and implemented

(f) **Personality**

3.4 **Immediate causes of resistance in any particular situation**

(a) **Self-interest:** if the status quo is perceived to be preferable

(b) **Misunderstanding and distrust:** if the reasons for, or the nature and consequences of the change have not been made clear

(c) **Contradictory assessments:** disagreement over the likely costs and benefits of the change

(d) **Low tolerance of change itself:** differences in tolerance of ambiguity, uncertainty and challenge to self-concept

3.5 **Reactions to proposed change**

(a) **Acceptance** whether enthusiastic espousal, co-operation, grudging co-operation or resignation

(b) **Indifference:** usually where the change does not directly affect the individual evidence is apathy, lack of interest, inaction

(c) **Passive resistance:** refusal to learn, working to rule; pleas of ignorance or defensiveness; procrastination

(d) **Active resistance:** deliberate 'spoiling', go-slows, deliberate errors, sabotage, absenteeism or strikes

---

Case example

Whether caused by mergers and acquisitions or the market, change has been at the top of management consciousness in the public and private sectors for a decade. Yet it remains the case that many change programmes will be either a disaster or an expensive joke. A disaster because so often they destroy value, cause share prices to tumble, force talent to walk out of the door, spark destructive rumours in the press and wreck carefully constructed networks. A joke because so often nothing fundamental changes as executives mouth platitudes and make big announcements while everyone else lets them have their fun and carries on exactly as before.

Indeed, in many offices, resistance becomes one of the satisfactions of work. It is common enough to blame 'human forces' for the failure of these initiatives. People do not do what they should, they do not show enthusiasm in the right measure at the right time, they do not buy in. But Jeanie Daniel Duck, who as senior vice-president of The Boston Consulting Group carries a certain battle-bloodied authority about her subject, has taken the understanding of the dynamics of those forces several stages on while serving up a timely, well-judged argument that few executives will care for.

First, change is essentially an emotional proposition. Second, it is very difficult. Third, it involves personal change. Oh, and there's nothing touchy-feely about it, either. There is a kind of silent consensus in business that if anyone disagrees with a management strategy, they are negative, hostile freeloaders who would quarrel with the sun for shinning on them. Ms Duck is withering about such attitudes. Any business leader who seeks to blame failure on people deserves to fail. Managers can have all the commercial logic and strategic vision in the world but if they cannot get employees to understand what they are doing and why, and voluntarily elicit their excitement, forget it.

Stephen Overell, Financial Times, 2 May 2001

Technological change and the working environment

3.6 The consequences of **technological changes** are particularly felt in the world of work.

(a) Unskilled and **semi-skilled jobs** will be automated.

(b) **Degrading of old skills**. New skills will be needed, and there will be more pressure on managers to provide training or re-training for staff.

(c) As equipment becomes simpler to use, there could be opportunities for **greater flexibility** in manning, with one worker able to carry out more varied tasks.

(d) Since more jobs will be **part-time**, there will be less need for full-time employees.

(e) Better communications systems, portable computers etc reduce the need for people to work together in an office. There will be more **working at home.**

(f) Working at home is likely to speed up the progression towards 'sub-contracting', and some managers might become self-employed **consultants**.

(g) Improved information systems should help managers to **plan and control** work more effectively.

(h) Better information systems open up opportunities for more **centralisation** of decision making by top management and a **reduced need** for **middle managers**.

3.7 **Areas of concern**

Issue	Comment
Job security	The threat of being out of work would unsettle the entire office staff.
Status loss	A new system might result in a loss of status for the individual or department concerned.
Promotions	A new system might damage **career prospects** by reducing the opportunities for promotion.
Social change in the office	Individuals who are used to working together might be separated into different groups, and individuals used to working on their own might be expected to join a group.
Bewilderment	It is easy for individuals to be confused and bewildered by change.
Fear of depersonalisation	Staff may resent losing the ability to introduce the 'human touch' to the work they do.

Case example

E-mail

Reports in the papers suggest that e-mail enhances informal communications, so much so that use of e-mail for items not directly related to work is a matter for disciplinary procedures.

Other reports are that e-mail is used to *avoid* personal communications - people have been bullied and even dismissed by e-mail.

3.8 Section summary

People resist change
• Psychological reasons
• Worries about job security and uncertainty.

Often, however, people welcome change.

4   MODELS OF THE CHANGE PROCESS   12/03

4.1   A systematic approach should be established, for planning and implementing changes.

Step	
1	Determine need or desire for change in a particular area.
2	Prepare a tentative plan. • Brainstorming sessions a good idea, since alternatives for change should be considered (Lippitt 1981)
3	Analyse probable reactions to the change
4	Make a final decision from the choice of alternative options • Decision taken either by group problem-solving (participative) or by manager on his own (coercive)
5	Establish a timetable for change • 'Coerced' changes can probably be implemented faster, without time for discussions. • Speed of implementation that is achievable will depend on the likely reactions of the people affected (all in favour, half in favour, all against etc). • Identify those in favour of the change, and perhaps set up a pilot programme involving them. Talk with the others who resist the change.
6	Communicate the plan for change • This is really a continuous process, beginning at Step 1 and going through to Step 7.
7	Implement the change. Review the change. • Continuous evaluation and modifications

The change process

4.2   In the words of John Hunt (*Managing People at Work*): 'Learning also involves re-learning - not merely learning something new but trying to unlearn what is already known.' This is, in a nutshell, the thinking behind Lewin/Schein's three stage approach to changing human behaviour, which may be depicted as follows.

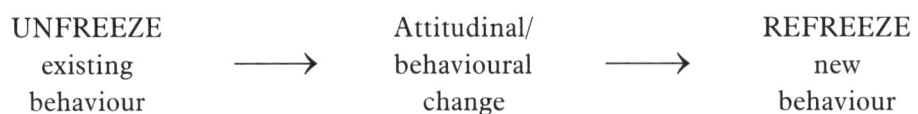

UNFREEZE		Attitudinal/		REFREEZE
existing	$\longrightarrow$	behavioural	$\longrightarrow$	new
behaviour		change		behaviour

Step 1.   **Unfreeze** is the most difficult stage of the process, concerned mainly with 'selling' the change, with giving individuals or groups a **motive** for changing their attitudes, values, behaviour, systems or structures.

(a)   If the need for change is immediate, clear and necessary for the survival of the individual or group, the unfreeze stage will be greatly accelerated.

(b)   Routine changes may be harder to sell if they are perceived to be unimportant and not survival-based.

(c)   Unfreezing processes need four things

• A trigger (eg a crisis).

• Someone to challenge and expose the existing behaviour pattern, by providing data about its negative effects.

• The involvement of outsiders.

• Alterations to power structure.

Step 2. **Change** is mainly concerned with identifying what the new, desirable behaviour should be, communicating it and encouraging individuals and groups to adopt it. The new ideas must be shown to work.

Step 3. **Refreeze** is the final stage, implying consolidation or reinforcement of the new behaviour. Positive reinforcement (praise, reward) or negative reinforcement (sanctions applied to those who deviate from the new behaviour) may be used. HRM practice is particularly important here.

Case example

Pascale, Milleman and Groga described change at *Shell Malaysia*. Its new chairman, who arrived in 1992, found an overstaffed organisation, facing declining revenues and increased competition, and offering poorer standards. The functional departments quarrelled a great deal but the culture did not encourage outright confrontation. Their way of dealing with impasses was 'smooth and avoid'.

'For more than a year, Knight (the new chief executive) tried to achieve authentic alignment among his eight-person executive team. Somehow the goal always eluded his grasp. In exasperation, he scheduled an event to which all 260 of Shell's mid-level and senior mangers were invited. At this unusual gathering:

(a) Knight proposed two new strategic changes.

(b) Managers were asked to deal with the issues in groups and come up with a response.

(c) Most lower level managers agreed with the plans, despite the fact they realised that their operating practices would have to change.

(d) This isolated the 'obstructionist' senior managers, one of whom was fired – 'a firing heard round the world'.

Systems intervention strategy

4.3 **Systems intervention strategy** (SIS) is a technique for bringing about change. It is a logical approach, not unlike the rational model of strategy. Like that model, it should be seen as **iterative** in nature: the complexity of human behaviour makes it necessary to revise and amend constantly.

4.4 SIS consists of three basic stages.
- Diagnosis
- Design
- Implementation

4.5 **Diagnosis.** There are three main processes in the diagnosis stage.
- Analysis and description of the current situation
- Definition of objectives and constraints
- Formulation of measures to control progress

4.6 **Design.** In the design stage possible ways of achieving the desired results are examined in detail. Consideration is given to likelihood of success and the implications of each option for all parts of the organisation are considered.

4.7 **Implementation.** In the implementation stage the progress of the chosen option is managed and monitored against the specified control measures.

Champion of change model: the role of the change agent

4.8 The **champion of change model** recognises the importance of change being led by a **change agent**, who may be an individual or occasionally a group.

Step 1. **Senior management** are the **change strategists** and decide in broad terms what is to be done. There is a need for **powerful advocacy** for change at the strategic apex. This will only occur if senior management are themselves agreed on the need for change. This is a role requiring a clear **vision** of what the change is to achieve.

Step 2. They appoint a **change agent** to drive it through. Senior management has three roles.

- Supporting the change agent, if the change provokes conflict between the agent and interest groups in the organisation

- Reviewing and monitoring the progress of the change

- Endorsing and approving the changes, and ensuring that they are publicised

Step 3. The change agent has to **win the support of functional and operational managers,** who have to introduce and enforce the changes in their own departments. The champion of change has to provide advice and information, as well as evidence that the old ways are no longer acceptable.

Step 4. The change agent **galvanises managers into action** and gives them any necessary support. The managers ensure that the changes are implemented operationally, in the field. Where changes involve, say, a new approach to customer care, it is the workers who are responsible for ensuring the effectiveness of the change process.

4.9 It is important to realise that successful change is not something exclusively imposed from above. There is a sense in which middle and junior managers are **change recipients** in that they are required to implement new approaches and methods. However, they are themselves also **change agents** within their own spheres of responsibility. They must be committed parts of the change process if it is to succeed.

4.10 New information systems developments often need management support and a management sponsor.

The Gemini 4Rs framework for planned strategic change

4.11 Management consultants *Gouillart and Kelly* describe a four-dimensional process for business transformation in their book 'Transforming the Organisation'. This approach aims to cover all the important components of the organisation's identity. Each of the four dimensions of the process has three components.

4.12 **Reframing** involves fundamental questions about what the organisation is and what it is for.

(a) **Achieve mobilisation**: create the will and desire to change.
(b) **Create the vision** of where the organisation is going.
(c) **Build a measurement system** that will set targets and measure progress.

4.13 **Restructuring** is about the organisation's structure, but is also likely to involve cultural changes.

(a) **Construct an economic model** to show in detail how value is created and where resources should be deployed.

(b) **Align the physical infrastructure** with the overall plan.

(c) **Redesign the work architecture** so that processes interact to create value.

4.14 **Revitalising** is the process of securing a good fit with the environment.

(a) Achieve market focus.
(b) Invent new businesses.
(c) Change the rules of competition by exploiting technology.

4.15 **Renewal** ensures that the people in the organisation support the change process and acquire the necessary skills to contribute to it.

(a) **Create a reward system** in order to motivate.
(b) **Build individual learning**.

(c) **Develop the organisation** and its adaptive capability.

4.16 Section summary

- Most changes require that the old ways are consciously abandoned (unfreeze - change - refreeze).

- Systems intervention strategy is a rational approach to change.

- Gemini 4Rs begins with fundamental questions.

- Some changes require the active support of a change agent, as inertia is common.

5 FORCE FIELD ANALYSIS

5.1 Current organisational practices and interest groups can embody a powerful inertia holding up the change process.

5.2 *Kurt Lewin* developed a simple technique of visualising the change process called **force field analysis**. In any group or organisational situation there is an interplay of driving and restraining forces. The balance between them keeps things as they are. The example below describes a public sector organisation whose management are introducing a performance review system.

Driving forces (for change)	Current state	Restraining forces (resistance)	Ideal position

A requirement of new legislation

Cynicism about change `another fad'

Existing systems are sufficient

Professional commitment to controlling the organisation

Trade Union concern over effects on jobs and working conditions

Requirement to report to external agencies

Complexity of producing such reviews

A concern for quality

Cost of carrying out reviews

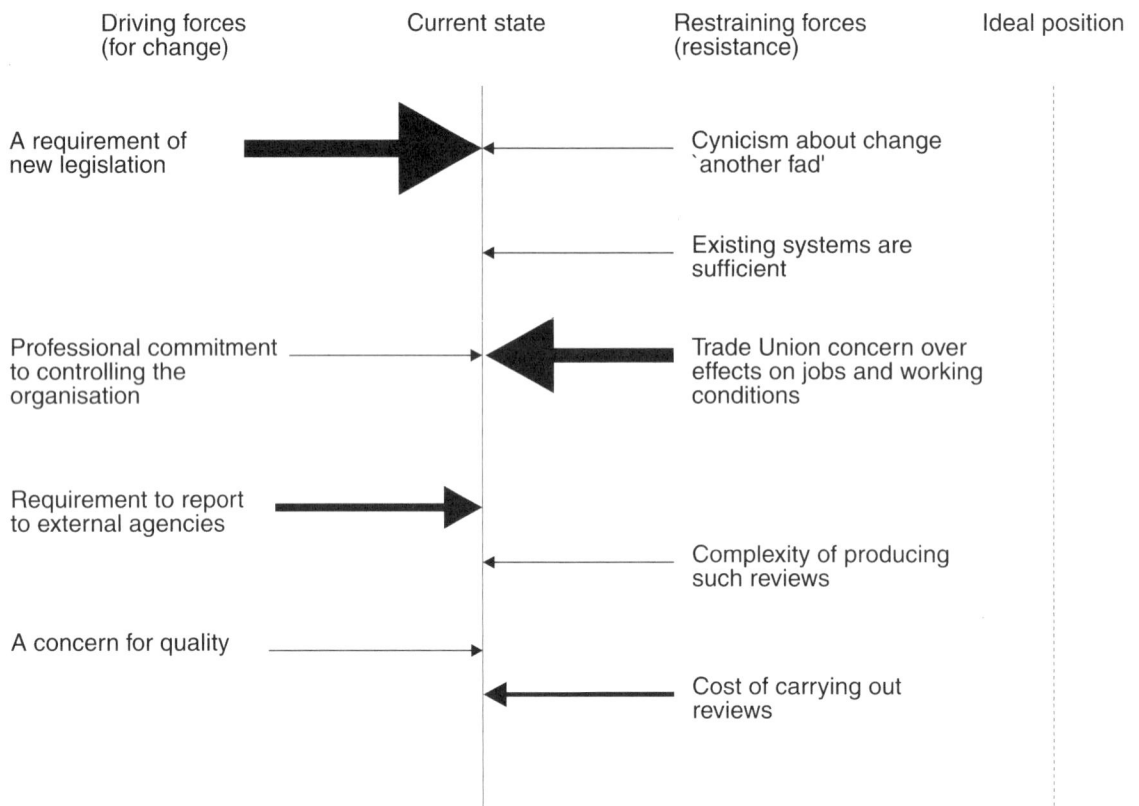

5.3 Forces can be impersonal (eg a new law, new technology), personal (the commitment of a new leader), institutional (trade union), or environmental (competitors). Lines of varying thickness to represent the probable strength of different forces.

5.4 *Senior* (drawing on the advice of *Carnall* and *Huczyuski and Buchanan*) suggests a practical route to applying the force field analysis idea.

(a) Define the problem in terms of the current situation and the desired future state.

(b) List the forces supporting and opposing the desired change and assess both the strength and the importance of each one.

(c) Draw the force field diagram.

(d) Decide how to strengthen or weaken the more important forces as appropriate and agree with those concerned. Weakening might be achieved by persuasion, participation, coercion or bargaining, while strengthening might be achieved by a marketing or education campaign, including the use of personal advocacy.

(e) Identify the resources needed.

(f) Make an action plan including event timing, milestones and responsibilities.

6 OVERCOMING RESISTANCE TO CHANGE

6.1 When dealing with resistance to change, managers should consider three aspects of the change.

- Pace
- Manner
- Scope

Pace of change

6.2 The more gradual the change, the **more time** is available for questions to be asked, reassurances to be given and retraining (where necessary) embarked upon.

6.3 Presenting the individual concerned with a **fait accompli** ('Let's get it over with - they'll just have to get used to it!') may short-circuit resistance at the planning and immediate implementation stages. It may cause problems later.

The manner of change

6.4 The **manner** in which a change is put across is very important.

(a) **Confront resistance.** Talking through areas of conflict may lead to useful insights and the adapting of the programme of change to advantage.

(b) **Keep people informed.** Information should be sensible, clear, consistent and realistic: there is no point issuing information which will be seen as a blatant misrepresentation of the situation.

(c) **Explanation.** The change can be sold to the people: people can be convinced that their attitudes and behaviours need changing.

(d) **Skills training.** Learning programmes for any new skills or systems necessary will have to be designed according to the abilities, previous learning experience etc of the individuals concerned.

(e) **Empathy.** Getting to know the people involved in and affected by changes enables their reactions to be anticipated.

(f) The degree to which **consultation or participation** will be possible (or genuine) will depend on management's attitude towards the competence and trustworthiness of its workforce.

When to start participation	*How participation is achieved in practice*
(a) From the beginning, discuss ideas. Gradually, acceptable ideas will emerge.	The desire of the manager for participation must be genuine. It won't work if participation is something the top orders the middle to do from the bottom'. (*Kanter* 1983)
(b) Make tentative plans for change, and then start to discuss them with subordinates.	1. Ask for input of ideas.
(c) Decide to make a change and then try to sell the idea to subordinates.	2. Seriously consider input and evaluate it objectively.
	3. Use good ideas.
Approaches (a) or (b) are preferred for real participation.	4. Reject bad ideas.
	5. Give credit/rewards to providers of good ideas.
	6. Convince the providers of bad ideas that their ideas were bad.

Coercion

6.5 Explicit or implicit **coercion**, that is, **autocratic** or **unilateral** imposition of change can be effective in some cases.

(a) Behavioural change or **compliance** is all that is required, and where resistance in attitudes can have no significantly detrimental effect on performance.

(b) The **balance of power** is heavily weighted in favour of the change agent.

(c) The **prevailing culture** is one of acceptance of dictatorial change, and there is little expectation of anything else.

Scope of change

6.6 The **scope of change** should also be carefully reviewed.

(a) **Total transformation** will create greater insecurity - but also greater excitement, if the organisation has the kind of innovative culture that can stand it - than moderate innovation.

(b) There may be **hidden changes** to take into account: a change in technology may necessitate changes in work methods, which may in turn result in the breaking up of work groups.

(c) Management should be aware of **how many different aspects** of their employees' lives they are proposing to alter - and therefore on how many fronts they are likely to encounter resistance.

Case example

The famous research by *Coch and French* into resistance to change in a pyjama factory provides evidence in favour of consultation. The company faced resistance to frequent changes to jobs and work methods necessitated by the product and production method development. This resistance showed in pay complaints, absenteeism and leaving, low efficiency (despite financial incentives), restriction of output and hostility to management. The main problem was that changes and transfers led to loss of status and earnings, through reduced efficiency ratings.

Coch and French designed an experiment in which changes were introduced in three production groups with different levels of participation.

(a) The *non-participative group* was informed about the change but not involved in the decision-making. Resistance was immediate; conflict flared, efficiency remained low, and some members left.

(b) The *representative group* was given a hand in the change to the extent that after a preliminary meeting of explanation, representatives were given appropriate training and subsequently trained fellow members. The group was co-operative and submissive and efficiency rose rapidly.

(c) The *total participation group* also had a preliminary meeting, but all members then took part in the design and standard-setting for the new job. The group recovered its efficiency rating very rapidly, and to a level much higher than before the change, without conflict or resignations.

(d) The *non-participative members* were later re-grouped and followed the total participation procedure - with the beneficial results of the latter. Coch and French concluded that it was not the people or personality factors that mattered, but the *way in which change was implemented*.

Acceptance

6.7 It takes time for changes to get accepted, in other words the 'Refreeze' steps. *Conner and Patterson* identified three phases and eight stages in the process of accepting change by the people affected.

Phase 1: Preparation phase

| Stage 1 | Contact | First knowledge that a change is imminent |
| Stage 2 | Awareness | Knowledge that change will happen |

Phase 2: Acceptance phase

| Stage 3 | Understanding | Gaining an understanding of the nature and purpose of the change |
| Stage 4 | Positive perception | Developing a positive view towards the change, and accepting the need for it |

Phase 3: Commitment phase

Stage 5	Installation	The change becomes operational
Stage 6	Adoption	The change has been in force for long enough and its value has become apparent
Stage 7	Institutionalisation	The change has been in for long enough to become routine and the norm
Stage 8	Internalisation	Individuals are highly committed to the change because it is now congruent with their personal interests, goals and value systems.

6.8 *Conner and Patterson* argued that **commitment** to change is necessary for its successful implementation.

(a) Getting commitment is **expensive,** and calls for an investment of time, effort and money, for instance providing information, involving subordinates in the planning and implementation process, rewarding them for their participation and so on.

(b) Strategies for commitment ought to be developed. For any change, management needs to decide how far through the eight stages the acceptance process needs to go. Some changes can stop at Stage 5; other must go to Stage 7 or Stage 8, otherwise the benefits of the change will be lost.

6.9 *Peter Honey* (quoted by *Robinson* in *Managing after the Superlatives*) suggests that each of the sources of resistance to change identified below can be dealt with in a different way.

Cause	How to deal with it
Parochial self-interest	**Negotiation** (eg offer incentives to those resisting on grounds of self-interest).
Misunderstanding	This is best dealt with by **educating and reassuring** people. Trust has to be earned.
Different viewpoints of the situation	Change can be promoted through participation and by **involving potential resisters**.
Low tolerance of change	Force the change through and then **support** the new behaviours it requires. In short, people have to be encouraged (by carrot and stick methods) to adopt the new methods.

6.10 Section summary
- The scope, manner and pace of change can cause problems.
- Participation can be valuable in winning over support, but coercion can be necessary and effective too.
- User involvement is needed in information systems projects.

BPP
PROFESSIONAL EDUCATION

7   MANAGING CONFLICT

Causes, symptoms and tactics of conflict

7.1   **Causes of conflict**

(a)   **Differences in the objectives** of different groups or individuals.

(b)   **Scarcity of resources**.

(c)   **Interdependence of two departments** on a task. They have to work together but may do so ineffectively.

(d)   **Disputes about the boundaries of authority.**

    (i)   The technostructure may attempt to encroach on line managers and usurp some of their authority.

    (ii)   One department might start **empire building** and try to take over the work previously done by another department.

(e)   **Personal differences**, as regards goals, attitudes and feelings, are also bound to crop up. This is especially true in **differentiated organisations**, where people employed in the different sub-units are very different.

7.2   **Symptoms of conflict**

- Poor communications
- Interpersonal friction
- Inter-group rivalry and jealousy
- Low morale and frustration
- Widespread use of arbitration and appeals to higher authority

7.3   **Tactics of conflict**

(a)   **Withholding information** from another.

(b)   **Distorting information**. This will enable the group or manager presenting the information to get their own way more easily.

(c)   **Empire building**. A group (especially a specialist group such as accounting) which considers its influence to be neglected might seek to **impose rules, procedures,** restrictions or official requirements on other groups.

(d)   **Informal organisation**. A manager might seek to by-pass formal channels of communication and decision-making by establishing informal contacts and friendships with people in a position of importance.

(e)   **Fault-finding** in the work of other departments: department X might duplicate the work of department Y - hoping to prove department Y 'wrong' - and then report the fact to senior management.

Managerial response to conflict

7.4   **Management responses to the handling of conflict** (not all of which are effective).

Response	Comment
Denial/withdrawal	If the conflict is very trivial, it may indeed blow over without an issue being made of it, but if the causes are not identified, the conflict may grow to unmanageable proportions.
Suppression	Smoothing over, to preserve working relationships despite minor conflicts.
Dominance	This creates all the lingering resentment and hostility of win-lose situations.
Compromise	Bargaining, negotiating, conciliating. To some extent, this will be inevitable in any organisation made up of different individuals. However, individuals tend to exaggerate their positions to allow for compromise, and compromise itself is seen to weaken the value of the decision, perhaps reducing commitment.
Integration/ collaboration	Emphasis must be put on the task, individuals must accept the need to modify their views for its sake, and group effort must be seen to be superior to individual effort.

7.5 *Handy* suggests two types of strategy which may be used to **turn conflict into competition or argument**, or to manage it in some other acceptable way.

(a) **Environmental ('ecological') strategies** involve creating conditions in which individuals may be better able to **interact co-operatively** with each other. Such strategies involve:

- Agreement of **common objectives**
- Reinforcing the **team nature** of organisational life, via culture
- Providing **feedback** information on progress
- Providing adequate co-ordination and communication **mechanisms**
- Sorting out territorial/role conflicts in the **organisational structure**

(b) **Regulation strategies**. These are directed to **control conflict**.

- The provision of **arbitration** to settle disputes.
- The establishment of **detailed rules and procedures**.
- A liaison/co-ordination officer or **committee.**
- Using **confrontation**, or inter-group meetings, to hammer out differences.
- **Separating** the conflicting individuals/departments.
- **Ignoring the problem**, if it is genuinely likely to 'go away'.

Changes and external stakeholders

7.6 The company's relationship with its stakeholders and other aspects of its boundaries with the environment has been presented so far as a passive and reactive process. Management respond to stakeholder demands. However there can be a number of conflicts in the relationship.

7.7 Management (and other internal stakeholders) are in possession of a lot more information about the company than any other group. Management are therefore in a position to **mould the expectations** of some stakeholder groups, to direct their demands in certain directions. In other words, management can craft stakeholder expectations in a similar way to that in which they might craft strategy.

(a) Customer expectations can be crafted by **clever marketing**. Also, the power of customers can be reduced by product differentiation, erecting barriers to entry, raising switching costs and so forth.

(b) Suppliers and distributors can be managed in a number of ways. Drawing them into a **closer operating relationship** (eg joint product development, just-in-time systems) can be a way of managing the relationship and controlling their influence.

(c) The public and the government can be **managed by advertising, public relations,** lobbying, and pre-empting legislation. Supermarkets, for example, sometimes promote healthy eating rather than protest about it.

(d) Some companies deliberately **cultivate good relations with members of the investment community** (eg pension fund managers, analysts working for securities firms).

8 CHANGING CORPORATE CULTURE

8.1 Any programme of cultural change involves identifying and exposing three things.

- The hidden assumptions of the new culture
- The conflicts hidden in the culture
- Cultural mechanisms for change

8.2 'Changing a culture to increase a corporation's effectiveness is a hazardous undertaking,' says *Hampden-Turner*. He recommends a number of steps that senior managers, perhaps with the advice of management consultants, should take.

Step 1. **Find the dangers ('locate the black sheep').** The best way to find out about how a culture works is to violate it, by doing something culturally shocking.

Step 2. **Bring conflicts into the open.** Interviewing and observation are the principal tools of cultural investigation. Interviews identify what people believe as *individuals*, as opposed to what they affirm as *employees*.

Step 3. **Play out corporate dramas.** The manager or consultant then discusses the culture with its members. 'A repressive culture may simply deny that remarks qualifying or criticising it were ever made.' 'A narrow or low context culture may agree that such remarks were made, but treat them as the utterances of private persons, irrelevant to the common task.' This can result in heated, but hopefully constructive argument.

Step 4. **Reinterpret the corporate myths.** Corporate stories passed round to recruits indicates something about competing value systems. Sometimes these corporate myths have to change. Hampden-Turner cites the experiences of Volvo in France. The French sales force considered the cars they were selling to be boring: after a long trip to Sweden, when they were shown around the factories, they changed their views.

Step 5. **Look at symbols, images, rituals.** An example quoted by Hampden-Turner is 'PepsiCo', where every month there is a formal meeting comparing Pepsi's sales with Coca-Cola's. Rituals are used to celebrate achievement, or to mark changes (eg in a merger): 'changing a corporate culture can mean that new symbols, rituals and approaches are devised.'

Step 6. **Create a new learning system.** Cultures filter and exclude information. They need to be modified to accept new types of data.

8.3 The norms in a culture include attitudes toward performance, teamwork, communication, leadership, profitability, staff relations, customer relations, honesty and security, training and innovation. A consistent approach is needed. Here are some essential features for a programme of cultural change.

- Top management commitment
- Modelling behaviour: managers should practice what they preach
- Support for positive behaviour and confrontation of negative behaviour
- Communication of desired norms
- Recruitment and selection of the right people
- Induction programmes for new employees on the desired norms of behaviour
- Training and skills development

8.4 Most research has shown that, in a large organisation, shifting the value system or culture can take between **three and eight years** to bring about. Strong cultures discourage the questioning of their basic assumptions, especially where they have been implemented successfully and reinforced in the recruitment of clones.

8.5 Section summary

- Cultures are hard to change.
- Their assumptions must be exposed and challenged.
- Managers have to lead by example.

Chapter roundup

- **Changes** occur within the environment, goods/services, technology, management organisation structure, and in an organisation's capacity to meet them. It may be **incremental** or **transformational** and management may take a **proactive** or **reactive** role.

- Gemini 4Rs is a framework for planned strategic change involving **reframing**, **restructuring**, **revitalising** and **renewal**.

- Management sometimes must **introduce change** to the organisation. A variety of forces will promote or resist the change. **Force field analysis** is a way of identifying these factors.

- People **resist change** because of uncertainty, fear, lack of confidence, and a sense of dissonance. The success of change can be promoted by taking these factors into account.

- The **change process** involves:
    - Determining the need for change
    - Preparing a plan
    - Analysing likely responses
    - Establishing a realistic timetable
    - Communicating the change
    - Implementing and reviewing the change

- It may be necessary to appoint a **change agent** who, with the public support of senior management, must promote the change to managers and workers, and ensure they implement it.

- **Systems intervention strategy** has three stages.
    - Diagnosis
    - Design
    - Implementation

- Lewin's **force field analysis** shows the forces driving and restraining change. It illustrates the idea that weakening the restraining forces is probably more appropriate than overwhelming them.

- Managing resistance to change requires consideration of the **pace, manner** and **scope** of the change.

- Change is often associated with conflict, but conflict may arise from several other sources. Conflict can lead to deliberately dysfunctional behaviour within the organisation and may evoke a range of managerial responses, not all of which are really productive. **Environmental** and regulatory strategies may be more effective.

- Cultural change is difficult and likely to be time-consuming. It requires an understanding of what the prevailing culture is and why it exists. Leadership, communication and training are essential elements.

Quick quiz

1   List five areas where change may occur.

2   What are the elements of Gemini 4Rs?

3   How may change affect an individual?

4   How do people react to proposed change?

5   What is the Lewin/Schein model?

6   What are the stages of systems intervention strategy?

7   How would you deal with parochial self-interest?

8   What is force field analysis?

9   Is coercion likely to work in a power culture?

10   What strategies for managing conflict were suggested by Handy?

Answers to quick quiz

1   Environment, products, manufacturing/service processes, management organisation structure/size

2   Reframing, restructuring, revitalising, renewal

3   Physiologically, psychologically, circumstantially

4   Acceptance, indifference, passive resistance or active resistance

5   Unfreeze-change-refreeze

6   Diagnosis, design, implementation

7   Negotiation, possibly using incentives

8   A visualisation of the forces driving and restraining a change

9   Yes

10   Environmental and regulational

Now try the question below from the Exam Question Bank

Number	Level	Marks	Time
Q11	Exam	20	36 mins

Chapter 12

OPERATIONS

Topic list	Syllabus reference
1 The importance of operations	5(f)
2 Business process re-engineering	5(f)
3 Benchmarking	5(f)
4 Production	5(f)
5 Service operations	5(f)
6 Quality	5(f)
7 Total quality management	5(f)
8 Purchasing and materials management	5(f)

Introduction

Operations are where strategies work or fail. They are inherently complex and they require people and processes to be co-ordinated at the customer interface. This chapter covers general operations planning issues, and then focuses on business processes. **Benchmarking** and **total quality management** are two recent trends, but remember that they are no substitutes for strategy.

Study guide

Section 5 – The nature of strategy implementation

- Project management issues

Exam guide

An understanding of the nature of operations management is essential if you are to put strategy into a practical context. The material in this chapter is therefore underpinning knowledge for the whole exam. Benchmarking, BPR and quality management could be the subjects of a question or part question in either section of the exam.

1 THE IMPORTANCE OF OPERATIONS

1.1 **Operations are the link between the strategy and the customer.** They appear lower in status than strategy formulation, but are critical in delivering customer satisfaction and profits. In **service industries**, in particular, the operational interface with the customer is the crux of the business.

1.2 **Link to mission.** The organisation's **mission** is only really meaningful if, at operational level, the mission is embodied in **policies and behaviour standards.**

1.3 Link to human resources management

(a) Operations management is linked to **job design**. Most jobs are designed around tasks to be done or roles to be played.

(b) **Changing** operations management can involve a major risk of process failure. Old ways of doing things have to be unlearnt.

KEY TERM

Operations plans are 'the fully detailed specifications by which individuals are expected to carry out the predetermined cycles of operations to meet sectional objectives.'

1.4 Operations plans are made for each department. They are **interrelated**.

(a) The **marketing plan** will detail expected selling quantities, and timings, advertising expenditure sales force activities.

(b) From the estimates of selling quantities, the required **production plan** can be formulated, stating what needs to be produced and at what cost, to match the volume and diversity of products that marketing expects to sell. The production programmes should include cost estimates (allowing for inflation) for direct materials, labour, energy and any other major expenditures, as well as overhead recovery.

1.5 There are potential snags in co-ordinating the efforts of the marketing and production departments to produce an optimal plan.

(a) **Marketing staff** are occasionally **over-optimistic** about what they can sell, and so might ask for too much production. This will result in excess stocks.

(b) **Inefficiencies in manufacture** might give rise to unnecessarily high costs, thereby denying the marketing function the chance to sell at a profit the goods for which there is demand at a given price.

(c) Many small companies fail through **over hasty expansion** or **over trading.** This can take the form of **pursuing volume sales as opposed to profitable sales** (ie selling a lot, at low and unsustainable margins). A large firm might see this as an investment in market share. An alternative route to insolvency is **getting one large order, and forsaking others**. A diverse customer base may be a better guarantee of long term success.

2 BUSINESS PROCESS RE-ENGINEERING

2.1 Many organisations have sought to improve performance by re-engineering their business processes.

KEY TERM

Business process re-engineering (BPR)

'the fundamental rethinking and radical redesign of business processes to achieve dramatic improvements in critical contemporary measures of performance, such as cost, quality, service and speed.' (*Hammer and Champy*)

2.2 Re-engineers start from the future and work backwards. They are unconstrained by existing methods, people or departments. In effect, they ask, 'If we were a new company, how would we run the place?'

Processes

2.3 'A collection of activities that takes one or more kinds of input and creates an output that is of value to the customer.' For example, order fulfilment is a process that takes an order as its input and results in the delivery of the ordered goods.

2.4 **Principles of BPR**

(a) **Processes should be designed to achieve a desired outcome** rather than focusing on **existing tasks**.

(b) **Personnel who use the output from a process should perform the process**. For example, a company could set up a database of approved suppliers; this would allow personnel who actually require supplies to order them themselves, perhaps using on-line technology, thereby eliminating the need for a separate purchasing function.

(c) **Information** processing should be **included in the work which produces** the information.

(d) **Geographically dispersed resources should be treated as if they are centralised**, for example, economies of scale through central negotiation of supply contracts, without losing the benefits of decentralisation, such as flexibility and responsiveness.

(e) **Parallel activities should be linked rather than integrated**. This would involve, for example, co-ordination between teams working on different aspects of a single process.

(f) **'Doers' should be allowed to be self-managing.** This is **empowerment.** Decision aids such as expert systems can be provided where they are required.

(g) Information should be captured **once, at source**.

2.5 BPR cannot be planned meticulously and accomplished in small and cautious steps.

(a) It tends to be an **all-or-nothing proposition**, often with an uncertain result. It is therefore a **high risk** undertaking.

(b) Many organisations trying BPR do not achieve good results because they **fail to think it through**, do not engage **hearts and minds** sufficiently, act on **bad advice** or cannot override established departmental/functional power groups which have a vested interest in the **status quo**, or in incremental change rather than radical revolution.

3 BENCHMARKING 6/03

3.1 **Benchmarking** generally involves comparing your operations to somebody else's.

KEY TERM

Benchmarking

'The establishment, through data gathering, of targets and comparators, through whose use relative levels of performance (and particularly areas of underperformance) can be identified. By the adoption of identified best practices it is hoped that performance will improve.

3.2 **Types of benchmarking**

(a) **Internal benchmarking,** is a method of comparing one operating unit or function with another within the same organisation.

(b) **Functional benchmarking** compares functions with those of the best external practitioners of those functions, regardless of the industry they are in (also know as operational benchmarking or generic benchmarking).

(c) **Competitive benchmarking,** gathers information about direct competitors, through techniques such as reverse engineering.

(d) **Strategic benchmarking** is a type of competitive benchmarking aimed at strategic action and organisational change.

Case example

British Airways

British Airways used benchmarking from 1987 to help transform itself from a stodgy, state-controlled enterprise to a leading world airline. Apparently BA managers analysed their own business processes to identify the weakest elements, and then visited other airlines with checklists and questions. Problems are often found to be shared and competitors are willing to pool information in pursuit of solutions.

3.3 **Advantages**

(a) **Position audit.** Benchmarking can **assess a firm's existing position.**

(b) The comparisons are carried out by **the managers who have to live with any changes** implemented as a result of the exercise.

(c) Benchmarking **focuses on improvement in key areas** and sets targets which are challenging but **achievable.** What is really achievable can be discovered by examining what others have achieved: managers are thus able to accept that they are not being asked to perform miracles.

(d) If **all firms provide the same standard of quality**, it **ceases to be a source of competitive advantage.**

3.4 **Dangers of benchmarking**

(a) It **implies there is one best way** of doing business - arguably this boils down to the difference between efficiency and effectiveness. A process can be efficient but its output may not be useful. Other measures such as developing the value chain may be a better way of securing competitive advantage.

(b) The benchmark may be **yesterday's solution to tomorrow's problem**. For example, a cross-channel ferry company might benchmark its activities (eg speed of turnround at Dover and Calais, cleanliness on ship) against another ferry company, whereas the real competitor is the Channel Tunnel.

(c) It is a **catching-up exercise** rather than the development of anything distinctive. After the benchmarking exercise, the competitor might improve performance in a different way.

(d) It **depends on accurate information** about competitors, in the case of competitor benchmarking, or an **appropriate analogies** in other industries, in the case of process benchmarking.

3.5 To make benchmarking work, it is important to **compare like with like.**

Case example

An article in *Management Accounting* (April 1997) by Ian Malcolm describes benchmarking applied to purchase/sales order processing.

	Best	Worst
Accounts payable Number of purchase invoices processed per full-time equivalent (FTE) accounts payable member of staff per annum	50,000	3,000
Accounts receivable Number of remittances processed per FTE remittance-processing staff per annum	750,000	12,000

The article then goes on to describe the *different processes* in which key billing tasks are divided. Clearly, automating some processes enhances efficiency, but also accuracy is important.

Accounts payable (A/P) - process options chart

Process tasks / Invoice type	Receive and sort post	Register	Authorise	Match with order or GRN	Code	Approve	Pay against terms	Advise payment
EDI invoice	Not required	Auto or manual	Auto or manual	Auto or manual	Auto or manual	Auto or manual	Auto or manual	Auto or manual
Self-billed invoice	Not required	Auto	Auto	Not required	Auto or manual	Auto or manual	Auto or manual	Auto or manual
Paper invoice	Manual	Manual	Manual	Auto or manual	Auto or manual	Auto or manual	Auto or manual	Auto or manual
Purchase card	Summary statement and file of receipts	Optional for statement	Pre-determined	Match statement with receipts	Auto or manual	Note required*	Auto	Not required
Cheque or cash paid by service/product recipient	Maintain file of receipts	Summary level only	Pre-determined	Not required	Manual	Not required*	Not required	Not required
	Sample audits are a necessary control to replace the payment-approval process in these cases							

Clearly, process failures have to be investigated.

3.6 Steps in a benchmarking process

Step 1. Identify items to be benchmarked.

Step 2. Identify suitable organisations for comparison.

Step 3. Collect data by an appropriate method.

Step 4. Determine the current performance gap.

Step 5. Project future performance levels.

Step 6. Tell people about benchmark findings.

Step 7. Establish goals for each business function.

Step 8. Develop action plans.

Step 9. Implement action plans.

Step 10. Re-set benchmarks to a higher level to encourage continuous improvement

4 PRODUCTION

4.1 The production function plans, organises, directs and controls the necessary activities to provide products and services.

Activity	Example
Obtain **inputs** to the production 'system', such as plant facilities, materials and labour.	Inputs: timber, screws, nails, adhesives, varnish, stain, templates, cutting tools, carpenters

Activity	Example
Adding of value The activities below occupy most of the production manager's attention: • Scheduling jobs on machines • Assigning labour to jobs • Controlling the quality of production and/or service delivery • Improving methods of work • Managing materials and equipment, to avoid waste	Operations: sawing, sanding, assembly, finishing
Create **outputs,** ie finished products and services	Outputs: tables, chairs, cabinets, and so on.

Intermediate activities in all three processes include processing, inspection and storage. The linkages in the process are usually provided by information. For example the stock control system will detail movements in and out of the warehouse. To control operations, a variety of records are required.

4.2 **Production management decisions**

(a) **Longer-term decisions**

These are related to setting up the production organisation.

- Selection of equipment and processes.
- Job design and methods.
- Factory location and layout.
- Ensuring the right number and skills of employees.

(b) **Short-term decisions**

These are concerned with the running and control of the organisation.

- Production and control
- Quality management
- Maintenance
- Labour control and supervision
- Stock control

Relationships with other functions

4.3 Longer term decisions, particularly relating to design and the innovation of improved products, cannot be taken by the production department alone; its activities must be **integrated with other functions** in the firm.

- **Product design** is co-ordinated with **R&D**. Production should advise R&D as to the consequences of particular designs for the manufacturing process.

- **Job design** will involve consultation with **human resources** specialists.

- The quantities needed to be produced will be notified by the **sales department**.

- The **human resources department** will be involved in managing the work force.

- The **finance department** might indicate the resources available for new equipment.

> **KEY TERM**
>
> **World Class Manufacturing (WCM)** is manufacturing excellence, achieved by developing a culture based on factors such as continuous improvement, problem prevention, zero defect tolerance, customer-driven JIT-based production and total quality management'

4.4 **Elements of WCM**

    (a) **A new approach to product quality**

    (b) **Just-in-Time manufacturing (JIT)**

    (c) **Managing people:** the aim of WCM is to utilise the skills and abilities of the work force to the full.

    (d) **Flexible approach to customer requirements** (eg mass customisation)

Features of an advanced factory environment.

4.5 **Machine cells.** Machine tools are grouped in heterogeneous clusters. Multi-skilled workers complete several processes on each work piece before passing it on to the next department. This reduces delays caused by routing and queuing between single process departments.

4.6 **Advanced manufacturing technology (AMT)**

    (a) **Computer aided design** (CAD) allows new products to be designed (and old ones modified) on a computer screen. 3D models can be created and rotated through any angle and there is infinite capacity for exploring the effects of changing product specifications.

    (b) **Computer aided manufacturing** (CAM) refers to the control of the physical production process by computers.

        (i) **Robots** typically comprise computer controlled arms and attachments that can perform tasks like welding, bolting parts together and moving them about.

        (ii) **Computer numerically controlled** (CNC) machines are programmable machine tools for punching holes, grinding, cutting, shaping and so on.

        (iii) **Automated guided vehicles** (AGVs) are used for materials handling, often in place of the traditional conveyor belt approach.

4.7 **Flexible manufacturing systems (FMS).** This is a highly automated manufacturing system, which is computer-controlled and capable of producing a broad family of parts in a flexible manner. It is characterised by **small batch** production, the ability to **change quickly** from one job to another and very **fast response times**, so that output can be produced quickly in response to specific orders.

Just-in-Time

4.8 Co-ordination of activities is necessary to ensure optimum use of resources. **Just-in-Time** (JIT) techniques are an example of long-linked technologies which have the effect of increasing technological interdependence by removing slack from the system.

KEY TERM

Just-in-time 'A system whose objective is to produce or to procure products or components as they are required by a customer or for use, rather than for stock. A just-in-time system is a pull system, which responds to demand, in contrast to a push system, in which stocks act as buffers between the different elements of the system, such as purchasing, production and sales.

(a) **Just-in-time production**. A production system which is driven by demand for finished products whereby each component on a production line is produced only when needed for the next stage.

(b) **Just-in-time purchasing**. A purchasing system in which material purchases are contracted so that the receipt and usage of material, to the maximum extent possible, coincide.

4.9 The most obvious physical manifestation of JIT is a small warehouse. In other words, there are few raw materials stocks, as these are only purchased when needed. There are few finished goods stocks, as effort is not expended on production that is not required. JIT makes a firm vulnerable to **interruptions** in supply, to **poor quality** in purchased inputs and to **defective production**. However, **quality management** can address these problems.

Operations planning for distribution

4.10 **Physical distribution management** is concerned with the physical transportation and warehousing of products.

- Transportation/type
- Materials handling in storerooms and warehouses
- Packaging
- Warehousing procedures
- Inventory levels and stock control
- The location of warehouses
- Order processing

4.11 Rising costs of freight, warehousing and stockholding, however, have forced attention towards physical distribution systems, and have stimulated the question as to how far distribution factors should influence marketing decisions, and how carefully should distribution activities be co-ordinated and integrated.

4.12 If a company is seeking to build or acquire a new warehouse, it must seek a general area and then a specific site in that area.

(a) Selecting the area will depend on its market potential.

(b) The choice of site *within* an area will depend on a range of factors.

- Sites available
- Delivery and collection arrangements
- Local transport facilities
- Future development in the area
- Tenure (lease or a freehold)
- Geographical position
- Size in relation to market potential

5   SERVICE OPERATIONS

Service quality

5.1   Many products have a service element: remember that a company's **value chain** has 'after sales service' as one of the elements. Service businesses include health care, restaurants, tourism, financial services, education and all the professions.

> **KEY TERM**
>
> **Service** '... any activity of benefit that one party can offer to another that is essentially intangible and does not result in the ownership of anything. Its production may or may not be tied to a physical product.' (P Kotler, *Social Marketing*)

5.2   **Characteristics of services**

(a)   **Intangibility.** Unlike goods there are no substantial material or physical aspects to a service. A service cannot be packaged in a bag and carried home, such as a live musical performance.

(b)   **Inseparability.** Many services are **created** at the same time as they are **consumed,** for example, dental treatment. Associated with this is **perishability**. Services cannot be stored. The services of a dentist are purchased for a **period of time**. The service they offer cannot be used later.

(c)   **Variability.** It may be hard to attain precise standardisation of the service offered. The quality of the service may depend heavily on **who** (or what) delivers the service, and exactly **when** it takes place.

(d)   **Ownership.** Services differ from consumer goods: they do **not normally result in the transfer of property**. The purchase of a service only confers on the customer access to or a right to use a facility, not ownership.

Deploying the marketing mix in services

5.3   Deploying the service marketing mix in services is a rather difficult task.

(a)   **Poor service quality on one occasion** (eg lack of punctuality of trains, staff rudeness, a bank's incompetence) is likely to lead to **widespread distrust** of everything the organisation does.

(b)   **Complexity.** If the service is intangible offering a complicated future benefit then attracting customers means promoting an attractive image and ensuring that the service lives up to its reputation, consistently.

(c)   **Pricing** of services is often complicated, especially if large numbers of people are involved in providing the service.

(d)   **Human resources management** is a key ingredient in the services marketing mix, as so many services are produced and consumed in a specific social context.

5.4   Service marketing involves three additional Ps: **people, processes and physical evidence**, as discussed in Chapter 7.

5.5 Dimensions of service operations

Determinants	Comments
Tangibles	The physical evidence, such as the quality of fixtures and fittings of the company's service area, must be consistent with the desired image.
Reliability	Getting it right first time is very important, not only to ensure repeat business, but, in financial services, as a matter of ethics, if the customer is buying a future benefit.
Responsiveness	The staff's willingness to deal with the customer's queries must be apparent.
Communication	Staff should talk to customers in non-technical language which they can understand.
Credibility	The organisation should be perceived as honest, trustworthy and as acting in the best interests of customers.
Security	This is specially relevant to medical and financial services organisations. The customer needs to feel that the conversations with bank service staff are private and confidential. This factor should influence the design of the service area.
Competence	All the service staff need to appear competent in understanding the product range and interpreting the needs of the customers. In part this can be achieved through training programmes.
Courtesy	Customers (even rude ones) should perceive service staff as polite, respectful and friendly. This basic requirement is often difficult to achieve in practice, although training programmes can help.
Understanding customers' needs	The use of computer-based customer databases can be very impressive in this context. The service personnel can then call up the customer's records and use these data in the service process, thus personalising the process. Service staff need to meet customer needs rather than try to sell products. This is a subtle but important difference.
Access	Minimising queues, having a fair queuing system and speedy but accurate service are all factors which can avoid customers' irritation building up. A pleasant relaxing environment is a useful design factor in this context.

Case example

Heathrow airport

The following example of a customer care programme was described in *People Management* (12 September 1996). Although focused on customer care it describes how marketing considerations go far further than adverts and logos.

'In 1994 Heathrow airport began a grassroots campaign to revolutionise engineers' attitudes to customer service. The project was modelled on an inverted organisational pyramid: the people nearest the customer would develop their own training programme, which managers would follow and support.

At Heathrow, the term 'engineering' covers a number of activities, from the specialised (for instance, aircraft jetty maintenance), to the more routine (plumbing, carpentry, etc).

The engineers' customers include airlines, airport franchises, airport control authorities plus colleagues at Heathrow airport. Representatives of these groups identified the eight key service elements that gave the programme its name: Aces High (standing for ability, communication, etiquette, speed of response, honesty, image, giving a little extra and Heathrow's representatives).

In a series of problem-solving workshops, front-line employees were asked to review their behaviour, customer service attitude and customer relationships against the Aces High elements.

The initial response was mixed. Some engineers rose to the challenge, while others felt they had 'seen it all before and nothing will change'. This reaction, from staff jaded by a series of company initiatives, was not unexpected, but it was a sad indication of how untapped talent can be driven into a rut.

So, while some engineers worked on their standards of behaviour towards customers, a different approach was needed for the cynics. When asked what would convince them of managerial commitment, they came up with a list of the major obstacles to good service. Senior management used these to prepare a statement offering extensive support.

The statement committed *managers* to *eight actions* including loosening the rules on overtime and releasing engineers from having to obtain three quotes before buying equipment. The speed and manner of this support produced an overwhelming response, and the role of engineering customer service representative (a title chosen by the engineers themselves) was born, as a number came forward to help move the programme onward.

The representatives produced a code of conduct; devised and ran special customer service workshops for their customers and contractors; and, most remarkably, composed a customer survey in which engineers were named and assessed by customers for their conduct and service attitude.

As Aces High moves through Heathrow's 14 engineering sections, front-line staff have continued to develop their own approaches to service improvement.

Perhaps the most disappointing problem was some senior managers' lack of responsibility for keeping in touch with customer service representatives.

Resisting the 'quick win' culture at Heathrow has also proved difficult. Productivity has clearly increased. In March 1996, 66 per cent of engineering faults were fixed in less than two hours, compared with 58 per cent a year earlier.

Some of the technicians who came forward to assist as customer service representatives were seen by their managers as lacking either the attitude or the skill for the role. Their involvement has perhaps been one of the most interesting results of using external facilitators who had no preconceptions and judged people on their contribution at the time, not on their history in the organisation.

5.6 Section summary

- Services are intangible, inseparable, variable and perishable.
- The service mix involves people, processes and physical evidence.
- Customer care is becoming a core strategic issue.

6 QUALITY

Case examples

Siebe, Motorola, General Electric

The case examples below (extracted from a Financial Times article, 24 February 1997) describe how three firms are using quality control to improve performance and save money.

When the UK engineering group Siebe [now merged with BTR, in the Invensys group] announced recently it was adopting a **six sigma** programme, the news caused little remark. Quality programmes under the six sigma banner absorb much time and money at such leading US companies as Motorola and General Electric. Siebe's announcement, in fact, was partly a rhetorical flourish: an application to join a world elite of super-efficient manufacturers.

Six sigma means reducing the defects in a process to just over three per million. It is thus a ferociously demanding target. The approach is particularly suited to the high-volume, high-precision electronics industry. For example, a mobile phone such as Motorola produces might contain 400 components. If the company operates to two sigma - 45,000 defects per million - on each part, the cumulative odds of the phone being defective are far too high.

Six sigma is part of a general shift in quality management. Where companies once measured quality by checking the final product, they now aim to control the processes at the outset. In the jargon, they have moved from **acceptable quality** levels to **statistical process controls**. Six sigma means tightening up the tolerance on processes to incredible levels.

Six sigma is by no means confined to manufacturing. GE Capital, the financial services division of General Electric, applies it to processes ranging from billing and the tracking of assets to various kinds of customer service.

The real question is whether you can put the right paradigm in place, so the process has fewer moving parts and less things to break down. It's very important to change the process fundamentally. You need to change the whole behaviour of the company, to become more responsive to the customer.

GE Capital surveys its customers regularly - some weekly, some monthly or quarterly, depending on their business - to check its performance.

At Siebe, the same emphasis on the customer crops up immediately. Jim Mueller, president of the company's temperature and appliance controls division, says: 'Customer satisfaction is very important for us, especially since we're mostly an OEM [original equipment manufacturer]. Someone else's name goes on the product, so if it fails, someone else gets a bad reputation.'

Siebe's adoption of six sigma, he says, follows the introduction of a lean manufacturing programme two years ago. 'We had to take inventory out of the system,' he says. 'When you do that, you have to have reliable processes. So going to six sigma, is part of the lean manufacturing puzzle.' Siebe's goal is a 25 per cent reduction in what Mueller calls the cost of quality: money spent on scrap, rework, inspection and warranty.

Six sigma is no good on its own. As Roy David of Arthur D Little says: 'Your company has to be applying total quality management already, including customer satisfaction, management commitment and employee involvement.'

KEY TERM

Quality has been defined by Ken Holmes *(Total Quality Management)* as 'the totality of features and characteristics of a product or service which bears on its ability to meet stated or implied needs.' It is fitness for use.

6.1 **Quality** is concerned with fitness for use, and quality management (or control) is about ensuring that products or services meet their planned level of quality and conform to specifications.

6.2 EXAMPLE

The postal service might establish a standard that 90% of first class letters will be delivered on the day after they are posted, and 99% will be delivered within two days of posting. Procedures would have to be established for ensuring that these standards could be met (eg frequency of collections, automated letter sorting, frequency of deliveries and number of staff employed etc). Actual performance could be monitored, perhaps by taking samples from time to time of letters that are posted and delivered. If the quality standard is not being achieved, the management of the postal service could take control action (eg employ more postmen or advertise again the use of postcodes) or reduce the standard of quality of the service being provided.

Traditional approaches to quality

6.3 In the past, quality control meant **inspection** of finished output (or goods inward). Quality was something assured **at the end** of the manufacturing process rather than being considered at the beginning.

6.4 **Problems with inspection**

(a) The **inspection process itself does not add value**. If no defective items were produced, there would be no need for an inspection function.

(b) The **production of substandard products is a waste** of materials and time.

(c) The **inspection department takes up expensive land** and warehousing space.

(d) **Working capital is tied up** in stocks which cannot be sold.

6.5 BS 6143 gives examples of each type of **quality cost.**

(a) **Prevention costs** are the 'cost of any action taken to investigate or reduce defects and failures'.

(b) **Appraisal costs** are 'the costs of assessing quality achieved'.

(c) **Internal failure costs** are 'costs arising within the organisation of failing to achieve quality'.

(d) **External failure costs**. These are 'costs arising outside the manufacturing organisation of failure to achieve specified quality (after *transfer* of ownership to the customer)'.

Developments in quality

6.6 **Fitness for use comes from** two things.

- **Quality of design:** the customer satisfactions incorporated into the product.
- **Quality of conformance:** a lack of defects in the finished goods.

(Juran)

6.7 **Zero defects and right first time**

(a) **Zero defects concept**. There should never be any *defects* in a finished product. Some hold it to be an impossible ideal, and invoke the concept of diminishing returns. Alternatively it can be seen as a slogan to employees.

(b) **Right first time:** a product should not have to be corrected once it is built. It is thus a corollary of the zero defects concept.

(Crosby)

6.8 **Design systems and products to reduce variation.** *Genichi Taguchi* focuses on the importance of functions and activities undertaken **before** the manufacturing process in determining product quality. The aim might be to ensure conformance quality and to reduce variation.

6.9 EXAMPLE

Compare two fast food outlets each selling hamburgers. Both *Gristle Prince* and *Greasy Mike's* sell burgers for £1 each and both outlets aim to serve *each* customer about 90 seconds after the customer has placed an order. Obviously certain times of the day are busier than others, so queues and hence serving times are slightly longer. There are no differences in the quality of the burgers served or in the layout of each shop. Both manage, on *average*, to serve a customer in the target 90 seconds, yet Gristle Prince is beginning to attract more customers. Greasy Mike's employ a quality consultant, who analyses both outlets using a Taguchi model. Here are the consultant's findings.

(a) 100 customers entered *Gristle Prince*. 50 of them were served in *less* than the 90 second target, and 50 of them in more. In fact 50 were served in 80 seconds and fifty in 100 seconds, leading to an average serving time of 90 seconds.

(b) At *Greasy Mike's* on the other hand the story was different. Again 100 customers entered the restaurant.

- Ten had to wait five minutes (300 seconds)
- Ten had to wait three minutes (180 seconds)
- Sixty had to wait one minute (60 seconds)
- Twenty had to wait 30 seconds

Again the average service time is 90 seconds.

The result of course is that *Gristle Prince's* service is much more predictable, which is why customers might prefer it. They know they will *never* have to wait more than 100 seconds for their meal.

Quality circles and employees' responsibilities

6.10 *Ishikawa* proposed **quality circles** (and the development of a few simple tools for quality improvement). Quality circles are groups of selected workers delegated with the task of analysing the production process, and coming up with ideas to improve it. Success requires a commitment from the circle's membership, and a management willingness to take a back seat.

Quality assurance and standards

6.11 The essentials of **quality assurance** are that the *supplier* guarantees the quality of goods supplied and allows the customers' inspectors access while the items are being manufactured. Usually agreed inspection procedures and quality control standards are worked out by customer and supplier between them, and checks are made to ensure that they are being adhered to.

(a) The **customer can eliminate goods inwards inspection** and items can be directed straight to production. This can give large savings in cost and time in flow production, and can facilitate JIT production.

(b) The **supplier produces to the customer's requirement**, thereby reducing rejects and the cost of producing substitutes.

6.12 Suppliers' quality assurance schemes are being used increasingly. One such scheme is BS EN ISO 9000 certification. This is a nationally promoted standard, only awarded after audit and inspection of a company's operations. The standard falls into three parts.

- Part 1 covers design manufacture and installation.
- Part 2 covers just manufacture and installation.
- Part 3 covers inspection and testing.

6.13 The **standard does not dictate the quality of individual goods and services**, but aims to ensure that **quality management systems of a suitable standard are in place**.

(a) The standards 'set out how you can establish, document and maintain an effective quality system which will demonstrate to your customers that you are committed to quality and are able to satisfy their quality needs'.

(b) While it provides feedback about performance, it cannot guarantee that control action is taken. It is 'an indicator of potential, not of achievement'.

(c) Certification can be withdrawn, if a firm does not live up to the requirement.

(d) BS EN ISO 9000 increasingly will become a factor in selecting suppliers. Customers wish to avoid the cost of inspecting goods inwards.

7 TOTAL QUALITY MANAGEMENT

> **KEY TERM**
>
> **Total quality management (TQM)** is 'a culture aimed at continually improving performance in all functions of a company'. (*Holmes*)
>
> '... The total composite product and service characteristics of marketing, engineering, manufacture and maintenance, through which the product and service in use will meet the expectations by the customer' (*Fiegenbaum*).
>
> 'A way of managing a business to ensure complete customer satisfaction internally and externally' (*Oakland*).

7.1 TQM takes on board many of the principles identified in the previous sections.

7.2 TQM programmes are aimed at identifying and then reducing/eliminating causes of wasted time and effort.

(a) **Core activities** are the reason for the existence of the work group and add value to the business.

(b) **Support activities** support core activities but do not themselves add value.

(c) **Discretionary activities** such as checking, progress chasing and dealing with complaints are **all symptoms of failure** within the organisation. These should be reduced.

Statistical techniques: conformance quality

7.3 **Statistical process control (SPC)** is a technique of TQM. Control charts might be used to record and monitor the accuracy of the physical dimensions of products. A typical control chart is shown below.

(a) The horizontal axis on the graph is time, the vertical axis is the physical dimension of the product in appropriate units.

(b) Above and below the level of the expected dimension of the product are the control limits. The graph shows inner warning limits and outer action limits.

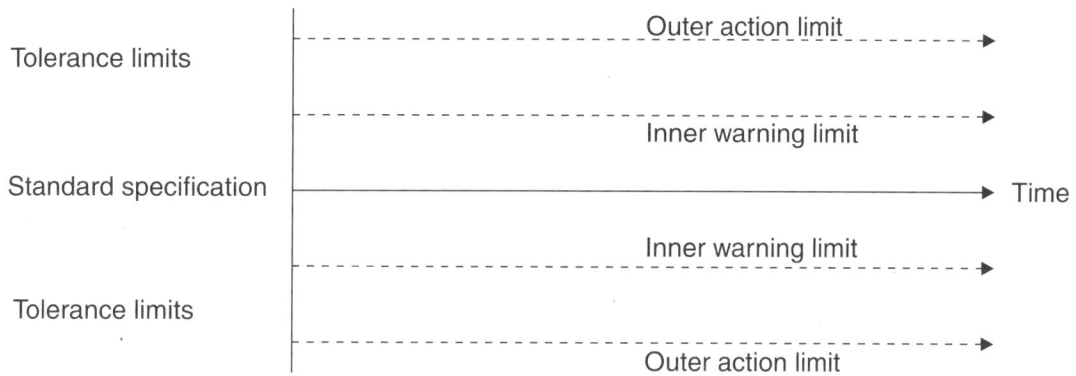

Quality function deployment (QFD): design quality

7.4 Quality function deployment (QFD) is a term to analyse how quality techniques can be used to cut across functional boundaries. QFD is aimed at getting quality right at an earlier time, and concentrates on design issues up front.

(a) '**Translate the voice of the customer**'. This means applying the marketing concept in assessing in detail the customer's needs and including them in a design specification, so that they are accurately translated **into relevant technical requirements.**

(b) **Obey the customer's voice**. Customer demands (eg that paper will not tear) are converted into quality requirements (paper must be of a minimum thickness). There is a matrix of relationships between customer demand and technical requirements.

Customer demand C has a strong relationship to quality characteristic W but a weak one to X.

(i) This matrix can determine where effort should be most expended

(ii) Furthermore, certain customer requirements might contradict each other, so the matrix identifies possible trade offs.

Assessing and auditing quality

7.5 Proper quality management depends on information.

KEY TERM

Quality assessment is the 'process of identifying business practices, attitudes, and activities that are either enhancing or inhibiting the achievement of quality improvement' (*Total Quality* Ernst and Young Quality Improvement Consulting Group).

7.6 **Quality assessment exercises**

(a) **Supply proof** that quality improvement measures are needed.

(b) **Provide a baseline for future measurement**, in other words to make a starting point from which you can measure your progress.

(c) **Build management** support for quality measures, by the power of the evidence collected.

(d) **Convince management**, particularly senior management, that the issue is important in the first place.

Continuous improvement

7.7 TQM is not a one-off process, but is the **continual examination** and improvement of existing processes. Continuous improvement applies both to the finished product, but also to the processes which make it.

(a) A philosophy of continuous improvement **avoids complacency**.

(b) **Customer needs change** so a continuous improvement enables these changes to be taken into account in the normal course of events.

(c) **New technologies or materials** might be developed, enabling cost savings or design improvements.

(d) Rarely do businesses know every possible fact about the production process. Continuous improvement **encourages experimentation** and a scientific approach to production.

(e) It is a way of **tapping employees' knowledge**.

(f) **Reducing variability** is a key issue for quality, if this is assessed on Taguchi's quality-cost model.

(g) Improvement on a continual, step by step basis is **more prudent** in some cases than changing things at one go.

7.8 **Model for improving quality**

Step 1. **Find out the problems** (eg from customer and employees).

Step 2. **Select action targets** from the number of improvement projects identified in *Step 1*, on the basis of cost, safety, importance, feasibility (with current resources).

Step 3. **Collect data** about the problem.

Step 4. **Analyse data** by a variety of techniques to assess common factors behind the data, to tease out any hidden messages the data might contain.

Step 5. **Identify possible causes** (eg using brainstorming sessions). No ideas are ruled out of order.

Step 6. **Plan improvement action.** Significant help might be required.

Step 7. **Monitor the effects of the improvement.**

Step 8. **Communicate the result.**

Total quality and customers (internal and external)

7.9 A **customer orientation** requires the firm to recognise that customers buy products for the benefits they deliver.

7.10 What constitutes a quality product or service must, it seems, be **related to what the customer wants.** Indeed, quality would have no commercial value unless it delivered benefits to the customer. The customer must be the final arbiter of the quality which a product possesses.

7.11 From a strategic point of view, then, **quality is in the eye of the consumer.** If quality is meeting the requirements of the consumer, then it should be recognised that throughout and beyond all enterprises, whatever business they are in, is a series of **quality chains**.

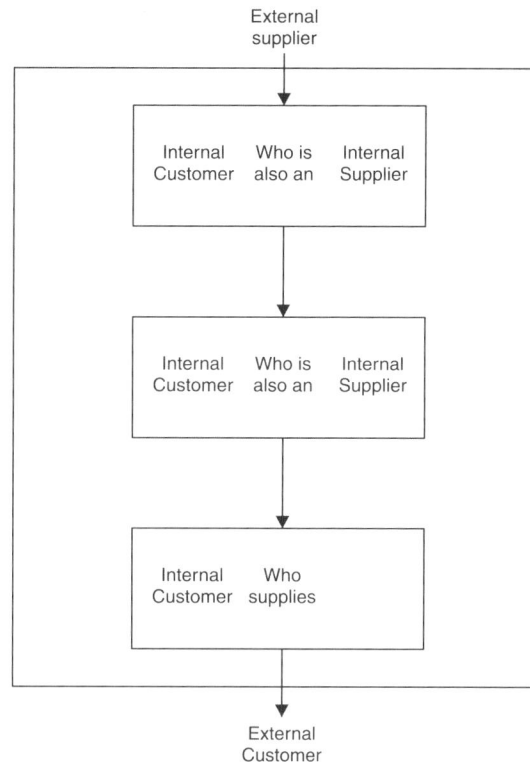

Oakland argues that meeting customer requirements is the main focus in a search for quality. (If the customer is outside the organisation, then the supplier must seek to set up a marketing activity to gather this information, and to relate the output of their organisation to the needs of the customer.)

7.13 **Internal customers** for services are equally important, but seldom are their requirements investigated. The quality implementation process requires that all the supplier/customer relationships within the **quality chain** should be treated as marketing exercises, and that each customer should be carefully consulted as to their precise requirements from the product or service with which they are to be provided.

7.14 Each link in the chain should prompt the following questions, according to Oakland.

Of customers

- Who are my immediate customers?
- What are their true requirements?
- How do or can I find out what the requirements are?
- How can I measure my ability to meet the requirements?
- Do I have the necessary capability to meet the requirements? (If not, then what must change to improve the capability?)
- Do I continually meet the requirements? (If not, then what prevents this from happening, when the capability exists?)
- How do I monitor changes in the requirements?

Of suppliers

- Who are my immediate suppliers?
- What are my true requirements?
- How do I communicate my requirements?
- Do my suppliers have the capability to measure and meet the requirements?
- How do I inform them of changes in the requirements?

Introducing TQM: organisational implications

7.15 Introducing TQM involves a significant shake up. TQM involves:

(a) **Giving employees a say** in the process (eg in the **quality survey**) and in getting them to suggest improvements.

(b) **Greater discipline** in the process of production and the establishment of better linkages between the business functions.

(c) **New relationships with suppliers,** which requires them to improve their output quality so that less effort is spent rectifying poor input. Long-term relationships with a small number of suppliers might be preferable to choosing material and sub-components on price.

(d) **Work standardisation** (with techniques perhaps introduced by the technostructure) and **employee commitment.**

(e) **Commitment over the long term.** It will fail if it is seen as just another fad.

(f) **All the organisation,** as the material on quality chains above suggests.

Case example

TQM

TQM is not just a body of techniques; it is a philosophy and movement that attracts followers. There are many alternative definitions of TQM, but the central concept is that quality is the key strategic variable in business and it is a variable that is amenable to organisational culture. The idea is that quality should be rooted in the structure of the organisation. It should influence the way the organisation is run and the way that staff are recruited, assessed, promoted and rewarded. The view that quality is something imposed on staff by inspectors is anathema to the TQM movement.

The main principles of a TQM-orientated organisation are:

- Top priority is given to satisfying customers and the organisation is structured to ensure that owners, employees, suppliers and management are all working to achieve this. Managers should act as facilitators rather than controllers.

- People are considered the key internal guarantors of success. Decision-making processes are participative. Management is both visible and accessible.

- Constant change is considered a way of life and the organisation is structured in a way that readily embraces change. That structure is flat, requiring employees to use initiative and communicate directly with customers and suppliers.

- The organisation pursues continuous improvement, not static optimisation. The concept of an optimum defects level is entirely alien to TQM. Performance is measured against an external benchmark and not against an internal standard.

- The emphasis is on prevention of problems and faults rather than on detection. Employees have a wide span of activity, but a short span of control.

Bob Scarlett, CIMA Insider, September 2001

8 PURCHASING AND MATERIALS MANAGEMENT

> **KEY TERM**
>
> **Purchasing** is 'the acquisition of material resources and business services for use by the organisation'.

8.1 Importance of purchasing

(a) **Cost**. Raw materials and subcomponents purchases are a major cost for many firms.

(b) **Quality**. The quality of input resources affects the quality of outputs and the efficiency of the production function.

(c) **Strategy.** In retailing, buying goods for resale is one of the most important activities of the business.

8.2 Position of purchasing within the organisation

(a) Where purchasing is of strategic importance, the purchasing officer may be on the **board of directors** or, at least, report to the managing director.

(b) Where raw materials are an important cost, the purchasing officer may work in the **production function**.

(c) In any event, the purchasing officer must **liaise with the finance department**, especially with regard to payment of creditors.

8.3 The purchasing manager's responsibilities

(a) **Inputs for production.** Acquiring raw materials, components, sub-assemblies, consumable stores and capital equipment for the production function.

(b) **Inputs for administration.** Purchasing supplies and equipment for all areas of the business (eg microcomputers, motor cars, telephone systems, office furniture, paper and other stationery items).

(c) **Cost control.** Ensuring that the organisation obtains value for money over the long term consistent with quality.

(d) **Liaison with the R&D** department to find suppliers for materials which are to the specifications required by the designers.

(e) **Supplier management**. Locating suppliers and dealing with them (eg discussing prices, discounts, delivery lead times, specifications; chasing late deliveries; sanctioning payments).

(f) Obtaining **information** on availability, quality, prices, distribution and suppliers for the evaluation of purchasing alternatives.

(g) Maintenance of **stock levels.**

The purchasing mix

8.4 The purchasing manager has to obtain the best purchasing mix.

- Quantity
- Quality
- Price
- Delivery

8.5 **Quantity**. The size and timing of purchase orders will be dictated by the balance between two things.

(a) Delays in production caused by insufficient stock

(b) Costs of stockholding: tied up capital, storage space, deterioration, insurance, risk of pilferage.

A system of stock control will set **optimum reorder levels** (the stock level at which supplies must be replenished so as to arrive in time to meet demand) to ensure **economic order quantities** (EOQ) are obtained for individual stock items.

8.6 **Quality**. The production department will need to be consulted about the quality of goods required for the manufacturing process, and the marketing department about the quality of goods acceptable to customers. Purchased components might be an important constituent of product quality.

8.7 **Price**. Favourable short-term trends in prices may influence the buying decision, but purchasing should have an eye to the best **value** over a period of time - considering quality, delivery, urgency of order, stock-holding requirements and so on.

8.8 **Delivery**. The **lead time** between placing and delivery of an order can be crucial to efficient stock control and production planning. The reliability of suppliers' delivery arrangements must also be assessed.

Question 1

If a company operates a **just in time production system**, what does this imply for purchasing?

Answer

(a) **Just in time** systems and stockless production require the receipt of goods from suppliers at the latest possible time, to avoid the need to carry any materials or components in stock.

(b) **Just in time** systems seek to avoid defects. Supplies must be of high quality to eliminate waste, as the quality of components can affect the quality of the end product.

Thus reliability of delivery and certainty of quality are as important as price.

Supply strategy

8.9 The **supply strategy** is a key task of the purchasing function.

Element of supply strategy	Comments
Sources of supply	What are the sources available? Where are they? Are they likely to treat you as a valued customer or not?
Spread of supply	Should there be just a single source of supply in order to get bulk purchase discounts, or should there be several to avoid the risk of lost production and supplier complacency?
Cost of supplies	How quickly can cost discounts through volume purchases be achieved?
The outsourcing (make or buy) decision	Is it more efficient to make the goods in house or buy them from outsiders?
The suitability of the existing supplier	Can existing suppliers produce goods to the required standard? If new standards of quality are required, can existing suppliers match them or not?
The image or reputation of the supplier	This could be a selling point for the buyer's own customers – major car rental firms are pleased to state that they rent Ford, GM or other makes of car
Building supplier relationships	Many companies value **long-term** relationships with suppliers, and offer help with product development, manufacturing processes and quality. This reduces the number of suppliers a firm deals with. This policy should ensure consistency of bought-in components quality, and facilitate just in time production

Materials management

8.10 Once materials are purchased they must be managed as any other resource. Materials management comprises the key functions of stock control, security and transportation to give the production **what** is needed **when** it is needed. It is also important to monitor the levels of wastage and to ensure that unused materials are returned to stock or disposed of (possibly in scrap sales) as appropriate.

Case example

Manufacturing

Traditionally motor cars have been designed by dedicated teams working on individual models. The result has been a proliferation of almost identical components, often produced by the same suppliers, being fitted into the different models.

Ford took a decision, starting with its European plants, to introduce a programme of commonality across the group, while ensuring that the intrinsic differences between its various models were maintained.

While he was head of Ford Europe, Nick Scheele, now overall chief operating officer, had appointed a 'commonality czar' to ensure production lines used the same parts were they could.

Mr Scheele recalls his astonishment, for example, on discovering that Ford Europe had been using about 100 different caps on its petrol tanks. By the end of the year there will be just two, a locking and a non-locking version.

Ford uses 40 different headlight switches on its models. 'We really don't need 40 headlight switches – we can run the business with eight.' In January 2000 Ford hired AT Kearney, the management consultant, to work on a pilot project that would demonstrate that the principle would work for a limited range of parts.

The team concentrated at first on the various components that went into the seats, including the headrest, and the mechanism and tracks that enable them to be adjusted. 'We identified that 50% of the value of a seat was made up of commonised parts. There was a further 30% where this was a possibility.'

An initial costing suggests that the rationalisation exercise could eventually save $1 billion (£710 million) over a six year lifespan of an average model, and allow a substantial increase in the number of new models brought to market.

Martin Waller, Financial Times, 5 March 2002

8.11 Section summary

The professionalism of the purchasing function affects profit in three ways. Effective purchasing does three things.

- It obtains the **best value for money,** giving the company more flexibility in its pricing strategy.

- It assists in meeting **quality targets,** with an impact on a firm's long-term marketing strategy if quality is an issue.

- It minimises the amount of purchased material held **in stock,** so minimising stock-holding costs.

Chapter roundup

- **Operations planning** involves the detailed procedures for creating and delivering products and services. Business processes can be re-engineered from a zero base.

- Operational effectiveness is vital in the delivery of customer satisfaction and maintaining profitability. This is why firms **benchmark** others in the same industry - although this may give an inappropriate emphasis on imitation where differentiation would be more appropriate.

- **Manufacturing** good practice has been transformed in recent years by advanced technology, flexible manufacturing systems and just-in-time techniques.

- Similar considerations also apply to **services**, where service quality is vital to ensure customer retention.

- Most significant has been the impact on **quality**.

- **Quality** is the totality of features which bears on a product's ability to meet stated needs. **Design quality** includes the degree to which customer satisfactions are built into a product. **Conformance quality** is an absence of defects in the finished goods.

- *Taguchi's* quality/cost model is important as it identifies the necessity of **reducing variation** in production processes as a means of reducing losses.

- **Quality assurance** is increasingly demanded of suppliers. Quality assurance standards include BS EN ISO 9000. Certification is granted to companies which have an adequate system of quality assurance.

- **TQM** is a concept which applies quality to the *whole* organisation. Relevant techniques concepts are **statistical process control** (for conformance quality) and **quality function deployment** (for design quality). Important aspects are **continuous improvement**, the fact that production has **employees take part** in controlling and improving quality, **internal marketing** and linking business activities in **quality chains.**

- Purchasing makes a major contribution to cost and quality management in any business and in retail is a vital element of strategy. The purchasing mix is:

  ° Quantity   ° Quality
  ° Price   ° Delivery

Quick quiz

1 What is the link of operations to mission?

2 Define operations plans.

3 What is business process re-engineering?

4 Identify four types of benchmarking

5 What is the difference between technical quality and functional quality in service operations?

6 Define quality.

7 Distinguish between design and conformance quality.

8 What is a quality circle?

9 Define TQM.

10 What is the purchasing mix?

Answers to quick quiz

1 Mission should be embedded in policies and behaviour standards at operational level

2 Specifications for individuals to enable sectional objectives to be achieved

3 Fundamental rethinking and radical redesign of business processes to achieve dramatic improvements

4 Internal, functional, competitive, strategic

5 Technical quality lies in the nature of the service provided. Functional quality lies in the customer's subjective assessment of the service encounter

6 Fitness for use

7 **Design** quality lies in the customer satisfactions incorporated into the product; **conformance** quality lies in the defect rate in the finished article

8 Groups of workers selected to analyse and discuss the production process with the aim of improving quality

9 Managing quality to ensure customer satisfaction both internally and externally

10 Quantity, quality, delivery, price

Now try the question below from the Exam Question Bank

Number	Level	Marks	Time
Q12	Introductory	n/a	32 mins

Chapter 13

HUMAN RESOURCE MANAGEMENT

Topic list	Syllabus reference
1　Personnel and human resources management	5(e)
2　The human resources plan	5(e)
3　Recruitment, selection and induction	5(e)

Introduction

Human resources management is about getting the right employees in the right place at the right time, and ensuring that they work effectively. As opposed to the administrative job of the personnel function, HRM is a set of management techniques designed to get the best out of employees. HRM strategy should derive from the **business strategy**, and HRM plans have to take factors such as labour turnover into account. **Recruitment** processes start with the plan, by identifying the jobs to be done, and then developing profiles of the people to fill them. Interviewing as a **selection** technique should be supplemented by other forms of assessment. The process of **induction** should form an effective introduction to the organisation and should include any essential initial training.

Study guide

Section 5 – The nature of strategy implementation

- HR issues

Exam guide

Human resource management is increasingly accepted as an aspect of strategic management and could therefore form part of the setting for a compulsory Section A question or a feature of a Section B question.

1　PERSONNEL AND HUMAN RESOURCES MANAGEMENT

Personnel management

1.1　The case example below shows some of the issues involved in the management of human resources in an organisation.

Case example

London bus drivers

The pressures faced by recruiters are exemplified by recruiting for the bus industry, here as described in the *Financial Times* (20 August 1997).

London bus drivers tend not to say in a job for more than a few months. The capital's bus companies are facing the highest levels of **staff turnover** since the 1950s. A combination of the reviving economy and the expanding London bus network means that some bus companies are having to replace up to 40 per cent of drivers a year.

Pay is one issue, shift work is another. A number of bus drivers, for instance, are skilled workers for whom the job was a welcome safety net during the recession of the early 1990s. But the **pay**, at £230 to £300 for a 40 hour week, is not enough to keep them now.

But the bus companies, competing in a deregulated market, are under pressure to **match their services to commuter needs, rather than the body clocks of their drivers.**

The squeeze on numbers of these semi-skilled workers - it takes six weeks to train a bus driver - is now so acute that some bus companies are looking outside London for staff. Go Ahead Group, which owns London General Transport with 1,400 drivers, has launched a scheme to recruit drivers from the provinces.

Some argue that what is really needed is a fundamental change of **culture** at London Transport. This is the authority that puts out to tender the coveted 400 London bus routes. The companies with the lowest cost base scoop the best routes as they require less public subsidy.

CentreWest, owed by FirstBus, believes that recruiting drivers from outside their local area spells trouble. Instead, it has broadened its **recruitment policy** to include significantly older and younger drivers, as well as more women.

Metroline hopes to keep its drivers by offering the prospect of virtually a job for life and very high staff share ownership as well as good pension schemes.

Bus bosses agree that the work has got tougher, with congestion now blocking London's roads from 7am to midnight.

1.2   It is easiest to understand HRM by contrasting it with the traditional model of **personnel management. Personnel management** is not directly involved in the business strategy. It is a collection of people-related support activities.

- Setting general and specific **management policy** for employment relationships
- **Administration:** writing job descriptions, managing the appraisal process
- **Policing:** ensuring all personnel follow company policies
- **Collective bargaining** and industrial relations
- **Staffing and organisation:** obtaining and retaining personnel
- **Implementing downsizing** or redundancy programmes
- Aiding the **self-development** of employees at all levels
- **Reviewing and auditing** manpower and management in the organisation

Human resources management (HRM)

1.3   **HRM aims to integrate personnel issues with the strategic planning of the business.**

> **KEY TERM**
>
> **Human resources management** (HRM) is 'a strategic and coherent approach to the management of an organisation's most valued assets: the people working there who individually and collectively contribute to the achievement of its objectives for sustainable competitive advantage'. (*Armstrong*)

1.4   **Goals of strategic HRM**

- Serve the **interests of management,** as opposed to employees.
- Suggest a **strategic approach to personnel issues.**
- Link **business mission to HR strategies.**
- Enable **human resource development to add value** to products and services.
- Gain **employees' commitment to the organisation's** values and goals.

Features

1.5 Distinctive features of HRM

Feature	Comment
Top management	Personnel was a staff function of limited impact. Top managers set direction, and so they must be involved in HRM.
Performance and delivery of HRM	Line managers are responsible for implementation of HRM. They do not carry out specialised instructions, but manage within the context of the organisation's HRM strategy.
Strategic fit	The right people in every respect must be chosen.
Cultures and values	HRM tries to inculcate the organisation's values into its employees.
Employee behaviour and commitment	HRM seeks to win hearts and minds rather than mere consent to management decisions.
Reward systems	These recognise good performance (eg performance related pay systems).
Employees are assets	People are a resource to be deployed. Assets need to be maintained though training. Degradation of human assets will harm competitiveness.

Management

1.6 HRM and personnel management compared

	HRM	**Personnel**
Purpose of activity	Strategic development of the business	Operations, policies and procedures; crisis management
Expertise	Serves the business strategy, and is spread throughout the organisation	A professional specialisation in one department
Responsibility	Everybody's, although the HR department still has an administrative and a 'teaching role'	The personnel department
Work focus	Employee roles in furthering the mission	Job descriptions

Human resources strategy

1.7 The HR strategy has to be related to the business strategy. Below we show how, using the example of an airline: most airlines are trying to become global companies to avoid dependence on one country.

Business strategy	HR implications	Airline example
What business are we in?	What people do we need?	Air transportation requires pilots, cabin crew, ground crew and so on.
What products/markets, level of output and competitive strategy, now and in future	Where do we need people what are they expected to do, and how many? Location and size of workforce. Productivity expected and output?	The airline is going global and therefore it needs cabin crew who are skilled in languages and are sensitive to cultural differences.
What is the culture and value system? Is it the right one?	The need to change culture and values	A cultural change programme; recruiting people to fit in with the right value system; attitudinal assessments
Tomorrow's strategies, demands and technologies	Tomorrow's personnel needs must be addressed **now**, because of lead times. New technology requires training in **new skills**	Recruitment, training, cultural education
Critical success factors	How far do these depend on staff?	Service levels in an aircraft depend very much on the staff, so HRM is crucial.

Values

1.8 **Human resource management** policies emphasise **values**. 'HRM places emphasis on finding people whose attitudes and behaviour are likely to be congruent with what management believes to be appropriate and conducive to success'.

(a) **Service industries** often involve direct personal interaction between an employee and the customer. Employees are ambassadors of the organisation. In a way they are part of the product (eg a troupe of actors in a play).

(b) **New organisational forms** which support autonomous teams and work groups require a **cultural glue** to replace direct management control. Asking employees to have a commitment to quality is an example.

2 THE HUMAN RESOURCES PLAN

2.1 The human resources plan arises out of the strategic plan.

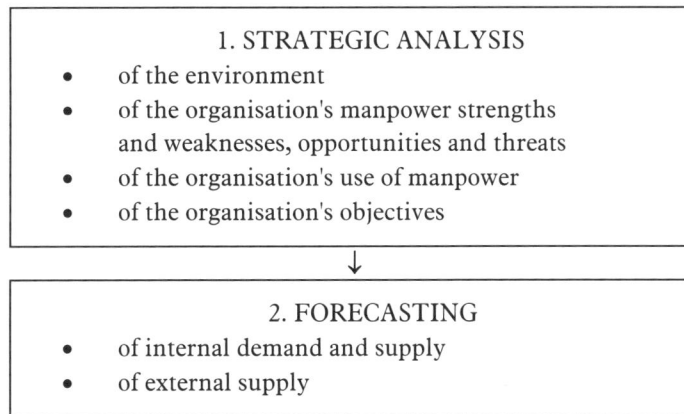

```
┌────────────────────────────────────────────────┐
│              1. STRATEGIC ANALYSIS               │
│     •   of the environment                       │
│     •   of the organisation's manpower strengths │
│         and weaknesses, opportunities and threats│
│     •   of the organisation's use of manpower    │
│     •   of the organisation's objectives         │
└────────────────────────────────────────────────┘
                        ↓
┌────────────────────────────────────────────────┐
│                2. FORECASTING                    │
│     •   of internal demand and supply            │
│     •   of external supply                       │
└────────────────────────────────────────────────┘
```

Strategic analysis

2.2 The current and future position should constantly be kept under review.

(a) **The environment**: population and education trends, policies on the employment of women and on pension ages, trends generally in the employment market.

(b) The organisation's HR **strengths, weaknesses, opportunities and threats** need to be analysed so as to identify skills and competence gaps and the level of innovation. Threats may involve competitors poaching staff.

(c) **Human resource utilisation**. An assessment should be made of how effectively the organisation is currently utilising its staff .

(d) **Objectives.** Core and subsidiary corporate objectives should be analysed to identify the manpower implications. New products, technology, sites, culture and structure will all make demands on staff.

2.3 **Timescales** are very important. An immediate gap may prompt instant recruitment while long-term corporate objectives will allow long-term plans for updating existing staff and providing them with the skills required.

Forecasting

2.4 **Estimating demand**. Planning future HR needs requires accurate forecasts of turnover and productivity (eg if fewer staff are required for the same output). The demand can be estimated after consideration of wide range of data.

- New venture details
- New markets (need new staff)
- New products/services
- New technology (new skills)
- Divestments
- Organisational restructuring (eg relocation)
- Cost reduction plans

2.5 **Estimating supply**

(a) **Current workers. A stocks and flows analysis** will define the **internal labour market**. It describes, not just aggregate quantities, but movements in and out of certain grades, by occupation and grade and according to length and service. This can be used in **modelling**.

(b) The **external labour market**. Labour **market research** has four functions.

- It measures potential employees' awareness of the organisation.
- It discerns attitudes of potential employees towards the organisation.
- It suggests possible segments for advertising purposes.
- It provides analysis of population trends for long-term forecasting.

2.6 A **position survey** compares demand and supply. Discrepancies between them in the numbers required/available, their grade, skills or location can be removed through the application of an integrated manpower strategy.

Closing the gap between demand and supply: the HR plan

2.7 The HR plan is prepared on the basis of personnel requirements, and the implications for productivity and costs. The HR plan breaks down into subsidiary plans.

Plan	Comment
Recruitment plan	Numbers; types of people; when required; recruitment programme
Training plan	Numbers of trainees required and/or existing staff needing training; training programme
Redevelopment plan	Programmes for transferring, retraining employees
Productivity plan	Programmes for improving productivity, or reducing manpower costs; setting productivity targets
Redundancy plan	Where and when redundancies are to occur; policies for selection and declaration of redundancies; re-development, re-training or re-location of redundant employees; policy on redundancy payments, union consultation
Retention plan	Actions to reduce avoidable labour wastage

The plan should include budgets, targets and standards. It should allocate responsibilities for implementation and control (reporting, monitoring achievement against plan).

Cost/benefit analysis

2.8 There may be a range of possible HR solutions to corporate problems. For example, if an expansion is planned the extra capacity could be provided in a variety of ways. Differential costs and benefits should, as always, be assessed and compared. Here are some possibilities.

(a) **Recruitment and/or training**
- Recruiting costs (advertisements, fees, management time)
- Training costs (money climbing the learning curve)
- Wages and related costs
- Other costs (eg requirements for factory space)

(b) **Outsourcing** the services or production to outsiders (eg getting a catering firm to run a canteen).

(c) **Buying capital equipment** or altering work processes in other ways to enhance productivity.

(d) Changing the **type of employment** offered.

(i) **Full-time salaried employment or part-time employment**. Part-time employees have been cheaper in the past because they are less likely to be eligible for benefits such as holiday pay or pensions. Recent EU legislation has significantly improved the lot of part-time workers.

(ii) **Temporary or permanent employment**.

2.9 Some firms are dividing their workforce into two sections.

(a) A **core workforce** of permanent full-time staff.

(b) A **peripheral workforce** consisting of part-timers, temporary staff, or staff on short-term contracts and subcontractors taken on for particular jobs.

2.10 This division was first identified in 1984. However, there are some contentious issues.

(a) Most people look for **secure** employment.

(b) Part time workers now have the same employment rights as full-time workers.

(c) Management issues include motivating part-timers to get the best out of them, **co-ordinating** their work and development so that they do not feel like second class citizens in the firm.

Succession planning

KEY TERM

Succession planning is undertaken in order to ensure continuity in the organisation's leadership. It involves the systematic identification, assessment and development of managerial talent at all levels.

2.11 Succession planning should be an integral part of the HR plan and should support the organisation's chosen strategy. The developed plan should also be compatible with any changes that that are foreseen in the way the organisation operates. It is likely that strategic objectives will only be obtained if management development proceeds in step with the evolution of the organisation.

2.12 **Benefits of succession planning**

(a) The development of managers at all levels is likely to be improved if it takes place within the context of a succession plan. Such a plan gives focus to management development by suggesting objectives that are directly relevant to the organisation's needs.

(b) Continuity of leadership is more likely, with fewer dislocating changes of approach and policy.

(c) Assessment of managerial talent is improved by the establishment of relevant criteria.

2.13 **Features of successful succession planning**

(a) The plan should focus on future requirements, particularly in terms of strategy and culture.

(b) The plan should be driven by top management. Line management also have important contributions to make. It is important that it is not seen as a HR responsibility.

(c) Management development is as important as assessment and selection.

(d) Assessment should be objective and preferably involve more than one assessor for each manager assessed.

(e) Succession planning will work best if it aims to identify and develop a leadership *cadre* rather than merely to establish a queue for top positions. A pool of talent and ability is a flexible asset for the organisation.

Case example

Succession planning

Few large companies approach their succession planning with care.

When Sir Richard Greenbury stepped down as chairman of Marks and Spencer last year, it took the retailer months to find a successor. Other companies that have struggled to find new leaders include Barclays and Reed Elsevier, the publisher.

When Bob Ayling was sacked as chief executive of British Airways earlier this year, one of the many criticisms directed at him was that he had sidelined any rivals and failed to groom a successor.

Michael Skapinker, Financial Times, 13 July 2000

3 RECRUITMENT, SELECTION AND INDUCTION

KEY TERMS

Recruitment is the part of the process concerned with finding the applicants: it is a positive action by management, going out into the labour market, communicating opportunities and information and generating interest.

Selection is the part of the employee recruiting process which involves choosing between applications for jobs: it is largely a negative process, eliminating unsuitable applicants.

3.1 A systematic approach to recruitment and selection

Step 1. Detailed personnel planning.

Step 2. Job analysis, so that for any given job a **job description** and a **person specification.**

(i) A job description is a statement of the purpose, component tasks, duties, objectives and standards and accountabilities of a job.

(ii) A person specification states the skills, knowledge, qualities and experience required to perform the job

Step 3. An identification of vacancies, by way of the personnel plan (if vacancies are created by demand for new labour) or requisitions for replacement staff by a department which has lost a current job-holder.

Step 4. Evaluation of the sources of labour, again by way of the personnel plan, which should outline personnel supply and availability, at macro- and micro-levels. Internal and external sources, and media for reaching both, will be considered.

Step 5. Review of applications, assessing the relative merits of broadly suitable candidates.

Step 6. Notifying applicants of the results of the selection process.

Step 7. Preparing employment contracts, induction, training programmes etc.

Job analysis, job design and competences

3.2 Procedures for recruitment should only be carried out in the context of a recruitment policy, which might cover issues such as internal/external applications of post, non-discrimination and so forth, courteous processing of applicants, the type of tests favoured.

> ### KEY TERM
>
> **Job analysis** is 'the process of collecting, analysing and setting out information about the content of jobs in order to provide the basis for a job description and data for recruitment, training, job evaluation and performance management. Job analysis concentrates on what job holders are expected to do.' (Armstrong)

Job analysis

3.3 The management of the organisation needs to analyse the sort of work needed to be done in order to recruit effectively. The type of information needed is outlined below.

Type of information	Comments
Purpose of the job	This might seem obvious. As an accountant, you will be expected to analyse, prepare or provide financial information; but this has to be set in the context of the organisation as a whole.
Content of the job	The tasks you are expected to do. If the purpose of the job is to ensure, for example, that people get paid on time, the tasks involve include many activities related to payroll.
Accountabilities	These are the results for which you are responsible. In practice they might be phrased in the same way as a description of a task.
Performance criteria	These are the criteria which measure how good you are at the job. These are largely taste related.
Responsibility	This denotes the importance of the job. For example, a person running a department and taking decisions involving large amounts of money is more responsible that someone who only does what he or she is told.
Organisational factors	Who does the jobholder report to directly (line manager)?
Developmental factors	Likely promotion paths, if any, career prospects and so forth. Some jobs are 'dead-end' if they lead nowhere.
Environmental factors	Working conditions, security and safety issues, equipment and so on.

Competences

3.4 A current approach to job design is the development and outlining of competences.

> ### KEY TERM
>
> A person's **competence** is 'a capacity that leads to behaviour that meets the job demands within the parameters of the organisational environment and that, in turn, brings about desired results'. (*Boyzatis*)

3.5 Some take this further and suggest that a competence embodies the ability to transfer skills and knowledge to new situations within the occupational area.

3.6 **Different sorts of competences**

(a) **Behavioural/personal** competences: underlying personal characteristics people bring to work (eg interpersonal skills); personal characteristics and behaviour for successful performance, for example, 'ability to relate well to others'. Most jobs require people to be good communicators.

(b) **Work-based/occupational competences** refer to 'expectations of workplace performance and the outputs and standards people in specific roles are expected to obtain'. This approach is used in NVQ systems (see below). They cover what people have to do to achieve the results of the job. For example, a competence of a Certified Accountant includes 'produce financial and other statements and report to management'.

(c) **Generic competences** can apply to all people in an occupation.

3.7 **Some competences for managers**

Competence area	Competence
Intellectual	• Strategic perspective
	• Analytical judgement
	• Planning and organising
Interpersonal	• Managing staff
	• Persuasiveness
	• Assertiveness and decisiveness
	• Interpersonal sensitivity
	• Oral communication
Adaptability	
Results	• Initiative
	• Motivation to achievement
	• Business sense

These competences can be elaborated by identifying **positive** and **negative** indicators.

Job description

> **KEY TERM**
>
> A **job description** sets out the purpose of the job, where it fits in the organisation structure, the context of the job, the accountabilities of the job and the main tasks they have to carry out.

3.8 **Purposes of job descriptions**

Purpose	Comment
Organisational	Defines the job's place in the organisational structure
Recruitment	Provides information for identifying the sort of person needed (person specification)
Legal	Provides the basis for a contract of employment
Performance	Performance objectives can be set around the job description

3.9 Contents of a job description

(a) **Job title** (eg Assistant Financial Controller). This indicates the function/department in which the job is performed, and the level of job within that function.

(b) **Reporting to** (eg the Assistant Financial controller reports to the Financial Controller), in other words the person's immediate boss. (No other relationships are suggested here.)

(c) **Subordinates** directly reporting to the job holder.

(d) **Overall purpose** of the job, distinguishing it from other jobs.

(e) **Principal accountabilities or main tasks**

  (i) Group the main activities into a number of broad areas.

  (ii) Define each activity as a statement of accountability: what the job holder is expected to achieve (eg **tests** new system to ensure they meet agreed systems specifications).

(f) The current fashion for multi-skilling means that **flexibility** is expected.

Alternatives to job descriptions

3.10 **Detailed** job descriptions are perhaps only suited for jobs where the work is largely repetitive and therefore performed by low-grade employees: once the element of **judgement** comes into a job description it becomes a straitjacket. Many of the difficulties that arise where people adhere strictly to the contents of the job description, rather than responding flexibly to task or organisational requirements.

3.11 Perhaps job descriptions should be written in terms of the **outputs and performance levels** expected. Some firms are moving towards **accountability profiles** in which outputs and performance are identified explicitly.

3.12 **Role definitions**. Whereas a **job** is a group of tasks, a role is more than this. A **role** is a part played by people in meeting their objectives by working competently and flexibly within the context of the organisation's objectives, structures and processes. A **role definition** is wider than a job description. It is less concerned with the details of the job content, but how people interpret the job.

Case example

Guinness

According to *People Management* (11 September 1997) in May 1996 Guinness Brewing Great Britain introduced a new pay system based on competences.

Restrictive job definitions, lengthy job descriptions and a 24-grade structure were replaced by broad role profiles and three pay bands. Roles are now specified in terms of 'need to do' (primary accountabilities), need to know (experience and knowledge requirements) and 'need to be' (levels of competence).

Competences are defined as the skill, knowledge and behaviours that need to be applied for effective performance. There are seven of them, including commitment to results and interpersonal effectiveness. Roles are profiled against each relevant competence and individuals' actual competences are compared with the requirements through the performance management process.

Person specification

3.13 A person specification identifies the **type of person** the organisation should be trying to recruit – character, aptitudes, educational or other qualifications, aspirations. It is an interpretation of the job specification in terms of the kind of person suitable for the job.

3.14 Research has been carried out into what a personnel specification ought to assess. *Munro Fraser's Five Point Pattern of Personality* directs the selector's attention to five aspects of the candidate.

- Impact on others
- Acquired knowledge or qualifications
- Innate ability
- Motivation
- Adjustment and emotional balance.

Advertising job vacancies

3.15 After a job description and a personnel specification have been prepared, the organisation should advertise the job vacancy. The job description and personnel specification can be used as guidelines for the wording of any advertisement or careers prospectus pamphlet. The choice of advertising medium will depend on **cost, frequency,** the frequency with which the organisation wants to advertise the job vacancy and its **suitability** to the target audience.

3.16 **Advertising media for recruitment**

- In-house magazines
- Professional journals
- National newspapers
- Local newspapers
- Local radio
- Job centres
- Recruitment agencies
- Schools careers officers
- University careers officers
- Careers/job fairs
- Open days
- The internet

Application forms

3.17 Applicants who reply to job advertisements are usually asked to fill in a job **application form,** or to send a letter giving details about themselves and their previous job experience (**their CV**) and explaining why they think they are qualified to do the job.

3.18 The application form should therefore help the selection officer(s) to **sift through the applicants**, and to reject some at once so as to avoid the time and costs of unnecessary interviews. It should therefore:

(a) **Obtain relevant information** about the applicant and which can be compared with the requirements (education and other qualifications, experience relevant to the job, age, interests even) of the job.

(b) Give applicants the **opportunity to write** about himself or herself, his or her career ambitions or why he or she wants the job.

The interview

3.19 Aims of the interview

- Finding the best person for the job, through direct assessment
- Giving the applicant the chance to learn about the firm

Testing

3.20 Tests are used supplement interviews or select applicants for interview.

3.21 **Types of test**

(a) **Psychological tests and personality tests**. An individual may be required to answer a long series of questions or score a variety of statements which indicate basic attitude profiles.

(b) **Intelligence tests** measure the applicant's general intellectual ability.

(c) **Proficiency tests** are perhaps the most closely related to an assessor's objectives, because they measure ability to do the **work involved.**

(d) **Aptitude tests** aim to provide information about the candidate's abilities. Aptitude tests can test mental ability (IQ tests, tests in mathematics, general knowledge or use of English) and physical dexterity.

(e) **Psychometric tests** contain features of all of the above. They are selection tests that seek to **quantify** psychological dimensions of job applicants, for example intelligence, personality and motivation. Candidates might be required to answer a list of questions. Those answers are then marked and the candidate is given a score.

3.22 **Advantage of tests**

- A test can be a sensitive measuring instrument.
- Tests are standardised, so that all candidates are assessed by the same yardstick.
- Tests always measure the same thing (eg IQ).

3.23 **Disadvantages**

(a) They give a spurious accuracy to complex issues.

(b) They are culturally-specific. Many tests for managers were developed in the US. The cultures in the UK and US differ in many respects.

Induction

3.24 Induction is a continuing process which might last for a few months. This is sometimes referred to as a **probationary period**.

(a) The supervisor must arrange for the recruit's training programme to start.

(b) The recruit will only gradually learn the job through continued on-the-job training.

(c) The person responsible for induction should keep checking up on the new recruit, to make sure that the recruit is settling in well and is learning the ropes.

(d) The senior manager should check on the recruit from time to time (in particular, find out how the training programme is progressing).

(e) The induction period should include training in essential aspects of organisational principles and practice such as health and safety awareness and equal opportunities policy.

Chapter roundup

- **Personnel management** in the past was never perceived to have a strategic role, dealing as it did with issues of hiring and firing, industrial relations and so forth.

- **Human resource management (HRM)** is based on the assumption that the management and deployment of staff is a key **strategic** factor in an organisation's competitive performance. HRM requires top management involvement and the promotion of culture and **values**, so that employees' **commitment**, as opposed merely to their consent, is obtained.

- **Resourcing** is about meeting the personnel needs of the organisation. HRM identifies the number of staff needed, the skills needed and the degree to which the staff's personalities and values are suited to the organisation culture.

- **Job analysis** determines the requirements for a job. The job's tasks are set out in a job description. A job specification describes the skills or competences required for the job. A **person specification** describes the sort of person suitable for a job.

- Job vacancies are often advertised in a number of ways. Market research is often useful so as to target recruitment efforts effectively. **Recruitment** advertising is still *advertising*, and so is a way in which the organisation shows its face to the world.

- **Interviews** are a widely used selection method. Many firms prefer to use tests as, for large numbers of candidates, they provide a more reliable prediction of performance on the job than interviews. **Tests** can assess intelligence, personality etc. Interviews are flawed because of bias and difficulties people have in interpreting a candidate's behaviour.

- New recruits need time to learn the job and settle in. Many organisations have formal procedures for **induction**.

Quick quiz

1. What was the role of personnel management, in traditional terms?
2. What is the overall aim of HRM?
3. Where does HR planning start?
4. What would a redevelopment plan deal with?
5. What is the purpose of application forms?
6. What is induction?
7. Distinguish between recruitment and selection.
8. What is a job description?
9. What is a role definition?
10. What are proficiency tests?

Answers to quick quiz

1   A collection of people related support activities

2   To integrate the management of the human resource with the organisation's strategy

3   With the overall organisational strategy

4   Programmes for retraining and redeploying staff

5   To eliminate obviously unsuitable candidates

6   A process of introduction to the organisation and initial training to ensure that the recruit settles into the role

7   Recruitment is obtaining candidates. Selection is choosing the most suitable candidate

8   A statement of the purpose, context, tasks and accountabilities of a job

9   A description of the part played by a person working competently and flexibly within the context of the organisation's objectives, structures and processes

10   Tests of ability to do particular work

Now try the question below from the Exam Question Bank

Number	Level	Marks	Time
Q13	Exam	20	36 mins

BPP
PROFESSIONAL EDUCATION

Chapter 14

MANAGING PERFORMANCE

Topic list	Syllabus reference
1 Performance management: an outline	5(e)
2 Motivating individuals	5(e)
3 Creating effective teams	5(e)
4 Appraisal and performance management	5(e)
5 Human resource development and organisational learning	5(e)
6 The management of diversity	5(e)

Introduction

The previous chapter described how the organisation obtains human resources, but HRM places great emphasis on how they are used. This chapter and the next deal with how to get the best out of the people who have been so expensively recruited.

Performance management is an active approach to defining what must be achieved and ensuring it is done. This sets the context for all the motivational, teamworking and appraisal activities in this chapter.

We also look at the concept of the learning organisation from the point of view of individual development and give a brief overview of the management of diversity and equal opportunities.

Study guide

Section 5 – The nature of strategy implementation

- HR issues

Exam guide

As with the previous chapter, the material in this chapter could be of use when dealing with any question in the exam.

1   PERFORMANCE MANAGEMENT: AN OUTLINE

KEY TERM

Performance management is: 'a means of getting better results…by understanding and managing performance within an agreed framework of planned goals, standards and competence requirements. It is a process to establish a shared understanding about what is to be achieved, and an approach to managing and developing people..[so that it]…will be achieved' (*Armstrong, Handbook of Personnel Management Practice*).

1.1 **The process of performance management**

Step 1. From the **business plan**, identify the requirements and competences required to carry it out.

Step 2. Draw up a **performance agreement**, defining the expectations of the individual or team, covering standards of performance, performance indicators and the skills and competences people need.

Step 3. Draw up a **performance and development plan** with the individual. These record the actions needed to improve performance, normally covering development in the current job. They are discussed with job holders.

- The areas of performance the individual feels in need of development
- What the individual and manager agree is needed to enhance performance
- Development and training initiatives

Step 4. **Manage performance continually throughout the year,** not just at appraisal interviews done to satisfy the personnel department. Managers can review actual performance, with more informal interim reviews at various times of the year.

- High performance is reinforced by praise, recognition, increasing responsibility; low performance results in coaching or counselling

- Work plans are updated as necessary.

- Deal with performance problems, by identifying what they are, establish the reasons for the shortfall, take control action (with adequate resources) and provide feedback

Step 5. Performance review. At a defined period each year, success against the plan is reviewed, but the whole point is to assess what is going to happen in future.

1.2 Organisations are introducing such systems for much the same reason as they pursued **management by objectives**, in other words to:

- Link the individual's performance with the performance of the organisation
- Indicate where training and development may be necessary

1.3 Success at work is based on a symbiotic relationship between the organisation and the employee. There are many factors which determine the work performance.

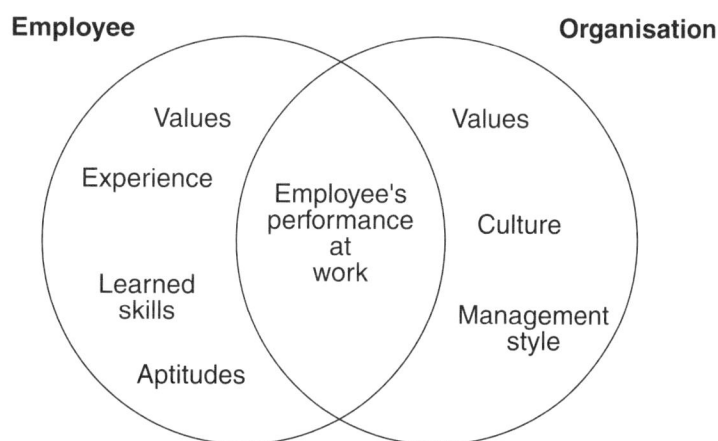

1.4 (a) An employee's **personality and ability** might be **fine for the task** but might **clash with the organisation's culture**. (A person who is a natural bureaucrat will not always fit in a culture where roles are not defined.)

(b) **Work organisation**: is the employee given a suitable job and are the employee's skills appropriately developed?

(c) **Motivation**: can an employee be persuaded to work hard, and well?

2 MOTIVATING INDIVIDUALS

2.1 Many managers have a crude idea of motivation, or of employees' attitudes to work. *Douglas McGregor* categorises managers' attitudes into two types. Most fall somewhere between these extremes.

(a) **Theory X**: most people **dislike work and responsibility and will avoid both if possible**. Because of this, most people must be coerced, controlled, directed and/or threatened with punishment to get them to make an adequate effort towards the achievement of the organisation's objectives.

(b) **Theory Y**: **physical and mental effort into work is as natural as play or rest**. The ordinary person does not inherently dislike work: according to the conditions, it may be a source of satisfaction or punishment. People learn not only to accept but to seek responsibility.

Psychological contracts

2.2 *Edgar Schein* believes that the **roots of motivation** at work can be found in the **psychological contract** an individual has with the organisation. A psychological contract might be thought of as a set of expectations.

(a) The individual expects to derive certain benefits from membership of the organisation and is prepared to expend a certain amount of effort in return.

(b) The organisation expects the individual to fulfil certain requirements and is prepared to offer certain rewards in return.

2.3 **Types of psychological contract**

(a) **Coercive contract**. The individual **considers that he or she is being forced** to contribute his or her efforts and energies **involuntarily**, and that the rewards received in return are inadequate compensation. (An individual might hate the job or be unable to leave; he or she might be forcibly transferred to another job he or she does not like.)

(b) **Calculative contract**. This is accepted **voluntarily** by the individual, who expects to do the job in exchange for a **readily identifiable set of rewards** (for example pay, status, or simply having a job of work to keep occupied).

(c) **Co-operative contract**. The individual voluntarily **identifies his or her goals** with the **organisation** and its goals, so that he/she actively seeks to contribute further to the achievement of those goals.

Motives

2.4 The words **motives and motivation** are used with several meanings.

(a) **Goals or outcomes** that have become desirable for a particular individual. Thus we say that money, power or friendship are motives for doing something. These outcomes satisfy **needs**.

(b) The **mental process of choosing desired outcomes**, deciding how to go about them and setting in motion the required behaviour.

(c) The **social process** by which the behaviour of an individual is influenced by others. Motivation in this sense apply to the attempts of organisations to get workers to put in more effort.

2.5 Many theories have tried to explain motivation.

(a) **Content theories** assume that human beings have a package of motives which they pursue: they have a set of needs or desired outcomes.

(b) **Process theories** explore the process through which outcomes **become** desirable and are pursued by individuals. This approach assumes that people are able to select their goals and choose the paths towards them, by a conscious or unconscious process of calculation.

Content theories

Maslow's hierarchy of needs

2.6 *Maslow's* theory is about motivation in general, not just motivation at work.

(a) An individual's needs are arranged in a hierarchy. They are satisfied in order, so that basic needs (eg for water) must be satisfied first.

(b) Each level of need is dominant until satisfied. Only then does the next level of need become a motivating factor.

(c) A need which has been satisfied no longer motivates an individual's behaviour. The need for self-actualisation can rarely be satisfied.

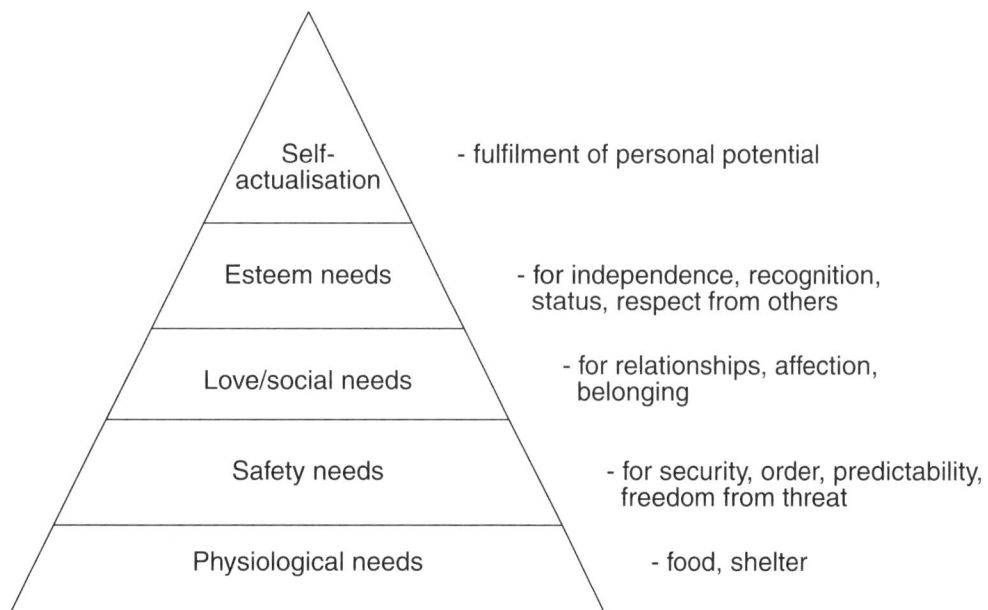

Self-actualisation	- fulfilment of personal potential
Esteem needs	- for independence, recognition, status, respect from others
Love/social needs	- for relationships, affection, belonging
Safety needs	- for security, order, predictability, freedom from threat
Physiological needs	- food, shelter

(d) Maslow described two other pervasive needs.

(i) Freedom of enquiry and expression needs (for social conditions permitting free speech, and encouraging justice, fairness and honesty)

(ii) Knowledge and understanding needs (to gain knowledge of the environment, to explore, learn)

2.7 **Problems in applying Maslow's theory**

(a) People seek to satisfy **several needs** at the same time.

(b) The **same need may cause different behaviour** in different individuals.

(c) It **ignores the concept of deferred gratification** by which people are prepared to accept current disadvantage for the promise of future benefits.

(d) **Empirical verification** of this theory is hard to come by.

McClelland

2.8 *David McClelland* also proposes a needs-based theory. It is not as wide ranging as Maslow's in that it does not take Maslow's very basic needs into account. McClelland identified three needs. They are not in any hierarchy.

Affiliation	*Power*	*Achievement*
People who need a sense of belonging and membership of a group tend to be concerned with maintaining personal relationships.	People who need power seek a leadership position to influence and control.	People have a strong desire for success and a fear of failure.

2.9 McClelland argued three points.

(a) Top managers have a strong need for power and a low need for affiliation.

(b) Entrepreneurs have a high need for achievement.

(c) It is possible to teach these needs in some cases, by teaching people to think with the right imagery so that they develop the needs.

Herzberg

2.10 *Herzberg's* two-factor theory identifies **hygiene factors** and **motivator factors**.

(a) **Hygiene factors** are those which, if inadequate, cause **dissatisfaction** with work. They work analogously to sanitation, which minimises threats to health. They are based on a **need to avoid unpleasantness.**

- Company policy and administration
- Salary
- The quality of supervision
- Interpersonal relations
- Working conditions
- Job security

(b) **Motivator factors** actively create job satisfaction and are effective in motivating an individual to superior performance and effort. They are based on a **need for personal growth**.

- Status (possibly a hygiene factor too)
- Advancement
- Gaining recognition
- Being given responsibility
- Challenging work
- Achievement
- Growth in the job

A lack of motivators at work will encourage employees to concentrate on bad hygiene (real or imagined) such as to demand more pay.

2.11 The job itself, on the other hand, can be interesting and 'exciting'. It can satisfy the desire for a feeling of accomplishing something, for responsibility, for professional recognition, for advancement, and the need for self-esteem.

2.12 Herzberg suggested means by which satisfactions could be supplied.

(a) **Job enrichment:** 'the planned process of up-grading the responsibility, challenge and content of the work' for example, by delegation.

(b) **Job enlargement:** increase the number of operations in which a worker is engaged and so moving away from narrow specialisation of work.

(c) **Job rotation:** this is the planned operation of a system whereby staff members exchange positions with the intention of breaking monotony in that work and providing fresh job challenge.

Process theories

Expectancy theory

2.13 *Victor Vroom* suggested that people will decide how much they are going to put into their work by considering two factors.

(a) **Valence.** The value that they place on the outcome (whether the positive value of a reward, or the negative value of a punishment). Valence is subjective.

(b) **Expectancy.** The strength of their **expectation** that behaving in a certain way will in fact bring about the desired outcome. **Expectation** is the individual's **subjective probability.** In other words, people differ in their estimates as to the outcome of an action.

> *Expectancy x Valence = Force of motivation.*

2.14 The theory holds that this is a **conscious decision making process.**

(a) If the outcome is worthless (ie has a Valence of 0) then according to Vroom, there will be no motivation. Similarly if the **expectation** of the result is 0, there will be no motivation either. Only when both **Expectancy and Valence have positive values** will individual be motivated.

(b) The **subjective** element of **Expectancy** and the fact that there is a **subjective element in Valence** mean that expectancy theory can account for **individual differences** in motivation.

(c) **Expectancy theory aims to measure motivation.** As it is based on the assumption that people are to a degree **rational,** it aims to be predictive. However, individuals can never have complete knowledge of outcomes nor do they soberly weigh up what they are doing.

2.15 *Drucker* (writing before Herzberg) suggested that motivation through **employee satisfaction** is not a useful concept because employee satisfaction is such a **vague idea.** His suggestion was that employee satisfaction comes about through encouraging – if need be, by pushing – employees to accept responsibility. There are four ingredients to this.

(a) **Careful placement of people in jobs** so that an individual is suited to the role.

(b) **High standards of performance in the job,** so that the employee should be encouraged to expect high standards of performance from himself or herself.

(c) **Providing the worker with regular feedback control information.**

(d) **Opportunities for participation,** to give managerial perspective.

2.16 **Improving motivation**

    (a) **Incentive schemes**. For some people such as piece workers or for those who are either in financial difficulties or see success in monetary terms, this might make a difference in encouraging higher output. Incentive schemes have become very popular, with reward tied to the profit of the firm. Problems arise, however.

- They are not fair when the performances of two people are linked.
- People might pursue their own goals to the detriment of organisation goals.
- Pay is usually a hygiene factor and does not give satisfaction.

    (b) **Fitting the job to the worker**? For example, people with **affiliation** needs can be organised in teams. Many companies now adopt team-based working because it is more effective operationally. Teams can have desirable characteristics.

- Self managing
- Multi-skilled
- Open, with negotiated production targets
- Able to share knowledge

    (c) Rewards can be based on **behaviours and attitudes** rather than mere output.

Developments in motivation research

2.17 According to *Robert McHenry* (*Spurring Stuff*, People Management, 24 July 1997):

    (a) Forty years ago, motivation at work tended to be tackled as single-issue psychology. Typical advice was 'people will work harder if you pay them more', or 'people will work harder if you give them more attention'.

    (b) A couple of decades later, a long list of single issues had emerged. The fashion then was to classify and combine them in relatively simple ways in order to create a good motivational climate. Perhaps Maslow's or Herzberg's theories are relevant here.

2.18 Recently, research has shifted from an external to an **internal perspective**: how employees **perceive** their job and the working environment. It has also explored the **relationships** *between* **the motivational variables,** to get inside the employee's mind.

2.19 Research by *Leigh and Brown* in the US identifies two key aspects of the psychological climate.

Psychological safety	Job meaningfulness
• Support: the boss backs you up	• Self-expression
• Role clarity	• Contribution: what you do makes a difference
• Recognition: praise for what you do	• Challenge

2.20 According to the research by *Kahn* these elements can be combined in different ways, into **job involvement**. This is when work is a major **satisfaction** in person's life.

2.21 Conclusions from the research.

    (a) **Perceptions** of the work environment are linked to job and effort. For many people a meaningful climate produces conditions under which involvement flourishes. People already involved **convince themselves** they are doing meaningful work.

(b) 'Distinctions between **intrinsic and extrinsic motivators may become less valuable**, if emphasis is put on employee perceptions, on the train of motivation-related thought, and on the blurred distinction between what is reality and what is created by people in their own minds. That is the true psychology of motivation.'

Setting performance targets

2.22 In April 2004, *Financial Management*, the CIMA members' magazine, reported on performance management in the NHS. The results of research supported the well-established idea that involving people in the setting of their work targets is beneficial.

(a) They generally know more about the processes they deal with then senior managers do.
(b) They know what can be improved and by how much.
(c) They tend to set higher targets than senior managers do.
(d) They set relevant targets.

2.23 The role of management in this situation is threefold.

(a) They contextualise improved performance by explaining the aims and benefits of initiatives in whole system terms.

(b) They provide the resources needed.

(c) They provide a framework for improved communication.

3 CREATING EFFECTIVE TEAMS

3.1 In your working life, though, you will generally find yourself working as part of a group or **team**; or, if you are a supervisor or a manager, you may direct a team. **A team is more than just a collection of individuals** - it has a specific purpose, a sense of identity and, in a work context, it has a task to perform. First of all, a team is a type of group.

> **KEY TERMS**
>
> A **group** is 'any collection of people who perceive themselves to be a group'. Unlike a random collection of individuals, a group of individuals share a common sense of identity and belonging.
>
> A **team** is a 'small number of people with complementary skills who are committed to a *common purpose*, performance *goals* and approach for which they hold themselves basically accountable'.

Teamworking

3.2 The basic work units of organisations have traditionally been specialised functional departments. In more recent times, organisations are adopting small, flexible teams. Teamworking allows work to be shared among a number of individuals, so it get done faster than by individuals working alone, without people either losing sight of their whole tasks or having to co-ordinate their efforts through lengthy channels of communication.

3.3 A **team may be called together temporarily**, to achieve **specific task objectives (project team)**, or may be more or less permanent, with responsibilities for a particular product, product group or stage of the production process (a **product or process team**). There are two basic approaches to the organisation of team work: multi-skilled teams and multi-disciplinary teams.

Multi-disciplinary teams

3.4 **Multi-disciplinary teams** bring together individuals with **different skills and specialisms**, so that their skills, experience and knowledge can be **pooled** or exchanged. Teamworking of this kind encourages freer and faster communication between disciplines in the organisation, which brings three advantages.

- It increases workers' **awareness of their overall objectives** and targets.
- It **aids co-ordination.**
- It **helps to generate solutions to problems**, and suggestions for improvements.

Multi-skilled teams

3.5 **Multi-skilled teams** bring together a number of **individuals who can perform *any* of the group's tasks** (eg each individual has many skills). These tasks can then be shared out in a more flexible way between group members.

The ideal team

3.6 **Characteristics of the ideal functioning team**

(a) Each individual gets the **support** of the team, a sense of identity and belonging which encourages loyalty and hard work on the group's behalf.

(b) Skills, information and ideas are **shared**, so that the team's capabilities are greater than those of the individuals.

(c) **New ideas** can be tested, reactions taken into account and persuasive skills brought into play in group discussion for decision making and problem solving.

(d) Each individual is **encouraged** to participate and contribute and thus becomes personally involved in and committed to the team's activities.

(e) **Goodwill, trust and respect can be built up** between individuals, so that communication is encouraged and potential problems more easily overcome.

Problems with teams

3.7 Unfortunately, team working is rarely such an undiluted success. There are certain constraints involved in working with others.

(a) Awareness of **group norms** and the desire to be acceptable to the group may **restrict individual personality** and flair.

(b) **Too much discord.** Conflicting **roles and relationships** (where an individual is a member of more than one group) can cause difficulties in communicating effectively.

(c) **Personality problems**, and will suffer if one member dislikes or distrusts another; is too dominant or so timid that the value of his ideas is lost; or is so negative in attitude that constructive communication is rendered impossible.

(d) **Rigid leadership** and procedures may strangle initiative and creativity in individuals.

(e) **Differences of opinion** and political conflicts of interest are always likely.

(f) **Too much harmony.** Teams work best when there is room for disagreement.

(i) They can become dangerously blinkered to what is going on around them and may confidently forge ahead in a completely wrong direction. The **cosy consensus of the group prevents consideration** of alternatives, constructive criticism or conflict.

(ii) Efforts to paper over differences leads to bland recommendations without meaning.

(g) **Corporate culture and reward systems.** Teams will fail if the company promotes and rewards the individual at the expense of the group.

(h) **Too many meetings.** Teams should not try to do everything together. Not only does this waste time in meetings, but team members are exposed to less diversity of thought.

(i) **Powerlessness.** People will not bother to work in a team or on a task force if its recommendations are ignored.

(j) **Suitability.** Teamworking does not suit all jobs.

3.8 *Belbin,* listed the most **effective character-mix** in a team.

Member	Role
Co-ordinator	Presides and co-ordinates; balanced, disciplined, good at working through others.
Shaper	Highly strung, dominant, extrovert, passionate about the task itself, a spur to action.
Plant	Introverted, but intellectually dominant and imaginative; source of ideas and proposals but with disadvantages of introversion.
Monitor-evaluator	Analytically (rather than creatively) intelligent; dissects ideas, spots flaws; possibly aloof, tactless - but necessary.
Resource-investigator	Popular, sociable, extrovert, relaxed; source of new contacts, but not an originator; needs to be made use of.
Implementor	Practical organiser, turning ideas into tasks; scheduling, planning and so on; trustworthy and efficient, but not excited; not a leader, but an administrator.
Team worker	Most concerned with team maintenance - supportive, understanding, diplomatic; popular but uncompetitive - contribution noticed only in absence.
Finisher	Chivvies the team to meet deadlines, attend to details; urgency and follow-through important, though not always popular.

The **specialist** joins the group to offer expert advice when needed.

The value of groups as work units

3.9 **Teams are not the solution to all problems**

(a) Some decisions and tasks are **better reached by individuals working alone** or having the final say.

(b) **Group norms** *may* work to lower effectiveness.

(c) Seeing people as a team – or expecting to work as one – is completely unrealistic in many cases (eg if they work in different countries) and **more formal co-ordination methods** may be necessary.

(d) Groups have been shown to produce **fewer ideas** - though better evaluated - than the individuals of the group working separately. A group will often produce a better solution to a quiz than its best individual, since 'missing pieces' can be added to his or her performance.

4 APPRAISAL AND PERFORMANCE MANAGEMENT

Appraisal: reviewing past performance to establish the current position

4.1 The process of appraisal is part of the system of performance management.

> **KEY TERM**
>
> Whilst performance management as a whole is forward looking, the process of **appraisal** is designed to review performance over the past period, with a view to identifying any deficiencies, and improving it in the future.

The purpose of appraisal

4.2 The general purpose of any appraisal system is to improve the efficiency of the organisation by ensuring that the individuals within it are performing to the best of their ability and developing their potential for improvement.

(a) **Reward review**: measuring the extent to which an employee deserves a bonus or pay increase

(b) **Performance review**: for planning and following-up training and development programmes, ie identifying training needs, validating training methods and so on

(c) **Potential review**, as an aid to planning career development and succession, by attempting to predict the level and type of work the individual will be capable of in the future

4.3 **Objectives of appraisals**

(a) Establishing what **the individual has to do** in a job in order that the objectives for the section or department are realised

(b) Establishing the **key or main results** which the individual will be expected to achieve in the course of his or her work over a period of time

(c) **Comparing the individual's level of performance against a standard**, to provide a basis for remuneration above the basic pay rate

(d) Identifying the individual's training and development **needs** in the light of actual **performance**

(e) Identifying **potential candidates for promotion**

(f) Identifying **areas of improvement**

(g) Establishing an **inventory of actual and potential performance** within the undertaking to provide a basis for manpower planning

(h) Monitoring the undertaking's **initial selection procedures** against the subsequent performance of recruits, relative to the organisation's expectations

(i) **Improving communication** about work tasks between different levels in the hierarchy

4.4 The need for appraisal

(a) Managers and supervisors may obtain **random impressions** of subordinates' performance (perhaps from their more noticeable successes and failures), but rarely form a coherent, complete and objective picture.

(b) They may have a fair idea of their subordinates' shortcomings - but may not have devoted **time and attention** to the matter of improvement and development.

(c) Judgements are **easy to make**, but **less easy to justify** in detail, in writing, or to the subject's face.

(d) **Different assessors** may be applying a **different set of criteria**, and varying standards of objectivity and judgement. This undermines the value of appraisal for comparison, as well as its credibility in the eyes of the appraisees.

(e) Unless stimulated to do so, managers rarely give their subordinates adequate **feedback** on their performance.

The process of appraisal

4.5 A typical appraisal system

Step 1. **Identification of criteria** for assessment, perhaps based on job analysis, performance standards, person specifications and so on

Step 2. An **appraisal report** is prepared by the manager. In some systems both the appraisee and appraiser prepare a report: these reports are then compared.

Step 3. An **appraisal interview**, for an exchange of views about the appraisal report, targets for improvement, solutions to problems and so on

Step 4. **Review of the assessment** by the assessor's own superior, so that the appraisee does not feel subject to one person's prejudices. Formal appeals may be allowed, if necessary to establish the fairness of the procedure.

Step 5. **Action plans** to achieve improvements and changes agreed are prepared and implemented

Step 6. **Follow-up:** monitoring the progress of the action plan

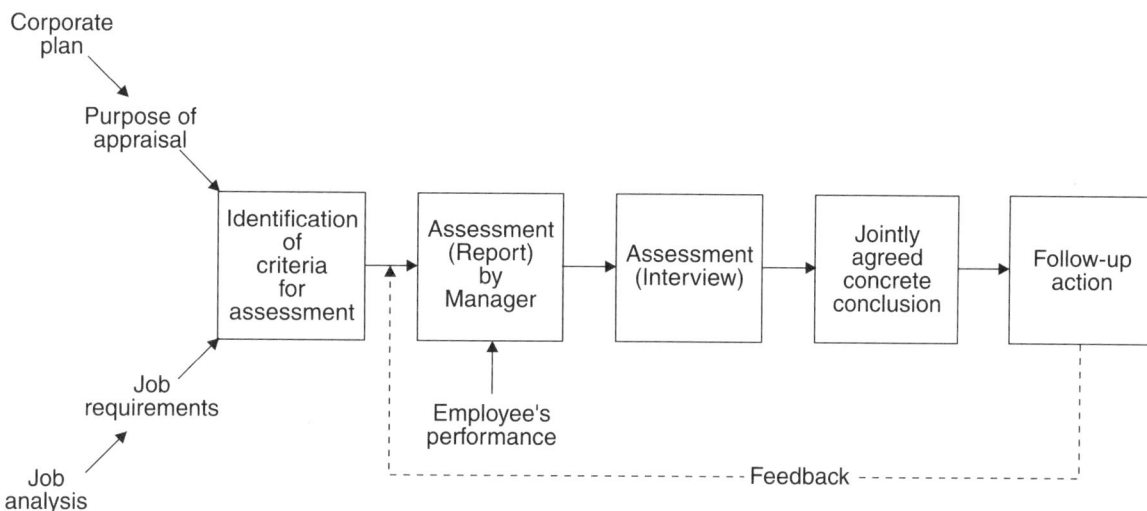

4.6
Most systems provide for appraisals to be recorded, and report forms of various lengths and complexity may be designed.

4.7 **Appraisal techniques**

(a) **Overall assessment**. The manager writes in narrative form his judgements about the appraisee. There will be no guaranteed consistency of the criteria and areas of assessment, however, and managers may not be able to convey clear, effective judgements in writing.

(b) **Guided assessment**. Assessors are required to comment on a number of specified characteristics and performance elements, with guidelines as to how terms such as 'application', 'integrity' and 'adaptability' are to be interpreted in the work context. This is more precise, but still rather vague.

(c) **Grading**. Grading adds a comparative frame of reference to the general guidelines, whereby managers are asked to select one of a number of levels or degrees to which the individual in question displays the given characteristic. These are also known as **rating scales**. There is a tendency to award average ratings.

(d) **Behavioural incident methods**. These concentrate on **employee behaviour**, which is measured against typical behaviour in each job, as defined by common **critical incidents** of successful and unsuccessful job behaviour reported by managers.

(e) **Results-orientated schemes**. This reviews performance against specific targets and standards of **performance agreed in advance by manager and subordinate together**. The effectiveness of the scheme depends on the targets set and the commitment of both parties to make it work. Targets must be realistic; clearly defined; wholly under the appraisee's control and relevant throughout the period of appraisal. These are difficult qualities to achieve.

Interviews and counselling

4.8 The extent to which any discussion or counselling interview is based on the written appraisal report varies in practice. Some appraisees see the report in advance.

4.9 *Maier (The Appraisal Interview)* identifies three types of approach to appraisal interviews.

(a) **The tell and sell method**. The manager tells the subordinate how he or she has been assessed, and then tries to sell (gain acceptance of) the evaluation and the improvement plan. This requires unusual human relations skills in order to convey constructive criticism in an acceptable manner, and to motivate the appraisee.

(b) **The tell and listen method**. The manager tells the subordinate how he or she has been assessed, and then invites the subordinate to respond. Moreover, this method does not assume that a change in the employee will be the sole key to improvement: the manager may receive helpful feedback about how job design, methods, environment or supervision might be improved.

(c) **The problem-solving approach**. The manager abandons the role of critic altogether, and becomes a counsellor and helper. The discussion is centred not on the assessment, but on the employee's work problems. The employee is encouraged to think solutions through, and to make a commitment to personal improvement.

Appraisal, management expertise and empowerment

4.10 There are particular difficulties in organisations where **empowerment** is practised and employees are given more responsibility.

(a) Many **managers may not have the time** to keep a sufficiently close eye on individual workers to make a fair judgement.

(b) In some jobs, **managers do not have the technical expertise** to judge an employee's output.

(c) Employees depend on **other people** in the workplace/organisation to be effective - in other words, an individual's results may not be entirely under his/her control.

4.11 Managers' influence on performance

A person's performance is often indirectly or directly influenced by the **management style** of the person doing the appraisal. However, given the disparity of power between the manager and the appraisee, key issues may not get raised. (An article in the Harvard Business Review was entitled 'Managing Your Boss': this suggests that an appraiser's own behaviour may be a factor in the appraisee's performance, but that such two-way discussions may not be appreciated.)

New approaches to appraisal

Upward appraisal

4.12 A notable modern trend, adopted in the UK by companies such as BP and British Airways and others, is **upward appraisal**, whereby employees are not rated by their superiors but by their subordinates. The followers appraise the leader.

4.13 Advantages of upward appraisal

(a) Subordinates tend to know their superior better than superiors know their subordinates.

(b) As all subordinates rate their managers statistically, these ratings tend to be more reliable – the more subordinates the better.

(c) Subordinates' ratings have more impact because it is more unusual to receive ratings from subordinates. It is also surprising to bosses because, despite protestations to the contrary, information often flows down organisations more smoothly and comfortably than it flows up. When it flows up it is qualitatively and quantitatively different. It is this difference that makes it valuable.

4.14 **Problems** with the method include fear of reprisals, vindictiveness, and extra form processing. Some managers in strong positions might refuse to act, even if a consensus of staff suggested that they should change their ways.

360 degree appraisal

4.15 Taking downwards, upwards and customer appraisals together, some firms have instituted **360 degree appraisal** (or multi-source appraisal) by collecting feedback on an individual's performance from the following sources (outlined by *Peter Ward* in *People Management*, 9 February 1995).

(a) The person's immediate boss

(b) People who report to the appraisee, perhaps divided into groups

(c) Co-workers

(d) Customers: (internal and external)

(e) The manager personally: all forms of 360 degree appraisal require people to rate themselves. Those 'who see themselves as others see them will get fewer surprises.'

4.16 Sometimes the appraisal results in a counselling session, especially when the result of the appraisals are conflicting. For example, an appraisee's boss may have a quite different view of the appraisee's skills than subordinates.

Appraisal and the organisation

4.17 'Any appraisal scheme can only be understood within the organisation structure of which it is a part' (Buchanan and Huczynski).

- They **reflect the values** an organisation seeks to promote.
- They clarify a person's job.
- They assess competence.
- They assume that feedback improves performance.
- They link performance with organisational goals.
- They aim to predict and control a person's behaviour.

4.18 A problem with many appraisal schemes in practice is that they concentrate exclusively on the **individual subordinate**. In other words they **reinforce hierarchy**, and are perhaps unsuitable to organisations where the relationship between management and workers is **fluid** or participatory. Upward, customer and 360° appraisals address this, but they are not widely adopted.

4.19 Appraisal systems, because they target the individual's performance, concentrate on the **lowest level of performance feedback**. They ignore the organisational and systems context of that performance. (For example, if an army is badly led, no matter how brave the troops, it will be defeated.) Appraisal schemes would seem to regard most **organisation problems** as a function of the **personal characteristics** of its members, rather than the **systemic problem** of its overall design.

4.20 A performance appraisal system is **designed by specialists** in the technostructure and **operated by managers** in the middle line. Its effectiveness depends on a range of factors.

(a) The **effort** line managers are prepared to put into the appraisal process.

(b) The **integrity** of line managers.

(c) The **ability** of line managers to do more than just give good appraisals to people who have a similar personality and background.

(d) The congruence between what the organisation **actually wants** and the behaviours it is **prepared to reward**.

4.21 If appraisal systems operate **successfully** as feedback control systems (in other words, if they do alter employees' performance) and identify behaviours to be encouraged, then, assuming organisational success is to some measure based on individual performance, they will influence the success of strategy.

5 HUMAN RESOURCE DEVELOPMENT AND ORGANISATIONAL LEARNING

KEY TERMS

Human resource development (HRD) is 'enhancing and widening ... skills by training, by helping people to grow within the organisation, and enabling them to make better use of their skills and abilities'.

Development is 'the growth or realisation of a person's ability and potential through the provision of learning and educational experiences'.

Training is 'the planned and systematic modification of behaviour through learning events, programmes and instruction which enable individuals to achieve the level of knowledge, skills and competence to carry out their work effectively'.

(Armstrong, *Handbook of Personnel Management Practice*)

5.1 Overall purpose of employee and management development

- **Ensure** the firm meets current and future performance objectives
- **Continuous improvement** of the performance of individuals and teams
- **Maximising people's** potential for growth (and promotion)

5.2 Development activities

- Training, both on and off the job
- Career planning
- Job rotation
- Appraisal (see previous chapter)
- Other learning opportunities

5.3 Organisations should have a **training and development strategy**, based on the overall strategy for the business. We can list the following steps.

Step 1. Identify the skills and competences are needed by the **business plan.**

Step 2. Draw up the **development strategy** to show how training and development activities will assist in meeting the targets of the corporate plan.

Step 3. **Implement** the training and development strategy.

This process is discussed in more detail below.

Developing skills and knowledge: the learning organisation

5.4 The **learning organisation** was discussed in Chapter 2 of this Study Text in the context of strategy formulation. Clearly, it is also relevant in training and development.

- It encourages continuous learning and knowledge generation at all levels.
- It has the processes to move knowledge around the organisation.
- It can transform knowledge into actual behaviour.

The justification for this is that knowledge can be created and exploited. Training is one part of this.

5.5   **Learning in the learning organisation**

Characteristics	Comments
Participative policy making	All members of a learning company have the chance to participate in the learning process.
Informating	This is the use of information not as a control mechanism, but as a resource for the whole organisation to exploit in order to develop new insights.
Enabling structures	Organisation structures are *temporary* arrangements that must respond to changed conditions and opportunities.
Boundary workers as environmental scanners	In a learning organisation, environmental monitoring is not restricted to specialists or managers. All employees dealing with the boundary should try and monitor the environment.
Inter-company learning	Learn from other firms.
Learning climate	The function of management in a learning organisation is to: • Encourage continuous learning and knowledge creation. • Create processes to move knowledge around the organisation. • Transform knowledge into actual behaviour, products and processes.

5.6   Training has a role in creating the learning organisation.

- Training enables skills to be disseminated.
- Training courses are an opportunity for people to get together.

The training process in outline

5.7   In order to ensure that training meets the real needs of the organisation, large firms adopt a planned approach to training. This has the following steps.

Step 1.   Identify and define the **organisation's training needs**. It may be the case that recruitment might be a better solution to a problem than training

Step 2.   **Define the learning required** – in other words, specify the knowledge, skills or competences that have to be acquired. For technical training, this is not difficult: for example all finance department staff will have to become conversant with the new accounting system.

Step 3.   **Define training objectives** – what must be learnt and what trainees must be able to do after the training exercise

Step 4.   **Plan training programmes**
   - Who provides the training
   - Where the training takes place
   - What resources are required and who provides them
   - Divisions of responsibilities between trainers, managers and trainees.

Step 5.   **Implement the training**

Step 6.   **Evaluate** the training: has it been successful in achieving learning objectives

Step 7.   Go back to Step 2 if more training is needed

6   **THE MANAGEMENT OF DIVERSITY**

6.1   This section reflects the social and legal situation in the UK, except where otherwise noted. This will serve as an example of practice in a developed country. All students should be aware of such practice, but may also find it relevant in the examination to discuss the situation in their own countries if it is different.

6.2 **Types of discrimination**

(a) **Direct discrimination:** one interested group is treated less favourably than another (except for exempted cases). This is illegal in the UK.

(b) **Indirect discrimination:** requirements or conditions are imposed, with which a substantial proportion of the interested group could not comply, to their detriment. This is also illegal.

(c) **Positive discrimination** gives **preference** to a protected person, regardless of comparative suitability and qualification for the job. British legislation does **not** (except with regard to training) **permit positive discrimination**. In particular, there is no quota scheme (except for registered disabled persons). The organisation may, however, set itself **targets** for the number of such persons that they will aim to employ – *if* the required number of *eligible* and *suitably qualified* people can be recruited.

(d) A number of countries in the world use **positive discrimination as an aspect of social policy to correct perceived disadvantages** endured by various ethnic and other groups in society. (For example, in India **scheduled castes** are entitled to a proportion of government jobs.)

Women in employment

6.3 Only in recent decades has there been a widespread challenge to **sex segregation** in employment; the idea that there are men's jobs and women's jobs, with only a few genuinely unisex categories of work persists. There are several reasons for this.

(a) There are cultural and social pressures on women to bear and rear children, and on men to make a lifetime commitment to paid work. Employers assumed that women's paid work would be short term or interrupted, and that training, development and promotion were wasted.

(b) The nature of earlier industrial work, which was physically heavy: legal restrictions were placed on women's employment in some areas.

(c) Lack of organisation of women at work and influence in trade unions.

(d) The reinforcing of segregation at home and at school.

(e) Career ladders which fail to fast-track women.

Ethnic minorities in employment

6.4 Unemployment rates differ amongst the various ethnic groups in the UK.

- The ethnic minority population is much younger than the population as a whole.
- Direct racial discrimination still exists in favour of white labour.
- Ethnic minorities are concentrated in certain industrial sectors, and occupations.

Other disadvantaged groups

6.5 Two further forms of discrimination are specifically legislated against.

(a) Failure to provide equal opportunities to suitably **qualified disabled persons**.

(b) Non-engagement or dismissal on the grounds of a **conviction for a criminal offence**, once the offender is rehabilitated and his conviction 'spent'.

Ageism

6.6 Most job advertisements specify age limits which make it difficult for older employees to find work. This is perfectly legal, but some groups are seeking to have it outlawed.

Legal rights to equal opportunity

6.7 In Britain, two main Acts have been passed to deal with inequality of opportunity.

   (a) The Sex Discrimination Act 1975, outlawing certain types of discrimination on the grounds of sex or marital status.

   (b) The Race Relations Act 1976, outlawing certain types of discrimination on grounds of colour, race, nationality, or ethnic or national origin.

   In both Acts, the obligation of **non-discrimination applies to all aspects of employment**, including advertisements, recruitment and selection programmes, access to training, promotion, disciplinary procedures, redundancy and dismissal.

Case example

In 2004 Stephanie Villalba sued bankers Merrill Lynch for £7.5 million for sexual discrimination, unfair dismissal and unequal pay. Merrill Lynch has paid £53 million in recent years to settle nearly 900 similar actions.

6.8 **Equal pay legislation** is intended 'to prevent discrimination as regards terms and conditions of employment between men and women' and covers equal pay for the same work and for work of equal value.

6.9 The **Disability Discrimination Act 1995** provides new rights for disabled people in relation to employment; access to goods, facilities and services; and buying or renting land or property.

6.10 The Act makes it unlawful for an employer who has 20 or more employees to discriminate against a disabled person in the field of employment, unless the discrimination is justified. As part of this protection, employers may have to make 'reasonable adjustments' to their premises or work arrangements.

6.11 Discrimination against disabled people can only be justified if the reason for it is both substantial and relevant to the circumstances of the individual case. It cannot be justified if the employer is under duty to make a reasonable adjustment, but fails (without reason) to do so – unless the treatment would have been justified even after that adjustment.

Rehabilitation of Offenders

6.12 **Rehabilitation of Offenders Act 1974.** A conviction for most criminal offences (earning less than 30 months in prison) is 'spent' after a period of time (which varies according to the severity of the offence). After this period, an offender (provided he or she is not a doctor, lawyer, teacher, accountant or police person) is 'rehabilitated' and is not obliged to disclose the nature of his offence or details of his conviction.

Management practice

6.13 The practical implications of the legislation for employers are set out in **Codes of Practice**, issued by the Commission for Racial Equality and the Equal Opportunities Commission. These do not have the force of law, but may be taken into account by Employment Tribunals, where discrimination cases are brought before them.

6.14 Organisations make minimal efforts to avoid discrimination, paying lip-service to the idea to the extent of claiming 'We are an Equal Opportunities Employer' on advertising literature! To turn such a claim into reality involves a range of policies and practices.

(a) **Support from the top** of the organisation for the formulation of a practical policy

(b) A **working party** drawn from, for example, management, unions, minority groups, the HRM department and staff representatives

(c) **Action plans and resources** (including staff) in order to implement and monitor the policy, publicise it to staff, arrange training and so on. Here are some possible measures.

- Appointing Equal Opportunities Managers
- Flexible hours or part-time work, including 'term-time' contracts
- Career-break or return-to-work schemes for women
- Training for women returnees
- Awareness training for managers
- The provision of workplace nurseries for working mothers
- Alteration of premises to accommodate wheelchair users

(d) **Monitoring**. The numbers of women and ethnic minority staff can easily be monitored at significant points.

- Entering (and applying to enter) the organisation
- Leaving the organisation
- Applying for transfers, promotions or training schemes

(e) **Positive action:** the process of taking active steps to **encourage** people from disadvantaged groups to apply for jobs and training, and to compete for vacancies.

Chapter roundup

- **Performance management** is a proactive approach to the management of people that breaks down strategic requirements into individual and team **targets** and seeks to obtain **commitment** to them.

- Managers' views as to what motivates employees vary between **Theory X** (employees are workshy) to **Theory Y** (employees like to work).

- Motivation theory is useful to managers as it exposes in a systematic way why or how people are or can be motivated. Some writers believe that employees' motivation can be raised if the job satisfies their **personal needs**. **Maslow's hierarchy** and **Herzberg's** two-factor theory (hygiene vs motivator factors) are examples.

- The roots of motivation, according to Schein, are found in the **psychological contract** an employee has with an organisation, underpinning basic attitudes to, and expectations of, the organisation and work.

- Others believe that motivation is a **process** in which individuals make partly rational choices based on the desirability of an outcome and the effort required to achieve it. **Expectancy theory** is an example.

- The development of **teamwork skills** is also a function of HRD. Teams go through four stages: forming, storming, norming, and performing. A team's effectiveness is contingent upon the personalities of its members, the task, the environment and the processes and procedures the team uses.

- **Appraisal schemes** exist to **monitor individual performance** in the hope that **feedback** can help **improve** it.

- Appraisal schemes can be subverted if managers (and staff) do not take them seriously, in particular with relation to **bias**.

- Appraisal schemes are part of the **organisation structure**. They work on the assumption that performance failures are the result of personal or communication problems, rather than overall organisation design. New methods of appraisal seek to overcome these problems.

- Human resource management seeks to enable people to grow within the organisation by equipping them with **enhanced skills and competences**. It can contribute to the development of the learning organisation.

- The training process begins with the definition of **training needs** and thence the definition of **training objectives**. The training itself must be planned and implemented to achieve those objectives and then evaluated to establish whether or not it has done so.

- Human resource management includes the management of **diversity and equal opportunities**. The UK has legislation forbidding discrimination in recruitment, promotion and reward against women and ethnic minorities.

Quick quiz

1. What is performance management?

2. What are the three types of psychological contract?

3. List the needs in Maslow's hierarchy.

4. Distinguish between multi-disciplinary and multi-skilled teams.

5. What are the purposes of appraisal?

6. How does management create a learning climate?

7. Why do employment rates differ among ethnic groups in the UK?

Answers to quick quiz

1   A proactive approach to the management of the human resource that breaks down strategic requirements into individual and team targets and seeks to obtain commitment to them

2   Coercive, calculative, co-operative

3   Physiological, safety, love/social, esteem, self actualisation

4   In multidisciplinary teams the members each have distinct skills. In multiskilled teams the members each have *several* skills

5   Generally, to improve organisational performance; individually, to review performance, potential and reward

6   Encourage continuous learning and knowledge creation; create processes to move knowledge around the organisation; transform knowledge into actual behaviour, products and processes.

7   Different age structure; racial discrimination; concentration of minorities in certain geographic and economic areas

Now try the question below from the Exam Question Bank

Number	Level	Marks	Time
Q14	Exam	20	36 mins

BPP
PROFESSIONAL EDUCATION

Chapter 15

INFORMATION TECHNOLOGY

Topic list		Syllabus reference
1	IT and strategic management: the case for planning	5(d)
2	The information resource	5(d)
3	Strategies for information systems	5(d)
4	Management of information systems	5(d)
5	Outsourcing IT	5(d)
6	End-user computing	5(d)

Introduction

Information technology affects all areas of a business. It is potentially so important that it is far more than a simple operational strategy. IT requires strategic management of its own, but there are special considerations. Arguably, IT shows some of the pitfalls of purely **emergent strategies**, and there are strong justifications for using the rational **planning** model in many areas. Throughout this text, you will see how IT can be integral to corporate, business and functional strategies. This is why we introduce it here.

Key models here include **McFarlan's grid**, which helps managers of a firm identify precisely where they stand in relation to IT and whether IT is going to be important strategically.

There are also practical, day to day problems to be solved in the management of IT. This is because it is a highly complex technology but it is most productive when it directly supports the individual work station. There is thus a tension between the need for highly skilled management of the resource and the need to make it widely available.

Study guide

Section 5 – The nature of strategy implementation

- IS/IT issues

Exam guide

The management of IS development has now been eliminated from the syllabus, according to the *Students' Newsletter* of January 2001. IS/IT management as such is therefore an unlikely theme for a question at all. However, IS/IT could well form part of the background to a compulsory question.

1 IT AND STRATEGIC MANAGEMENT: THE CASE FOR PLANNING

Case example

The Millennium Bug

When many old computer programs were written, few people anticipated they would still be in use by the year 2000; but they were, patched up and modified.

At one time, computer memory was a scarce resource, and so programmers saved space by limiting the digits used to contain the date. Many old computer programmes were unable to cope with the change of year from 1999 to 2000 as they assumed that going from 99 to 00 meant changing from 1999 to 1900, not 2000. *For some systems, every line of computer code had to be examined.*

(a)   A *rectification cost* of £31bn was given as the estimate for the *UK as a whole*.

(b)   *Individual companies*

(i)   Resources which could have been spent on new products or marketing programmes, were spent on curing this problem.

(ii)   There was possibility of severe disruption to the activities of *service organisations* which used IT extensively, such as transportation (eg timetabling) and the NHS.

(iii)   Organisational functions and systems with direct customer contact such as accounts departments were expected to be adversely affected.

(iv)   Not only information systems were affected, but also factory machinery, lifts, security systems and control devices of all kinds.

The government suggested that most firms seriously *underestimated* the severity of the situation. In the event, there were few breakdowns, but a huge amount of expensive programmer and management time was spent to achieve this.

1.1   With this sobering example in mind, it is easy to understand why managers should pay proper attention to IT.

1.2   **The case for a planned strategy for IT**

- **Costs**
- IT is **critical** to the success of many organisations.
- IT is a **strategic weapon** for competitive advantage can come from IT.
- IT affects all levels of **management**.
- IT changes how **information** is created and presented to management.

Costs

1.3   **IT is a high cost activity.** There are several key issues.

- The total amount spent on IT
- How much is spent on other areas of the business
- How well the funds are spent
- The time-lag between the expenditure and the benefits received
- The difficulty of quantifying the benefits
- The relative proportions of fixed costs and variable costs

Criticality: McFarlan's grid

1.4   **IT is critical to the success** of **some** organisations.

(a)   **IT has brought some industries into being.** For example, it is unlikely that global financial markets would have developed the current range and sophistication of financial instruments, and the possibility for trading at any time of day, without IT.

(b)   **Security.** Banks and other firms go to extraordinary lengths to protect themselves from a breakdown in their current systems. A failure of computer systems to work would result in a failure of some organisations to function at all. (On the other hand, many organisations are not dependent on IT.)

1.5   *McFarlan* analysed the strategic importance of IT as follows.

Strategic impact of future systems

		Low	*High*
Strategic impact of existing systems	*Low*	Support	Turnround
	High	Factory	Strategic

(a)   **Support role.** Information systems have **little relevance to a firm's existing or future** success.

(i)   IT thus requires below average investment and little management attention.

(ii)   *Earl* quotes the example of a cement manufacturing company. IT might be used to speed up administration and to make occasional improvements to the manufacturing process. IT is not vital or critical to the manufacture or distribution of cement.

(b)   **Factory role. Existing IT applications are important.** However, future IT developments are not anticipated to be relevant. Earl mentions a steel works, with an existing on-line real-time system for controlling production. It is **production** technology, not **information** technology, that will be most important.

(c)   **Strategic role. Existing and future developments** are at the heart of the company's future success. In fact, the business **operation depends on IT**: without IT it would not exist at all. Many finance/service companies depend on computers, telecommunications and databases.

(d)   **Turnround role. Existing IT is not important**, but **future developments** are likely to **have a significant impact.** In this case, IT is becoming *more* important. Its role and profile in the organisation is being enhanced. An example would be a firm which moved its computer system from back operation (eg administration) to front operation (providing the service).

1.6   **Moving round the grid.** A firm can be pushed by three forces.

(a)   The fit between IT's potential and the firm's strategy (and resources). Managers may exaggerate IT's benefit.

(b)   The strategic choices actually made by management about IT **in the past. Legacy** systems are those which are hard or too costly to change and which therefore affect strategic choice.

(c) The firm's **environment**. For example, competitors might exploit IT and the firm might have to copy them.

Question 1

Readyware Clothes makes clothes. IT spending has been strictly controlled, and IT is used mainly for accounting, processing sales orders, and printing invoices. One of its major customers, Keaton and Lamarque, has sent the firm the following letter: 'It has always been our intention to source most of our clothes for sale from domestic suppliers - we've always valued speed and responsiveness. We have recently, however, received interesting offers from a supplier in Hong Kong who has offered a wider ranging flexibility in design with new production technology. Can you offer anything similar? At the least, we would advise you to automate your sales order processing system so it can become interlinked with our purchasing systems for greater responsiveness'.

(a) In view of the original IT configuration, what square on the grid did the company find itself in?

(b) If the company's management made a decision to introduce the new ordering systems and the new production technology, what square on the grid would it occupy?

(c) What forces were driving it round the grid, if any?

Answer

(a) Support

(b) Turnround (the new ordering system was becoming critical to keep the customer)

(c) The main forces driving it round were:

    (i)   the competitive environment (the overseas producer, and the customer's demand);

    (ii)   the management decision to respond to this by using an IT-based strategy.

Strategic weapon

1.7 IT can be used as a strategic weapon to gain competitive advantage for the organisation

(a) It can improve productivity and performance (eg in design and manufacturing).

(b) It can be used to alter the management and organisational structure of the business (eg electronic mail, telecommuting).

(c) It can lead to the development of entirely new businesses (eg Reuters created an electronic market place where subscribers could trade via Reuter terminals).

The value chain

1.8 IT can be used at each stage in the value chain.

1.9 **Operations**

(a) IT can be used to **automate and improve physical tasks** in the operating core. Examples include robots.

(b) IT also **provides information** about operational processes.

1.10 **Inbound and outbound logistics**

(a) **Warehousing.** *Parcelforce* uses IT to track the progress of different parcels through the system.

(b) Create **virtual warehouses** of stock actually held at **suppliers**. For example an organisation with several outlets might have each connected to a system which indicates the total amount of stock available at different sites.

1.11 **Marketing and services**

(a) **Internet websites** can be used as an advertising medium and to gather information about customers.

(b) **Customer databases** enable firms to monitor consumers' buying habits and to identify new segments.

(c) Supermarkets use **EPOS** systems to give them a precise hour-by-hour idea of how products are selling to enable speedy ordering and replenishments.

1.12 **Support**

(a) **Procurement**. IT can automate some purchasing decisions and save paperwork if the organisation's purchase systems are linked directly to the sales order systems of its suppliers (eg by electronic data interchange).

(b) **Technology development.** *Computer automated design (CAD)* enables design modification and simulation, saving money.

(c) **Human resources** applications in the office include the maintenance of a **skills database**, staff planning (eg using network analysis), computer based training, time attendance systems, payroll systems and pension systems. HR applications include homeworking, now that powerful PCs the Internet and ISDN are affordable.

1.13 **Scoping models** respond to the difficulty in assessing how information can be exploited for competitive advantage. *Porter and Miller* produced an **information intensity matrix** which analyses the **amount of information** in the **product** itself and in the **value chain.**

(a) The **product:** (For example, oil has a low information content, a newspaper has a high information content). Where this is high, IT can be used to process or present it more effectively. For example, many newspapers have Internet websites.

(b) The **value chain:** (For example, low in the case of a cement maker making a simple product in bulk in a simple process, high in the case of a complex, technologically sophisticated product such as aircraft). Where information content in the value chain is high, IT can result in radical changes to business processes to ensure that the linkages in the value chain are managed effectively.

		Information in product	
		Low	*High*
Information in value chain	*Low*	Cement maker	Text books
	High	Oil (refined)	Newspaper

Question 2

The management of the *Globe*, a national daily newspaper, is considering the introduction of radically new technology to enhance its internal processes and the services it gives its distributors and readers. The management wishes to encourage researchers and business planners to access its archive of historical data.

Can you think of any possible IT applications? What framework could be used to analyse the suitability of these ideas? Use the models suggested in this and the previous chapter.

Answer

This exercise tries to get you to apply some of these models to a knowledge based industry, newspaper publishing. Here are some suggestions.

(a)   The **information intensity matrix** describes newspapers as having a high information content (by definition). The Globe's value chain also has a high information content (eg buying in inputs or stories, sub-editing them, arranging them on the pages, printing them, distributing them to wholesalers, and newsagents, in a very short time). This would imply a significant use of IT, as information is so important.

(b)   **Applications search tools** are also useful, as they can identify the possible uses of information technology.

  (i)   What do distributors actually want (eg speed of delivery)?

  (ii)   What do customers require (eg better graphics in maps and visual presentation)?

  (iii) New distribution systems (eg by fax).

  (iv)   Using IT to create a database of archive material which can be accessed over the telecommunications network.

  (v)   Store data on CD ROM.

(c)   Futuristically, technology might be used to supplement print-based newspapers. Some writers argue that customers will be able to dial up the stories they are interested in, which will be distributed over a communications network. Some newspapers are already exploring such a service.

Economic/industry context

1.14   IT is an **enabling technology,** and can produce dramatic changes in individual businesses and whole industries, especially where there are other major forces for change. Just under 50% of UK companies in a recent DTI survey use the internet.

Case example

The Internet has implications for the structure and strategies of some industries. Take telecommunications. The telephone tariff system is 'fundamentally a fixed cost system, but we pay for it on the basis of a variable - mainly voice minutes. What is more, where the charges are levied bears no relation to where the costs occur.'

The Internet is undermining this. Access to the Internet is normally charged at *local* call rates. It is now possible to hold conversations over the Internet, which 'will undermine the 'price per distance' business model' which allows telephone companies to charge more for long distance calls.

Levels of management

1.15   IT permeates the different layers of management, as a routine feature of office life and a facility for everyone to use.

(a)   Senior managers can see more precisely what goes on at operational level.

(b)   Operational management can be empowered by IT (eg expert systems) to take decisions, which computers can support.

(c)   **Delayering.** IT renders redundant the information processing role of middle managers.

(d)   Use of IT requires so-called **intellective** skills, the ability to analyse and manipulate abstract data. These used to be management's concern.

(e)   Email systems and diary planning systems enable managers to **co-ordinate** their activities better. 63% of UK companies in a recent survey by the DTI use email.

Technical issues

1.16 A strategic view of IT must take detailed **technical issues** into account. Ignoring the technology-based choices in IT is rather like ignoring interest rates when you are borrowing money. (Two UK building societies abandoned a merger because of incompatibility between their computer systems.)

1.17 The **security** of IT-based systems can be compromised by **technological** as well as management failures. Some organisations, especially those whose IT systems are important or critical, have to be concerned with security issues (hence some banks have fault-tolerant systems).

Case example

It is now possible to make payment over the Internet, but banks and credit card companies are still worried about possible fraud. However, solutions are being developed – but hackers always seem to be able to crack any encryption technology developed.

The importance of management

1.18 Success or failure in implementing IT depends on the systems themselves and the management effort behind them. IT will fail under certain conditions.

(a) When it is used to tackle the wrong problem, that is, the use of IT has not been thought through in the wider organisational context. Often those applications which are **easiest to computerise** are chosen in preference to those which are **most important**.

(b) If senior management are not interested in and do not appreciate the significance of IT based choices.

(c) If users are ignored in design and development.

(d) when no attention is given to behavioural factors in design and operation.

1.19 IT requires proper planning and management attention, because IT can affect the long-term performance of the enterprise in many ways.

Case example

An example of the importance of the wider organisational processes for the success of information technology is provided by the *Taurus project.*

This was a project, funded by various institutions in the City of London and managed by the Stock Exchange, to computerise certain aspects of share trading and *registration.* There was an existing computer system, Talisman, but for various reasons it was regarded as being no longer suitable.

(a) A new system was felt to be necessary because of large trading volumes in *shares* expected after the Big Bang.

(b) Stock markets and bourses elsewhere in Europe use computerised settlement systems. These are giving increasing competition to London as a financial centre.

However, the plans to develop a computer system failed, at a substantial cost to City institutions and damage to London's reputation as a financial centre. What went wrong? There was nothing inherently impossible about the task: automated settlement has been achieved in other financial centres. A number of reasons were suggested.

(a) Poor project management with inadequate control.

(b) The system was designed to *replicate* existing structures. Rather than use *one* central database, it was decided to use a system of separate but linked databases. Not to do so would have taken away business (and profits) from *share registrar* companies. The design was made unnecessarily complex in order to cater for all the vested interests. This then is an instance of the neutralisation of technology's possible benefits by wider social and organisational choices.

Reconciling planning and emergent strategies

1.20 That said, it is short-sighted to ignore the value and **creativity** of emergent strategies.

- Opportunities for the use of IT cannot always be identified in advance.
- Creative thinking should be encouraged.
- There should be many inputs as possible to the planning process.
- Users are becoming more powerful, as this becomes technologically possible.

1.21 **Successful IT development tendencies**

- **User-driven**, with the active support of superiors in user departments
- **Evolutionary developments** of existing approaches, rather than revolutionary change
- Developed outside the **information system function**
- **Marketed extensively** throughout the organisation and to customers
- Developed in **consultation with customers**

1.22 Indeed, IT departments are now enabled, within the framework of the plan, to offer user-friendly systems to help users devise their own applications.

1.23 Section summary

- Planning for IT is important because of cost, criticality, potential strategic importance and **technical** issues.
- **Relying on** planning alone fails to exploit the value of emergent strategies.

2 THE INFORMATION RESOURCE

Types of information

2.1 Information is a key business resource. *Drucker* suggests the executive's tool kit has four **types of information**.

(a) **Foundation information** (eg profitability, cash flow) is only useful insofar that, if abnormal, it tells us something is wrong.

(b) **Productivity information** is exemplified by traditional measures of productivity. Such information is only slowly being developed for **knowledge** and **service** work.

(c) **Competence information**. A firm should meticulously analyse what it does best (eg it might find unexpected uses for its products, which it can exploit).

(d) **Resource-allocation information** tells us how resources are used.

2.2 These four kinds of information relate to **tactics** and the **current business. For strategy** organised information about the **environment** is necessary: 'at least half the important new technologies that have transformed an industry in the past 50 years came from outside the industry itself'. Such information is unpredictable, informal or unstructured.

Levels of information

2.3 We can categorise information as strategic, tactical and operational.

2.4 EXAMPLE

Finance subsystem

- The **operational level** would deal with cash receipts and payments, bank reconciliations and so forth.

- The **tactical level** would deal with cash flow forecasts and working capital management.

- **Strategic level** financial issues are likely to be integrated with the organisation's commercial strategy, but may relate to the most appropriate source of finance (eg long-term debt, or equity).

2.5 The type of information at each level can be seen in the table below.

	Inputs	*Process*	*Outputs*
Strategic	Plans, competitor information, overall market information	Summarise Investigate Compare Forecast	Key ratios, ad hoc market analysis, strategic plans
Management/tactical	Historical and budget data	Compare Classify Summarise	Variance analyses Exception reports
Operational	Customer orders, Programmed stock control levels, cash receipts/payments	Update files Output reports	Updated file listings, invoices

Types of information system

2.6 These information requirements can be met, to a greater or lesser degree, by a firm's information systems.

Transaction processing systems

2.7 Transaction processing systems (TPS) are used at operational level for routine processing of data items and transactions. They provide the raw material for management information systems (MIS).

- Process: updating master files using transactions files
- Examples: ledgers, stock, payroll, order processing.

Management information systems

> **KEY TERM**
>
> **Management information system**: 'a system to convert data from internal and external sources into information and to communicate that information, in an appropriate form, to managers at all levels in all functions to enable them to make timely and effective decisions for planning, directing and controlling the activities for which they are responsible'. (*Lucey*).

2.8 An MIS cannot deal with:

- Qualitative data/information

- Informal information: Many managers express preference for 'grapevine' in information gathering

- Unprogrammed information

Decision support systems

2.9 Decision support systems (DSS) are a type of MIS which deal with semi-structured problems.

   (a) **Features**

- User-friendly
- Flexible
- Analytical capabilities
- Do not make decisions, but support decision maker

   (b) **Components**

- **Language module** for communication with user
- **Problem processing** module for analysis
- **Knowledge module** providing data storage

The best known and most widely used example of a DSS is the **spreadsheet**.

Expert systems

2.10 An expert system does make decisions. Its advantages include a learning ability, span of knowledge and use of fuzzy logic to overcome gaps. Expert systems are used in specific applications, including diagnosis in medicine and credit approval in banking.

2.11 Specific components of an expert system are as follows.

- **Knowledge base:** a collection of facts and rules
- **Knowledge acquisition program:** captures data to add to knowledge base
- **Inferencing engine:** processes rules and establishes which apply
- **Explanation program:** provides the user interface

Executive information systems

2.12 An executive information systems (EIS) is a system which provides information to senior management. It is designed to be very easy to use.

- It provides summary level data from organisation's MIS/TPS.
- It allows executive to drill down to supporting data.
- It provides flexible data manipulation facilities
- It incorporates graphics for user-friendly presentation
- A template system may be used for pro-forma/consistent reports

Data warehousing and data mining

2.13 IT systems can be used to store vast amounts of data in accessible form. A **data warehouse** receives data from operational systems, such as a sales order processing system, and stores it in its most fundamental form, without any summarisation of transactions. Analytical and query software is provided so that reports can be produced at any level of summarisation and incorporating any comparisons or relationships desired.

2.14 The value of a data warehouse is enhanced when **datamining** software is used. True datamining software **discovers previously unknown relationships** and provides insights that cannot be obtained through ordinary summary reports. These hidden patterns and relationships can be used to guide decision making and to predict future behaviour. Datamining is thus a contribution to **organisational learning**.

Case example

The American retailer *Wal-Mart* discovered an unexpected relationship between the sale of nappies and beer. Wal-Mart found that both tended to sell at the same time, just after working hours, and concluded that men with small children stopped off to buy nappies on their way home, and bought beer at the same time. Logically, therefore, if the two items were put in the same shopping aisle, sales of both should increase. Wal-Mart tried this and it worked.

Question 3

What do you consider is the importance of some of the management information systems discussed above for organisation hierarchy?

Answer

(a) Expert systems bring the power of expertise to the desk. Say a person wants a loan from a bank. An expert system can be used for credit scoring, so the request will not have to be directed back to a superior.

(b) Executive information systems mean that senior management can focus easily on operations so the middle management function of information processing might disappear.

All in all, this points to delayering of management hierarchies, but counterbalanced by the creation of new jobs in information management.

2.15 Section summary
- Different types of information are needed at different levels.
- Information systems aim to provide them.

3   STRATEGIES FOR INFORMATION SYSTEMS

Integrating IT and business objectives

3.1   A firm's IT strategy should support the overall strategy of the business.

3.2   IT *can* be considered a functional strategy, in other words a preserve of the data processing department, but IT might also be viewed as an aspect of **corporate strategy**: The strategy for information systems deals with the deployment of a **crucial resource throughout the whole business**. IT should therefore be considered during the strategic planning process in the same way that financial resources or human resources are considered.

Business objectives and IT resources

3.3   The **identification of business needs** and the information technology framework to satisfy them is at the **heart of a strategy for information systems** and information technology. This is not always feasible, especially if an organisation's use of IT has grown in a haphazard fashion, and the purpose of the strategy is to impose some sort of order on an already chaotic situation.

3.4   **Critical success factors** (CSFs) can translate business into IT objectives. We have already discussed them in the preparation of resource plans.

   (a)   **Define business objectives** (eg raise earnings per share, develop new businesses).

   (b)   **Identify the CSFs** whose success is necessary for the organisation to flourish (eg new markets, new products, core activities).

   (c)   **Develop the information systems to support the CSFs** (eg develop customer information systems, improve the financial control reporting system).

3.5   Critical success factors (CSFs) function as linking pins between IT and business planning even without a formal business strategy. Don't think, however, that going from a critical success factor to the relevant information strategy is easy.

Plans for information systems

3.6   An organisation might draw up a **strategic information systems plan.** An information strategy for an organisation can be said to cover three areas: systems, technology, management.

> **KEY TERM**
>
> The **information systems strategy** is the 'long-term directional plan...seen to be business-led, demand-oriented and concerned to exploit IT either to support business strategies or create new strategic options'.

3.7   The **information systems** strategy therefore deals with the integration of an organisation's information requirements and information systems planning with its long-term overall goals such as (customer service). The IS strategy determines **what applications should** be developed and **where resources** should be deployed.

3.8   We can draw another grid to help decide what to do with our systems once we have reviewed them.

Technical quality

	Low	High
Low	Divest system	Reassess system
High	Renew/upgrade the system	Maintain and enhance system

Business Value (row labels on left)

(a) **Technical quality** depends on the cost, reliability, speed and functionality of the system.

(b) **Business value** depends on the usefulness of the system output and the ease with which it can be used. This can be measured by the intensity of usage.

3.9 **Information technology strategy** follows on from the IS strategy above.

(a) It deals with four main **technologies**

- Computing
- Communications
- Data
- Application systems.

(b) This provides a **framework** for the analysis and design of the **technological infrastructure** of an organisation. For example, this might involve guidelines for makes of computers and software purchased (eg must support Windows IT) and so forth. This strategy basically indicates how the information systems strategies will be implemented.

3.10 **Information management strategy** is the basic approach an organisation has to the management of its information systems IT has a number of elements.

- Planning information systems developments

- Organisational management of information systems (eg the role of the information director)

- Control (eg cost control)

- Technology (eg systems development methodologies)

Question 4

Babbage and Newman plc is a company with an established base of IT applications. The finance department has a fully computerised accounting system. The marketing department has developed a primitive customer modelling package. The production department does not need IT.

The Finance Director is in charge of IT at Babbage and Newman. He proposes in the annual corporate budget a 10% increase in IT expenditure based on last year, for the relevant departments. This will enable system upgrades.

Comment.

Answer

There is no strategy at all. The Finance Director regards IT as a cost. Moreover the IT strategy is directed to enhancing its existing base (eg in the accounts department) rather than areas where it might prove competitively valuable (eg in marketing).

3.11 Section summary

The relationship between the three elements is summarised in the table below.

	Information systems strategy	*Information management strategy*	*Information technology strategy*
Subject	What?	Context?	How?
Basis	Divisional/product-market	Organisational	Processes/activities
Orientation	Demand (for applications)	Relationships (between people)	Supply (of technology)
Focus	Business (product - market)	Management	Technology (new developments, designs etc)

4 MANAGEMENT OF INFORMATION SYSTEMS

4.1 IT requires **strategic management**, because of its cost, criticality to the organisation's operations and its capacity to promote competitive advantage.

4.2 **Organisational response**

(a) **Raising the level of IT staff**, sometimes to the extent of appointing **information directors**

(b) Setting up **information centres** to aid users to develop their own applications

(c) Developing overall **strategies** for information systems

(d) Setting **standards** for hardware and software acquisition

(e) **Increasing resources** devoted to information systems security

The information director

4.3 The **information director** (ID) should be a member of the Board of Directors, or occupy a position of similar executive seniority.

4.4 **The role of the information director**

Role	Comment
Integrating	Ensuring the organisation's acquisition and use of IT fits in with the goals of the organisation.
Controlling	Ensure that *users* operate IT for the benefit of the organisation; this covers: • Technical standards (eg only buy from one supplier) • Software standards (eg only use Excel for spreadsheet applications) • Establishment of *corporate* as opposed to *departmental* databases • Providing an information systems service function.
Designing	The information director may be responsible for the overall design of an organisation's information systems. This responsibility is likely to be delegated on a day to day basis.

Role	Comment
Liaison	Liaison between information systems professionals and the rest of the organisation, eg *technical assistance*, discussions with users as to their needs, advice on the impact of information systems on organisational structure, working environment and so forth.
Environmental scanning	This is essential for a strategic perspective. IT affects ways of doing business, supplier-customer relationships etc. The information director will seek to dovetail these types of facility into the organisation's overall commercial strategy. The legal environment is also complex: data protection legislation, the vexed status of copyright on the Internet, virus problems and so on.

4.5 **Problems facing the information director**

(a) Shortages of skilled staff

(b) Backlogs in application development caused by (a) above, and also the fact that much programming time is spent repairing old applications rather than developing new ones

(c) Ensuring continued expansion

4.6 **Responsibilities entailed in information systems management**

Role	Comment
Administration	Secretarial work, accounting and library services of the information function. These support services are likely to be provided by other business functions. The IS manager's administrative responsibilities include budgeting (for capital and revenue expenditure) and personnel selection, training and welfare.
Strategic control and planning	IS plans should be tied into the overall business plan of the organisation. Planning activities include development of procedures and standards for guidance of staff (eg choice of systems development methodologies and control) and assigning development work to subordinates, and liaising with users to assess their needs.
Information systems development	This includes systems design, programming and so forth. The IS manager is likely to be a member of any steering committee for a project and will probably be instrumental in the choice of a project manager.
User support	This is the development and operation of applications. Information systems personnel can aid users to develop their own applications. Also, they can provide advice, help lines, and other services. (This is the role of the Information Centre.)
Service management computer operations and data centres	Currently, these contain complex and powerful systems, and are similar in function to the old style computer centres. The IS manager will review the operation of services provided to user departments.

Role	Comment
Network management	Ensure that networks are secure, with protection from viruses, operational (enough capacity on the file server) and that appropriate confidentiality (eg through passwords, user profiles restricting access to certain files) is maintained, new users are added, there are adequate connections.

5 OUTSOURCING IT

5.1 Rather than maintain a computing department, some organisations choose to contract out their computer operations to a private company, which might be paid a fee to provide a service.

- A computer bureau is an **external** service.

- **Facilities management** (FM) companies operate **within** the organisation. The FM company must work to a contract and will bear any losses.

5.2 FM companies are contracted to take over part or all of an organisation's computing facilities. Facilities management can take a variety of forms.

- Project management assistance
- Control of systems development
- Running an organisation's entire computing function

5.3 **Advantages of facilities management**

(a) A small organisation may have substantial IT requirements, but may not have the staff, management time or expertise.

(b) Facilities management is an effective form of **cost control**, as there is a **contract** where services are specified in advance for a fixed price. If the facilities management supplier is inefficient, the extra costs will not be borne by the 'host' organisation.

(c) A facilities management company has **economies of scale**. If two organisations employ the same FM company, the FM company's research into new products or technologies can be shared between its clients.

(d) Similarly, FM companies can employ staff with specific **expertise** which can be shared between several clients. FM is a way of coping with the skills shortage widely felt to be a feature of the IS labour market.

5.4 **Disadvantages**

(a) **Key role of information.** Unlike office cleaning or catering, an organisation's computing and information services are too important to be contracted out.

(b) **Different objectives. Technologies which play a strategic role** in an organisation's success cannot be handed over to outsiders. Also the **FM company has strategic objectives of its own,** which are different from the strategic objectives of the host. An IS function run by an FM company will be even more separate from the overall business functions than an organisation's own IS department.

(c) **No going back.** Once an organisation has handed over its computing to an FM company, it is locked in to the arrangement. The decision is very difficult to reverse. Should the FM company supply unsatisfactory levels of service, then the effort and expense an organisation would have to incur to rebuild its own computing function and expertise would be enormous.

(d) **IT awareness.** The use of FM does not encourage a proper awareness of the potential costs and benefits of IT amongst managers '...many managers naturally lean towards FM because they are technophobic and frightened by their jargon-spouting DP departments. The result is that they opt for the easy if short-sighted route'.

6 END-USER COMPUTING

KEY TERM

End-user computing: 'the direct, hands-on use of computers by users - not indirect use through systems professionals or the data processing staff. End-users include executives, managers, professional staff, secretaries, office workers, salespeople and others' (*Sprague and McNurlin: Information Systems Management in Practice*).

6.1 End-user computing has been fuelled by several trends.

- The introduction of PCs and networking to user departments
- User-friendly software (eg Windows)
- Greater awareness of computers and what they can do
- The applications backlog: most information systems departments do not have the resources to cope with all the demands for new applications pressed on them.

Question 4

List some uses of IT by end-users.

Answer

Uses of computers by end-users

- Accounting and calculating (eg spreadsheets)
- Writing (word processing)
- Search and retrieval of information (interrogating a database)
- Aiding communications (computer networks, electronic mail)
- Presentation of information (graphics)
- Planning, scheduling and monitoring (project management)
- Personal organisation (electronic diary facilities)
- Routine transaction processing
- Learning and education (computer based training)
- End-user programming (developing new programs)
- Decision support

6.2 **Management issues related to end-user computing**

(a) Responsibility for the **development of applications**: user departments or the IS department?

(b) **Duplication of effort**. Development of similar applications in different departments can occur, duplicating programming effort.

(c) **Security** may be a problem if access to the system is easy to obtain.

6.3 **Advantages of user-developed systems**

(a) Relieves shortage of systems development personnel

(b) Eliminates the problem of information requirements determination by information systems personnel

(c) Transfers the information system implementation process to users

6.4 **Disadvantages of user developed systems**

(a) The elimination of the separation of the functions of user and analyst

(b) The limits on user ability to identify correct and complete requirements for an application

(c) Lack of user knowledge and acceptance of application quality assurance procedures for development and operation

(d) Unstable user systems

(e) The dangers of private information systems

(f) The possibility of undesirable information behaviour

6.5 An approach to dealing with these problems is the **information centre**, which enables a proper convergence of intended strategies and emergent strategies in the use of IT, and is described below.

Centralisation or decentralisation?

6.6 Technological changes have shifted the balance of power over processing from the information systems department to user departments. The issues of **centralisation** and **decentralisation** relate both to **technical matters** and **managerial issues.**

Issue	Comment
Data management	Decentralisation can result in a riot of minor applications, with subtly different definitions of data reducing the ability to compare like with like or use for generating information. This might mean that the organisation's data resource as a whole is insufficiently transparent.
Hardware	Compatibility is less of a problem than in the past, if only because 'Windows' has become a *de facto* standard.
Software	If, say, two departments set up their own databases using different software, this would inhibit sharing data, or require complex programs.
Security	Networked PCs are less secure than mainframes. (However they are much more flexible to use.)
Cost	Networks of PCs are not always cheaper than central servers (mainframes). This is because the cost of 'add-ons', maintenance and so forth for PCs are much greater than that for mainframes.
Corporate vs functional	Looking at the **value chain** means considering the organisation as a **whole**. A decentralised approach to IT applications can result in IT being reduced to functional control: potentially revolutionary applications for reconfiguring **business processes** will not be identified.
Organisation structure	The degree of centralisation is not only influenced by technical issues, but by organisation structure. An organisation which is decentralised for most strategic issues will probably have a decentralised approach to IT.

Chapter roundup

- **Information technology** links computers with communications.

- IT is of **strategic importance** owing to its **cost**, its **critical** role to the success of some organisations, its potential as a **strategic weapon** and its effect on all **management levels**. Organisations need to assess both existing and future uses of IT.

- McFarlan's grid outlines four uses for IT: factory, support, turnround, strategic. Management can move a firm around the grid.

- Information is tactical, operational and strategic.

- An information strategy should be integrated with the business strategy of the organisation.

- Strategies should be developed for applications, system and technology.

- Information systems pose unique management problems of co-ordination, direction and cost.

- The **information director** is responsible for ensuring that IT issues are discussed at Board level and for developing the strategy.

- The **information systems department** is involved in administration, strategic control of IT, development of IS user support and service management.

- Some **central control** is necessary to ensure that the organisation as a whole benefits from IT.

- IT may be outsourced to obtain expertise and cost control.

- End-user computing puts the IT resource in the hands of users.

Quick quiz

1   Why should IT be planned?

2   How does a firm move around McFarlan's grid?

3   How does IT affect management?

4   Why is relying on top-down planning inappropriate to IT?

5   What are four types of information?

6   What is an EIS?

7   How can IT be incorporated into business strategies?

8   What is the information systems strategy?

9   What are the advantages of outsourcing the IT resource?

10 Define end-user computing.

Answers to quick quiz

1 It may be critical to organisational success; it is costly; it affects all levels in the organisation; it influences the way information is used.

2 It is pushed by three forces.

- The potential of IT to support the strategy
- Past management choices
- The environment

3 Information processing by managers is largely eliminated, while information use is more effective, especially among higher management, though there is a possibility of information overload.

4 IT is empowering users; the rapid pace of change means that opportunities cannot always be identified in advance; IT's flexibility promotes creativity among users.

5 Foundation, productivity, competence and resource-allocation

6 Executive information system

7 By making it support CSFs

8 Integration of IT with long-term overall goals

9 Cost control, expertise, economies of scale, convenience

10 Direct, hands-on use of computers by users

Now try the question below from the Exam Question Bank

Number	Level	Marks	Time
Q15	Exam	20	36 mins

BPP
PROFESSIONAL EDUCATION

Chapter 16

STRATEGIC OUTCOMES

Topic list	Syllabus reference
1　Strategic control systems	8(c)
2　The balanced scorecard	8(c)
3　Corporate decline	8(d)

Introduction

To monitor its own strategic performance a firm needs to establish a number of performance indicators, relevant to different aspects of the business. Over-reliance on **financial results** alone can mean that managers do not address longer term strategic issues hence measures such as the **balanced scorecard** to redress the emphasis. Other operational **performance indicators** are needed as well.

Corporate decline is a test of managerial skill, either to turn round an underperforming company or to pull out from a product market area in permanent decline.

Note that the theory of the **learning organisation**, **sustainable competitive advantage** and **critical success factors** are relevant to strategic outcomes. They are discussed elsewhere in this Study Text.

Study guide

Section 8 – Outcomes of the strategic management process

- Alternative performance measures

- Strategic failure

Exam guide

The material in this chapter could form an essential part of the setting for a question in either part of the exam. It is, perhaps, most likely to be dealt with in detail in the lengthy setting to a compulsory Section A question.

1　STRATEGIC CONTROL SYSTEMS

1.1　Control is the final element of the strategic management process, the review of actual performance in the light of planned performance.

1.2　**Problems with relying solely on budgetary control**

(a)　Financial results appear to provide proof that the strategy is working. But it is possible to **overlook important indicators of strategic success**.

(b)　Too much emphasis on budgetary control and short-term profit can **disguise strategic problems**.

(c) Strategic control measures might **require complicated trade-offs** between current financial performance and longer-term competitive position, and between different desirable ways of building competitive strength.

Strategic control systems

1.3 To encourage the measurement of the right things, firms can institute formal or informal systems of **strategic control**. There are four **influences on a strategic control system.**

- The **time-lag** between **strategic control** measures and **financial results**
- The **linkages** with the other businesses in a group
- The **risks** the business faces
- The **sources** of competitive advantage.

1.4 **Formal systems of strategic control**

Step 1. **Strategy review.** Review the progress of strategy.

Step 2. Identify **milestones of performance** (strategic objectives) both quantitative and qualitative (eg market share, quality, innovation, customer satisfaction).

- Milestones are identified **after** the business's **critical success factors** have been outlined.

- Milestones are **short-term steps** towards **long-term goals**.

- Milestones enable managers to monitor **actions** (eg whether a new product has been launched) and results (eg the success of the launch).

Step 3. **Set target achievement levels** These need not be exclusively quantitative.

(i) Targets must be reasonably precise.
(ii) Targets should suggest strategies and tactics.
(iii) **Competitive benchmarks** are targets set **relative to the competition**.

Step 4. **Formal monitoring of the strategic process.** Reporting is less frequent than for financial reporting.

Step 5. **Reward.** For most systems, there is little relationship between the achievement of strategic objectives and the **reward system**, although some companies are beginning to use measures of strategic performance as part of the annual *bonus* calculations.

1.5 Many companies do not 'define explicit strategic objectives or milestones that are regularly and formally monitored as part of the ongoing management control process'.

(a) Choosing one objective (eg market share) might encourage managers to ignore or downgrade others (eg profitability), or lead managers to ignore wider issues.

(b) Informality promotes flexibility.

(c) Openness of communication is necessary.

(d) Finite objectives overlook nuances especially in human resource management. In other words, an objective like 'employee commitment' is necessary for success, but hard to measure quantitatively.

1.6 Informal control does not always work because it enables managers to skate over important strategic issues and choices.

Guidelines for a strategic control system

1.7 The characteristics of strategic control systems can be measured on two axes.

(a) How **formal** is the process?

(b) How many **milestones** are identified for **review**?

1.8 As there is no optimum number of milestones or degree of formality, *Goold and Quinn* suggest these guidelines.

Guideline	Comment
Linkages	If there are **linkages** between businesses in a group, the formality of the process should be low, to avoid co-operation being undermined.
Diversity	If there is a great deal of **diversity**, it is **doubtful whether any overall strategic control system is appropriate**, especially if the critical success factors for each business are different.
Criticality	Firms whose strategic stance depends on decisions which can, if they go wrong, destroy the company as a whole (eg launching a new technology) need strategic control systems which, whether formal or informal, have a **large number of milestones so that emerging problems in any area will be easily and quickly detected**.
Change	Fashion-goods manufacturers must respond to relatively high levels of environmental turbulence, and have to react quickly. If **changes are rapid**, a system of **low formality and few measures** may be appropriate, merely because the control processes must allow decisions to be taken in changed contexts.
Competitive advantage	(i) **Businesses with few sources of competitive advantage**. Control can easily focus on perhaps market share or quality with high formality.
	(ii) **Businesses with many sources of competitive advantage**. Success over a wider number of areas is necessary and the firm should not just concentrate on one of them.

1.9 EXAMPLE: STRATEGIC CONTROL REPORT

Date: March 20X4
Source: January 20X0 planning document
Mission: Market share

1.   *Long-term targets, to be achieved by 20X9*

   (a)   X% value of market share
   (b)   Y% profitability over the decade

   Status: March 20X4. Market share lower than anticipated, owing to unexpected competition. Profits lower than expected because of loss of scale economies and increased marketing costs.

   Outlook. Profit will be improved thanks to cost-cutting measures. Market share target might be missed.

2.   *Assumptions*

   The home market is growing only slowly, and is becoming mature. There are limited opportunities for segmentation.

   Overseas markets are likely to expand by Z% as some are reducing tariffs.

   Status March 20X4. The home market has matured more quickly than expected. Overseas market growth can compensate for this.

3.   *Critical success factors*

   Although market share and hence profit are lower than expected, as a result of loss of scale economies, we have become more efficient. Defects per 1,000 have been reduced to 0.3, which allows us to bid for the Japanese contract.

4.   *Key tasks*

   - Launch of budget products for overseas markets
   - Setting up of a computerised distribution system to enhance speedy response to demand and to cut warehousing costs
   - Get BS EN ISO 9000 certification

1.10 Desirable features of strategic performance measures

Role of measures	Comment
Focus attention on what matters in the long term	Shareholder wealth?
Identify and communicate drivers of success	How the organisation generates shareholder value over the long term.
Support organisational learning	Enable the organisation to improve its performance.
Provide a basis for reward	Rewards should be based on strategic issues not just performance in any one year.

1.11   Strategic performance measures should be:

- Quantifiable
- Meaningful
- Defined by the strategy and relevant to it
- Consistently measured
- Re-evaluated regularly
- Acceptable

1.12   Section summary

- Strategic control is needed as over-dependence on purely financial measures leads to gaps and false alarms, and ignores long-term features of the business.

- Strategic control systems can be formal or informal, and have any number of measures of performance, depending on the business.

2 THE BALANCED SCORECARD

2.1 Although financial measurements do not capture all the strategic realities of the business, a failure to attend to the 'numbers' can rapidly lead to a failure of the business, if there is a liquidity crisis.

The balanced scorecard

> **KEY TERM**
>
> The **balanced scorecard** is:
>
> 'a set of measures that gives top managers a fast but comprehensive view of the business. The balanced scorecard includes financial measures that tell the results of actions already taken. And it complements the financial measures with **operational** measures on customer satisfaction, internal processes, and the organisation's innovation and improvement activities - operational measures that are the drivers of future financial performance.' (Robert Kaplan, January-February 1992, *Harvard Business Review.*)

2.2 The reason for using such a system is that 'traditional financial accounting measures like return on investment and earnings per share can give misleading signals for continuous improvement and innovation - activities today's competitive environment demands'. The balanced scorecard allows managers to look at the business from **four important perspectives**

- **Customer**
- **Financial**
- **Internal business**
- **Innovation and learning**

Customer perspective

2.3 '**How do customers see us?**' Given that many company mission statements identify customer satisfaction as a key corporate goal, the balanced scorecard translates this into specific measures. Customer concerns fall into four categories.

(a) **Time**. Lead time is the time it takes a firm to meet customer needs from receiving an order to delivering the product.

(b) **Quality**. Quality measures not only include defect levels - although these should be minimised by TQM - but accuracy in forecasting.

(c) **Performance** of the product. (How often does the photocopier break down?)

(d) **Service**. How long will it take a problem to be rectified? (If the photocopier breaks down, how long will it take the maintenance engineer to arrive?)

2.4 In order to view the firm's performance through customers' eyes, firms hire market researchers to assess how the firm performs. Higher service and quality may cost more at the outset, but savings can be made in the long term.

Internal business perspective

2.5 The **internal business perspective** identifies the **business processes that have the greatest impact on customer satisfaction,** such as quality and employee skills.

(a) Companies should also attempt to identify and measure their **distinctive competences** and the critical technologies they need to ensure continued leadership. Which processes should they excel at?

(b) To achieve these goals, **performance measures must relate to employee behaviour,** to tie in the strategic direction with employee action.

(c) An information system is necessary to enable executives to measure performance. An **executive information system** enables managers to drill down into lower level information.

Innovation and learning perspective

2.6 The question is '**Can we continue to improve and create value?**' Whilst the customer and internal process perspectives identify the *current* parameters for competitive success, the company needs to learn and to innovate to **satisfy future needs**.

- How long does it take to develop new products?
- How quickly does the firm climb the experience curve to make new products?
- What percentage of revenue comes from new products?
- How many suggestions are made by staff and are acted upon?
- What are staff attitudes?
- The company can identify measures for training and long-term investment.

Financial perspective

2.7 '**How do we appear to shareholders?**' Financial performance indicators indicate 'whether the company's strategies, implementation, and execution are contributing to bottom line management.'

2.8 **Financial performance indicators**

Measure	For	Against
Profitability	Easy to calculate and understand.	Ignores the size of the investment.
Return on investment (profit/ capital)	Accounting measure: easy to calculate and understand. Takes size of investment into account. Widely used.	• Ignores risk • Easy to manipulate (eg managers may postpone necessary capital investment to improve ratio) • What are 'assets'? (eg do brands count?) • Only really suited to products in the maturity phase of the life cycle, rather than others which are growing fast.
Residual income	Head office levies an interest charge for the use of asset.	Not related to the size of investment except indirectly
Earnings per share	Relates the firm's performance to needs of its shareholders	Shareholders are more concerned about future expectations; ignores capital growth as a measure of shareholders' wealth

Measure	For	Against
DCF measures	Relates performance to investment appraisal used to take the decision; cash flows rather than accounting profits are better predictors of shareholder wealth	• Practical difficulties in predicting future cash flows of a whole company • Difficulty in separating cash flows for products which share resources

Linkages

2.9 **Disappointing results** might result from a **failure to view all the measures as a whole**. For example, increasing productivity means that fewer employees are needed for a given level of output. Excess capacity can be created by quality improvements. However these improvements have to be exploited (eg by increasing sales). The **financial element** of the balanced scorecard 'reminds executives that improved quality, response time, productivity or new products, benefit the company only when they are translated into improved financial results', or if they enable the firm to obtain a sustainable competitive advantage.

2.10 **The balanced scorecard only measures strategy. It does not indicate that the strategy is the right one.** 'A failure to convert improved operational performance into improved financial performance should send executives back to their drawing boards to rethink the company's strategy or its implementation plans.'

2.11 EXAMPLE: A BALANCED SCORECARD

Balanced Scorecard

Financial Perspective

GOALS	MEASURES
Survive	Cash flow
Succeed	Monthly sales growth and operating income by division
Prosper	Increase market share and ROI

Customer Perspective

GOALS	MEASURES
New products	Percentage of sales from new products
Responsive supply	On-time delivery (defined by customer)
Preferred supplier	Share of key accounts' purchases
	Ranking by key accounts
Customer partnership	Number of cooperative engineering efforts

Internal Business Perspective

GOALS	MEASURES
Technology capability	Manufacturing configuration vs competition
Manufacturing excellence	Cycle time
	Unit cost
	Yield
Design productivity	Silicon efficiency
	Engineering efficiency
New product introduction	Actual introduction schedule vs plan

Innovation and Learning Perspective

GOALS	MEASURES
Technology leadership	Time to develop next generation of products
Manufacturing learning	Process time to maturity
Product focus	Percentage of products that equal 80% sales
Time to market	New product introduction vs competition

2.12 Many firms use profit or investment centre organisation to control the performance of different divisions. A profit centre is where managers are responsible for revenues and costs; an investment centre is a profit centre in which managers have some say in investment decisions. Always keep in mind the following.

(a) Different divisions may offer different risk/return profiles.

(b) Managers will take dysfunctional decisions if these put their performance in a better light.

(c) An economically efficient, fair transfer pricing system must be devised.

(d) There are problems in assessing how shared fixed assets or head office costs should be charged out.

3   CORPORATE DECLINE   6/03

3.1 It is easy to rattle off a list of successful companies, and to ascribe to them a whole variety of factors which have fuelled their success. It is less easy, however, to assess precisely those factors which cause industries and companies to fail. Decline has two aspects.

(a) What should a company do to be successful in a **declining industry**, if it cannot realistically withdraw?

(b) How do **corporations 'go bad'** and what can be done to turn them round?

Declining industries

3.2 There are two types of industrial decline, as identified by *Kathryn Harrigan*.

(a) **Product revitalisation** occurs when the decline is temporary (eg owing to a genuine recession in consumer demand).

(b) **Endgame**. A firm (and the industry) is confronted with substantially lower demand for its products.

3.3 **Declining industries**

(a) In **endgame** conditions, firms which had not competed with each other were drawn into **price wars**. This knee-jerk response should encourage managers to consider their competitive behaviour before the endgame.

(b) The **characteristics of declining industries differ** (eg some have high exit barriers, some are concentrated, others are fragmented), so **different strategies** are appropriate.

(c) The **expectations** of competitors about future demand, and the expectations of their customers about future supplies, can have a powerful **influence** on the nature of the **competitive environment**.

(d) Forecasting techniques can help firms identify the **type** of competitor that will leave the industry and the types most likely to remain.

(e) If the industry is falling to a **substitute product**, then firms should innovate to capture the new technology.

(f) If products become commodity-like (ie differentiation is not all that significant) then **all but the lowest cost competitor will lose market share**. In these conditions a cost leadership strategy is appropriate. On the other hand, it might be a good idea to **differentiate** a product, if this is feasible, to build the security of a niche.

(g) Unless a company has the lowest costs, a strong distribution system relative to competitors, or a loyal niche of customers, it might be **worth selling the business to a competitor** who can make better use of it.

(h) Finally, a firm which is part of a **conglomerate** might be retained because of strategic relationships with other areas of the conglomerate.

Declining companies

3.4 *Stuart Slatter*, from an analysis of UK companies during the severe recession of the early 1980s identifies ten **symptoms of corporate decline**.

- Declining profitability
- Decreasing sales volume (ie sales revenue adjusted for inflation)
- An increase in gearing (debt as a proportion of equity)
- A decrease in liquidity, as measured by accounting ratios
- Restrictions on the dividend policy
- Financial engineering (eg changes in accounting policies and periods)
- 'Top management fear'
- Frequent changes in senior executives
- Falling market share
- Evidence of a lack of planning

Z scores

3.5 *E I Altman* researched into the simultaneous analysis of several financial ratios as a combined predictor of business failure. Altman analysed 22 accounting and non-accounting variables for a selection of failed and non-failed firms in the USA and from these, five key indicators emerged. These five indicators were then used to derive a **Z score**. Firms with a Z score above a certain level would be predicted to be financially sound, and firms with a Z score below a certain level would be categorised as probable failures. Altman also identified a range of Z scores in between the non-failure and failure categories in which eventual failure or non-failure was uncertain.

3.6 Altman's Z score model (derived in 1968) emerged as:

$$Z = 1.2X_1 + 1.4X_2 + 3.3X_3 + 0.6X_4 + 1.0X_5$$

where

$X_1 = $ working capital/total assets
$X_2 = $ retained earnings/total assets
$X_3 = $ earnings before interest and tax/total assets
$X_4 = $ market value of equity/book value of total debt (a form of gearing ratio)
$X_5 = $ sales/total assets

Other researchers have developed similar models.

3.7 The severity of any crisis depends on the behaviour of managers. Slatter identifies four stages in the crisis.

Step 1. **Crisis denial.** Managers are complacent, ignore warning signs or do not appreciate their significance.

Step 2. **Hidden crisis.** When the signs of crisis appear, managers explain them away, or say that there is nothing they can do. If they admit something *is* wrong they will be blamed. If radical change is required, it might adversely affect their position.

Step 3. **Disintegration.** Managers decide that things are amiss and act to do something about them - too little, usually. Management becomes more autocratic.

Step 4. **Collapse.** Slatter says that, in the end, action is impossible. An expectation of failure increases, the most able managers leave, and there are power struggles for the remaining spoils. Eventually, usually after the prompting of a bank, the receiver is called in.

Argenti's A score

3.8   *John Argenti* developed a management-scoring approach which explicitly sought to rate the risks of poor management's causing corporate failure. The model takes the qualitative problems associated with management and assigns a score for each problem area. These scores are judgemental, but aim to provide a means of comparing the situation with the possible worse-case scenario.

Source of problem	Observed variable	Score
Group A		
Management defects		
• Chief Executive is an autocrat		8
• Chief Executive also holds position of Chairman		4
• Passive Board of Directors		2
• Unbalanced Board of Directors, not representing all business functions or overweight in one discipline		2
• Weak Finance Director		2
• Poor management in depth		1
Accounting defects		
• No budgets or budgetary controls		3
• No cash flow forecasts, or not up to date		3
• No costing system: costs and contribution of each product or service are not known		3
• Poor response to change: old-fashioned product or service, obsolete production facilities, out-of-date marketing methods; old directors		15
	Σ	= 43
Group B		
Management mistakes		
• High leverage		15
• Overtrading: company expanding faster than funding; capital base too small for level of activity, or capital base unbalanced for type and nature of the business		15
• Big project that has gone wrong; any obligation that the company will be unable to meet if something goes wrong		15
	Σ	= 45

Source of problem	Observed variable	Score
Group C		
Symptoms of trouble		
• Financial analysis appear to indicate failure or difficulties (eg poor Z-score)		4
• Creative accounting		4
• Any non-financial signs of problems: uncleaned and untidy offices and factory, high turnover, low moral, rumours and so on		4
	Σ	= 12

The criteria require that, for a firm to be cleared as healthy, it meets certain standards.

Category of score	Maximum	Minimum
Group A	43	10
Group B	45	15
Group C	12	N/a
Total score	100	25

3.9 The system sets a minimum acceptable score of 25 overall with minimum of 10 and 15 in problem areas A (defects) and B (mistakes).

A firm that scored more than 25 overall but failed to reach the minimum for Group A or Group B would still be considered to be at risk.

Strategic failure

3.10 Failure of strategic management is likely to lead to rapid corporate decline. A common route to failure is **strategic drift**. Ironically, this often derives from success. Unfortunately, success can have the effect of making the organisation over-confident. The **paradigm** comes to revolve around what worked in the past, hampering innovation and reducing flexibility. *Miller* calls this the **Icarus paradox**. The organisation develops its strategy in accordance with its unchanged assumptions and gradually drifts away from environmental fit. It is very difficult to detect the difference between the deployment of core competences to achieve competitive advantage and the constraining effect of an obsolete paradigm.

The Icarus paradox

3.11 Miller suggests that when companies succeed, their success can lead to a kind of dislocated feedback of the qualities that made them succeed; this distortion then leads to failure.

3.12 Miller diagnoses four important aspects of this distortion.

(a) **Leadership failures** occur when success reinforces top management's pre conceptions, makes them over confident, less concerned for the customer's views, conceited and obstinate.

(b) **Cultural domination** by star departments and their ideologies leads to intolerance of other ideas and reduces the capacity for innovative and flexible response.

(c) **Power games and politics** are used by dominant managers and departments to resist change and amplify current strategic thinking.

(d) **Corporate memory**, consisting of processes, habits and reflexes, is substituted for careful thought about new problems.

3.13 The interplay of these factors leads to decline, usually along one of four **trajectories**.

  (a) **Craftsman become tinkerers**. Quality driven engineering farms become obsessed with irrelevant technical detail.

  (b) **Builders become imperialists**. Acquisitive, growth driven companies over-expand into areas they cannot manage properly.

  (c) **Pioneers become escapists**. Companies whose core competence is technically superb innovation and state-of-the-art products lose focus and waste their resources on grandiose and impractical projects.

  (d) **Salesman become drifters**. Marketing oriented companies with stables of valuable brands become bureaucratic pursuers of sales figures whose market offerings become stale and uninspired.

3.14 The **learning approach** to strategy-making, discussed in Chapter 2, with its emphasis on challenging assumptions by means of wide discussion can help to prevent strategic drift.

3.15 Companies which recovered did so largely because of the way in which the recovery strategy was implemented.

  (a) **Contraction** in order to cut the cost base while maintaining revenue
  (b) **Reinvestment** in organisational capability and efficiency
  (c) **Rebuilding** with a concentration on innovation

Case example

In May 2004, *Levi Strauss* announced the sale of its *Dockers* casual clothing brand. The rationale given by the chief financial officer was to reduce debt, improve financial strength and increase competitiveness. Dockers contributes about $US 1.4 billion to Levi's global turnover of $US 4.1 billion. The company lost $US 2 million in the quarter to February 2004 and has debt of $US 2 billion. In 2003, Levi's cut 1415 jobs and withdrew from manufacturing in the USA.

3.16 Turning a company round requires an able top management, with the right mix of skills and experience, to stand outside of the culture of the organisation. Substantial changes at the top (eg as at Barings) may be needed, and one of the most important **symbols of a new order is the change of personnel**. The development of an effective top management team depends on three things.

  (a) What resources does the team have to work with, in the **context** of the industry and of the firm.

  (b) What is **the ideal management** team given the nature of the crises facing the organisation? For example a firm with poor financial controls may require a team with a financial or systems bias, whereas a firm whose problem was lacklustre products may need a team with a marketing bias.

  (c) Against this **ideal team**, how does the **current team** shape up? New expertise may need to be imported, or a plan may be needed to enhance the capability of the existing team.

3.17 **Leadership roles**

  (a) **Charismatic leaders** lead by force of personality, which will only be exercised in difficult situations.

  (b) **Transformational leaders** not only have charisma, but use it to some purpose.

- To create a new vision for the organisation
- To gain acceptance of the new vision
- To force through and 'refreeze' the change

3.18 There are, of course, **corporate governance** issues involved. An overly-powerful leader can be a danger to the good governance of the firm. This is why the Cadbury committee recommended that the **roles of Chairman and Chief Executive should be split.**

(a) The **Chairman** should have no day-to-day operating responsibilities but should represent the interests of shareholders, deal with the audit committee and so forth.

(b) The chief executive officer has direct responsibility for the operations of the company.

3.19 Such an arrangement has four useful features.

- It avoids **over-concentration** of power.
- Two senior members offer **different perspectives** on the businesses.
- The chairman represents the **shareholders**.
- The chairman deals with **key external stakeholders**.

Exam focus point
The potential for corporate decline within a currently successful business was the topic of a 10 mark part-question in June 2003.

Chapter roundup

- The purpose of **strategic control systems** is to shift management attention away from sole reliance on financial performance indicators towards longer-term strategic milestones which eventually determine financial performance. The **balanced scorecard** is an example of how this might be put into practice.

- **Competitive advantage** results from providing value to customers in a way not provided by competitors. Various **value activities** can drive cost or differentiation strategies. Buyers do not always appreciate the value they are acquiring, so cannot assess a product by this criterion alone.

- Competitive advantage is therefore **relative** and to sustain it firms have to pre-empt the actions of their competitors.

- The **balanced scorecard** is a comprehensive set of measures intended to give a rounded picture of corporate progress and achievement. It extends beyond traditional financial accounting measures to provide information from four **perspectives**.

  - Customer
  - Financial

  - Internal business
  - Innovation and learning

- **Corporate decline** arises from the decline in the industry and from poor management. It is still possible to make money in declining industries, just as it is possible to '**turn round**' declining companies.

- The **Icarus paradox** arises when a successful paradigm becomes over-rigid, hampering innovation and reducing flexibility.

- *Altman* developed the first **Z-score**, an attempt to predict corporate failure by combining significant financial ratios into a single measure of performance.

- Argenti's A score is a wider ranging index of risk.

- Recovery from corporate failure depends to a great extent on **leadership** and **corporate governance**. It may involve **contraction** and heavy **investment**.

Quick quiz

1   What influences the strategic control system?

2   What is the basic principle behind the balanced scorecard?

3   What four perspectives are found on the balanced scorecard?

4   State two types of industrial decline.

5   Give the four stages of inadequate management reaction to crisis.

6   Give four typical causes of corporate decline.

Answers to quick quiz

1 Timelag between control measures and response
  Linkages with other group businesses
  Business risks
  Sources of competitive advantage

2 A range of measures gives a more useful picture than a single financial measure.

3 Customer, financial, internal business, innovation and learning

4 Temporary and endgame

5 Crisis denial; hidden crisis; disintegration; collapse

6 Poor financial controls; high cost structure; a big project; high gearing

Now try the question below from the Exam Question Bank

Number	Level	Marks	Time
Q16	Exam	12	22 mins

Part D
Global strategy

Chapter 17

GLOBALISATION

Topic list	Syllabus reference
1 Economic fundamentals	7(a)
2 The economics of international trade	7(a)
3 Protectionism in international trade	7(b)
4 The competitive advantage of nations	7(b)
5 Global strategic management	7(b)

Introduction

Many large commercial organisations confine their operations to a single country. This is quite easy in a large economy, such as the USA. However, for most growing companies, an entry into some form of **international trade** is an almost inevitable development. This brings a large number of opportunities and equally numerous complications. Not only is the basic cultural and social **environment** likely to be quite different from the domestic market, international trade has its own distinct body of rules, both economic and legal.

In this chapter we introduce the background to international trade. As there is no longer a foundation examination involving basic economics, we start with a consideration of the economic forces that tend to govern trade between nations.

The remainder of the chapter covers some of the basic economic and strategic management ideas that are relevant to international operations. This material is fundamental to your ability to analyse the information given in exam questions on global strategy. Pay particular attention to sections 4 and 5.

Study guide

Section 7 – The nature of global competition

- The internationalisation of business
- The development of the global business

Exam guide

There is a great deal of material in this chapter and the next and it would be very easy for the examiner to produce questions exclusively concerned with global strategy. Note, however, that the economic material in Sections 1 and 2 is unlikely to be examined in detail: it is essential foundation material for what follows. The remaining sections are very likely to form the background to a global strategy scenario.

1 ECONOMIC FUNDAMENTALS

1.1 It is a fact of life that there are limits to available **resources**.

(a) For the world as a whole, resources available to serve human consumption are limited. For example, the supply of non-renewable energy resources is, by definition, limited.

(b) For the individual **consumer,** the scarcity of goods and services might seem obvious enough. No matter what they already have, most people would like to have more, or better: perhaps a faster car, or longer holidays, or a house of their own.

(c) Each country is endowed with natural resources of limited quantity and of different types. For example, some countries have plentiful mineral resources while others have hardly any, or none. Some countries have more skilled labour than others. Some countries have a relatively undeveloped manufacturing infrastructure. We shall see later how such differences provide a basis for international trade.

> **KEY TERMS**
>
> A **scarce resource** is a resource for which the quantity demanded at a nil price would exceed the available supply.
>
> **Scarcity** is the excess of human wants over what can be produced.

1.2 We can identify four types of scarce productive resource, which are also called **factors of production. Land** is the natural resources which a firm uses, including land itself and products such as oil and minerals. The definition of **capital** in economics is different from that used in accounting: as well as money, it means plant and buildings. **Entrepreneurship** or **enterprise** is the role of management and finance providers in organising production.

1.3 Since resources for production are scarce and there are not enough goods and services to satisfy the total potential demand, **choices** must be made. **Choice is only necessary because resources are scarce.**

(a) **Consumers** must choose what goods and services they will have.

(b) **Producers** must choose how to use their available resources, and what to produce with them.

Economics studies the nature of these choices. What will be produced? What will be consumed? And who will benefit from the consumption?

The production possibility curve: illustrating the limits of production

1.4 We can approach the central questions of economics by looking first at the possibilities of production. Suppose that a society can spend its money on either of two types of products, A and B. The society's resources are limited. Therefore there are restrictions on the amounts of A and B that can be made; this can be shown by a **production possibility curve**.

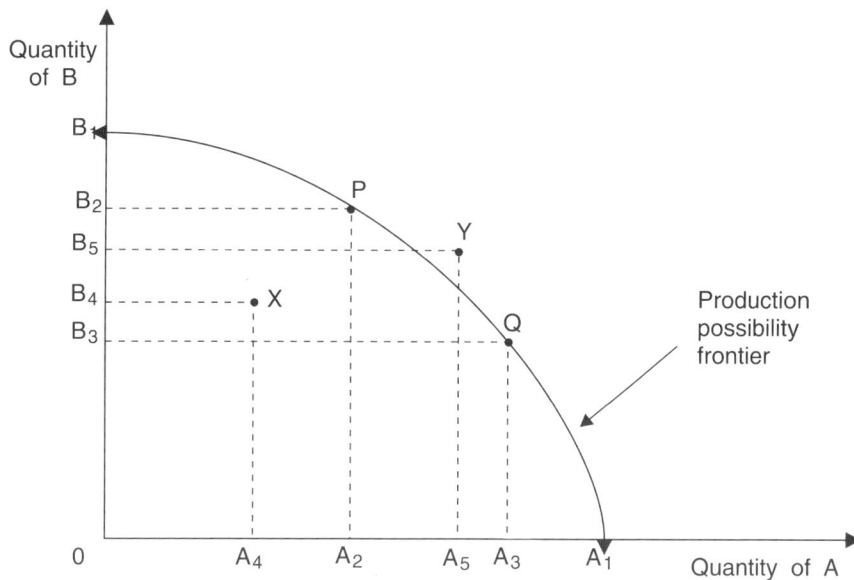

Production possibility curve

1.5 The curve from A_1 round to B_1 in Figure 1 shows the various combinations of A and B that a society can make, if it uses its limited resources efficiently.

- A_1 units of A and no B
- B_1 units of B and no A
- A_2 units of A and B_2 of B (point P on the curve)
- A_3 units of A and B_3 of B (point Q on the curve).

The combination of A_4 units of A and B_4 units of B plotted at point X is within the production possibility curve. More than these quantities can be made of either or both of A and B. Point X is therefore an inefficient production point for the economy, and if the society were to make only A_4 of A and B_4 of B, it would be using its limited resources inefficiently.

Question 1

What can you say about the combination of A and B indicated by point Y in Figure 1?

Answer

Point Y lies outside the production possibility curve. Even with efficient use of resources it is impossible to produce this combination of A and B. To reach point Y either current resources must be increased or production methods must be improved - perhaps by developments in technology.

1.6 The production possibility curve is an important idea in economics which illustrates the **need to make a choice about what to produce when it is not possible to have everything** – that is, when there is scarcity. Although we have characterised the products of our hypothetical economy as A and B, we can generalise the production possibility curve to show the production possibilities for some 'good X' on one axis and 'all other goods' on the other axis.

Opportunity cost: the cost of one use for resources rather than another

1.7 Choice involves sacrifice. If there is a choice between having A and having B, and a country, chooses to have A, it will be giving up B in order to do so. The **cost** of having a certain amount of A can therefore be regarded as the **sacrifice** of not being able to have a certain amount of B. There is a sacrifice involved in the choices of consumers and firms, as well as the choices of governments at the level of national economy.

1.8 The cost of an item measured in terms of the **alternatives forgone** is called its **opportunity cost**. A production possibility curve illustrates opportunity costs. For example, if in Figure 1 it is decided to switch from making A_3 units of A and B_3 units of B (point Q) to making A_2 units of A and B_2 units of B (point P), then **the opportunity cost of making the extra units of B would be the reduction in the output of A**.

1.9 The production possibility line is a **curve** and not a straight line because opportunity costs change as we move away from a situation in which production is wholly devoted to either A or B. Thus, as we move away from point A_1, and introduce an increasing level of production of B, the amount of B that we gain from losing each unit of A progressively diminishes.

2 THE ECONOMICS OF INTERNATIONAL TRADE

2.1 Economists distinguish the concepts of **comparative advantage** and **absolute advantage** in international trade. Our explanation of this distinction makes the following assumptions.

- There are only two countries, country X and country Y.
- Only two goods are produced, lorries and wheat.
- There are no transport costs and no barriers to trade.
- Resources within each country are easily transferred from one industry to another.

Absolute advantage

2.2 A country is said to have an **absolute advantage** in the production of a good when it is **more efficient than another country** in the production of that good, that is, when it can produce more of the good with a given amount of resources than the other country. It is a fairly common situation for one country to be more efficient than another in the production of a particular good.

2.3 Assuming that country Y produces wheat more efficiently than country X, while country X has an absolute advantage in producing lorries, a simple arithmetical example can illustrate the potential gains from trade. The table below shows the amounts of lorries and wheat that each country can produce in year 0, assuming that each country has an equal quantity of resources and devotes half of its resources to lorry production and half to wheat production.

Year 0

	Lorries	Wheat (tons)
Country X	20	100
Country Y	10	150
World total	30	250

2.4 The relative cost of lorry production is lower in country X than in country Y, but the situation is reversed in the case of wheat production. Country X has an absolute advantage in lorry production and country Y has an absolute advantage in wheat production. Greater specialisation will, however, increase total output.

Question 2

Suppose that each country devotes its entire production resources to the product for which it enjoys an absolute advantage. What will be the total output of lorries and wheat?

Answer

Total world output will be 40 lorries (produced by country X) and 300 tons of wheat (produced by country Y).

2.5 By specialising, total world output is now (see Exercise 1 solution) greater with ten more lorries and 50 tons more wheat now available for consumption. In order to obtain the benefits of specialisation these countries can exchange some part of their individual outputs.

Comparative advantage

KEY TERM

The law of **comparative advantage** states that two countries can gain from trade when each specialises in the industries in which it has lowest opportunity costs.

2.6 When two countries produce the same two goods, and each has an absolute advantage in the production of *one* good, then it is easy to show that specialisation will lead to an increase in their combined output. Specialisation and trade can still be mutually advantageous, however, even if one country has an absolute advantage in the production of *both* goods. This situation will arise if the countries find they can obtain the good they produce *less* efficiently at lower **opportunity cost** by importing them.

2.7 The principle of comparative advantage can be shown by an arithmetical example. Assume that in year 10 country X is more efficient in the production of both lorries and wheat. If each country devotes half its resources to each industry the assumed daily production totals are as shown below.

Year 10

	Lorries	*Wheat (tons)*
Country X	20	200
Country Y	10	150
World total	30	350

2.8 In terms of resources used, the costs of production in both industries are lower in country X: it has an *absolute* advantage in the production of both kinds of good. If we consider the **opportunity costs**, however, the picture is rather different. In country X the cost of one lorry is ten tons of wheat: that is, in devoting resources to the production of one lorry, country X must sacrifice the production of ten tons of wheat. In country Y, the opportunity cost of one lorry is **fifteen** tons of wheat, so country X has a *comparative* advantage in the production of lorries (as well as an absolute advantage).

2.9 However, country Y has a *comparative* advantage in the production of wheat. In terms of the *output of lorries forgone*, wheat is cheaper in country Y than in country X. Country X could produce another 10 tons of wheat by giving up 1 lorry. However, if country Y reduced its production of lorries by one, it could obtain an extra *fifteen* tons of wheat with the resources released. Thus, country X would better off if it exchanged one lorry for 15 tons of wheat from country Y, rather than increasing its own wheat production.

2.10 If it produces 15 tons of wheat itself it will have to forgo the production of $1\frac{1}{2}$ lorries: the opportunity cost of domestic production of wheat is higher than the opportunity cost of importing.

2.11 Country X could transfer some of its resources from the production of wheat to the production of lorries, while country Y could put all of its resources into the production of wheat. Total production would now look like this.

	Lorries	Wheat(tons)
Country X	30	100
Country Y	0	300
World total	30	400

There is an increase in the world output of wheat.

2.12 Alternatively, country X might buy 150 tons of wheat from country Y in exchange for 15 lorries. Country X would transfer even more resources to the production of lorries and the total production figures would change again.

	Lorries	Wheat(tons)
Country X	35	50
Country Y	0	300
	35	350

There has now been an increase in the world output of lorries.

2.13 Clearly, the two countries could adjust their trade between these extremes, achieving overall increases in **both** types of good.

2.14 There are other advantages to the countries of the world in encouraging free international trade.

(a) Some countries have **raw materials** surplus to their needs and others have a deficit. A country with a surplus can export them. A country with a deficit must either import them or accept restrictions on its economic prosperity.

(b) International trade **increases competition** amongst suppliers in the world's markets, which benefits consumers, undermining monopolies and promoting the pressure to be efficient.

(c) International trade creates **larger markets** for a firm's output and so some firms can benefit from **economies of scale**.

(d) There are **political advantages** because the development of trading links provides a foundation for economic and political links. An example is the European Union and its single market programme.

(e) From the consumer's point of view, international trade should provide **greater choice, lower prices** and **better quality** products.

Why do countries often try to avoid specialisation?

2.15 In practice many countries try to avoid **specialisation**. Where there is a major export industry already in existence, the country's government might actively encourage the growth of other unrelated industries.

2.16 **Arguments against specialisation**.

(a) **Comparative advantage is never stable.** Technological change might mean that other countries can compete more effectively.

(b) **Diversification** protects against a possible **fall in world demand** for a particular product, with a consequent fall in export earnings and deterioration in the balance of trade.

(c) Agriculture is subject to the **uncertainties of climate**. A poor harvest or a crop disease might be disastrous if the country relies on that product alone.

(d) **Market segmentation** and **product differentiation** have enabled suppliers to develop markets so that countries producing variants of the same product are able to sell their goods to each other.

(e) Multinational companies may choose to site some **manufacturing or assembly activity** in each country in which they operate for political or logistical reasons.

(f) A country may find itself a victim of **import restrictions** in the rest of the world and this may make it cautious about over specialisation.

(g) Governments might wish to develop **self-sufficiency** in some industries. An example would be the defence industry.

(h) **Special interest groups** can influence the government to restrict imports; this is often in the interest of industries which are subject to import competition and

Money and trade

2.17 International trade implies international remittances and therefore currency exchange. An exchange rate is the rate at which one country's currency can be traded in exchange for another country's currency. **Exchange rate risk** is the risk that future receipts in a foreign currency will exchange into a smaller amount than expected of the domestic currency. This can arise under any type of exchange rate system, whether fixed, managed or floating.

(a) A **fixed exchange rate** depends upon the intervention of national central banks to support it. When there is great pressure on a fixed exchange rate, a devaluation may result, despite government attempts to avoid it.

(b) A **managed exchange rate** is supported in the same way as a fixed one, but is allowed to vary within preset bounds. The movement within the bounds and the bounds themselves may be subject to the same pressures as a fixed exchange rate.

(c) A **floating exchange rate** depends entirely upon supply and demand for its level. Supply and demand depend in turn upon trade volumes and values between the countries concerned and their interest rates. These are subject to fluctuation.

Case example

In 2003, *Rio Tinto*, the world's second-largest mining group, reported a 10 per cent fall in underlying profit, as the benefits of higher commodities prices were cancelled out by the negative effects of currency fluctuations.

2.18 A variety of financial hedging devices exists for the management of exchange rate risk. A company can also minimise its exposure to the risk associated with any given exchange rate by managing its affairs in such a way that it has money flowing in both directions between the countries concerned. If the flows are initially of equal value and the exchange rate changes, what is lost by exchange in one direction is gained by the opposite transaction. Exchange rate risk thus motivates companies to both buy from and sell to the same countries if possible.

2.19 Currencies can be maintained for quite long periods at artificial rates by government intervention in the market. Official exchange rates do not always, therefore, give a true indication of global resource costs. This is particularly the case when the countries concerned have different rates of inflation. Decisions relating to international operations may be more informed if they are made using **purchasing power parity exchange rates**. These rates attempt to remove the distorting effects of inflation. The purchasing power parity approach is to calculate an exchange rate based on the relative cost of purchasing the same basket of goods in the two countries. *The Economist* regularly publishes purchasing power parity exchange rates based on the price of McDonalds' Big Mac hamburger. This was chosen because of McDonald's well-known dedication to achieving standardisation of their product. The Economist Big Mac index indicates some quite wide discrepancies in official exchange rates.

Case example

The Big Mac Index

From the *Economist*, Dec 20th 2001.

The Economist's Big Mac Index is based on the theory of 'purchasing-power parity'. Under PPP, exchange rates ought to adjust to equalise the price of a basket of goods and services across countries. Our basket is the Big Mac. Dividing the American price of a Big Mac, $2.59, by the British price, £1.99, implies a PPP exchange rate of $1.30. The market rate is $1.45, making sterling 12% overvalued. By this measure, the South African rand is undervalued by 68%.

---

3 PROTECTIONISM IN INTERNATIONAL TRADE

KEY TERM

Protectionism is the discouraging of imports by government action.

3.1 Some governments seek to protect their home producers from foreign competition by making it harder to import from overseas. A wide variety of methods is used.

- **Tariffs** or customs duties
- **Non-tariff** barriers
- Exchange **controls**
- Exchange rate **policy**

Tariffs or customs duties

3.2 A **tariff** is a **tax on imports**.

(a) The importer is required to pay either a percentage of the value of the imported good (an *ad valorem* duty), or per unit of the good imported (a **specific duty**).

(b) The government **raises revenue** and domestic producers may expand sales, but **consumers** pay higher prices if they buy imported goods. They may have to buy domestic goods of a lesser quality.

Non-tariff barriers

Import quotas

3.3 **Import quotas** are **restrictions** on the quantity of product allowed to be imported into a country.

(a) The restrictions can be imposed by **import licences** (in which case the government gets additional revenue) or simply by granting the right to import only to certain producers.

(b) **Prices will rise** because the supply of goods is artificially restricted. The consumer pays more while foreign producers benefit from the higher price available but the volume of their sales is restricted.

Case example

Chicago became the USA's 'candy capital' a century ago when sweet makers bought gelatine from meat packers in the city's stockyards. However, there is now a steady exodus of sweet manufacturers from Chicago, and the USA generally, because of the high cost of sugar. US import quotas, which protect domestic sugar producers, mean that sugar costs twice as much in the US as on the international market.

The total number of jobs in the US sweet industry declined by 8.9 per cent between 1991 and 2000, while in Chicago the fall was 24.6 per cent.

Minimum local content rules

3.4 Related to quotas is a requirement that, to avoid tariffs or other restrictions, products should be made **in** the country or region in which they are sold. In the EU the product must be of a specified **minimum local content** (80% in the EU) to qualify as being 'home' or 'EU-made'. This is one of the reasons Japanese and Korean manufacturers have set up factories in Europe.

Minimum prices and anti-dumping action

3.5 **Dumping** is the sale of a product in an overseas market at a price lower than charged in the domestic market. **Anti-dumping measures** include establishing quotas, minimum prices or extra excise duties.

Embargoes

3.6 An embargo on imports from one particular country is a **total ban**, a zero quota. An embargo may have a political motive, and may deprive consumers at home of the supply of an important product.

Subsidies for domestic producers

3.7 An enormous range of government **subsidies** and assistance for exporters is offered, such as **export credit guarantees** (insurance against bad debts for overseas sales), financial help and assistance from government departments in promoting and selling products. The effect of these grants is to make unit production costs lower. These may give the domestic producer a **cost advantage** over foreign producers in export as well as domestic markets.

Exchange controls and exchange rate policy

3.8 Many countries have **exchange control regulations** designed to make it difficult for importers to obtain the currency they need to buy foreign goods.

3.9 If a government allows its currency to depreciate, imports will become more expensive. Importers may cut their profit margins and keep prices at their original levels for a while, but sooner or later prices of imports will rise. A policy of exchange rate depreciation in this context is referred to as a **competitive devaluation**.

Case example

In the last several years whilst European countries were preparing to meet the criteria to establish a common currency, the Euro, there were considerable changes in the relative valuations of the individual country currencies. In particular, the pound sterling has strengthened making it more difficult for British exporters to sell their products abroad.

Unofficial non-tariff barriers

3.10 The governments of some countries are accused of establishing or tolerating **unofficial barriers to trade**. Here are some examples.

(a) Onerous **quality and inspection procedures** for imported products impose time and cost penalties on companies selling them.

(b) **Packaging and labelling** requirements may be rigorous, **safety and performance** standards difficult to satisfy and **documentation procedures** very laborious.

(c) Restrictions may be imposed on **physical distribution**, such as the use of display facilities and transport systems.

Regional trading groups

3.11 Currently, a number of **regional trading arrangements** exist. These regional groups generally attempt to promote trade within the region while protecting it against imports from countries outside it. These regional trading groups take three forms.

- Free trade areas
- Customs unions
- Common markets

Types of trading group

Free trade areas

3.12 Members in these arrangements agree to lower barriers to trade amongst themselves. They enable free movement of **goods** and **services,** but not always the factors of production.

Customs unions

3.13 **Customs unions** provide the advantages of free trade areas and agree a common policy on tariff and non-tariff barriers to **external countries.** Internally they attempt to harmonise tariffs, taxes and duties amongst members.

Economic unions/common markets

3.14 In effect the members become one for economic purposes. There is free movement of the factors of production. The EU is attempting to move towards this condition.

3.15 The major regional trade organisations are as follows.

(a)   North American Free Trade Agreement (NAFTA) – US, Canada and Mexico.

(b)   European Free Trade Association (EFTA) – Norway, Switzerland, Iceland, Liechtenstein.

(c)   European Union (EU) – Ireland, Britain, France, Germany, Italy, Spain, Portugal, Finland, Sweden, Denmark, Luxembourg, Belgium, the Netherlands, Austria, Greece. A number of other countries have applied to join.

4   THE COMPETITIVE ADVANTAGE OF NATIONS

4.1   *Michael Porter's The Competitive Advantage Of Nations,* suggests that some nations' industries are more internationally competitive than others. For example, UK leadership in many heavy industries, such as ship-building, has been overtaken by Japan and Korea.

4.2   Porter does not believe that countries or nations as such are competitive, but rather that the conditions within a country may help firms to compete.

4.3   The original explanation for **national** success was the theory of **comparative advantage**, discussed earlier in this chapter. This held that relative opportunity costs determined the appropriateness of particular economic activities in relation to other countries.

4.4   Porter argues that comparative advantage is **too general a concept** to explain the success of individual companies and industries. He suggests that industries which require **high technology** and **highly skilled employees** are less affected than low technology industries by the relative costs of their inputs of raw materials and basic labour as determined by the national endowment of factors of production.

4.5   We must therefore look elsewhere for the determinants of national competitive advantage

4.6   Porter identifies four principal factors, which are outlined in the diagram below. Porter refers to this as the **diamond.**

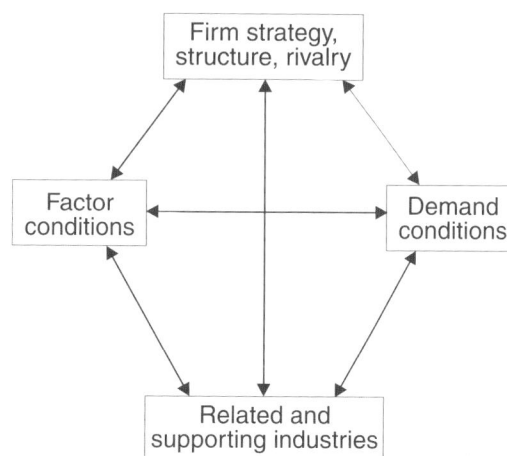

Analysing the diamond

Factor conditions

4.7   **Factor conditions** are a country's endowment of inputs to production.

- Human resources (skills, price, motivation, industrial relations)
- Physical resources (land, minerals, climate, location relative to other nations)
- Knowledge (scientific and technical know-how, educational institutions)
- Capital (amounts available for investment, how it is deployed)

- Infrastructure (transport, communications, housing)

Porter distinguishes between **basic** and **advanced** factors.

(a) **Basic factors** are natural resources, climate, semiskilled and unskilled labour. They are inherent, or at best their creation involves little investment. They are **unsustainable** as a source of national competitive advantage, since they are widely available. For example, the wages of unskilled workers in industrial countries are undermined by even lower wages elsewhere.

(b) **Advanced factors** are associated with a well-developed scientific and technological infrastructure and include modern digital communications infrastructure, highly educated people (eg computer scientists), university research laboratories and so on. They are necessary to achieve high order competitive advantages such as differentiated products and proprietary production technology.

An abundance of factors is not enough. It is the efficiency with which they are deployed that matters. The former USSR has an abundance of natural resources and a fairly well educated workforce, but was an economic catastrophe.

4.8 Porter also notes that **generalized factors**, such as transport infrastructure do not provide as decisive and sustainable bases for competitive advantage as **do specialized factors**. These are factors that are relevant to a limited range of industries, such as knowledge bases in particular fields and logistic systems developed for particular goods or raw materials. Such factors are integral to innovation and very difficult to move to other countries.

Demand conditions: the home market

4.9 The **home market determines how firms perceive, interpret and respond to buyer needs.** This information puts pressure on firms to innovate and provides a launch pad for global ambitions.

(a) There are **no cultural impediments** to communication.

(b) The **segmentation** of the home market shapes a firm's priorities: companies will be successful globally in segments which are similar to the home market.

(c) **Sophisticated and demanding buyers** set standards.

(d) **Anticipation of buyer needs:** if consumer needs are expressed in the home market earlier than in the world market, the firm benefits from experience.

(e) The **rate of growth.** Slow growing home markets do not encourage the adoption of state of the art technology.

(f) **Early saturation** of the home market will encourage a firm to export.

Related and supporting industries

4.10 **Competitive success in one industry is linked to success in related industries.** Domestic suppliers are preferable to foreign suppliers, as they offer continuing close co-operation and co-ordination. The process of innovation is also enhanced when suppliers are of high quality, since information is transmitted rapidly and problems are solved by joint effort.

Firm strategy, structure and rivalry

4.11 **Management style and industrial structure.** Nations are likely to display competitive advantage in industries that are culturally suited to their normal management practices and industrial structures. For example, German managers tend to have a strong bias towards engineering and are best at products demanding careful development and complex manufacturing processes. They are less successful in industries based on intangibles such as fashion and entertainment.

4.12 **Strategy.** Industries in different countries have different **time horizons**, funding needs and so forth.

(a) **National capital markets** set different goals for performance. In Germany and Switzerland, banks are the main source of capital, not equity shareholders. Short-term fluctuations in share prices are not regarded as of great importance as funds are invested for the long term. In the USA, most shares are held by financial institutions whose own performance indicators emphasise short-term earnings growth.

(b) National attitudes to **wealth** are important. The egalitarian Swedes are rarely successful in industries that have the potential to create individual fortunes but depend on new start-ups.

(c) National culture affects industrial priorities through the relative prestige it allots to various industries and their leaders. Italy values fashion and furnishings, for instance, while in Israel the most prestigious industries are agriculture and those related to defence.

4.13 **Domestic rivalry** is important for several reasons.

- There can be no special pleading about unfair foreign competition.
- With little domestic rivalry, firms are happy to rely on the home market.
- Tough domestic rivals teach a firm about competitive success.
- Domestic rivalry forces firms to compete on grounds other than basic factors.
- Each rival can try a different strategic approach.

4.14 The promotion of one or two '**national champions**' who can reap major economies of scale in the domestic market is undermined by the vigorous domestic competition among high-performing companies. Examples are the Swiss pharmaceutical industry and the US IT industry.

Influencing the diamond

4.15 A nation's competitive industries tend to be **clustered**. Porter believes clustering to be a key to national competitive advantage. A cluster is a linking of industries through relationships which are either vertical (buyer-supplier) or horizontal (common customers, technology, skills). For example, the UK financial services industry is clustered in London.

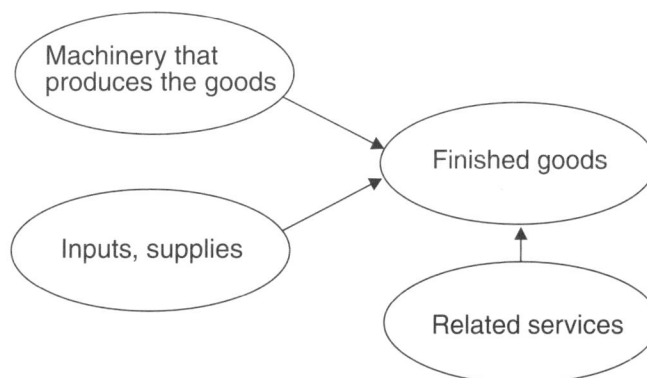

4.16 **How does a country create a diamond of competitive advantage?** Governments cannot compete, only firms can do that. Governments can influence the **context** in which an industry operates and can create opportunities and pressures for innovation.

(a) Factors of production provide the seed corn. A large endowment of easily mined iron ore would suggest metal-working industries.

(b) Related and supporting industries can also be a foundation, if the competences within them can be configured in a new way.

(c) Government policy should support cluster development and promote high standards of education, research and commercially relevant technologies

(d) Extraordinary demand in the *home market* based on national peculiarities and conditions can set the demand conditions determinant in the diamond.

It must be remembered that the creation of competitive advantage can take many years.

Case example

The Swedish and Danish governments are co-operating to form a 'Medicon valley', comprising the areas either side of the Oresund, a waterway which forms the border between them. The Oresund is due to be linked shortly by a 16km bridge. They hope to develop a medical industrial complex. A Medicon Valley Academy has been set up to promote the region 'as a centre of medical and biotechnical research and production. The area boasts two universities, three university hospitals and forty pharmaceutical and medical-technical manufacturing companies.' (*Financial Times*, 4 April 1997)

4.17 The **individual** firm will be more likely to succeed internationally if there is a **supporting cluster.** Firms should be prepared to invest in co-operative ventures in such fields as training, infrastructure and research.

4.18 However, if, say a UK firm wishes to compete in an industry in which there is no national competitive advantage, it can take a number of steps to succeed.

(a) **Compete in the most challenging market,** to emulate domestic rivalry and to obtain information. If a firm can compete successfully in such a market, even if this only means carving out a small niche, it should do well elsewhere.

(b) **Spread research and development** activities to countries where there is an established research base or industry cluster already.

(c) Be prepared to **invest heavily in innovation**.

(d) **Invest in human resources**, both in the firm and the industry as a whole. This might mean investing in training programmes.

(e) **Look out for new technologies** which will change the rules of the industry. The UK with its large efficient research base should have some creative ideas.

(f) **Collaborate with foreign companies.** American motor companies, successfully learned Japanese production techniques.

(g) **Supply overseas companies**. Japanese car plants in the UK have encouraged greater quality in UK components suppliers. Inward investment provides important **learning opportunities** for domestic companies.

(h) **Source components from overseas**. In the UK crystal glass industry, many firms buy crystal glass from the Czech Republic, and do the cutting and design work themselves. Conversely, firms can sell more abroad.

(i) **Exert pressure on politicians** and opinion formers to create better conditions for the diamond to develop (eg in education).

5 GLOBAL STRATEGIC MANAGEMENT 12/01, 12/02

Globalisation

5.1 Since 1945, the volume of world trade has increased. There have been several factors at work.

(a) **Import substitution.** A country aims to produce manufactured goods which it previously imported, by protecting local producers. This has had limited success.

(b) **Export-led growth.** The success of this particular strategy has depended on the existence of open markets elsewhere. Japan, South Korea and the other Asian 'tiger' economies (eg Taiwan) have chosen this route.

(c) **Market convergence.** Transnational market segments have developed whose characteristics are more homogeneous than the different segments within a given geographic market. **Youth culture** is an important influence here.

5.2 This has meant a proliferation of suppliers exporting to, or trading in, a wider variety of places. In many domestic markets it is now likely that the same international companies will be competing with one another. However, the existence of global markets should not be taken for granted in terms of **all** products and services, or indeed in **all** territories.

(a) Some **services** are still subject to managed trade (for example, some countries prohibit firms from other countries from selling insurance). Trade in services has been liberalised under the auspices of the World Trade Organisation.

(b) **Immigration.** There is unlikely ever to be a global market for labour, given the disparity in skills between different countries and restrictions on immigration.

(c) The market for some goods is much more globalised than for others.

(i) Upmarket luxury goods may not be required or afforded by people in developing nations.

(ii) Some goods can be sold almost anywhere, but to limited degrees. Television sets are consumer durables in some countries, but still luxury or relatively expensive items in other ones.

(iii) Other goods are needed almost everywhere. In oil a truly global industry exists in both production (e.g. North Sea, Venezuela, Russia, Azerbaijan, Gulf states) and consumption (any country using cars and buses, not to mention those with chemical industries based on oil).

Management orientation

5.3 *Perlmutter* identifies four orientations in the management of international business.

Ethnocentrism

KEY TERM

Ethnocentrism is a **home country orientation**. The company focuses on its domestic market and sees exports as secondary to domestic marketing.

5.4   This approach simply ignores any inter-country differences which exist. Ethnocentric companies will tend to market the same products with the same marketing programmes in overseas countries as at home. Marketing management is centralized in the home country and the marketing mix is standardized. There is no local market research or adaptation of promotion. As a result, market opportunities may not be fully exploited and foreign customers may be alienated by the approach.

Case example

Pepsi experienced customer alienation when it attempted to mechanically import its global 'younger challenger to Coke' image into Russia. It lost ground to an obscure Swiss rival, Herschi, which used Russian sports stars and celebrities in its campaign.

Polycentrism

KEY TERM

With **polycentrism**, objectives are formulated on the assumption that it is necessary to adapt almost totally the product and the marketing programme to each local environment. Thus the various country subsidiaries of a multinational corporation are free to formulate their own objectives and plans.

5.5   The polycentric company believes that each country is unique. It therefore establishes largely independent local subsidiaries and decentralizes its marketing management. This can produce major increases in turnover but the loss of economies of scale can seriously damage profitability. Such companies tend to think of themselves as **multinationals**. (Later in this chapter we introduce a slightly different polycentric company: the **transnational**.)

Geocentrism and regiocentrism

KEY TERM

Geocentrism and **regiocentrism** are syntheses of the two previous orientations. They are based on the assumption that there are both similarities and differences between countries that can be incorporated into regional or world objectives and strategies.

5.6   **Geocentrism** and **regiocentrism** differ only in geographical terms: the first deals with the world as a unity while the second considers that there are differences between regions. Bearing this in mind, we will speak in terms of geocentrism only, for simplicity.

5.7   **Geocentrism** treats the issues of standardisation and adaptation on their merits so as to formulate objectives and strategies that exploit markets fully while minimising company costs. The aim is to create a global strategy that is fully responsive to local market differences. This has been summed up as: 'think globally, act locally'.

5.8   **Geocentric** companies use an integrated approach to marketing management. Each country's conditions are given due consideration, but no one country dominates. A great deal of experience and commitment are required to make this approach work. A strong, globally recognised brand is a major aspect of the marketing approach. Geocentrically oriented companies both promote and benefit from **market convergence**.

Developing the global business

5.9 Following *Ohmae*, we may describe five stages in the evolution of global business operations. These may be related to Perlmutter's classification of orientations.

(a) **Exporting**. The product is saleable in overseas markets and they are exploited by means of foreign intermediaries such as agents and distributors. Foreign sales are a profitable extension of domestic operations. Little or no adjustment is made to the product in order to reap economies of scale. This is a low risk strategy, since there is little financial commitment, but the company is very much dependent on the effort and motivation of its foreign intermediaries. The management orientation in **ethnocentric**.

(b) **Overseas branches**. Existing and potential export sales are high enough to justify largely replacing the foreign intermediaries with the company's own foreign sales and service branches. The company aims for a stronger presence in its overseas markets and to be more responsive to their requirements. Financial commitment increases with increasing business, as does exchange rate and political risk. If the company is aiming to achieve globalisation, it is at this stage that it begins to acquire the local knowledge and experience that it will need. However, the management orientation is still **ethnocentric**.

(c) **Overseas production**. Export sales are now so high that shipping and other exporting-related costs represent a substantial opportunity for savings by establishing overseas production. At the same time, overseas production can exploit cheap labour and other resources. The company's management orientation is still largely **ethnocentric**. Some functions, such as R&D and marketing are centralized and there is centralized control of manufacturing operations with regular reports to headquarters. World-wide synergies and economies of scale are sought and decisions on adapting to local conditions are made at headquarters. Products are still largely standardized.

(d) **Insiderisation**. The company clones itself in its overseas markets, completing the corporate functionality in each location rather than restricting itself to marketing. The aim is to develop a full marketing capability and offer products suited to local requirements. The management is shifting to a **polycentric** orientation and likes to think of itself as a **multinational**. This approach reduces exchange rate and political risk but requires substantial financial commitment. Economies of scale are likely to be lost and there may be inefficiencies of co-ordination.

(e) **The global company**. The global company differs from the multinational in that it has a **geocentric** management orientation. It takes a world view while recognizing local differences and similarities. It minimises its local adaptation of product and the rest of the marketing mix to those things that actually add customer value and it makes use of the best of its global facilities and people to promote overall excellence. It is likely to centralize functions such as R&D, finance and HR, though not necessarily all in the same place. At the same time its operations will be controlled locally. The primary skill of the global company is to integrate learning, skills, competences and technologies in order to achieve global efficiencies combined with local responsiveness. It manages the value chain so that each part is centred in an optimal location. It is subject to a number of problems.

- Differing cultural values may undermine the global corporate identity.

- Senior executives with the right mix of attitudes and skills are likely to be scarce.

- It is subject to a wide range of environmental risks, particularly political ones.

5.10 Ohmae suggests there are five reasons why companies are moving towards the global stage. He calls these the **5Cs**.

(a) **Customer**. Market convergence is driven by widespread customer demand for products with similar characteristics.

(b) **Company**. The search for economies of scale drives expansion towards the global scale.

(c) **Competition**. The very existence of global competitors motivates companies to expand for reasons of prestige and competitiveness. They may also be amenable to cost-reducing strategic alliances.

(d) **Currency**. Exchange rate risk can be managed most easily when a company has major cash flows in the countries in which it operates.

(e) **Country**. Multiple locations enable a company to exploit both absolute and comparative advantage. They also enable it to promote itself as locally oriented in each country, thus enhancing its image with the local government and markets.

> ### Exam focus point
> The December 2002 examination offered 12 marks for a discussion of polycentrism and geocentrism.

5.11 There are other factors encouraging the globalisation of world trade.

(a) **Financial factors** such as Third world debt; often lenders require the initiation of economic reforms as a condition of the loan. This can lead to a reduction in local protectionism and a consequent increase in trade

(b) **Country/continent** connections, such as that between the UK and the Commonwealth which foster trade and tourism.

(c) **Legal and regulatory factors** such as industrial standards and protection of intellectual property, which encourage the development and spread of standardised technology and design.

(d) **Markets** trading in international commodities; commodities are not physically exchanged, only the rights to ownership. A buyer can, thanks to efficient systems of trading and modern communications, buy a commodity in its country of origin for delivery to a specific destination at some future time.

(e) **The Internet**; major companies are developing on line systems of internal co-ordination and procurement.

(f) **Government policy** in many countries seeks to control the balance of payments by discouraging imports. Government policy towards importers will also reflect their quite proper desire to expand their economies and hence employment and the local standard of living. Local manufacture may thus be the only way to access some markets.

Designs for global businesses

5.12 *Bartlett and Ghoshal* find that the pressures driving globalisation exist independently of the need for local responsiveness; and that both vary from industry to industry. The relationship between these pressures influences both the management orientation and the structure of the company that operates internationally.

(a)   The global company, if active in more than one industry, is likely to be organized in product divisions with global scope.

(b)   Companies operating in industries that require little local differentiation but at the same time are not subject to pressure for globalisation will tend to be structured with an international or export division.

(c)   The multinational environment drives a polycentric orientation, with largely autonomous local operating companies.

(d)   The transnational environment is particularly difficult to respond to. Global scale is desirable but local conditions require differentiated approaches. The structural response may be the **global heterarchy**. Each regional or national unit achieves global scale and influence within the overall organization by exploiting its specialized competences on behalf of the whole company. Some headquarters functions, such as R&D may be diffused across the organization. The role of the global strategic apex is to promote a corporate culture and shared values that will promote co-operation and co-ordination.

	Low requirement for local adaptation and responsiveness	**High requirement for local adaptation and responsiveness**
High pressure to globalise	**Global environment** Geocentric orientation Global product divisions (Chemicals, construction)	**Transactional environment** Polycentric orientation Integrated systems and structures (Pharmaceuticals, motor vehicles)
Low pressure to globalise	**International environment** Ethnocentric orientation International division (Paper, textiles)	**Multinational environment** Polycentric orientation National or regional divisions (Fast food, tobacco)

Case example

British Airways is one of the world's most respected companies. It is been transformed from a state-owned airline into a profitable company against the background of the rapidly changing world of aviation. It faces numerous international competitive pressures.

- New alliances being formed, creating larger networks
- Emergence of budget carriers such as Easy-Jet
- Competition from other forms of transport such as high speed railways
- High fleet maintenance costs
- Government regulations

Such pressures add up to a series of challenges which the company can only face by rigorous planning. Strategic decisions to cut the workforce have had to be made.

The two examples below suggest the varying pressures underlying the structure of a business on a worldwide scale.

Shell

In March 1995 (*Financial Times*, 30.3.95) Shell announced the end of its old matrix organisation. For historical reasons the firm had a complicated structure. Each country or region had its own operating companies.

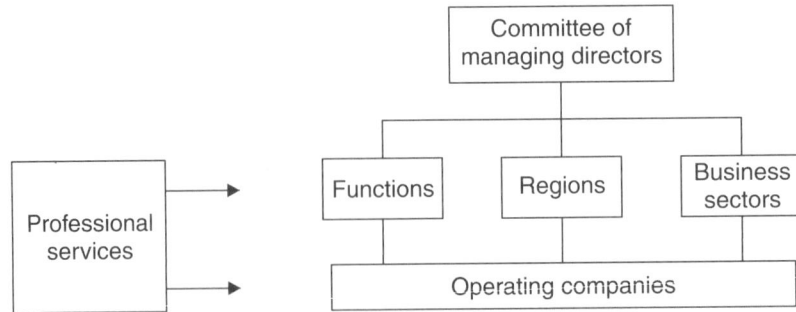

A given operating company could be defined by geography, or business sector for example. The structure was very elaborate and required the support of large groups of executives, representing 'national or regional units, business sections (or divisions) and functions such as finance. It is felt that the company can no longer afford the army of coordinators to "police" such a matrix'. This old structure is all to go. The change will 'cut the larger regional baronies'. It should speed decision making.

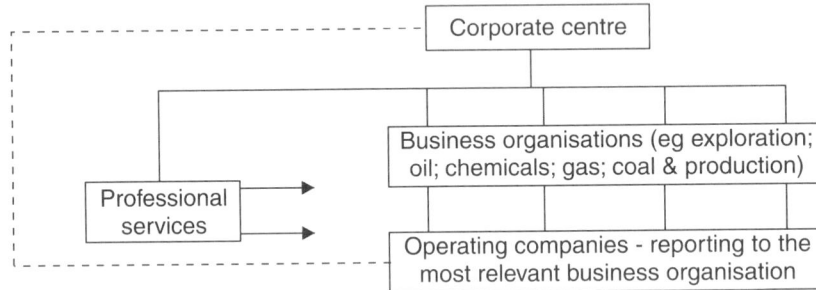

The operating companies are unchanged, so a local basis is maintained and the operating companies still have a link to the corporate centre.

Ford

However, whilst many firms are trying to reduce their head offices and have dismantled their matrices and others such as IBM are streamlining them, some companies have decided to *install* them. Ford has announced a matrix structure to avoid duplication of effort.

Ford had suffered for a long time from duplication: for example the North American and European Escorts were quite separate cars. However, the Mondeo was launched as a world car, and the lessons learned from that exercise have been absorbed elsewhere. The following comes from the *Financial Times* 3 April 1995.

- First of all, its previously independent automotive operations have been integrated into one.

- There is one worldwide product development organisation with five 'vehicle centres' for different ranges of car.

- A matrix management system will replace the old 'functional chimneys' of the old organisation.

Chapter Roundup

- International trade brings benefits to all concerned because of **absolute** and **comparative advantage.** The basis of comparative advantage is **opportunity cost**. Many countries try to avoid specialisation, however.

- **International markets** offer firms opportunities to trade, to acquire resources and investment, but also offer threats in that other companies from overseas can do the same.

- Although trade has benefits, many countries have sought to limit its effects in order to **protect** local producers. In the long term this serves to harm economic welfare as resources are not allocated where they are most productive.

- **Regional trading blocks** promote trade between countries in groups. The environment of world trade is becoming freer, globally, with the influence of the World Trade Organisation.

- **Exchange rates** are determined by demand for goods and services, interest rates and inflation rates. Co-ordination in economic policy is necessary to fix or manage these rates.

- A currency's **exchange rate** is determined by **supply and demand.** They in turn are determined by inflation, speculation, interest rates, government policy and the balance of payments. **Purchasing power parity** theory attempts to explain exchange rate fluctuations by reference to relative **inflation** rates. Governments may try to support the exchange rate of their currency by **protectionist** measures.

- Porter identifies four principal determinants of national competitive advantage.

  - **Factor conditions**
  - **Firm strategy structure and rivalry**
  - **Demand conditions**
  - **Related and supporting industries**

- Perlmutter identifies four orientations in the management of international business.

  - **Ethnocentrism** is a home country orientation
  - **Polycentrism** adapts totally to local environments
  - **Geocentrism** adapts only to add value. It 'thinks globally, acts locally'.
  - **Regiocentrism** recognises regional differences.

- Ohmae describes five stages in the evolution of a global business.

  - **Exporting** is an extension of home sales, using foreign intermediaries. It is low risk and **ethnocentric.**

  - **Overseas branches** arise when turnover is large enough. It requires greater investment and is still **ethnocentric.**

  - **Overseas production** exploits cheap labour and reduces exporting costs. The orientation is still **ethnocentric** and the business is still largely run from its HQ.

  - **Insiderisation** is a shift to **polycentrism**, with full functional organisations being set up overseas. This reduces exchange rate and political risk but economies of scale may be lost and there may be problems of co-ordination. The company is a **multinational**.

  - **The global company** takes a world view while recognising total differences: it has a **geocentric** orientation. It integrates learning, skills and competences to achieve global efficiencies while retaining local responsiveness.

- Ohmae offers five reasons for globalisation.

  - **Customer:** market convergence
  - **Company:** economies of scale
  - **Competition:** keeping up
  - **Currency:** exchange rate risk
  - **Country:** absolute and comparative advantage; local orientation

BPP
PROFESSIONAL EDUCATION

Chapter Roundup (continued)

- Bartlett and Ghoshal discern four types of organisations, depending on the strength or weakness of pressure to globalise and need for local adaptation.

  o Global environment; geocentric; global product divisions
  o International environment; ethnocentric; international division
  o Transnational environment; polycentric; integrated systems and structures
  o Multinational environment; polycentric; national or regional divisions

Quick Quiz

1 What are the fundamental ideas behind the principle of comparative advantage?

2 What determines the level of a floating exchange rate?

3 What is insiderisation?

4 What is a global heterarchy?

5 What is ethnocentrism?

6 What are the elements of Porter's diamond?

7 What is a tariff?

8 What is the difference between a free trade area and a customs union?

9 A global company has a polycentric orientation: true or false?

10 What are Ohmae's 5Cs?

Answers to quick quiz

1 Specialisation and opportunity cost

2 Supply and demand

3 The building up of a production and distribution system in a foreign country

4 A form of organisation adopted by transnational organisations

5 A home country business orientation in which international marketing is subordinated to domestic marketing

6 Factor conditions; demand conditions; firm strategy, structure and rivalry; related and supporting industries

7 A tax on imports

8 Members of a free trade area lower barriers to trade between themselves. Members of a customs union do this and also adopt a common set of tariffs on and barriers to imports from other countries.

9 False

10 Customers, company, competition, currency, country

Now try the question below from the Exam Question Bank

Number	Level	Marks	Time
Q17	Introductory	n/a	27 mins

Chapter 18

GLOBAL STRATEGY

Topic list	Syllabus reference
1 The international planning process	7(c)
2 International marketing research	7(e)
3 Modes of entry to overseas markets	7(c)
4 Standardisation or adaptation	7(c)
5 Human resources issues	7(d)
6 Culture and the organisation	7(d)
7 The strategic importance of distribution	7(c)
8 International physical distribution	7(c)
9 Controlling global performance	7(e)
10 Social and cultural behaviour	7(e)

Introduction

This chapter continues our examination of global strategy and deals with some of the more practical aspects of international operations. We commence with the planning process and continue with international market research. The study guide emphasises a critical approach to this topic, so we look at it in some detail.

The human dimension is a particularly problematical aspect of international operations, largely because of the extended range of national cultures that must be considered. National culture affects both the internal organizational practices of the global company and its approach to its markets.

The practical aspects of **distribution** and **logistics** are particularly important in international operations so we devote two sections to this topic. Distribution is often thought of as being no more than a technical service. Always remember that it can be an important source of competitive advantage.

Finally, we consider the problems of performance management in a global economy.

Study guide

Section 7 – The nature of global competition
- The development of the global business
- Global strategies
- Managing a global company
- Reaching global customers

Exam guide

This is a large chapter. Be aware that it could be a fruitful source of questions for either part of the exam. In particular, modes of entry and standardisation or adaptation are fundamental topics.

1 THE INTERNATIONAL PLANNING PROCESS

1.1 Companies can venture into exporting for a variety of reasons, sometimes without a clear strategic vision.

(a) **Chance**. An executive may see an opportunity when abroad or the firm may receive chance orders or requests for information from potential foreign customers.

(b) **Mature or declining home market**. Products are often in different stages of the product life cycle in different countries.

(c) **Intense competition** at home sometimes induces firms to seek markets overseas where rivalry is less keen.

(d) **Reduction of dependence** on a single domestic market: export sales may provide useful **counter-cyclic** business.

(e) **Need for volume**: a large volume of sales may be needed to cover high fixed overheads (high operational gearing) or to obtain economies of scale.

(f) **Disposal of discontinued products** or **excess production**: these can be sold abroad without spoiling the home market.

(g) **Opportunism**: higher profit margins, depreciation in foreign currency values, corporate tax benefits offered by particular countries and the lowering of import barriers abroad

(h) **Counter-cyclical trade patterns**, either in terms of seasonal markets each year, or the longer term business cycle.

1.2 An unplanned or uncontrolled international venture runs a high risk of failure. There are a large number of important differences between doing business in a well-known domestic environment, where the basic rules and assumptions are well known, and tackling the very different international arena.

1.3 **Differences between domestic and international business**

Factor	Domestic	International
Cultural factors	Few language problems	Many language barriers
	Homogeneous market	Fragmented, diverse markets
	'Rules of the game' understood	Rules diverse, changeable and unclear
	Similar purchasing habits	Purchasing habits may vary by nation or region.
Economic factors	National price	Diverse national prices
	Uniform financial climate	Variety of financial climates, ranging from very conservative to highly inflationary
	Single currency	Currencies differing in stability and real value
	Stable business environment	Multiple business environments, some unstable

Factor	Domestic	International
Competitive factors	Data available, usually accurate and easy to collect.	Formidable data collection problems
Political factors	Relatively unimportant	Often significant
Technological factors	Use of standard production and measurement systems	Training of foreign personnel to operate and maintain equipment
		Adaptation of parts and equipment
		Different measuring systems

Objectives

1.4   The starting point for all successful strategic planning must be the formulation of **objectives**. Failure to define objectives clearly may lead to a firm attempting activities that conflict with or detract from the firm's principal objectives. If there is a mismatch between corporate objectives and foreign market opportunities then either plans must be modified or objectives reconsidered.

Modelling the strategic planning process

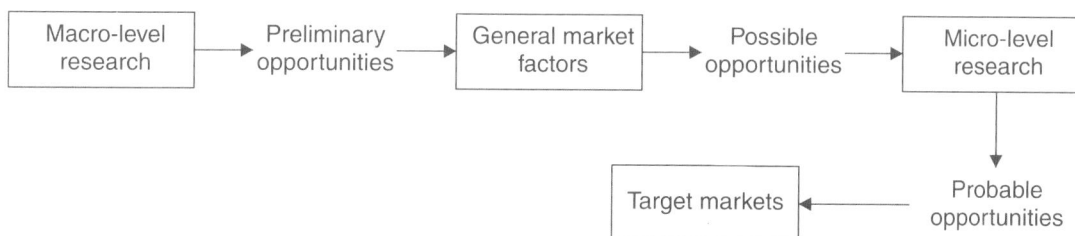

Information derived from each phase, market research and evaluation of performance

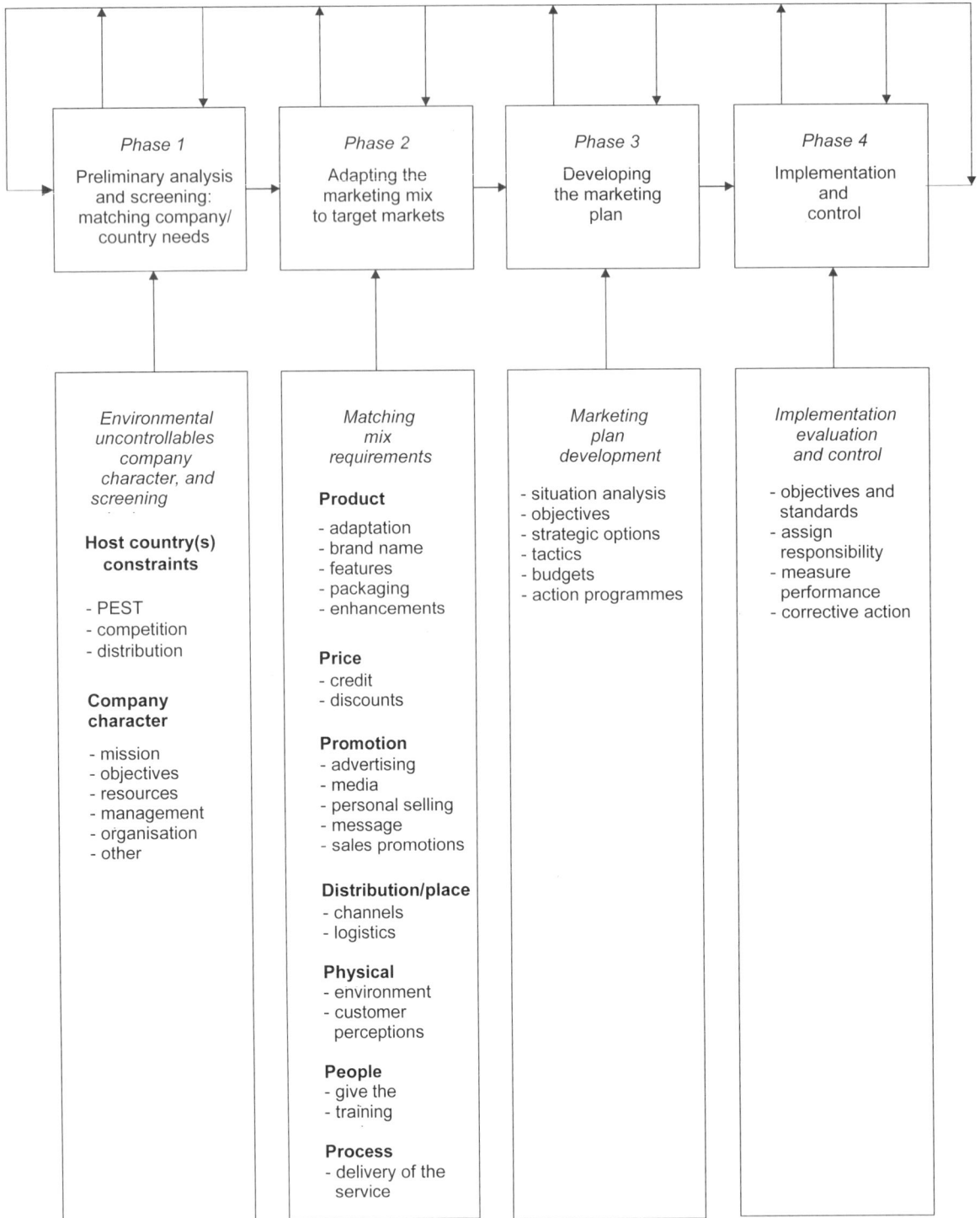

Phase 1 Preliminary analysis and screening: matching company/ country needs	Phase 2 Adapting the marketing mix to target markets	Phase 3 Developing the marketing plan	Phase 4 Implementation and control
Environmental uncontrollables company character, and screening **Host country(s) constraints** - PEST - competition - distribution **Company character** - mission - objectives - resources - management - organisation - other	*Matching mix requirements* **Product** - adaptation - brand name - features - packaging - enhancements **Price** - credit - discounts **Promotion** - advertising - media - personal selling - message - sales promotions **Distribution/place** - channels - logistics **Physical** - environment - customer perceptions **People** - give the - training **Process** - delivery of the service	*Marketing plan development* - situation analysis - objectives - strategic options - tactics - budgets - action programmes	*Implementation evaluation and control* - objectives and standards - assign responsibility - measure performance - corrective action

Phase 1: preliminary analysis and screening: matching company and country needs

1.5 The first step is an **evaluation of available markets**. The purpose here is to identify which countries, on the basis of very rough screening criteria, are obviously not suitable for investment. For example, a company marketing downhill skiing holidays would automatically rule out Holland and Egypt as locations for its activities.

Screening criteria

1.6 The next step in Phase 1 is the development of further screening criteria against which to evaluate the prospects of the remaining alternatives. Such criteria vary from company to company, being determined by their own objectives, strengths and weaknesses. Central to the evaluation are the company's reasons for entering a foreign market and the returns expected from it. Here are some typical **screening criteria**.

- Specified minimum acceptable levels of profits
- Market share and volume
- Acceptable levels of competition
- Acceptable legal conditions
- Political risks

1.7 When screening criteria have been outlined, the next step of Phase 1 is a thorough analysis of the **environmental conditions** prevailing in each prospective country At this stage, the company must consider any links between its domestic environment and its ambitions for overseas markets. For example, domestic laws may forbid exporting to a particular country or company language capabilities may favour a particular market. The results of Phase 1 yield the following information.

- Obviously inappropriate countries are identified.
- The potential of each overseas market is assessed.
- Areas for further environmental research and analysis are identified.
- The most appropriate overseas markets are selected.
- Changes to the marketing mix to meet local needs are determined.

1.8 Note that one of the consequences of globalisation might be market segmentation across national boundaries; however we should always be aware that national borders do exist.

Choosing countries

1.9 That said, it is unlikely that a firm would export to its chosen segment in **every country**. After all there are practical and logistical problems in exporting everywhere, the political and currency risk profiles of the various countries may differ and the competitive environments may vary.

1.10 So, it is worth having a screening process for new **country markets**, if of course such a screening process is carried out rationally. The scanning process should give information on the existing state of markets.

- **Existing markets,** where customer needs are already serviced

- **Incipient markets** where potential customers are currently recognised but are not being serviced

- **Latent markets** where there is a foreseeable, but not a present, market for products

1.11 In practice, the segmentation and screening process will be based on economic factors, and might follow a number of stages. *Jeannet and Hennessy* suggest a four-stage approach to screening.

(a) **Macrolevel research** considers the overall PEST factors in the overseas market. Indicators of the total size of the market might include area, climate, demographic factors or gross domestic product.

(b) The next level is the **general market** relating to the product.

(i) Market size can be estimated by proxy statistics. For example, if telephone ownership is widespread, there is likely to be a bigger market for answering machines than if telephones are a rarity.

(ii) Specific regulations controlling the market must be known. For example, trade in financial services is still widely protected.

(iii) Products must be culturally acceptable.

(c) **Microlevel research** identifies specific factors relating to the product.

(i) **Competition**, existing and potential must be considered. For example, some markets might be very open and host to a large number of competitors. Others may be closed, arising to regulation, or foreigners may have restricted access. Air travel is heavily regulated, for example.

(ii) The market might be similar to the domestic market in certain key respects. Measures of similarity include production and transportation, personal consumption, trade, health care and education.

(iii) Finally this leads to **target markets** or segments which are screened for their suitability.

Financial issues

1.12 **Financial issues** are always of vital importance.

(a) Will the company make profits? Which mode of entry will be profitable?

(b) Will the profit be acceptable given the risk? Normally, the higher the risk, the higher the return required.

(c) What is the size of the investment required, and how much will it cost to finance the investment? Is money being taken away from other, potentially more profitable, investments?

(d) How will the international trade be financed and how will the international cashflows be managed? There are a number of sophisticated techniques available to manage international credit control.

- Irrevocable letter of credit
- Documentary collection
- Bill of exchange
- Forfeiting

(e) Will the firm be able to repatriate dividends and cash from the country? Restrictions on the export of cash make an investment less attractive.

(f) What is the extent of exchange rate risk?

Without an extensive search and appraisal programme, firms entering IM are liable to make major and costly mistakes.

Case example

The Tandy Corporation, a US firm, did without such an exercise and consequently made many errors when attempting to enter the Western European Market. For example, in Holland, Tandy staged its first Christmas promotion for December 25 unaware that the Dutch exchange Christmas presents on December 6 (St Nicholas). Tandy also launched citizen band radios as a product only to find that in many European countries it was illegal to use them.

Phase 2: adapting the marketing mix to target markets

1.13 When target markets have been chosen it is necessary to examine the blend of mix elements in greater detail. Specifically the company should be seeking answers to two major questions.

(a) What cultural or other environmental **adaptations** are needed to ensure customer satisfaction with the mix offered?

(b) Will adaptation **costs** prevent profitable market entry?

Often the answers to either of these questions indicate that the marketing mix requires such major **adaptation** that a decision is taken to eliminate the country from any further consideration. However, further research in this phase may suggest ways in which the marketing programme can be **standardised** for two or more countries.

Phase 3: developing the marketing plan

1.14 At this point a marketing plan is formulated for a specific country or target market. As in the earlier phases, the firm may decide to drop a particular country if it becomes evident that it cannot design a marketing plan that will result in the achievement of marketing objectives for the country.

Phase 4: implementation and control

1.15 Finally, specific marketing actions are implemented, co-ordinated and controlled. The last of these is very important, being much neglected despite the fact that effective monitoring and control enhances performance substantially. Control requires continuing monitoring of performance against targets to identify when remedial action is needed, in what form and by whom.

Planning problems

1.16 There are difficulties to be encountered in the strategic planning process. As far as the **management structure and culture** are concerned, the following issues may pose problems.

(a) **Domestic headquarters**

(i) Managers may be ignorant of overseas markets, and their decisions might be taken with little regard to local attitudes or feelings.

Case example

In the early 1990s, managers of Johnson and Johnson in the Philippines discovered that young Filipino women were using Johnson and Johnson baby talcum powder to freshen their makeup during the day, carrying a small amount in a knotted handkerchief.

Johnson and Johnson Philippines developed a compact holder for the talcum powder, and an advertising campaign was devised.

A few days before the product launch, corporate HQ in the US asked that it be cancelled, because 'we are not in the cosmetics business'. It was only after the chief marketer in the Philippines flew to headquarters and pleaded for the product's life that it was allowed to go ahead.

Adapted from *Harvard Business Review*

    (ii)   Furthermore, if the organisation is centralised, all the 'political' battles within its leadership will be focused around the domestic agenda.

(b) Local level problems

- Resentment at being bossed around.
- Unclear goals.
- Different ways of doing business.
- Inadequate control.
- A lack of a strategic outlook and marketing expertise.
- A completely different attitude to the product and marketing task.

(c) International marketing planning also involves human resources considerations. The local subsidiary will have its own human resource needs, and these will be met by and large by local personnel.

1.17 **Management processes and decision making**

(a) Poor information systems and communications. However, the rapidly falling costs of telecommunications in real terms, the development of e-mail and video-conferencing facilities make this less excusable than before.

(b) **Interpretation of information**. Culture filters information. It can also determine the priorities of the planners. By **failing to allow for diversity**, planners can make marketing on the ground more difficult.

    (i)   Managing a local market in a large country with a low population density and whose main source of earnings is natural resources would be different from marketing to a small country with a high population density.

    (ii)   High tech products may not be suitable to a country with a poorly developed educational and technological infrastructure as there might be no-one to service the equipment. So a high tech strategy at home would not work abroad.

    (iii)   Consumers in countries with very high rates of inflation will have different priorities to those who live in countries with low inflation. Managers' priorities will be to minimise any holdings of local currency, by converting it into a harder currency or into tangible assets. However, this makes financial reporting difficult.

Distance and implementation problems

1.18 The gap between the corporate plan and its implementation is greater for the international company than it is for a company which only deals with one market.

(a) **Physical**

    (i)   The degree of variation in environmental conditions is so much greater. Managers, in trying to get a global picture, may **aggregate data** from very dissimilar markets.

(ii) In order to compete effectively, local management must be able to respond to differing environmental conditions.

(b) **Psychological.** Corporate planners may not share the same assumptions as local managers.

1.19 As a consequence of the greater variety of factors involved in planning, any attempt at central control is likely to be much less certain.

(a) **Lack of experience.** The expertise and experience of head office planners might be limited by their careers in the 'head office' or by a gradual loss of a feel for their local roots.

(b) **Time horizons.** Corporate planners will be seeking to satisfy the firm's **investors**, whose desire for a return might be dominated by their local considerations. This is typically a problem when a long term investment is required in an overseas market.

2 INTERNATIONAL MARKETING RESEARCH 6/02

2.1 The most important requirement of effective international marketing is thorough **market analysis**, both before entering the market and also once the market has been entered, in order to maintain continuous awareness of opportunities, threats and trends.

2.2 **Objectives of international marketing research**

- Identify attractive **new markets**
- Enhance profitability by pinpointing **opportunities and threats**
- Facilitate awareness of **general market trends**
- Monitor changes in **customer needs and preferences**
- Knowledge of **competitor plans and strategies**
- Identify new **product opportunities** in the marketplace
- Monitor **political, legal, economic, social** and **technological** trends
- Enhance the level and quality of **information** available for planning

2.3 It is obvious that international marketing research (IMR) is more complex than domestic marketing research because of its focus on more than one country. It requires additional efforts to overcome a lack of empathy with a market. Thus there is a need to gather information about foreign customer preferences, languages, customs, beliefs and so on which in a domestic market could be assumed to be largely known and understood.

Strategic questions for IMR

(a) **Should the company look to foreign markets at all?** This will involve an assessment of overseas market demand and the firm's potential share in it compared to domestic opportunities.

(b) **Which market(s) should it enter?** Potential foreign markets need to be ranked according to size, competition, investment and risk.

(c) **How should the company enter the selected markets?** Detailed analysis is required of market size, international trade barriers, transport systems and costs, local competition, government regulations and political stability.

(d) **What marketing programme is best suited to the selected market?** For each selected market a detailed knowledge of buyer behaviour, competitive practices, distribution channels, promotional methods and media will be required.

Information sources

2.4 Before considering the IMR process in detail it is important to consider the types of data source available to the international marketer.

Human sources

2.5 **Human sources** provide the largest source of information to international marketers.

2.6 For well established international marketing companies, the principal human information source is the **managers** of subsidiaries, branches and associates abroad. Not only do they live in the foreign cultural environments but they also appreciate the company's business objectives.

- They can distinguish relevant from irrelevant information
- They can use **personal contacts** to acquire unpublished information

2.7 **Consumers**, **customers**, **distributors**, **suppliers** and even **competitors** are all important sources of information.

Documentary sources

2.8 **Documentary sources** are compiled without any knowledge of the reader or the precise purposes for which the information is required.

2.9 The biggest problem in using documentary sources is that there are simply so many of them, whilst none may **specifically address** the point of interest.

Direct sources

2.10 Direct sources provide information without any intermediate analysis that could reduce its levels of accuracy and relevance. There are three general types.

   (a) Direct observation and specialist knowledge.
   (b) Direct observation and background information.
   (c) Personal experience supporting indirect information.

2.11 **Examples of UK documentary sources**. The **DTI** maintains a collection of overseas market information. This is complemented by numerous trade publications, directories, statistical material and published market research. This information is a great help to exporters.

2.12 **Export Market Information Centre**. EMIC is a self-help research and library facility. Information available in EMIC includes foreign statistics on trade, production, prices, employment, population and transport as well as development plans of many countries which are useful guides to the current and future state of specific economies as well as highlighting specific opportunities.

2.13 **Export publications**. The **DTI** publishes a wide range of country and sector reports.

2.14 **Export intelligence**. Exporters can arrange to be kept up to date with export intelligence from the DTI, the EU and the World Bank. Export intelligence includes selling opportunities such as enquiries from overseas buyers and agents and market information on tariff changes, forthcoming projects, aid and loan agreements.

The IMR process

2.15 The international market research (IMR) process can be divided into three processes: monitoring, investigation and research.

2.16 **Monitoring** involves **passive information gathering** in which the organisation has identified a particular market on which information needs to be collected but, as yet, does not warrant active measures.

2.17 The most important aspect of **investigation** is the accurate assessment of **market opportunity.**

(a) **Existing demand** concerns current purchases of the type of product. The level of existing demand alone may be enough to justify entry to that market, to win a share.

(b) **Latent demand** is demand which exists in the market but is currently **untapped** because of a defect in the marketing mix used by existing suppliers.

Case example

The success of mountain bikes depended on new product features. Although in industrially advanced economies bicycles were regarded as a product of the leisure market rather than as a means of transport, their design gave them a rather 'tame' image, perhaps a two-wheeled version of rambling! The introduction of a more rugged design and other product features (such as styling and colour) designed to appeal to the youth market opened up a whole new segment of the bike market.

(c) **Incipient demand** requires wealth levels in an economy to be above a certain minimum before the volume of demand becomes sufficiently great for the market to become profitable.

2.18 Investigation is often done informally and information may be collected as part of other activities; market **research** proper is **proactive.** In the international context, this can be expensive.

2.19 A vital part in any research exercise is to plan it properly. Although no entirely standard plan can be drawn up, it is likely to have the following elements.

- Define the scope of the project
- Define the project's information needs
- Evaluate the available sources for the required information
- Undertake the desk research and evaluate its findings
- Undertake field research

Case example

Both McDonalds and Kelloggs suffered setbacks when trying to penetrate the Indian market. McDonalds has had to come to terms with a market that considers killing cows to be sacrilege, is averse to pork, is 40% vegetarian, hostile to frozen meat and fish, and very fond of spices.

Kelloggs was unsuccessful in persuading Indians that its cereals were a healthier alternative to traditional heavy Indian breakfasts.

Using IMR data

2.20 IMR data can be used in the following ways to identify market opportunities.

    (a) To estimate **patterns** of demand/or consumption in individual markets.

    (b) To **compare** patterns of demand or consumption in different markets.

    (c) To identify **clusters** of markets with similar characteristics, which can be targeted with similar mix.

    (d) To identify **strategically equivalent** segments, across country boundaries.

Predicting patterns of demand

Demand pattern analysis

2.21 **Demand pattern analysis** involves analysing production patterns (as a surrogate for demand) over time. It helps in identifying general marketing opportunities and, because it uses **production** statistics, it can indicate potential markets.

Income elasticity of demand

2.22 Income elasticity of demand describes the relative changes in demand for a product with changes in income levels.

    (a) Demand for some goods is **income inelastic.** As people get richer, demand for such goods does not increase proportionately. For example, poor people might spend over 50% of their income on basic foodstuffs. In wealthy countries such as the UK, food accounts for about 11%. British people do not eat less, but food takes up a lower proportion of their income.

    (b) Goods for which demand is **income elastic** are very sensitive to changes in people's income. These include leisure products and some consumer durables.

Comparing patterns of demand/consumption in different markets

Comparative analysis

2.23 **Comparative analysis** assumes that if market potential is equivalent in two markets then marketing performance should be comparable too. It usually takes the form of comparison of the same company's performance in two (or more) national markets. If the economies are broadly similar but performance is not (or vice-versa) it suggests that marketing performance is not being optimised and thus raises questions to be addressed.

Inter-market timing differences

2.24 This technique uses the premise that certain markets have **similar demand patterns** for similar goods but that one leads and the other lags. Clearly this technique is useful only for comparing countries that can be assumed to have similar economic, social and cultural conditions. The diagram below shows the similarity in the rate of acquisition of television in the 1950s and 1960s between the UK and West Germany. At its simplest, the technique enabled the prediction of growth or decline in the then West German market by taking that of the UK market a few years earlier and adjusting for the different numbers on households in the two markets.

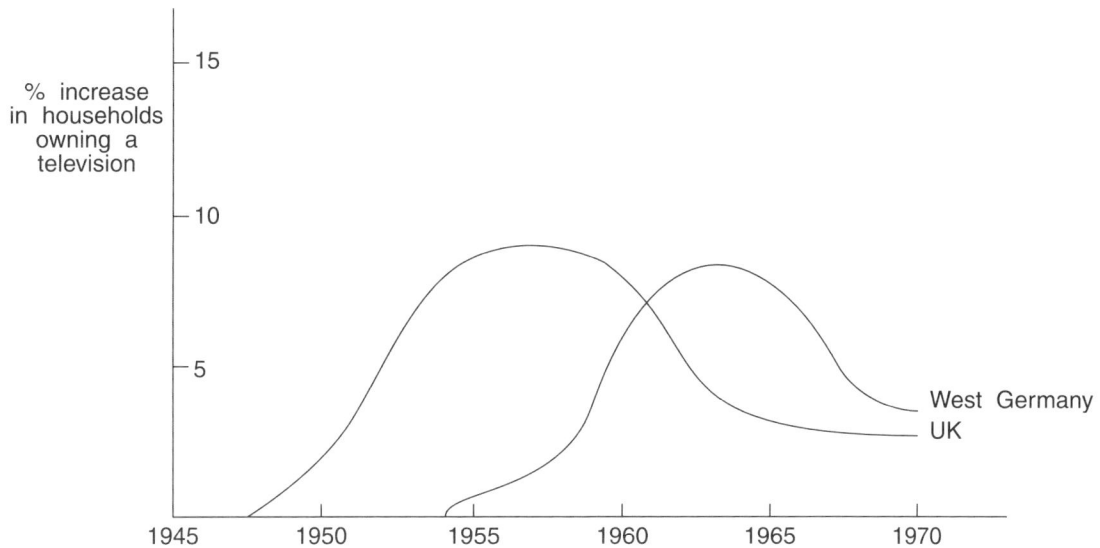

% increase in households owning a television (y-axis, marked 5, 10, 15)

x-axis: 1945, 1950, 1955, 1960, 1965, 1970

West Germany
UK

Identifying clusters of markets with similar characteristics

2.25 A logical extension of using one market to predict the behaviour of another is to identify **clusters of markets** with the same characteristics. **Cluster analysis** involves mathematical techniques - too complex to describe here - to identify similar markets.

Identifying strategically equivalent segments

2.26 In addition to identifying clusters of countries, it is possible that a firm may wish to segment each market and pursue these segments only.

2.27 In international marketing, as in domestic marketing, firms can use more than one segmentation variable, a **primary segmentation** variable and a **secondary segmentation** variable. For example, for wet shaving equipment, the primary segmentation variable might be sex (Gillette produces different razor blade holders for men and women), and secondary segmentation variables might be age or lifestyle.

2.28 In international marketing, using **country** as the **primary** segmentation variable would seem common sense, certainly for consumer products, given the cultural influences, political risk factors and so forth identified earlier. If a firm pursues a multi-domestic strategy it will almost certainly use country as the primary segmentation variable. Even a global firm, to whom the world is a single market, will develop country-based segments in **consumer markets.**

2.29 Take the example of a firm selling walking sticks in the EU. Using country as the prime segmentation variable may cause confusion. The country markets for walking sticks are each **naturally** segmented by **age.** Consequently, rather than using country as a primary segmentation variable, it might be sensible to use **age** instead to avoid separately targeting segments whose needs are very similar.

2.30 This leads us to the notion of **strategically equivalent segments,** which transcend national boundaries. Here are some possible examples.

(a) In South East Asia, people of Chinese ethnic extraction form the business elite in many countries (eg Malaysia) despite government attempts to reduce imbalances. Therefore, for certain types of goods and services, overseas Chinese (eg in Malaysia, Singapore, Thailand and so on) could be considered a strategically equivalent segment.

(b) Geodemographic segmentation can also be used. CCN **EuroMosaic** analyses ten classifications of European consumers as shown below.

- Wealthy suburbs
- Average-income areas
- Flats - luxury
- Low income inner city
- Municipal/social housing estates

- Industrial communities
- Dynamic families
- Low income families
- Farming/rural
- Holiday/retirement areas

2.31 Such worries may not exist for many **industrial markets,** where there are fewer buyers, and where purchase decisions are in theory taken according to rational criteria. The market for aircraft engines comprises the world's airlines, and it may not be possible or necessary to segment this market.

Case example

Japan's population profile is ageing more rapidly than that of most other countries. Thus, Shiseido, the cosmetics company, launched Acteaheart, a range of cosmetics specially aimed at women over 40. This might also be considered a strategically equivalent segment in other markets which Shiseido may wish to target - the US and the wealthy Asian countries.

Some problems in IMR

Secondary data problems

2.32 There are normally three critical deficiencies regarding secondary data that are important to the international market researcher.

(a) **Lack of data.** Without doubt, the USA has the best documented commercial information. But few countries come close to matching the sheer volume and diversity of data collected in the USA. Until the United Nations began assimilating world economic data, there was often little available other than very rough estimates for many lesser developed countries.

(b) **Comparability** and **timeliness.**

(i) This problem is at its most acute in less economically developed countries. Data is often many years out of date and collected on an infrequent and unpredictable schedule.

(ii) More specific problems involve different definitions used in data collection, the fact that different base years have been used for comparative purposes and that gaps may exist. As an example a television is classified as household furniture in the USA but not in Germany (where it is treated as a recreational purchase) leading to problems of comparability of data collected in different countries.

(c) **Lack of reliability** of some of the secondary data that are collected. Much of it has to be analysed with great care.

(i) In many economically underdeveloped countries, national pride takes precedence over statistical accuracy.

(ii) Moreover, companies have been known to reduce their production statistics so that they reconcile to sales reported to the tax authorities!

2.33 As a practical matter, before basing a marketing strategy on the analysis of secondary data, it is worthwhile asking the following questions.

(a) **Who** collected the data? Would there be any reason for deliberately misrepresenting the facts?

(b) For what **purpose** was data collected?

(c) **How** was the data collected (ie what was the survey methodology used?)

(d) Is the data **consistent with one another** and are they logical (in the light of known data sources or market factors)?

Case example

One of the problems of doing market research in Russia is identifying groups of consumers. Official statistics leave a lot to be desired, given the enormous social changes over the past few years.

Researchers have begun, however, to identify new segments, from wealthy entrepreneurs to poorer people dependent on state pensions. Rather than outlining a simple rich/poor divide, a number of groups have been identified.

Response problems

2.34 People's unwillingness to provide information is a feature of many countries. Several reasons can be suggested for this.

(a) **Tax evasion and avoidance of responsibility.** Anyone asking questions may be suspected of being a government employee.

(b) **Wish to preserve secrecy.** Many business managers regard data relating to their company or markets as potential help to competitors and accordingly response rates are low when they concern anything that might be regarded as an aid to a competitor.

(c) **Cultural taboos and norms**

(i) Topics that are freely discussed in some countries (for example birth control methods) are taboo for discussion in others except in the most intimate situations.

(ii) Similarly the authority to respond may not be the same in all cultures. Thus whilst in one country a female head of household may feel authorised to discuss a topic with a researcher, in other countries there may be a marked reluctance to give information.

2.35 In carrying out surveys, firms in the UK take many things for granted that may not exist in other countries, particularly less developed ones.

(a) There may be no suitable lists (**sampling frames**) from which a representative sample can be selected.

(b) Inadequate **communication infrastructure** can be a severe practical handicap.

(c) Low levels of **literacy**.

(d) Problems of **language and comprehension** are widespread in IMR. Differences in idiom and problems of precise translation lead to great misunderstandings. In large countries such as India the researcher has to be prepared to deal with some fourteen languages and 200 dialects when planning a survey.

2.36 This discussion should make it clear that there is a greater necessity for **care, understanding and skill** in IMR data analysis.

(a) Thus the analyst requires an extensive understanding of the cultural environment of the countries being researched and a talent for interpolating data that contains gaps or has other deficiencies.

(b) A final requirement would be a **healthy scepticism** towards both primary and secondary data since they are very likely to be imperfect, resulting in a desire to cross check and substantiate data wherever possible.

3 MODES OF ENTRY TO OVERSEAS MARKETS 12/01, 12/03

3.1 If an organisation has decided to enter an overseas market, the way it does so is of crucial strategic importance. Broadly, three ways of entering foreign markets can be identified: **indirect exports**, **direct exports** and **overseas manufacture**.

3.2 The most suitable mode of entry varies:

(a) **Among firms in the same industry** (eg a new exporter as opposed to a long-established exporter)

(b) **According to the market** (eg some countries limit imports to protect domestic manufacturers whereas others promote free trade)

(c) **Over time** (eg as some countries become more, or less, hostile to direct inward investment by foreign companies).

3.3 Choice of mode of entry

Consideration	Comment
The firm's marketing objectives	These relate to volume, time scale and coverage of market segments. Thus setting up an overseas production facility would be inappropriate if sales are expected to be low in volume.
The firm's size	A small firm is less likely than a large one to possess sufficient resources to set up and run a production facility overseas.
Mode availability	Some countries only allow a restricted level of imports, but will welcome a firm if it builds manufacturing facilities which provide jobs and limit the outflow of foreign exchange.
Mode quality	All modes may be possible in theory, but some are of questionable quality or practicality. The lack of suitably qualified distributors or agents would preclude the export, direct or indirect, of high technology goods needing installation, maintenance and servicing by personnel with specialist technical skills.
Personnel requirements	When a firm is unable to recruit suitable staff either at home or overseas, indirect exporting or the use of agents based overseas may be the only realistic option.
Market feedback information	In some cases a firm can receive feedback information about the market and its marketing effort from its sales staff or distribution channels. In these circumstances direct export or joint ventures may be preferred to indirect export.
Learning curve requirements	Firms which intend a heavy future involvement in an overseas market might need to gain the experience that close involvement in an overseas market can bring. This argues against the use of indirect exporting as the mode of entry.
Risks	Firms might prefer the indirect export mode as assets are safer from

Consideration	Comment
	expropriation.
Control needs	Production overseas by a wholly owned subsidiary gives a firm absolute control while indirect exporting offers virtually no control to the exporter.

Exporting

3.4 Goods are made at home but sold abroad. It is the easiest, cheapest and most commonly used route into a new foreign market.

3.5 **Advantages of exporting**

(a) Exporters can **concentrate production** in a single location, giving **economies of scale** and **consistency of product quality**.

(b) Firms lacking experience can try international marketing on a **small scale**.

(c) Firms can **test** their international marketing plans and strategies before risking investment in overseas operations.

(d) Exporting **minimises operating costs**, administrative overheads and personnel requirements.

Indirect exports

3.6 **Indirect exporting** is where a firm's goods are sold abroad by other organisations who can offer greater market knowledge.

(a) **Export houses** are firms which facilitate exporting on behalf of the producer. Usually the producer has little control over the market and the marketing effort.

(b) **Specialist export management firms** perform the same functions as an in-house export department but are normally remunerated by way of commission.

(c) **UK buying offices of foreign stores and governments**.

(d) **Complementary exporting** ('piggy back exporting') occurs when one producing organisation (the carrier) uses its own established international marketing channels to market (either as distributor, or agent or merchant) the products of another producer (the rider) as well as its own.

Direct exports

3.7 **Direct exporting** occurs where the producing organisation itself performs the export tasks rather than using an intermediary. Sales are made directly to customers overseas who may be the wholesalers, retailers or final users.

(a) **Sales to final user**. Typical customers include industrial users, governments or mail order customers.

(b) Strictly speaking an **overseas export agent** or distributor is an overseas firm hired to effect a sales contract between the principal (ie the exporter) and a customer. Agents do not take title to goods; they earn a commission (or profit).

(c) **Company branch offices abroad**. A firm can establish its own office in a foreign market for the purpose of marketing and distribution as this gives greater control.

3.8 A firm can manufacture its products overseas, either by itself or by using an overseas manufacturer.

Overseas production

3.9 **Benefits of overseas manufacture**

- A **better understanding of customers** in the overseas market.
- **Economies of scale** in large markets.
- **Production costs are lower** in some countries than at home.
- **Lower storage and transportation costs**.
- **Overcomes the effects of tariff and non-tariff barriers**.
- Manufacture in the overseas market **may help win orders from the public sector**.

Contract manufacture

3.10 **Licensing** is a quite common arrangement as it avoids the cost and hassle of setting up overseas.

3.11 In the case of **contract manufacture** a firm (the contractor) makes a contract with another firm (the contractee) abroad whereby the contractee manufactures or assembles a product on behalf of the contractor. Contract manufacture is suited to **countries** where the **small size of the market** discourages investment in plant and to **firms** whose main **strengths are in marketing** rather than production.

  (a) **Advantages of contract manufacture**

- No need to invest in plant overseas
- Lower risks associated with currency fluctuations
- Lower risk of asset expropriation is minimised
- Control of marketing is retained by the contractor
- Lower transport costs and, sometimes, lower production costs

  (b) **Disadvantages of contract manufacture**

- Suitable overseas producers cannot always be easily identified
- The need to train the contractee producer's personnel
- The contractee producer may eventually become a competitor
- Quality control problems in manufacturing may arise

Joint ventures

3.12 Some governments discourage or even prohibit foreign firms setting up independent operations. so joint ventures are the only option. That said, a joint venture with an indigenous firm provides local knowledge, quickly.

Wholly owned overseas production

3.13 Production capacity can be built from scratch, or, alternatively, an existing firm can be acquired.

  (a) **Acquisition** has all the benefits and drawbacks of acquiring a domestic company.

  (b) **Creating new capacity** can be beneficial if there are no likely candidates for takeover, or if acquisition is prohibited by the government.

3.14 **Advantages**

- The firm does **not have to share its profits** with partners of any kind.
- The firm does **not have to share or delegate decision-making**.
- There are **none of the communication problems** that arise in joint ventures.
- The firm is able to operate completely **integrated** international systems.
- The firm gains a more **varied experience** from overseas production.

3.15 **Disadvantages**

(a) The **investment** needed prevents some firms from setting up operations overseas.

(b) Suitable **managers** may be **difficult to recruit** at home or abroad.

(c) Some overseas **governments discourage**, and sometimes prohibit, **100% ownership** of an enterprise by a foreign company.

(d) This mode of entry **forgoes the benefits of an overseas partner's market knowledge**, distribution system and other local expertise.

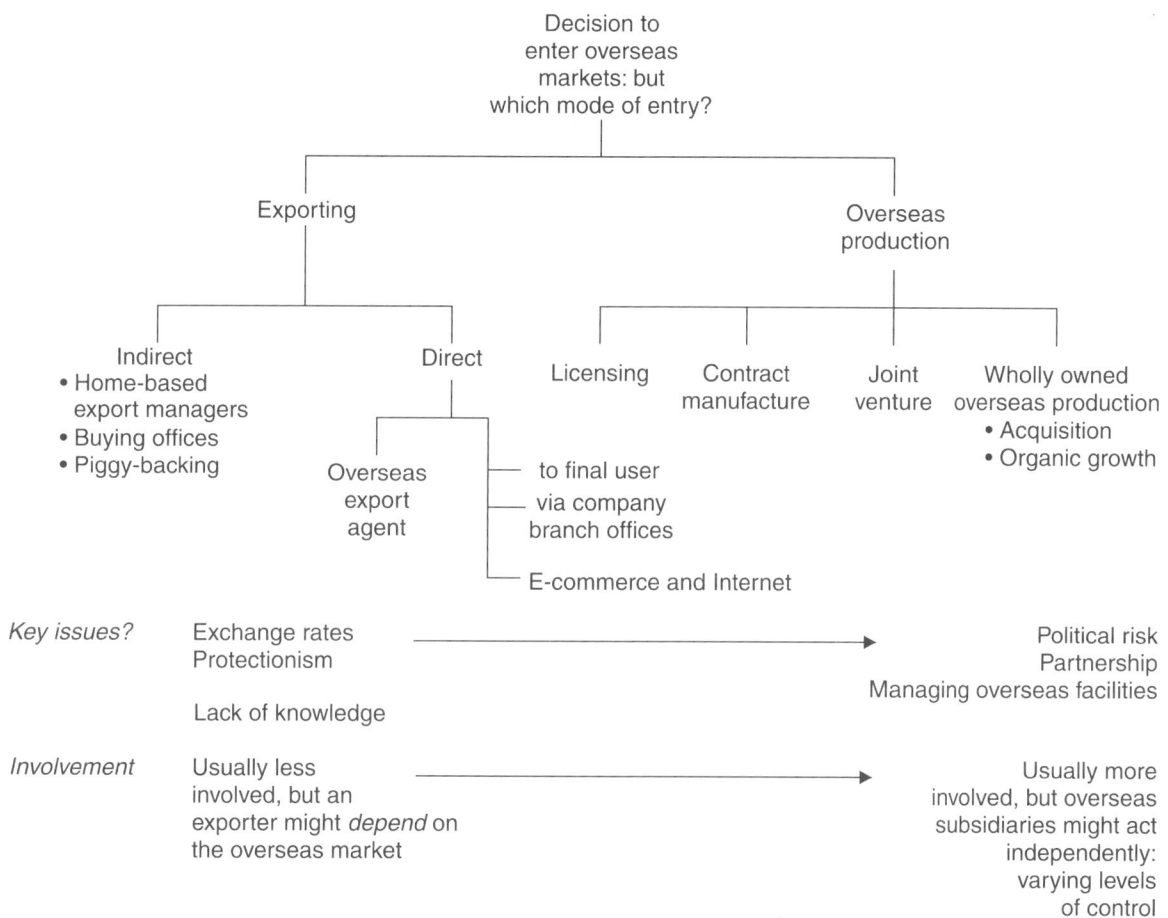

The criteria for selecting a method of entry

3.16 The most suitable method of entry varies.

(a) Among firms in the same industry (eg a new exporter as opposed to a long-established exporter)

(b) According to the market (eg some countries limit imports to protect domestic manufacturers whereas others promote free trade)

(c) Over time (eg as some countries become more, or less, hostile to direct inward investment by foreign companies)

3.17 To choose a method of entry to a particular market, a firm should consider the following issues.

  (a) **Firm's marketing objectives,** in relation to volume, timescale and coverage of market segments. Thus setting up an overseas production facility would be inappropriate if sales are expected to be low in volume, or if the product is only to be on sale for a limited period.

  (b) **Firm's size**. A small firm is less likely than a large one to possess sufficient resources to set up and run a production facility overseas. Not only would the firm have to provide investment capital and organisational ability, but it would also have to support the costs of continuing operations.

  (c) **Mode availability.** A firm might have to use different methods of entry to enter different markets. Some countries only allow a restricted level of imports, but will welcome a firm if it builds manufacturing facilities which provide jobs and limit the outflow of foreign exchange. In this case, overseas manufacture is a better option than direct export.

  (d) **Method quality**. In some cases, all modes may be possible in theory, but some are of questionable quality or practicality. The lack of suitably qualified distributors or agents would preclude the export, direct or indirect, of high technology goods needing installation, maintenance and servicing by personnel with specialist technical skills.

  (e) **Human resources requirements**. These vary according to which method of entry is used. When a firm is unable to recruit suitable staff either at home or overseas, indirect exporting or the use of agents based overseas may be the only realistic option.

  (f) **Market information feedback**. In some cases a firm can receive feedback information about the market and its marketing effort from its sales staff or distribution channels. In these circumstances direct export or joint ventures may be preferred to indirect export.

  (g) **Learning curve requirements**. Firms which intend a heavy future involvement might need to learn from the experience that close involvement in an overseas market can bring. This argues against the use of indirect exporting as the method of entry.

  (h) **Risks**. Some risks, such as political risk or the risk of the expropriation of overseas assets by foreign governments, might discourage firms from using overseas production as the method of entry to overseas markets. Instead, firms might prefer the indirect export mode as it is safer. On the other hand, the risk of losing touch with customers and their requirements would encourage either direct export or overseas production.

  (i) **Control needs**. Control over the marketing mix and the distribution channel varies greatly by method of entry. Production overseas by a wholly owned subsidiary gives a firm absolute control while indirect exporting offers virtually no control to the exporter.

4 STANDARDISATION OR ADAPTATION

4.1 Once a firm has decided on which markets it is going to operate in and the level of involvement in each market, it has to determine its marketing mix.

Standardisation

4.2 A business has three broad possibilities for its international marketing mix.

KEY TERMS

Undifferentiated marketing. The company offers to the whole market a standard product with a standard price and promotional activities. It aims to minimise both production and marketing costs.

Differentiated marketing. Here the company segments its market. It sells in a large number of markets, but adjusts its product and marketing programmes to the needs and environmental variables of each.

Concentrated marketing. With this approach a company devotes all its marketing effort to one or a very few markets. It will choose a market where its standardised product and marketing programme will be best suited. It is the best approach for a company with limited resources.

Case example

In Europe, surprisingly few products are sold from one end of the continent to the other. People in Finland simply do not eat the same foods, wear the same clothes or buy the same furniture as people in Greece. And even where brand names do travel, the products that carry them are often adjusted to suit local preferences, making comparisons difficult.

Take a product as mundane as laundry detergent. In the US, soap powder is the same wherever you go: it comes in a big red box and it is called Tide. In Europe, there are more laundry detergent brands than there are countries; and even two boxes with the same name on the outside can have different products within.

For example, Unilever, the Anglo-Dutch consumer goods company, makes Persil with higher-quality ingredients for the UK market than for France, where it sells the product as a low-end brand; and in the rest of Europe, Persil is owned by a completely different company, Germany's Henkel, which varies the formula from country to country to suit local conditions. "Stains in the south of Europe are different from Scandinavian stains because the Spanish and Italians eat different foods," Henkel says, referring to the special challenges of olive oil and tomatoes.

Richard Tomkins, Financial Times, 5 January 2002

4.3 Most firms would prefer to sell the same product at the same price through similar distribution channels, using the same means of communication in all its markets. The diagram below shows examples of barriers to such **standardisation** caused by environmental differences.

Barriers to standardisation

Environmental variable	Product	Price	Distribution	Promotion
Economy	Usage	Varied income level	Different retail structures	Media availability
Culture	Consumer tastes and Habits	Price negotiating habits	Buying habits	Language and attitude differences
Competition	Nature of existing products	Competitors' objectives, costs and prices	Competitors' monopoly and use of channels	Competitors' budgets appeals
Law	Product regulation	Price controls	Restriction on distribution	Advertising and media restrictions

Product and communications

Standardisation vs adaptation

4.4   The question of whether or not to adapt the product is often considered in conjunction with the **promotion/communication** issue. This gives us four possible product and communication strategies.

	Product standardised	Product adapted
Communications standardised	Standardisation worldwide of both product and communications	Adaptation of product only
Communications adapted	Adaptation of communications only	Both product and communications adapted

Source: Keegan

Standardised product and communications

4.5   This is the obvious strategy for the occasional exporter but also some major international companies seeking economies of scale.

Case example

PepsiCo has been successful with this strategy. Many perfumes and cosmetics are marketed in this way. (For example, the actress Elizabeth Hurley was adopted to be the 'face of Estée Lauder' worldwide.) Polaroid, however, failed in France with their instant picture camera because of failure to modify their product and communications activities from the successful USA version. This failure was due to the fact that the product was at a different stage in its product life cycle in France and the United States.

Standardised product/adapted communication

4.6 This strategy is used where a product meets different needs in different countries, as with bicycles for example. The product is the same, but communications can suggest different uses.

- France/Belgium - sport-recreation
- UK - recreation
- Third World - means of transport

Adapted product/standardised communication

4.7 This strategy is relevant where the product satisfies the same need (or solves the same problem) in many markets but conditions of use vary.

(a) Petrol companies adapt their fuel to climactic conditions but standardise their advertising and other promotional activities.

(b) Car manufacturers need different tyres and temperature control systems in Saudi Arabia than they do in the UK.

Adaptation of both product and communications

4.8 This strategy is the most costly one but may be necessary to exploit a market fully. For example, take these two stereotypes.

(a) US product - can be made or packaged in plastic and be disposable.

(b) German product - must be made or packaged in metal and must be durable and repairable because of German concern for environmental issues. Promotional activities must reflect these product attributes.

Exam focus point
Factors encouraging a policy of customisation were asked for in an 8 mark part question in December 2002.

5 HUMAN RESOURCES ISSUES

Expatriates or locals?

5.1 For an international company, which has to think globally as well as act locally, there are a number of problems.

- Do you employ mainly **expatriate staff** to control local operations?
- Do you employ **local managers**, with the possible loss of central control?
- Is there such a thing as the **global manager**, equally at home in different cultures?

5.2 Expatriate staff are sometimes favoured over local staff.

(a) Poor **educational opportunities** in the market may require the import of skilled technicians and managers. For example, expatriates have been needed in many western firms' operations in Russia and Eastern Europe, simply because they understand the meaning of profit.

(b) Some senior managers believe that a business run by expatriates is easier to **control** than one run by local staff.

(c) If the firm is a macropyramid, expatriates might be better able than locals to **communicate** with the corporate centre.

(d) The expatriate may **know more about the firm** overall, which is especially important if he or she is fronting a sales office.

5.3 The use of expatriates in overseas markets has certain disadvantages.

(a) They **cost** more (eg subsidised housing, school fees).

(b) **Culture shock**. The expatriate may fail to adjust to the culture (eg by associating only with other expatriates). This is likely to lead to poor management effectiveness, especially if the business requires personal contact.

(c) A substantial training programme might be needed.

(i) **Basic facts** about the country will be given with basic language training, and some briefings about cultural differences.

(ii) **Immersion training** involves detailed language and cultural training and simulation of field social and business experiences. This is necessary to obtain an intellectual understanding and practical awareness of the culture.

5.4 Employing local managers raises the following issues.

(a) A **glass ceiling** might exist in some companies. Talented local managers may not make it to board levels if, as in many Japanese firms, most members of the board are drawn from one country.

(b) In some cases, it may be hard for locals to assimilate into the corporate culture, and this might led to communication problems.

(c) They will have greater local knowledge - but the difficulty of course is to get them to understand the wider corporate picture, but this is true of management at operational level generally.

5.5 Firms that export sporadically might employ a home-based sales force. However, their travel expenses may be high, and recruitment might be difficult.

Human resources management

5.6 **Relevant issues to keep in mind**

(a) **Recruitment and training**. In countries with low levels of literacy, more effort might need to be spent on basic training.

(b) **Career management**. Can overseas staff realistically expect promotion to the firm's highest levels if they do well?

(c) **Appraisal schemes**. These can be a minefield at the best of times, and the possibilities for communications failure are endless. For example, in some cultures, an appraisal is a two way discussion whereas in others arguing back might be considered a sign of insubordination.

(d) **Communications**. HRM tries to mobilise employees' commitment to the goals of the organisation. In far-flung global firms, the normal panoply of staff newsletters and team briefings may be hard to institute but are vital. Time differences also make communication difficult.

(i)   **E-mail** and satellite linkages between branch offices can be used for routine messages: e-mail is especially useful, as it allows swift access to a person's electronic mailbox.

(ii)   Major conferences are also necessary.

(iii) Firms with many subsidiaries face additional problems of **language.** What language should be used for business communications? Some multinational firms have decreed English the language of official internal communications, even if they are not headquartered in the English speaking world.

Case example

An example of the role of communications in managing a business is provided by British Airways (as reported in the Guardian).

After privatisation, BA cut its staff by almost 20,000 to 35,000 although since that staff levels have increased as airline traffic has expanded.

BA attaches great important to internal corporate communications, as it wishes to make staff feel involved.

At a series of business seminars, costing £750,000, senior board members made detailed presentations to 4,500 junior and senior managers, and, as importantly, invited - and received - feedback and criticism. BA's senior managers 'say they benefit enormously from hearing how staff feel that BA can continue to improve its performance.'

---

6   CULTURE AND THE ORGANISATION

6.1   We have already discussed culture in society generally as a factor of a firm's wider environment. The issue of **corporate culture** is particularly important for multinational businesses because of the variety of national cultures that its members may bring to it. Corporate culture can set common values, overcoming misunderstandings and conflicts.

Management cultures

6.2   **Management culture** resides in the views about managing held by the organisation's managers. Obviously, this reflects wider cultural influences.

6.3   The world leadership survey conducted by the *Harvard Business Review* asked a variety of questions to managers in different countries. Although the respondents were self-selected, the survey indicated that managers in different countries do not have the same priorities. When asked what they thought of as the three most important factors in organisation success, these were listed as follows, in order of priority.

Japan: product development, management, product quality
Germany: workforce skills, problem solving, management
USA: customer service, product quality, technology

6.4   The existence of these different systems of priorities and ways of doing business affects the competitive environment, the marketing plan and the success of joint ventures. An important problem is to ensure that the corporate culture is strong enough to withstand any potential clashes caused by cultural differences between Head Office and subsidiaries.

Case example

The following case is drawn from *Corporate Culture: From Vicious to Virtuous Circles*, by Charles Hampden-Turner.

The attitude of the staff of Volvo in France to the product they were selling was this. 'The Swedish people who make Volvo don't understand the French. We are hot-blooded Latins, with dash, romance and style. We like cars that perform and are in fashion. Volvos are too sober, too safe, too pedestrian, too cerebral and too practical, consisting of largely old models, which have not changed noticeably in years. Scandinavians have a temperament that dwells on accidents and upon keeping warm. The French have more joie de vivre. Despite heroic efforts to move these melancholy motors, we have not been very successful.' A crucial aspect of changing a culture is to retell, reinterpret or transform a story which otherwise spells defeat. Goran Carstedt did that in Volvo France. By taking the dealers and their wives to Sweden and giving them the grand tour, the story of moody Scandinavians and dull cars was totally recast to read as follows. 'Volvos are made in Sweden by small, dedicated groups of craftsmen who make and sign each entire car and who manage themselves. Volvo symbolises for the world an individualism married to social concern, to which the virtues of safety and reliability are the key. There are enough French people of discernment and good sense to think of their families and future responsibilities. With the new support we are getting, the Volvo message is one we can deliver with pride and success.'

The Hofstede model of national cultures

6.5 A model was developed in 1980 by Professor Geert Hofstede in order to explain national differences by identifying 'key dimensions' which represent the essential 'programmes' forming a common culture in the value systems of all countries. Each country is represented on a scale for each dimension so as to explain and understand values, attitudes and behaviour. In particular, Hofstede pointed out that countries differ on the following dimensions.

(a) **Power distance**. This dimension measures how far superiors are expected to exercise power. In a high power-distance culture, the boss decides and people do not question.

(b) **Uncertainty avoidance**. Some cultures prefer clarity and order, whereas others are prepared to accept novelty. This affects the willingness of people to **change** rules, rather than simply obey them.

(c) **Individualism**. In some countries individual achievement is what matters. A collectivist culture (eg people are supported - and controlled - by extended families) puts the interests of the group first.

(d) **'Masculinity'**. In 'masculine' cultures, gender roles are clearly differentiated. In 'feminine' ones they are not. 'Masculine' cultures place greater emphasis on possessions, status, and display as opposed to quality of life and concern for others.

6.6 Hofstede grouped countries into eight 'clusters'.

Group		Power distance	Uncertainty avoidance	Individualism	'Masculinity'
I	'More developed Latin' (eg Belgium, France, Argentina, Brazil, Spain)	High	High	Medium to high	Medium
II	'Less developed Latin' (eg Portugal, Mexico, Peru)	High	High	Low	Whole range
III	'More developed Asian' (eg Japan)	Medium	High	Medium	High
IV	'Less developed Asian' (eg India, Taiwan, Thailand)	High	Low to medium	Low	Medium
V	Near Eastern (eg Greece, Iran, Turkey)	High	High	Low	Medium

Group		Power distance	Uncertainty avoidance	Individualism	'Masculinity'
VI	'Germanic' (eg Germany)	Low	Medium to high	Medium	Medium to high
VII	Anglo (eg UK, US, Australia)	Low to medium	Low to medium	High	High
VIII	Nordic (eg Scandinavia, the Netherlands)	Low	Low to medium	Medium to high	Low

6.7 There are dangers in using these models. In the management of individual businesses, other factors may be more important.

(a) **Type of industry**: people working in information technology from two countries might have more in common with each other than they might with people working in a different industry.

(b) **Size of company.** Some people may be accustomed to working in a **bureaucracy**.

7 THE STRATEGIC IMPORTANCE OF DISTRIBUTION

7.1 The distribution channel is of strategic importance.

(a) It is **hard to change** in the short term, unlike the price or promotion elements in the marketing mix.

   (i) A distribution channel often involves **contractual arrangements** with the distributor which cannot be changed easily.

   (ii) There is a substantial **physical infrastructure** involved, of warehouses, lorry fleets, containers etc.

   (iii) In many respects, **distributors are 'customers'** whose needs should be considered, and with whom a **long-term relationship** should be built.

(b) A firm's **marketing communications** will be strongly influenced by the extent to which the firm is able to obtain wide distribution.

(c) Distribution can offer competitive advantage.

Case example

Japanese firms

Following the success of Japanese firms worldwide in motor vehicles and consumer electronics it was assumed that no Western companies were safe from Japanese competition. However, wider domination by Japanese companies has not occurred. For example, Japanese pharmaceutical firms, such as Green Cross, have not achieved the world domination anticipated. US and European firms are still dominant in this industry.

Perhaps cars and consumer electronics are the exception rather than the rule. The reason for this might be distribution. Normally, outsiders do not find it easy to break into established distribution patterns. However distribution channels in cars and consumer electronics offered outsiders an easy way in.

(a) The car industry is vertically integrated, with a network of exclusive dealerships. Given time and money, the Japanese firms could simply build their own dealerships and run them as they liked, with the help of local partners. This barrier to entry was not inherently complex.

(b) Consumer electronics

   (i) In the early years, the consumer electronics market was driven by technology, so innovative firms such as Sony and Matsushita could overcome distribution weaknesses.

(ii)   Falling prices changed the distribution of hi if goods from small specialist shops to large cut-price outlets, such as Comet. Newcomers to a market are the natural allies of such new outlets: existing suppliers prefer to shun'discount retailers to protect margins in their current distribution network.

Japanese firms have not established dominant positions

- In healthcare, where national pharmaceuticals wholesalers are active as gatekeepers
- In household products, where there are strong supermarket chains
- In cosmetics, where department stores and specialist shops offer a wide choice

---

7.2   **Key issues in distribution**

(a)   **Coverage and density**: the number of sales outlets

(i)   Countries like the UK and US allow large stores.

(ii)   In Japan, there have been restrictions on store size, to protect the livelihoods of small retailers.

(b)   **Channel length**: the number of intermediaries between producer and consumer

(c)   **Power and alignment.** The international marketer has to realise that distribution channel power is not equal in each country. Different roles are played by retailers, wholesalers and agents in each country. For example, wholesalers are most important where retailing is fragmented.

(d)   **Logistics** and physical distribution

Distribution channels

7.3   The participants in a **trading channel** have to provide certain services to the customer. A good trading channel will provide the following.

- Research and information feedback about the market
- Promotion of the goods and services
- Contact and negotiation with prospective buyers
- Storage, sorting, assembling and processing of orders
- Physical distribution
- Financing operations
- Speculative risk taking

The producer's problem is in ensuring that these activities will be carried out. It can be seen that where a weak distributive infrastructure exists within a country, the duties will fall on the exporter and the selected entry organisation, and thus care must be taken in the selection of any partner in international marketing.

Consumer trading channels

7.4   **Consumer trading channels** generally require a variety of goods in small quantities, and the trading channel both accumulates a wider variety of goods and breaks down the trade quantities to smaller units. Thus whilst an importer may import wine in bulk and then sell it by the case to the retailer, the retailer will sell wine by the bottle and other associated goods that will appeal to the consumer, and provide a sufficiently large order to make the cost of trading worthwhile. Consumer trading channels tend to be longer, with more intermediaries.

Business trading channels

7.5 Unlike consumer trading channels, trading on a **business to business** basis usually requires a narrow variety of goods from specialist suppliers in larger quantities. Thus the problems of discrepancy of assortment are less and the **trading channels shorter**, often involving only one or two intermediaries between the originator and the end user.

Case example

The distribution system in Japan has been considered as an impediment to imports, in that planning regulations and trading practices are prejudiced against the sort of independent and powerful retailers which exist in the UK. While there are a few large department stores in Japan, there are far more small 'corner shops' with semi-dependent relationships with either manufacturers directly or wholesalers. As the system is so fragmented, it is costly and difficult to reach customers.

Recent reports have indicated some relaxation to permit the construction of larger stores, enabling imported goods to be distributed more easily.

Buyer behaviour and culture

7.6 The social, demographic and economic profile of the target customer varies from country to country. Each segment exhibits different purchasing habits. A key determinant of this behaviour is the **purchasing culture** prevalent in the target market. This affects the following.

(a) The end user preference as to **where** to buy, **frequency** of purchase and **services** required

(b) The services that the **intermediary** both expects and is capable of providing, and their purchasing patterns

7.7 Thus, whilst UK retailers, through their economic concentration and power, have generally thrust most of the duties outlined above back onto the manufacturer, in other countries stocking and promotion may be regarded as the legitimate activity of the importing wholesaler/ distributor rather than the manufacturer.

7.8 In some countries, local legislation may prohibit the ownership of trading organisations by foreign companies and international companies are either forced into some form of joint ownership or to select a local intermediary to act on their behalf.

Product features

7.9 The nature of the product being sold will affect the choice of channel members in a particular country. Perishable goods need short quick turnover channel systems to retain their value. Some goods require presales surveys, advice, installation, aftersales service, maintenance and local spares and accessory availability. The distribution channel must be able to provide these enhancements efficiently and quickly. In other cases the intermediary will only be required to collect and pass on orders with few other demands or restrictions. Financial services may be required to offer credit in the cases of some high value goods, and the intermediary may be required to provide such a service.

Competition

7.10   **Established competition** in a market will indicate the usual form of trading channel.

(a)   Where strong and concentrated competitors exist, this may mean that it will be difficult to attract the better dealers in a trading channel. Typically the competitors will have offered exclusive dealerships in return for an undertaking not to stock competitive goods (eg computers, cars, machine tools etc). Thus the new entrant will find it difficult to attract quality dealers to stock and trade in their goods or services.

(b)   The international marketer may then be forced to consider new and innovative approaches to trading in a market where the traditional outlets are blocked.

- Other traders selling to same market
- Catalogue selling
- Direct mail

Company objectives in the market

7.11   The choice of trading channel will also depend on what the company wants to achieve in a particular market. Three types of distribution objective are generally considered: **coverage**, **market share** and **commitment** required from intermediaries.

Coverage

7.12   There are three approaches to coverage.

> **KEY TERMS**
>
> **Exclusive distribution** involves the selection of high quality intermediaries, who in return for providing local stocks and services are given an exclusive territorial trading right, ensuring that no outlet carrying the same product range will be trading nearby. This approach is used when the international marketeer requires most of the functions to be carried out locally to a high standard, through a reputable dealer. It results in a few, strategically located, main dealers in a country giving wide coverage, service and support. (It applies to most high value goods requiring good pre and post sales support.)
>
> **Selective distribution.** This strategy involves the use of premium quality dealers selected area by area, and whilst not given any 'rights', involves the avoidance of too many competitive dealers in an area. (Luxury consumer goods, designer clothes, perfumes, high quality durables fall into this category.)
>
> **Intensive distribution.** In this situation the goods or services involved require little or no pre or post sales support and have wide appeal (eg most fast moving consumer goods). Sales can be increased by engaging as many dealers as possible in the distributive network, and the exporter seeks to get as high a market coverage as possible.

Market share

7.13   Where a company is content with a **small share** of the market, the use of a **local distributor** in a region of the market may be appropriate. In the UK most trading channels can provide national coverage, but in large countries such as the USA and India, the availability of national coverage through one or two organisations is almost impossible. Region by region dealerships need to be developed to obtain nationwide coverage.

Commitment

7.14 **The degree of commitment desired**. Where an exporter either has little financial resources, or prefers not to invest that resource in a particular country, the preference will be for independent dealers that have no financial tie with the exporter. On the other hand, a greater degree of control in the channel can be exercised if the exporter has some degree of investment in the dealer network.

E-commerce

7.15 The growing importance of **e-commerce** will revolutionise channel design. Direct access to customers and businesses via the Internet will speed up delivery times and improve communications. A company that wishes to use e-commerce as a channel for business will have to satisfy itself that customers and business partners are sufficiently equipped. Alternatively it may be forced to accept e-commerce as a channel because customers insist on doing business that way.

Case example

A study by the DTI in Britain has revealed that many British manufacturers are not using the Internet to its full potential for areas such as speeding up design work, selling products and services, forming closer links and even gaining payment. Setting up links with parts suppliers to assist JIT production is another area that could be developed. Lack of technological knowledge and security fears mean that Britain lags behind Germany and the US. The DTI believes use of the internet for business-to-business activity is a key area where competitive edge can be gained.

7.16 E-commerce will facilitate corporate buying and selling when companies post their requirements on a website. Looking through company websites may also help companies seeking distribution channel partners to link up with appropriate contacts.

Motivating agents

7.17 A major problem for exporters is gaining the **motivation and full commitment** of agents and distributors. They usually carry the products of many firms and they are tempted to commit most of their resources to the products which provide the quickest returns.

7.18 There are various methods for motivating overseas agents, of which the following are the most important.

(a) **Regular and fairly frequent personal contact with the agent**. This enables both parties to communicate their needs, problems, philosophies, objectives and mutual responsibilities. Moreover, it allows good personal relationships to be developed among the two sets of personnel.

(b) Assuring agents of **long term business relationships** with the exporter

(c) Provision of attractive **commission** and other financial incentives

(d) Exclusivity

7.19 **Controlling agents** and distributors can be difficult.

- Realistic expectations of performance are necessary
- Contracts should be clear and mutually understood
- Performance should be analysed in the light of changing environmental conditions
- Attention will need to be paid to the culture of the negotiating situation

8 INTERNATIONAL PHYSICAL DISTRIBUTION

8.1 The **cost** of physically transporting goods between countries has been estimated to be as high as 25% of the **landed price** of an item (more typically 15%), and thus represents a significant part of the cost structure of the item involved. But international logistics provide services to the customer in terms of availability, speed of delivery and convenience, which provide significant added value to the goods themselves. Logistics involves the following.

- Order processing
- Transportation
- Stock management
- Warehousing
- Customer services

8.2 In international marketing, the longer distances involved and the problem of dealing with alien cultures mean that the time between order and delivery can be considerable when compared to locally sourced supplies, and the cost significantly higher.

Transportation

8.3 **Transport between markets** is often the easier part of the problem, with good transport systems and infrastructure (roads, ports, airports, railheads etc) between nations. Within a particular country however both the transport systems and the infrastructure may vary in quality considerably. As we look to the lesser developed countries, the quality of communications, availability of transport facilities, and the physical infrastructure may pose significant problems.

Logistics management

> **KEY TERM**
>
> **Logistics management** includes **physical distribution and materials management**. It encompasses the inflow of raw materials and goods together with the outflow of finished products.

8.4 Logistics management has developed for three main reasons.

(a) **Customer benefits** that can be incorporated into the overall product offering because of efficient logistics management

(b) The **cost savings** that can be made when a logistics approach is undertaken

(c) Trends in **industrial purchasing** that necessarily mean closer links between buyers and sellers, for example just-in-time purchasing and computerised purchasing.

8.5 Logistics managers organise inventories, warehouses, purchasing and packaging to produce an efficient and effective overall system. There are benefits to consumers of products that are produced by companies with good logistic management. There is less likelihood of goods being out of stocks, delivery should be efficient and overall service quality should be higher.

9 CONTROLLING GLOBAL PERFORMANCE

9.1 Standards and targets should be **clearly defined**, understood and accepted by those whose activities are being controlled.

What standards should be adopted?

Corporate objectives

9.2 Corporate objectives include matters of **financial performance**.

- Profit
- Return on capital
- Cash flow
- Earnings per share

Marketing objectives are usually determined to satisfy these corporate concerns and **local marketing activities** will be designed accordingly.

9.3 Where an organisation is decentralised, each subsidiary may be given its own **profit targets**, and **cash flow targets**.

Marketing objectives

9.4 The following are some examples of standards for local marketing activities.

- Market research (number and types of studies)
- Sales volume (by product line/quarter/year etc)
- Market share (by product/quarter/year)
- Product (quality control standards)
- Distribution (market coverage, dealer support)
- Pricing (levels, margins and rigidity or flexibility)
- Branch (volume and nature of local advertising/sales promotion)
- Selling (local sales force standards)
- Customer returns
- Number of complaints
- 'Share of voice' in international promotions
- Consumer awareness

How are standards established?

9.5 Where practical, headquarters should not impose standards arbitrarily but should use local input, because this will be more up to date and will ensure morale and motivation is maintained.

9.6 There are many ways of establishing standards.

(a) **Job specifications** of marketing personnel give the basic performance requirements.

(b) **The annual planning process** will indicate more specific corporate standards.

(c) **Communication** (both personal and impersonal) between HQ and subsidiary staff (such as meetings, task forces, internal publications).

Financial performance

9.7   The task of setting financial objectives within a multinational is complex, and several problems must be resolved. The company may decide that a single objective should be applied, so that every subsidiary must earn, for example, a specified return on capital employed or profit margin.

9.8   On the other hand, because of **differing local conditions** (such as government policies, taxation, exchange rate fluctuations) it might be more appropriate to apply a different financial target to each subsidiary. For example, the same product may be at different stages in its life cycle in each country.

International comparisons

9.9   If the firms being compared operate in different countries there will be certain problems for performance measurement.

   (a)   **Realistic standards** need to be set, taking account of local conditions.

   (b)   **Controllable cash flows**. Care must be taken to determine which cash flows are controllable.

   (c)   **Currency conversion**. Care must be exercised to ensure that conversion rates are valid. A firm can lock itself into a particular exchange rate by hedging. Jaguar used this when, as an independent British company, most of its sales were in the US. Hedging instruments were used to protect its profits from any deterioration caused by weakening of its currency receipts.

Obtaining performance information

9.10   Monitoring of international marketing performance is difficult since it generally relies more on indirect methods such as reports, as well as direct meetings.

Reports

9.11   • **Standardised** to allow comparative analysis between subsidiaries
   • Use an agreed **common language** and currency
   • **Frequent** as necessary to allow proper management
   • Cover all the **information needs** of headquarters

Meetings

9.12   Gatherings between HQ executives and subsidiary management allow for more intensive information exchange and monitoring; and minimise misunderstandings. They do however take up time and resources, and are generally not as regular as reports.

Information technology

9.13   Information technology makes it much easier for marketing and financial performance to be monitored closely, given the speed of transmission of e-mail and Internet communications.

9.14   Meetings can even be conducted by video-conferencing - this might prove cheaper than flying.

Control of intermediaries

9.15 The problem with controlling 'outsiders' is that there is no control by **ownership**. In the final analysis **negative controls** such as legal pressures or threats to discontinue relationships can be used, resulting perhaps in loss of business. The best control is through good selection and by making it clear to intermediaries that their interests and the company's coincide.

10 SOCIAL AND CULTURAL BEHAVIOUR

Demographic issues in overseas markets

10.1 **Demographics** is the study of populations and their characteristics.

10.2 **Purpose of studying a country's population and trends within it**

(a) People create a demand for goods and services.

(b) If economic growth exceeds population growth you would expect to see enhanced **standards** of living. **Quality of life** measures would also include pollution measures, life expectancy rates, infant mortality and so on.

(c) Population is a source of labour, one of the **factors of production.**

(d) Population creates demands on the physical environment and its resources, a source of increased international political concern. (the Kyoto conference in Japan at the end of 1997 agreed reductions in carbon dioxide).

10.3 The higher rate of population growth in **less-developed countries** compared with developed countries has arisen due to a continuing high birth rate and a declining death rate although some populations are being threatened by the HIV virus (for example in Botswana). Social change in such matters as the prevailing attitude to large families has not accompanied medical advances imported from developed societies. People are living longer.

(a) **Growing populations**

- Require fast economic growth just to maintain living standards
- Result in overcrowding and a decline in the quality of life
- Require more resources for capital investment
- Stimulate investment (as the market size is increasing)
- Lead to enhanced labour mobility

(b) **Falling populations**

- Require more productive techniques to maintain output
- Make some scale economies harder to achieve
- Put a greater burden on a decreasing number of young people
- Exhibit changing consumption patterns

Age structure and distribution

10.4 **Age structure**

(a) The effect of greater life expectancy is that a larger proportion of the population will be senior citizens and unlikely to be working. These offer significant opportunities to international marketers. The UK, Europe and Japan all face an ageing population.

(b) The proportion of old people is lower in developing countries. In Egypt and Iran, over half the population is below the age of 30.

Geographic distribution

10.5 A country may suffer the problems of overpopulation in some areas and underpopulation in others. Industrialisation has usually meant a shift of population from the countryside to the towns.

Sex

10.6 There is often an imbalance in the population between the numbers of men and the numbers of women. This has arisen for a number of reasons.

(a) Males tend to die younger.

(b) In some countries male children are more valued than female children, and female children are more likely to suffer infanticide.

10.7 The **work roles of the sexes** in different societies vary, even within the industrial world. In different societies, women and men have distinct purchasing and social powers.

Ethnicity

10.8 Only a few societies are homogenous, with populations of one culture and ethnic background. Japan is an example, although the population includes descendants of Koreans. On the other hand, societies like the USA and the UK have populations drawn from a variety of different areas.

Buying patterns

10.9 Buying behaviour is an important aspect of marketing. Demography and the **class structure** (the distribution of wealth and power in a society) are relevant in that they can be both **behavioural determinants** and **inhibitors**.

(a) **Behavioural determinants** encourage people to buy a product or service. The individual's personality, culture, social class, and the importance of the purchase decision (eg a necessity such as food or water, or a luxury) can predispose a person to purchase something.

(b) **Inhibitors** are factors, such as the individual's income, which will make the person less likely to purchase something.

10.10 **Socio-economic status** can be related to buying patterns in a number of ways, both in the amount people have to spend and what they spend it on. It affects both the quantity of goods and services supplied, and the proportion of their income that households spend on goods and services.

Case example

(a) India has a large peasantry and an industrial proletariat, but its huge population size means that its wealthy middle class is bigger than the populations of many developed countries. With import liberalisation and economic deregulation, this should be an attractive segment for marketers.

(b)   The level of inequality in society also influences its attractiveness to the marketer. Brazil has the greatest degree of inequality in the world. Japan, famously, has low inequality.

(i)   In societies of high inequality, wealth is concentrated, hence the buying power of the majority is limited. This might suggest more success in selling luxury goods.

(ii)   Where equality is higher, there may be a higher demand for mass market goods as more people will have access to them.

Family structure

10.11 The role of the family and family groupings varies from society to society.

(a)   In societies such as India, the **caste system** still exists and family structures can be part of this wider network.

(b)   **Extended families** are still strong in many countries, especially where the family is to assume most of the burden of looking after the elderly: many countries do not have a welfare state.

(c)   Family size varies.

10.12 Marketers have often used the model of the **family life cycle** model purchase and consumption patterns. You will have encountered it before.

- Bachelor - single people
- Newly-weds - household and childcare products
- Full nest
- Empty-nest: children have left home
- Solitary survivor

10.13 This model may not hold.

(a)   Quite often, households contain three generations (grand-parents, parents, children).

(b)   People leave home later in life. In countries such as Italy and Spain it is common for adult children to live at home.

(c)   Purchase and consumption decisions vary.

Chapter roundup

- Global operations must be carefully planned and have clear objectives. These must support the company's overall mission.

- International market research (IMR) requires extensive resources since it deals with more than one country. Government bodies assist organisations with their IMR **Strategically equivalent segments** may be discerned where market homogeneity transcends national boundaries.

- **Comparative analysis** of markets assumes that if market potential is similar in two markets, then market performance should also be similar.

- **IMR problems** include lack of secondary data, poor comparability and timeliness of secondary data and response problems.

- Modes of entry to foreign markets vary widely and include:

  - Direct and indirect exporting
  - Wholly owned overseas production
  - Contract manufacture
  - Joint ventures

  The most suitable mode of entry depends on:

  - Marketing objectives
  - Mode availability
  - HR requirements
  - Risks
  - Firm size
  - Mode quality
  - Market research feedback
  - Control needs

- **Undifferentiated marketing** offers all markets a standard product at a standard price to minimise production and marketing costs.

- **Differentiated marketing** adjusts products and marketing for each market.

- **Concentrated marketing** brings standardised product and marketing to those markets for which they are suitable.

- HR policy must be established in connection with the employment of local and expatriate staff. Expatriates can bring expertise, experience and internal communication advantages. However, they are expensive, may suffer culture shock and will probably require training in local ways.

- Writers differ on the international applicability of **management principles**.

- The *Hofstede* model of national management culture identifies difference on four axes:

  - Power distance
  - Individualism
  - Uncertainty avoidance
  - 'Masculinity'

- The **distribution channel** is of strategic importance, with important contractual obligations, physical infrastructure and the need to build long term relationships with partners. Key issues are:

  - Coverage and density
  - Power and alignment
  - Channel length
  - Logistics

- **Exclusive distribution** give exclusive rights to a high quality intermediary within its territory.

- **Selective distribution** also uses high quality distributors and minimises competition by means of territorial split, but does not give exclusive rights.

- **Intensive distribution** engages as many dealers as possible to obtain high coverage.

- **Logistics** includes order processing, transportation, stock management, warehousing and customer services.

- **Global performance** is controlled by setting marketing objectives and measuring performance. International comparisons must incorporate realistic standards and currency conversion. Special features of international performance management are the need for **meetings** and dealing with independent intermediaries.

Quick quiz

1 What cultural differences are there between domestic and international business?

2 What basic screening criteria might be applied to a potential foreign market?

3 How is income elasticity of demand calculated?

4 What are strategically equivalent segments?

5 What is indirect exporting?

6 What is the great advantage of a joint venture?

7 What is concentrated marketing, in the context of export marketing?

8 What is immersion training?

9 What is power distance?

10 What is selective distribution?

Answers to quick quiz

1 Language, market homogeneity/fragmentation, 'rules of the game', purchasing habits

2 Profit level, market share and volume, level of competition, legal conditions, political risk

3 $\dfrac{\text{\% Change in product demand}}{\text{\% Change in income}}$

4 Market segments whose homogeneity transcends national differences

5 Exporting where the firm's goods are sold abroad by other organisations

6 The local partner's local knowledge

7 Devotion of marketing resources to a few markets where a standardised product will do well

8 Extensive familiarisation with all aspects of life in a foreign country, including language, culture and society

9 A measure of the extent to which superiors are expected to exercise power

10 Use of premium dealers selected area by area but not given exclusive rights

Now try the questions below from the Exam Question Bank

Number	Level	Marks	Time
Q18	Introductory	n/a	27 mins
Q19	Exam	60	108 mins

Exam
question bank

438

Questions with mark allocations are in the style of full examination questions

1 ✓ FOUR STAR PRODUCTS
36 mins

Four Star Products plc is a major manufacturing organisation with a range of consumer products. Founded over seventy years ago and run for many years by the founder and his family, the company was rather traditional in its strategy, tending to stick to the hardware and other household goods that it understood. A formal system of strategic planning was introduced in 1962 and remains in place today, with a 47 person strong planning department reporting to a Planning Director.

Since a financial crisis in 1994, the dominance of the founding family has been diluted by banker power and the appointment from outside of a new CEO, a new CFO and three non-executive directors. The CEO has a reputation for turning companies around and his strategy has been to move into the IT and telecommunications sectors in force. He has made little use of the work of the planning department, preferring to commission research externally. Unfortunately, the recent collapse of the Internet bubble and fall in interest in IT and telecomms shares has led to Four Star suffering significant losses and a fall in its share price. One of the CEO's plans for cost reduction is to abolish the planning department.

Required

(a) Is the CEO justified in his attitude towards the planning department? **(15 marks)**

(b) Explain how the formal planning process is intended to deal with events such as the collapse of the Internet business model. **(5 marks)**

(20 marks)

Approaching the question

You must learn to read question settings critically. Look for hints and keywords and ask questions of the information given to you. This is illustrated here.

Four Star Products plc is a major manufacturing organisation with a range of consumer — How quickly does the market move? Is rapid introduction of new products required?

products. Founded over seventy years ago and run for many years by the founder and his

family, the company was rather traditional in its strategy, tending to stick to the hardware — Culture? Flexibility? Innovation?

and other household goods that it understood. A formal system of strategic planning was

introduced in 1962 and remains in place today, with a 47 person strong planning department — Rational model

reporting to a Planning Director. | That is a lot of people and likely to be a major overhead |

Since a financial crisis in 1994, the dominance of the founding family has been diluted by — Concern for financial performance

banker power and the appointment from outside of a new CEO, a new CFO and three non-

executive directors. The CEO has a reputation for turning companies around and his — Change of sector – how practical? Expertise?

strategy has been to move into the IT and telecommunications sectors in force. He has

made little use of the work of the planning department, preferring to commission research — Why?

externally. Unfortunately, the recent collapse of the Internet bubble and fall in interest in IT

and telecomms shares has led to Four Star suffering significant losses and a fall in its share — Requirement for cost reduction

price. One of the CEO's plans for cost reduction is to abolish the planning department.

2/ **EMPIRE CHEMICALS** *36 mins*

> *Tutorial note.* The data in this case is based on the experience of ICI; however, names and certain key details have been changed. You should concentrate on the data in the case study itself, rather than ICI's subsequent history. Remember that Empire Chemicals is a fictitious company, although based on a real one.

Empire Chemicals is one of the UK's largest companies with several divisions including paints, pharmaceuticals, bulk chemicals, and agrochemicals such as fertiliser. Empire Chemicals detected three years ago that the financial performance of its paints business was deteriorating. Profits were steady, but its return on capital was falling. Mr Matthew Black, the main board director responsible for paints, reacted quickly to cut costs. Despite a 6% fall in turnover in the last two years, profits of the division have been rising, albeit modestly. Unfortunately, not all the divisions had such foresight. Empire's total profits are falling sharply. Mr Scott Wallace, a chemical industry analyst, says that Empire neglected to keep its costs under control in the past. Management controls are 'relatively undisciplined'. This is the legacy of a complicated management structure, which divided financial responsibilities confusingly between territorial and business managers. The autonomy of divisional heads is considerable.

Sir Denis Mack Smith created Empire's first globally organised businesses – first a world-wide pharmaceuticals operation and then, in 1984, a global agrochemical division. An increasing number of Empire's operations were set up to operate on an international basis, to meet the trans-national requirements of so many of its clients. However, Sir Denis did not streamline the organisation completely. A parallel power structure, based on geography rather than products, has been kept in place. Because Empire is ahead of the pack in running divisions on a global basis, analysts believe that it must be careful not to neglect the differing needs of European, Japanese and US purchasers. A director points out that only 20% of Empire's business is purely domestic, but the Chairman and main board executives spend a disproportionate amount of time on UK matters.

Empire itself has long considered itself virtually bid-proof. It is one of the UK's biggest employers with 53,700 employees in Britain and it spends some 70% of its £679m R&D budget at home. However Cobb Holdings plc has purchased a stake with a view to a takeover.

Despite years of efforts by Empire to refashion itself, which did make it more international and produced a gush of profits when times were good, the company is still spread thinly across an array of separate products and markets ranging from research-intensive products to PVC (which goes to make plastic buckets). Empire has many products, in many different markets.

The company's embattled chairman, Sir Henry Sanderson has had to eat his words about the company being recession-proof. 'When I suggested that I saw no return to the dark days of recession, I was clearly wrong,' he acknowledges.

Required

To what extent do you think strategic planning has succeeded or failed at Empire Chemicals? Briefly outline an alternative model. **(20 marks)**

3/ **MISSION STATEMENTS**

The managing director of TDM plc has recently returned from a conference entitled 'Strategic planning beyond the '90s'. Whilst at the conference, she attended a session on Corporate Mission Statements. She found the session very interesting but it was rather short. She now has some questions for the accountant.

'What does corporate mission mean? I don't see how it fits in with our strategic planning processes.'

'Where does our mission come from and what areas of corporate life should it cover?'

'Even if we were to develop one of these mission statements, what benefits would the company get from it?'

You are required to prepare a memorandum which answers the managing director's questions.

4

NADIR PRODUCTS: ETHICS (Pilot paper amended) *36 mins*

John Staples is the Finance Director of Nadir Products plc, a UK-based company which manufactures and sells bathroom products – baths, sinks and toilets – to the UK market. These products are sold through a selection of specialist shops and through larger 'do-it-yourself' stores. Customers include professional plumbers and also ordinary householders who are renovating their houses themselves. The company operates at the lower end of the market and does not have a strong reputation for service. Sales have been slowly declining whereas those of competitors have been improving. In order to encourage increased sales the Board of Directors have decided to pay senior staff a bonus if certain targets are achieved. The two main targets are based on profit levels and annual sales. Two months before the end of the financial year the Finance Director asks one of his staff to check through the orders and accounts to assess the current situation. He is informed that without a sudden improvement in sales before the year end the important sales targets will not be met and so bonuses will be adversely affected.

The Finance Director has proposed to other senior staff that this shortfall in sales can be corrected by taking one of the following decisions.

1. A significant discount can be offered to any retail outlet which takes delivery of additional products prior to the end of the financial year.

2. Scheduled orders due to be delivered at the beginning of the next financial year can be brought forward and billed before the end of this year.

3. Distributors can be told that there is a risk of price increases in the future and that it will be advisable to order early so as to circumvent this possibility.

The Board is not sure of the implications associated with such decisions.

Required

(a) As a consultant, prepare a report for the Board of Nadir Products examining the commercial and ethical implications associated with each of the proposed options mentioned above. **(8 marks)**

(b) Assess the significance of the corporate social responsibility model for Nadir Products.

(12 marks)

(20 marks)

5 **FIREBRIDGE TYRES LTD** *36 mins*

Firebridge Tyres Ltd (FTL) is a wholly owned UK subsidiary of Gonzales Tyre Corporation (GTC) of the USA. FTL manufactures and sells tyres under a number of different brand names.

(a) Firespeed, offering high product quality, at a price which offers good value for money
(b) Freeway, a cheap brand, effectively a standard tyre
(c) Tufload, for lorries and commercial vehicles

FTL has good relationships with car firms and distributors.

GTC is rather less focused; not only does it make tyres and some other components, but it also owns a chain of car service centres specialising in minor maintenance matters such as tyre replacement, exhaust fitting, and wheel balancing.

FTL has experienced a fall in sales revenue, partly as a result of competition from overseas producers, in what is effectively a mature market. Moreover, sales of new cars have not been as high as had been hoped, and consumers are more reluctant than before to part with their money.

FTL's managers have had meetings with GTC's managers as to how to revive the fortunes of the company. FTL would like to export to the US and to Asia. GTC has vetoed this suggestion, as FTL's tyres would compete with GTC's. Instead, GTC suggests that FTL imitate GTC's strategy by running a chain of service stations similar to GTC's service stations in the US. GTC feels that vertical integration would offer profits in its own right and provide a distribution network which would reduce the impact of competition from other tyre manufacturers. GTC has no shortage of cash.

You are a strategic consultant to FTL.

Required

(a) What are the principal factors in the external environment that would influence FTL's strategic choice? **(6 marks)**

BPP
PROFESSIONAL EDUCATION

(b) Describe the barriers to entry that FTL might face if it decided to enter the service centre business. **(6 marks)**

(c) Can FTL's distinctive competences satisfy the critical success factors of the service business?
(8 marks)
(20 marks)

6 TOROIDAL TOOLING
36 mins

Toroidal Tooling manufactures a range of highly specialized cutting tools for the engineering industry. It also acts as exclusive UK selling agent for three complementary product ranges manufactured overseas. Toroidal tooling has been in the machine tool industry for 107 years and is still largely family owned. Perhaps as a result, it is rather sleepy and vulnerable to competition from the major global players. Recently, Toroidal has seen its annual turnover stagnate at about £27M and is aware that its competitors are cutting deep into its market. Profitability is falling.

Toroidal has never had a very sophisticated accounting system, so its knowledge of its costs is rudimentary. However, its salespeople have good knowledge of the market and they suggest that prices are not the most important consideration among customers. Delivery, after sales service and product reliability seem to be more important. Toroidal's product reliability is generally good, but it is often late with deliveries and customers complain that they can rarely obtain accurate information on the progress of their orders. The sales force also note that the overall product range contains several important gaps that are not compensated for by overlaps elsewhere. The overlaps are caused by Toroidal's well-established agency policy of accepting their overseas principals' complete product ranges. There are four basic sales categories: buffing and polishing wheels; grinding wheels; taps and dies; and high speed steel cutting tools. Within each of these main categories, however, there are up to seven distinct product groups and five brand names.

Required

The Managing Director of Toroidal has asked your advice about two principal areas of concern.

(a) With regard to the company's product portfolio, explain a technique that could be used to assess the commercial value of the various product groups. **(10 marks)**

(b) With regard to the company's business systems, explain a technique that could be used to provide a broad overview of the way it operates. **(10 marks)**
(20 marks)

7 ACKLINGTON ANTENNAS
36 mins

Acklington Antennas Ltd is a UK company that designs and manufactures antennas for airborne navigation and communication systems. The industry is characterised by dedication to high technical standards because of the demands of aircraft safety. There are three main parts to the business: design and integration of antennas for new aircraft; aftermarket spares for existing systems; and sub-contract manufacture of other firms' designs.

Design of new installations is highly technical and very time consuming since it depends on extensive tests, including test flying. Globally, there are only three other manufacturers capable of this work.

The aftermarket operation includes spares for Acklington's own products and for antennas the company has designed to replace the other three manufacturers' own proprietary designs. Sales of the latter are somewhat price sensitive, but the aircraft spares market generally is characterised by the high prices charged to captive customers for approved spares.

Demand for subcontracting work tends to be intermittent but forms a profitable supplement to the manufacture of the company's own designs. Nobody in the industry thinks it odd that Acklington should both manufacture for and compete with other firms.

Acklington's market is now being threatened by Wizzomatic Inc, which is a subsidiary of a major US armaments group. Wizzomatic is offering a family of standardised antennas derived from its work for the US government. The antennas offer a substantial price advantage over most proprietary designs and are being promoted as suitable for most applications.

Required

(a) Assess the strategic options available to Acklington Antennas. **(12 marks)**

(b) Briefly describe how you would expect Acklington Antennas' marketing mix to be made up.

(8 marks)

(20 marks)

8 ✓ **NEW PARTNERSHIP (Pilot paper)** *36 mins*

Karen Lee has been a qualified accountant for several years and currently works for a large partnership with international links. Although successful in her career she feels that there is still more she could achieve. Being part of a large organisation can be limiting. There is a tendency for large partnerships to become increasingly specialised. This is understandable because such a move can lead to efficiencies. However the disadvantage with this is that the employees tend to find their work becoming repetitive and occasionally boring. Also, because the client base consists of very large firms, Karen tends to concentrate her activities on only two or three firms. Her line manager has told her that although the work she does is specialised the benefit to her and the organisation is that she can now focus on the issues in greater depth. However Karen is looking for a breadth of experience rather than increased depth in specialist areas. She is not alone in feeling this way and knows a number of colleagues and friends who are also seeking a greater challenge.

Despite the tendency towards 'big being beautiful' Karen is also aware that a number of clients prefer to deal with smaller accountancy firms. Rather than dealing with several accountants employed by one large firm, each dependent upon the type of service required, these clients would like to develop a business relationship with smaller accountancy firms who could provide a more integrated and friendly service. Karen has decided that the opportunities are available to set up more local partnerships, which will meet both the requirements of clients and the aspirations of some of the accountancy staff. She and five other friends and colleagues have decided to set up their own partnership. She realises that initially she will have to market the partnership vigorously if the venture is to prove successful. This is an area where she has little experience. She approaches a colleague who works in marketing and seeks their advice.

Required

(a) As the colleague, explain in report format, the major issues which the proposed partnership must address if it is to be successfully launched. **(12 marks)**

Karen is proposing to base her partnership's pricing strategy on costs, because she feels that she and her colleagues lack knowledge of the market and therefore cannot make any other informed judgement.

(b) Evaluate cost-based pricing as a suitable pricing strategy for Karen's proposed partnership.

(8 marks)

(20 marks)

9 ✓ **UNITED PRODUCTS** *36 mins*

United Products (UP) was formed 46 years ago by the merger of two large commercial organisations: Bulk Foods and Rowbotham Enterprises. Over the years it has acquired and disposed of several businesses and now has operations in Europe and North America. It has wholly owned subsidiaries operating in flour milling; vineyards; grocery retailing; agricultural machinery manufacturing and distribution; chemicals (particularly fertilisers); publishing; film production; and forestry. It is also involved via joint ventures and partnerships in quarrying, electronics design and clothes retailing.

The company is regarded by investors as fairly safe but dull. Its growth has not kept pace with its competitors and some of its divisions' performance is distinctly poor.

UP is organised into divisions, some of which are product based and some geographically based. Control is devolved to the CEOs of each division, subject to the compilation and submission of detailed monthly performance reports to the corporate HQ in Fazackerley, near Liverpool in the UK. Corporate HQ requires that each division has identifiable managers responsible for production, sales and finance. These managers are frequently visited by senior members of the relevant head office staff. It is corporate policy to promote from within, and all divisional CEOs must have experience of working both at corporate HQ and in at least three divisions.

There has been a history of disputes between HQ and the divisions. Many have complained about the complexity of the monthly reports and the cost of compiling them. Some have said that they find HQ requirements and visits to be disruptive and counter-productive. However, the Corporate CEO, is very concerned about the tendency of the divisions to go their own way.

BPP
PROFESSIONAL EDUCATION

Required

(a)   Is the way UP is currently organised a sensible one?   **(12 marks)**

(b)   What is a virtual organisation? Would such an approach be suitable for any of UP's operations?
                                                                                                    (8 marks)
                                                                                                    (20 marks)

10   **FLEET WATER SERVICES LTD**   *27 mins*

Fleet Water Services Ltd (FWSL) has been formed by centralising a number of regional management units of *Fleet Water*, the holding company. FWSL, which provides a variety of technical services, has been formed so that Fleet Water will benefit from economies of scale. FWSL will sell its services to other companies in the water industry, firms in industries such as brewing and chemicals, and public sector organisations such as hospitals. Water is to be priced according to usage. Water firms need to introduce metering technology; user firms are seeking to manage their use of water more effectively, and FWSL is there to help them.

A major issue to be faced relates to information. FWSL requires a strategy for the use of the information resource. FWSL also needs to install new information systems to get up and running; of these, an accounting system is felt to be most urgent.

Required

FWSL's managers are aware that project management techniques will need to be used in introducing new systems.

(a)   What are the distinguishing characteristics of project management and how can its success be defined?   **(6 marks)**

(b)   Describe the project management techniques which can be used to introduce new information systems to FWSL, and to minimise the risk of the project failing to meet its objectives.   **(9 marks)**
                                                                                                    (15 marks)

11   **SIMON CLARK**   *36 mins*

Simon Clark is Head of the Department of Business at a local public sector college which provides professional training on a part-time basis for students who are already in employment. The students are mainly studying for professional qualifications in either accountancy, marketing or personnel. A number of students are also studying for general management qualifications. Increasingly this college is experiencing competition from a newly established private sector organisation. This private sector organisation is able to deliver programmes more efficiently and effectively than the older established college because of its more flexible work contracts and working practices. The traditional method of tuition has been on a part-time day release basis (one day or one half-day a week) away from work, studying within the college. With local companies becoming more reluctant to give their staff time off on a regular basis to study, Simon is proposing that more of the training should be carried out on a distance-learning basis, often being supplemented by taught weekend programmes. This will involve the staff in writing study materials and working weekends.

Simon's college has a teaching staff who, in recent years, have had to adapt to new situations including organisational structure changes and syllabus changes. However they are most unhappy about the current proposals which could result in their conditions of service worsening. They are reluctant to work on a weekend basis without additional payments. This would make the college uncompetitive. The private sector college, although it employs high quality staff, is able to absorb the high costs by employing lecturers on a freelance basis and by having larger class sizes, the students being drawn from a larger catchment area. Simon is becoming frustrated by his staff's apparent opposition to accept the proposed changes, and he is contemplating what to do next.

Required

Simon has arranged a meeting with his staff to discuss weekend working and study material production.

(a)   Identify and discuss the different tactics which Simon could make use of in dealing with this conflict. — *Par, EWa - fewas ---, Unfrere --*   **(10 marks)**

(b)   Discuss how Simon might encourage his staff to be more supportive of the proposed change in work practice.   **(10 marks)**
                                                                                                    (20 marks)

12 RUS PLC

RUS plc operates a chain of hotels. Its strategy has been to provide medium-priced accommodation for business people during the week and for families at weekends. The market has become increasingly competitive and RUS plc has decided to change its strategy. In future, it will provide 'a high-quality service for the discerning guest'.

(a) Explain the relevance of a programme of 'total quality management' for RUS plc in the implementation of its new strategy.

(b) Summarise the financial and organisational implications of RUS plc's new strategy.

(c) Discuss the contribution that RUS plc's management accountant could make to the new strategy.

13 PERSONNEL MANAGEMENT
36 mins

You have recently been appointed to a management position in a high-technology enterprise that has expanded very rapidly during the last few years. You have quickly discovered that the personnel policies and procedures used in the organisation are haphazard and unsystematic. The administrative, professional, engineering and managerial staff employed by this company all seem to vary greatly in their quality and performance. The few statistics that are available to you also indicate high levels of labour turnover and employee dismissals amongst all grades of staff. You have therefore decided that the establishment of a systematic recruitment and selection policy and procedure is an urgent priority. The implementation of this policy and procedure would require the appointment of appropriate professional staff, and would involve additional administrative, clerical and information technology costs. In making the case for implementation, you should explain the financial benefits to be gained from the operation of a more effective recruitment and selection procedure. You are required to write a report to the managing director. In this report you should both describe the characteristics of such a recruitment and selection policy and procedure and make the case for implementing it. **(20 marks)**

14 COXFORD DOORS (Pilot paper)
36 mins

Coxford Doors is a family owned wood products company, specialising in producing doors and windows to be sold directly to house builders. There are currently no sales directly to homeowners who may wish to purchase doors and windows to replace their existing ones. In recent years the industry has become much more competitive. Most of the customers are now large nationwide builders, the industry having gone through a period of consolidation. These customers generally require standardised products in large volume, and they buy on the basis of low prices and guarantees of regular delivery. This has put great pressure on companies such as Coxford Doors. This company is still operating as if it were dealing with the fragmented market of twenty years ago. The family, in seeking uninterrupted growth, has permitted the workforce to have a substantial degree of self-management. This has avoided industrial unrest but there have been disadvantages to this approach. This delegated decision-making has led to delays in manufacturing and problems with quality. There has appeared to be a lack of focus. Consequently the company has lost important contracts and is gradually seeing its sales volume and profits decline.

The family has employed Andrew Smith as the new Managing Director, giving him the responsibility for turning the company around. He has decided that power and control must now return to the centre. The passive style of management pursued in the earlier years is now giving way to a more centralised and autocratic approach. However it is obvious that such a change in management style could create even further problems for the company.

Required

(a) Discuss the benefits and problems which this more direct style of management might bring to Coxford Doors. **(10 marks)**

(b) It is apparent that such a change in management style could bring opposition from the workforce. How might this change be implemented with minimal disruption? **(10 marks)**
(20 marks)

15 NATIONAL FREIGHT DISTRIBUTION COMPANY
36 mins

AB plc is a national freight distribution company with a head office, five regional offices and a hundred local depots spread throughout the country. It is planning a major computerisation project. The options which are being considered are as follows.

BPP PROFESSIONAL EDUCATION

(a) A central mainframe system with terminals at each depot.

(b) Distributed minicomputers at each regional office.

Required

Draft a report to the board of AB plc describing the ways in which each of the options would suit the company's structure and explaining the advantages and disadvantages of each.

(20 Marks)

16 NADIR PRODUCTS: INDICATORS (Pilot paper)   *22 mins*

This question is based on the same scenario as question 4.

Required

Identify the main weaknesses of using profits and sales as the sole indicators of performance and suggest other indicators which may be more appropriate.   **(12 marks)**

17 GLOBALISATION

Many key authors like Levitt, Keegan, Ohmae and others state the necessity to develop a global strategy. State what you consider to be the definition of 'globalisation' and outline the forces driving its development.

18 STANDARDISATION

In an ideal world, companies would like to manufacture a standardised product. What are the factors that support the case for a standardised product and what are the circumstances that are likely to prevent its implementation? Support your argument with examples.

19 GLOBAL INDUSTRIES (Pilot paper)

108 mins

Angus Cairncross has recently been appointed as Head of Strategic Operations to the main board of Global Industries plc. This company is a UK-based conglomerate organisation, which had achieved significant expansion during the 1960s and 1970s when focusing on core businesses was not the fashion. The company has managed to maintain a leading position with the UK but is increasingly meeting competition from foreign competitors, both at home and abroad. Angus, prior to this recent appointment, had been Managing Director of one of Global Industries' subsidiary companies, Control Systems Ltd. This subsidiary company had focused on building control systems, including central heating, air conditioning and security equipment. The market had been mainly in the industrial sector as distinct from the general housing market. This subsidiary had traditionally not been a significant profit earner for Global Industries but Angus had been able to radically improve the position by his ability to control costs and, with judicious capital investment, improve the output per employee. He had also identified new markets overseas, particularly in China, and the rapidly developing countries of South East Asia. The recent economic problems faced by these countries had only marginally affected Control Systems' business and now sales are again following an upward trend.

The Chairman and Managing Director of Global Industries are both impressed with Angus and are hoping that his proven abilities in managing a focused company can be transferred to managing a conglomerate. Recently Global Industries has experienced a downturn in profits. The variety of businesses incorporated in the Company is large. The presence in industrial markets is considerable, ranging from design and construction within the nuclear power industry, railtrack construction, components for the motor vehicle assembly industry and the building control systems. As can be imagined the demand for these products is volatile and depends upon the state of economic activity within a country. So as to avoid over-dependence on one market Global Industries has set up sales and manufacturing facilities in overseas markets. This has enabled Global Industries to break into new foreign markets. Without a manufacturing presence the company would find it difficult to overcome trade barriers, and transport costs. It is also benefiting from access to cheaper labour and from local government grants so as to attract foreign investment.

Apart from the industrial sector Global Industries is also heavily involved in the defence industry, particularly in weapon systems and avionics. This is also an uncertain environment with demand being mainly determined by government policy which is highly dependent on the state of public finances. Finally Global Industries has a significant position within the consumer durable industry. It manufactures electric cookers and refrigerators within its kitchen appliance subsidiary, and also has recently purchased a number of franchises in the automobile distribution sector.

The problem which Global Industries is facing is that it appears to be exposed in too many markets and product areas. Its strategy of diversification has enabled it to be less dependent upon one market or one industrial sector. However it has created a difficult control system for management. Most of the technologies in which it operates are complex and the markets are dynamic, responding to increasing social, technological and political change. It has proved impossible to manage these industries from the centre, because no central organisation could possibly cope with the complexities of such a widespread business. Consequently the business is organised on divisional lines with each subsidiary reporting to the centre on a financial basis only. Each subsidiary is given financial targets by the centre (after consultation with the subsidiary) and then strategy formulation, implementation and control are delegated to the subsidiary companies. Because there appears to be little synergy between the companies their corporate and brand names are not even related to each other. At the end of a financial year most of the profits are returned to the Global Industries Headquarters, with a proportion being available for re-investment. The company acts in a shareholder role. It takes no active part in management but if profits from a subsidiary are considered to be inadequate then the likelihood of funds for investment in innovation or on new capital equipment will be low. In the final resort the subsidiary may be sold off. Angus has sympathy with this management philosophy. Its attitude towards delegation and the freedom to develop strategies had benefited him at Control Systems. However he also is concerned with a lack of support from the centre. Each subsidiary, by acting as an independent company has to provide its own support infrastructure - R&D, marketing and sales, finance and human resources. He believes that there must be some benefit in developing an organisational structure which can provide some direction and help, other than the Global Industries' Headquarters controlling the subsidiaries only through financial discipline.

However Angus appears to have a more urgent task to attend to as The Board has become very concerned about the performance of its kitchen appliance subsidiary. Over the past few years the performance of this company has deteriorated. This subsidiary originally produced and marketed these appliances within the UK market. However over time it acquired five foreign companies with their own product brands - two in Europe, two in the Far East and one in South America. The management at that time decided that it would be worthwhile continuing to promote these products under their original brand names. It also believed that by maintaining separate production facilities the kitchen appliance subsidiary could still appear to be a local company, so customising products for distinctive markets. Initially this had seemed to be a sensible strategy. Sales actually increased for a short time. However over the past three years sales have fallen significantly. Competition is mainly from one major global company who has grown rapidly over the past few years by pursuing a focus strategy. Its strategy has been to concentrate on a restricted number of models, both of cookers and refrigerators, promoted under a single corporate brand name. It has also decided to source its products from just two manufacturing sites. Its marketing strategy has also been centralised, with apparently little reference to local demand conditions. Initially the Global Industries' kitchen appliance subsidiary attempted to correct its position by increasing its promotion. However the inability of the company to halt the slide in sales, and the resultant loss in profits now means that Global Industries is now unwilling to finance any increased expenditure. Whereas Angus still believes there is profit potential within the kitchen appliance industry the majority of the members of the Board of the Global Industries plc do not believe that the subsidiary can be turned around and are considering disposing of the company. Unless the Board can see an improvement in sales or at least be presented with a strategic plan which will identify opportunities to turn around the situation then it will look for a buyer or starve the subsidiary of cash, milk the current operations and then withdraw from that sector.

Angus has analysed the company accounts and has been able to draw up the following table. The figures for the competitor's internal costs are estimates based on media expenditure statistics and assessment on costs for new product development. Whilst these figures cannot be guaranteed they should give a sound guide to the current situation and the relative competitive positions. Table 1 shows selected data and is not intended as a comprehensive set of accounts.

Table 1 £ million

	1998	1999	2000	2001 (forecast)
Sales of Global Industries' kitchen appliances				
domestic	14.2	13.5	12.8	11.4
overseas	8.5	7.5	7.2	7.0
total	22.7	21.0	20.0	18.4
Cost of Sales of Global Industries				
domestic	8.8	8.2	7.8	7.5
overseas	4.8	4.9	5.0	5.2
total	13.6	13.1	12.8	12.7
Gross profit (domestic and overseas)	9.1	7.9	7.2	5.7
Expenses	6.4	6.9	7.4	8.0
of which				
marketing	2.0	2.2	2.5	2.7
R&D	3.0	3.1	3.2	3.4
administration	1.4	1.6	1.7	1.9
Operating Profit (Loss)	2.7	1.0	-0.2	-2.3
Number of employees	1,300	1,350	1,250	1,250
Work in progress	3.5	3.7	4.0	4.2
Stock	2.4	2.9	3.2	4.1
Competitor:				
Sales revenue	18.0	19.5	22.5	25.0
Cost of sales	10.4	11.1	12.6	13.8

Table 1 £ million

Gross profit	7.6	8.4	9.9	11.2
Expenses	4.6	4.9	5.4	6.3
of which				
marketing	1.4	1.5	1.7	2.0
R&D	2.2	2.2	2.4	2.8
administration	1.0	1.2	1.3	1.5
Operating profit	3.0	3.5	4.5	4.9
Number of employees	800	850	950	1,000
Work in progress	2.7	2.4	2.2	1.9
Stock	1.9	1.8	2.0	2.1

Required

(a)   As Angus Cairncross prepare a report identifying the main problems which the kitchen appliance subsidiary has, particularly when compared with its major competitor.

(20 marks)

(b)   Examine the factors which should be considered before a company decides to dispose of a subsidiary. Consider how each of these factors might relate to the disposal of the kitchen appliance subsidiary by Global Industries plc.   **(15 marks)**

(c)   Discuss the benefits and problems which Global Industries plc is likely to experience, operating as a decentralised group of companies, using mainly financial controls as the major management control system. Suggest how the company can provide more help from the Headquarters, without becoming over-involved in day-to-day operations.

(25 marks)

(60 marks)

Approaching the question

Angus Cairncross has recently been appointed as Head of Strategic Operations to the main board of Global Industries plc. This company is a UK-based conglomerate organisation, | Pros and cons of this organisational form

which had achieved significant expansion during the 1960s and 1970s when focusing on | Experience - culture

core businesses was not the fashion. The company has managed to maintain a leading

position with the UK but is increasingly meeting competition from foreign competitors, both | Globalisation of competition

at home and abroad. Angus, prior to this recent appointment, had been Managing Director

of one of Global Industries' subsidiary companies, Control Systems Ltd. This subsidiary | Useful experience

company had focused on building control systems, including central heating, air conditioning

and security equipment. The market had been mainly in the industrial sector as distinct from | Industrial marketing

the general housing market. This subsidiary had traditionally not been a significant profit

earner for Global Industries but Angus had been able to radically improve the position by his | Performance measure

ability to control costs and, with judicious capital investment, improve the output per

employee. He had also identified new markets overseas, particularly in China, and the

rapidly developing countries of South East Asia. The recent economic problems faced by | Political implications

449   BPP
PROFESSIONAL EDUCATION

these countries had only marginally affected Control Systems' business and now sales are again following an upward trend.

> Emerging markets entry method? Stage of development

> Financial pressure eg from banks

The Chairman and Managing Director of Global Industries are both impressed with Angus and are hoping that his proven abilities in managing a focused company can be transferred to managing a conglomerate. Recently Global Industries has experienced a downturn in

> Heavily regulated industries – very predictable

profits. The variety of businesses incorporated in the Company is large. The presence in industrial markets is considerable, ranging from design and construction within the nuclear power industry, railtrack construction, components for the motor vehicle assembly industry

> Quality, JIT Global Market

and the building control systems. As can be imagined the demand for these products is volatile and depends upon the state of economic activity within a country. So as to avoid over-dependence on one market Global Industries has set up sales and manufacturing

> Cost advantages

facilities in overseas markets. This has enabled Global Industries to break into new foreign markets. Without a manufacturing presence the company would find it difficult to overcome trade barriers, and transport costs. It is also benefiting from access to cheaper labour and from local government grants so as to attract foreign investment.

> Organisational implications – structure? Culture?

Apart from the industrial sector Global Industries is also heavily involved in the defence industry, particularly in weapon systems and avionics. This is also an uncertain environment

> Very high technology

with demand being mainly determined by government policy which is highly dependent on the state of public finances. Finally Global Industries has a significant position within the consumer durable industry. It manufactures electric cookers and refrigerators within its

> Rather low technology

kitchen appliance subsidiary, and also has recently purchased a number of franchises in the automobile distribution sector.

> Standard

The problem which Global Industries is facing is that it appears to be exposed in too many markets and product areas. Its strategy of diversification has enabled it to be less dependent upon one market or one industrial sector. However it has created a difficult control system

> Problem of diversification

for management. Most of the technologies in which it operates are complex and the markets are dynamic, responding to increasing social, technological and political change. It has proved impossible to manage these industries from the centre, because no central organisation could possibly cope with the complexities of such a widespread business.

Consequently the business is organised on divisional lines with each subsidiary reporting to the centre on a financial basis only. Each subsidiary is given financial targets by the centre (after consultation with the subsidiary) and then strategy formulation, implementation and control are delegated to the subsidiary companies. Because there appears to be little synergy between the companies their corporate and brand names are not even related to each other. At the end of a financial year most of the profits are returned to the Global Industries Headquarters, with a proportion being available for re-investment. The company acts in a shareholder role. It takes no active part in management but if profits from a subsidiary are considered to be inadequate then the likelihood of funds for investment in innovation or on new capital equipment will be low. In the final resort the subsidiary may be sold off. Angus has sympathy with this management philosophy. Its attitude towards delegation and the freedom to develop strategies had benefited him at Control Systems. However he also is concerned with a lack of support from the centre. Each subsidiary, by acting as an independent company has to provide its own support infrastructure - R&D, marketing and sales, finance and human resources. He believes that there must be some benefit in developing an organisational structure which can provide some direction and help, other than the Global Industries' Headquarters controlling the subsidiaries only through financial discipline.

Effect on motivation?

A missed opportunity

Fits with lack of synergy

Fragmented effort

Cost?

However Angus appears to have a more urgent task to attend to as The Board has become very concerned about the performance of its kitchen appliance subsidiary. Over the past few years the performance of this company has deteriorated. This subsidiary originally produced and marketed these appliances within the UK market. However over time it acquired five foreign companies with their own product brands - two in Europe, two in the Far East and one in South America. The management at that time decided that it would be worthwhile continuing to promote these products under their original brand names. It also believed that by maintaining separate production facilities the kitchen appliance subsidiary could still appear to be a local company, so customising products for distinctive markets. Initially this had seemed to be a sensible strategy. Sales actually increased for a short time. However over the past three years sales have fallen significantly. Competition is mainly from one

Getting down to specifics now

Five brands – differential approach

Loss of economies of scale

Why?

Should leave plenty of market available

If they can do it, why not Global?

major global company who has grown rapidly over the past few years by pursuing a focus strategy. Its strategy has been to concentrate on a restricted number of models, both of cookers and refrigerators, promoted under a single corporate brand name. It has also decided to source its products from just two manufacturing sites. Its marketing strategy has also been centralised, with apparently little reference to local demand conditions. Initially the Global Industries' kitchen appliance subsidiary attempted to correct its position by increasing

Increasing cost

its promotion. However the inability of the company to halt the slide in sales, and the resultant loss in profits now means that Global Industries is now unwilling to finance any increased expenditure. Whereas Angus still believes there is profit potential within the kitchen appliance industry the majority of the members of the Board of the Global Industries plc do not believe that the subsidiary can be turned around and are considering disposing of

Why not?

the company. Unless the Board can see an improvement in sales or at least be presented

Implies reasonably long term plan acceptable

with a strategic plan which will identify opportunities to turn around the situation then it will look for a buyer or starve the subsidiary of cash, milk the current operations and then withdraw from that sector.

Angus has analysed the company accounts and has been able to draw up the following table. The figures for the competitor's internal costs are estimates based on media

Note of caution – but the best estimate we have

expenditure statistics and assessment on costs for new product development. Whilst these figures cannot be guaranteed they should give a sound guide to the current situation and the relative competitive positions. Table 1 shows selected data and is not intended as a comprehensive set of accounts.

Table 1   £ million   Overall %

	1998	1999	2000	2001 (forecast)	Change 98-00
Sales of Global Industries' kitchen appliances					
domestic	14.2	13.5	12.8	11.4	-10
overseas	8.5	7.5	7.2	7.0	-15
total	22.7	21.0	20.0	18.4	-12
Cost of Sales of Global Industries					
domestic	8.8	8.2	7.8	7.5	-11
overseas	4.8	4.9	5.0	5.2	+4 Why?
total	13.6	13.1	12.8	12.7	-6
Gross profit (domestic and overseas)	9.1	7.9	7.2	5.7	-11
Expenses	6.4	6.9	7.4	8.0	+16 Why?
of which					
marketing	2.0	2.2	2.5	2.7	Rising!
R&D	3.0	3.1	3.2	3.4	Rising!
administration	1.4	1.6	1.7	1.9	Rising!
Operating Profit (Loss)	2.7	1.0	-0.2	-2.3	
Number of employees	1,300	1,350	1,250	1,250	-4
Work in progress	3.5	3.7	4.0	4.2	Rising!
Stock	2.4	2.9	3.2	4.1	Rising!
Competitor:					
Sales revenue	18.0	19.5	22.5	25.0	+34
Cost of sales	10.4	11.1	12.6	13.8	+21
Gross profit	7.6	8.4	9.9	11.2	
Expenses	4.6	4.9	5.4	6.3	
of which					
marketing	1.4	1.5	1.7	2.0	Rising
R&D	2.2	2.2	2.4	2.8	slowly

administration	1.0	1.2	1.3	1.5	}
Operating profit	3.0	3.5	4.5	4.9	
Number of employees	800	850	950	1,000	
Work in progress	2.7	2.4	2.2	1.9	} Falling
Stock	1.9	1.8	2.0	2.1	} steady

Note!

Required

A wide brief

Rational assessment of a potential strategy

(a) As Angus Cairncross prepare a report identifying the main problems which the kitchen appliance subsidiary has, particularly when compared with its major competitor.

(20 marks)

Theory: advantages and disadvantages of divisional diversified conglomerate form. Mintzberg **Fact**: examples from the scenario of how Global Industries does things

(b) Examine the factors which should be considered before a company decides to dispose of a subsidiary. Consider how each of these factors might relate to the disposal of the kitchen appliance subsidiary by Global Industries plc. **(15 marks)**

(c) Discuss the benefits and problems which Global Industries plc is likely to experience, operating as a decentralised group of companies, using mainly financial controls as the major management control system. Suggest how the company can provide more help from the Headquarters, without becoming over-involved in day-to-day operations.

What can they do? **Value chain** is a good checklist of possibilities

Exam answer bank

1   FOUR STAR PRODUCTS

Part (a)

Answer plan

NB Q not so much about the planning department as about what it does. Therefore answer requires critique of formal planning approach.

Against

Difficulty of forecasting discontinuities
Linear approach - annual cycle
Isolation of planners from operations
Politics
Implementation
Learning

For

Systematic approach
Sets targets
Co-ordination of objectives, departments, activities
Organised attention to environment

Criticisms of the rational model concern both the theory behind it and how it has worked in practice. Empirical studies have not proved that formal planning processes contribute to success.

Planning theory assumes that the development of the business environment can be forecast, and to some extent controlled. In conditions of stability, forecasting and extrapolation make sense. But forecasting cannot cope with sudden **discontinuities** and **shocks**, such as the change from mainframe computing to PCs, which nearly destroyed IBM.

Part of the problem is the **linear approach** sometimes adopted, using an annual cycle. Unfortunately, strategically significant events outside the organisation are rarely synchronised with the annual planning cycle. Four Star's financial crisis in the early 1990s is, perhaps, an example.

Another problem is that formal planning can **discourage strategic thinking** among operational managers. Once a plan is locked in place, people are unwilling to question it. The internal significance of the chosen performance indicators leads managers to focus on fulfilling the plan rather than concentrating on developments in the environment. Strategy becomes something for specialists.

A complementary problem arises when the planners are separated from the operational managers; the implication is that the planners do not really need day-to-day knowledge of the product or market. However, small-scale developments can have important strategic influence and should not be ignored.

The rational model by definition assumes that an **objective approach** prevails. Unfortunately, no account is taken of the essentially political processes that determine many plans. There also problems of implementation. Managers are not all-knowing, and there are limits to the extent to which they can control the actual behaviour of the organisation. This places limits upon what can be achieved. Discovering strengths and weaknesses is a learning process. Implementing a strategy is necessary for learning - to see if it works.

On the other hand, we can discern an important role for **formal planning activities**. Apart from anything else, a desire to do things in a systematic way naturally leads to rational planning; deciding what to do, and when and how it should be done. Such an approach can make management control more effective by developing detailed and explicit targets. This shows managers at all levels where they fit in and forces them to confront the company's expectations of them

The development of a plan for a large organisation such as Four Star includes an important element of **co-ordination**. Long-term, medium-term and short-term objectives, plans and controls must be made consistent with one another. Similarly, the activities of the different business functions must be directed towards a common goal.

Also, companies cannot remain static: they have to cope with and exploit changes in the **environment**. It is clear from the CEO's use of external agencies and his new strategy for Four Star that he understands this. We may speculate that he is not so much an enemy of strategic planning as much as he is unimpressed with the performance of the Four Star planning department.

Part (b)

> **Tutorial note**. This part of the question is fairly unusual in that there is pretty much a single correct approach to a good answer; that is, this question is about the environmental analysis aspect of the rational planning model and not very much else will do. However, notice that a good answer will point out the weakness of the forecasting process: the future is essentially unknowable and the danger of detailed research is that we forget this and come to believe that we do indeed know just what is going to happen.

Answer plan

Nature of environmental analysis
The environment - divisions
Desk research
Market research
Informal research
Technical nature of Internet boom
Importance of judgement
Relationship of formal planning to strategic decision making-support

Environmental analysis is a fundamental part of strategic business management. The aim of the analysis is to identify opportunities and threats and to assess their significance. The environment itself may be divided both according to its proximity to the organisation and according to its inherent features. Thus, the task environment, dealing with suppliers, customers, competitors and so on, may be differentiated from the wider, general environment and, indeed, from the global physical environment. The general, or macro, environment is often analysed under such headings as political, economic, social and technological.

The work of analysis can be carried on to a great extent by **desk research**. This may be quite adequate for keeping abreast of the more general aspects of the macro environment, and even for some parts of the task environment, such as changing labour costs and the fortunes of competitors. However, more complex and expensive methods, such as market research surveys may be required for some aspects of the task environment, and more intuitive ones, such as personal contact between senior managers for others.

In the case of the Internet business model, which was given enormous publicity, it should have been easy to obtain a full understanding of both principle and technique by the methods outlined above. The problem with the collapse of confidence in the model was that foretelling was very much a matter of **judgement**. Extremely large sums of money were invested on quite rational grounds and very few commentators took a pessimistic view.

This is not a failure of the formal planning process as such, but rather a failure of strategic judgement at the highest levels of the organisations concerned. Planning techniques cannot foretell exactly what the future holds, let alone control it. Their purpose is to support those who must take strategic decisions, not to replace them.

2   EMPIRE CHEMICALS

Strategic planning at Empire Chemicals

Although Empire Chemicals has a large range of businesses, there is always the danger that like any conglomerate business it can lose its sense of direction.

Empire includes diverse product-market mixes such as paints, fertiliser and agrochemicals, pharmaceuticals, bulk chemicals. Each of these products has different characteristics. The synergies, between for example paints and pharmaceuticals are hard to see. However, it is probable that profits from bulk chemicals are much more volatile than, say, pharmaceuticals, which perhaps require a higher research base. The business synergies might be financial.

The question what business are we in? is therefore hard to answer, other than in the most general terms.

Sir Henry Sanderson's statement that at one time the business had been thought of as recession-proof seems complacent. Each individual business might have conducted SWOT analyses, but as the group operates in so many different environments, it might have been hard to conduct an analysis for the group as a whole. The fact that the effects of recession were not anticipated does indicate at group level at least, a failure of analysis.

The overall strategic choice for the group as a whole has obviously been made. It functions largely by conglomerate diversification, like Cobb. The admittedly poor cost control, and Cobb's bid, suggests that tactical plans allow for too much corporate flab. Possible economies of scale in accounting and other overheads are avoided.

The only way to judge the success or failure of strategic plans is with hindsight, which is not available to the planners.

Emergent strategies are those which develop out of patterns of behaviour. They do not develop from management's explicit control or from planning. The result from operational decisions and their unintended consequences exploiting sudden insights, and develop in the process of business itself, rather than as a separate planning exercise. Mintzberg holds that this is how many business strategies actually developed in practice.

The past history of the company suggests a freewheeling approach to entering different product-market areas. Freewheeling opportunism has perhaps seduced the company into spreading itself too thinly as a pattern of decision making. It is significant that the chairman and main board spend too much time on purely UK matters. Clearly, they have not achieved a global perspective.

The planning process failed to take the fluctuations of the business cycle into account. The existence of the business cycle is not an uncertainty, although the exact timing and severity of any down turn cannot be predicted. It is hard to see how any major environmental discontinuities have affected Empire. The bid by Cobb, however, could not be predicted. Perhaps the firm regarded itself as secure from any takeover.

Arguably, there is insufficient planning. An internal appraisal would have revealed the excess costs sooner. Bad planning, rather than an excess of planning, would seem to be evident.

3   MISSION STATEMENTS

To: Managing Director
From: Anne Accountant
Date: 29 February 20XX
Subject: Mission Statements

Contents: Introduction
              Mission statement and strategic planning
              Originating a mission statement
              The scope of mission statements
              The benefits of mission statements

Introduction

A *mission* can be defined as a business's basic function in society. It is often visionary, open-ended and has no time limit for achievement. It is possible however to reach a more expanded definition of mission to include four elements.

(a)   *Purpose*. Why does the company exist, or why do its managers and employees feel it exists?

    (i)   To create wealth for shareholders, who take priority over all other stakeholders.

    (ii)   To satisfy the needs of all stakeholders (including employees, society at large, for example).

    (iii)   To reach some higher goal and objective ('the advancement of society' and so forth).

(b)   *Strategy*. This provides the commercial logic for the company, and so defines:

    (i)   the business the company is in;
    (ii)   the competence and competitive advantages by which it hopes to prosper.

(c)   *Policies and standards of behaviour*. Policies and strategy need to be converted into everyday performance. For example, a service industry that wished to be the best in its market must aim for standards of service, in all its operations, which are at least as good as those found in its competitors. In service businesses, this includes simple matters such as politeness to customers, speed at which phone calls are answered, and so forth.

(d)   *Values*. These relate to the organisation's culture, and are the basic, perhaps unstated beliefs of the people who work in the organisation. For example, a firm's moral principle might mean not taking on an assignment if it believes the client will not benefit, even though this means lost revenue. An example of this can be found in the standards of professional ethics required of accountants.

A *mission statement* is a document embodying some of the matters noted above. A mission statement might be a short sentence, or a whole page. It is intentionally unquantified and vague, and is sometimes seen as a statement of the guiding priorities that govern a firm's behaviour. Mission statements are rarely changed, as otherwise they have less force, and become mere slogans.

(a)   *Purpose*

    (i)   The firm's purpose might be described in terms of more than just self interest. A pharmaceutical company might define its corporate mission as 'the well-being of humanity'.

    (ii)   The firm's responsibility to its stakeholders.

(b)   *Strategy*

    (i)   The statement should identify the type of business the firm is engaged in.

    (ii)   The statement should perhaps identify the strategy for competitive advantage the firm intends to pursue.

(c)   *Values*

    (i)   The statement should identify values that link with the firm's purpose.
    (ii)   The values should reinforce the corporate strategy.

(d)   *Behaviour standards*

    (i)   Defined standards of behaviour can serve as benchmarks of performance.
    (ii)   Individual employees should be able to apply these standards to their own behaviour.

(e)   *Character*

    (i)   The statement should reflect the organisation's actual behaviour and culture, or at least its aspirations for improved behaviour and culture.

    (ii)   The statement should be easy to read.

Objectives, on the other hand, are the embodiment of a mission statement in a commercial context. They specify the meaning of a mission in a particular period, market, or situation.

Mission statements and strategic planning

The relationship between mission statements and strategic planning is an ambiguous one. In some cases, the mission statement is prepared after the strategic plan is drawn up as a sort of summary of it. However this would only be done if there was a major change in the company's direction.

Whilst the mission inspires corporate objectives, the strategy is a means for fleshing them out. The strategy also provides directions for specific context. The mission statement cannot institute particular strategies but it can indicate priorities. Say an investment company prided itself on investing funds in companies which it regarded as behaving ethically, and its mission statement contains a clause which says that the company is 'to invest clients' funds in companies whose products promote health'. It would be unlikely to invest in tobacco firms, but no indication is given as to which shares to buy, on which stock exchanges, when to sell, what returns to expect, and so forth.

Originating a mission statement

A mission statement originates at the highest levels of the organisation. It is possible that, given a mission statement is meant to inspire as well as direct, a process of consultation with employees should take place to determine what the mission statement should be, or to assess what would be laughed out of courts. A company which declared its commitment to customer service in a mission statement, but whose practices for years had been quite the opposite, would have problems in persuading employees to take it seriously. The fact that the employees were consulted about the current ethos in a formal procedure would make the mission statement more effective. The mission statement would be introduced as part of an attempt to change the culture of the organisation.

The scope of mission statements

All areas of corporate life can be covered by a mission statement. This is because it is broadly based, and as a statement of an organisation's values and objectives, it should affect everyone in the organisation. That means its scope is wide-ranging. If it did not affect everybody in each department, from managing director to clerk, then its power would be lessened, and its purpose poorly satisfied.

For example, if a company's mission highlights the provision of *good quality* products and services, then this does not only include the way in which products are made and services delivered, but the way in which commercial relationships are conducted. Given that a successful business requires, in the long term, good commercial relationships, quality applies to these as well.

The benefits of mission statements

(a) They describe what the company is about.

(b) They provide a guiding philosophy where there are doubts about the direction a company should take, or a decision an individual manager or employee should make.

(c) They display the area in which the company is operating.

(d) They enable the communication of a common culture throughout the whole organisation.

(e) They stimulate debate as to how the mission can be implemented.

4   NADIR PRODUCTS: ETHICS

Part (a)

> **Tutorial note**. While this question clearly has an important ethical slant, it is important to deal with the commercial impact of the proposed courses of action. If you feel your experience has not prepared you to do this, think in terms of stakeholder theory and ask yourself what connected stakeholders like customers are reasonably entitled to expect and how *you* would react to these ploys.
>
> Do not spend more than a minute on dealing with the report form requirement: a suitable heading and, perhaps, numbered paragraphs are all that are required. A short introductory paragraph giving the reason for the report is a good way to get started.

REPORT

To: Board Members, Nadir Products plc

From: A Consultant

Date: December 2001

Subject: Proposed adjustments to turnover reporting

You asked me to comment on the commercial and ethical implications of suggestions that had been made about the value of this year's turnover. There was concern that a current decline in sales will adversely affect the level of bonuses paid to senior staff.

My first comment is that the assumption behind the suggestions appears wrong. The aim of the bonus scheme was surely to provide an incentive for senior staff to take appropriate action to improve performance. If performance has not improved, it would be perverse to adjust the numbers so that they receive the bonuses anyway. There is an element of moral hazard here: if the bonuses are in effect guaranteed and not dependent on improved performance, the incentive effect disappears and the scheme might as well be abandoned.

I understand that there is concern that staff will be adversely affected by the downturn in sales value. However, I must point out the questionable nature of the suggestions from an ethical point of view. It is likely that the detailed proposals will create a conflict of interests since each has the potential to disadvantage shareholders. It would be ethically inappropriate to pursue any course of action that reduced shareholder value in order to enrich senior staff.

I will now examine the individual proposals.

Discount for additional sales. A discount is an unexceptional sales promotional device that may be used, for instance, to increase or defend market share or to shift excess stock. It has a cost, in the form of reduced margin, and it is a matter of commercial judgement to decide whether the benefit is greater than the cost. It may also have the effect of merely bringing sales forward in time, so that later trading periods suffer.

Of the three suggestions, this is the most defensible. However, it is quite *indefensible* if it is undertaken solely in order to boost bonuses, because of the conflict of interest discussed above.

Bringing forward scheduled orders is a form of window dressing. Your auditors will deploy checks on such activities as a matter of course, and may succeed in detecting this. The accounts would then have to be adjusted, since there is no commercial justification for the practice. It can be seen as detrimental to shareholders since the reported profit would be overstated and, while this may have a positive effect on share value in the short term, were it ever discovered, it would bring into question the company's corporate governance. Such a scheme is also likely to irritate customers who may respond by delaying payment and even seeking a new supplier. This would clearly disadvantage the company.

This suggestion is unacceptable on both ethical and practical grounds.

Warning of possible price rises. I take it as read that there are no actual plans to raise prices? If this is the case, to say that such plans exist is untruthful and therefore inappropriate for a company that wishes to maintain high ethical standards. Further, to hide behind a form of words such as 'there *may* be price rises' would be equally dishonest, since the intention would be to create a specific, incorrect impression in customers' minds. When the warning is eventually shown to be spurious, customers' estimation of the company will fall, with an eventual knock-on effect on turnover.

This ploy is comparable to the previous one in its potential effect on shareholders and customers but is even more unethical

Conclusion. None of the suggestions is acceptable ethically or commercially as a solution to the senior staff bonus problem.

Part (b)

The original part (b) of Nadir Products appears as question 16. We have introduced this part to give you a more comprehensive exercise on Chapter 4. You will have realised that there is very little in the scenario that is directly related to the issue of social responsibility.

One of our aims in preparing the suggested solution below was to demonstrate how it is possible to relate an answer to such a question. You will notice that we have used a little deduction and suggestion to achieve this effect. It is perfectly in order to talk about matters the setting is silent on if you use this technique.

However, use it with care! You must stick to the point and not wander off into regions you like the look of but which have no connection to the question as set!

The stakeholder view is that many groups have a stake in what the organisation does. This is particularly important in the business context, where shareholders own the business but employees, customers and government also have particularly strong claims to having their interests considered. It is suggested that modern corporations are so powerful, socially, economically and politically, that unrestrained use of their power will inevitably damage other people's rights. Under this approach, the exercise of corporate social responsibility constrains the corporation to act at all times as a good citizen. Particular emphasis is laid on the preservation of employment and protection of the environment.

We are not told the extent of Nadir Products operations. If as seems likely, they are largely confined to the UK, or at least to the EU, the company's activities will be subject to fairly demanding legal requirements concerning such basic aspects of good corporate citizenship. They must conform or court legal sanctions.

Another argument points out that corporations exist within society and are dependent upon it for the resources they use. Some of these resources are obtained by direct contracts with suppliers but others are not, being provided by government expenditure. Examples are such things as transport infrastructure, technical research and education for the workforce. Clearly, Nadir Products contributes to the taxes that pay for these things, but the relationship is rather tenuous and the tax burden can be minimised by careful management. The company can do as much or as little as it cares to in this connection.

Mintzberg suggests that simply viewing organisations as vehicles for shareholder investment is inadequate, since in practice, he says, organisations are rarely controlled effectively by shareholders. Most shareholders are passive investors. We do not know whether or not this is the case with Nadir Products.

Many organisations regard the exercise of corporate social responsibility as valuable in promoting a positive corporate image. The management of Nadir Products therefore may feel that it is appropriate to take an instrumental approach to such matters as sponsorship and charitable giving. Charitable donations and artistic sponsorship are useful media of public relations and can reflect well on the business. They can be regarded as another form of promotion, which like advertising, serves to enhance consumer awareness of the business. It would be necessary for the company to ensure that the recipients of its generosity were appropriate to its operations at the bottom end of the market: grand opera would probably be inappropriate.

The arguments for and against social responsibility are complex ones. However, ultimately they can be traced to different assumptions about society and the relationships between the individuals and organisations within it. It is unlikely to be something that need occupy a great deal of the time of Nadir Products' directors.

5 FIREBRIDGE TYRES LTD

> **Tutorial note**. This is a fairly straightforward question on the environment and how an organisation can ensure environmental fit.

Part (a)

Main factors in the external environment

The environment of an organisation is everything outside the boundaries of the organisation. Organisations are by definition open to the environment: it is the source of their inputs; it is the destination of their outputs; and it sets constraints over what the organisation can do. Some argue that the environment is increasingly a source of uncertainty for organisations, and that it is becoming harder to read. The degree of uncertainty it causes results from its complexity and the rate of change.

Hofer and Schendel argue that the very purpose of strategy is to secure some sort of environmental fit. This might be an extreme position, as it implies reaction to the environment rather than activity to shape environmental forces. However, any formal strategic planning process takes the environment into account.

As far as the general environment is concerned, we can analyse PEST and competitive factors.

Political and legal factors. Firebridge Tyres Ltd (FTL) operates in a stable political environment. Agreements between governments on the single European market and GATT have opened up international markets, not only to FTL but to its competitors: however GTC does not want FTL to increase its exports outside Europe. There is no shortage of car service stations, a fragmented industry, so political interference is unlikely. Local government might determine the siting of certain activities. FTL is indirectly affected by government transport policy, if this affects the demand for and use of cars.

Economic factors. In the UK, tyres must be checked annually, as part of the MOT testing process. The overall level of economic activity determines transport use, which influences wear and tear of tyres. However, in times of hardship, people will be less likely to buy the premium brand range preferring to go for the lower cost Freeway range, cheaper overseas tyres, or even retreads. The general level of prosperity also influences the number of people in the population who use cars; rising incomes and wealth mean rising numbers of cars purchased, hence greater demand for tyres. People will also move to lower cost service options in hard times: FTL does not want a service business lumbered with heavy overheads. The UK market is much smaller than the US: GTC might be unrealistic in assuming that the same formula, which might depend on economies of scale, would work over in the UK.

Social factors influence demand indirectly, via political pressure for legislation or changing patterns of demand. For examples, governments are more concerned with ecological issues. There are disposal problems with used tyres. This might affect what they are made of. Some can be burnt as fuel, but with landfill taxes increasing, recyclable tyres may be preferred. The proposed service business depends on patterns of car use. It may be that many drivers and will prefer a garage.

Technological factors. Tyres are a fairly mature technology, although there are improvements to be made to increase their grip, their longevity, and their recyclability. Any changes in the plastics and materials industry might be relevant. Also, if cars become lighter, lighter tyres will be needed.

The main factor in the environment is competition, which is impinging directly on FTL.

A number of service chains already exist in the UK, but otherwise the industry is fairly fragmented. Competition on price is important, but also on quality. However, FTL needs to assess how the competition will respond.

The competitive environment can be described using Porter's five forces model (barriers to entry- see below, substitute products, customer bargaining power, supplier bargaining power, competitive rivalry). There are few substitute products, but competitive rivalry is intense. Suppliers have low bargaining power probably.

Part (b)

Barriers to entry discourage new competitors to an industry. If they are low, it is easy to set up shop, but hard to discourage other people from doing so too. The main barriers to entry are described below.

Economies of scale. For some firms, a barrier to entry is the size of the operation needed to be profitable. Tyres are high volume, low margin products on the whole, and for most cases, the best way to make money is to manufacture in large quantities. A large plant implies high fixed costs and a high breakeven point. There is little evidence that significant economies of scale can be achieved in *servicing*. There are some service chains, but the industry seems fragmented.

Product differentiation. FTL already pursues this strategy by producing different tyres, directed at different segments. In service, differentiation might be achieved on the basis of FTL's brand name, and a promise of service quality. Advertising costs might be considerable, however, to build the brand.

Capital requirements. No new factories need to be built, of course, but FTL will have to acquire leases or freeholds of a number of properties in which to set up its service stations. Many of the prime spots might be taken over by petrol stations. Ideally FTL will be positioned near residential areas or near roads, to make them easy to find. The cost of this depends on the size of the operation that GTC is proposing.

Switching costs are minimal; new customers are easy to find, but hard to keep, unless service quality is better.

Distribution. The chain is basically a distribution outlet for FTL's tyres. The importance of choosing the right sites for distributing the service was identified in (iii) above.

Existing service providers know the market, but otherwise they have no special advantages.

Barriers to entry are fairly low. This will make it easy to set up business, but hard to make a profit perhaps, unless some unique lessons can be transferred from GTC, operating in a very different transport infrastructure.

Part (c)

Distinctive competences and critical success factors

A distinctive competence is those activities which a firm carries out uniquely or distinctly well. To be an enduring source of competitive advantage, a distinctive competence should be hard to imitate.

Critical success factors, on the other hand, are aspects of a business's performance which are essential to its success. Some of these relate to internal processes, others to the basic infrastructure of the business.

What is FTL's distinctive competence. FTL is a manufacturing business, making what is essentially a commodity products, tyres, with a stab at product differentiation. This competence is not truly distinctive, as there are other tyre manufacturers in the world, but FTL has built up a market presence in Europe. The distinctive competences in such a business might be the ability:

(a)   To build a brand which customers recognise

(b)   To make incremental technical innovations, to encourage new sales

(c)   To keep costs under control, to support the brand, and to prevent its erosion by competition

(d)   To win the support of distributors and garages for the tyres, as opposed to competitors

How do these relate to the service business? A key problem is that services are a very different proposition to products. There are several possible critical success factors for the service business.

(a)   A brand which customers recognise (eg as with McDonald's for hamburgers) and choose, having realistic and satisfied expectations of what it offers

(b)   A number of well chosen sites for people to choose and access easily, which make the experience not too unpleasant (eg by offering customers a lounge or coffee bar)

(c)   Well trained staff who not only know how to change wheels and tyres, and do other repairs but who are able to demonstrate higher standards of customer care

(d)   To be seen as preferable to the local garage in terms of the processes by which the service is provided

FTL's existing competences at best cover brand building. It has no experience in choosing and managing properties: US conditions are different, so a transfer of skills between the US and the UK firm may be hard to achieve. FTL runs a manufacturing business; a service business, based on a variety of intangibles such as staff courtesy, is a different proposition. The required cultures of the two businesses might conflict.

The firm might have to spend a lot of money on training, both technically and in terms of customer care. Also money would have to be spent on building the brand. However, GTC should be able to provide some expertise in building the service aspects.

In short, FTL's distinctive competences are not sufficient to make a go of this plan, given the fragmented nature of the industry. GTC may be able to provide some help, but GTC might end up investing more money and making short term losses, rather than the profits it is looking for.

FTL is in a difficult situation, because its managers are tied by the priorities of the US parent.

6   **TOROIDAL TOOLING**

> **Tutorial note**. This is not an original ACCA question; however, it is in the style of the Paper 3.5 questions, if a little easier to answer than most. We have used the BCG matrix in part (a) as it is the simplest and possibly the most useful of the portfolio analysis matrices. It is certainly one you should be completely familiar with. We mention other approaches in our suggested solution.
>
> In part (b), we use the value chain. There are certainly other approaches that the company could use to improve its systems, such as business process re-engineering, but the value chain is an ideal route to the overview the question asks for. In fact, the value chain is widely applicable in the exam as a framework for answering many questions, because it offers a comprehensive framework for analysing business problems.

Part (a)

Portfolio analysis examines the current status of the organisation's products and their markets. A variety of techniques may be used, including the product lifecycle concept, the GE business screen and the Shell matrix. One of the best established is the BCG matrix

The Boston Consulting Group (BCG) developed a matrix based on empirical research that assesses a company's products in terms of potential cash generation and cash expenditure requirements. Products (or even complete product divisions) are categorised in terms of market growth rate and relative market share.

(a)   Assessing rate of market growth as high or low depends on the conditions in the market. No single percentage rate can be set, since new markets may grow explosively while mature ones grow hardly at all. Toroidal's sales force seems to be well informed about its market and its collective judgement will be useful here.

(b)   Relative market share is assessed as a ratio: it is market share compared with the market share of the largest competitor. Thus a relative market share greater than unity indicates that the product or SBU is the market leader. It has been established empirically that market leaders tend to be more profitable than their competitors. This is felt to be due largely to economies of scale. Obtaining this information requires Toroidal to do some desk research in industry publications: their marketing staff are probably best placed to do this.

The matrix offers guidance as to appropriate strategy for each category of product.

Four major strategies can be pursued with respect to products, market segments and, indeed, SBUs.

(a)   **Build**. A build strategy forgoes short term earnings and profits in order to increase market share.

(b)   **Hold**. A hold strategy seeks to maintain the current position.

(c)   **Harvest**. A harvesting strategy seeks short-term earning and profits at the expense of long-term development.

(d)   **Divest**. Divestment reduces negative cash flow and releases resources for use elsewhere.

Market share

		High	Low
Market growth	High	Stars	Question marks
	Low	Cash cows	Dogs

(a)   **Stars**. In the short term, these require capital expenditure in excess of the cash they generate, in order to maintain their market position, but promise high returns in the future. Strategy: build.

(b)   In due course, stars will become **cash cows**. Cash cows need very little capital expenditure and generate high levels of cash income. Cash cows can be used to finance the stars. Strategy: hold or harvest if weak.

(c)   **Question marks**. Do the products justify considerable capital expenditure in the hope of increasing their market share, or should they be allowed to die quietly as they are squeezed out of the expanding market by rival products? Strategy: build or harvest.

(d)   **Dogs** may be ex-cash cows that have now fallen on hard times. Although they will show only a modest net cash outflow, or even a modest net cash inflow, they are cash traps which tie up funds and provide a poor return on investment. However, they may have a useful role, either to complete a product range or to keep competitors out. Strategy: divest or hold.

Toroidal has a wide range of products and product groups. It may be advisable to preface the portfolio analysis exercise with an assessment of the appropriateness of the existing classification. This might save a great deal of work in those areas where brand ranges overlap.

Part (b)

The value chain model of corporate activities, developed by Michael Porter, offers a bird's eye view of the firm and what it does. Competitive advantage, says Porter, arises out of the way in which firms organise and perform value activities. These are the means by which a firm creates value in its products

Activities incur costs, and, in combination with other activities, provide a product or service which earns revenue.

Porter grouped the various activities of an organisation into what he calls a value chain, which is illustrated below .

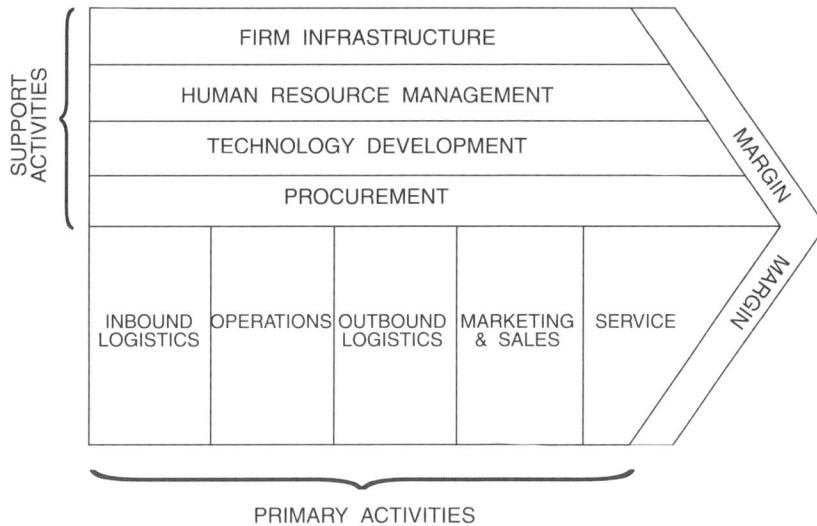

PRIMARY ACTIVITIES

The margin is the excess the customer is prepared to pay over the cost to the firm of obtaining resource inputs and providing value activities. It represents the value created by the value activities themselves and by the management of the linkages between them.

Primary activities are directly related to production, sales, marketing, delivery and service.

(a) Inbound logistics includes receiving, handling and storing inputs to the production system: warehousing, transport, stock control and so on. Toroidal's apparent poor performance in meeting orders promptly is a weakness that would be highlighted here.

(b) Operations convert resource inputs into a final product. Resource inputs are not only materials. People are a resource especially in service industries. Toroidal has two kind of operations: manufacturing its own products and dealing those produced by its agency principals. This area will therefore bear close examination in case the two types of operation come into conflict, for example over stock holding and packing (which take us into the next activity).

(c) Outbound logistics includes storing the product and its distribution to customers: packaging, testing, delivery and so on.

(d) Marketing and sales activities include informing customers about the product, persuading them to buy it, and enabling them to do so: advertising, promotion and so on. There is much scope for thought here, concerning the multiplicity of brands that Toroidal deals in.

(e) After sales service includes installing products, repairing them, upgrading them, providing spare parts and so forth. Clearly, Toroidal has problems in this area.

Support activities provide purchased inputs, human resources, technology and infrastructural functions to support the primary activities.

(a) Procurement acquires the resource inputs to the primary activities (eg purchase of materials, subcomponents equipment).

(b) Technology development includes such activities as product design, improving processes and resource utilisation.

(c) Human resource management activities include recruiting, training, developing and rewarding people.

(d) Management planning activities include planning, finance and quality control. Porter believes that these activities are crucially important to an organisation's strategic capability in all primary activities.

Linkages connect the activities of the value chain.

(a) Activities in the value chain affect one another. For example, more costly product design or better quality production might reduce the need for after-sales service.

(b) Linkages require co-ordination. For example, Just In Time requires smooth functioning of operations, outbound logistics and service activities such as installation.

The variety of Toroidal's products, brands and business relationships may make the management of linkages a fruitful area for investigation.

7 **ACKLINGTON ANTENNAS**

Part (a)

> **Tutorial note**. We answer the first part of this question largely in terms of *Porter's* **generic strategies**. This is because of the nature of the scenario. There is mention of price sensitivity, to which cost is related; the market is clearly highly specialised, so the idea of a niche approach is relevant; and finally, the products tend to be highly differentiated.
>
> It would be possible to take a product-market growth vector approach, but that model would not be so appropriate. We are given no information relevant to market penetration; product development is clearly going on anyway; market development and diversification are high-risk strategies for such a specialised company working in such high technology. Generally, *Ansoff's* model is most useful for less specialised companies, particularly those working in consumer products and services.
>
> The possible solution of a reorganisation of the industry, however, could be applied just as easily to an analysis using the product-market model.

Acklington Antennas is under threat from a new entrant that appears likely to enjoy a substantial cost advantage because of high volumes and the prior amortisation of development costs. However, Wizzomatic's products, being standardised, are unlikely to be suitable for many specialised applications.

Wizzomatic appear to be seeking to establish themselves as the cost leaders within the industry, using their cost advantage to build up volume. Cost leaders tend to seek as much product standardisation as possible in order to obtain economies of scale and Wizzomatic seem to have a major advantage here.

It would therefore not be advisable for Acklington to meet the new entrant head on. The price cuts necessary to build the necessary volume would be likely to starve the company of cash, thus prejudicing its new design work. It would find itself in the classic 'stuck in the middle' trap, subject to continuing high costs but unable to raise its prices.

A much safer option for Acklington would be to pursue two specific target market segments.

- The new design market, where they have expertise and a reputation that Wizzomatic cannot challenge with its standardised products

- Those parts of the spares market that require more specialised products than Wizzomatic can supply.

The first of these options represents a strategy of differentiation, while the second is a niche strategy.

It is likely that if Wizzomatic succeeds in establishing itself in the market it has chosen, Acklington will see its volumes falling. This need not lead to a fall in turnover if it is able to penetrate its chosen segments more deeply. However, a fall in volume of standard antennas will mean an increase in fully absorbed cost per unit, with a knock-on effect on margin. It may be that Acklington will have to withdraw from the volume part of its business. This will lead to concomitant downsizing of its production capacity unless it succeeds in retaining much of its existing aftermarket business.

To expand its share of the new systems market, Acklington will have to increase its sales effort and its design and test capacity. We have no way of knowing how easy this will be, but we may speculate that the highly skilled staff required will be fairly difficult to find, while the design and test facilities are likely to be quite expensive. Depending on the company's access to investment funds, therefore, this strategy may require a long period of time to implement.

The niche spares market will probably be easier to expand initially, since Acklington is likely to have the manufacturing capacity available, as discussed above. An immediate problem here is likely to be that the other three established players may also be planning a similar strategy.

It is possible that the other three principal suppliers in the industry will also feel the heat of Wizzomatic's arrival. This is all the more likely if they too are unable to meet the challenge head on. It may be that this could be a cue for restructuring the industry, by merger or takeover. The aim would be to accumulate the resources necessary to compete with Wizzomatic rather than ceding dominance in the volume sales segments of the market.

A strategy of consolidation would not be easy to implement. It would probably involve painful rationalisation of several functions, with job losses and other staff upheaval. There would also be a probability of conflict between perceived winners and losers, which would be exacerbated if the rationalisation took the form of takeover rather than merger.

The aim of the consolidation would be for a larger, more efficient company to emerge, retaining the best of the products, people, markets and resources of its parents. A careful strategic analysis would be necessary to ensure that the new strategy built on strengths and avoided weaknesses. It may be, for example, that even a merged company would not dispute the volume market but would aim to dominate the new design market.

Part (b)

> **Tutorial note**. Acklington Antennas is a manufacturing company, so the basic 4 Ps mix is what is required here. With a question like this, which is only worth 8 marks, do not dwell too much on background explanations. Cut to the chase and make as many good valid points as you can. You don't need to know anything about aircraft communication systems. But you do need to be generally aware of the differences between consumer and industrial marketing.

Product

The product element of Acklington's marketing mix is relatively simple. A firm's product may be viewed as a solution to a customer's problem. Acklington's products are therefore of two basic types: the newly developed and very high-value added antennas designed for new aircraft; and the standard antennas produced either for use as spares or for supply to other businesses.

Quality is clearly a major issue affecting both types of product, because of the requirements of aircraft safety. The standard antennas must be produced to existing precise specifications, while the new designs must satisfy strict performance requirements before they are released to service.

Packaging is also likely to be important. Spares, in particular, must have a long shelf life and may be transported to any part of the world. The packaging will have to provide substantial protection against climatic variables such as heat and humidity, as well as against impact and abrasion.

Price

We are told that prices in the industry are generally high and that co-operation between suppliers is not unusual. While presumably not engaging in price-fixing, it seems that the small group of suppliers in the industry tend not to compete on price. It is likely that winning contracts for new systems design is likely to depend far more on long-term relationships with customers and proven technical quality. In the spares market, it would seem that Wizzomatic's arrival may shake up the existing rather cosy arrangements, both as far as supplies direct to users and subcontract manufacturing are concerned. So long as variable costs can be covered, Acklington may feel it can cut its prices in these markets in order to maintain its manufacturing capacity in being.

Acklington will have to establish exactly which of Wizzomatic's products are acceptable substitutes for its own and where there are gaps in Wizzomatic's standardised range. Those gaps can then be exploited with higher prices.

Promotion

Acklington's products are complex, expensive and sold to industrial buyers, so the company's main promotional effort is likely to go into personal selling by experienced sales engineers. There is also likely to be attendance at trade fairs and a small amount of reminder advertising in the specialist press. Public relations effort is likely to be minimal and also concentrated on the specialist press.

Distribution

Distribution to aircraft manufacturers is likely to be direct to the end user, without any use of intermediaries. The subcontract work will also go direct to the purchasers. Distribution of aftermarket spares may involve the use of intermediaries, since the products are highly standardised technically and may be sold globally without modification. Since the products are expensive, regional or national intermediaries may be able to provide a service by investment in spares inventories.

8   NEW PARTNERSHIP

Part (a)

> **Tutorial note.** The implication of the last three sentences of the setting is that this part of the question is about major issues of *marketing*. Similarly, taking the requirement at face value, one could answer the question in terms of *launch* considerations, such as publicity, premises and internal administration. However, it is clear from the mark scheme and the Examiner's own suggested solution that he was actually thinking of wider strategic considerations. In fact, 50% of his suggested solution consists of a mini-strategic analysis.
>
> Do not be discouraged by this: refer to our comments on question 19, part (c), which was question 1(b) in the Pilot Paper.

To: Karen Lee
From: A Marketeer
Date: December 2001

REPORT – PROPOSED PARTNERSHIP

You asked me to advise on your new partnership project. As you know, my main area of expertise is marketing, so I have concentrated on marketing aspects of the project, though this inevitably includes some consideration of wider strategic matters.

Strategy

As an accountant working in practice you are no doubt familiar with the requirements of a business plan. You seem to have a firm idea of the satisfactions you intend to offer your target market, in the form of a variety of professional accountancy services. You also seem to have identified a gap in the market for such services provided by a small but integrated practice. No doubt your financial planning has been careful and you are assured of sufficient capital and liquidity to enable you to build up your business.

It would probably be appropriate at this stage to carry out an analysis of your group's strengths and weaknesses and the opportunities and threats present in the market. For instance, while I have no doubt that you have an appropriate mix of professional skills available, are you happy that the mundane administration of the practice will be carried on well enough to support rather than hinder your professional efforts? To what extent will your cash flow depend on the prosperity of any single client or industry?

Your aim should be to exploit the strengths and opportunities you identify, while avoiding the threats and converting the weaknesses into strengths.

Marketing

We have already considered the **product** aspect of the marketing mix, and, to some extent, **price. Place**, or distribution, is not really an issue for the type of services you are proposing to supply. I would merely suggest that you give proper consideration to the almost subliminal messages your premises will send to your clients, and ensure that they are in keeping with the overall image you wish to promote.

Promotion, as you realise will be an important input to the success of your venture. You are subject to professional rules governing promotion, but I would urge you to budget considerable resources, not least your own time, to the promotion of your practice.

You will be engaged in the supply of services and there are therefore three further marketing elements to consider: **people**, **processes** and **physical evidence**.

Your colleagues will no doubt be aware of the importance of the impression made by the staff of any service business. They must give a lead in matters such as appearance, friendly attitude and reliability so that your support staff form the correct impression of what is required. We both know how easy it is to regard the clients as an annoying distraction from the real work of the practice!

Your working processes and administrative procedures must also be designed to provide the maximum satisfaction to your clients. You will know better than I what is involved here.

Finally, because services are so intangible, you must give serious consideration to the physical evidence you actually put into your clients' hands. This is likely to consist largely of communications of one sort and another. Remember that you will be judged by such things as the correctness of your grammar and spelling and the quality of your notepaper. I suggest that you consult a trained designer before having your letterheads and so on printed.

Part (b)

> **Tutorial note**. This part of the question allows you to make use of material from other parts of your ACCA studies, since you will have covered pricing as an aspect of financial management. Also, if you have experience of how accountancy practices work, you can use that knowledge as background input into your answer.

We are told that Karen is a qualified accountant and we may assume that she and her colleagues intend to trade as members of their professional body, or bodies. If this is the case, it is important to point out that their conduct in relation to their fees, as with so much else, will be subject to the appropriate rules of professional conduct. These are such that most practices do in fact base their fees largely on cost, charging on the basis of time spent and degree of skill deployed.

That said, there is wide discretion available to the practitioner as to the size of any fee note issued, so other considerations other than cost may be introduced into the fee by adjusting the mark-up.

There are many factors that may be considered in setting a price. Fortunately, many of them, such as market skimming and penetrating are not really relevant to professional services. For Karen and her colleagues, the main considerations are economic: supply and demand will determine what price the market will bear.

There is likely to be competition from both qualified and unqualified accountants. While Karen's practice will have an advantage over the latter in professional credibility and the capacity to provide audit opinions, it is likely that they will be in competition with them for at least some of their business. Similarly, though they hope to serve a niche market, there is no guarantee that larger competitors will not try to attract the same clients. All this will tend to drive their fees down.

The level of demand in the market will also affect the prices they can charge. This may well differ between the various professional specialities Karen and her colleagues offer. For instance, there is currently a gradual erosion of demand for audit services because of changes to the law relating to audit of smaller limited companies. On the other hand, there is an expanding market for taxation services resulting from the introduction of self-assessment and an increase in the number of people falling into the higher tax bracket.

9   UNITED PRODUCTS

Part (a)

> **Tutorial note**. This is a wide ranging question and, perhaps, therefore, somewhat daunting. Remember that with this type of question there will be a lot of easy marks for explaining the basics. For example, a list of strengths and weaknesses would glean quite a few marks, though not 50%.
>
> In order to score well on this question you must do two slightly different things when you are applying your knowledge to the scenario: use the setting to illustrate your theory; and suggest ways in which the theory might be used to make improvements.
>
> Thus, for example, we say that the internal transfer and promotion from within policy is an example of the way that relatively junior managers can obtain good experience of real business problems. Similarly, we say that the detailed monthly reporting might be over-restrictive in its effects and, on examination, might prove to be unnecessarily expensive.
>
> Notice also that we begin with a comment about the very nature of UP's business, which you might think is a matter over and above the question of its organisation. Don't forget that there is scope in this exam for this sort of digression if you make it relevant to the scenario.

Divisionalisation is a common form of organisation structure in large organisations, especially those that encompass a wide variety of products, technologies and geographical locations. UP seems to qualify under all three of these categories. The form has been found to allow for overall control from the corporate headquarters without drowning it in the detail of micromanagement at long range.

The diversity of the company's operations is itself worthy of comment from a strategic point of view. There is obviously a tradition of having widely different operations and it is possible to

BPP
PROFESSIONAL EDUCATION

discern some potential for synergy, in agriculture and retailing, for instance. However, the organisation is committed to managing a very wide range of technologies and markets and it may be that its lacklustre financial performance is linked to a lack of specialist knowledge among its senior managers. The policy of moving managers from division to division, while generally good for their personal development may   actually hamper the progress of the more specialised operations.

It is generally considered that conglomerate diversification only adds value when the expertise of the corporate headquarters is such that its allocation of capital is more effective than would be achieved by a normally efficient capital market. Whether this is the case with United Products must be subject to some doubt. The less profitable divisions are protected from the disciplines of the market by the corporate HQ, while those with good prospects may find themselves starved of funds.

UP clearly displays one disadvantage of the divisional form. There is a tendency for the divisions to be more bureaucratic than they would be as independent organisations in order to service the demands of the corporate HQ's control procedures. UP takes this to an extreme, with monthly reports and frequent functional inspections. The probable effect of this is to stifle the creativity and sense of ownership that flow from greater autonomy. This is most likely to be visible in the divisions that operate in complex, unstable environments, such as film-making, publishing and fashion retailing. A side effect is the absorption of an excessive degree of divisional revenue in management charges for HQ and in the divisional bureaucracies themselves.

Another problem of divisionalisation was referred to by Mintzberg as the pull to balkanise. This is the natural desire of the division heads for independence from central control. In an organisation like UP, with its rather bureaucratic approach, this might take the form conforming to the letter of the rules but manipulating activities and finances. So long as the reporting parameters fall within set limits, it may be possible to conceal unauthorised ventures for a long time, possibly with unfortunate consequences.

A final comment might be made about the mixture of divisional types: there are both product divisions and geographical divisions. This might be a sensible response to UP's geographical range and variety of products. On the other hand it might be a source of confusion and conflict between geographical and product based managers for control of particular operations. This will be particularly apparent when new markets are entered. The problem may be exacerbated by the management structures put in place for the various joint ventures. Overall, the potential for complexity and confusion is significant.

Part (b)

> **Tutorial note**. The idea of virtuality has become very fashionable and people tend to use the term rather loosely. The definition we give is academically correct. Be sure that you do not confuse the virtual organisation with *Handy's* concept of the **shamrock organisation**, which is merely an organisation that makes extensive use of self-employed and temporary staff in order to be able to control its labour costs in times of economic slowdown.

The idea of a virtual organization or cybernetic corporation has attracted considerable attention as the usefulness of IT for communication and control has been exploited. The essence of the virtual organization is the electronic linking of spatially dispersed components.

Such an organization is a temporary or permanent collection of geographically dispersed individuals, groups, organizational units (which may or may not belong to the same organization), or entire organizations that depend on electronic linking in order to complete the production process.

However, an organization is not a virtual organization merely because it uses IT extensively and has multiple locations. Many organisations fall into that category.

Also, organisations that make extensive use of temporary and self-employed labour are not necessarily virtual organisations because of that, though they may   have some virtual characteristics.

UP almost certainly uses extensive IT systems for its internal communications. It would be surprising if it did not have an internal e mail system and it may well have a corporate intranet. However, it clearly has activities that are very real as opposed to virtual, such as its agricultural, extractive, manufacturing and retailing operations.

Of the activities we are told about, electronic design is perhaps the one most suited to the virtual approach. It may be possible for design engineers to work in isolation, using computer aided design equipment and communicating by e mail. However, where the design work requires a team effort, co-ordination may become a problem.

Publishing may also be a candidate, depending on the nature of what is published. Authors of books are likely to work alone, and editors may be able to do the same, as may their assistants and other specialists such as proof readers and indexers. The transmission of entire texts by electronic means is quite feasible and some specialist books are published by being printed on demand from computer memory.

10   FLEET WATER SERVICES LTD

Part (a)

Project management

Project management is directed at an end. It is not directed at maintaining or improving a continuous activity. It thus has a limited objective within a limited time span. All projects involve, according to Dennis Lock, the 'projection of ideas and activities into new endeavours. No project can ever be exactly the same as anything which has gone before.' The steps and tasks leading to completion can never be described accurately in advance. Therefore, according to Lock, 'the job of project management is to foresee as many dangers as possible, and to plan, organise and control activities so that they are avoided.'

There are therefore some special management problems.

(1)   The work is carried out by a team of people usually assembled for one project, who must be able to communicate effectively and immediately with each other.

(2)   There can be many novel *expected* problems, each one of which should be resolved by careful design and planning prior to commencement of work.

(3)   There can be many novel *unexpected* problems, particularly with a project working at the limits of existing and new technologies. There should be mechanisms within the project to enable these problems to be resolved during the time span of the project without detriment to the objective, the cost or the time span.

(4)   There is normally no benefit until the work is finished. The 'lead in' time to this can cause a strain on the eventual recipient who feels deprived until the benefit is achieved (even though in many cases it is a major improvement on existing activities) and who is also faced with increasing expenditure for no immediate benefit.

(5)   Contributions made by specialists are of differing importance at each stage. Assembling a team working towards the one objective is made difficult due to the tendency of specialists to regard their contribution as always being more important than other people's and not understanding the inter-relationship between their various specialities in the context of the project.

(6)   If the project involves several parties with different interests in the outcome, there might be disputes between them.

Part (b)

Project management techniques

Objectives of project management

(1)   *Defining the project*. The project has a task which it must achieve. A technique for making this clear is the specification prepared by or with the client; constantly changing client specifications can increase the cost of the project and lead to its failure. This defines the scope of the project.

(2)   *Quality* (in the sense of conformance to client specifications, and any appropriate safeguards). The result of the project should achieve what it is supposed to do. Some information systems methodologies have a series of steps which specifically relate to ones which have gone before, right back to the specification.

To ensure the right level of quality is achieved, a systems project will require specific documentation to ensure there have been no short cuts taken. Tests should be carried out and fully documented. For greatest benefit, the quality controls over the project should relate to BS EN ISO 9000. This will also give additional assurance to the client.

(3) *Budget and timescale* can be dealt with together. In order to plan the project effectively, a number of techniques are used. *Work breakdown structure* is an approach which determines the tasks needed to complete the project, which are then broken down into sub-tasks. These can then by mapped on Gantt charts, or even on critical path networks, to find the optimal allocation of resources to activities. Some activities can be crashed or shortened by throwing more resources at them; of course playing around with the critical path in this way might have the effect of increasing the cost of the project. Other activities might be less urgent, depending on the critical path. Estimating the timescale is quite important; for many commercial contracts there are penalties for late delivery.

Some of the cost aspects relate to the work breakdown structure, in that costs can be ascribed to the resources used by each activity. Generally speaking, estimates are prepared, based on the work breakdown structure. A standard costing system might be relevant here.

A further issue to be considered is that of *risk*. There is the risk that the project will be late or over budget. This can be managed by ensuring that the specification is as accurate as possible. Effective project management should minimise the risk. Insurance might compensate for some of the immediate financial problems.

In other cases, a project may have to be over-specified with fail-safe mechanisms. In other cases risks can be dealt with by means of contingency plans. Some firms have back-up computer systems if an application is judged to be critical.

11 SIMON CLARK

Part (a)

> **Tutorial note**. This is a very easy question if you have studied your BPP Text conscientiously, since the Examiner's marking scheme and suggested solution follow closely the relevant paragraph in Chapter 11. However, as always, knowing the theory is not enough; it must be related to the setting, as we relate it in our answer below.
>
> Also, be aware that after his suggested solution, the Examiner inserted a note saying that candidates who used Lewin's models to approach this question would be awarded appropriate marks so long as they demonstrated the pressures and influences on Simon Clark and integrated their answers with the case scenario.
>
> The marking scheme for this question is based on four possible approaches to managing conflict. We include a fifth, integration/collaboration for completeness. This is covered in the Study Text.

Simon has a range of possible responses to his problem of potential conflict with his staff.

Some essentially trivial problems blow over without particular management effort. This type of problem can be ignored. If Simon feels that this is the case here, he can effectively deny that a problem exists and withdraw from considering it further. However, the proposed changes would require very important changes to working practices at the college and conditions of service and the staff are 'most unhappy'. It seems unlikely that denial and withdrawal would be a satisfactory response, since teaching as an occupation is particularly demanding of individual motivation.

A more active policy would be to suppress the problem by smoothing over any overt disputes, if possible, in order to preserve working relationships. This approach is unlikely to produce the changes evidently required at the College, so Simon may have to combine it with a certain amount of coercion, imposing necessary changes unilaterally. This is a recipe for continuing dispute and the lingering hostility of 'win-lose' situations. The effect on motivation is likely to be even more dire than a policy of denial and withdrawal. Indeed, the teaching staff may retaliate by withdrawing their co-operation and working to rule.

A more positive approach for Simon to take would involve a willingness to make compromises *via* a process of bargaining, negotiation and conciliation. It is likely that there is some room for manoeuvre in the matter of weekend working, perhaps by offering time off *in lieu*. The staff are no doubt well aware of the potential threat to their interests from the private college and may be prepared to adjust their initial position.

This approach may, perhaps, be extended into a more sophisticated process of integration and collaboration, in which a continuing dialogue can establish both common ground and general agreement as to what is necessary for the achievement of the overall task. To achieve this, Simon must overcome his frustration and attempt to bring the staff into full participation in the changes that affect them.

Part (b)

Tutorial note. Generating support is an important aspect of change management generally. This question is about one department in quite a small organization, so more complex change management strategies, such as the Gemini 4Rs and the Systems Intervention Strategy are probably over complex. We are concerned here with management techniques that would be useful to the head of a single department in such an organization.

This is essentially a problem of practical leadership. Some aspects of the solution, such as providing resources, are easy both to specify and to implement. Other, less concrete, measures related to human behaviour, such as the importance of communication are less easy to describe and, indeed, to perform. Do not shy away from these less material things and do cover them in as precise a way as you can. It is very easy to be vague and woolly about such matters. Try to be definite. For example, don't just say 'communicate' say 'hold a meeting' as well.

It seems likely from the staff's initial reaction to Simon's proposals that he has not given sufficient thought to enlisting their support. This may reflect his managerial technique, or lack of it. If he is to succeed with his plan to change the way things are done, he will have to improve the way he deals with his staff in both material and intangible ways.

The highest priority is to improve his overall relations with the staff. He must make more effective communication a continuing personal target in order to improve motivation and mutual understanding. He must ensure that the staff see him as approachable and sympathetic to their concerns, within the limitations set by reality.

Simon Clark should ensure that his staff understand that his proposals are a response to a serious commercial threat that affects them all and not an arbitrary decision. He should point out the potential effects upon them of failing to respond to the commercial competition and the opportunities and rewards that success will bring. He should encourage the staff to think for themselves about the situation the college is in, invite them to debate it among themselves and make alternative proposals if they can. Such participation, even if it does not produce any feasible new ideas, will make whatever solution is eventually decided upon more acceptable.

However, Simon must not abdicate responsibility. It is his role to make the final decision and to implement it. There are several measures he can take to promote acceptance of change.

He may be able to enlist the support of more senior staff who have the respect of their peers as change agents. Their role would be to lend their credibility to the new arrangements, to assist with its planning and implementation and to provide practical day-to-day leadership in the context of change.

He should support positive responses to change with praise and reward and deal firmly with negative behaviour such as murmuring and absenteeism.

The need for change has been forced upon the College and the Department and it may be that time and resources are limited. However, Simon's aim should be to introduce change at a measured pace and avoid the rush and panic that is sure to upset the staff and provoke hostility.

Similarly, he should make a case for the provision of resources to the change process, so that for instance, some promotions might result, or working conditions be improved. Quite small enhancements such as decorating the staff common room or providing a new photocopier would help to present the change in a positive light.

12   **RUS PLC**

Part (a)

Relevance of TQM

TQM is relevant to both the previous and the new strategy. It is a way of managing a business to achieve continually improving performance.

TQM is more than just a set of techniques. Developed in manufacturing industry, it is an approach to dealing with production, which involves getting things right first time and achieving zero defects. It tries to involve the customer's needs in the very process of production. This is obviously relevant to service industries, with the proviso that bad service cannot be inspected and scrapped after it is delivered: services are generally consumed as they are produced. As much of the success in a service industry depends on repeat business, getting things right first time (as that is, indeed, the only time) must be a priority.

TQM also involves a detailed analysis of the process of production. An aspect of TQM is *reduction in variation*. Restaurant service should be predictable; food quality must be consistently good, not outstanding one day and mediocre the next, otherwise the hotel will get a reputation for being unreliable.

The culture of TQM also must be considered. Employees must be encouraged to come forward with suggestions, and they must be engaged in the process of improving service. An almost obsessional interest in service quality should be encouraged.

There is no reason why these considerations should not apply to the family and medium-priced business accommodation as well as to the hotel's new strategy. However, as the new guests will be paying more, their expectations will be so much more exacting than before. The design quality of the service (what these new customers actually want) is paramount, and conformance quality (what is actually given) must be faultless.

Part (b)

Financial and organisational implications

RUS is chasing a different market, targeting high spending customers whose requirements will be different. Investment in buildings and fixtures includes:

(i)   decoration;
(ii)   changes to room sizes (eg conversion of pairs of single rooms into suites);
(iii)   more luxurious furnishings;
(iv)   perhaps expanded restaurant and kitchen facilities;
(v)   swimming pool, gymnasium etc;
(vi)   more opulent spaces;
(vii)   enhancing the hotel's grounds and gardens;
(viii) carparking facilities;

Other expenditure will arise from:

(i)   more staff, to provide the service required;
(ii)   more training;
(iii)   the greater variety of food offered to guests (hence kitchen costs will rise);
(iv)   advertising to reach the target segment.

There will be few customers but they will be paying more.

Organisationally, the increased numbers in staff must be given more training, and existing staff will have to learn to cater differently for the new customers. Furthermore, there is unlikely to be the same deployment of staff as before, catering for family and business customers at different times. More effort will need to be spent on management and marketing. Quality circles could be introduced.

Part (c)

The management accountant's contribution to the new strategy is as follows.

(i)   To provide cost and revenue information in the initial research and planning phase, and to forecast future income and expenditure.

(ii)   To cost any improvements to buildings and furnishings.

(iii)   To suggest an appropriate pricing policy.

(iv)   To raise external finance (eg from the bank) if substantial capital investment is needed and borrowing is necessary.

(v)   To draw up tactical plans and budgets for the changeover.

(vii)   To set up and operate new management accounting systems to monitor and control the hotel's performance.

(viii)   To suggest appropriate non-financial performance measures, in particular with relation to quality of service.

(ix)   To consider if the hotel's new clients will need services such as travellers cheques encashment etc, if they are from overseas.

(x)   To provide regular and suitable management information.

13   PERSONNEL MANAGEMENT

To: Managing Director
From: A Newbodd

Date: X/X/20XX

POLICIES AND PROCEDURES FOR RECRUITMENT AND SELECTION

Contents

1.   Introduction
2.   Summary of findings
3.   Current personnel performance
4.   Suggested recruitment and selection policy
5.   The case for implementation

1.   INTRODUCTION

1.1   This report has been written in response to the company's current personnel performance.

1.2   It assesses the current situation and makes some suggestions for improving it.

2.   EXECUTIVE SUMMARY OF FINDINGS

2.1   There is currently no personnel policy worth speaking of. This situation is costly in the long term, and strategically unwise in the long term.

2.2   In order to benefit from the investment in personnel, the company should do three things.

- Appoint a personnel manager
- Institute a formal policy and procedures for recruitment
- Implement review of current staff

Such proposals are financially justified.

3.   CURRENT PERSONNEL PERFORMANCE

3.1   *Staff profile*

There is a mixture of staff. High technology skills are relatively rare, and it takes a while to train them on the company's projects. Staff display different levels of competence.

3.2   The high levels of labour turnover are disruptive, especially if a leaver occupies an important position in a project. Newcomers have to be trained, which takes up time which could be better spent working. The high turnover does not encourage a sense of commitment, and has had an adverse effect on morale.

3.3   There is also resentment, as the better performing staff feel they are carrying others who are less productive.

4.   SUGGESTED RECRUITMENT AND SELECTION POLICY

4.1   A series of objectives should be defined.

- A reduced rate of staff turnover

- The establishment of proper job descriptions according to the company's requirements
- The recruitment of suitable personnel

4.2 A management structure should be put in place as, inevitably, there will be a lot of work to do.

- A personnel department should be set up under the control of an experience personnel manager. The personnel manager should be given a brief.

- Suitable information systems should be provided to collate knowledge of staff, perhaps in an employee database.

4.3 The personnel manager should be given the following brief.

- Assess formally the type of jobs the company offers.

- Assess the skills needed to fill those jobs.

- Draw up a profile of the sort of people the company is looking for in each of the various capacities. This will include professional expertise, and personality.

- Draw up guidelines for employee development.

- Draw up guidelines for the use of recruitment consultants and outside agencies.

- Determine a selection method that is best needed for the diversity of skills the company requires, to give a systematic and objective case for employing a particular candidate.

- Design application forms that properly draw out the biographical information from candidates.

- Assess reasons (eg through exit interviews) for the current rate of staff turnover.

4.4 It is recommended that the method of selection should be more scientific than currently to date. Interviews are generally a poor predictor of performance in a particular job, so *aptitude tests* and *personality* profiles should be used to ensure both the candidate's suitability and that the person will fit into the group.

4.5 The personnel manager should seek actively to promote the company in the relevant job markets, through advertising, and the development of recruitment documentation.

5. *THE CASE FOR IMPLEMENTATION*

5.1 Clearly introducing such a policy would mean incurring costs, in financial terms, and also a reduction in the autonomy which perhaps some managers have enjoyed in recruiting staff.

5.2 However, a cost benefit analysis which looked at the wider issues would take the following into account.

1 *Costs of new system*

- Salary of a personnel manager and perhaps an assistant at some stage.
- Cost of information technology to support the new personnel function.

2 *Against these costs must be set the costs of doing nothing*

- *Staff turnover:* quantifiable costs. The cost of recruiting a new member of staff is sometimes equivalent to a quarter of their annual salary if recruitment consultants are used. Even a small reduction in staff turnover caused by this policy would probably justify pay for the salary of the personnel manager.

- *Staff turnover:* non-quantifiable costs means disruptions to projects and production, time lost in training, and managerial time lost in advertising and recruiting for new staff. In short this results in lost productivity and output.

- *Boundary management.* The company is not in a position to promise a standard of performance quality with such a rapidly changing staff.

14   COXFORD DOORS

> **Tutorial note**. This rather unrealistic scenario turns the situation in the typical UK family run business on its head: one would normally find such a business falling behind because its autocratic management style and **power culture** were unsuited to a rapidly changing environment. Nevertheless, this question is a gift to the reasonably well prepared candidate. It is *almost* an invitation to write down all you know about participation and change management. Almost - but not quite: you must *always* relate your answer to the scenario!

Part (a)

This company seems to have operated more like a soviet than a business. No doubt there has been much job-satisfaction, but the company's ability to compete and add value has deteriorated.

A participatory style of management has been shown in many studies to enhance personal **motivation** and **commitment** to the organisation's mission. This occurs via the process of **internalisation**, whereby the members of the workforce adopt the corporate goal as their personal goal. This can lead to better industrial relations, higher quality and better service. However, there is no conclusive evidence that such an approach necessarily leads to improved overall performance. This is borne out by the situation at Coxford Doors.

Andrew Smith's style of management is likely to bring the focus that has been missing in the past. He will no doubt speed up the decision making process (probably by making most decisions himself) plan effectively and issue clear instructions. Confusion and delay should be reduced and control enhanced. This will improve the business's responsiveness and ability to satisfy customers.

However, Andrew Smith is likely to encounter resistance from a work force used to proceeding according to its own ideas of what is appropriate. Morale and loyalty are both likely to suffer from the loss of autonomy. There is likely to be a lack of co-operation and, possibly, active resistance to the new order. The commercial position might deteriorate further as a result.

Even if there is acceptance that the trading position demands change it is unlikely to be wholehearted. A strong undercurrent of resentment may be created, resurfacing at some time in the future, perhaps when the commercial situation has improved.

Part (b)

> **Tutorial note**. We use the Lewin/White model of the change process in our answer to this part of the question. Be aware that the **systems intervention strategy** would be just as appropriate.

Any significant change in the workplace is likely to provoke a mixture of reactions including resigned acceptance, hostility and outright opposition. Many people are simply naturally averse to change of any kind, being happiest with what they know and understand. With a change of the kind proposed here, many workpeople will lose a degree of independence in their working practices and are likely to object. The danger is that Andrew Smith's gathering up of the reins will provoke serious disruption perhaps extending to a strike.

The theoretical models proposed for the management of change offer no magical solutions to the problems of human behaviour. They simply provide a rational framework within which reason, diplomacy, tact and communication skills may be deployed to the best advantage. The general idea is to obtain agreement about the **need** for change and to manage it in as harmonious a manner as possible.

Lewin and White's model divides the change process into three stages: **unfreeze, change, refreeze**.

Unfreeze is the most difficult stage of the process. The aim is to **sell** both the need for change and the proposed changes themselves. Individuals and groups must be provided with **motives** for changing their attitudes, systems and behaviour. If the need for change is immediate, clear and perceived to be associated with the survival of the individual or group (for example change in reaction to an organisation crisis), the unfreezing process will be eased. Andrew Smith should use the decline in financial performance to illustrate the necessity for change at Coxford Doors, since it seems likely that without change, the organisation is doomed to ultimate failure. This may involve takeover or winding-up but is certain to be more inimical to the interests of the workforce than any possible change to working practices.

Routine changes are harder to sell than **transformational** ones if they are perceived to be unimportant and not survival-based.

Culture change is perhaps hardest of all, especially if it involves basic assumptions. This is certainly the case at Coxford Doors. However, the necessary precondition for change are in place. Andrew Smith is himself an **outsider**, prepared to challenge and expose, in a visible way, the existing behaviour pattern; his appointment will act as a **trigger**; and **alterations to the power structure** will be an inherent part of his actions.

The unfreeze stage is likely to include extensive **communication** and **consultation processes**, but the objective must be kept in sight; concern for proper treatment of employees must not be allowed to subvert the overall aim.

Change is the second stage of the process and is mainly concerned with introducing the new, desirable behaviours and approaches. This will involve retraining and practice to build up familiarity and experience. Individuals must be encouraged to take ownership of the new ways of doing things. For this to happen they must be shown to work.

Refreeze is the final stage, involving consolidation and reinforcement of the new behaviour. Positive or negative reinforcement may be used, with praise, reward and sanctions applied as necessary.

It will be important for Andrew Smith to retain **control of the process** at all times, since the company's history of participative management will tend to undermine his move towards a firmer style. He must make it clear from the outset that change must take place, while remaining flexible on the detail and the style of its introduction. It would be advisable to aim for an intermediate style of management, in which the workforce retain a voice. Operational control must be improved, but it should not be necessary to move to a completely autocratic way of doing things.

15   NATIONAL FREIGHT DISTRIBUTION COMPANY

To: The Directors, AB plc
From: A Consultancy
Date: 30 March 20X1
Subject: Configuration options for the new computer systems

Terms of reference and executive summary

Further to your letter of instruction of 28 January 20X1, we were asked to produce a report for the half year board meeting specifying the reasons for and against using different computer systems. The current manual system was documented, and a number of options discussed with management. This report summarises the results.

The two options being actively considered are the following.

(a)   A central mainframe with terminals at each depot (the 'centralised system').

(b)   Minicomputers such as IBM AS/400s at each regional depot connected together over a network (the 'distributed system').

The second option, using a network of minicomputers, is better suited to the organisation's requirements. We recommend that this option be actively considered. Further consideration should be given to financing methods and we will be happy to advise on this if required.

Centralised system

This will involve setting up a room at head office or a central location in which to run the mainframe-based system. This room will have to have good environmental control, together with security. In addition you should consider establishing a back-up computer facility which could be used in the advent of a breakdown or catastrophe on the main machine.

The centralised system will be linked to the depots by leased telephone links. These will be expensive to run, but in the case of the larger depots will provide voice facilities, allowing you to save on the current voice phone charges.

The system will require specialised staff to run it. This will impose a new department on the organisation, and will result in an additional headcount of approximately fifteen. There will be a small loss of jobs at the regional level.

The centralised system will facilitate the keeping of all the figures up to date, and will allow for economic production, in batches, of the printouts which will come off the system. Data would be entered at the depots and reports produced either at the depots or at the head office computer.

Advantages of the centralised system include:

(a)   having a central up-to-date set of data which will be accessible by all depots;

(b)   maintaining a single set of data, which will eliminate inconsistencies in data used for different purposes;

(c)   providing the head office with the centralised control which the current system lacks, as freight can be tracked from one depot to another;

(d)   setting up of a centralised and specialised DP team with expert knowledge focused in one department.

The disadvantages, however, include:

(a)   capital costs. The back-up system and the high cost of the main computer are both major factors;

(b)   operating costs, for example, high telecommunications costs;

(c)   the problem of being entirely dependent on one machine. Computers do fail, and the impact on the business of the central machine failing would be great.

Distributed system

This would involve installing a minicomputer at each region, and another at the head office. Although space would have to be found for each they can be installed and run in standard office environments. Some staff would have to be trained at each site to work the machines, but staff could back up different regions in the event of others being off on leave or ill, which would largely do away with the need for specialist staff.

Advantages of this approach would include:

(a)   keeping the responsibility for the system with the regions. This would encourage the regions to adopt the computers and would also encourage them to keep the data accurate;

(b)   in the event of any single machine failing it would be reasonably easy to acquire another on a short-term basis, and it would be able to be installed with a minimum of work;

(c)   lower communication costs, as most line usage will be within individual regions;

(d)   speed of processing is improved and local priorities can be better satisfied.

The disadvantages of this approach would include:

(a)   control would require on-going monitoring and effort. A supervisor at each region would have to be designated as the person responsible for ensuring procedures were adhered to by whoever was actually running the computers.

(b)   installation of, and training on, new versions of software would take more time and cost more. In addition, the logistics of installing later releases of software would require careful monitoring;

(c)   capital costs, involving acquisition of six minicomputers, will be high, although with phased regional implementation this can be spread more easily than a single mainframe purchase;

(d)   operating costs, particularly staff costs, will be high as it will be necessary to maintain a certain level of expertise at each regional office, resulting in some duplication;

(e)   it is not clear how this solution would embrace the individual depots, and tracking freight could be problematic.

16   NADIR PRODUCTS: INDICATORS

> **Tutorial note**. You may suppose that performance measurement is a mainstream management accounting topic and be surprised to see it in a strategy paper. First, don't forget that the professionally qualified accountant should be able to bring significant breadth of knowledge to bear. Real life problems do not fall neatly into separate, syllabus relevant categories. Second, remember that **control** is an important aspect of strategic management and control implies measurement. The **balanced scorecard** is an obvious solution to the second part of the question requirement but if you are able to discuss some other suitable scheme, perhaps from experience, do not hesitate to do so. Markers are always ready to give credit for practical solutions from real life.

There are two main categories of problem connected with restricting performance measurement to consideration of turnover and profit.

- Concentration on these two measures can actually be counter-productive and encourage **dysfunctional decision making**.

- There are many **other aspects of business activity** that are critical to the continued health and success of the organisation and that should be monitored.

While both turnover and profit are clearly important aspects of performance measurement, senior managers must be aware that both are subject to manipulation. A **trade-off** between the two can often be achieved, as when margin is sacrificed by discounting to increase volume or promotion budgets are cut to boost profitability. The latter example is also an instance of the way short-term profitability can be increased by cost cutting that actually prejudices longer-term results. Similar **tensions between short-term and long-term results** may be observed when considering the costs of R&D, training, market research and equipment upgrades.

Turnover and profit are respectively the top and bottom lines of the profit statement. The lines in between are not merely costs: they represent the varied activities that any business must undertake, and each activity has two aspects: it represents a **cost** and it **adds value** to output. Each activity must be managed so that the value it adds is greater than its cost: this means that a wide range of measures of performance is required. Some of these will be of departmental importance only, but some will be strategic in nature.

Kaplan and Norton suggested that attempting to run a business by reference to a single performance measure such as profit was like trying to fly an aircraft by reference to a single instrument. They proposed the adoption of a **balanced scorecard** that provided information on four strategically vital perspectives.

- Customer concerns
- Financial performance
- Internal processes
- Innovation and learning

Effective performance from the **customer perspective** may be assessed by measures such as failure rates for products, delivery times, reliability of service and changes in market share.

Internal processes should all create value, though some, such as legal compliance requirements are more concerned with avoiding the long-term *destruction* of value through infringements. Other internal processes may have significant impact on customer satisfaction. These include order handling, service staff training and quality procedures. Performance measures must relate to staff behaviour and proficiency; they may be particularly difficult to establish.

The internal process perspective may also include consideration of **core competences** where these are process based.

The **innovation and learning perspective** considers the organisation's potential to achieve **future success**. This is another area in which performance measures are difficult to design. Possible indicators include the percentage of revenue generated by products introduced during the last three years and the average time taken to bring a new product to market.

The **financial perspective** shows how the business appears to shareholders. Performance measures are well-established here and include ROE, EPS, dividend cover and capital growth as measured by market valuation. This perspective is the acid test of performance. Successful innovation and learning and efficient internal processes are only useful if they are translated into customer satisfaction; similarly, success with customers is only worthwhile if it leads to satisfactory financial performance.

17 GLOBALISATION

Theodore Levitt first put forward the term 'globalisation' in 1983. The debate as to whether such a thing as a **global company** exists goes on, but there is certainly ancedotal evidence that world markets are converging. If a **definition** of **globalisation** is accepted as being:

'*the process by which the world becomes more homogeneous with regard to the products and services demanded*'

then the forces driving its development are as follows.

- Developments in **global telecommunications** using satellite broadcasting are helping to establish English as the international language for interpersonal and business communications.

- Global telecommunications are helping to establish **global brands** that are killing off local brands in certain product categories. The global dominance of Kodak and Fuji in the 35mm film market is an example.

- The emergence of a **global consumer**, particularly amongst young people, is a reality exploited by many multinationals such as Nike and Reebok, who have developed both a global product range and a global brand and image, targeted at a global consumer.

- **Multinational** car companies (GM and Ford) are exploiting developments in transportation systems to source components for their assembly plants in the US and Europe from suppliers all over the world. This is improving the wealth creating (value adding) activities of the developing world, and creating consumers with discretionary money to spend in places where previously no spare money existed.

- Developments in **transportation systems**, particularly air transport, have brought global travel within the reach of increasing numbers of people. Increased travel brings increased demand for goods to be available in places visited by the travellers.

- Increasing **affluence** of consumers, as the global economy grows due to the relaxation of trade barriers through agreements negotiated by WTO and the actions of the multinational companies, encourages spending on travel. This fuels the need for more homogeneous products and services. For instance, airports around the world are beginning to look the same, with similar check-in and baggage processing facilities, retail outlets, and styled restaurants offering food and refreshments from around the world. This reflects the convergence of consumer needs.

- The **convergence of consumer needs** on a global scale re-defines concepts of **economies of scale** and the **competitive** and **absolute advantages** these can generate. The car companies, led by Ford with its Mondeo, are designing and building cars with a global consumer in mind.

- The acquisition and merger activities of companies to ensure profit growth contributes significantly to the process of globalisation, as management teams are forced to abandon their **ethnocentric** 'comfort zones' and adopt **regiocentric, geocentric or polycentric** approaches to managing increasingly global businesses.

For many companies in an increasing number of industries survival will be dependent upon them taking a **global perspective**. There are many ways to achieve the objective of being a global company with the right way for any particular company being the way which achieves the **objectives** set for globalisation.

18 STANDARDISATION

The factors encouraging and supporting **standardisation** of products are, principally, **economies of scale** in production, **research and development** and **marketing communications**. With standardised products, and a belief that an ethnocentric approach to the markets of the world is appropriate, then standardised marketing plans can be used in all markets.

Standardised marketing communications enable single images to be created, and for some products competitive advantage can be extracted from country of origin effect. With standardised products produced in a number of plants around the world, production can be shared amongst the plants and markets supplied from any or all of the plants to take advantage of prevailing favourable conditions.

The use of satellite broadcasting by advertisers encourages the use of standardised advertising due to the very large footprints of the satellite transmissions. Thus, in the medium term developments in global communications technology could give greater impetus to standardisation. In the recent past Ford have announced that the Mondeo is to be their first 'world car', and historically a number of product such as 35mm film, blank VHS tapes and certain designer goods have become standardised throughout the world.

The circumstances that prevent or hinder standardisation are legion. Differing **usage conditions** for example due to differing climates make standardisation of some products difficult. Differences in **taste, income and level of sophistication** will also impact on standardisation.

Intervention by government in the form of tariffs and non-tariff barriers together with pressure from **regulatory bodies** can prevent a standardisation strategy being effective. Markets will vary dramatically in their **development cycles**, and correspondingly, products will be at a different stage of their life cycles in differing markets. For instance, bicycles are leisure products in the developed world but vital transport products in the developing world. This demonstrates that the global standardisation of bicycles will be difficult, but regional standardisation may be practical.

Technology differences will also hinder standardisation. Computer users in the developed world are more likely to operate with the latest versions of micro processors in their PC's. Users in the developing world will invariably use the older technology. It is in the interests of both the micro processor manufacturers and the PC manufacturers to maintain these differentials, in order to re-coup the investments in the respective technologies.

The standardisation of **global brands** is a far more frequently encountered phenomenon with many brands being targeted at the emerging **world youth culture**, for instance Nike and Reebok. These companies appear to be exploiting the global communication of sport and the desire of young people world-wide to be associated with the brands worn by their sporting heroes.

19 GLOBAL INDUSTRIES

Part (a)

> **Tutorial note.** The question asks for an answer in the form of a personalised report. Do not get carried away with the format of your answer. At this level there are very few marks for it.

Answer plan

Part (a)

Report format

Current indicator of failure

Strategic management

   Failure of customisation

   Competitor – economies of scale – prices?

   Value of differential product?

   Niche or compete on price

Operations

   Costs especially R&D and admin

   Rise in stock and WIP

Achievement of competitor

Part (b)

Evaluating strategy

Suitability – mission?

   PV of costs and benefits

   Effect on portfolio

  Feasibility

Financial analysis

Acceptability

  Risk – minimal?

  Return – financial analysis

  Stakeholder expectations

    Employees

    Governments (nb nuclear and rail industries)

Part (c)

Goold & Campbell – financial controller

Chief executive autonomy – motivation - training

Performance measures

Coordination – synergy – value system links

Economies of scale – purchasing materials

  - marketing – brand economies and presence

Dysfunctional effects of financial performance measures eg ROI

Strategic guidelines

Rationalisation of kitchen equipment subsidiary

  structure and marketing

Other: ethics; treasury; investment

Answer

Part (a)

To: Board Members, Global Industries plc
From: Head of Strategic Operations
Date: 1 December 2001

Kitchen Appliance Subsidiary

Scope of the report: Analysis of the problems faced by the kitchen appliance subsidiary

Introduction

1.1   The kitchen appliance subsidiary (KAS) has suffered falling sales and profits in its global operations for the last three years and the downward trend is forecast to continue next year. This is despite increases in promotional expenditure of about 10% each year. KAS lost £200K in 2000 and a loss of £2.3M is forecast for 2001.

Analysis

1.2   There appear to have been failures of management at both the strategic and operational levels at KAS. The strategy of market customisation has not led to increased turnover. At the same time, there has been a lack of control over manufacturing and costs.

Strategy

1.3   Global turnover has fallen by 12% over three years, at the same time as the major competitor (MC) has increased turnover by 25%. Their strategy is in marked contrast to ours. We have retained separate brand names and manufacturing plants in each of our markets as part of our polycentric strategy. MC have consolidated manufacturing on two sites and market a standardised range under a single brand name. On the face of it, it would seem that theirs is the more appropriate strategy. I do not have any data on selling prices; however, it is safe to assume that MC have reaped economies of scale from their policies, both in manufacturing and in promotion, and are probably the cost leader. I anticipate, therefore, that we will find that their competitive advantage lies at least partly in lower prices.

1.4   There are two possibilities to consider here.

    1.4.1   The market for differentiated products exists in each of our markets, but is smaller and more demanding than we had anticipated. If this is the case, we may only be able to pursue our present policy by reducing the scale of our operations still further and moving upmarket.

1.4.2 Kitchen appliances have become commodities, with no significant market for differentiation at all. If this is the case, we may choose to compete on price and promotion or to withdraw completely.

Operations

1.5 There appears to be poor cost control at KAS. While I accept that there was a conscious decision to increase spending on promotion, I am concerned about the increases in R&D and administrative costs. I accept that R&D, if focused and controlled, is as important in lean times as in good, but I feel an actual increase in R&D spending is inappropriate.

1.6 Stock rose from 39 days in 1998 to 50 days in 1999 and then to 58 days in 2000. Again, I accept that if turnover slumps, some increase in stock is to be expected. However, it should not be allowed to go on accumulating for two years. There has clearly been insufficient attempt to control output. This is borne out by the 14% increase in WIP since 1998 and the fall in turnover per person from £17462 in 1998 to £16000 in 2000. I am alarmed to observe that stock is actually forecast to *increase* to 81 days in 2001, more than double the level in 1998.

Comparison with MC

1.7 At the same time as KAS has been faltering, MC has increased turnover by 39% and operating profit by 163%, WIP has fallen in absolute terms while stock has fallen from 39 days to 31, and turnover per person has increased from £22500 to £25000.

Conclusion

1.8 Our product market strategy for KAS has been proven unsatisfactory. While improvements in operational management may enable us to contain our short-term losses, for the longer term we must reassess our strategy of differentiation. It may be that we must either accept a market niche or compete on price.

Angus Cairncross

Part (b)

> **Tutorial note.** The most important thing about answering this question is to do what it tells you and **relate your discussion to Global Industries' kitchen appliance subsidiary**.
>
> The Examiner's suggested solution to this question was a largely unstructured sequence of short discussion paragraphs. We conclude that he will regard such an approach as satisfactory in answering a question like this. We think it is possible to add value by answering in terms of the appropriate part of the rational model: strategy evaluation and selection.

Disposal of a subsidiary is an important strategy option and should be subject to the same assessment for suitability, feasibility and acceptability applied to other possible courses of action.

Suitability

A strategy is suitable if it supports the organisation's mission and overall strategic stance. Global Industries plc is a highly diversified conglomerate operating internationally in a wide range of markets. We are not told how it has defined its mission, if at all, but it seems that it would be difficult to identify a type of business that was unsuitable for Global Industries plc to undertake. Probably, the only real criterion for suitability in this sense is that the component parts of the organisation should achieve an acceptable return on investment over the long term.

It would be appropriate therefore to carry out a full financial analysis of the disposal in terms of the present value of the **relevant costs and benefits** involved.

Another aspect of suitability is the extent to which the strategy supports other strategic activities. A strategy's suitability is enhanced if it enhances the balance of the organisation's portfolio of activities, for instance by selling into the same markets or complementing existing products. In the case of this disposal, Global Industries plc should be sure that it will not be left with a rump of associated activities that will wither without the presence of the kitchen appliance subsidiary. This seems unlikely from the information we are given, however.

Feasibility

Feasibility is usually assessed in financial terms, so the analysis mentioned above would cover this.

Acceptability

Johnson and Scholes say that acceptability may be assessed in terms of **risk**, **return** and **stakeholder reactions**. Return will be dealt with by financial analysis. Risk may be considered to be minimal given that the strategy involves withdrawal. Stakeholder reactions, however, are a very important consideration. There are two main groups of stakeholders to consider: employees and governments.

Employees will inevitably see the disposal as a threat to their employment. This will probably lead at least to a bad press and possibly to strikes and more violent unrest. There will be an interaction with the response of governments, who will be equally concerned about the possible economic impact of the disposal. As Global Industries plc operates in the nuclear power, railway and defence industries, its relations with governments are particularly important since they are either the major customers in those markets or have major influence over them.

Part (c)

> **Tutorial note.** In the main part of our answer we cover much the same ground as the Examiner's own suggested solution. However, we do not reach the same conclusion as he does about the best role for the Global Products plc headquarters. He suggested that the HQ could act as a provider of optional corporate services. You should understand that **there is unlikely to be a single correct answer** to any question in this paper and that a large part of what you must be able to do is to argue sensibly from theory and the scenario in order to reach a **reasonable conclusion**. Note that the introduction to the marking scheme for the Pilot Paper says:
>
> 'Scope is given to markers to award marks for alternative approaches to a question, including relevant comment, and where well reasoned conclusions are provided. This is particularly so in case scenario questions where there may be more than one acceptable solution.'

Global Industries plc is highly diversified and its subsidiaries are spread over the world. It is involved in a variety of complex technologies and dynamic markets. It is almost inevitable, therefore, that its approach to strategic management should be that identified by *Goold and Campbell* as **'financial controller'**. This allows the individual businesses to develop their own longer-term plans, requiring only that they produce a proper return on their assets.

This approach has its advantages.

Each operating company can exploit its knowledge of the market fully and rapidly, without the need for regular reference to the global headquarters. Market developments and opportunities can be exploited and tactics tailor-made for local conditions.

The senior managers of each SBU should be **motivated** by their independence and freedom of action, which may have a positive effect on their commitment and efforts.

Devolution of power and responsibility will **provide experience in general and strategic management for the senior managers**. This will provide an element of practical training and also act as a proving-ground, creating a pool of candidates for appointment to more demanding roles. These include the most senior posts in the global organisation and 'trouble-shooting' or 'turn-round' posts in under-performing subsidiaries.

The financial control approach means that the global headquarters can be a **small and therefore inexpensive** organisation, perhaps concentrating on overall group performance and structure through acquisitions and disposals.

Assessment against financial targets is the simplest way of making **performance comparisons** between diverse subsidiaries. Indeed it may be the only practical way of doing so. There may be similar elements that can be compared directly, such as the operation of a road transport fleet, but the core operations of businesses as diverse as the manufacture of refrigerators and the construction of railways cannot really be compared except in terms of financial outcomes.

However, this approach is not perfect. In particular, it makes little attempt to co-ordinate across companies in order to **exploit synergies and value chain** linkages.

One obvious area where performance could be improved is the achievement of **economies of scale**. It is likely that large savings could be made in the purchasing of supplies and raw materials, for instance. This does not mean that all purchasing would have to be done centrally, imposing delays and reducing flexibility. Rather, a small centralised staff could negotiate appropriate discounts with favoured suppliers, on a global or country basis, that individual companies could then exploit. A more sophisticated approach would be the creation of a global computer database of suppliers and terms that could then be rationalised and exploited.

Economies of scale could also be achieved in other functional areas such as marketing, by the rationalisation of brands and in R&D by means of a global review of what was being done and the most efficient means of doing it. There may well be elements of duplication that could be avoided also.

An important disadvantage of financial controls is that they tend to encourage a short-term approach, with possible dysfunctional effects. The tension between the short-term and the long-term is easily seen in the area of **maintenance**, where a cost cutting approach brings an immediate improvement to short-term financial performance, but at the risk of degraded performance or even major failure in the future.

A similar dysfunctional outcome can be seen in investment decisions where ROI is used as the main performance measure, as is common. ROI varies according to two quantities: profit and the value of the investment base. A fall in profit will reduce ROI, but so will a rise in the value of the assets in use. The use of ROI therefore discourages investment, since capital expenditure increases the value of the asset base.

Global Industries plc can overcome these problems by instituting a more comprehensive system of reporting and performance assessment, with regular meetings between SBU and HQ staff.

Where SBUs operate autonomously, a dysfunctional lack of cohesion may arise between them. This is apparent in Global Industries plc's kitchen appliance subsidiary, where the national operating companies have been allowed to go their own way without any overall guidance.

If Global Industries plc is to continue as a multi-national conglomerate, it should almost certainly continue its policy of operational independence for subsidiaries. However, the global HQ must **lay down the rules** by which they operate, providing a strategic framework for them to work within. This means using its privileged access to detailed information to take an overview of the SBUs themselves and the relationships between them.

In the case of the kitchen appliance subsidiary, for instance, this is as much a problem of **structure** as of anything else. There is a clear need for rationalisation of both production and marketing effort, with realignment of brands, standardisation of design and concentration of manufacturing. This would be a major strategic change, but once it has been done, devolved management may recommence.

Other areas in which the corporate HQ should be involved include long term investment plans, corporate ethics and treasury operations. These all form part of the strategic framework for operations. More detailed operational input should be kept to a minimum and should concentrate on detecting and exploiting potential synergistic effects such as economies of scale and value chain linkages.

It is probably inappropriate for the HQ to undertake the provision of services such as marketing on an optional, consultancy basis. Such things can be bought in by the operating companies as they find they need them. This approach eliminates all the problems of overhead absorption and charge-out rates.

Index

490

Note: **Key Terms** and their references are given in **bold**

BPP
PROFESSIONAL EDUCATION

REVIEW FORM & FREE PRIZE DRAW

All original review forms from the entire BPP range, completed with genuine comments, will be entered into a draw on 31 January 2005 and 31 July 2005. The names on the first four forms picked out will be sent a cheque for £50.

Name: _____   **Address:** _____

_____

How have you used this Text? *(Tick one box only)*	**During the past six months do you recall seeing/receiving any of the following?** *(Tick as many boxes as are relevant)*
☐ Home study (book only)	☐ Our advertisement in *ACCA Student Accountant*
☐ On a course: college _____	☐ Our advertisement in *Pass*
☐ With 'correspondence' package	☐ Our advertisement in *PQ*
☐ Other _____	☐ Our brochure with a letter through the post

Why did you decide to purchase this Text?
(Tick one box only)

Which (if any) aspects of our advertising do you find useful?
(Tick as many boxes as are relevant)

☐ Have used complementary Kit	☐ Prices and publication dates of new editions
☐ Have used BPP Texts in the past	☐ Information on Text content
☐ Recommendation by friend/colleague	☐ Facility to order books off-the-page
☐ Recommendation by a lecturer at college	☐ None of the above
☐ Saw advertising	
☐ Other _____	

Which BPP products have you used?

Text	☑	Success CD	☐	i-Learn	☐
Kit	☐	Success Tape	☐	i-Pass	☐
Passcard	☐	Big Picture Poster	☐	Virtual Campus	☐

Your ratings, comments and suggestions would be appreciated on the following areas of this Text.

	Very useful	Useful	Not useful
Introductory section (Key study steps, personal study)	☐	☐	☐
Chapter introductions	☐	☐	☐
Key terms	☐	☐	☐
Quality of explanations	☐	☐	☐
Case examples and other examples	☐	☐	☐
Questions and answers in each chapter	☐	☐	☐
Chapter roundups	☐	☐	☐
Quick quizzes	☐	☐	☐
Exam focus points	☐	☐	☐
Question bank	☐	☐	☐
Answer bank	☐	☐	☐
List of key terms and index	☐	☐	☐
Icons	☐	☐	☐

	Excellent	Good	Adequate	Poor
Overall opinion of this Text	☐	☐	☐	☐

Do you intend to continue using BPP Products?   ☐ Yes   ☐ No

Please note any further comments and suggestions/errors on the reverse of this page. The BPP author of this edition can be e-mailed at: glennhaldane@bpp.com

Please return to: Catherine Watton, ACCA Range Manager, BPP Professional Education, FREEPOST, London, W12 8BR

REVIEW FORM & FREE PRIZE DRAW (continued)

TELL US WHAT YOU THINK
Please note any further comments and suggestions/errors below.

FREE PRIZE DRAW RULES

1 Closing date for 31 January 2005 draw is 31 December 2004. Closing date for 31 July 2005 draw is 30 June 2005.

2 No purchase necessary. Entry forms are available upon request from BPP Professional Education. No more than one entry per title, per person. Draw restricted to persons aged 16 and over.

3 Winners will be notified by post and receive their cheques not later than 6 weeks after the draw date.

4 The decision of the promoter in all matters is final and binding. No correspondence will be entered into.

See overleaf for information on other
BPP products and how to order

ACCA Order

To BPP Professional Education, Aldine Place, London W12 8AW

Tel: 020 8740 2211 — Fax: 020 8740 1184

email: publishing@bpp.com — website: www.bpp.com

Order online www.bpp.com

Mr/Mrs/Ms (Full name)

Daytime delivery address

Postcode

Daytime Tel

Date of exam (month/year)

Scots law variant Y / N

Occasionally we may wish to email you relevant offers and information about courses and products. Please tick to opt into this service. ☐

	6/04 Texts	1/04 Kits	1/04 Passcards	***Success CDs	Big Picture Posters	8/04 i-Learn	8/04 i-Pass	Virtual Campus
PART 1								
1.1 Preparing Financial Statements	£24.95 ☐	£10.95 ☐	£6.95 ☐	£14.95 ☐	£6.95 ☐	£34.95 ☐	£24.95 ☐	£90 ☐
1.2 Financial Information for Management	£24.95 ☐	£10.95 ☐	£6.95 ☐	£14.95 ☐	£6.95 ☐	£34.95 ☐	£24.95 ☐	£90 ☐
1.3 Managing People	£24.95 ☐	£10.95 ☐	£6.95 ☐	£14.95 ☐	£6.95 ☐	£34.95 ☐	£24.95 ☐	£90 ☐
PART 2								
2.1 Information Systems	£24.95 ☐	£10.95 ☐	£6.95 ☐	£14.95 ☐	£6.95 ☐	£34.95 ☐	£24.95 ☐	£90 ☐
2.2 Corporate and Business Law **	£24.95 ☐	£10.95 ☐	£6.95 ☐	£14.95 ☐	£6.95 ☐	£34.95 ☐	£24.95 ☐	£90 ☐
2.3 Business Taxation FA2003 (12/04 exams)	£20.95 ☐	£10.95 ☐	£6.95 ☐	£14.95 ☐	£6.95 ☐			£90 ☐
2.3 Business Taxation FA2004 (8/04 for 6/05 exams)†	£24.95 ☐				£6.95 ☐			£90 ☐
2.4 Financial Management and Control	£24.95 ☐	£10.95 ☐	£6.95 ☐	£14.95 ☐	£6.95 ☐	£34.95 ☐	£24.95 ☐	£90 ☐
2.5 Financial Reporting (7/04)	£24.95 ☐	£10.95 ☐	£6.95 ☐	£14.95 ☐	£6.95 ☐	£34.95 ☐	£24.95 ☐	£90 ☐
2.6 Audit and Internal Review (12/04 exams)	£24.95 ☐	£10.95 ☐	£6.95 ☐	£14.95 ☐	£6.95 ☐	£34.95 ☐	£24.95 ☐	£90 ☐
2.6 Audit and Internal Review (9/04 for 6/05 exams)†	£24.95 ☐				£6.95 ☐			£90 ☐
PART 3								
3.1 Audit and Assurance Services	£24.95 ☐	£10.95 ☐	£6.95 ☐	£14.95 ☐	£6.95 ☐		£24.95 ☐	
3.2 Advanced Taxation FA2003 (12/04 exams)	£20.95 ☐	£10.95 ☐	£6.95 ☐	£14.95 ☐	£6.95 ☐		£24.95 ☐	
3.2 Advanced Taxation FA2004 (9/04 for 6/05 exams)†	£24.95 ☐				£6.95 ☐			
3.3 Performance Management	£24.95 ☐	£10.95 ☐	£6.95 ☐	£14.95 ☐	£6.95 ☐		£24.95 ☐	
3.4 Business Information Management	£24.95 ☐	£10.95 ☐	£6.95 ☐	£14.95 ☐	£6.95 ☐		£24.95 ☐	
3.5 Strategic Business Planning and Development	£24.95 ☐	£10.95 ☐	£6.95 ☐	£14.95 ☐	£6.95 ☐		£24.95 ☐	
3.6 Advanced Corporate Reporting (7/04)	£24.95 ☐	£10.95 ☐	£6.95 ☐	£14.95 ☐	£6.95 ☐		£24.95 ☐	
3.7 Strategic Financial Management	£24.95 ☐	£10.95 ☐	£6.95 ☐	£14.95 ☐	£6.95 ☐		£24.95 ☐	
INTERNATIONAL STREAM								
1.1 Preparing Financial Statements	£24.95 ☐	£10.95 ☐	£6.95 ☐		£6.95 ☐	£34.95 ☐	£24.95 ☐	
2.2 Corporate and Business Law	£24.95 ☐	£10.95 ☐	£6.95 ☐		£6.95 ☐			
2.5 Financial Reporting	£24.95 ☐	£10.95 ☐	£6.95 ☐		£6.95 ☐	£34.95 ☐	£24.95 ☐	
2.6 Audit and Internal Review	£24.95 ☐	£10.95 ☐	£6.95 ☐		£6.95 ☐	£34.95 ☐	£24.95 ☐	
3.1 Audit and Assurance Services	£24.95 ☐	£10.95 ☐	£6.95 ☐		£6.95 ☐			
3.6 Advanced Corporate Reporting	£24.95 ☐	£10.95 ☐	£6.95 ☐		£6.95 ☐			
Success in Your Research and Analysis								
Project - Tutorial Text (10/04)	£24.95 ☐							
Learning to Learn (7/02)	£9.95 ☐							

SUBTOTAL £ ☐

POSTAGE & PACKING

Study Texts

	First	Each extra	Online
UK	£5.00	£2.00	£2.00 £ ☐
Europe*	£6.00	£4.00	£4.00 £ ☐
Rest of world	£20.00	£10.00	£10.00 £ ☐

Kits

	First	Each extra	Online
UK	£5.00	£2.00	£2.00 £ ☐
Europe*	£6.00	£4.00	£4.00 £ ☐
Rest of world	£20.00	£10.00	£10.00 £ ☐

Passcards/Success Tapes/CDs

	First	Each extra	Online
UK	£2.00	£1.00	£1.00 £ ☐
Europe*	£3.00	£2.00	£2.00 £ ☐
Rest of world	£8.00	£8.00	£8.00 £ ☐

Grand Total (incl. Postage) £ ☐

I enclose a cheque for
(Cheques to BPP Professional Education)

Or charge to Visa/Mastercard/Switch

Card Number ☐☐☐☐ ☐☐☐☐ ☐☐☐☐ ☐☐☐☐

Expiry date ☐☐☐☐   Start Date ☐☐☐☐

Issue Number (Switch Only) ☐☐

Signature

We aim to deliver to all UK addresses inside 5 working days; a signature will be required. Orders to all EU addresses should be delivered within 6 working days. All other orders to overseas addresses should be delivered within 8 working days. * Europe includes the Republic of Ireland and the Channel Islands.† **For 6/05 exam, New edition Kit, Passcard, i-Learn and i-Pass available 2005.** ** For Scots law variant students, a free **Scots Law Supplement** is